Criminal Law

Third Edition

Criminal Law

Third Edition

Joel Samaha

University of Minnesota

WEST PUBLISHING CO.
St. Paul • New York • Los Angeles • San Francisco

Copyeditor: Cheryl Drivdahl
Composition: Carlisle Communications
Cover Art: Stephen Flanagan, "Law & Order", (detail), acrylic on canvas,
      66" × 72", 1987, courtesy of Littlejohn-Smith Gallery,
      New York.

COPYRIGHT ©1983, 1987, 1990 By WEST PUBLISHING COMPANY
                     50 W. Kellogg Boulevard
                     P.O. Box 64526
                     St. Paul, MN 55164–1003

97 96 95 94 93 92 91 90   8 7 6 5 4 3 2 1

Library of Congress Cataloging-in-Publication Data

Samaha, Joel.
    Criminal law / Joel Samaha. — 3rd ed.
       p.   cm.
    Includes index.
    ISBN 0-314-56394-6
      1.Criminal law—United States—Cases.   I. Title.
KF9218.S26   1990
345.73—dc20
[347.305]   89-33626
                                   CIP

For Adam and Lucas

Contents

Chapter Three   The General Principles of Criminal Liability   74

Chapter Four   Parties to Crime: The Doctrine of Complicity   120

Chapter Five   *Uncompleted Crimes: Attempt, Solicitation, and Conspiracy*   *154*

Chapter Six   Defenses to Criminal Liability: Justifications   192

Chapter Seven   Defenses to Criminal Liability: Excuses   232

Chapter Ten   Crimes against Habitation: Burglary and Arson   378

Chapter Eleven   Crimes against Property   412

Chapter Twelve   Crimes against Public Order and Morals   *454*

Table of Cases

Preface

Twenty years ago, when I started teaching criminal law to undergraduate liberal arts students, criminal justice professionals, and law students, I decided to take the broad approach to the topic. That approach I adopted in the first two editions to *Criminal Law*. The success of both editions has convinced me to continue that approach. Writing the third edition provided me the opportunity to incorporate new scholarship, new cases, and suggestions both from undergraduate, graduate, and law students at the University of Minnesota and from instructors around the country who have used the second edition of *Criminal Law*. Despite changes, the third edition retains all that I consider central to teaching criminal law.

Criminal law examines the ordinary phenomena of life in extraordinary circumstances. The basic principles of criminal liability—the physical and mental elements in crime, the relationship between them, and when appropriate the harmful result—all look at the most basic activities and relationships in human society: bodily movements, mental activity, cause and effect. Similarly, the doctrines of criminal law bring into bold relief incomplete action, teamwork, justification, and excuse. Ordinary activities and relationships under ordinary circumstances go largely, if not totally, unnoticed. Who pays attention to a moving arm, the intention to move it, the relationship between the moving arm and the intent that prompted it? Who pays attention to the consequences of such action? Or to the reasons why the actor moved the arm?

Under ordinary circumstances, no one wonders about the answers to these questions, no one even asks them. When an arm hurts, however, its movement—at least to its possessor—takes on great significance. The person whose arm hurts will contemplate before moving, will wonder whether the results of moving it justify or excuse doing so. So, too, in criminal law, when a moving arm strikes a blow at another person, the movement and all that surrounds it take on moral and legal significance. The blow, the mental state associated with it, and the harm it caused, as well as the possible justification or excuse for moving the arm that struck the blow, determine whether the person was "wrong" in the moral sense, or committed a crime, or both. The principles of *actus reus, mens rea,* concurrence, and causation, as well as the defenses of justification and excuse, address ordinary phenomena and relationships when they constitute violations of the criminal law.

Teamwork, another feature of organized society, can work for good or bad. Individuals in groups can accomplish what alone they may never even attempt, or what alone they can never accomplish to the same degree. Society encourages and rewards teamwork for individual and social good. The criminal law deals with teamwork for criminal purposes. Crimes that individuals never attempt alone they not only embark upon but often make worse when they join with or prod others. The law of accomplices and vicarious liability deals with teamwork in crime.

This third edition of *Criminal Law* retains what I consider central to the subject of criminal law. It stresses general principles and doctrines, not rules applicable to a single jurisdiction. Criminal law's diversity according to place and its changes over time require students to concentrate on basic principles that apply widely over space and time. This book also invites students to participate actively in learning rather than to absorb information passively. It emphasizes that reasonable minds can interpret and apply the general principles and doctrines of criminal law differently. Hence, the text not only explains the principles and doctrines but also presents various formulations and applications among the jurisdictions. This approach demonstrates to students that criminal law offers no single "right" or "wrong" application of principles and doctrines, no uniform interpretation of rules.

Cases highlight and illustrate the general principles and doctrines in real-life situations. They demonstrate how courts arrive at different decisions, according to how they interpret and apply the principles and doctrines to particular facts. By seeing criminal law in action, students can think about, formulate, and apply the principles themselves. I require students to act both as legislators and as judges, first formulating their own statutes and then applying them to cases. In my criminal law class discussions and examinations, students must demonstrate that they understand the principles and doctrines by writing rules, explaining how the rules accord with the principles and doctrines, and then applying the rules to real or hypothetical cases. Stressing the general principles and doctrines variously formulated and applied remains fundamental in this text.

Changes in *Criminal Law* enhance this approach. The third edition reflects new developments that call for **reinterpreting and applying the general principles and doctrines of criminal law.** In the second edition, I took into account the importance of family violence and corporate crime in elaborating the subject of criminal law. In the third edition, I have added text and cases that demonstrate how legislatures and courts have adapted the general principles and doctrines of criminal law to respond to date rape, the battered-woman syndrome, gang activities, computer crime, and other recent social problems. These new developments clearly demonstrate the viability of the ancient principles and doctrines of criminal law in the face of challenging modern problems.

I have edited the **cases,** many of them new in this edition, to suit the needs of undergraduates and other nonlaw students. The cases remain distinct from the text, which stands on its own as an unbroken narrative. Each case follows immediately after the main point in the text that it elucidates. Instructors can either omit the cases entirely, or use them as examples of the text's main points. A case question introduces each case to focus attention on the point the case addresses. The case excerpt names the crime charged and, if known, the sentence the defendant received. The excerpt uses the exact language from the reported case to set out the facts of the case, the court's decision, and the arguments to support the decision. A case discussion follows the excerpted facts, decision, and opinion. The case discussion should provoke students to think about the principles, doctrines, and rules that the case addresses, to assess the court's decision and arguments, and where appropriate to propose alternative decisions and arguments to the court's.

In this edition, **chapters have been rearranged.** The new arrangement combines into chapters 1 through 7 the whole of the general part of criminal law: the overarching principles; the principles of criminal liability; and the doctrines that can, but do not always, apply to all crimes, or classes of crimes. Chapter 1 introduces the nature and historical origins of modern criminal law. It expands on the earlier editions' treatments of the common-law origins of American criminal law, and revises the existing material where appropriate. Chapter 2 now includes the overarching principles of criminal law: legality, punishment, and proportionality. In both earlier editions, these principles appeared piecemeal as they applied to special topics. In this edition, I have collected them into one place, expanding on each so that students will have a good basic understanding of the principles that apply to the whole of criminal law. Then follow the general principles of criminal liability in chapter 3: *actus reus, mens rea,* concurrence, and causation. Chapters 4 and 5 focus on the main doctrines of criminal law: the parties to crime (accomplices, accessories, and vicarious liability) and the inchoate crimes (attempt, conspiracy, and solicitation). Chapters 6 and 7 elucidate the defenses of justification and excuse, respectively. The remaining chapters examine the special part of the criminal law: the rules that apply the general principles and doctrines to specific offenses. Chapters 8 and 9 analyze the crimes against *persons;* chapter 10, the crimes against *habitation;* chapter 11, the crimes against *property;* and chapter 12, the crimes against public morals and order. Roughly, chapters 8 through 12 range from the most serious felonies against persons in chapter 8 to the minor misdemeanors in chapter 12.

The logic of the arrangement is to treat the general materials first, then to discuss the specific crimes to which those general principles and doctrines apply. The special part moves from the most serious to the least serious offenses embodied in the criminal law. However, the chapters in the text all stand alone. Instructors can teach them in any order to fit varying logic. They can treat specific crimes first, then read the general part to put the particular crimes within the context of general principles and doctrines. They can move from the least serious crimes to the most serious within the chapters that treat the individual offenses. Furthermore, they can cover the doctrines of complicity and the incomplete crimes before or after the defenses, depending on how they organize their courses. I have found that the arrangement established in this text works well, but I have utilized the others described here with equal effectiveness. The text's flexibility allows for any arrangement that suits individual instructors' needs.

In *Criminal Law*, second edition, the relevant sections of the Model Penal Code were distributed throughout the text. In *Criminal Law*, third edition, in order to improve readability I have placed all relevant Model Penal Code sections into an Appendix. These sections are summarized and referenced in the text.

Chapter outlines, main points, and key terms make the basic topics, the important points, and the key terms clear to students. My students tell me that they find these useful both as an introduction to what to look for and as a review after reading the chapter. A list of **review and discussion questions** provides another aid to learning the main points in the chapter. The **suggested readings** guide students to deeper and broader issues and topics related to the material in each chapter. I have tried to include works that students can easily find in most libraries, that will provoke them to think about the major points, and that will stimulate their interest in reading and learning more about criminal law. A completely revised **test bank** and **instructor's manual** accompany this edition.

I want to acknowledge those who have read and commented on this edition and earlier editions: Jerry Dowling; Richard Gwen; Robert Harvie; Julius Koefoed; James Maddex; Leon Manning; William Michalek; William Pelkey; Gregory Russell; Susette Talarico; James Todd; Donald Wallace; and Wayne Wolff. The text's improvement owes much to them, and I appreciate their suggestions. I would also like to acknowledge the following people from West Publishing Company who worked hard to see this book through all of its stages: Terry Casey, text designer; Kristen McCarthy, promotion manager; Poh Lin Khoo, production assistant; John Och, senior graphic arts specialist; and Mary Schiller, acquiring editor.

Finally, listening to my students' questions about the book and seeing their reactions to it have improved this edition as well. I am happy to record my debt both to other instructors and to my students. I also accept, as my own, the book's shortcomings—shortcomings that seem all the more painful in a subject I have loved to teach, think, learn, read, and write about since 1958 when I took criminal law as a freshman law student at Northwestern University Law School.

Joel Samaha
University of Minnesota

Chapter One

The Nature and Origins of Criminal Law

CHAPTER OUTLINE

CHAPTER MAIN POINTS

1. Criminal law defines, prohibits, and prescribes punishment for *some* harms to society.

2. The general part of criminal law consists of principles and doctrines that apply to all specific crimes.

3. The special part of criminal law defines specific crimes.

4. American criminal law originates in Anglo-American common law, in statutes, and in judicial opinions interpreting common law and statutes.

5. Crimes are classified according to several schemes having to do with harm, ethical and moral values, and penalties attached to them.

6. Several theories explain why some harms but not others are crimes.

7. There is no single American criminal law. All states, the federal government, and most municipalities have their own criminal laws.

8. The Model Penal Code is a comprehensive statement of principles, doctrines, and rules of criminal law.

CHAPTER KEY TERMS

common law all the statutes and case law background of England and the colonies before the Revolution based on principles and rules that derive from usages and customs of antiquity

defendant the person against whom a civil or criminal action is brought

discretion freedom to decide outside written rules

felonies serious crimes generally punishable by one year or more in prison

misdemeanor minor crimes, for which the penalty is usually less than one year in jail, or a fine

Model Penal Code the code developed by the American Law Institute to guide reform in criminal law

plaintiff the person who sues another party in a civil action

stare decisis the policy of courts to stand by prior decisions and to not disturb settled points of law

statutes rules or doctrines enacted by legislatures

torts private lawsuits brought to collect money for injuries

INTRODUCTION

Consider the following hypothetical cases. Put aside what you know about actual criminal law. Suppose you have been appointed to a legislative commission charged with drafting a rational criminal code for your state. If you were defining the criminal law, who in the examples have committed crimes? Should any who have not committed crimes still be subject to some kind of state control? Should any be subject to private lawsuits by injured parties? Who should suffer social condemnation by families and friends, even though they are not subject to criminal or other legal action? Who deserves no sanction? Do any deserve praise or other reward? Can you state specifically why you answered the questions the way you did?

1. Sheila hates Rosemary. She has always hated her because Rosemary is rich, charming, and beautiful, but most of all because she is more intelligent, aggressive, and successful than Sheila. Sheila reaches the breaking point in a long, controlled hostility when a prestigious medical school accepts Rosemary, while the law school at the same university rejects Sheila. Enraged, Sheila decides to murder Rosemary. Sheila carefully awaits the appropriate time to carry out her intention; her opportunity arises when Rosemary invites Sheila to a celebration party. Sheila takes a deadly drug from the medical center where she works, conceals it in her pocket, and puts it in Rosemary's

drink. Then she watches with immense pleasure as Rosemary writhes in pain and dies a slow, agonizing death.

2. Tom's father suffers excruciating pain from terminal bone cancer. The family has exhausted its insurance coverage and savings in order to keep him alive. Tom's father pleads with Tom to put him out of his misery. Tom, who loves his father and cannot bear to see him in pain, buys a fast-working poison to end his father's misery. As a medical student, Tom has access to hypodermic syringes. He takes one from the supply room. While his father sleeps, Tom injects him with the poison. His father dies painlessly.

3. David is driving his car down an icy city street. As he approaches a particularly slick spot, he accelerates rapidly. His car does just as he hopes it will—it skids out and around in a circle. Enjoying the skidding immensely, David glances up and sees a pedestrian, a frail ninety-year-old man, crossing the street in front of him. He tries to swerve away but cannot. He hits the old man, who is killed instantly. "Oh, my God," moans David. "This is the last thing I wanted to happen."

4. Kim is drowning in a lake. Steve, his lifetime rival, sees Kim struggling but walks on, laughing at the thought of getting Kim out of the way. Kim drowns.

5. Gretchen hates her law professor for constantly making a fool of her in class. She imagines all kinds of horrible deaths that might befall the man. In class one day—in the middle of a fantasy that Gretchen is strangling the professor—the hated teacher staggers, gasps, and falls dead upon the floor from a heart attack. Gretchen rejoices at his demise.

6. Jesse, extremely jealous, attacks and wounds his former lover, Marie, with a knife after he discovers she has married another man. Marie runs to her bedroom to get a gun she keeps hidden there. Jesse follows her, threatening to finish the job. Just as he is about to stab her again, she shoots him in the head. He dies.

7. Every night when he gets home from work, Marty goes to his room alone and takes out a brown paper bag. Inside the bag are pornographic pictures, which he studies for hours. Sometimes Marty gets so excited he can hardly calm down.

8. Michael really likes women and is a demonstrative person. He goes into a singles' bar, where he is immediately drawn to Theresa. Michael puts his arm around her and introduces himself. Theresa is extremely upset because it greatly offends her to be touched by strangers.

9. Adam sees a radio he much admires lying on a department store counter. "Just what I need," he thinks. When the clerk walks away, Adam goes to the counter and reaches out to take the radio. But just as he is about to pick it up, a store detective grabs his hand.

10. Bill is addicted to cocaine.

11. Kristen purposely tries to win Luke's love. As soon as she succeeds, she rejects Luke, telling him she never could stand him. She hates

men and will take any opportunity to destroy them. Luke is so distraught that he cannot concentrate on his highly successful video business. He goes bankrupt, acquires enormous medical bills for treatment of a nervous breakdown, and ends up alcoholic.

12. A major pharmaceutical corporation introduced to the American market a drug used to treat hypertension. The company knew the drug had been reported to cause death and liver damage in French patients. The corporation labeled the product saying that no cause and effect relationship existed between the drug and liver damage. After the drug was linked to thirty-six deaths and more than five hundred cases of liver and kidney damage, the corporation withdrew the drug from the market.

13. At about 9:30 P.M., Ms. Goff left her two children, aged eight years and twenty-two months, respectively, to attend a Halloween party with her friends at a nearby tavern. She did not return until about 2:00 A.M. She drank eight or nine beers while at the party. A fire broke out while Ms. Goff was at the party, and both children were killed.

These hypothetical cases present, in capsule form, the major dimensions of the subject of criminal law. They illustrate the general principles and doctrines discussed in chapters 2 through 5, some specific crimes analyzed in chapters 6 through 12, and the nature and sources of criminal law, the main concern of chapter 1.

THE DEFINITION OF CRIMINAL LAW

Rape, cancer, child abuse, poverty, misleading advertising, cheating, lying, mistreatment of friends, and rejection of lovers all cause harm to their victims. Private and public social control mechanisms protect society and individuals against only some harms. Private social control operates at the individual level through personal integrity, courage, and responsibility. Peer groups, churches, clubs, schools, and other nonlegal agencies also exercise social control by means of their teachings and informal power to exclude and expel undesirable members.[1]

Law is the primary public social control mechanism. Civil law focuses on lawsuits in which one person sues another to recover money. Criminal law centers on the government's power to define, prosecute, and punish crime. Criminal law is the harshest, most cumbersome, and most expensive social control mechanism; it is not, however, always necessary, appropriate, or effective. It is a last resort in the effort to prevent, prohibit, and punish social harms.

Rational Criminal Law and the Model Penal Code

The phrase "rational criminal law" appears frequently in this text. It refers to a criminal law that satisfies several criteria: (1) it is based on general principles and doctrines; (2) the general principles apply to all specific crimes; (3) it grades punishment according to the seriousness of the harm and the blameworthiness of the conduct; and (4) it prescribes no greater penalty than punishment and prevention require. Rational criminal law prefers informal to public sanctions, civil actions to criminal actions, and lesser criminal penalties to greater ones, if the lesser penalties punish and prevent crime effectively.

The American Law Institute's **Model Penal Code** has greatly advanced the pursuit of a rational criminal code. The American Law Institute (ALI) is a private association whose members are eminent lawyers, judges, and professors. Founded in 1923, it works to clarify and improve the law. In 1950, with Rockefeller Foundation aid, it undertook a major effort to guide reform in American criminal law. The ALI created a large advisory committee drawn from all disciplines concerned with criminal justice and charged it with drafting a model penal code. For ten years, these specialists met and drafted, redrafted, and finally in 1961 completed the *Model Penal Code and Commentaries*, a learned and influential document.[2]

As its title indicates, the code is a model to guide actual legislation. Jurisdictions vary in what specific provisions meet their needs. By 1980 and 1985, when the ALI published an updated code and commentary, thirty-four states had enacted widespread criminal law revision and codification based on its provisions; fifteen hundred courts had cited its provisions and referred to its commentary. The Model Penal Code fulfills the criteria outlined above for a rational criminal code, but it is not the final word on the subject. Feel free to disagree with it; when you do, devise your own scheme for a rational criminal law.

The General and Special Parts of Criminal Law

Criminal law is divided into a general part and a special part. The general part covers the general principles and doctrines that apply to all crimes. The principles relate to punishment, legality, and requirements for criminal liability. The doctrines refer to tenets that *may* apply to all crimes, but are not necessarily present in all cases. The doctrines include defenses to criminal liability, such as insanity; liability in incompleted crimes, such as attempt and conspiracy; and liability of complicity, such as that exhibited by accomplices and accessories.

The special part of criminal law defines specific crimes—murder, rape, robbery, theft, and disturbing the peace, for example. These definitions must agree with the principles and, where relevant, the doctrines set out in the general part. For example, the general principle *actus reus* bases criminal liability on action—on what people *do*, not what they *think* or who they *are*. The acts in specific crimes manifest this general principle, such as the act of killing in the crime of murder, breaking and entering in burglary, taking another's property in theft. Similarly, criminal liability requires a *mens rea*, or a mental element. Particular crimes have individual mental element requirements, such as the intent to kill in the crime of murder, to permanently deprive another of property in theft, to take property by fear or force in robbery.[3]

Criminal Law Close-Up

WHAT ARE THE CHARACTERISTICS OF SOME SERIOUS CRIMES?

Crime	Definition	Facts
Homicide	Causing the death of another person without legal justification or excuse, including Uniform Crime Reports, crimes of murder and nonnegligent manslaughter and negligent manslaughter.	• Murder and nonnegligent manslaughter occur less often than other violent UCR index crimes. • 58% of the known murderers were relatives or acquaintances of the victim. • 20% of all murders in 1985 occurred or were suspected to have occurred as the result of some felonious activity.
Rape	Unlawful sexual intercourse with a female, by force or without legal or factual consent.	• Most rapes involve a lone offender and a lone victim. • About 32% of the rapes recorded by National Crime Survey in 1985 were committed in or near the victim's home. • 73% of the rapes occurred at night, between 6 P.M. and 6 A.M. • 58% of the victims of rape in 1985 were under 25 years old.
Robbery	The unlawful taking or attempted taking of property that is in the immediate possession of another, by force or threat of force.	• Robbery is the violent crime that most often involves more than one offender (in almost half of all cases in 1985). • About half of all robberies reported by NCS in 1985 involved the use of a weapon.
Assault	Unlawful intentional inflicting, or attempted inflicting, of injury upon	• Simple assault occurs more frequently than aggravated assault.

	the person of another. Aggravated assault is the unlawful intentional inflicting of serious bodily injury or unlawful threat or attempt to inflict bodily injury or death by means of a deadly or dangerous weapon with or without actual infliction of injury. Simple assault is the unlawful intentional inflicting of less than serious bodily injury without a deadly or dangerous weapon or an attempt or threat to inflict bodily injury without a deadly or dangerous weapon.	● Most assaults involve one victim and one offender.
Burglary	Unlawful entry of any fixed structure, vehicle, or vessel used for regular residence, industry, or business, with or without force, with the intent to commit a felony or larceny.	● Residential property was targeted in 2 out of every 3 reported burglaries; nonresidential property accounted for the remaining third. ● In 1985, 42% of all residential burglaries occurred without forced entry. ● About 37% of the no-force burglaries were known to have occurred during the day between 6 A.M. and 6 P.M.
Larceny theft	Unlawful taking or attempted taking of property other than a motor vehicle from the possession of another, by stealth, without force and without deceit, with intent to permanently deprive the owner of the property.	● Less than 5% of all personal larcenies involve contact between the victim and offender. ● Pocket picking and purse snatching most frequently occur inside nonresidential buildings or on street locations. ● Unlike most other crimes, pocket picking and purse snatching affect the elderly about as much as other age groups.

Motor vehicle theft	Unlawful taking or attempted taking of a self-propelled road vehicle owned by another, with the intent of depriving him or her of it, permanently or temporarily.	● Motor vehicle theft is relatively well reported to the police. In 1985 89% of all completed thefts were reported. ● The stolen property is more likely to be recovered in this crime than in other property crimes.
Arson	The intentional damaging or destruction or attempted damaging or destruction by means of fire or explosion of property without the consent of the owner, or of one's own property or that of another by fire or explosives with or without the intent to defraud.	● Single-family residences were the most frequent targets of arson. ● 16% of all structures where arson occurred were not in use.

SOURCES: *Dictionary of Criminal Justice Data Terminology,* 2nd ed., Bureau of Justice Statistics, 1981; *Criminal Victimization in the US,* Bureau of Justice Statistics, 1985; *Crime in the United States,* Federal Bureau of Investigation, 1985.

SOURCES OF CRIMINAL LAW

Criminal law stems from three main sources: the common law, statutes, and judicial decisions interpreting and applying the common law and statutes. The matter is complicated because there is a three-tiered criminal law system: federal, state, and local. Criminal law is further complicated because American government is separated into three branches, two of which—legislatures and courts—both generate criminal law. Legislatures enact criminal statutes, the greatest bulk of which are state criminal codes. Municipal ordinances and federal statutes are also sources of criminal laws, but they produce fewer criminal laws than do state codes. Judicial decisions create criminal law both indirectly by interpreting criminal statutes and, occasionally, by expanding the common law.

The Common-Law Origins of Criminal Law

Today, legislatures create most crimes. This was not always so. Before legislatures existed, social order depended on obedience to unwritten rules—the *lex non scripta*—based on customs and mores. These traditions were passed on from generation to generation, altering to meet changed conditions and times. In England, from which American law descended, these unwritten rules were eventually incorporated into court decisions. These incorporated traditions became the **common law.**

English jurist Sir William Blackstone, whose *Commentaries on the Laws and Customs of England* was the only law book most American lawyers read until well into the nineteenth century, described the common law as follows:

> As to general customs, or the common law, properly so called, this is that law, by which proceedings and determinations in the king's ordinary courts of justice are guided and directed. This, for the most part, settles . . . the several species of temporal offenses, with the manner and degree of punishment . . . [A]ll these are doctrines that are not set down in any written statute or ordinance, but depend merely upon immemorial usage, that is, upon the common law, for their support.[4]

The common law covered the whole field of law, including the criminal law. By the seventeenth century, the courts had created a substantial list of crimes, called common-law felonies and misdemeanors. Most have familiar names today, and many have retained their original core of meaning, although adapted to meet modern conditions. The common-law **felonies** created by the common-law courts were murder, suicide, manslaughter, burglary, arson, robbery, larceny, rape, sodomy, and mayhem. The common-law **misdemeanors** included (and in some jurisdictions still include) assault, battery, false imprisonment, libel, perjury, corrupting morals, and disturbing the peace.[5]

No one knows exactly how it developed, like the traditions it incorporated, the common law grew and changed to meet new conditions. At first, its growth depended mainly on judicial decisions. The courts formulated basic principles, rules, and standards based on the common law. They considered these the law of the land. Judges felt bound to follow these common-law principles, standards, and rules, and interpreted new cases according to them. As judges decided more cases according to them, the law became more elaborate and complete. These prior decisions are called **precedents,** and being bound to follow them is called the rule of *stare decisis.*

As legislatures became more established, **statutes** were added to the common law, partly in response to new conditions, partly to clarify existing common law, and partly to fill in blanks left by the common law. Court decisions interpreted these statutes according to common-law principles and past decisions. These judicial decisions interpreting the statutes became part of the growing body of precedent making up the common law.

When the British colonized North America, they brought this body of common law—tradition, judicial opinions, statutes, and judicial decisions interpreting the legislation—with them. Hence, American criminal law included common-law crimes, legislation adding to common-law crimes, and judicial decisions interpreting common-law crimes and legislation.

Criminal Codes

Periodically, reformers have called for abolishing the common law in America. *The Laws and Liberties of Massachusetts,* appearing shortly after the

British came to America, codified the criminal law and prescribed definite penalties for violating it. Following the American Revolution, when hostility to all things English ran strong, reformers again called for codes to replace the "English" common law.

The eighteenth-century Enlightenment, with its emphasis on natural law and order, inspired reformers to put aside the piecemeal, incomplete common law scattered throughout judicial decisions, and to replace it with rational criminal codes that implemented the natural law of crimes. Despite anti-British feeling, Blackstone's well-written, orderly *Commentaries* remained popular with reformers who hoped to emulate the well-arranged outline of criminal law into criminal codes. Reformers also believed that judge-made law was antidemocratic; that legislatures, which reflect the popular will, should make laws, not judges who are aloof and out of touch with public opinion. Thomas Jefferson's proposed reforms in Virginia's penal code reflected these influences. The Proposed Virginia Code never passed the Virginia legislature, however, because it recommended too many drastic reductions in criminal punishments.[6]

Reformers' fears of judicial oppression were realized in a Connecticut Court's effort to create a new common law of libel early in the nineteenth century. In *United States v. Hudson and Goodwin*, the United States Supreme Court, reflecting this fear in part, denied the *federal* courts the power to create common-law crimes. The defendants were indicted for

> a libel against the President and Congress of the United States, contained in the Connecticut Courant of 7th May, 1806, charging them with having in secret voted $2,000,000 as a present to Bonaparte, for leave to make a treaty with Spain.

No statute made such conduct an offense. The Supreme Court held that federal courts were not

> vested with jurisdiction over any particular act done by an individual in supposed violation of the peace and dignity of the sovereign power. The legislative authority of the Union must first make an act a crime, affix a punishment to it, and declare the court that shall have jurisdiction over the offense.

United States v. Hudson and Goodwin does not, however, prohibit *state* courts from creating common-law crimes.[7]

The codification movement had an uneven history, but the concept of common-law crimes retreated throughout the nineteenth century. During the twentieth century, the codification movement strengthened. The American Law Institute strongly supported codification, and the earliest drafts of the Model Penal Code abolished common-law crimes:

§ 1.05 All Offenses Defined by Statute
    (1) No conduct constitutes an offense unless it is a crime or violation under this Code or another statute of this State.

Since the American Law Institute adopted § 1.05, twenty-five jurisdictions have abolished the common-law crimes and ten others have proposed abolition legislation. Moreover, although New York's legislature has not abolished the common-law crimes, its judicial decisions have done so. On the other hand, since § 1.05 was introduced three states—Florida, New Mexico, and Washington—have enacted statutes that specifically preserve the common-law offenses. Most of the remaining states appear to have abolished the common-law crimes, but pertinent legislation and judicial decisions are not altogether clear on the point.[8]

Common-Law Crimes and Modern Criminal Law

Abolishing the common-law crimes does not render the common law irrelevant. Most states that have abolished common-law offenses (these states are called code jurisdictions) retain the common-law defenses, such as self-defense and insanity. Furthermore, statutes frequently contain the terms murder, manslaughter, robbery, burglary, rape, and assault without defining them, and courts turn to the common law to determine the meanings of those terms. For example, the 1975 Alabama Criminal Code provides as follows:

> Any person who commits . . . voluntary manslaughter, shall be guilty of a felony. Voluntary manslaughter is punishable as a Class 5 felony.[9]

Jurisdictions that retain the common-law crimes (these are called common-law jurisdictions) have created many offenses, particularly misdemeanors, that extend beyond the well-established common-law felonies. All of the following are crimes without statutes in some states: committing conspiracy, attempt, and solicitation; uttering grossly obscene language in public; burning a body in a furnace; keeping a house of prostitution; maliciously killing a horse; using blasphemy; negligently permitting a prisoner to escape; discharging a gun near a sick person; being drunk in public; using libel; committing an indecent assault; and eavesdropping.[10]

Three problems arise in common-law jurisdictions. First, statutes do not prescribe penalties for individual common-law crimes. In some states, statutes prescribing general penalties for felonies and misdemeanors alleviate this problem. The problem remains when the common law does not designate whether an offense is a felony or misdemeanor. Some states solve this problem with statutes providing that all common-law offenses are misdemeanors.

Second, if both statutes and common law cover the same conduct, which takes precedence? Some states construe statutes narrowly, declaring that they repeal the common law only to the extent that they specifically so state, or unless by their language they preempt the entire field covered by the common-law crimes. So, where a state conspiracy statute listed five criminal conspiracies while the common law listed many more, the court held that the statute was not meant to take over the whole field of conspiracy; hence, the common-law conspiracies not listed in the statute remained criminal.[11]

Third, what conduct constitutes common-law crimes? Courts approach this subject from two perspectives. Some courts eagerly create new crimes without precedent; others do so only reluctantly. The perspective that courts adopt depends upon their view of the common law itself. If decided cases merely illustrate the unwritten common

FIGURE 1   Courts at Various Levels of Government Interact in Many Ways

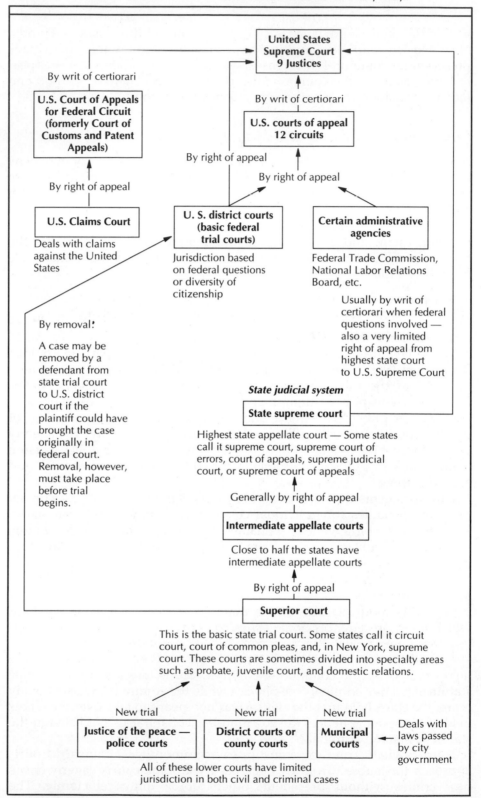

SOURCE: Updated and reprinted by permission from *The American Legal Environment* by William T. Schantz. Copyright © 1976 by West Publishing Company. All rights reserved.

Criminal Law Close-Up

HOW TO ANALYZE CASES

Cases bring criminal law to life because they are about real people accused of actual crimes. In them, general principles and doctrines as well as specific rules are applied to particular events. They show the criminal law in action, as opposed to in books. Most cases in this book are appellate cases, or cases that have been appealed from lower courts. American criminal courts are two-tiered. Trial courts adjudicate or try criminal cases, accept defendants' guilty pleas, and convict or acquit defendants.

Convicted defendants (and occasionally states) may appeal trial court decisions to appellate courts, in most cases state supreme courts. These appeals are called appellate cases, those who appeal them are called appellants, and parties appealed against are called appellees. Convicted defendants are most often appellants in criminal cases.

Most case excerpts in this book are appellate cases in which convicted defendants are appellants and states are appellees. Defendants have appealed their convictions; they are asking appellate courts to overturn, or reverse, their convictions. The appellate case excerpts included in the text raise questions about the principles, doctrines, and rules of criminal law. (See Figure 1.)

To benefit most from your reading, answer the following four questions about each case excerpt.

1. What are the facts? To determine the facts relevant to criminal law, answer these questions:
   a. What did the defendant do?
   b. What did the defendant intend to do?
   c. What harm befell the victim?
   d. Did the defendant's acts cause the harm to the victim?
   e. Was there a justification or excuse for what the defendant did?
2. What is the legal issue in the case? That is, what question or problem regarding the principles, doctrines, and rules of criminal law does the case raise?
3. What are the court's reasons for its decision? How did it arrive at the conclusions it reached? The court's reasoning, or opinion, applies the general principle, doctrine, and rule to the facts of the case.
4. Did the court *affirm* (agree with and uphold) the trial court's decision, or *reverse* it (set it aside) and substitute its own decision, or *remand* it (send the case back to the trial court for further proceedings in accord with the appellate opinion)?

> You probably cannot answer all these questions at first because the answers depend on knowledge you will accumulate as the text introduces new principles, doctrines, and rules. Furthermore, courts do not follow the same order as the questions do.
>
> Developing the skills needed to sort out the elements of court cases requires practice but is worth the effort. Answering the questions given here can challenge you to think not only about the basic principles, doctrines, and rules of criminal law but also about your values touching life, property, privacy, and morals.

law's broad principles, then creating new offenses requires no precedent. According to this view, the common law can expand to meet new conditions; in fostering that expansion, the courts do not invent new crimes, they only apply existing common-law principles to new problems. Courts following this view of the common law are more likely to create new crimes without precedent. On the other hand, some courts have held that American courts are not empowered to create new crimes; such courts are more likely to look for precedent to justify creating common-law crimes.

CASE

Is There a Common Law of Crimes?

Pope v. State

38 Md. App. 520, 382 A. 2d 880 (1978)

[Justice Lowe delivered the opinion.]

FACTS

Following a Friday evening service at the Christian Tabernacle Church, the appellant, Joyce Lillian Pope, agreed to permit Melissa Norris and her 3-month-old child, Demiko, to stay at appellant's home. During that evening and the following morning appellant assisted Melissa with the child by assuming some of the maternal functions such as preparing its bed (in a dresser drawer) and changing the child and feeding him.

Melissa's conduct that evening and the following day sporadically indicated some sort of mental distress. She would at times seem caught up in religious frenzy with a wild look about her, trying to preach and declaring that she was God. She would as quickly resume her normal self without ever seeming to notice her personality transitions. This changing back and forth continued throughout the following day, Saturday, even during a "shower" party that evening attended by the mother, the child and the appellant. Because of this strange conduct, appellant admitted some concern for the child's safety and watched it "like it was [her] own," prevailing upon Melissa to let the child sleep in a dresser drawer, rather than in bed with the mother, as Melissa had suggested, because she feared the mother might roll over on the child during the night.

The following morning Melissa's episodes of "changing to God" became more and more pronounced. She stomped and gestured as she strode back and forth, putting crosses on doors and demanding the departure of the evil which she claimed to see. She kicked and banged at the door of appellant's son, and fearful that by breaking in Melissa would frighten him, appellant unfastened the door to permit entry. Loudly exhorting Satan to leave the premises, Melissa "anointed" appellant's son with oil, placing some of the oil in this child's mouth. She subsequently repeated the process with appellant's daughter. When dressed, appellant's children left the house expeditiously, lingering only long enough to embrace their mother.

Melissa's changing process continued. Finally, while still appearing to be herself, she prepared the water tub to bathe the baby. Then, from her suddenly changed voice and appearance, appellant knew Melissa had changed again to "God." Calling out that Satan had hidden in the body of her son, Melissa began to verbally exorcise that spirit and physically abuse the child by punching and poking him repeatedly about the stomach, chest, and privates. After she undressed the child, that which ensued was hardly describable. In her religious frenzy and apparent exorcism, Melissa poled the child's vitals and beat the child about the head. She reached her fingers down its throat, wiping mucous and blood on diapers at hand, and even lifted the child by inserting her hands in its mouth, and shook him like a rag.

Appellant, Joyce Lillian Pope, watched but did nothing else during this entire episode. She never participated in the abuse nor tried to prevent it. Whether from fear or fervor, her abstinent conduct manifested total indifference. Her testimony sought to indicate that her passivity was motivated by fear but other evidence belied that inference. Her sister, Angela, came to the door as Melissa's frenzy diminished, and was let in by appellant who tried to tell Angela what had happened—but couldn't. Appellant, on advice from Angela, locked the door so that Angela's children would stay in the yard with appellant's. Angela wrapped the dead or dying child in a towel, held the comatose body over her head and prayed. Although the record is not clear as to when, sometime during or soon after its ordeal, the child mercifully expired.

The three adults (appellant, her sister and Melissa) left with the child, destined ultimately for the church located in the District of Columbia. . . .

At the church the child was given to, or taken by, the Reverend Leon Hart who gave him to Mother Dorothy King for her prayers. Mother King discovered the child's body was cool and sent for ambulance assistance from the firehouse across the street. Police and rescue personnel arrived and determined that the child was dead. . . .

A detective from the District of Columbia Homicide division arrived and interviewed Melissa and appellant together. . . .

> Q Did you have any . . . conversation with Melissa Norris?
> A Yes. I explained to her that an autopsy would be performed, and where the body was going and the arrangements she was to make with the funeral home in regards to picking the baby up and burying it.
> Q Throughout the course of this period of time, other than the statements with reference to feeding, did Joyce Pope give you any information with reference to your investigation?
> A No, sir.

The following day the Montgomery County police began their investigation and appellant was brought to the station. At that interview, for the first time, appellant disclosed what had happened.

OPINION

Most lawyers know, if only vaguely from law school recollection, that misprision of felony is the concealment and/or nondisclosure of the known felony of another. . . . The crime has never been recognized in the appellate courts of Maryland, however, and we are confronted here with the question of whether it is an indictable offense in this State. Since there is no statute here so proclaiming, we must look to the Common Law of England or her statutes as they existed on July 4, 1776, for that is the law to which the inhabitants of Maryland are entitled. . . .

The primary question asked in this case is whether misprision of felony is "an indictable offense under the constitution and laws of this State." The argument raises the questions of whether that crime was one recognized under the Common Law of England when Maryland adopted that body of law, and if so, has the crime since been abandoned for obsolescence by its apparent non-use here. There is no argument made that this crime which is in the nature of a criminal cover-up is "inconsistent with the spirit of the Constitution and the nature of our political institutions," or that it is:

> " . . . inconsistent with or repugnant to the spirit and principles of republican institutions, whose strength lies in the virtue and integrity of the citizens to correct the morals and protect the reputation, rights, and property of individuals, . . . "

. . . Nearly every author of any note . . . has said there is an offense of misprision of felony and described it in much the same terms . . . Indeed, the United States has statutorily enacted such a crime in language not dissimilar to that describing the common law crime:

Misprision of felony.—Whoever, having knowledge of the actual commission of a felony cognizable by a court of the United States, conceals and does not as soon as possible make known the same to some judge or other person in civil or military authority under the United States, shall be fined not more than $500 or be imprisoned not more than three years, or both. 18 U.S.C.

. . . Furthermore, language in our own Court of Appeals indicating that an agreement to prevent the apprehension of a criminal would be illegal in Maryland provides some philosophical direction concordant with the philosophy of misprision of felony. . . .

In the light of this history, it is plain that there is and always has been an offence of misprision of felony and that it is not obsolete.

We hold, therefore, that misprision of felony was a crime at common law given life in Maryland by Art. 5 of the Declaration of Rights. The contention that it has become obsolete or abandoned by disuse is without merit.

CASE

Should the Common Law Influence Statutory Definitions?

State v. Forsman

260 N.W. 2d 160 (Minn. 1977)

[Justice Peterson delivered the opinion.]

FACTS

Defendant, David Forsman, was found guilty by jury verdict of two counts of distributing heroin and one count of third-degree murder for the death of Randy Winters, who died after defendant allegedly injected heroin into his body. . . .

On October 3, 1975, Miles Miller brought decedent, Randy Winters, to the emergency room at St. Joseph's Hospital in Mankato, where Winters was pronounced dead. The time of his death was estimated at 10 P.M. that day. An autopsy revealed the morphine content in his blood but no morphine in his urine, which placed the time of the injection at around 9 P.M. The autopsy also revealed 6 needle marks in the bend of the right arm, 6 on the back of the left hand, and 23 on the front of the left knee.

Miller was the prosecution's major witness at trial and gave this version of the relevant events. On October 3, 1975, Miller drove Winters to the farmhouse rented by defendant and Pam Johnson about 16 miles southeast of Mankato. Miller and Winters arrived some time between 7 and 9 P.M., with the purpose of purchasing some heroin from defendant. They waited while a woman delivering Tupperware spoke with defendant. When she left, defendant came into the room where Miller and Winters were waiting. After a brief discussion regarding how much heroin they desired, defendant left and returned to the room with three small paper packages containing heroin, for which Miller and Winters paid him $150. There was a package of needles and syringes in the room. Defendant suggested that Miller and Winters split one of the bags of heroin. He placed approximately half of one package on a spoon, added water, held a match under it until it boiled, "took the needle off the syringe and wadded up a little piece of cotton and filtered it into the syringe and then put the needle back on." Defendant injected Winters in the arm, and within seconds Winters "pass[ed] out." Upon Miller's request, the defendant injected Miller with a little less than the remaining solution. Defendant and Miller carried Winters to Miller's automobile and Miller drove off. He returned several minutes later, worried about Winters, whose breathing had slowed. Defendant told Miller to take Winters to the hospital in Mankato but declined to accompany them and advised Miller not to mention where they had been. When later informed of decedent's death, defendant stated, "Yes, I thought he would."

OPINION

The first issue we reach is defendant's contention that a drug distribution felony, voluntarily solicited by a person whose death results therefrom, should not invoke the felony-murder rule, because the felony is not "inherently dangerous." In his brief, defendant writes: "This issue arises not from a reading of the third degree murder statute, but from a review of the common law in the United States out of which the felony-murder rule has developed."

Defendant's argument is misdirected. Because common-law crimes were abolished by adoption of our criminal code, any analysis of the applicability of a penal statute must begin with a reading of the statute. No act is a crime unless so defined by a statute. It is the exclusive province of the legislature to define by statute what acts shall constitute a crime and to establish sanctions for their commission . . .

The statute at issue in this case, Minn. St. 609.195, provides:

> Whoever, without intent to effect the death of any person, causes the death of another by either of the following means, is guilty of murder in the third degree and may be sentenced to imprisonment for not more than 25 years: (2) Commits or attempts to commit a felony upon or affecting the person whose death was caused by another, except rape or sodomy with force or violence within the meaning of section 609-185.

The language of this provision is unambiguous and incorporates no common-law terms. The distribution of heroin by direct injection into the body of another is a felony "upon or affecting the person whose death was caused" thereby. Because the statutory language applies to the act for which defendant was convicted, we need not decide how the rule which developed at common law to limit the felony-murder doctrine to felonies "inherently dangerous" to human life would apply to this case.

CASE DISCUSSION

The principle advantage to common-law jurisdictions, some say, is that there are no gaps in the law. If particular conduct should be a crime, but the legislature forgot or overlooked it, then the courts can step in and make the conduct criminal. On the other hand, the criminal law ought to be clear and certain, warning citizens in advance that their conduct is criminal. Which view do you favor? How would you decide the two cases presented here? If citizens do not know in advance that what they do is criminal, is the law fair? Will it deter crime? Will it protect society?

CLASSIFYING AND GRADING CRIMES

Criminal law covers a broad range of conduct, encompassing everything from murder to spitting on the street. In Palo Alto, California, for example, "harboring overdue library books" is punishable by thirty days in jail!

Crime and Social Harm

Despite its breadth, criminal law punishes only some harms to people and their property, reputations, and relationships. Many injuries, deaths, and property losses are not included in the criminal law (see table 1). Most harms caused by corporations do not fall within the scope of the criminal law. They are considered "business matters," best managed by informal, or at least non-criminal, proceedings, such as private lawsuits. Reformers have long recommended extending the criminal law to corporations, and one recent development in criminal law is expanding corporate criminal liability.[12]

Furthermore, criminal justice officials have traditionally treated harms that individuals inflict on their relatives and friends as "family matters," even though they are formally crimes. Counselors, social service agencies, or families themselves have had to deal with them. Recently, attitudes and criminal law enforcement practices have begun to change. Crimes committed against friends, lovers, and family are no longer so widely considered family matters; increasingly, police arrest, and prosecutors charge, the perpetrators of such crimes.

Table 1   How do Crime Rates Compare with the Rates of Other Life Events?

Events	Rate per 1,000 Adults per Year[*]
Accidental injury, all circumstances	242
Accidental injury at home	79
Personal theft	72
Accidental injury at work	58
Violent victimization	31
Assault (aggravated and simple)	24
Injury in motor vehicle accident	17
Death, all causes	11
Victimization with injury	10
Serious (aggravated) assault	9
Robbery	6
Heart disease death	4
Cancer death	2
Rape (women only)	2
Accidental death, all circumstances	0.5
Pneumonia/influenza death	0.3
Motor vehicle accident death	0.2
Suicide	0.2
Injury from fire	0.1
Homicide/legal intervention death	0.1
Death from fire	0.03

NOTE: These rates approximate your chances of becoming a victim of these events. More precise estimates can be derived by taking account of such factors as your age, sex, race, place of residence, and life-style. Findings are based on 1982–84 data, but there is little variation in rates from year to year.

[*]These rates exclude children from the calculations (those under age 12–17, depending on the series). Fire injury/death data are based on the total population, because no age-specific data are available in this series.

SOURCES: *Current estimates from the National Health Interview Survey; United States, 1982,* National Center for Health Statistics; "Advance Report of Final Mortality Statistics, 1983," *Monthly Vital Statistics Report,* National Center for Health Statistics; *Estimates of the Population of the United States, by Age, Sex, and Race: 1980 to 1984,* United States Bureau of the Census; *The 1984 Fire Almanac,* National Fire Protection Association; *Criminal Victimization 1984,* Bureau of Justice Statistics Bulletin, October 1985.

Despite these new developments, in practice criminal law still emphasizes interpersonal harms between strangers. Corporate harms and harms inflicted upon friends, lovers, and family are largely dealt with outside criminal law. Most, if not all, public efforts—legislatures defining crime; police investigating crime and apprehending suspects; prosecutors, defense attorneys, and courts adjudicating cases; and corrections administering punishment—are devoted to interpersonal stranger-to-stranger harms.[13] (See Table 2 and Figure 2.)

Crime, Tort, and Nonlegal Responses to Social Harms

Fair and effective social control calls for both grading social harms and establishing a measured response to them. Not all immoral, reprehensible,

Table 2   35 Million Victimizations Occurred in 1985 According to NCS Data

Personal Crimes	
Crimes of violence	
Rape	138,000
Robbery	985,000
Aggravated assault	1,605,000
Simple assault	3,094,000
Crimes of theft	
Larceny with contact	523,000
Larceny without contact	12,951,000
Household Crimes	
Burglary	5,594,000
Larceny	8,703,000
Motor vehicle theft	1,270,000
Total	34,864,000

SOURCE: *Criminal Victimization, 1985*, Bureau of Justice Statistics Bulletin, United States Justice Department, October 1986.

FIGURE 2   Victimization Rates are Well Below the Levels of 1979

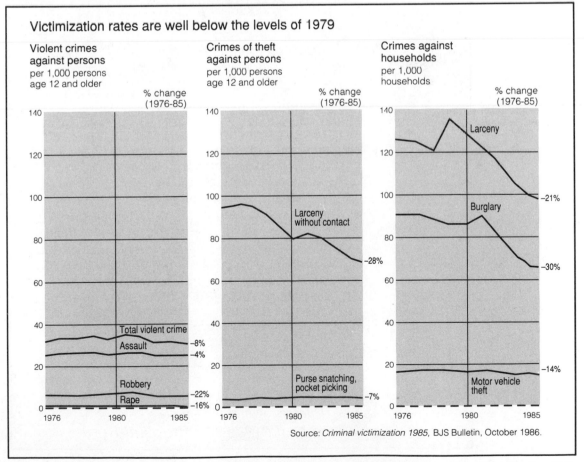

Victimization rates are well below the levels of 1979

Source: *Criminal victimization 1985*, BJS Bulletin, October 1986.

SOURCE: *Criminal Victimization, 1985*, Bureau of Justice Statistics Bulletin, United States Justice Department, October 1986.

Criminal Law Close-Up

Degrees of Felonies

Model Penal Code, Art. 6 § 6.01

Distribution of Offenses. The Model Code contains 141 crimes and violations, divided as follows: 50 felonies, 84 misdemeanors and petty misdemeanors, and 7 violations. The 50 felonies are distributed among the three classes authorized by this section in the following manner:

First-Degree Felonies

Offenses Involving Danger to the Person
Murder
Kidnapping
Rape

Offenses against Property
Robbery

Second-Degree Felonies

Offenses Involving Danger to the Person
Manslaughter
Causing or aiding suicide
Aggravated assault
Kidnapping
Rape
Deviate sexual intercourse by force

Offenses against Property
Arson
Causing catastrophe
Burglary
Robbery
Forgery

Offenses against the Family
Abortion

Third-Degree Felonies

Offenses Involving Danger to the Person
Negligent homicide
Aggravated assault
Terroristic threats
Felonious restraint
Interference with custody of children
Criminal coercion
Gross sexual imposition
Deviate sexual intercourse by imposition
Corruption of minors

Offenses against Property
Reckless burning or exploding
Causing catastrophe
Criminal mischief
Burglary
Theft
Forgery
Fraudulent destruction, removal or concealment
of recordable instruments
Credit card fraud

Offenses against the Family
Polygamy
Incest
Abortion
Self-abortion
Pretended abortion

Offenses against Public Administration
Bribery in official and political matters
Threats and other improper influence in official
and political matters
Perjury
Tampering
Witness or informant taking bribe
Tampering with public records or information
Hindering apprehension or prosecution
Aiding consummation of crime
Escape
Bail jumping, and so on

Offenses against Public Order and Decency
Riot
Promoting prostitution

and indecent conduct is criminal, nor should it be. Society draws lines between mere immoralities, **torts** (private wrongs), and crimes. A measured response calls for leaving some wrongs entirely to wrongdoers' consciences. Evil thoughts, such as Gretchen's wish for her professor's death in the hypothetical case at the beginning of the chapter, fall into this category.

Some conduct, while reprehensible, does not demand a criminal law response; private sanctions suffice. Appropriate private sanctions include suspending students who cheat on exams, exacting a penance for churchgoers who lie to their friends, and censuring peers who maliciously reject their lovers.

Some harms may call for legal redress, but not a criminal law response. Law is divided into two basic parts: civil law and criminal law. Civil law provides private and individual redress, by which injured persons sue those who have injured them. The formal title to a civil action reflects these individual and private qualities—for example, *Marconi* (**plaintiff,** or injured person who brings the suit) *v.* (versus or against) *Yu* (**defendant**, or person who is being sued). Torts or civil actions award damages. Damages are not fines; damages compensate injured individuals, and fines are penalties paid to the state. Although there are punitive damages in tort actions, the primary purpose of damages is to restore injured persons to their position before injury, not to punish defendants for hurting plaintiffs. Damages cover medical expenses, lost wages, disability, and sometimes pain and suffering.

Criminal law treats society as a whole as the injured party because harms to individuals and their property undermine social security, harmony, and well-being. The government prosecutes criminal defendants to protect the social interest in harmony, order, and security. The titles of criminal cases—*State v. Wenz, People v. Twohy, Commonwealth v. McDonald,* or *United States v. Storlie*—denote the societal nature of criminal prosecution. The stigma attached to criminal conviction and incarceration is far greater than that associated with losses in private lawsuits, even though the financial cost may be lower.

Civil actions and criminal prosecution are not mutually exclusive responses to social harms. States may prosecute, injured parties sue, friends censure, and conscience pang the same person, all for a single event. Most crimes are also torts: burglary is the tort of trespass, theft is the tort of conversion, and assault is both civil and criminal. Burglary victims can sue burglars for trespass, and states can prosecute burglars for burglary. The double jeopardy clause in the United States Constitution— "no person shall . . . be subject for the same offence to be twice put in jeopardy of life or limb"—does not prohibit tort and criminal actions for the same conduct. Tort actions do not put defendants in danger of "life or limb"; defendants in tort actions can only lose money.

Keep this range of alternative responses—personal and private sanctions, tort, and criminal prosecution—in mind throughout your study of criminal law. Rational law appropriately grades social harm among crimes, torts, and private condemnation. The most serious harms are designated crimes. Murder, rape, robbery, and burglary are obvious examples; they call for society's strongest response. Imprisonment and sometimes death, the consequences for committing serious crimes, evidence criminal law's gravity. Criminal law is society's last resort in dealing with social harms. Where something less will do, then common sense requires that something less be done. Thus, if friends' disapproval will make avaricious people less greedy, then making avarice a crime does not make sense.[14]

Felony, Misdemeanor, and Violation

Crimes are graded according to various standards. One standard focuses on the penalties imposed. From most severe to least severe penalties, the categories are capital felonies, felonies, gross misdemeanors, petty misdemeanors, and violations.

Capital felonies include those punishable by death, or in some jurisdictions by life imprisonment. The only remaining death penalty felony in America is aggravated murder. The broad distinction between felonies and misdemeanors is that felony convictions are punishable by incarceration in state prisons, while misdemeanors are punishable by incarceration in local jails or by fines. Noncapital **felonies** in most jurisdictions are punishable by imprisonment for between one year and life.[15] **Misdemeanors** are punishable by jail sentences, fines, or both. Although staggering disparity exists among jurisdictions, gross misdemeanors typically carry maximum penalties of close to one year, ordinary misdemeanors are usually punishable in the ninety-day range, and petty misdemeanors receive up to thirty days. In most jurisdictions, violations that are punishable by fines only—mainly traffic offenses—are not criminal convictions.[16]

One problem with grading is the large number of offenses and penalties that exist in most jurisdictions' criminal codes. Oregon, for instance, had 1,413 separate offenses and 466 different sentencing levels in 1960. Some maintain that this multitude of crimes and penalties creates "anarchy in sentencing." It also inhibits rational thinking about sentencing, builds sentencing disparities in practice, and prevents systematic sentencing reform. Furthermore, chaotic sentencing patterns undermine public confidence in, and respect for, the criminal law and its administration.[17]

One expert labels the multitude of offenses nonsense:

> The human mind cannot draw an infinite number of distinctions about crime. You can see the most serious crimes and the less serious ones, and you can see some gradations in between. And there may be some difference of opinion whether you can see three or four or six or seven categories. But there is a finite number that it is prudent to attempt to perceive.[18]

The Model Penal-Code divides crimes into three degrees of felonies, misdemeanors, petty misdemeanors, and violations.

Wrongs Mala in Se *and* Mala Prohibita

Another classification scheme divides crimes between inherently evil conduct, *malum in se*, and merely prohibited conduct, *malum prohibitum*. The serious felonies—murder, rape, robbery, burglary, arson, larceny— are wrong by their very nature. Killing another without justification or excuse, raping, robbing, burglarizing, and stealing would be wrong whether or not the law prohibited and punished them. On the other hand, the long list of violations that attend regulating modern urban industrial society, such as traffic codes, building codes, and health regulations, are not inherently bad; they are wrong only because the law declares that they are illegal. Society does not label drivers who make illegal left turns or park in no-parking zones bad, even though they have broken the law.

Criminal Law or Criminal Laws?

Throughout this chapter, the term criminal law appears in the singular. This is not strictly accurate because there are fifty state criminal codes, a federal criminal code, and innumerable city ordinances containing criminal provisions. Jurisdictions agree about the kinds of crimes; they all include murder, rape, robbery, burglary, arson, theft, and assault, for example. They vary greatly, however, as to what specific conduct these crimes encompass and the penalties they attach to them. For example, in some jurisdictions, the act of burglary requires actual unlawful breaking and entering; in others, it requires only entering without breaking; and in still others, it requires merely unlawfully remaining in a building entered lawfully, such as hiding until after closing time in a department store restroom lawfully entered during business hours.

Criminal penalties also differ widely among jurisdictions. Some states prescribe death for some convicted murderers; others prescribe life imprisonment. Hence, where murderers happen to kill their victims can determine whether those murderers will live or die. It also determines how they will die: by electrocution, lethal injection, the gas chamber, hanging, or even the firing squad.

The death penalty may illustrate the disparity in penalties most graphically, but it affects only a few individuals. Other examples affect more people. Some states subject those who engage in "open and notorious" sexual intercourse to possible fines; others make the mere fact of cohabitation outside marriage punishable by three to five years of imprisonment. Some states send individuals who possess even small quantities of marijuana to prison; others protect marijuana use at home as a constitutional right that the state cannot make a crime.

These disparities in crime and punishment among jurisdictions stem from several sources having to do with the type of community, the period in time, and the social problems of particular localities. In Texas, for example, stealing property valued between $750 and $20,000 is a third-degree felony. It is also a third-degree felony theft to steal crude petroleum oil "regardless of the value."[19]

≡ PERSPECTIVES AND THEORIES OF CRIMINAL LAW

The great disparity in crimes and punishments in American jurisdictions has generated several explanations. The theories and general perspectives outlined in this section represent some basic explanations for the nature and origins of American criminal law. Each perspective provides a different view of criminal law; often, ideology as much as objective analysis informs these perspectives. Nonetheless, they help to make sense of the principles, doctrines, and rules that the text addresses.

The Legal Perspective

The legal perspective focuses on crimes already defined in criminal law. It stresses three principles governing the definitions of crimes. First, only conduct that the law specifically prohibits is a crime; the Latin maxim *nullum crimen sine lege* expresses this principle. Second, the law must prescribe punishments for crimes; this principle is expressed in another Latin maxim, *nulla poena sine lege*. Third, the *ex post facto* clause in the United States Constitution forbids making conduct criminal retroactively; citizens must have advance notice that their conduct may be criminal.

According to the legal theory, therefore, crimes consist of whatever the law clearly defines and prohibits in advance, and for which it prescribes a punishment. Notice three important parts to this definition: A specific law must *define* the crime, *prohibit* the conduct, and *prescribe* a penalty for violating the prohibition. Excluded are harms that are not so defined and that are left to other social control devices, such as private lawsuits, peer group condemnation, and individual conscience. The following statute embodies all three elements of this definition of crime as criminal law.

> Whoever, in any matter within the jurisdiction of any department or agency of the United States knowingly and willfully falsifies, conceals or covers up by any trick, scheme, or device a material fact, or makes any false, fictitious or fraudulent statement or representations, or makes or uses any false writing or document knowing the same to contain any false, fictitious or fraudulent statement or entry, shall be fined not more than $10,000 or imprisoned not more than 5 years, or both.[20]

The law therefore explains how to define criminal conduct. It does not, however, explain *why* the law makes some conduct criminal and not other.

Political Perspectives

All crimes are political in the sense that the legislatures that enact criminal codes are not neutral bodies. Community standards and pressures also influence judges when they interpret the law. Statutes outline broad categories of conduct, permitting judges room in which to fit particular cases. In applying broad categories to individual cases, judges' own ideas and community standards influence their decisions; applying criminal law to individual cases is never a value-neutral exercise.[21]

Two opposing theories inform the political perspective. The democratic-consensus theory holds that elected representatives define crime. The criminal law expresses the will of the people through their elected representatives. Criminal law represents society's stand against conduct that violates its values and describes what punishments society will inflict on those who flout its values. This reading of the legislative process rests on two assumptions. First, politics and laws reflect consensus; people work together and compromise their individual interests so the state can work efficiently and effectively to satisfy the majority's collective needs. Second, criminal statutes embody the people's will. Recent research suggests that criminal codes express neither the will of the people nor the will of their legislators; instead, criminal justice professionals write most criminal laws.[22]

The conflict-elitist theory assumes that society operates according to conflict, not consensus. Interest groups, each ensconced in a bailiwick, come out fighting for their selfish interests—interests promoted only at the expense of other groups' interests. The most powerful interest group wins every major contest and then imposes its values on the rest of society. The rich and powerful use the legal system to protect their wealth and secure their dominant position of power. The ruling elite brandish the criminal laws as weapons to coerce weaker elements of society into submission.[23]

The conflict-elitist theory is considerably more complicated than this brief summary suggests. The criminal process is rarely so personal and purposely exploitative. Furthermore, the ruling elite often disagree over which criminal laws best serve their interests; nor do all laws by any means promote the dominant class's interests, at least not in the short term.[24]

Both political theories are true to some extent. Without question, much criminal law exhibits consensus. Most people, for example, agree that murder, rape, and robbery should be crimes; in fact, widespread agreement exists about the seriousness of more than one hundred crimes. Legislatures represent most people when they enact these statutes, as do judges when they apply them. Much criminal law, however, does not represent consensus. Historically, the powerful have used vagrancy laws to keep in their place certain elements of society—the poor, the unattached, and others on the fringes of "respectable" society. Vagrancy legislation therefore supports the claim of the conflict-elitist theory that criminal law results from the ruling class's effort to keep the "lower orders" in line. Similarly, recent ordinances against "aggressive panhandling," sleeping on park benches, and camping within city limits represent middle-class efforts to control the growing numbers of homeless people.[25]

Both theories are naive in some respects. The democratic-consensus theory fails to take into account the powerful effects that money, class, race, and other social factors have on both the political and the legal processes. Decisions throughout every stage of the criminal process— reporting crimes; arresting suspects; prosecuting, trying, and convicting defendants; and sentencing or releasing offenders—require judgments. The amount of freedom that victims, police officers, prosecutors, judges, or juries have in making these decisions is called **discretion**.[26]

A debate as old as law itself exists concerning how much leeway law officers and the public should have in enforcing criminal law. Good reasons support tempering the letter of the law with flexibility to do justice in individual cases. In his advice to new judges, Sir Nicholas Bacon, a sixteenth-century English lord chancellor, stressed that legislators could not possibly write statutes clear enough or complete enough to cover all cases. Because of this,

> the judge is not always so narrowly to weigh the words of the law, but sometimes in respect of the person, place, time and occasion or other circumstance to qualify and moderate such extremeties as the particular words of the law written may offer.

Sir Nicholas was no fool. Realizing that discretion was equally a means to evil as well as good, he warned his new judges accordingly:

> For albeit his knowledge be never so great and his discretion equal to it, if he will suffer them to be subject and governed by fear, by love, by malice or gain, then shall all his judgments be such as his affections be and not such as knowledge and discretion doth require.[27]

Class, wealth, power, and prejudice influence the operation of the law, perhaps even more than they influence its formulation. Selective enforcement has characterized the administration of criminal law from as early as the sixteenth century. For example, in one English town in the 1570s, poor, wandering people without family or other community ties were arrested more often, prosecuted more vigorously, and punished more harshly than were "respectable," established residents.[28]

Discretion creates a gap between what law books *say* and what law officers *do* because it is influenced by class, race, economics, and politics. Victims who never report crimes, suspects whom police could arrest but do not, arrested suspects whom prosecutors could charge but do not, and offenders who could be punished but are not—they, as much as any statute or universal moral code, determine the nature of criminal law. Commenting on social forces and their current impact upon the administration of justice, criminologist Donald R. Cressey concluded that

> [t]here is a great deal of evidence that current statutes calling for punishment of lawbreakers are not administered uniformly, or with celerity or certainty. This suggests that the actual reactions to crime are not really reflected in the laws governing the administration of justice. Statutes are so severe they must be mitigated in the interests of justice, and in order to maintain the consent of the governed. The following conclusions have been drawn by so many investigators that they may be accepted as factual:
> (1) Blacks are more likely to be arrested than whites.
> (2) Blacks are more likely to be indicted than whites.
> (3) Blacks have a higher conviction rate than whites.
> (4) Blacks are usually punished more severely than whites, but this is not true for all crimes, especially those in which a black person victimizes a black person.
> (5) Blacks are less likely to receive probation and suspended sentences.
> (6) Blacks receive pardons less often than do whites.
> (7) Blacks have less chance of having a death sentence commuted than do whites.[29]

The conflict-elitist theory, no more than the democratic-consensus theory, fully explains criminal law's origins and nature. Just as the democratic-consensus theory minimizes the pluralistic conflict of interests in society, the conflict-elitist theory ignores the very real core of values about which wide agreement exists. The same sixteenth-century English town that favored established members of the community over poor, wandering strangers also exhibited wide consensus on some values. Town officials adhered to the principle of legality in the administration of justice, enforcing procedural safeguards such as rules of proof requiring reliable witnesses to bring charges and testify in court against the accused. They also firmly recognized that despite the letter of the law prescribing death as a punishment for all felonies—from murder to the theft of a chicken—only murderers and some other violent criminals should hang for their crimes. This consensus persists today.

The Irrational Forces Perspective

Both the conflict-elitist and the democratic-consensus theories possess one major flaw. Neither allows room for chance or for the irrational or emotional elements in human behavior. Behaviorists cannot accurately predict what people will do; individuals rarely act strictly according to democratic-consensus and conflict-elitist theories. Police officers on patrol, for example, may arrest citizens as much because they are tired, irritable, or bored as because they revere law and order.

Irrational forces give rise to more than erratic individual decisions. They affect criminal codes as well, as sex psychopath laws illustrate. Shortly after World War II, a small spate of brutal sex crimes generated public fear. One ghoulish man dismembered and killed several young girls after sexually assaulting them. In response, most states hastily passed sex psychopath statutes, enabling states to confine potential sex offenders indefinitely without a trial. Some experts questioned the effectiveness, propriety, and constitutionality of these statutes. Critics argued that the statutes were unconstitutional because they denied procedural safeguards to those affected by them. Furthermore, they rested on shaky confidence in predictive capacity, since identifying in advance who will commit sex offenses is virtually impossible.[30]

Considerable empirical evidence since the passage of sex psychopath legislation has demonstrated its shortcomings. Despite this knowledge, the laws remain largely in force today. Fear and panic explain their enactment. Any complete explanation of the nature and origins of criminal law must account for the unpredictable, irrational, and chance elements in human behavior.[31]

The Historical Perspective

The great jurist Oliver Wendell Holmes maintained that in understanding the law, a page of history is worth volumes of logic. He meant that real life experience, not abstract reasoning, creates law. Most crimes originate in the circumstances of time and place. In addition to law's response to time and place, lawyers' reverence for precedent enhances history's strength. Imbued with the importance of precedent, lawyers approach change in the law cautiously. As a result, the present criminal law retains laws that were once believed necessary but are no longer relevant. One legal historian noted that the ghosts of the past stalk silently through our courts and legislatures, ruling our modern law by means of outdated and irrelevant but venerated ancient principles and doctrines. Thus, history plays a powerful part in maintaining, in today's criminal law, that which yesterday's social, economic, political, and philosophical considerations created.

The development of the modern law of theft illustrates the historical perspective on criminal law. In early times, larceny—forcibly taking and carrying away another's cattle—was the only theft. The original crime resembles the modern law of robbery—taking another's property by force or by threat of force (see chapter 11). Later, larceny came to include taking another's property by stealth (from which our word *stealing* descends). Getting another's property by trickery was not a crime; it was shrewd or clever. Neither was taking property left for safekeeping (examples would be taking a car left in an attended parking lot, or clothes left at a dry cleaner's); it was the owner's folly. Hence, only stealing or forcibly taking another's property constituted larceny; cheating was not a crime.[32]

Such was the law of theft in medieval England before commerce and industry had advanced beyond the most rudimentary stages. Most people lived in small communities, rarely dealt with strangers, and had few personal property items available to misappropriate. Furthermore, larceny was a felony, punishable by death. Judges were reluctant to expand the definition of larceny if doing so meant hanging more property offenders.

The complexities of modern life changed all this. More people, personal property, and strangers; a greater need to leave property and money with strangers; and less bloody punishments for larceny all led to alterations in theft law. Larceny came to include the theft of most movable personal property, such as jewels, furniture, clothing, and utensils. Then it was expanded to include the stealing of paper instruments representing ownership, such as checks, bank notes, and deeds. Finally, new crimes were created to embrace more misappropriations than the taking of property by force and stealth. Misappropriating money entrusted to another became embezzlement; tricking another out of money became false pretenses; both became felonies.

Theft law developed both to meet the needs of a complex society and to ameliorate a harsh criminal law; these historical facts explain theft law. In the past twenty years, thirty states have overcome this history by consolidating larceny, embezzlement, false pretenses, and other theft offenses into one crime. The remaining twenty states cling to a host of theft offenses of which the arcane larceny, embezzlement, fraud, and false pretenses are only the most common.

To cite one more example, the criminal law enacted in seventeenth-century New England to secure Puritan religious values, despite its clear irrelevance to modern behavior, remains surprisingly intact. For example, until their recent demise in the face of a constitutional assault on their validity, vagrancy statutes were based on the needs of sixteenth-century England. Yet, as recently as 1971, American vagrancy statutes copied their sixteenth-century English legal forebearers *verbatim*. Fornication, profanity, and curfews still remain on the books, although they are rarely enforced. The retention of these "morals" offenses demonstrates that the past rules the present in criminal law.[33]

The Ethical Core Theory

The historical, irrational, political, and legal theories all rest on the assumption that environment determines criminal law. Crime does not reflect permanent values; it is relative to time and place. In other words, irrational outbursts, ideology, social conditions, and other circumstances shape what society condemns in its criminal law. What one age considers evil, another may tolerate, even promote as good.

A fundamentally different approach assumes that crime represents universal, permanent, inherent evil in codified form. According to this theory, lawmaking, politics, history, and emotional outbursts do not affect this ethical core of criminal law.

The ethical core theory stems in part from religion. For example, some proponents maintain that criminal law reflects the Ten Commandments— "Thou shalt not kill" and "Thou shalt not steal" illustrate this. Other commandments, however, do not comport with modern criminal law. "Thou shalt not covet thy neighbor's wife" violates the basic principle that the state cannot punish thoughts unaccompanied by action. Moreover, consensus supports only some commandments; deep controversy surrounds others (see chapter 3).

The ethical core theory is not always articulated in strictly religious form; sometimes it is cast in general moral terms. For instance, criminal law manifests the universally high value placed on the rights to life, liberty, and property. Initially, the English common law enshrined these rights, then Americans entrenched them in constitutions, statutes, and court decisions. The ethical core theory strikes a responsive chord in those who accept that life, liberty, and property are widely valued, uniformly defined, and universally protected by law. But the theory does not fully match reality. The enormous body of regulatory offenses—traffic offenses, for example—do not fit the theory. Driving seventy-five miles per hour in a sixty-five mile-per-hour zone may violate the law, but few would call it inherently evil, violating some ethical core of values. On the other hand, although Gretchen's wish for her law professor's demise was evil (recall the earlier hypothetical case), the law does not make it a crime.

Some critics argue that equating values or notions of good and bad with crime, as the ethical core theory does, is both dangerous and improper. Professor Louis B. Schwartz criticized the statement of purpose in the Federal Criminal Justice Reform Act of 1973 on the ground that

> the bill injects a new, false, and dangerous notion that the criminal code "aims at the articulation of the nation's public values" and its vindication through punishment. A criminal code necessarily falls far short of expressing the nation's morality. Many things are evil or undesirable without being at all appropriate for imprisonment: lying, overcharging for goods and services, marital infidelity, lack of charity or patriotism. Nothing has been more widely recognized in modern criminal law scholarship than the danger of creating more evil by ill-considered use of the criminal law than is caused by the target misconduct. Accordingly, the failure to put something under the ban of the penal code is not an expression of a favorable "value" of the non-penalized behavior. It is a fatal confusion of values to see the Criminal Code as anything but a list of those most egregious misbehaviours, which

according to a broad community consensus, can be usefully dealt with by social force.[34]

Several of the hypothetical cases presented at the chapter's outset illustrate other weaknesses in the ethical core theory. For example, they demonstrate that the meaning of life, liberty, and property is by no means settled. Controversy surrounds whether looking at pornography, smoking marijuana, or even using heroin should be crimes. What constitutes life and property, not to mention liberty, whether these should be protected by the criminal law and to what extent—the answers vary from place to place and over time.

One major theme in criminal law is the need to reconcile stability with change. Changed conditions, new knowledge, and shifts in ideals all require that in the late twentieth century the law advance beyond what it was in the eighteenth or nineteenth centuries. Stealing a chicken was once a capital offense. Wives who scolded their husbands were considered criminals in the not-too-distant past. Most of the adult population in India can remember a time when a widow's burning herself to death after her husband died was considered the highest form of love. Recent cases involving people whose hearts are beating and who are still breathing but whose brains have stopped functioning have raised new questions about the meanings of life and death. A term has even been created to describe the new dilemma: brain death. Equally controversial is the heated debate over whether a fetus is property subject to contract law, and whether it is a life for purposes of criminal law (see chapter 8).

≡ SUMMARY

Criminal law has two main parts. The general part deals with principles and doctrines that apply to all crimes. These include the general principles of legality, harm, punishment, criminal liability and the doctrines governing the defenses to crime, complicity, and incomplete crimes. The special part refers to specific crimes and formulates rules—defining individual crimes and prescribing punishments for them—that apply the general principles and doctrines to particular crimes.

Criminal law is the formal, public response to *some* social harms. Formally, crime is a legal phenomenon—the law defines and prohibits it, and prescribes punishment for it. Criminal harms have a large range and occur under many conditions, but they do not by any means encompass all social harms. The range and conditions of social harms are illustrated in the hypothetical cases at the chapter's outset.

Crimes are classified and graded according to several schemes. First, they may be classified according to the social harm they cause: harm to persons, families, habitation, property, public order, and morals. Second, they can be arranged according to the legal procedures and consequences that attend them: felony, misdemeanor, and petty violations. Third, they may be divided between inherently evil conduct (*malum in se*) and merely illegal behavior (*malum prohibitum*). There is no single American criminal law. All states, the federal government, and most municipalities have their own criminal laws, which vary in how they define and punish particular crimes.

Several influences determine what harms constitute crime. The varied perspectives and theories of criminal law explain, and to some extent reflect, these influences. Legal theories emphasize the principles, doctrines, statutes, and court decisions that articulate, apply, and interpret them. Political theories stress how ideology, community values, power structure, and the processes of consensus and conflict resolution contribute to defining crime and enforcing criminal law. Historical theories stress the developmental forces that shape the content of criminal law. Historical theory demonstrates that experience and the felt needs of particular places and times, rather than some universal logic, determine what is criminal. Related to the historical theory is the theory of irrational forces, in which passion, chance, and other influences that are difficult to predict and organize put their mark on the criminal law.

All these theories rely on the environment to explain the nature and origins of criminal laws. Criminal law is determined by political, social, and psychological forces that change from time to time and from place to place. In striking contrast to these theories is the ethical core theory, which relies heavily on the idea that criminal law embodies not relative norms but absolute, universal values. The criminal law merely codifies moral principles that are good for all seasons and places. It assumes that murder, rape, robbery, and so on are inherently evil and authorizes state action to deal with the evils these embody.

As a result of the complicated nature of criminal law, the American Law Institute undertook a major effort to guide reform and improvement in criminal law. Its Model Penal Code, which covers every aspect of criminal law, sets out general purposes and principles of criminal law, classifies types of offenses, defines particular crimes, and creates a simplified structure of sentencing levels. Although only a model, it has influenced actual criminal law revision and reform in thirty-four states and more than one thousand judicial opinions in all jurisdictions. Much of the text compares the Model Penal Code provisions and the reasoning behind them with representative state statutes, the common law, and judicial opinions applying the codes and common law. Throughout the remainder of the book, the Model Penal Code's provisions are compared with the common law, representative state statutes, and court decisions applying them. As you read, evaluate in your own mind what a "rational" criminal code and accompanying definitions ought to include.

▬▬ QUESTIONS FOR REVIEW AND DISCUSSION

1. What is criminal law?
2. Does it make sense to speak of a criminal law? Or should we say criminal laws? Explain your answer.
3. With which theory of criminal law do you agree? Do you have your own theory?

4. What are the proper criteria for classifying and grading conduct that is made criminal? What types of conduct, if any, should be excluded from the criminal law? Why?
5. Define common law.
6. Distinguish between code jurisdictions and common jurisdictions. What are the strengths and weaknesses of each? Which, in your opinion, is better? Why?

≡ SUGGESTED READINGS

1. Jeffrey H. Reiman, *The Rich Get Richer and the Poor Get Prison*, 2d ed. (New York: Wiley, 1984), is a lively, forcefully argued presentation of the conflict-elitist theory.
2. Rollin M. Perkins and Ronald N. Boyce, *Criminal Law*, 3d ed. (Mineola, N.Y.: Foundation Press, 1982), is a law school hornbook (textbook) covering the general and special parts of criminal law. It is an excellent and up-to-date reference book for anyone who wishes to pursue in further detail topics suggested here.
3. George P. Fletcher, *Rethinking Criminal Law* (Boston: Little, Brown, 1978), is a provocative effort to write a comprehensive theory of criminal law. It is challenging and difficult but well worth the serious student's efforts.
4. Lawrence M. Friedman, *A History of American Law* (New York: Simon and Schuster, 1973), is an interesting history of American law written for the general public. Although it covers all law, sections on criminal law are clearly set apart and can be read separately without difficulty.
5. American Law Institute, *Model Penal Code* (Philadelphia: American Law Institute, 1954–61), and American Law Institute, *Model Penal Code and Commentaries* (Philadelphia: American Law Institute, 1980, 1985), are excellent works full of the latest scholarship, thoughtful analyses, and commentary by some of the leading judges, lawyers, and academics in American law. The works present, in imposing fashion, the democratic-consensus approach to criminal law, but their value stretches well beyond. They are the most comprehensive coverage of American criminal law in existence.
6. Lawrence M. Friedman, *American Law* (New York: Norton, 1984), is a general introduction to American law, filled with anecdotes and discussion intended to explain the nature and processes of American law to the general reader. It is a vivid picture of American law and its role in American life, well worth the time spent reading it.
7. Jerome Hall, *General Principles of Criminal Law*, 2d ed., (Indianapolis: Bobbs-Merrill, 1960) covers the general principles and doctrines of criminal law, arranging them into a theory of criminal law. This text is a classic in the literature of criminal law.
8. Leo Katz, *Bad Acts and Guilty Minds* (Chicago: University of Chicago, 1987), presents an interesting, thought-provoking look at the philoso-

phy of criminal law. It focuses on the basic problems of criminal law, using real cases from several countries, many challenging hypothetical cases, and critical suggestions.

═══ NOTES

1. Joel Feinberg, *Harm to Others* (New York: Oxford University Press, 1984), chapter 1, elaborates on the concept of harm and its relation to the criminal law.

2. A useful survey of the Model Penal Code written by its leading light can be found in Herbert Wechsler, "The Model Penal Code and the Codification of American Criminal Law," Roger Hood, ed., *Crime, Criminology, and Public Policy* (London: Heineman, 1974), pp. 419–68; American Law Institute, *Model Penal Code*, tentative drafts 1–13 (Philadelphia: American Law Institute, 1954–61).

3. Jerome Hall, *General Principles of Criminal Law*, 2d ed. (Indianapolis: Bobbs-Merrill, 1960), pp. 17–19.

4. Blackstone's *Commentaries*, book IV.

5. Wayne R. LaFave and Austin W. Scott, Jr., *Criminal Law* (St. Paul: West Publishing Co., 1972), p. 59.

6. This proposed code and Jefferson's fascinating notes about it can be found in Julian P. Bond, ed., *The Papers of Thomas Jefferson*, vol. 2 (Princeton: Princeton University Press, 1950). A recent informative discussion about Jefferson's code is Kathryn Preyer, "Crime, the Criminal Law and Reform in Post-Revolutionary Virginia," *Law and History Review*, 1(1983):53–85.

7. 11 U.S. (7 Cranch) 32, 3L.Ed. 259 (1812).

8. American Law Institute, *Model Penal Code and Commentaries*, part I, §§1.01 to 2.13 (Philadelphia: American Law Institute, 1985), p. 77.

9. §13A-1-4, Code of Alabama 1975.

10. Wayne R. Lave and Austin Scott, Jr., *Criminal Law* (St. Paul: West Publishing Co., 1972), pp. 62–63.

11. *State v. McFeely*, 25 N.J. Misc. 303, 52 A.2d 823 Quar.Sess. 1947).

12. See, for example, "Business and the Law: Criminal Onus Executives," *New York Times* (March 5, 1985); "Can a Corporation Commit Murder?" *New York Times* (May 19, 1985).

13. For useful introductions to this problem, see Jeffrey H. Reiman, *The Rich Get Richer and the Poor Get Prison*, 2d ed. (New York: Wiley, 1984), and William Chambliss and Robert Seidman, *Law, Order, and Power*, chapter 7.

14. For two excellent discussions of rational grading, see American Law Institute, *Model Penal Code and Commentaries*, vol. 1 (Philadelphia: American Law Institute, 1985), pp. 1–30, and for the general reader, Norval Morris and Gordon Hawkins, *The Honest Politician's Guide to Crime Control* (Chicago: University of Chicago Press, 1969), chapter 1.

15. For an excellent discussion of capital crimes and punishment, see Hugo Adam Bedau, ed., *The Death Penalty in America*, 3d ed. (New York: Oxford University Press, 1982).

16. For a thorough summary of the wide disparity in existing misdemeanor classification, see American Law Institute, *Model Penal Code and Commentaries* (Philadelphia: American Law Institute, 1985), pp. 1–30.

17. American Law Institute, *Model Penal Code and Commentaries*, vol. 3 (Philadelphia: American Law Institute, 1985), part I, pp. 34–38.

18. Ibid, p. 34.

19. *Texas Penal Code*, § 31.03(5) (a)(i) (St. Paul: West Publishing Co., 1988).

20. U.S.C.A., Title 18, § 1001 (as amended to May 1, 1988).

21. An excellent discussion of some of these matters is David W. Neubauer, *Criminal Justice in Middle America* (Morristown, NJ: General Learning Press, 1974), pp. 86–105. For an earlier but provocative analysis, see Jerome Frank, *Courts on Trial: Myth and Reality in American Justice* (Princeton: Princeton University Press, 1949), chapter 14.

22. This conclusion is based on Timothy Lenz's doctoral dissertation research on criminal justice policy formulation in the Department of Political Science, University of Minnesota, as yet not complete.

23. George B. Vold and Thomas J. Bernard, *Theoretical Criminology*, 3d ed. (New York: Oxford University Press, 1986); chapters 14–16 develop these points fully.

24. For good introductions to this theory, see Richard Quinney, *Criminology*, 2d ed. (Boston: Little, Brown, 1979), pp. 120–25, and William Chambliss and Robert Seidman, *Law, Order, and Power*, 2d ed. (Reading, Mass.: Addison-Wesley, 1982), pp. 171–207.

25. Peter Rossi et al., "The Seriousness of Crimes: Normative Structure and Individual Differences," *American Sociological Review*, 39 (1974): 224–37; William J. Chambliss, "The Law of Vagrancy," in *Criminal Law in Action*, 2d ed., edited by William J. Chambliss (New York: Macmillan, 1984), pp. 33–42.

26. The definitive work on discretion is Kenneth Culp Davis, *Discretionary Justice* (Baton Rouge, La.: Louisiana State University Press, 1969).

27. Sir Nicholas Bacon, quoted in Joel Samaha, "Hanging for Felony," *Historical Journal* (1979): 775.

28. Ibid, pp. 769–71.

29. Edwin H. Sutherland and Donald R. Cressey, *Criminology*, 10th ed. rev. (Philadelphia: Lippincott, 1978), pp. 333–34.

30. Edwin Sutherland, "The Sexual Psychopath Laws," *Journal of Criminal Law, Criminology, and Police Science*, 40 (1950): 543–54.

31. Francis A. Allen, *The Borderland of Criminal Justice* (Chicago: University of Chicago Press, 1964), p. 15.

32. This section is based on Perkins and Boyce, *Criminal Law*, pp. 289–92, and American Law Institute, *Model Penal Code and Commentaries*, vol. 2 (Philadelphia: American Law Institute, 1980), pp. 128–30. For a full and interesting treatment of the relationship of history and society to theft, see Jerome Hall, *Theft, Law, and Society* (Indianapolis: Bobbs-Merrill, 1952).

33. Joel Samaha, "John Winthrop and the Criminal Law," *William Mitchell Law Review* (1989):217.

34. Quoted in Sanford Kadish and Manfred Paulson, *Criminal Law and Its Processes*, 3d ed. rev. (Boston and Toronto: Little, Brown, 1975), p. 40.

Chapter Two

The General Principles of Criminal Law

CHAPTER OUTLINE

CHAPTER MAIN POINTS

1. General principles are overarching norms that apply to all crimes.

2. The principle of legality requires that criminal laws must proscribe conduct and prescribe punishments clearly and in advance of prosecution.

3. The *ex post facto* prohibition protects against both making conduct criminal after it occurs and arbitrary government power.

4. Vague laws violate the Fourteenth Amendment.

5. Equal protection prohibits only classifications based upon unacceptable criteria, such as race.

6. The right to privacy is based on the idea that citizens in free societies should be "left alone" from government interference.

7. The principle of punishment requires both that it rest upon proper purposes and that it be proportionate to the crime committed.

CHAPTER KEY TERMS

criminal punishment special meaning that criminal law gives to punishment, containing four elements: (1) pain or other unpleasant consequence (2) inflicted for breaking a specific law and (3) administered by the state (4) for the primary purpose of hurting criminal offenders, not helping them.

culpability blameworthiness, or the notion that someone can be blamed and therefore punished for committing crimes.

ex post facto **laws** laws passed after the occurrence of the conduct constituting the crime.

general deterrence the utilitarian purpose of punishment; aims to prevent crime by threatening would-be lawbreakers with punishment.

incapacitation sometimes called special deterrence; aims to prevent crime by restraint, mutilation, and even death.

material elements the parts of a crime that prosecutors must prove beyond a reasonable doubt if they are to convict defendants.

nulla poena sine lege the principle that no punishment is administered without specific authority in law.

nullum crimen sine lege the principle that nothing is a crime without a specific law defining it as such.

opinion the reasons given for an appellate court decision.

principle of legality the assumption that government cannot punish citizens without specific laws forewarning that particular conduct will be punished in a particular manner.

proportionality the nature and amount of punishment in relation to the person and conduct punished.

rehabilitation the prevention of crime by altering criminals' behavior, usually by "treating" offenders instead of punishing them.

retribution the paying back of criminals for the harm they have done; sometimes called just deserts.

≡ INTRODUCTION

The general principles in criminal law apply to all crimes. Some principles govern the **material elements** in crime—the physical elements, mental element, concurrence, causation, and resulting harm. These general principles of criminal liability are discussed in chapter 3. Some of the principles that overarch the material elements in criminal liability are discussed here. The overarching principles include legality and punishment.

☰ THE PRINCIPLE OF LEGALITY

The essence of the **principle of legality** is that the government cannot punish citizens without specific laws forewarning citizens that particular conduct will be punished in a particular manner. Legality encompasses all the following: (1) *nullum crimen sine lege* (the principle that nothing is a crime without a specific law defining it as such); (2) the constitutional void-for-vagueness principle; (3) the constitutional prohibition against **ex post facto laws** (laws passed after the occurrence of the conduct); and (4) *nulla poena sine lege* (the principle that no punishment is administered without specific authority in law). Because it establishes norms embracing both crime and punishment, the principle of legality is the most fundamental principle in criminal law.

The United States Constitution's prohibitions against *ex post facto* laws and vagueness in criminal statutes embody most of the principle of legality. These constitutional principles reflect the eighteenth-century Enlightenment's philosophical commitment to the rule of law, particularly to codification. However, the basic idea that the law must define the crime and penalty in advance enjoys a long history. The ancient Greeks prohibited *ex post facto* laws, and the Roman Civil Law read: ". . . a penalty is not inflicted unless it is expressly imposed by law, or by some other authority." In the fierce struggle between king and Parliament in seventeenth-century England, the great jurist Lord Edward Coke said:

> [I]t is against the law, that men should be committed [to prison], and no cause shewed . . . it is not I, Edward Coke, that speaks it, but the Records that speak it; we have a national appropriate Law to this nation . . ."[1]

The Ex Post Facto *Prohibition*

The Constitution's framers considered the *ex post facto* principle so important that they wrote it into the main body of the Constitution several years before they added most constitutional provisions relating to the criminal law in the Bill of Rights. According to the Supreme Court, which addressed the question as early as 1798, *ex post facto* prohibits all of the following: (1) laws that make a crime of and punish conduct done before their passage; (2) laws that aggravate a crime after it was committed; (3) laws that increase the punishment for a specific crime after the crime was committed; and (4) laws that alter the rules of evidence to convict a defendant, receiving less or different testimony than the law required when the offense was committed.[2]

The *ex post facto* prohibition has two major goals: to give fair warning to citizens and to prevent arbitrary action by government. Since ignorance of the law does not excuse criminal liability, guarding against arbitrary government action is the more important purpose. The *ex post facto* prohibition does not apply to changes in the law that *help* defendants. For example, if a law reduces from first- to second-degree murder killings that occur during the commission of other felonies, that law can be retroactive because it benefits defendants. Similarly, laws that reduce the penalty for particular crimes can have retroactive effect. For example, a defendant who committed a capital murder before the enactment of a statute abolishing capital punishment cannot suffer the death penalty. Some statutes have "savings clauses" specifically excluding retroactivity. In these cases, reductions in crime and punishment do not benefit defendants; the law that was in effect when the crime was committed governs.[3]

Void for Vagueness

The Constitution does not have a clause like the *ex post facto* clause to specifically prohibit vague laws. The Supreme Court, however, has ruled that vague laws violate the Fifth and Fourteenth Amendments, which prohibit the federal government and the states, respectively, from denying citizens life, liberty, or property without due process of law.

> [A] statute which either forbids or requires the doing of an act in terms so vague that men of common intelligence must necessarily guess at its meaning and differ as to its application, violates the first essential of due process of law.[4]

The principle applies to both criminal statutes and common-law crimes. Vagueness may refer to the conduct prescribed by the statute, the persons within the statute's scope, or the punishment imposed.

Vague laws do not give fair warning to defendants; hence, they create the opportunity for the government to abuse its power.

> No one may be required at peril of life, liberty or property to speculate as to the meaning of penal statutes. All are entitled to be informed as to what the State commands or forbids.[5]

What constitutes a law vague enough to violate the due process clause is difficult to determine. Words are not precise like numbers; they cannot define as clearly. Furthermore, lawmakers cannot foresee all the variations that might arise under statutes; some ambiguity inheres in all laws. As a result, there is no litmus test to determine when a law is too vague.

The standard for vagueness is that a law is not unconstitutionally vague if reasonable persons know when they are approaching the line—admittedly not clearly drawn—between criminal and noncriminal. For example, statutes prohibiting reckless driving do not define reckless, but reasonable people know that exceeding the speed limits approaches the line between careful and reckless.

The court in *Metzger v. State* addressed the problem of vagueness.

CASE

Was the Statute "Vague?"

State v. Metzger
211 Neb. 593, 319 N.W.2d 459 (1982)

[Chief Justice Krivosha delivered the opinion.]

FACTS

The appellant, Douglas E. Metzger, was convicted in the municipal court of Lincoln, Nebraska, of violating § 9.52.100 of the Lincoln Municipal Code. The judgment was affirmed by the District Court for Lancaster County, Nebraska, and Metzger has appealed to this court. . . . [W]e reverse and dismiss. . . .

Metzger lived in a garden-level apartment. . . . A large window in the apartment faces a parking lot which is situated on the north side of the apartment building. At about 7:45 A.M., on April 30, 1981, another resident of the apartment, while parking his automobile in a space directly in front of Metzger's apartment window, observed Metzger standing naked with his arms at his sides in his apartment window for a period of 5 seconds. The resident testified that he saw Metzger's body from the thighs on up.

The resident called the police department and two officers arrived at the apartment at about 8 A.M. The officers testified that they observed Metzger standing in front of the window eating a bowl of cereal. They testified that Metzger was standing within a foot of the window and his nude body, from the mid-thigh on up, was visible.

The pertinent portion of § 9.52.100 . . . under which Metzger was charged, provides as follows: "It shall be unlawful for any person within the City of Lincoln . . . to commit any indecent, immodest or filthy act in the presence of any person, or in such a situation that persons passing might ordinarily see the same." . . .

OPINION

The . . . basic issue presented to us by this appeal is whether the ordinance, as drafted, is so vague as to be unconstitutional. We believe that it is. There is no argument that a violation of the municipal ordinance in question is a criminal act. Since the ordinance in question is criminal in nature, it is a fundamental requirement of due process of law that such criminal ordinance be reasonably clear and definite. Moreover, a crime must be defined with sufficient definiteness and there must be ascertainable standards of guilt to inform those subject thereto as to what conduct will render them liable to punishment thereunder. The dividing line between what is lawful and unlawful cannot be left to conjecture. A citizen cannot be held to answer charges based upon penal statutes whose mandates are so uncertain that they will reasonably admit of different constructions. A criminal statute cannot rest upon uncertain foundation. The crime and the elements constituting it must be so clearly expressed that the ordinary person can intelligently choose in advance what course it is lawful for him to pursue. . . .

The ordinance in question makes it unlawful for anyone to commit any "indecent, immodest or filthy act." We know of no way in which the standards required of a criminal act can be met in those broad, general terms. There may be those few who believe persons of opposite sex holding hands in public are immodest, and certainly more who might believe that kissing in public is immodest. Yet, the fact that it is immodest does not thereby make it illegal, absent some requirement related to the health, safety, or welfare of the community. The dividing line between what is lawful and what is unlawful in terms of "indecent," "immodest," or "filthy," is simply too broad to satisfy the constitutional requirements of due process. Both lawful and unlawful acts can be embraced within such broad definitions. That cannot be permitted. One is not able to determine in advance what is lawful and what is unlawful.

Reversed and dismissed.

Boslaugh, Justice, Dissenting.

DISSENT

The ordinance in question prohibits indecent acts, immodest acts, *or* filthy acts in the presence of any person. Although the ordinance may be too broad in some respects, it would seem the defendant in this case lacks standing to raise the issue. The exhibition of his genitals under the circumstances of this case was, clearly, an indecent act.

Statutes and ordinances prohibiting indecent exposure generally have been held valid. I do not subscribe to the view that it is only "possible" that such conduct may be prohibited by statute or ordinance.

CASE DISCUSSION

Does the dissent have a point when he argues that displaying genitals when others can see them is clearly an indecent act? Or does the ordinance refer to intentionally exposing genitals, or "flashing"? Should courts guess what legislatures mean, or should they construe the words as narrowly as possible, or strike down laws, as this court did? Explain.

Equal Protection of the Laws

The Fourteenth Amendment to the United States Constitution prohibits states from denying citizens the equal protection of the laws. This does not mean that the government must treat all citizens exactly alike. The common law and numerous statutes classify (that is, single out for special treatment) certain persons and conduct. For example, statutes in some jurisdictions classify embezzlement by public officials as a more serious crime than embezzlement by private citizens; virtually every state labels premeditated killings as more heinous than negligent homicides; and several states punish habitual offenders more severely than first-time offenders. Hence, the criminal law distinguishes according to occupation, state of mind, and type of person. Other statutes *exempt* certain conduct or groups from criminal liability. For example, Sunday closing laws typically exempt from coverage small businesses or sales of necessary items. All these and many more classifications comport with the equal protection clause. The clause does not prohibit distinctions, but it forbids distinguishing on unacceptable criteria. Hence, all criminal laws based on racial distinctions offend the equal protection clause, as do most gender and class distinctions.

The Supreme Court upholds most classification schemes embodied in the states' criminal laws, striking down such laws only when the classification has no "reasonable basis." Furthermore, defendants who challenge a classification must prove that the classification rests on no reasonable basis. Referring to this deference to state laws and the heavy burden of proof placed on defendants who challenge their equality of protection, the Court calls the equal protection challenge "the usual last resort of constitutional arguments."[6]

In *Michael M. v. Superior Court of Sonoma County*, the Supreme Court addressed a classification based on gender in California's statutory rape law.

CASE

Was the Gender Classification "Reasonable?"

Michael M. v. Superior Court of Sonoma County

450 U.S. 464, 101 S.Ct. 1200, 67 L.Ed.2d 437 (1981)

[Justice Rehnquist announced the judgment of the Court and delivered an opinion, in which Chief Justice Burger, Justice Stewart, and Justice Powell joined. Justice Blackmun filed an opinion concurring in the judgment. Justice Brennan filed a dissenting opinion, in which justices White and Marshall joined. Justice Stevens filed a dissenting opinion.]

FACTS

. . . In July 1978, a complaint was filed in the Municipal Court of Sonoma County, Cal., alleging that petitioner, then a 17½-year-old male, had had unlawful sexual intercourse with a female under the age of 18, in violation of § 261.5 [California's statutory rape law, which defines unlawful sexual intercourse as "an act of sexual intercourse accomplished with a female not the wife of the perpetrator, where the female is under the age of 18 years"]. The evidence adduced at a preliminary hearing showed that at approximately midnight on June 3, 1978, petitioner and two friends approached Sharon, a 16½-year-old female, and her sister as they waited at a bus stop. Petitioner and Sharon, who had already been drinking, moved away from the others and began to kiss. After being struck in the face for rebuffing petitioner's initial advances, Sharon submitted to sexual intercourse with petitioner. Prior to trial, petitioner sought to set aside the information on both state and federal constitutional grounds, asserting that § 261.5 unlawfully discriminated on the basis of gender. The trial court and the California Court of Appeal denied petitioner's request for relief and petitioner sought review in the Supreme Court of California.

The Supreme Court held that [the compelling state interest in reducing the "tragic human costs of illegitimate teenage pregnancies" justified the discrimination in § 261.5 in which "only females may be victims, and only males may violate the section"]. . . . For the reasons stated below, we affirm the judgment of the California Supreme Court. . . .

OPINION

A legislature may not "make overbroad generalizations based on sex which are entirely unrelated to any differences between men and women or which demean the ability of social status of the affected class." But because the Equal Protection Clause does not "demand that a statute necessarily apply equally to all persons" or require "things which are different in fact . . . to be treated in law as though they were the same," this Court has consistently upheld statutes where the gender classification is not invidious, but rather realistically reflects the fact that the sexes are not similarly situated in similar circumstances. As the Court has stated, a legislature may "provide for the special problems of women."

Applying these principles to this case, the fact that the California Legislature criminalized the act of illicit sexual intercourse with a minor female is a sure indication of its intent or purpose to discourage the conduct. . . .

The justification for the statute offered by the State, and accepted by the Supreme Court of California, is that the legislature sought to prevent illegitimate teenage pregnancies. . . .

We are satisfied not only that the prevention of illegitimate pregnancy is at least one of the "purposes" of the statute, but also that the

State has a strong interest in preventing such pregnancies, which have increased dramatically over the last two decades, have significant social, medical, and economic consequences for both the mother and her child, and the State. Of particular concern to the State is that approximately half of all teenage pregnancies end in abortion. And of those children who are born, their illegitimacy makes them likely candidates to become wards of the State.

We need not be medical doctors to discern that young men and young women are not similarly situated with respect to the problems and risks of sexual intercourse. Only the women may become pregnant, and they suffer disproportionately the profound physical, emotional, and psychological consequences of sexual activity. The statute at issue here protects women from sexual intercourse at an age when those consequences are particularly severe.

The question boils down to whether a State may attack the problem of sexual intercourse and teenage pregnancy directly by prohibiting a male from having sexual intercourse with a minor female. We hold that such a statute is sufficiently related to the State's objectives to pass constitutional muster.

Because virtually all of the significant harmful and inescapably identifiable consequences of teenage pregnancy fall on the young female, a legislature acts well within its authority when it elects to punish only the participant who, by nature, suffers few of the consequences of his conduct. . . .

Accordingly the judgment of the California Supreme Court is affirmed. . . . Justice Stevens, dissenting.

DISSENT

Local custom and belief—rather than statutory laws of venerable but doubtful ancestry—will determine the volume of sexual activity among unmarried teenagers. The empirical evidence cited by the plurality demonstrates the futility of the notion that a statutory prohibition will significantly affect the volume of that activity or provide a meaningful solution to the problems created by it. Nevertheless, as a matter of constitutional power, . . . I would have no doubt about the validity of a state law prohibiting all unmarried teenagers from engaging in sexual intercourse. The societal interests in reducing the incidence of venereal disease and teenage pregnancy are sufficient, in my judgment, to justify a prohibition of conduct that increases the risk of these harms.

My conclusion that a nondiscriminatory prohibition would be constitutional does not help me answer the question whether a prohibition applicable to only half the joint participants in the risk-creating conduct is also valid. . . .

In my judgment, the fact that a class of persons is especially vulnerable to a risk that a statute is designed to avoid is a reason for making a statute applicable to that class. The argument that a special need for protection provides a rational explanation for an exemption is one I simply do not comprehend.

In this case, the fact that a female confronts a greater risk of harm than a male is a reason for applying the prohibition to her—not a reason for granting her a license to use her own judgment on whether or not to assume the risk. Surely, if we examine the problem from the point of view of society's interest in preventing the risk-creating conduct from occurring at all, it is irrational to exempt 50% of the potential violators. . . .

If pregnancy or some other special harm is suffered by one of the two participants in the prohibited act, that special harm no doubt would constitute a legitimate mitigating factor in deciding what, if any, punishment might be appropriate in a given case. But from the standpoint of fashioning a general preventive rule—or, indeed, in determining appropriate punishment when neither party in fact has suffered any special harm—I regard a total exemption for the members of the more endangered class as utterly irrational. . . .

[E]ven if my logic is faulty and there actually is some speculative basis for treating equally guilty males and females differently, I still believe that any such speculative justification would be outweighed by the paramount interest in evenhanded enforcement of the law. A rule that authorizes punishment for only one of two equally guilty wrongdoers violates the essence of the constitutional requirement that the sovereign must govern impartially.

I respectfully dissent.

CASE DISCUSSION

Do you agree that distinguishing between men and women in statutory rape cases is a reasonable device to protect against teenage pregnancies? Or does the classification deny men the equal protection of the laws?

The Right to Privacy

The Bill of Rights to the United States Constitution and bills of rights in state constitutions limit the administration of criminal justice through prohibitions against self-incrimination, double jeopardy, unreasonable search and seizure, and so on. The Bill of Rights also imposes limitations on the substantive criminal law; in particular, the First Amendment prohibits state infringement upon free speech, association, and religion. Laws that make crimes out of practicing these guarantees cannot stand.

A right not specifically mentioned in the Bill of Rights to the United States Constitution but sometimes utilized in limiting the reach of the criminal law is the right to privacy. The constitutional right to privacy arises out of an amalgam of the First Amendment right to free expression and association, and the Fourth Amendment right to be secure in one's person, house, and effects. These amendments protect "against all governmental invasions of the sanctity of a man's home and the privacies of life." The right to privacy reflects the notion that a free society guarantees that its citizens will be "left alone," particularly by the government.

The right to privacy applies with greatest force to activities in private homes related to intimate family relationships. Hence, in the leading case on the point, *Griswold v. Connecticut*, the Court struck down a statute making it a crime for married couples to use contraceptives. Justice Douglas, writing for the majority, said that the prohibition against contraceptives

> operates directly on an intimate relation of husband and wife. . . . The present case . . . concerns a relationship lying within the zone of privacy created by several different fundamental constitutional guarantees. And it concerns a law which, in forbidding the *use* of contraceptives rather than regulating their manufacture or sale, seeks to achieve its goals by means having a maximum destructive impact upon that relationship. Such a law cannot stand . . .[7]

Four years later, the Supreme Court struck down a statute that made it a crime to possess pornography within the privacy of a home. It appeared to some that the Court would lock the criminal law out of private homes, essentially ruling that whatever citizens do within their own homes is not the law's business. The Court has not, however, so restricted the criminal law.

In 1986, the Court upheld Georgia's sodomy statute against a challenge that what consenting adult homosexuals do in the privacy of their own homes cannot be made a crime by the state. In *Bowers v. Hardwick*, the Atlanta police followed Hardwick home. They entered Hardwick's home with a houseguest's permission but without Hardwick's knowledge. The police surprised Hardwick in his bedroom, where he was engaged in sodomy with another adult man. Hardwick argued that

> the Georgia statute violated [Hardwick's] fundamental rights because his homosexual activity is a private and intimate association that is beyond the reach of state regulation by reason of the Ninth Amendment [The enumeration . . . of certain rights shall not be construed to deny or disparage others retained by the people.] and the Due Process Clause of the Fourteenth Amendment.[8]

The Court held that the right to privacy did not prevent states from making homosexual conduct criminal, even within the privacy of homes. (See case excerpt in Chapter 12.)

Some state constitutions specifically protect the right of privacy. For example, the Alaska Constitution provides that

> [t]he right of the people to privacy is recognized and shall not be infringed.[9]

In *Ravin v. State*, the Alaska Supreme Court addressed the question of whether Alaska's statute making the possession of marijuana a crime applied to possession within the privacy of the home.

CASE

Does He Have a "Right" to Possess Marijuana?

Ravin v. State

537 P.2d 494 (Alaska 1975)

[Chief Justice Rabinowitz delivered the opinion.]

FACTS

. . . Ravin was arrested . . . and charged with violating AS 17.12.010 [which provides] . . . it is unlawful for a person to manufacture, compound, counterfeit, possess, have under his control, sell, prescribe, administer, dispose, barter, supply or distribute in any manner, a depressant, hallucinogenic or stimulant drug. [Section 17.12.150 defines marijuana as such a drug.] Before trial Ravin attacked the constitutionality of . . . [the statute] by a motion to dismiss in which he asserted that the State had violated his right of privacy under both the federal and Alaska constitutions. . . . Ravin's motion to dismiss was denied. . . . The superior court then granted review and after affirmance by the superior court, we, in turn, granted Ravin's petition for review from the superior court's affirmance. . . .

OPINION

. . . Alaska Constitution, Article I, section 22 reads:

> The right of the people to privacy is recognized and shall not be infringed.

The legislature shall implement this section. The effect of this amendment is to place privacy among the specifically enumerated rights in Alaska's constitution. But this fact does not, in and of itself, yield answers concerning what scope should be accorded to this right of privacy. We have suggested that the right to privacy may afford less than absolute protection to "the ingestion of food, beverages or other substances." For any such protection must be limited by the legitimate needs of the state to protect the health and welfare of its citizens. . . .

This leads us to a more detailed examination of the right to privacy and the relevancy of where the right is exercised. At one end of the scale of the scope of the right to privacy is possession or ingestion in the individual's home. If there is any area of human activity to which a right to privacy pertains more than any other, it is the home. . . .

In Alaska we have also recognized the distinctive nature of the home as a place where the individual's privacy receives special protection. . . . The privacy amendment to the Alaska Constitution was intended to give recognition and protection to the home. Such a reading is consonant with the character of life in Alaska. Our territory and now state has traditionally been the home of people who prize their individuality and who have chosen to settle or to continue living here in order to achieve a measure of control over their own life-styles which is now virtually unattainable in many of our sister states.

The home, then, carries with it associations and meanings which make it particularly important as the situs of privacy. Privacy in the home is a fundamental right. . . . We do not mean by this that a person may do anything at anytime as long as the activity takes place within a person's home. There are two important limitations to this facet of the right to privacy. First, we agree with the Supreme Court of the United States, which has strictly limited the . . . guarantee to possession for purely private, noncommercial use in the home. And secondly, we think this right must yield when it interferes in a serious manner with the health, safety, rights and privileges of others or with the public welfare. No one has an absolute right to do things in the privacy of his own home which will affect himself or others adversely. . . .

Thus, we conclude that the citizens of the State of Alaska have a basic right to privacy in their homes under Alaska's constitution. This right to privacy would encompass the possession and ingestion of substances such as marijuana in a purely personal, non-commerical context in the home unless the state can meet its substantial burden and show that proscription of possession of marijuana in the home is supportable by achievement of a legitimate state interest. . . .

[The court surveyed a wide range of empirical and medical findings regarding the economic, medical, and social costs arising out of marijuana possession and use.]

The state is under no obligation to allow otherwise "private" activity which will result in numbers of people becoming public charges or otherwise burdening public welfare. But we do not find that such a situation exists today regarding marijuana. It appears that effects of marijuana on the individual are not serious enough to justify widespread concern, at least as compared with the far more dangerous effects of alcohol, barbiturates and amphetamines. Moreover, the current patterns of use in the United States are not such as would warrant concern that in the future consumption patterns are likely to change. . . .

Thus we conclude that no adequate justification for the state's intrusion into the citizen's right to privacy by its prohibition of possession of marijuana by an adult for personal consumption in the home has been shown. The privacy of the individual's home cannot be breached absent a persuasive showing of a close and substantial relationship of the intrusion to a legitimate governmental interest. Here, mere scientific doubts will not suffice. The state must demonstrate a need based on proof that the public health or welfare will in fact suffer if the controls are not applied. . . .

> [W]e wish to make clear that we do not mean to condone the use of marijuana. The experts who testified . . . were unanimously opposed to the use of psychoactive drugs. We agree completely. It is the responsibility of every individual to consider carefully the ramifications for himself and for those around him of using such substances. With the freedom which our society offers to each of us to order our lives as we see fit goes the duty to live responsibly, for our own sakes and for society's.

CASE DISCUSSION

Is it true that possessing marijuana at home does not harm anyone? If you were compiling a list, what could citizens do in the privacy of their homes without government intrusion? What criteria would you establish for determining what falls within the right to privacy, and what does not? Would you extend the privacy right to motor homes? to motel rooms?

≡ THE PRINCIPLE OF PUNISHMENT

Fundamental to criminal law is the notion that the law not only *pro*scribes conduct, but it also *pre*scribes punishment. Two dimensions to the principle of punishment in criminal law are the purposes that justify punishment and **proportionality** (the nature and amount of punishment in relation to the person and conduct punished).

The Purposes of Punishment

Punishment takes many forms. A parent who grounds a teenager, a club that expels a member, a church that excommunicates a parishioner, a friend who rejects a companion—all punish because they *intentionally* inflict pain or other unpleasant consequences on their objects. None of these examples involve criminal punishment. **Criminal punishment** requires the following elements: (1) pain or other unpleasant consequences (2) prescribed by law and (3) administered intentionally (4) by the state. The last three elements are self-explanatory; the first requires elaboration.

The phrase "pain or other unpleasant consequences" is both broad and vague. It does not define the kind and amount of pain. A violent mental patient indefinitely confined to a padded cell in a state security hospital suffers more pain than a person incarcerated for five days in the county jail for disorderly conduct. Nevertheless, only the jail sentence is criminal punishment. The difference lies in the purpose. Hospitalization, at least formally, aims to treat and cure; the pain accompanying treatment is incidental to, not a reason for, the hospitalization. On the other hand, punishment—the intentional infliction of pain—lies behind the jail inmate's incarceration.

Criminal Law Close-Up

CURRENT SENTENCING ALTERNATIVES REFLECT MULTIPLE OBJECTIVES

What Types of Sentences Usually Are Given to Offenders?

Death Penalty In most states for the most serious crimes such as murder, the courts may sentence an offender to death by lethal injection, electrocution, exposure to lethal gas, hanging, or other method specified by state law.

- As of 1985, 37 states had laws providing for the death penalty.
- Virtually all death penalty sentences are for murder.
- As of year-end 1985, 50 persons had been executed since 1976, and 1,591 inmates in 32 states were under a sentence of death.

Incarceration The confinement of a convicted criminal in a federal or state prison or a local jail to serve a court-imposed sentence. Confinement is usually in a jail, administered locally, or a prison, operated by the state or federal government. In many states offenders sentenced to 1 year or less are held in a jail; those sentenced to longer terms are committed to a state prison.

- More than 4,200 correctional facilities are maintained by federal, state, and local governments. They include 47 federal facilities, 922 state-operated adult confinement and community-based correctional facilities, and 3,300 local jails, which usually are county operated.
- On any given day in 1985 about 503,000 persons were confined in state and federal prisons. About 254,000 were confined in local jails on June 30, 1985.

Probation The sentencing of an offender to community supervision by a probation agency, often as a result of suspending a sentence to confinement. Such supervision normally entails specific rules of conduct while in the community. If the rules are violated a sentence to confinement may be imposed. Probation is the most widely used correctional disposition in the United States.

- State or local governments operate more than 2,000 probation agencies.
- At year-end 1985, nearly 1.9 million adults were on probation, or about 1 of every 95 adults in the nation.

Split Sentences, Shock Probation, and Intermittent Confinement A penalty that explicitly requires the convicted person to serve a brief period of confinement in a local, state, or federal facility (the "shock") followed by a period of probation. This penalty attempts to combine the use of community supervision with a short incarceration experience. Some sentences are periodic rather than continuous; for example, an offender may be required to spend a certain number of weekends in jail.

■ In 1984 nearly a third of those receiving probation sentences in Idaho, New Jersey, Tennessee, Utah, and Vermont also were sentenced to brief periods of confinement.

Restitution and Victim Compensation The offender is required to provide financial repayment or, in some jurisdictions, services in lieu of monetary restitution, for the losses incurred by the victim.

■ Nearly all states have statutory provisions for the collection and disbursement of restitution funds. A restitution law was enacted at the federal level in 1982.

Community Service The offender is required to perform a specified amount of public service work, such as collecting trash in parks or other public facilities.

■ Many states authorize community service work orders. Community service often is imposed as a specific condition of probation.

Fines An economic penalty that requires the offender to pay a specified sum of money within limits set by law. Fines often are imposed in addition to probation or as alternatives to incarceration.

■ The Victims of Crime Act of 1984 authorizes the distribution of fines and forfeited criminal profits to support state victim-assistance programs, with priority given to programs that aid victims of sexual assault, spousal abuse, and child abuse. These programs, in turn, provide assistance and compensation to crime victims.

■ Many laws that govern the imposition of fines are being revised. The revisions often provide for more flexible means of ensuring equity in the imposition of fines, flexible fine schedules, "day fines" geared to the offender's daily wage, installment payment of fines, and the imposition of confinement only when there is an intentional refusal to pay.

■ A 1984 study estimated that more than three-fourths of criminal courts use fines extensively and that fines levied each year exceed $1 billion.

SOURCE: *Report to the Nation on Crime and Justice: The Data*, Bureau of Justice Statistics, United States Justice Department, Washington, D.C., 1988, page 96.

This distinction between criminal punishment and treatments is rarely clear-cut. Many persons in maximum-security hospitals are convicted criminal offenders, but the government sentences other convicted criminals to prison for "treatment" and "cure." Furthermore, pain and pleasure do not always distinguish punishment from treatment. Shock treatment and padded cells inflict more pain than confinement in some minimum-security federal prisons with their "country club" atmospheres. When measured by pain, punishment may often be preferable to treatment. Indeed, some critics maintain that treatment's major shortcoming is that "helping" a patient justifies extreme measures: massive surgery, castration, and lobotomy.[10]

Professor Herbert Packer resolved the dilemma of treatment and punishment by adding a fifth element to criminal punishment, suggesting that its dominant purpose is not to make offenders better, but to inflict "deserved pain" and prevent crimes. Although criminal punishment's primary aim is to hurt and not help offenders, this does not mean that treatment cannot deter further crime. Deterrence has always been assumed, and has sometimes been specifically articulated, as a utilitarian aim of rehabilitation.[11]

New York clearly asserted this aim in its 1967 Revised Penal law:

> The general purposes of this chapter are to insure public safety by preventing the commission of offenses through the deterrent influence of the sentences authorized, [and] the rehabilitation of those convicted. . . .[12]

Two basic justifications underlie all criminal punishment: retribution and prevention. Prevention encompasses three divisions: general deterrence, incapacitation, and rehabilitation.

RETRIBUTION. Striking out to hurt what hurts us is a basic human impulse. In one commentator's words, "It is what makes us kick the table leg on which we stub our toe." This impulse captures the idea of **retribution,** which is at least as old as the Old Testament:

> When one man strikes another and kills him, he shall be put to death. When one man injures and disfigures his fellow-countryman, it shall be done to him as he had done; fracture for fracture, eye for eye, tooth for tooth.[13]

Retribution rests on the assumption that hurting the wicked is right. As forcefully stated by Sir James F. Stephen, a nineteenth-century judge and historian of the criminal law, the wicked deserve to suffer for their evil deeds.

> [T]he infliction of punishment by law gives definite expression and a solemn ratification and justification to the hatred which is excited by the commission of the offense. The criminal law thus proceeds upon the principle that it is morally right to hate criminals, and it confirms and justifies that sentiment by inflicting on criminals punishments which express it. I think it highly desirable that criminals should be hated, that the punishments inflicted upon them should be so contrived as to give expression to that hatred, and to justify it so far as the public provision of means for expressing and gratifying a healthy natural sentiment can justify and encourage it. The forms in which deliberate anger and righteous disapprobation are ex-

pressed, and the execution of criminal justice is the most emphatic of such forms, stand to the one set of passions in the same relation in which marriage stands to sexual passion.[14]

Retribution's proponents contend that it benefits not only society, as Stephen emphasized, but also criminals. Just as society feels satisfied in retaliating against, or paying back, criminals, offenders themselves benefit through expiating their evil, or paying their debt to society. Retaliation, by which society pays back criminals, and expiation, through which criminals pay back society, are both central to retribution. Retribution assumes that offenders are free to choose between committing and not committing crimes. Because offenders have this choice, society can blame them for making the wrong choice. This blameworthiness is called **culpability**. Culpability means that offenders are responsible for their actions and must suffer the consequences if they act irresponsibly.

Retribution has several appealing qualities. First, it assumes free will, or human autonomy. This assumption upholds a basic value—that individuals have the power to determine their own destinies and are not at the mercy of uncontrollable forces. Retribution also makes sense because it seems to accord with human nature. Hurting that which hurts and hating wrongdoers—especially murderers, rapists, robbers, and other violent criminals—appear to be natural impulses.[15]

From the Old Testament's philosophy of taking an eye for an eye, to the nineteenth-century Englishman's claim that it is right to hate and hurt criminals, to the modern idea of "lock 'em up and throw away the key," the desire for retribution has run strong and deep in both religion and criminal justice. This long tradition endorses retribution, especially in the average person's mind. The principle's sheer tenacity seems to validate its use in modern criminal justice.

Retributionists maintain that retribution rests not only on long use but also on a firm jurisprudential (legal philosophical) foundation. Two reasons support this claim, the first centering on culpability, the second on justice.

Retribution requires culpability—it requires that criminals choose and intend to harm their victims. Accidents do not qualify for retribution. Hence, people who load, aim, and fire guns into their enemies' chests deserve punishment; hunters who lay down and leave loaded guns that fire and kill companions who bump them do not deserve punishment. Civil law can deal with careless people; the criminal law ought to punish only people who purposely perpetrate harm. Retribution focuses the criminal law on culpable behavior.

Retributionists also claim that justice is the only proper measure of punishment. Justice is a philosophical concept whose application depends on culpability. Only those who deserve punishment can receive it, or it is unjust. Similarly, only justice qualifies to determine the quality and quantity of punishment—the culpable defendant's just deserts.

It is difficult to translate abstract justice into concrete penalties. What are a rapist's just deserts? Is castration justice? How many years in prison is robbery worth? How much offender suffering will repay the pain of a maimed aggravated assault victim? The pain of punishment cannot be equivalent to the suffering caused by the crime. Furthermore, critics contend that retribution is barbarism's last holdout.

> All of this abstract philosophizing about punishment as requital for crime has a musty smell about it, a smell of the professor's study. The people who have the responsibility for fighting crime and dealing with criminals have learned that it is pointless to talk about "how much punishment" is deserved. In the nineteenth century [it] had its appeal. [But] the modern behavioral sciences have shown that armchair abstractions about the "justice" of retribution by philosophers who reject human experience are sadly defective in human understanding, not to say human sympathy. The retributive approach is too subjective and too emotional to solve problems that have their roots in social conditions and the consequent impact on individual personality.[16]

The author of the preceding statement denies that the urge to retaliate inheres in human nature; the law ought to reject any demand for vengeance. Furthermore, he argues that retributionists merely assume, but do not have proof, that a bloodthirsty human nature craves vengeance.

The determinists reject the freewill assumption that underlies retribution. They suggest that forces beyond human control determine individual behavior. Social scientists have shown the relationship between social conditions and crime. Psychiatrists point to subconscious forces, beyond the conscious will's control, that determine criminal conduct. A few biologists link violent crime to an extra Y chromosome. Determinism undermines the theory of retribution because it forecloses blame, and punishment without blame is unjust.[17]

PREVENTION. Retribution justifies punishment on the ground that it is right to inflict pain on criminals. Prevention inflicts pain not for its own sake but to prevent future crimes. **General prevention,** also called **general deterrence**, aims to prevent the general population who have not committed crimes from doing so. **Special deterrence,** or **incapacitation,** prevents convicted criminals from committing future crimes. **Rehabilitation** hopes to achieve prevention by changing individuals so that they will obey the law. These all have in common the aim of preventing future crime; inflicting pain for its own sake is not the aim of prevention.

General Deterrence Jeremy Bentham, an eighteenth-century English law reformer, promoted deterrence. Bentham was part of, and was heavily influenced by, the intellectual movement called the Enlightenment. At the movement's core was the notion that natural laws govern the universe and, by analogy, human society. One of these laws, hedonism, posits that human beings seek pleasure and avoid pain. A related law, rationalism, states that individuals can, and ordinarily do, act to maximize pleasure and minimize pain. Rationalism also permits human beings to apply natural laws mechanistically (that is, according to rules, not discretion).

These ideas, which are much oversimplified here, led Bentham to formulate classical deterrence theory. It states that rational human beings will not commit crimes if they know that the pain of punishment outweighs the pleasure gained from committing crimes. Prospective criminals weigh the pleasure derived from present crime against the pain from the threat of future punishment. According to the natural law of hedonism, if prospective criminals fear future punishment more than they derive pleasure from present crime, they will not commit crimes.

Deterrence is considerably more complex than Bentham's useful but oversimplified crime prevention model suggests. Threatened punishment does not always deter—it goads some to do the very thing it aims to prevent. During the Vietnam War, for example, Congress made burning draft cards a crime. Instead of avoiding such conduct, protesters turned out in scores to flout the law. Deterrence, then, has two dimensions.[18]

Deterrence proponents argue that the principle of utility—permitting only the minimum amount of pain necessary to prevent crime—better limits criminal punishment than retribution does. English playwright George Bernard Shaw, a strong deterrence supporter, put it this way: "Vengeance is mine saith the Lord; which means it is not the Lord Chief Justice's." According to this argument, divinity enables only God, the angels, or some other divine being to measure just deserts, while social scientists can determine how much pain, or threat of pain, deters crime. With this knowledge, the state can scientifically inflict the minimum pain needed to produce the maximum crime reduction.

Deterrence proponents concede that impediments to implementing deterrence exist. The emotionalism surrounding punishment impairs objectivity. Often, prescribed penalties rest more on faith than on evidence. For example, one economist's study shows that every execution under capital punishment laws saves about eight lives by deterring potential murderers. This finding sparked a controversy having little to do with the study's empirical validity. Instead, the arguments turn to ethics—whether killing anyone is right, no matter what social benefits it produces.[19]

Deterrence proponents do not argue against the need for an inquiry into the ethics, wisdom, and humaneness of punishment, but they do maintain that empirical research necessarily precedes answers to those questions. The problem of punishment involves a division of labor. Researchers answer the empirical question What works? Policymakers answer the questions Is it wise? Is it humane? Is it legal? For instance, research might demonstrate that the death penalty for rape prevents rape, but the United States Supreme Court has declared that capital punishment for rape violates the Eighth Amendment.[20]

Even if particular punishments are constitutional, they may still be unwise public policy. For example, suppose it is found that a statute authorizing surgery to prevent erections deters male sex offenders. Even if the statute were constitutional (an issue about which there are grave doubts), the humaneness of this draconian measure should be raised. Amputating thieves' hands, an effective deterrent in some countries, is rejected on humanitarian grounds in America.

Critics find several faults with deterrence theory and its application to criminal punishment. The wholly rational, freewill individual that deterrence theory assumes exists is as far from reality as the eighteenth-century world that spawned the idea. Complex forces within the human organism and in the external environment, both of which are beyond individual control, strongly influence behavior.[21]

Human beings and their behavior are too unpredictable to reduce to a mechanistic formula. For some people, the criminal law's existence suffices to deter them from committing crimes; others require more. Information about just who these others are and of what the more consists has not been determined sufficiently so that policy can rest upon it. Furthermore, severity is not the only influence on punishment's effectiveness. Tentative conclusions are that certainty and celerity (speed) have a greater deterrent effect than severity.[22]

Moreover, threats do not affect all crimes or potential criminals equally. Crimes of passion, such as murder and rape, are probably little affected by threats, whereas speeding, drunken driving, and corporate crime are probably greatly affected by threats. The leading deterrence theorist, Johannes Andenaes, sums up the state of our knowledge about deterrence:

> There is a long way to go before research can give quantitative forecasts. The long-term moral effects of the criminal law and law enforcement are especially hard to isolate and quantify. Some categories of crime are so intimately related to specific social situations that generalizations of a quantitative kind are impossible. An inescapable fact is that research will always lag behind actual developments. When new forms of crime come into existence, such as highjacking of aircraft or terrorist acts against officers of the law, there cannot possibly be a body of research ready as a basis for the decisions that have to be taken. Common sense and trial by error have to give the answers.[23]

Finally, critics maintain that even if getting empirical support for criminal punishment is possible, deterrence is unjust because it punishes for example's sake. Supreme Court Justice Oliver Wendell Holmes described the example dimension to deterrence:

> If I were having a philosophical talk with a man I was going to have hanged (or electrocuted) I should say, "I don't doubt that your act was inevitable for you but to make it more avoidable by others we propose to sacrifice you to the common good. You may regard yourself as a soldier dying for your country if you like. But the law must keep its promises."[24]

Punishment should not be a sacrifice to the common good, according to retributionists; it is just only if administered for the redemption of particular individuals. According to critics, punishment is personal and individual, not general and societal. Deterrence proponents respond that so long as offenders are in fact guilty, punishing them is personal; hence, it is just to use individual punishment for society's benefit.

Incapacitation Incapacitation means to restrain offenders from committing further crimes. At the extreme, incapacitation means mutilation—castration, amputation, and lobotomy, for example—or even death in capital punishment. Less extreme and most common is imprisonment. Incapacitation works; dead people do not commit crimes, and prisoners cannot commit crimes, at least not outside prison walls. Incapacitation, then, offers much to a society determined to repress crime.

> [T]he chances of a persistent robber or burglar living out his life, or even going a year, with no arrest are quite small. Yet a large proportion of repeat

offenders suffer little or no loss of freedom. Whether or not one believes that such penalties, if inflicted, would act as a deterrent, it is obvious that they could serve to incapacitate these offenders and, thus, for the period of the incapacitation, prevent them from committing additional crimes.[25]

Like deterrence and retribution, incapacitation has its share of critics. Some stress the distant relationship between offense and punishment. The basic problem with incapacitation is predicting behavior, particularly violent criminal conduct. Kleptomaniacs will almost surely steal again, exhibitionists will expose themselves, and addicts will continue to use chemicals. But when will murderers, rapists, or bank robbers strike again? Nobody really knows. Therefore, punishment is based, empirically, on a poor guess concerning future danger.[26]

Furthermore, critics argue, incapacitation merely shifts criminality from outside prisons to inside prisons. Sex offenders and other violent criminals can and do still find victims among other inmates; property offenders abound in trading contraband and other smuggled items. Incarceration is also expensive. According to current estimates, it costs approximately $50,000 to construct prison cells and in some states another $20,000 to feed, house, and clothe every prisoner. Finally, critics maintain that several incapacitative measures—death, psychosurgery, mutilation, and long-term incarceration—violate the Eighth Amendment.[27]

Rehabilitation In a widely acclaimed essay on criminal law, Professor Herbert Packer succinctly stated the rehabilitative aim:

> The most immediately appealing justification for punishment is the claim that it may be used to prevent crimes by so changing the personality of the offender that he will conform to the dictates of law; in a word, by reforming him.[28]

Rehabilitation borrows much from medicine. Indeed, it is based on what has been called the medical model. In this model, crime is a "disease" that criminals have contracted. The major purpose in punishment is to "cure" criminal patients through "treatment." The length of imprisonment depends upon how long it takes to effect this cure. On its face, rehabilitation is the most humane justification for criminal punishment. Its proponents contend that treating offenders is much more civilized than punishing them.

Two assumptions underlie rehabilitation theory. The first is that external and internal forces beyond offenders' control determine criminality. Rehabilitationists are determinists when it comes to crime causation. Since offenders do not freely choose to commit crimes, they cannot be blamed for doing so. The second assumption is that experts can modify subjects' behavior to prevent further crimes. After treatment or rehabilitation, former criminals will control their own destinies, at least enough so that they will not commit crimes. In this respect, rehabilitationists subscribe to free will: criminals can choose to change their life habits and often do, after which society can hold them responsible for their actions.

The view that criminals are sick has had a profound effect on criminal law and has generated acrimonious debate. The reason is not that reform and rehabilitation are new ideas; quite the contrary. Victorian Sir Francis

Palgrave summed up a seven-hundred-year-old attitude when he stated that medieval church's position on punishment: it was not to be "thundered in vengeance for the satisfaction of the state, but imposed for the good of the offender; in order to afford the means of amendment and to lead the transgressor to repentance, and to mercy." Sixteenth-century Elizabethan pardon statutes were laced with the language of repentance and reform; the queen hoped to achieve a reduction in crime by mercy rather than by punishment. Even Jeremy Bentham, most closely associated with deterrence, claimed that punishment would "contribute to the reformation of the offender, not only through fear of being punished again, but by a change in his character and habits."[29]

Despite its long history, rehabilitation has suffered serious attacks. The most fundamental criticism is that rehabilitation is based on false, or at least unproven, assumptions. The causes of crime are so complex, and the wellsprings of human behavior as yet so undetermined, that sound policy cannot rest on treatment. A second criticism is that it makes no sense to brand everyone who violates the criminal law as sick and needing treatment.[30]

Some critics call rehabilitation inhumane because cure justifies administering large doses of pain. Noted British philosopher C. S. Lewis argued as follows:

> My contention is that good men (not bad men) consistently acting upon that position would act as cruelly and unjustly as the greatest tyrants. They might in some respects act even worse. Of all tyrannies a tyranny sincerely exercised for the good of its victims may be the most oppressive. It may be better to live under robber barons than under omnipotent moral busybodies. The robber baron's cruelty may sometimes sleep, his cupidity may at some point be satiated; but those who torment us for our own good will torment us without end for they do so with the approval of their own conscience. They may be more likely to go to Heaven yet at the same time likelier to make a Hell of earth. Their very kindness stings with intolerable insult. To be "cured" against one's will and cured of states which we may not regard as disease is to be put on a level with those who have not yet reached the age of reason or those who never will; to be classed with infants, imbeciles, and domestic animals. But to be punished, however severely, because we have deserved it, because we "ought to have known better," is to be treated as a human person made in God's image.[31]

TRENDS IN PUNISHMENT Historically, retribution, deterrence, incapacitation, and rehabilitation have all been used to justify criminal punishment. But the weight given to each has changed over the centuries. Retribution and reformation, for example, run deep in English criminal law from at least the year 1200. The church's emphasis on atoning for sins and reforming sinners affected criminal law variously. Sometimes the aims of punishment and reformation conflict in practice. In Elizabethan England, for example, the letter of the law was retributionist: the penalty for all major crimes was death. Estimates show that in practice, however, most accused persons never suffered this extreme penalty. Although some escaped death because they were innocent, many were set free based on their chances for rehabilitation. The law's technicalities, for example, made death a virtually impossible penalty for first-time property offenders. In addition, the queen's general pardon, issued almost annually, gave blanket clemency in the hope that criminals, by this act of mercy, would reform their erring ways.[32]

Gradually retribution came to dominate penal policy, until the eighteenth century, when deterrence and incapacitation were introduced to replace what contemporary humanitarian reformers considered ineffective, brutal, and barbaric punishment in the name of retribution. By the turn of the twentieth century, humanitarian reformers concluded that deterrence was neither effective nor humane. Rehabilitation replaced deterrence as the aim of criminal sanctions, and remained the dominant justification for criminal punishment throughout the twentieth century's first sixty years. Most states enacted indeterminate sentencing laws that made prison release dependent on rehabilitation. Most prisons created treatment programs intended to reform criminals so they could become law-abiding citizens. Nevertheless, considerable evidence indicates that rehabilitation never really won the hearts of most criminal justice professionals despite their strong public rhetoric to the contrary.[33]

By the early 1970s, little evidence existed to show that rehabilitation programs reformed offenders. "Nothing works" dominated reform discussions, prompted by a highly touted, widely publicized, and largely negative study evaluating the effectiveness of treatment programs. At the same time that academics and policymakers were becoming disillusioned with rehabilitation, public opinion was hardening into demands for severe penalties in the face of steeply rising crime rates. The time was clearly ripe for retribution to come once again to the fore as a dominant aim of punishment.[34]

California, a rehabilitation pioneer in the early twentieth-century, reflected this shift in attitude in 1976. In its Uniform Determinate Sentencing Law, the legislature abolished the indeterminate sentence, stating boldly that "the purpose of imprisonment is punishment," not treatment or rehabilitation. Called just deserts or even simply deserts, retribution was touted as "right" by conservatives who believed in punishment's morality and as "humane" by liberals convinced that rehabilitation was cruel and excessive. Public opinion supported it, largely on the ground that criminals deserve to be punished.[35]

By the middle of the 1980s, reformers heralded retribution and incapacitation as the primary criminal punishments. There were, to be sure, some powerful holdouts. One was the Model Penal Code, first written in 1961 while rehabilitation dominated penal policy. After reviewing current research and debate thoroughly, its reporters decided to retain rehabilitation as the primary purpose of punishment in 1981.[36]

Proportionality

The Eighth Amendment declares that

[e]xcessive bail shall not be required, nor excessive fines imposed, nor cruel and unusual punishments inflicted.

The Supreme Court has ruled that the phrase "cruel and unusual punishments" means "not only barbaric punishments, but also sentences that are disproportionate to the crime committed."[37]

The principle of proportionality of punishment is much older than the Eighth Amendment. In 1215, three articles in the Magna Carta prohibited "excessive" fines. The principle was repeated and extended in the First Statute of Westminster in 1275. The royal courts relied on these provisions to enforce the principle in actual cases. When imprisonment became a common-law sanction, the courts extended the principle to prison terms. The English Bill of Rights in 1689 repeated the principle of proportionality in the language that later appeared in the Eighth Amendment. Three months later, the House of Lords, the highest court in England, declared that a fine of 30,000 pounds

> was excessive and exorbitant, against magna charta, the common right of the subject, and the law of the land.[38]

The Supreme Court first applied the constitutional principle of proportionality in *Weems v. United States*, in 1910. Weems was convicted of falsifying a public document. The trial court sentenced him to fifteen years in prison at hard labor in chains and permanently deprived him of his civil rights. The Supreme Court ruled that the punishment violated the Eighth Amendment's proportionality requirement. In the 1960s, the Court reaffirmed its commitment to the principle in *Robinson v. California*, ruling that a ninety-day sentence for drug addiction was disproportionate because addiction is an illness, and it is cruel and unusual to punish persons for being sick (see chapter 3).

> Even one day in prison would be a cruel and unusual punishment for the "crime" of having a common cold.[39]

During the 1970s, the Court considered proportionality mainly in capital cases. For example, it held that the death penalty is disproportionate for raping an adult woman. Not until the 1980s did the Court take up the application of the principle to the length of imprisonment, which it addressed in *Solem v. Helm*.[40]

CASE

Was the Punishment Proportionate to the Crime?

Solem v. Helm

463 U.S. 277, 103 S.Ct. 3001, 77 L.Ed.2d 637 (1983)

[Justice Powell delivered the opinion of the Court, in which justices Brennan, Marshall, Blackmun, and Stevens joined. Chief Justice

Burger filed a dissenting opinion, in which justices White, Rehnquist, and O'Connor joined.]

FACTS

By 1975 the State of South Dakota had convicted respondent Jerry Helm of six nonviolent felonies. In 1964, 1966, and 1969 Helm was convicted of third-degree burglary. In 1972 he was convicted of obtaining money under false pretenses. In 1973 he was convicted of grand larceny. And in 1975 he was convicted of third-offense driving while intoxicated. The record contains no details about the circumstances of any of these offenses, except that they were all nonviolent, none was a crime against a person, and alcohol was a contributing factor in each case.

In 1979 Helm was charged with uttering a "no account" check for $100. The only details we have of the crime are those given by Helm to the state trial court:

> "I was working in Sioux Falls, and got my check that day, was drinking and I ended up here in Rapid City with more money than I had when I started. I knew I'd done something but I didn't know exactly what. If I would have known this, I would have picked the check up. I was drinking and I didn't remember, stopped several places."

After offering this explanation, Helm pleaded guilty.

Ordinarily the maximum punishment for uttering a "no account" check would have been five years' imprisonment in the state penitentiary and a $5,000 fine. As a result of his criminal record, however, Helm was subject to South Dakota's recidivist statute:

> "When a defendant has been convicted of at least three prior convictions [sic] in addition to the principal felony, the sentence for the principal felony shall be enhanced to the sentence for a Class 1 felony."

The maximum penalty for a Class 1 felony was life imprisonment in the state penitentiary and a $25,000 fine. . . .

Immediately after accepting Helm's guilty plea, the South Dakota Circuit Court sentenced Helm to life imprisonment. . . . The Court explained

> I think you certainly earned this sentence and certainly proven that you're an habitual criminal and the record would indicate that you're beyond rehabilitation and that the only prudent thing to do is to lock you up for the rest of your natural life, so you won't have further victims of your crimes, just be coming back before the Courts. You'll have plenty of time to think this one over.

The South Dakota Supreme Court, in a 3–2 decision, affirmed the sentence, despite Helm's argument that it violated the Eighth Amendment. . . .

In November, 1981, Helm sought habeas relief in the United States District Court. . . . Helm argued . . . that his sentence constituted cruel and unusual punishment. . . . Although the District Court recognized that the sentence was harsh, it . . . denied the writ. The United States Court of Appeals . . . reversed. The Court of Appeals examined the nature of Helm's offense, the nature of his sentence, and the sentence he could have received in other states for the same offense. It concluded . . . that Helm's sentence was "grossly disproportionate to the nature of the offense. . . . We granted certiorari to consider the Eighth Amendment question. . . . We now affirm.

OPINION

The Eighth Amendment declares: "Excessive bail shall not be required, nor excessive fines imposed, nor cruel and unusual punishment inflicted." The final clause prohibits not only barbaric punishment, but also sentences that are disproportionate to the crime committed.

The principle that a punishment should be proportionate to the crime is deeply rooted and frequently repeated in common-law jurisprudence. In 1215 three chapters of Magna Carta were devoted to the rule that "amercements" may not be excessive. . . .

The constitutional principle of proportionality has been recognized explicitly in this Court for almost a century. . . . [The Court discussed *Weems v. United States*.]

[W]e hold as a matter of principle that a criminal sentence must be proportionate to the crime for which the defendant has been convicted. Reviewing courts, of course, should grant substantial deference to the broad authority that legislatures necessarily possess in determining the types and limits of punishments for crimes, as well as to the discretion that trial courts possess in sentencing convicted criminals. But no penalty is *per se* constitutional. . . . [A] single day in prison may be unconstitutional in some circumstances.

When sentences are reviewed under the Eighth Amendment, courts should be guided by objective factors that our cases have recognized. First, we look to the gravity of the offense and the harshness of the penalty. . . . Second, it may be helpful to compare the sentences imposed on other criminals in the same jurisdiction. If more serious crimes are subject to the same penalty, or to less serious penalties, that is some indication that the punishment at issue may be excessive. . . . Third, courts may find it useful to compare sentences imposed for commission of the same crime in other jurisdictions. . . . In sum, a court's proportionality analysis under the Eighth Amendment should be guided by objective criteria, including (i) the gravity of offense and the harshness of the penalty; (ii) the sentences imposed on other criminals in the same jurisdiction; and (iii) the sentences imposed for commission of the same crime in other jurisdictions. . . .

It remains to apply the analytical framework established by our prior decisions to the case before us. We first consider the relevant criteria, viewing Helm's sentence as life imprisonment without possibility of parole. We then consider the State's argument that the possibility of commutation is sufficient to save an otherwise unconstitutional sentence.

Helm's crime was "one of the most passive felonies a person could commit." It involved neither violence nor the threat of violence to any person. The $100 face value of Helm's "no account" check was not trivial, but neither was it a large amount. One hundred dollars was less than half the amount South Dakota required for a felonious theft. . . .

Helm, of course, was not charged simply with uttering a "no account" check, but also with being a habitual offender. And a State is justified in punishing a recidivist more severely than it punishes a first offender. Helm's status, however, cannot be considered in the abstract. His prior offenses, although classified as felonies, were all relatively minor. . . .

Helm's present sentence is life imprisonment without possibility of parole. Barring executive clemency, Helm will spend the rest of his life in the state penitentiary. . . . Helm's sentence is the most severe punishment that the State could have imposed on any criminal for any crime. Only capital punishment, a penalty not authorized in South Dakota when Helm was sentenced, exceeds it.

We next consider the sentence that could be imposed on other criminals in the same jurisdiction. When Helm was sentenced, a South Dakota court was required to impose a life sentence for murder, and was authorized to impose a life sentence for treason, first-degree manslaughter, and kidnapping. No other crime was punishable so severely on the first offense. Attempted murder, placing an explosive device on an aircraft, and first-degree rape were only Class 2 felonies. Aggravated riot was only a Class 3 felony, and aggravated assaults were only Class 4 felonies. . . .

In sum, there were a handful of crimes that were necessarily punished by life imprisonment: murder, and, on a second or third offense, treason, first-degree murder, first-degree manslaughter, first-degree arson, and kidnapping. There was a larger group for which life imprisonment was authorized in the discretion of the sentencing judge, including: treason, first-degree manslaughter, first-degree arson, and kidnapping; attempted murder, placing an explosive device on an aircraft, and first-degree rape on a second or third offense; and any felony after three prior offenses. Finally, there was a large group of very serious offenses for which life imprisonment was not authorized, including a third offense of heroin dealing or aggravated assault.

Criminals committing any of these offenses ordinarily would be thought more deserving of punishment than one uttering a "no account" check—even when the bad-check writer had already committed six minor felonies. . . . Helm has been treated in the same manner as, or more severely than, criminals who have committed far more serious crimes.

Finally, we compare the sentences imposed for commission of the same crime in other jurisdictions. The Court of Appeals found that "Helm could have received a life sentence without parole for his offense in only one other state, Nevada." . . . At the very least, therefore, it is clear that Helm could not have received such a severe sentence in 48 of the 50 States. . . .

The Constitution requires us to examine Helm's sentence to determine if it is proportionate to his crime. Applying objective criteria, we find that Helm has received the penultimate sentence for relatively minor criminal conduct. He has been treated more harshly than other criminals in the State who have committed more serious crimes. He has been treated more harshly than he would have been in any other jurisdiction, with the possible exception of a single State. We conclude that his sentence is significantly disproportionate to his crime, and is therefore prohibited by the Eighth Amendment. The judgment of the Court of Appeals is accordingly.

Affirmed

Chief Justice Burger, with whom Justice White, Justice Rehnquist, and Justice O'Connor join, dissenting.

DISSENT

The controlling law governing this case is crystal clear, but today the Court blithely discards any concept of *stare decisis*, trespasses gravely on the authority of the states, and distorts the concept of proportionality of punishment by tearing it from its moorings in capital cases. Only three Terms ago, we held in *Rummel v. Estelle*, that a life sentence imposed after only a *third* nonviolent felony conviction did not constitute cruel and unusual punishment under the Eighth Amendment. Today, the Court ignores its recent precedent and holds that a life sentence imposed after a *seventh* felony conviction constitutes cruel and unusual punishment. Moreover, I reject the fiction that all Helm's crimes were innocuous or nonviolent. Among his felonies were three burglaries and a third conviction for drunken driving. By comparison Rummel was a relatively "model citizen." Although today's holding cannot rationally be reconciled with *Rummel*, the Court does not purport to overrule *Rummel*. I therefore dissent. . . .

Although historians and scholars have disagreed about the Framers' original intentions, the more common view seems to be that the Framers viewed the Cruel and Unusual Punishments Clause as prohibiting the kind of torture meted out during the reign of the Stuarts. . . . The prevailing view up to now has been that the Eighth Amendment reaches only the *mode* of punishment and not the length of a sentence of imprisonment. . . .

This Court has applied a proportionality test in extraordinary cases. The Court's reading of the Eighth Amendment as restricting legislatures' authority to choose which crimes to punish by death rests on the finality of the death sentence. Such scrutiny is not required where a sentence of imprisonment is imposed after the State has identified a criminal offender whose record shows he will not conform to social standards. . . .

The Court's traditional abstention from reviewing sentences of imprisonment to ensure that punishment is "proportionate" to the crime is well founded in history, in prudential considerations, and in traditions of comity. Today's conclusion by five Justices that they are able to say that one offense has less "gravity" than another is nothing other than a bald substitution of individual subjective moral values for those of the legislature. . . .

It is indeed a curious business for this Court to so far intrude into the administration of criminal justice to say that a state legislature is barred by the Constitution from identifying its habitual criminals and removing them from the streets. Surely seven felony convictions warrant the conclusion that respondent is incorrigible. . . .

CASE DISCUSSION

In a portion not included here, the dissent argued that proportionality should not apply to the length of sentence because it usurps the legislature's power to prescribe penalties and allows a majority of the Supreme Court to define what is cruel and unusual. Do you agree? The dissent also argued that sentencing Helm to prison was not extraordinary since Helm's "record shows that he will not conform to societal standards." Do you agree? What standards would you adopt for determining when prison sentences are disproportionate to the crimes for which the legislature prescribes them? for when judges apply them in their sentences?

≡ SUMMARY

The general principles of criminal law overarch the entire criminal law. They are different from the general principles of criminal liability discussed in chapter 3. The principles of liability govern the material elements of crimes—the physical, mental, concurrence, causation, and resulting harm requirements—not the punishments or doctrines. The doctrines, such as necessity and responsibility, may or may not arise in individual cases. The general principles of criminal law, on the other hand, encompass all the elements, doctrines, and penalties.

The first principle of criminal law is legality. The principle of legality requires that for a behavior to qualify as criminal, the law must define its conduct and prescribe a penalty. The principle of legality encompasses at least three other principles: (1) the *ex post facto* prohibition against making conduct criminal after it occurs; (2) the void-for-vagueness principle, which requires the law to state with precision what conduct it prohibits; and (3) equal protection of the laws. The purposes underlying the principle of legality are to forewarn citizens about the conduct the law proscribes and to protect against abuse of state power.

The Constitution protects a number of individual rights from criminal prohibition. For example, the right to privacy protects conduct that does not harm others from criminal sanctions. The underlying purpose of the right to privacy and other civil rights is that conduct that affects only the individuals who engage in it ought to be left alone, especially by the government. Limits on making crimes out of conduct that is included in civil rights reflect the positive side of criminal law—that it ought to promote behavior that it does not prohibit.

The principle of punishment refers both to the purposes of punishment and to punishment's proportionality—the nature and amount of punishment in relation to the crime committed. The two basic purposes for punishment are retribution—to inflict pain on the person who harmed another in order to give offenders their just deserts—and prevention. The major types of prevention are (1) general deterrence, or using the threat of punishment to deter people generally from future crime; (2) incapacitation, or preventing specific offenders from committing future crimes; and (3) rehabilitation, or changing individual offenders' behavior so that they will not commit crimes in the future. Throughout history, criminal law has reflected these purposes, but the emphasis has shifted among them. During most of early history, retribution predominated; during the first sixty years of the twentieth century, rehabilitation held sway; during the last two decades, retribution and incapacitation have returned to prominence.

Proportionality prohibits excessive punishment. Punishments that are out of proportion to the conduct they penalize violate the Eighth Amendment. Proportionality might refer to types of penalty, such as hard labor or capital punishment, or to the degree of a particular penalty, such as the length of imprisonment or the amount of a fine.

QUESTIONS FOR REVIEW AND DISCUSSION

1. Distinguish between general principles of criminal law, general principles of criminal liability, and doctrines of criminal law.
2. Define and state the two major purposes of the *ex post facto* prohibition.
3. What part of the Constitution is violated by vague laws? Why?
4. What kinds of classifications are prohibited by the equal protection clause? Explain.
5. Is there a right to privacy in the United States Constitution? Explain.
6. Describe the major purposes of criminal punishment. What are the strengths and weaknesses of each? Which purpose or purposes do you favor? Why?
7. Explain the principle of proportionality and describe its historical background.

SUGGESTED READINGS

1. Herbert L. Packer, *The Limits of the Criminal Sanction* (Palo Alto, Calif.: Stanford University Press, 1968). Professor Packer's book is a necessary starting point for anyone seriously interested in the aims and purposes of criminal law in general and in criminal punishment in particular. Packer takes the approach that he is writing for the generalist, not the

criminal justice specialist. He especially addresses what he calls the rational lawmaker, one who "stops, looks, and listens" before passing laws. The book is written in a thoughtful, clear, easy-to-read style.

2. Lois G. Forer, *Criminals and Victims* (New York: Norton, 1980). Written by a judge with many years of experience in sentencing criminal defendants, this book explores the difficulties in applying general purposes to concrete cases. Judge Forer analyzes the few alternatives judges have in sentencing, particularly the heavy emphasis on imprisonment, which she believes satisfies neither victims nor society. Well documented with interesting, challenging cases from her courtroom, the book is lively, easy to read, and provocative.

3. Andrew von Hirsch, *Doing Justice* (New York: Hill and Wang, 1976), is a brief, clear, and concise argument for just deserts. Based on deliberations by the Committee for the Study of Incarceration, it resulted from serious consideration of returning to retribution as the proper aim of punishment.

4. Norval Morris, *The Future of Imprisonment* (Chicago: University of Chicago Press, 1974), is an influential book written by a criminal justice expert. Morris recommends a set of principles upon which punishment should rest. His principles are aimed at preserving what is best of the rehabilitative ideal in the realities of twentieth-century prisons. These ideas are argued convincingly and written clearly, so that general readers can profit from reading the book.

5. David J. Rothman, *Conscience and Convenience* (Boston: Little, Brown, 1980). Professor Rothman, a historian, surveys the origins and historical development of rehabilitation in the early years of the twentieth century. This book is excellent for anyone interested in the history of the rehabilitative ideal.

6. Johannes Andenaes, "Deterrence," in *Encyclopedia of Crime and Justice*, vol. 2, ed. Sanford H. Kadish (New York: Free Press, 1983). This is a brief, excellent summary of deterrence theory, research, and the problems of applying deterrence theory in practice, written by the world's leading deterrence theorist. The article includes a valuable bibliography on deterrence, which can lead to fruitful examination of this basic justification for criminal punishment.

7. Jerome Hall, *General Principles of Criminal Law*, 2d ed. (Indianapolis: Bobbs-Merrill, 1960), is the most comprehensive treatment of the general principles of legality and proportionality. Hall, a law professor, writes for the specialist, but his challenging arguments and his knowledge of history, law, and philosophy make the book well worth the effort to read it.

═══ NOTES

1. Quotes from Roman Civil Law and Lord Coke in Jerome Hall, *General Principles of Criminal Law*, 2d ed. (Indianapolis: Bobbs-Merrill, 1960), pp. 31–32.

2. United States Constitution, Art. 1, § 9, cl. 3 prohibits the federal government from passing *ex post facto* laws; Art. 10, § 10, cl. 1 prohibits the states from doing so; *Calder v. Bull*, 3 U.S. (3 Dall.) 386, 390, 1 L.Ed. 648 (1798) defined *ex post facto*.

3. *People ex rel. Lonschein v. Warden,* 43 Misc. 2d 109, 250 N.Y.S.2d 15 (1964) (change from death penalty to life imprisonment retroactively effective).

4. *Lanzetta v. New Jersey,* 306 U.S. 451, 453, 59 S.Ct. 618, 619, 83 L.Ed. 888 (1939).

5. Ibid.

6. *Buck v. Bell,* 274 U.S. 200, 208, 47 S.Ct. 584, 585, 71 L. Ed. 1000 (1927) (equal protection argument the last resort).

7. *Griswold v. Connecticut,* 381 U.S. 479, 85 S.Ct. 1678, 14 L.Ed.2d 510 (1965).

8. *Bowers v. Hardwick,* 478 U.S. 186, 106 S.Ct. 2841, 92 L.Ed.2d 140 (1986).

9. Art. 1, § 22.

10. Thomas Szasz, M.D., *Law, Liberty, and Psychiatry* (New York: Collier Books, 1963).

11. Herbert Packer, *The Limits of the Criminal Sanction* (Palo Alto, Calif.: Stanford University Press, 1968), pp. 33–34.

12. *McKinney's New York Criminal Law Pamphlet* (St. Paul: West Publishing Co., 1988), New York Penal Code, § 1.05(6).

13. *Leviticus* 24: 20.

14. *A History of the Criminal Law of England,* vol. 3 (London: Macmillan, 1883), pp. 81–82.

15. James Q. Wilson and Richard Herrnstein thoroughly discuss free will in *Crime and Human Nature,* chap. 19 (New York: Simon and Schuster, 1985); psychiatrist Willard Gaylin also develops the point at length in his fascinating *The Killing of Bonnie Garland* (New York: Simon and Schuster, 1982).

16. Henry E. Wiehofen, "Retribution Is Obsolete," in *Responsibility,* ed. C. Friedrich, Nomos series, no. 3 (New York: Lieber-Atherton, 1960), pp. 116, 119–20.

17. These theories are discussed at length in James Q. Wilson and Richard Herrnstein, *Crime and Human Nature.* An intriguing case study applying the theories to one criminal homicide is Andre Mayer and Michael Wheeler, *The Crocodile Man: A Case of Brain Chemistry and Criminal Violence* (Boston: Houghton Mifflin, 1982).

18. Joseph Goldstein, "Psychoanalysis and Jurisprudence," *Yale Law Journal,* 77 (1968), pp. 1071–72.

19. This topic is explored fully in Bedau, ed., *The Death Penalty in America,* chap. 4.

20. *Coker v. Georgia,* 433 U.S. 584, 97 S.Ct. 2861, 53 L.Ed.2d 982 (1977).

21. See Wilson and Herrnstein, *Crime and Human Nature,* for a full discussion.

22. Johannes Andenaes, "Deterrence," *Encyclopedia of Crime and Justice,* ed. Sanford H. Kadish (New York: Free Press, 1983), 2, p. 593.

23. Ibid., p. 596, 97 S.Ct. at 2868.

24. Mark DeWolfe Howe, ed., *Holmes-Laski Letters* (Cambridge, Mass.: Harvard University Press, 1953), p. 806.

25. James Q. Wilson, *Thinking about Crime* (New York: Basic Books, 1975), p. 1.

26. A good survey of the current state of knowledge on the subject is Mark H. Moore et al., *Dangerous Offenders: The Elusive Target of Justice* (Cambridge, Mass.: Cambridge University Press, 1984).

27. Sandra Gleason, "Hustling: The 'Single' Economy of a Prison," *Federal Probation* (June 1978), pp. 32–39; Samuel Walker, *Sense and Nonsense about Crime: A Policy Guide* (Monterey, Calif.: Brooks/Cole, 1985), p. 59–61.

28. *The Limits of the Criminal Sanction,* p. 50.

29. For these early reformation ideas, see Joel Samaha, "Hanging for Felony" *Historical Journal* 21 (1979); and "Some Reflections on the Anglo-Saxon Heritage of Discre-

tionary Justice," in *Social Psychology and Discretionary Law*, ed. Lawrence E. Abt and Irving R. Stuart (New York: Van Nostrand, 1979), p. 4–16.

30. These points are summarized in Richard D. Schwartz, "Rehabilitation," in *Encyclopedia of Crime and Justice*, ed. Sanford H. Kadish (New York: Free Press, 1983), 4, pp. 1364–73.

31. "The Humanitarian Theory of Punishment," *Res Judicatae*, 6 (1953), p. 224.

32. Joel Samaha, *Law and Order in Historical Perspective* (New York: Academic Press, 1974), passim; Samaha, "Hanging for Felony".

33. See David J. Rothman, *Conscience and Convenience* (Boston: Little, Brown, 1980), for the history of rehabilitation during the early twentieth century.

34. Robert Martinson, "What Works? Questions and Answers about Prison Reform," *The Public Interest* 35 (Spring 1974), pp. 22–54.

35. Quoted in Malcolm M. Feeley, *Court Reform on Trial* (New York: Basic Books, 1983), p. 139; Walker, *Sense and Nonsense about Crime*, chap. 1, 5, 6, and 11.

36. See the excellent review of these issues in American Law Institute, *Model Penal Code and Commentaries* (Philadelphia: American Law Institute, 1985), 3, pp. 11–30.

37. *Solem v. Helm*, 463 U.S. 277, 284, 103 S.Ct. 3001, 3006, 77 L.Ed.2d 637 (1982).

38. Ibid., 285, 103 S.Ct. at 3007.

39. *Weems v. United States*, 217 U.S. 349, 30 S.Ct. 544, 54 L.Ed. 793 (1910); *Robinson v. California*, 370 U.S. 660, 82 S.Ct. 1417, 8 L.Ed.2d 758 (1962).

40. *Coker v. Georgia*, 433 U.S. 584, 97 S.Ct. 2861, 53 L.Ed.2d 982 (1977) (capital punishment in rape cases).

Chapter Three

The General Principles of Criminal Liability

CHAPTER OUTLINE

CHAPTER MAIN POINTS

1. Every crime consists of several material elements that the prosecution must prove beyond a reasonable doubt to convict.

2. The general principles of criminal liability are *actus reus, mens rea,* concurrence, causation, and resulting harm.

3. Acts must be voluntary, and they include more than mere bodily movements; failure to act and possession also qualify.

4. The four mental states that constitute *mens rea* are purpose, knowledge, recklessness, and negligence.

5. Strict liability crimes require no mental element.

6. Criminal acts must join (concur with) criminal mental states, and in some cases, conduct must concur with harmful results.

7. Causation includes both *sine qua non,* or but-for, causation, and proximate or substantial cause.

8. *Mens rea* determines the seriousness of an offense; purposeful wrongdoing is the most serious, followed by recklessness, negligence, and liability without fault.

KEY TERMS

actus reus the criminal act or the physical element in criminal liability; one of the material elements in criminal liability.

concurrence the requirement that *actus reus* must join with *mens rea* to cause a harmful result in order to impose criminal liability.

culpability blameworthiness; a culpable individual acts with one of the criminal mental states—purpose, knowledge, recklessness, or negligence—and can therefore be blamed for the harmful result.

general principles of criminal liability the theoretical foundation for the material elements: *actus reus, mens rea,* causation, and harm.

material elements the parts of a crime that the prosecution must prove beyond a reasonable doubt, such as *actus reus, mens rea,* causation, and harmful result.

mens rea the mental element in crime, of which there are four mental states: purpose, knowledge, recklessness, and negligence.

negligence the unconscious creation of risk, or the mental state in which actors create risks of harm but are not aware they are creating them.

recklessness the conscious creation of risk, or the state of mind in which actors know they are creating risks of harm.

strict liability liability without fault.

INTRODUCTION

The prosecution must prove five **material elements** beyond a reasonable doubt in order to convict defendants in most criminal cases. Proof of these material elements affects not only guilt in criminal trials but also decisions to prosecute in the first place and sentencing following conviction. For example, if prosecutors believe enough facts exist to conclude that defendants committed a crime, they have *factual* guilt. If they do not have sufficient admissible, credible evidence to prove that guilt, however, they do not have *legal* guilt, and ordinarily they will not prosecute. If they do prosecute, they either reduce the charge or negotiate a plea with defendants and their lawyers.[1]

The principal material elements are as follows: (1) the physical element (the criminal act, or *actus reus*) must (2) concur or join with (3) the mental element (the criminal mind, or *mens rea*) and, where relevant, to (4) cause or produce a (5) harmful result. Statutes do not often define the material elements in detail because most crimes derive from well-established common-law meanings. The material elements constitute the **general principles of criminal liability.** This chapter treats *actus reus, mens rea,* concurrence, causation, and harmful result as they apply to all crimes. Later chapters analyze the material elements of particular offenses, such as the *mens rea* of murder, the act in larceny, and the harm in statutory rape.[2]

ACTUS REUS

Status

The first principle of criminal liability is the requisite of an act—the *actus reus.* In American law, criminal liability rests on action. Many axioms illustrate this principle: "Thoughts are free," "We are punished for what we do, not for who we are," "Criminal punishment depends on conduct, not status," "We are punished for what we have done, not for what we might do." The principle is easy to state, but exceptions to the general rule complicate its apparent simplicity.

Several problematic extensions to the common meaning of *act* appear in criminal laws. *Robinson v. California* confronts the problem of whether the Constitution prohibits making the status of drug addiction a crime.

CASE

Is "Illness" a Crime?

Robinson v. California

370 U.S. 660, 82 S.Ct. 1417, 8 L.Ed. 2d 758 (1962)

FACTS

A California statute makes it a criminal offense for a person to "be addicted to the use of narcotics."[1] This appeal draws into question the constitutionality of that provision of the state law, as construed by the California courts in the present case.

The appellant was convicted after a jury trial in the Municipal Court of Los Angeles. . . . Officer Brown testified that . . . he had observed "scar tissue and discoloration on the inside" of the appellant's right arm, and "what appeared to be numerous needle marks and a scab which was approximately three inches below the crook of the elbow" on the appellant's left arm. The . . . appellant . . . admitted to the occasional use of narcotics.

OPINION

The broad power of a State to regulate the narcotic drugs traffic within its borders is not here in issue. More than forty years ago, this Court explicitly recognized the validity of that power: "There can be no question of the authority of the State in the exercise of its police power to regulate the administration, sale, prescription and use of dangerous and habit-forming drugs. The right to exercise this power is so manifest in the interest of the public health and welfare, that it is unnecessary to enter upon a discussion of it beyond saying that it is too firmly established to be successfully called in question."

Such regulation could take a variety of valid forms. A State might impose criminal sanctions, for example, against the unauthorized manufacture, prescription, sale, purchase, or possession of narcotics within its borders. In the interest of discouraging the violation of such laws, or in the interest of the general health or welfare of its inhabitants, a State might establish a program of compulsory treatment for those addicted to narcotics. Such a program of treatment might require periods of involuntary confinement. And penal sanctions might be imposed for failure to comply with established compulsory treatment procedures. Or a State might choose to attack the evils of narcotics traffic on broader fronts also—through public health education, for example, or by efforts to ameliorate the economic and social conditions under which those evils might be thought to flourish. In short, the range of valid choice which a State might make in this area is undoubtedly a wide one, and the wisdom of any particular choice within the allowable spectrum is not for us to decide. Upon that premise we turn to the California law in issue here.

This statute . . . is not one which punishes a person for the use of narcotics, for their purchase, sale or possession, or for antisocial or disorderly behavior resulting from their administration. It is not a law which even purports to provide or require medical treatment. Rather, we deal with a statute which makes the "status" of narcotic addiction a criminal offense, for which the offender may be prosecuted "at any time before he reforms." California has said that a person can be continuously guilty of this offense, whether or not he has ever used or possessed any narcotics within the State, and whether or not he has been guilty of any antisocial behavior there.

It is unlikely that any State at this moment in history would attempt to make it a criminal offense for a person to be mentally ill, or a leper, or to be afflicted with a venereal disease. A State might determine that the general health and welfare require that the victims of these and other human afflictions be dealt with by compulsory treatment, involving quarantine, confinement, or sequestration. But, in the light of contemporary human knowledge, a law which made a criminal offense of such a disease would doubtless be universally thought to be an infliction of cruel and unusual punishment in violation of the Eighth and Fourteenth Amendments.

We cannot but consider the statute before us as of the same category. In this Court counsel for the State recognized that narcotic addiction is an illness. Indeed, it is apparently an illness which may be contracted innocently or involuntarily. We hold that a state law which imprisons a person thus afflicted as a criminal, even though he has never touched any narcotic drug within the State or been guilty of any irregular behavior there, inflicts a cruel and unusual punishment in violation of the Fourteenth Amendment. To be sure, imprisonment for ninety days is not, in the abstract, a punishment which is either cruel or unusual. But the question cannot be considered in the abstract. Even one day in prison would be a cruel and unusual punishment for the "crime" of having a common cold.

We are not unmindful that the vicious evils of the narcotics traffic have occasioned the grave concern of government. There are, as we have said, countless fronts on which those evils may be legitimately attacked. We deal in this case only with an individual provision of a particularized local law as it has so far been interpreted by the California courts.

Reversed.

CASE DISCUSSION

Robinson v. California asks the question Is status or condition a basis for criminal liability? Earlier in this chapter, the maxim "We are punished for what we do, not for who we are" was mentioned. It is not always followed in actual criminal statutes. Prostitution, vagrancy, and drug addiction have all been criminal conditions not related to any specific acts. Not until the two landmark cases *Robinson v. California* and *Papachristou v. City of Jacksonville* did the United States Supreme Court rule that the Constitution limited how far condition or status may replace or supplement act as a requisite for criminal liability. *Robinson* makes it clear that basing criminal liability on "illness" violates the Eighth Amendment prohibition. Vagrancy and prostitution statutes are also open to constitutional challenge. Would you make drug addiction a crime? prostitution? vagrancy? Why or why not?[3] (See chapter 12 for vagrancy discussion.)

---

[1]The statute is § 11721 of the California Health and Safety Code. It provides: "No person shall use, or be under the influence of, or be addicted to the use of narcotics, excepting when administered by or under the direction of a person licensed by the State to prescribe and administer narcotics. It shall be the burden of the defense to show that it comes within the exception. Any person convicted of violating any provision of this section is guilty of a misdemeanor and shall be sentenced to serve a term of not less than 90 days nor more than one year in the county jail. The court may place a person convicted hereunder on probation for a period not to exceed five years and shall in all cases in which probation is granted require as a condition thereof that such person be confined in the county jail for at least 90 days. In no event does the court have the power to absolve a person who violates this section from the obligation of spending at least 90 days in confinement in the county jail."

Thoughts

Consider a statute that makes it a crime to *intend* to kill another person. Why does such a statute strike us as absurd? Several reasons come to mind. It is impossible to enforce. Those who intend to kill can simply deny they ever had such an intention. The mere intention is not subject to proof without a confession. "The thought of man is not triable, for the devil himself knoweth not the thought of man," said one medieval English judge. Furthermore, no harm to another comes from mere intentions. The moral law may condemn those who have immoral thoughts; the criminal law requires conduct—a combination of act and intention. Hence, punishing intention, even if it were possible, does not punish the harm contemplated by the statute: the death of another person.[4]

In addition, rarely can daydreaming or fantasy be distinguished from intention. The intention to act practically never accompanies an angry thought such as "I'll kill him for what he just did!" Therefore, punishment must await sufficient action to prove that intention accompanies the expression of angry thoughts.

Finally, punishing thoughts expands the meaning of crime to encompass a "mental state that the accused might be too irresolute even to begin to translate into action." Criminal liability awaits action sufficient to demonstrate the resolution and will to harm another. In short, punishing thoughts is impractical, inequitable, and unjust; hence, thoughts are not criminal acts. (See also chapter 5 on incomplete crimes.[5]

Voluntariness

Actus reus excludes not only thoughts and condition but also some physical movements as well. Several criteria determine what acts are criminal. First, criminal acts must be voluntary; they must stem from the actor's free will. The criminal law imposes liability on those who consciously and freely act, not on those who are acted upon by outside (or even internal) forces. The bizarre case *The King v. Cogdon* deals with sleepwalking as a criminal act.

CASE

Is Killing while Asleep a Criminal Act?

The King v. Cogdon[6]

FACTS

Mrs. Cogdon was charged with the murder of her only child, a daughter called Pat, aged nineteen. Pat had for some time been receiving psychiatric treatment for a relatively minor neurotic condition of which, in her psychiatrist's opinion, she was now cured. Despite this, Mrs. Cogdon continued to worry unduly about her. Describing the relationship between Pat and her mother, Mr. Cogdon testified: "I don't think a mother could have thought any more of her daughter. I think she absolutely adored her." On the conscious level, at least, there was no reason to doubt Mrs. Cogdon's deep attachment to her daughter.

To the charge of murdering Pat, Mrs. Cogdon pleaded not guilty. Her story, though somewhat bizarre, was not seriously challenged by the Crown, and led to her acquittal. She told how, on the night before her daughter's death, she had dreamt that their house was full of spiders and that these spiders were crawling all over Pat. In her sleep, Mrs. Cogdon left the bed she shared with her husband, went into Pat's room, and awakened to find herself violently brushing at Pat's face, presumably to remove the spiders. This woke Pat. Mrs. Cogdon told her she was just tucking her in. At the trial, she testified that she still believed, as she had been told, that the occupants of a nearby house bred spiders as a hobby, preparing nests for them behind the pictures on their walls. It was these spiders which in her dreams had invaded their home and attacked Pat. There had also been a previous dream in which ghosts had sat at the end of Mrs. Cogdon's bed and she had said to them, "Well, you have come to take Pattie." It does not seem fanciful to accept the psychological explanation of these spiders and ghosts as the projections of Mrs. Cogdon's subconscious hostility towards her daughter; a hostility which was itself rooted in Mrs. Cogdon's own early life and marital relationship.

The morning after the spider dream she told her doctor of it. He gave her a sedative and, because of the dream and certain previous difficulties she had reported, discussed the possibility of psychiatric treatment. That evening Mrs. Cogdon suggested to her husband that he attend his lodge meeting, and asked Pat to come with her to the cinema. After he had gone Pat looked through the paper, not unusually found no tolerable programme, and said that as she was going out the next evening she thought she would rather go to bed early. Later, while Pat was having a bath preparatory to retiring, Mrs. Cogdon went into her room, put a hot water bottle in the bed, turned back the bedclothes, and placed a glass of hot milk beside the bed ready for Pat. She then went to bed herself. There was some desultory conversation between them about the war in Korea, and just before she put out her light Pat called out to her mother, "Mum, don't be so silly worrying there about the war, it's not on our front door step yet."

Mrs. Cogdon went to sleep. She dreamt that "the war was all around the house," that soldiers were in Pat's room, and that one soldier was on the bed attacking Pat. This was all of the dream she could later recapture. Her first "waking" memory was of running from Pat's room, out of the house to the home of her sister who lived next door. When her sister opened the front door Mrs. Cogdon fell into her arms, crying "I think I've hurt Pattie."

In fact Mrs. Cogdon had, in her somnambulistic state, left her bed, fetched an axe from the woodheap, entered Pat's room, and struck her two accurate forceful blows on the head with the blade of the axe, thus killing her.

OPINION

Mrs. Cogdon's story was supported by the evidence of her physician, a psychiatrist, and a psychologist. The jury believed Mrs. Cogdon, the presumption that the natural consequences of her acts were intended as being completely rebutted by her account of her mental state at the time of the killing, and by the unanimous support given to it by the medical and psychological evidence. She was acquitted. It must be stressed that insanity was not pleaded as a defence—she was acquitted because the act of killing itself was not, in law, regarded as her act at all.

CASE DISCUSSION

Was Mrs. Cogdon's act of killing Pattie involuntary? Could she have done anything to prevent her killing Pattie? It is widely held that it is wrong to punish those who cannot be blamed. Would it be "right" to punish Mrs. Cogdon? Why or why not?[7]

Acts occurring during sleepwalking are not the only involuntary acts. Spasms associated with neurological disorders are also involuntary acts. So, a person whose hand or leg suddenly and uncontrollably jerks, striking and injuring another, has not acted voluntarily. Acts occurring under hypnosis are also involuntary. In a Danish case, Bjorn Nielson masterminded a robbery by hypnotizing his friend Palle Hardrup. While in the hypnotic trance, Hardrup held up a Copenhagen bank, shooting and killing a teller and director. Nielson was sentenced to life imprisonment because he masterminded the holdup, even though he was nowhere near the bank when the robbery took place. Hardrup was sent to a mental hospital. He was not tried for robbery because his acts during the holdup were not considered voluntary.[8]

Involuntary acts do not give rise to criminal liability because punishment in such cases does not satisfy criminal law's general purposes. Retribution does not apply because involuntary acts are not blameworthy and hence do not deserve punishment. Furthermore, punishment does not deter those who act without conscious choice. The government can incapacitate "dangerous" involuntary actors, but civil commitment more appropriately serves this purpose in the absence of blameworthiness.

On the other hand, threatened punishment might induce individuals susceptible to involuntary acts to take precautions against harming others. Hypnotized persons can refuse hypnosis; sleepwalkers can lock their bedroom doors at night; and spastics might take many of the "new" drugs to control movement disorders. If individuals can take measures to control involuntary movements and do not, then they are arguably blameworthy; they have committed voluntarily induced involuntary acts, a complex concept explored later in this chapter under *mens rea*.

Voluntarily induced involuntary states that are less bizarre than hypnosis include unconscious states that individuals know beforehand might occur. These arise frequently in the driving of cars: drivers who are drowsy continue to drive until they fall asleep; persons who are intoxicated to the point that they do not know what they are doing continue to drive; persons with dangerously high blood pressure suffer strokes while driving; or epileptics have seizures while driving. Chapter 6 analyzes some of these situations under negligent homicide.

Verbal Acts

In common usage, *act* means bodily movement; however, in *actus reus,* the term encompasses more than moving arms, legs, hands, feet, and the entire body. Words constitute criminal acts in some crimes. Crimes consisting of **verbal acts** include conspiracy, solicitation, terroristic threats, some kinds of assault, and inciting to riot. These crimes are discussed in chapters on specific crimes; here it suffices to note that they constitute criminal acts under the general principle of *actus reus.*

Omission

Voluntary bodily movements, voluntarily induced involuntary conduct, and words are not the only acts that may qualify as criminal under the general principle of *actus reus.* Under some circumstances, omissions, or failures to act, are also criminal. But the law imposes liability on omissions only reluctantly, preferring to punish those who act affirmatively, not those who allow something to happen, as is the case in omissions.

Only the failure to perform *legal* duties is a criminal omission. Legal duties to act might arise out of relationships or contracts, or might be imposed by statutes. Failure to perform *moral* duties does not constitute the *actus reus.* Lord Macauley, a nineteenth-century English law reformer, stated the idea this way:

> It is, indeed most highly desirable that men should not merely abstain from doing harm to their neighbors; but should render active service to their neighbors. In general, however, the penal law must content itself with keeping men from doing positive harm, and must leave to public opinion, and to the teachers of morality and religion, the office of furnishing men with motives for doing positive good. It is evident that to attempt to punish men by law for not rendering to others all the service which it is their [moral] duty to render to others would be preposterous. We must grant impunity to the vast majority of these omissions which a benevolent morality would pronounce reprehensible, and must content ourselves with punishing such omissions only when they are distinguished from the rest by some circumstance which marks them out as peculiarly fit objects of penal legislation.[9]

Moral duties include the obligation for neighbors to help neighbors in need, passersby to aid injured pedestrians, and friends to help friends, fellow students, co-workers, and associates. These are not the same as legal duties.

Certain relationships impose legal duties. Most common of these are the parent-child relationship, the marital relationship in some jurisdictions, the doctor-patient relationship, the employer-employee relationship, and the carrier-passenger relationship. Statutes also give rise to legal duties. Examples include duties to file income tax returns, to report accidents and child abuse, and to register firearms. Contracts create other legal duties. Police officers, for example, agree to perform certain public duties; failure to perform those duties, such as not saving a victim's life when present and able to do so, creates criminal liability.

Limiting criminal omissions to failure to perform legal duties is based on the proposition that individual conscience, peer pressure, and other informal mechanisms sanction and prevent behavior more effectively than does criminal prosecution. Furthermore, prosecuting omissions unduly burdens an already overburdened criminal justice system. Finally, the criminal law cannot compel Good Samaritans to help those in need.[10]

CASE

Did She Criminally Fail to Act?

Commonwealth v. Konz

498 Pa. 639, 450 A.2d 638 (1982)

[Mrs. Konz was convicted of involuntary manslaughter. She appealed. Justice Flaherty delivered the opinion.]

FACTS

In September, 1973, Reverend Konz, while serving as a teacher, counselor, and chaplain at United Wesleyan College, became acquainted with Erikson, a student at the College. A close friendship, based on their common interest in religion, formed between Erikson and Reverend Konz as the former became a regular visitor at the latter's residence.

Reverend Konz was a thirty-four year old diabetic and had, for seventeen years, administered to himself daily doses of insulin. On March 4, 1974, however, following an encounter on campus with a visiting evangelist speaker, Reverend Konz publicly proclaimed his desire to discontinue insulin treatment in reliance on the belief that God would heal the diabetic condition. He assured the president of the College and members of the student body that he would carefully monitor his condition and would, if necessary, take insulin.

. . . On March 18, 1974, however, Erikson and Reverend Konz formed a pact to pray together to enable the latter to resist the temptation to administer insulin.

Mrs. Konz was informed of the prayer pact, and, on the morning of Saturday, March 23, 1974, when her husband evidenced symptoms of insulin debt, she removed his insulin from the refrigerator and concealed it. Later that day, the Reverend attempted to obtain insulin from the refrigerator, and, upon discovering that the medicine had been removed, strongly indicated that it should be returned. He then attempted to proceed from room to room but his passage was blocked by Erikson. Harsh words were exchanged, and Erikson, after kneeling in prayer, forced the Reverend into a bedroom where, accompanied by Mrs. Konz, Erikson and the Reverend conversed for approximately one half hour. During that time, the Reverend tried to telephone police to obtain assistance but was prevented from doing so by Erikson and Mrs. Konz, who, during a struggle with the Reverend, rendered at least that telephone permanently inoperable.

Immediately after this confrontation, the Reverend, his wife, and Erikson returned amicably to the kitchen for coffee, and no further request for insulin was ever made. In addition, the Reverend approached his aunt who resided in the same household and stated, in an apparent reference to the preceding confrontation with Erikson, that "It's all settled now," and told her that there was no cause for concern. He also told his eleven year old daughter that "Everything is fine," and indicated to her that he did not intend to take insulin. The Reverend then departed from the house, accompanied by Erikson, and returned an hour later. As the day progressed, Reverend Konz cancelled his speaking commitment for the following day and drove his wife to an institution having hospital facilities to pick up a close friend who was a practical nurse. Late on Saturday night, while waiting inside the institution for the nurse to complete her duties, the Reverend appeared very fatigued and complained that he was developing an upset stomach. Both of these conditions were symptomatic of lack of insulin, but neither the Reverend nor his wife requested that insulin, which was available at the institution, be administered. With regard to the Reverend's condition at that time, the nurse observed that he travelled with unimpaired mobility, and that he was conversant, rational, and cognizant of his environs. Nevertheless, he made no mention of a need for insulin, and the nurse made no inquiry as to such a need because the Reverend had on a previous day become very upset at her inquiry as to his diabetic condition.

Upon returning home from this errand, Reverend Konz experienced increasing illness, vomiting intermittently Saturday night and Sunday morning, and remained in bed all day Sunday except for trips into the bathroom. On Sunday afternoon visitors arrived at the Konz residence. The Reverend, recognizing their voices, called to them from his room to inquire whether they wished to see him; having been informed of the Reverend's nausea, however, the visitors declined to stay. As the Reverend's condition worsened and he became restless, his wife and Erikson administered cracked ice but did not summon medical aid. The Konz's eleven year old daughter then inquired as to why a doctor had not been summoned but Mrs. Konz responded that her husband was "going to be getting better." Late Sunday night or early Monday morning everyone in the household fell asleep. On Monday morning at approximately 6 A.M., while the others were still asleep, Reverend Konz died of diabetic ketoacidosis.

Appellants were found guilty by a jury of the crime of involuntary manslaughter pursuant to Section 2504 of the Pennsylvania Crimes Code, which provides: "A person is guilty of involuntary manslaugh-

ter when as a direct result of the doing of an unlawful act in a reckless or grossly negligent manner, or the doing of a lawful act in a reckless or grossly negligent manner, he causes the death of another person."
. . .

OPINION

To impose criminal liability for an omission as opposed to an act, the omission must be "expressly made sufficient by the law defining the offense" or "a duty to perform the omitted act otherwise imposed by law." The . . . issue on appeal, therefore, is whether Mrs. Konz had a duty to seek medical attention for her spouse. Under the circumstances of this case, we find no such duty to have been present; hence, the conviction of Mrs. Konz, and that of Erikson as her accomplice, cannot be sustained.

Courts have, in limited circumstances, departed from the long-standing common law rule that one human being is under no *legal* compulsion to take action to aid another human being. One such circumstance is where there exists a requisite relationship between the parties, as is present in the relationship of parent to child. Hence, a parent has been held guilty of involuntary manslaughter for failure to seek medical assistance for his sick child. . . . The inherent dependency of a child upon his parent to obtain medical aid, i.e., the incapacity of a child to evaluate his condition and summon aid by himself, supports imposition of such a duty upon the parent.

The Commonwealth argues that the marital relationship gives rise to a similar duty to aid one's spouse. Spouses, however, do not generally suffer the same incapacity as do children with respect to the ability to comprehend their states of health and obtain medical assistance. We reject, therefore, the holding of the Superior Court that the marital relationship gives rise to an unrestricted duty for one spouse to summon medical aid whenever the other is in a serious or immediate need of medical attention. Recognition of such a duty would place lay persons in peril of criminal prosecution while compelling them to medically diagnose the seriousness of their spouses' illnesses and injuries. In addition, it would impose an obligation for a spouse to take action at a time when the stricken individual competently chooses not to receive assistance. The marital relationship gives rise to an expectation of reliance between spouses, and to a belief that one's spouse should be trusted to respect, rather than ignore, one's expressed preferences. That expectation would be frustrated by imposition of a broad duty to seek aid, since one's spouse would then be forced to ignore the expectation that the preference to forego assistance will be honored.

Reversed and appellants discharged.

CASE DISCUSSION

Rev. Konz died following Mrs. Konz's failure to give him insulin. According to the law, her omission was only criminal if Mrs. Konz had a duty to give Rev. Konz insulin. Do you agree that spouses do not have a legal duty to provide emergency aid, or at least to summon a doctor when their spouses need it? Criminal omission—the *actus reus*—is only one element in criminal liability. The prosecution must also prove *mens rea*, concurrence, causation, and harmful result in order to convict Mrs. Konz. However, since *actus reus* was not proved, the court did not need to address these other elements.

Not all failures to perform legal duties constitute criminal omissions. A criminal omission consists of an *unreasonable* failure to fulfill a legal duty to act. It would not apply if a sea captain allowed a crew member who had fallen overboard to drown in order to save other crew members and passengers from a dangerous storm. It would also not apply if a babysitter did not dive into deep water to save the child he was watching because the sitter could not swim.

An excerpt from an article on the case of Kitty Genovese follows. In this case, if there was a legal duty to act, what was the duty—to rescue her from her assailant? chase the assailant? call the police?

CASE

Was Their Omission a Crime?

37 Who Saw Murder Didn't Call the Police

New York Times (March 17, 1964). Copyright © 1964 by the New York Times Company. Reprinted by permission.

For more than half an hour 38 respectable, law-abiding citizens in Queens watched a killer stalk and stab a woman in three separate attacks in Kew Gardens.

Twice the sound of their voices and the sudden glow of their bedroom lights interrupted him and frightened him off. Each time he returned, sought her out and stabbed her again. Not one person telephoned the police during the assault; one witness called after the woman was dead. But Assistant Chief Inspector Frederick M. Lussen, in charge of the borough's detectives and a veteran of 25 years of homicide investigations, is still shocked.

He can give a matter of fact recitation of many murders. But the Kew Gardens slaying baffles him—not because it is a murder, but because the "good people" failed to call the police.

"As we have reconstructed the crime," he said, "the assailant had three chances to kill this woman during a 35-minute period. He returned twice to complete the job. If we had been called when he first attacked, the woman might not be dead now."

This is what the police say happened beginning at 3:20 A.M. in the staid, middle-class, tree lined Austin Street area:

Twenty-eight-year-old Catherine Genovese, who was called Kitty by almost everyone in the neighborhood, was returning home from her job as manager of a bar in Hollis. She parked her red Fiat in a lot adjacent to the Kew Gardens Long Island Rail Road Station, facing Mowbray Place. Like many residents of the neighborhood, she had parked there day after day since her arrival from Connecticut a year ago, although the railroad frowns on the practice.

She turned off the lights of her car, locked the door and started to walk the 100 feet to the entrance of her apartment at 82–70 Austin Street, which is in a Tudor building, with stores on the first floor and apartments on the second.

The entrance to the apartment is in the rear of the building because the front is rented to retail stores. At night the quiet neighborhood is shrouded in the slumbering darkness that marks most residential areas.

Miss Genovese noticed a man at the far end of the lot, near a seven-story apartment house at 82–40 Austin Street. She halted. Then, nervously, she headed up Austin Street toward Lefferts Boulevard, where there is a call box to the 102d Police Precinct in nearby Richmond Hill.

She got as far as a street light in front of a bookstore before the man grabbed her. She screamed. Lights went on in the 10-story apartment house at 82–67 Austin Street, which faces the bookstore. Windows slid open and voices punctured the early morning stillness.

Miss Genovese screamed: "Oh, my God, he stabbed me! Please help me! Please help me!"

From one of the upper windows in the apartment house, a man called down: "Let that girl alone!"

The assailant looked up at him, shrugged and walked down Austin Street toward a white sedan parked a short distance away. Miss Genovese struggled to her feet.

Lights went out. The killer returned to Miss Genovese, now trying to make her way around the side of the building by the parking lot to get to her apartment. The assailant stabbed her again.

"I'm dying!" she shrieked. "I'm dying!"

Windows were opened again, and light went on in many apartments. The assailant got into his car and drove away. Miss Genovese staggered to her feet. A city bus, Q_i10, the Lefferts Boulevard line to Kennedy International Airport, passed. It was 3:35 A.M.

The assailant returned. By then, Miss Genovese had crawled to the back of the building, where the freshly painted brown doors to the apartment house held out hope of safety. The killer tried the first door; she wasn't there. At the second door, 82–62 Austin Street, he saw her slumped on the floor at the foot of the stairs. He stabbed her a third time—fatally.

It was 3:50 by the time the police received their first call, from a man who was a neighbor of Miss Genovese. In two minutes they were at the scene. The neighbor, a 70-year-old woman and another woman were the only persons on the street. Nobody else came forward.

The man explained that he had called the police after much deliberation. He had phoned a friend in Nassau County for advice and then he had crossed the roof of the building to the apartment of the elderly woman to get her to make the call.

"I didn't want to get involved," he sheepishly told the police.

The police stressed how simple it would have been to have gotten in touch with them. "A phone call," said one of the detectives, "would have done it." The police may be reached by dialing "0" for operator or SPring 7–3100.

Today, witnesses from the neighborhood, which is made up of one-family homes in the $35,000 to $60,000 range with the exception of the two apartment houses near the railroad station, find it difficult to explain why they didn't call the police.

Lieut. Bernard Jacobs, who handled the investigation by the detectives, said: "It is one of the better neighborhoods. There are few reports of crimes." . . .

The police said most persons had told them they had been afraid to call, but had given meaningless answers when asked what they had feared.

"We can understand the reticence of people to become involved in an area of violence," Lieutenant Jacobs said, "but where they are in their homes, near phones, why should they be afraid to call the police?"

Witnesses—some of them unable to believe what they had allowed to happen—told a reporter why.

A housewife, knowingly if quite casual, said, "We thought it was a lover's quarrel." A husband and wife both said, "Frankly, we were afraid." They seemed aware of the fact that events might have been different. A distraught woman, wiping her hands in her apron, said, "I didn't want my husband to get involved." . . .

A man peeked out from a slight opening in the doorway to his apartment and rattled off an account of the killer's second attack. Why hadn't he called the police at the time? "I was tired," he said without emotion. "I went back to bed."

It was 4:25 A.M. when the ambulance arrived for the body of Miss Genovese. It drove off. "Then," a solemn police detective said, "the people came out." Citizens who failed to come to Miss Genovese's aid were clearly under a moral duty to do so, and they should receive the moral condemnation of society for failing to perform that duty. But should they be punished for criminal omission?

Consider two other incidents. In the first, an assailant raped and beat an eighteen-year-old switchboard operator. The victim ran naked and bleeding from the building onto the street screaming for help. A crowd of forty people gathered and watched, in broad daylight, while the rapist tried to drag her back into the building. No onlooker intervened; two police officers happened on the scene and arrested the assailant. In the second incident, eleven people watched while an assailant stabbed seventeen-year-old Andrew Melmille in the stomach on a subway. The assailant left the subway at the next stop. Not one of the eleven people on the train helped Melmille. He bled to death. Is there a legal duty to act in either of these incidents? What is the duty? How, if at all, do these incidents differ from the Genovese incident?[11]

Possession

In addition to voluntary acts and the failure to reasonably perform legal duties, the passive state of possessing some items and substances sometimes qualifies as a criminal act. Although possession itself is passive, acquiring possession requires action. If the possessor performs that action, then the possessor's act produces the possession. If a third person places an item or substance in another's possession without the receiver's knowledge, the possessor has, of course, not committed a voluntary act. Once possession is discovered, however, retaining it instead of disposing of it involves an omission. Thus, having pornography in my house is not an act, but buying it and putting it there is. Furthermore, finding heroin in my house and not disposing of it after discovery is an omission.

Jurisdictions differ on two questions regarding criminal possession: (1) What constitutes possession? and (2) Does criminal possession require *knowing* possession, or is constructive possession sufficient? **Constructive possession** is not physical or **actual possession;** it is legal possession or custody. An owner has custody over a home but does not physically possess the cocaine that a weekend guest keeps in the host's closet. One who buys cocaine in order to use it has **knowing possession** of the cocaine. One who does a friend a favor by carrying a brown paper bag without knowing that the bag contains stolen money has what the law designates as **mere possession** of the money.

Constructive possession and mere possession give rise to difficult problems in criminal law. Constructive possession increases the chance that innocent people will be convicted. In the strongest possession cases, the defendant physically possesses the prohibited item or substance; constructive possession requires only that the prohibited item or substance fall under the constructive possessor's control. Having cocaine in my pocket more clearly demonstrates guilt than having cocaine found in my houseguest's room. Mere possession creates the possibility that the law may punish people who do not intend harm. For example, postal carriers constructively possess narcotics they are carrying for delivery. If your professor asks you to deliver an envelope to her office, and you do so, do you criminally possess the cocaine it contains? A long line of cases rules that you do on the ground that mere possession constitutes the *actus reus.*[12]

CASE

Did He Criminally Possess the Heroin?

State v. Weaver
24 Wn. App. 83, 600 P.2d 598 (1979)

[Leon Weaver was convicted of possessing heroin. He appealed. Chief Justice Callow delivered the opinion.]

FACTS

During the evening of April 5, 1977, Seattle police detectives executed a search warrant on a 3-bedroom house in Seattle. During the search, one of the detectives recovered a yellow balloon from a small trash can. This was analyzed and found to contain a residue of heroin. Also seized from the kitchen were funnels, a dietitian scale, lactose, sandwich bags, a coffee mill containing lactose, a strainer, a recently washed playing card, some balloons, and a letter addressed to the defendant. No one was at home during the course of the search, although at one point the defendant's mother stopped by. The defendant was later arrested on the basis of the materials seized.

The State brought out at trial that 8 months before the search a prior search of the house revealed photographs depicting the defendant, his sister, and a juke box with the name "Mr. Leon" on it. The pictures were taken at the house in the bar area between the kitchen and living room. Personal property, mail addressed to the defendant at that address, and other documents belonging to the defendant were also found in the living room. The defendant's cousin, Johnie Weaver, was arrested upon his arrival at the house during the course of the earlier search. The defendant was not present at that time. Approximately 5 months before the search of April 5, 1977, the defendant was awakened and arrested at the house. A detective testified that the defendant went into the southeast corner bedroom and dressed. Another detective testified that over a period of several months up to April 5, 1977, he observed the defendant at the residence about a dozen times.

The defendant presented testimony that legal title to the house was held by the defendant's Aunt Ruth, and that the defendant's brother, Vernon, held equitable title to the house. The defendant's mother and aunt are twins, as are his father and uncle. According to Johnie Weaver, the defendant's first cousin, the juke box was owned by all of the Weavers who stayed at the house from time to time, of which there were six. He also stated that the southeast corner bedroom was used by whoever was staying there, and that unrelated overnight visitors frequently stayed at the house. Vernon Weaver was said to have been residing at the house on April 5, 1977. Johnie Weaver also testified that the house was sometimes used as an after-hours place, that he was there maybe every other night, and that the defendant was there about the same number of times. Both Johnie and Vernon Weaver indicated that Leon stayed at times at his mother's house, at his aunt's house, and at the Empire Way house; he received correspondence at all three adresses. Both also testified that the defendant did not use drugs, but that Vernon did.

At the close of the State's case and again at the close of all the evidence, the defendant moved to dismiss for failure of the State to prove prima facie the elements of possession and knowledge. The motion was denied.

The trial court found, . . . that "the defendant and members of his family contrived a system with the predetermined purpose to make it appear that the defendant did not reside at [the] residence," and that the accumulation of all the evidence showed that the defendant had dominion and control over the heroin. The trial court made no finding as to the defendant's knowledge of the presence of the drug.

OPINION

The defendant first assigns error to the trial court's failure to find that the defendant had guilty knowledge of the heroin's presence on the premises searched. The State contends that this was proper because guilty knowledge is not an element of the crime of possession of a controlled substance. Therefore, the issue presented is whether it must be proven, and the trial court must find, that the defendant had knowledge of the presence of the illicit drug.

> Under the . . . Uniform Controlled Substances Act, . . . it was declared unlawful for any person to manufacture, possess, have under his control, sell, prescribe, administer, dispense, or compound any narcotic drug, except as authorized in this chapter.

. . . The language of the statute . . . provides no guidance on the issue before us. However, without the mental element of knowledge, even a postal carrier would be guilty of the crime were he innocently to deliver a package which in fact contained a forbidden narcotic. Such a result is not intended by the legislature. Accordingly, absent express legislative language to the contrary, we find in the context of this statute, its history and language, that guilty knowledge is intrinsic to the definition of the crime itself. Guilty knowledge must be proven beyond a reasonable doubt in conviction of this defendant under the statute. . . .

Reversed.

CASE DISCUSSION

If you were writing a criminal code, would you adopt the constructive or actual possession definition? the knowing or mere possession definition? Under your definitions, did Leon Weaver criminally possess the heroin? Why would you adopt the definitions and apply them in the way that you did here?

Criminal possession punishes *potential* harm. It aims to prevent possessors from putting prohibited items and substances to use; for example, from taking drugs, shooting guns, and using burglary tools. The law of criminal possession resembles the idea that, as the doctors say, prevention is better than cure. Some jurists believe that preventive justice is the best justice. Possession also increases the risk that criminal law will punish status and condition. People who possess drugs, burglary tools, and the like are considered dangerous. The law of criminal possession punishes them for being burglars or drug addicts, not because they have burgled a house or used marijuana.[13]

Problems with criminal possession have led to suggestions that it should encompass only knowingly possessing substances and objects that unambiguously threaten serious bodily harm. The criminal law appropriately includes possessing guns and explosives, although this should be a minor crime because possession itself does not harm. On the other hand, some argue that possessing marijuana and obscene materials does not threaten serious bodily harm and should not be included in criminal law. In addition, they maintain that substances or items that possessors may use for either harmless or harmful purposes should be excluded. These include burglary tools, such as lock picks, and drug paraphernalia like hypodermic needles and pipes.

Summary

The *actus reus*, or criminal act, includes voluntary bodily movements; omissions, or failures to perform legal duties; and possession. This definition is cumbersome, but it covers the essential characteristics of the *actus reus*. The meanings of these aspects of *actus reus* vary from jurisdiction to jurisdiction. Whether sleepwalking or hypnosis are voluntary movements, whether harms resulting from failures to act on moral duties are crimes, and whether criminal possession must be knowing—these questions appreciably alter criminal law's scope. Hence, they bear heavily on criminal policy, reflecting the basic values that a jurisdiction's criminal law hopes to uphold and protect.

═══ *MENS REA*

Perhaps nothing is more basic to criminal law than the principal of **mens rea,** the idea that some kind of blameworthy state of mind must accompany *actus reus*. The child's "I didn't mean to . . . " captures this idea, as does Justice Holmes's pithy "Even a dog distinguishes between being stumbled over and being kicked." Since at least 1600, common-law judges required that some sort of "bad state of mind" accompany criminal acts. The Latin maxim *"actus not facit ream nisi mens sit rea"* ("An act is not bad without an evil mind") expresses this idea.

Mens rea is complex, perhaps the most complex concept in criminal law. Various terminology conceptualizes and expresses it, and proving it gives rise to difficult problems. Furthermore, it encompasses several mental states, and some mental states are more blameworthy—more culpable, or more deserving of punishment—than others.[14]

Determining Mens Rea

The only direct evidence of *mens rea* is defendants' confessions; no instruments can measure it. Electroencephalograms can record brain waves and Xrays can photograph brain tissue, but the medieval judge's words are still true: "The thought of man is not triable, for the devil himself knoweth not the thought of man." St. Thomas Aquinas put it even more pointedly:

> Now man, the framer of human law, is competent to judge only of outward acts, because man seeth those things that appear . . . while God alone, the framer of the Divine law, is competent to judge of the inward movement of wills.[15]

Since defendants rarely confess their *mens rea*, the criminal law determines *mens rea* mainly by circumstantial or indirect evidence. Action supplies the indirect evidence. Inferring intent from actions substitutes for observing the mind directly; we can know indirectly what actors intend by observing directly what they did. General human experience permits accurate inferences about intent from actions. For example, most people do not break into strangers' houses at night unless they intend to commit crimes. Thus, the acts of breaking into and entering another person's house permit the reasonable inference that the intruder intends to commit a crime while inside.

Do not confuse questions of whether and how to discover intent with the question What mental states suffice to impose criminal liability? The principle of *mens rea*, when stated properly, defines the mental states required for criminal liability.

Defining Mens Rea

Until recently, courts and legislatures did not define *mens rea* precisely. Instead, they used a host of vague terms to identify the mental element. For example, the United States Criminal Code used seventy-nine words and phrases to define *mens rea*—a staggering number according to the researcher who compiled the list.[16]

The cases, statutes, and commentators accepted four mental states that qualify as *mens rea:* general, specific, transferred, and constructive intent. **General intent** has various meanings. Sometimes it simply means *mens rea*, or all the mental states encompassed in *mens rea*. It can also mean an intent to do something at an undetermined time or directed at an unspecified object, such as to fire a gun into a crowd, intending to kill whomever the bullet strikes, or to set a bomb to explode in a plane without regard to whom it kills. Most commonly, general intent refers to the *actus reus*—that is, to the intent to commit the act required in the definition of the crime. For example, the required act in burglary is breaking and entering, in larceny the taking and carrying away of another's property, and in rape sexual penetration. General intent refers to the intent to commit those acts.

Specific intent designates the requirement to do something in addition to the *actus reus*. For example, burglary requires an intent to commit a crime after breaking and entering, and larceny the intention to steal in addition to the taking and carrying away. Rape is sometimes called a general intent crime because its *mens rea* requires no more than the intent to penetrate. Specific intent also refers to crimes requiring an intent to cause a particular result, such as homicide, which requires the intent to cause death.[17]

Transferred intent refers to cases in which actors intend to harm one victim but instead harm another. For example, if Brent shoots at his enemy Tony but kills Tony's friend Lisa when she steps in front of Tony to block the shot, the law transfers Brent's intent to kill Tony to an intent to kill Lisa. Some refer to transferred intent cases as bad-aim intent cases because so many involve misfired guns or rocks and other objects thrown at others. However, the law also transfers intent in a wide variety of other situations. If Karen intends to burn down Kent's house but mistakenly burns down Carmen's instead, Karen has committed arson. Only the intent to accomplish similar harms transfers; hence, an intent to assault a man does not transfer to the breaking of a window by throwing a rock intended to injure the victim.

Constructive intent refers to cases in which actors do not intend any harm but should have known that their behavior created a high risk of injury. For example, if one drives above the speed limit on an icy city street and the car veers out of control, killing a pedestrian, one has the constructive intent to kill.

The Model Penal Code has refined these four types of intent in its *mens rea* provision (see Section 2.02 of the Model Penal Code in the Appendix). After enormous effort and sometimes heated debate, the drafters sorted out, identified, and defined four criminal mental states: purposeful, knowing, reckless, and negligent. These are roughly equivalent to but more elaborate and precise than general, specific, transferred, and constructive intent. The Code specifies that all crimes requiring a mental element (some do not) must include one of these mental states. Most *mens rea* discussions throughout the text rely on the Model Penal Code's *mens rea* formulation.

The facts in actual cases often blur the distinctions among these four mental states, particularly between recklessness and negligence. Furthermore, the Model Penal Code requires that the state prove **culpability,** or *mens rea,* with respect to all three of the following: (1) the act, or the nature of the forbidden conduct; (2) the attendant circumstances; (3) the result of the conduct. Hence, under the Model Penal Code, a single offense may require purpose for the nature of the conduct, recklessness with respect to the attendant circumstances, and negligence with respect to the result.[18]

PURPOSE. The mental state of purpose means the intention to commit a crime. Some crimes require purpose with respect to engaging in specific conduct. For example, common-law burglary requires that the burglar purposely break and enter a dwelling house, and larceny requires that the thief purposely take and carry away another's property. Other crimes require a purpose to produce a particular result; for example, in murder, the murderer's "conscious object" is the victim's death. *Godfrey v. Georgia* addresses the question of purpose.

CASE

Did Godfrey Kill on Purpose?

Godfrey v. Georgia

446 U.S. 420, 100 S.Ct. 1759, 64 L.Ed. 2d 398 (1980)

[Godfrey was convicted of murder and aggravated assault. He appealed. Justice Stewert delivered the opinion, in which justices Blackmun, Powell, and Stevens joined. Justice Marshall filed a concurring opinion, in which Justice Brennan joined. Chief Justice Berger filed a dissenting opinion. Justice White also filed a dissenting opinion, in which Justice Rehnquist joined.]

FACTS

On a day in early September in 1977, Godfrey and his wife of 28 years had a heated argument in their home. During the course of this altercation, the petitioner, who had consumed several cans of beer, threatened his wife with a knife and damaged some of her clothing. At this point, the petitioner's wife declared that she was going to leave him, and departed to stay with relatives. That afternoon she went to a Justice of the Peace and secured a warrant charging the petitioner with aggravated assault. A few days later, while still living away from home, she filed suit for divorce. Summons was served on the petitioner, and a court hearing was set on a date some two weeks later. Before the date of the hearing, the petitioner on several occasions asked his wife to return to their home. Each time his efforts were rebuffed. At some point during this period, his wife moved in with her mother. The petitioner believed that his mother-in-law was actively instigating his wife's determination not to consider a possible reconciliation.

In the early evening of September 20, according to the petitioner, his wife telephoned him at home. Once again they argued. She asserted that reconciliation was impossible and allegedly demanded all the proceeds from the planned sale of their house. The conversation was terminated after she said that she would call back later. This she did in an hour or so. The ensuing conversation was, according to the petitioner's account, even more heated than the first. His wife reiterated her stand that reconciliation was out of the question, said that she still wanted all the proceeds from the sale of their house, and mentioned that her mother was supporting her position. Stating that she saw no further use in talking or arguing, she hung up.

At this juncture, the petitioner got out his shotgun and walked with it down the hill from his home to the trailer where his mother-in-law lived. Peering through a window, he observed his wife, his mother-in-law, and his 11-year-old daughter playing a card game. He pointed the shotgun at his wife through the window and pulled the trigger. The charge from the gun struck his wife in the forehead and killed her instantly. He proceeded into the trailer, striking and injuring his fleeing daughter with the barrel of the gun. He then fired the gun at his mother-in-law, striking her in the head and killing her instantly.

The petitioner then called the local sheriff's office, identified himself, said where he was, explained that he had just killed his wife and mother-in-law, and asked that the sheriff come and pick him up. Upon arriving at the trailer, the law enforcement officers found the petitioner seated on a chair in open view near the driveway. He told one of the officers that "they're dead, I killed them" and directed the officer to the place where he had put the murder weapon. Later the petitioner told a police officer: "I've done a hideous crime, but I have been thinking about it for eight years. I'd do it again."

The petitioner was subsequently indicted on two counts of murder and one count of aggravated assault. He pleaded not guilty. . . . The jury returned verdicts of guilty on all three counts.

OPINION

[The Supreme Court's opinion is omitted. The issue was not Godfrey's intent but whether he should receive the death penalty for it; the lower courts had decreed that he should, and the Supreme Court upheld. Capital murder is discussed in chapter 6.]

CASE DISCUSSION

What was Godfrey's conscious object in the case? to pull the trigger on the gun? to shoot the gun? to kill his wife? all three? What facts demonstrate his purpose? Do they prove his purpose beyond a reasonable doubt? Defend your answer.

KNOWING. Wrong done purposely is always done knowingly. It is impossible to intend a wrong without knowing it, but it is possible to knowingly act without that action being one's conscious object. Awareness of conduct or knowledge that a result is practically certain to follow from conduct is not the same thing as having the conduct or result as a conscious object. For example, a telephone answering service owner provided service to women he knew were prostitutes; hence, he knowingly provided the service. However, his purpose, or conscious object, was not to promote prostitution, it was to make a profit; hence, he did not conspire to promote prostitution. A surgeon who removes a cancerous uterus to save a pregnant woman's life knowingly, but not purposely, kills the fetus in the womb. The fetus's death is an unwelcome, if necessary, side effect to removing the cancerous uterus. Similarly, in treason, defendants may knowingly provide aid and comfort to United States' enemies without intending to overthrow the government. Such defendants are not guilty of treason, even though they know their conduct is practically certain to contribute to overthrowing the government. Hence the need for a separate crime—providing secrets to the enemy—that requires only that defendants purposely provide such secrets. The need to distinguish between knowledge and purpose arises most frequently in attempt, conspiracy, and treason.[19]

SUBJECTIVE AND OBJECTIVE STANDARDS. Most jurisdictions measure knowledge and purpose *subjectively*; that is, they depend on the actor's actual state of mind. These jurisdictions reject an *objective* standard based on what defendants *should have* believed, or on what "most people would have intended." Those who support the subjective standard argue that fairness requires that culpability for serious criminal conduct rest on defendants' actual intentions, not on what reasonable people would have intended. The Washington code is an exception:

> A person acts knowingly or with knowledge when:
>   (i) he is aware of a fact, facts, circumstances or result . . . ; or
>   (ii) he has information which would lead a reasonable man in the same situation to believe that facts exist . . .[20]

Recently, Michigan proposed introducing objective criteria into the *mens rea* determination, but only for the purpose of drawing inferences about defendants' actual intent. A person acts "intentionally" with respect to a result or conduct . . . when his conscious objective is to cause that result or engage in that conduct. In finding that a person acted intentionally with respect to a result the finding of fact may rely upon proof that such result was the natural and probable consequence of the person's act.[21]

RECKLESSNESS. Reckless people do not purposely or knowingly do harm; they consciously create risks of harm. Recklessness resembles knowledge in that both require consciousness. However, something less than certainty establishes conscious risk creation; recklessness rests on probabilities. The conscious risk creation may refer to the nature of the actor's conduct, to material attendant circumstances, or to the result.

Recklessness requires consciousness of *substantial* and *unjustifiable* risks. To reduce the unavoidable imprecision in the terms *substantial* and *unjustifiable*, the Model Penal Code proposes that fact finders determine **recklessness** according to a two-pronged test: (1) To what extent were defendants actually aware of how substantial and unjustifiable the risks they took were? (2) Does the disregard constitute so "gross [a] deviation from the standard" that a law-abiding person would observe that it deserves criminal condemnation in that situation? This standard has both a subjective and an objective component. Question 1 focuses on defendants' actual awareness; question 2 measures conduct according to how it deviates from what most people do.

Reckless wrongdoers do not have harm as a conscious objective (indeed, they may hope that no harm befalls anyone), yet they consciously create risks. A large drug company knew that a medication it sold had been linked to deaths and liver damage but sold the drug anyway. The company's officers who made the decision to sell the drug did not want to hurt anyone (indeed, they hoped no one would die or suffer liver damage), they only wanted their company to make a profit. They were prepared to risk death for profit.[22]

CASE

Is It Reckless to Shoot a Gun You Forgot Was Loaded?

State v. Ingle

20 N.C. App. 50, 200 S.E.2d 427 (1973).

[Ingle was convicted of involuntary manslaughter. He appealed. Chief Justice Brock delivered the opinion.]

FACTS

Defendant and Cordell were friends, and on the night in question Cordell and his wife were visiting defendant in his home. The two men were in the kitchen, sitting at a table, drinking intoxicants and talking. Cordell asked defendant if he could still do his "fast draw" trick, the trick being explained by witnesses thusly: a person, while sitting or standing, would hold his hands extended forward several inches apart; defendant, with a pistol in a holster strapped to his body, would attempt to draw his pistol and place it between the hands of the other person before that person could clap his hands together. Defendant replied that he could still do the trick and proceeded to try it with a .22 caliber pistol. The pistol discharged, a bullet struck Cordell in the front of his head and killed him almost instantly. When police recovered the pistol shortly after the tragedy, it contained four live cartridges and one spent cartridge. Defendant told police that he had forgotten that he loaded the pistol some three or four days earlier. The court submitted the case to the jury on the question of involuntary manslaughter. From a verdict of guilty and judgment imposing prison sentence of not less than four nor more than five years, with recommendation for work release, defendant appealed.

OPINION

. . . It seems that, with few exceptions, it may be said that every unintentional killing of a human being proximately caused by a reckless use of firearms, in the absence of intent to discharge the weapon, or in the belief that it is not loaded, and under circumstances not evidencing a heart devoid of a sense of social duty, is involuntary manslaughter. Conviction upheld.

CASE DISCUSSION

Notice that Ingle was found guilty because he recklessly used his gun, according to the court. However, if Ingle was telling the truth, and the court appears to believe him when he said he forgot the gun was loaded, was Ingle reckless? Remember that reckless wrongdoers consciously create risks. Could he consciously create the risk that he would kill his friend if he forgot the gun was loaded? How would you apply the Model Penal Code's two-pronged test to the facts of this case? Many courts confuse reckless with negligent wrongdoing, an issue taken up in the next section of this chapter. After reading the definition of negligence, do you think Ingle is reckless or negligent? Does it make a difference? Should it make a difference?

NEGLIGENCE. Negligent wrongdoers do not consciously create risks. They *should* know they are creating substantial and unjustifiable risks, but they do not. Recklessness is conscious risk creation; **negligence** is *un*conscious risk creation. The standard for negligence is objective—actors *should have* known, even though in fact they did not know, that they were creating risks. For example, a reasonable person should know that driving fifty miles per hour down a crowded street can cause harm, even though in fact the driver does not know it. The driver who should know this but does not is negligent. The driver who knows it but drives too fast anyway is reckless.

CASE

Reckless or Negligent?

People v. Warner-Lambert Co.

51 N.Y.2d 295, 434 N.Y.S.2d 159, 414 N.E.2d 660 (1980)

[The Warner-Lambert Company was indicted for second-degree manslaughter. Justice Jones delivered the opinion.]

FACTS

Defendant Warner-Lambert Co. is a manufacturing corporation which produces, among other items, Freshen-Up chewing gum. The individual defendants were officers or employees of the corporation. Defendant Kraft was vice-president in charge of manufacturing; defendant Harris was the director of corporate safety and security; defendants O'Mahoney and O'Rourke were, respectively, plant manager and plant engineer of the Warner-Lambert facility located at 30–30 Thompson Avenue in Long Island City, New York, which was the situs of the events out of which this indictment arose. The indictment charges each defendant with six counts of manslaughter in the second degree in violation of section 125.15 of the Penal Law and six counts of criminally negligent homicide in violation of section 125.10 of the Penal Law in consequence of the deaths of six employees which resulted from a massive explosion and fire at the Long Island City Warner-Lambert plant about 2:30 A.M. on November 21, 1976.

On the day on which the explosion occurred, Freshen-Up gum, which is retailed in the shape of a square tablet with a jellylike center, was being produced at the Warner-Lambert plant by a process in which filled ropes of the gum were passed through a bed of magnesium stearate (MS), a dry, dustlike lubricant which was applied by hand, then into a die-cut punch (a Uniplast machine) which was sprayed with a cooling agent (liquid nitrogen), where the gum was formed into the square tablets. Both the MS (normally an inert, organic compound) and the liquid nitrogen were employed to prevent the chicle from adhering to the sizing and cutting machinery, the tendency to adhere being less if a dry lubricant was used and the punch was kept at a low temperature. The process produced a dispersal of MS dust in the air and an accumulation of it at the base of the Uniplast machine and on overhead pipes; some also remained ambient in the atmosphere in the surrounding area.

Both MS and liquid nitrogen are considered safe and are widely used in the industry. In bulk, MS will only burn or smoulder if ignited; however, like many substances, if suspended in the air in sufficient concentration the dust poses a substantial risk of explosion if ignited. The minimum concentration at which an explosion can occur is denominated the "lower explosion level" (LEL). Liquid nitrogen, with a boiling temperature of minus 422 degrees Fahrenheit, is an effective cryogenic which might play a part in the process of "liquefaction"—here, the production of liquid oxygen in the course of the condensation of air on its exposure to a source of intense cold. Liquid oxygen is highly volatile, is easily ignited and, if ignited, will explode. Among possible causes of such ignition of either liquid oxygen or ambient MS are electrical or mechanical sparks.

On November 21, 1976 defendant Warner-Lambert was operating six Uniplast machines in the production of Freshen-Up gum on the fourth floor of its Long Island City plant. The machines were in almost constant operation; however, at the time of the catastrophic explosion near the end of one of the work shifts only one machine (designated the "D" machine) was in operation and employees were engaged in removing settled MS dust from the base of that machine and from overhead pipes by broom sweeping and by the use of airhoses. Suddenly an explosion occurred in the area of the operating machine, followed almost immediately by a second, much larger explosion accompanied by flames which caused injuries to more than 50 workers in the area (six of whom did not survive) and extensive damage to the building and equipment, which was attributed to burning of ambient dust and explosion rather than general fire. Thorough postcatastrophe investigation eliminated intentional or "man-caused" ignition as the origin of the event.

A New York City Fire Marshal and an investigator for the United States Occupational Safety and Health Administration, both of whom examined the scene, testified before the Grand Jury that a primary explosion had occurred at the "D" machine which dispersed added MS dust into the atmosphere and could have caused the second, greater explosion. There was testimony that the ceiling of the floor below the "D" machine had been covered with peeling paint, indicating that the temperature of that machine was colder than the others and that an examination of the machine itself after the explosion had shown that its base, made of cast iron, had cracked, perhaps by reason of the cold. An employee present at the time of the occurrence testified that he had observed a spark in the area of the "D" machine immediately prior to the event. Although there was no direct proof as to what had triggered the early morning disaster, the People introduced expert testimony hypothesizing that there might have been a mechanical sparking induced by a breakup of metal parts of the Uniplast machine. Also presented was testimony by one of the People's experts who theorized that liquid oxygen produced through liquefaction occurring in the Uniplast machine was ignited by the impact of a moving metal part and that this touched off the dispersed MS dust present.

With respect to the quantity of ambient MS dust in the area of the Uniplast machines (the presence of which was the basis for the People's submission to the Grand Jury of evidence against the defendants ultimately indicted), there was proof that an inspection of the plant by Warner-Lambert's insurance carrier in February, 1976 had resulted in advice to the insured that the dust condition in the Freshen-Up gum production area presented an explosion hazard and that the MS concentration was above the LEL, together with recommendations for installation of a dust exhaust system and modification of electrical equipment to meet standards for dust areas. Although a variety of proposals for altering the dust condition were considered by the individual defendants in consultations and communications with each other and some alterations in the MS application were made, both ambient and settled MS dust were still present on November 21, 1976, as the result of an executive decision to work toward the eventual elimination of MS entirely by modification of the Freshen-Up equipment. This modification had been accomplished with respect to only one Uniplast machine at the date of the explosion, when approximately 500 pounds of MS a day were still being used in Freshen-Up production. Employees were wearing face masks and goggles to protect their eyes and breathing passages, and just prior to the tragedy, when sweeping and airhosing of accumulated MS were in progress, there was rising dust and a "heavy fog" or "mist" all around.

OPINION

The charges of manslaughter in the second degree and criminally negligent homicide laid against the corporate and individual defendants are each dependent on two interrelated provisions of the Penal Law. As to manslaughter in the second degree, the following provisions are pertinent:

> 125.15 Manslaughter in the second degree
>
> A person is guilty of manslaughter in the second degree when:
>
> 1. He recklessly causes the death of another person.

> 15.05 Culpability; definitions of culpable mental states
>
> The following definitions are applicable to this chapter:
>
> 3. "Recklessly." A person acts recklessly with respect to a result or to a circumstance described by a statute defining an offense when he is aware of and consciously disregards a substantial and unjustifiable risk that such result will occur or that such circumstance exists. The risk must be of such nature and degree that disregard thereof constitutes a gross deviation from the standard of conduct that a reasonable person would observe in the situation. A person who creates such a risk but is unaware thereof solely by reason of voluntary intoxication also acts recklessly with respect thereto.

As to criminally negligent homicide the following provisions are pertinent:

> § 125.10 Criminally negligent homicide
>
> A person is guilty of criminally negligent homicide when, with criminal negligence, he causes the death of another person.

> § 15.05 Culpability; definitions of culpable mental states
>
> The following definitions are applicable to this chapter:
>
> 4. "Criminal negligence." A person acts with criminal negligence with respect to a result or to a circumstance described by a statute defining an offense when he fails to perceive a substantial and unjustifiable risk that such result will occur or that such circumstance exists. The risk must be of such nature and degree that the failure to perceive it constitutes a gross deviation from the standard of care that a reasonable person would observe in the situation.

For each of these crimes there must be "a substantial and unjustifiable risk," and "[t]he risk must be of such nature and degree that disregard thereof [or, the failure to perceive it] constitutes a gross deviation from the standard of conduct [or, care] that a reasonable person would observe in the situation." The essence of manslaughter in the second degree is awareness accompanied by disregard of the risk; for criminally negligent homicide the essence is failure to perceive the risk. With respect to each crime the culpable conduct of the defendant must have been the cause of the death of the other person or persons.

There have been relatively few reported cases (other than those involving vehicular homicide) in which judicial attention has been focused on the proof required to establish the commission of the crimes of manslaughter in the second degree or criminally negligent homicide. None has been drawn to our attention and our research has disclosed none in which the statutory provisions were applied to deaths occurring in the course of manufacturing operations.

There can be no doubt that there was competent evidence before the Grand Jury here which, if accepted as true, would have been sufficient to establish the existence of a broad, undifferentiated risk of explosion from ambient MS dust which had been brought to the attention of defendants. It may be assumed that, if it be so categorized, the risk was both substantial and unjustifiable. Reversed on other grounds. [See the section entitled "Causation" later in this chapter.]

CASE DISCUSSION

As *Ingle* showed, distinguishing between recklessness and negligence is not always easy. The court in *People v. Warner-Lambert* admirably states the distinction, but then avoids coming to grips with applying it in the case by deciding the case on other grounds, discussed in the later section on causation. The court did acknowledge that there was sufficient evidence in the case to find either negligence or recklessness. If you were a juror and had to decide whether Warner-Lambert was reckless or negligent, what would you conclude? What would be your arguments to interpret the facts as negligence or recklessness?

Warner-Lambert illustrates an important point about the principles of criminal liability, the doctrines, and the specific crime definitions. Defining standards—in *Warner-Lambert*, recklessness and negligence—is distinct from applying standards to specific cases. Hence two questions: (1) What is the standard? (2) Do the facts of the case fit within it? Question 1 is a question of law for the judge to decide; question 2 is a question of fact for the fact finder (the jury, or the judge in bench trials or trials without juries). The Anglo-American idea that judges decide the law and juries the facts arises upon this distinction. The ultimate fact is whether defendants are guilty—whether prosecutors have proven them guilty beyond a reasonable doubt. Thus, the legal question "Should Warner-Lambert be held to a standard of negligence or recklessness?" must not be confused with the factual question "Was Warner-Lambert negligent or reckless?"

STRICT LIABILITY, OR LIABILITY WITHOUT FAULT. **Strict liability** offenses constitute a major exception to the principle that every crime consists of both a physical and a mental element. Strict liability crimes require no *mens rea;* they impose liability without fault. Hence, whether a defendant's conduct was purposeful, knowing, reckless, or negligent is neither relevant nor material to criminal liability.

Two main arguments support strict liability. First, a strong public interest sometimes justifies eliminating *mens rea*. Strict liability arose during the industrial revolution when manufacturing, mining, and commerce exposed large numbers of the public to death, disability, and disease in the form of noxious gases, unsafe railroads and other work places, and adulterated foods and other products. Second, strict liability offenses carry minimum penalties, usually fines. The combined strong public interest and moderate penalty justify extending criminal liability to cases where there is no *mens rea*, according to supporters.[23]

Despite these arguments, strict liability has strong critics. They maintain that it is too easy to expand strict liability beyond public welfare offenses that seriously endanger the public. They also contend that strict liability weakens criminal law's force because too many people acting innocently are caught within its net. This brings disrespect to criminal law, which properly should punish only the blameworthy. It does no good, and probably considerable harm, to punish those who have not purposely, knowingly, or recklessly harmed others. In the end, critics maintain, strict liability does not fit well into the criminal law because it is not consistent with the law's basic nature: to serve as a stern moral code. To punish those who accidentally injure others violates that moral code.

CASE

Can You Commit a Crime without Intending Harm?

State v. Lucero

98 N.M. 204, 647 P.2d 406 (1982)

[Lucero was convicted of child abuse. She appealed. Justice Riordan delivered the opinion.]

FACTS

Defendant is the unmarried mother of two children, Arthur almost five years old and Jose six months. At the time of the trial, Defendant was pregnant with her third child. Defendant gave birth to Arthur when she was sixteen years old. Two years later, Arthur's father died in an automobile accident. About six months later, Defendant met

Eddie Lucero (Eddie). Several months thereafter, Defendant and Eddie began living together; however, they have never married. Defendant claims that while they were living together Eddie beat her. On one occasion, he broke her jaw. However, Defendant continued to live with Eddie.

Neither Defendant nor Eddie were employed. They lived on Defendant's "income" which came from public assistance. Defendant, however, testified that she would never give Eddie any of her money, which she believed is why Eddie always beat her up. After defendant gave birth to Jose, Eddie's child, Eddie began hitting Arthur. Defendant admitted knowing about this, but denied seeing the abuse take place. She stated that she would "yell" at Eddie after such an incident. She also testified that she could not contact the police or get help for Arthur because Eddie threatened to inflict more harm on her and Arthur.

Defendant's mother, who took care of Arthur frequently, finally took Arthur to the hospital's emergency room to have some marks on his body evaluated. Dr. Sidney Schnidman, who examined Arthur, found:

1. a partial thickness burn on the left ear, and the hair around the burn singed; he surmised that a flame or fire had caused the burn to his ear.
2. multiple bruises on both cheeks.
3. laceration/cut of the lower lip that was partially healed.
4. scratches in the middle of the neck under the jaw.
5. three small round bruises on the left upper arm.
6. bruises on the right shoulder.
7. bruises on the thigh and knee cap.
8. multiple reddened areas on and between his buttocks.
9. circumferential marks/abrasions on both ankles.
10. peeled and cracked skin on both feet; the doctor testified that he has seen this injury before in relation to emersion into a hot liquid.

The doctor was of the opinion that the bruises were not caused at the same time, because of the color of the different bruises. As a result, Defendant was charged with child abuse of Arthur.

Section 30–6–1(C) reads:

Abuse of a child consists of a person . . . without justifiable cause, causing or permitting a child to be: (1) placed in a situation that may endanger the child's life or health; or (2) tortured, cruelly confined or cruelly punished.

Whoever commits abuse of a child is guilty of a fourth degree felony, unless the abuse results in the child's death or great bodily harm, in which case he is guilty of a second degree felony.

OPINION

"A strict liability statute is one which imposes criminal sanction for an unlawful act without requiring a showing of criminal intent." Thus, the sole question for the jury in a strict liability offense is whether the jury believes the defendant committed the act prescribed by the statute. If it finds that the defendant did commit the act, then the jury is obliged to bring a guilty verdict.

At common law, crimes involved a showing of criminal intent. However, the Legislature may forbid the doing of an act and make its commission criminal without regard to the intent of the wrongdoer.

The rationale for a strict liability statute is that the public interest in the matter is so compelling or that the potential for harm is so great, that public interests override individual interests. Lucero, supra. Lucero held the child abuse statute to be a strict liability statute because of the obvious public interest of prevention of cruelty to children. Therefore, in the strict liability crime of child abuse it makes no difference whether a defendant acted intentionally or negligently in committing the act.

Since child abuse is a strict liability offense, a defendant's criminal intent is not required to be proven as an element of child abuse. Defendant asserts that she acted under duress in not obtaining help for Arthur. Duress is defined as "[a]n act committed under compulsion, such as apprehension of serious and immediate bodily harm, is involuntary and, therefore, not criminal." Apprehension in the mind of a defendant, is obviously a mental state. Defendant claims that her failure to act was a result of the fear and belief that Eddie would hurt her and Arthur to a greater extent if she obtained help for Arthur. However, duress is not a defense to child abuse because the mental state of the defendant is not essential. Child abuse does not require an intent. Therefore, duress is not a defense to the crime of child abuse.

We reverse the Court of Appeals and reinstate the Defendant's conviction. It is so ordered.

CASE DISCUSSION

Do you agree with the court that child abuse should constitute an exception to the *mens rea* requirement? Explain. What strong public interest justifies putting the mental element aside? What penalty would you prescribe? The court says strict liability is warranted because the public interest in protecting children is so strong that *mens rea* may be removed in order to do so.

≡ CONCURRENCE

The principle of **concurrence** requires that *mens rea* set the criminal act in motion; acts not generated by *mens rea* do not constitute criminal conduct. The Model Penal Code and jurisdictions following it subsume concurrence in causation. Some jurisdictions, however, provide specifically for concurrence in their criminal codes. California provides as follows:

> In every crime or public offense there must exist a union, or joint operation of act and intent, or criminal negligence.[24]

Therefore, if I plan to kill my enemy during a hunting expedition, and carry out my plans, I have committed murder—the intent to kill set my act of shooting her into motion. It is not murder if I shoot my enemy accidentally and rejoice afterwards because I am happy she died—the *mens rea* following the act; hence, there is no concurrence because the *mens rea* did not set the fatal shot in motion. Even if *mens rea* precedes action, it does necessarily constitute concurrence. For example, if I break the lock of my friend's house with her permission in order to wait for her to come home, but once inside decide to steal her new VCR, I have not committed common-law burglary because I decided to steal *after* breaking and entering her house. Burglary requires that the intent to steal motivate the breaking (see chapter 9).[25]

In cases where causing a particular result is an element in the crime, concurrence requires a fusion not only of act and *mens rea* but also of *mens rea* and resulting harm. This dimension to concurrence requires that the harm flowing from a defendant's conduct concur with the defendant's intent. For example, a man who ripped out a gas meter from a house in order to steal the coins in it did not batter a woman living in the house who became ill from the escaping gas fumes. Similarly, throwing a rock at another person is not malicious damage to property if that rock instead breaks a window. In addition, setting fire to the hold of a ship with a lighted match is not arson if the match was intended to illuminate an area so the defendant could see the rum he intended to steal. The felony murder doctrine, discussed in chapter 8, constitutes an exception to the rule that harms differing in kind from those intended do not satisfy concurrence.[26]

Actual harm that differs from intended harm only in degree satisfies the concurrence requirement. For example, if I intend to beat my enemy within an inch of her life, and she dies, then *mens rea* and harm concur. Furthermore, harm intended for one victim that falls upon another (transferred intent) also fits within the principle of concurrence. For example, shooting with the intent to kill Ellen but striking and killing Tim instead satisfies concurrence (see the following section on causation).[27]

CAUSATION

The principle of causation applies to crimes that require that conduct cause a particular result, such as death in homicide, fear in assault, injury in battery, and a burned building in arson. For a large number of crimes where conduct alone constitutes the crime, causation does not pose problems. For example, it is forgery to make a false writing, even if no one but the maker ever sees it; it is reckless driving to drive carelessly, whether or not the driver injures anyone; it is perjury to lie under oath, even if no one believes the lie. Crimes requiring injury to persons, property, reputation, public order, and morals do not pose problems if actors either harm persons or property other than those contemplated (as in the transferred intent cases discussed earlier), or cause less harm than they intend (as in attempt, discussed in chapter 6).

The law expresses the relationship between conduct and resulting harm in two ways: factual and legal. In **factual cause** (but-for or *sine qua non* causation), the conduct sets in motion a chain of events that eventually leads to the harmful result; hence, "but for" the actor's conduct, the harm would not have occurred. **Legal cause**, or proximate cause (phrased variously as the direct, substantial, next, or efficient cause), is the cause recognized by the law. Both factual and legal cause apply whether conduct is purposeful, knowing, reckless, negligent, or without fault (strict liability). (See Section 2.03 of the Model Penal Code, Appendix.)

Most cases satisfy the but-for standard. For example, if I strike and kill a pedestrian while driving recklessly, the pedestrian would be alive but for my reckless driving. Similarly, if I purposely shoot and kill my enemy, but for the shooting my victim would be alive. Problems arise, however, when something in addition to the actor's conduct contributes to the result. For example, if I recklessly injure a pedestrian who dies at the hospital during negligent surgery to save her life, what caused the pedestrian's death? But for my injury she would not be in surgery; however, without the negligent surgery she might not have died. Both my reckless driving and the surgeon's negligence contributed to the death. In these cases, the question becomes Was the defendant's conduct a sufficient—proximate—cause to impose criminal liability?[28]

Factual cause is necessary to impose criminal liability. Suppose I ask Peter to meet me in a dark park where I plan to assault him. On the way, Doug, who does not know what I have planned, attacks Peter. Owing to the injuries Doug inflicted on him, Peter never comes to meet me. I have not, in fact, caused the injury I wished to inflict; hence, I am not criminally liable, even though I intended to cause such injury. In other words, factual cause does not encompass what *would* have happened.

Factual cause is necessary but not sufficient; the government must also prove legal cause, or the cause recognized by the law. Proximate cause suggests nearness in time and place; legal cause is described more accurately by nearness in relation. The law draws the line flexibly where nearness in relation satisfies the legal cause requirement. Three primary policy considerations determine where to draw the line: expedience, justice, and fairness. These considerations might lead to drawing the line differently depending on the type of offense, such as more remotely in intentional harm than in reckless harm. For example, in purposeful homicide, the law may define legal cause as almost congruent with factual cause. In negligent homicide, the law may look to a less remote cause. In establishing liability for the tort of wrongful death, the law may recognize a more remote cause than it would for criminal homicide.

Commonsense guidelines inform how to approach deciding whether legal cause exists in particular cases. First, the cause must be substantial. The legal maxim *"de minimus non curat lex"* ("The law does not care for trifles") expresses this idea. For example, if two assailants stab a victim simultaneously, the law will not inquire into which wound spilled the blood that actually killed the victim. On the other hand, suppose one assailant stabbed the victim in the jugular vein and blood gushed forth, while the other stabbed the victim in the hand and only a tiny amount of blood oozed out. Both wounds have hastened death, but the law ignores the wound in the hand's minimal contribution to the death, relying rather on the substantial cause of the stab to the jugular.[29]

Second, the law does not follow the consequences set in motion by an act beyond the point where the consequences have "come to rest in a position of apparent safety." In one case, a man drove his wife out of their house into the subzero weather. She walked to her father's house, but when she arrived it was late. Not wishing to awaken her father, she curled up outside his front door, fell asleep, and froze to death. Since the husband's act in forcing his wife out into the cold had results that came to rest in a position of apparent safety, his actions did not legally cause her death.[30]

Several other commonsense considerations inform the decision about proximate cause. The search for a dominant—proximate—legal cause might uncover an intervening cause, one that either sufficiently interrupts the chain of events set in motion by the defendant's actions or that at least contributes to the death of the victim. Again suppose I injure a pedestrian while negligently driving my car. While the pedestrian is in the hospital seeking treatment, an inexperienced intern injects her with a fatal dose of a painkiller given to him by a drunken nurse. The intern's inexperience and the drunken nurse's action at least contributed to the death, and perhaps supervened to become themselves the main, dominant, or proximate cause.

CASE

What Caused Stafford's Death?

People v. Kibbe

35 N.Y.2d 407, 362 N.Y.S.2d 848, 321 N.E.2d 773 (1974)

FACTS

. . . During the early evening the defendants were drinking in a Rochester tavern along with the victim, George Stafford. The bartender testified that Stafford was displaying and "flashing" one hundred dollar bills, was thoroughly intoxicated and was finally "shut off" because of his inebriated condition. At some time between 8:15 and 8:30 P.M., Stafford inquired if someone would give him a ride to Canandaigua, New York, and the defendants, who, according to their statements, had already decided to steal Stafford's money, agreed to drive him there in Kibbe's automobile. The three men left the bar and proceeded to another bar where Stafford was denied service due to his condition. The defendants and Stafford then walked across the street to a third bar where they were served, and each had another drink or two.

After they left the third bar, the three men entered Kibbe's automobile and began the trip toward Canandaigua. Krall drove the car while Kibbe demanded that Stafford turn over any money he had. In the course of an exchange, Kibbe slapped Stafford several times, took his money, them compelled him to lower his trousers and to take off his shoes to be certain that Stafford had given up all his money; and when they were satisfied that Stafford had no more money on his person, the defendants forced Stafford to exit the Kibbe vehicle.

As he was thrust from the car, Stafford fell onto the shoulder of the rural two-lane highway on which he had been traveling. His trousers were still down around his ankles, his shirt was rolled up towards his chest, he was shoeless and he had also been stripped of any outer clothing. Before the defendants pulled away, Kibbe placed Stafford's shoes and jacket on the shoulder of the highway. Although Stafford's eyeglasses were in Kibbe's vehicle, the defendants, either through inadvertence or perhaps by specific design, did not give them to Stafford before they drove away. It was some time between 9:30 and 9:40 P.M. when Kibbe and Krall abandoned Stafford on the side of the road. The temperature was near zero, and, although it was not snowing at the time, visibility was occasionally obscured by the heavy winds which intermittently blew previously fallen snow into the air and across the highway; and there was snow on both sides of the road as a result of previous plowing operations. The structure nearest the point where Stafford was forced from the defendants' car was a gasoline service station situated nearly one half of a mile away on the other side of the highway. There was no artificial illumination on this segment of the rural highway.

At approximately 10:00 P.M. Michael W. Blake, a college student, was operating his pickup truck in the northbound lane of the highway in question. Two cars, which were approaching from the opposite direction, flashed their headlights at Blake's vehicle. Immediately after he had passed the second car, Blake saw Stafford sitting in the road in the middle of the northbound lane with his hands up in the air. Blake stated that he was operating his truck at a speed of approximately 50 miles per hour, and that he "didn't have time to react" before his vehicle struck Stafford. After he brought his truck to a stop and returned to try to be of assistance to Stafford, Blake observed that the man's trousers were down around his ankles and his shirt was pulled up around his chest. A deputy sheriff called to the accident scene also confirmed the fact that the victim's trousers were around his ankles, and that Stafford was wearing no shoes or jacket.

At the trial, the Medical Examiner of Monroe County testified that death had occurred fairly rapidly from massive head injuries. In addition, he found proof of a high degree of intoxication with a .25%, by weight, of alcohol concentration in the blood.

OPINION

. . . [T]he defendants were convicted of murder, robbery in the second degree and grand larceny in the third degree. However, the defendants basically challenge only their convictions of murder, claiming that the People failed to establish beyond a reasonable doubt that their acts "caused the death of another." . . . They contend that the actions of Blake, the driver of the pickup truck, constituted both an intervening and superseding cause which relieves them of criminal responsibility for Stafford's death. . . . [T]o be sufficiently direct cause of death so as to warrant the imposition of a criminal penalty . . . it is not necessary that the ultimate harm be intended by the actor. It will suffice if it can be said beyond a reasonable doubt, as indeed it can be here said, that the ultimate harm is something which should have been foreseen as being reasonably related to the acts of the accused.

In People v. Kane, the defendant inflicted two serious pistol shot wounds in the body of a pregnant woman. The wounds caused a miscarriage; the miscarriage caused septic peritonitis, and the septic peritonitis, thus induced, caused the woman's death on the third day after she was shot. Over the defendant's insistence that there was no causal connection between the wounds and the death and, in fact, that the death was due to the intervention of an outside agency, namely, the negligent and improper medical treatment at the hospital, this court affirmed the conviction "even though the medical treatment may also have had some causative influence."

We subscribe to the requirement that the defendants' actions must be a *sufficiently direct cause* of the ensuing death before there can be any imposition of criminal liability, and recognize, of course, that this standard is greater than that required to serve as a basis for tort liability. Applying these criteria to the defendants' actions, we conclude that their activities on the evening of December 30, 1970 were sufficiently direct cause of the death of George Stafford so as to warrant the imposition of criminal sanctions. In engaging in what may properly be described as a despicable course of action, Kibbe and Krall left a helplessly intoxicated man without his eyeglasses in a position from which, because of these attending circumstances, he could not extricate himself and whose condition was such that he could not even protect himself from the elements. The defendants do not dispute the fact that their conduct evinced a depraved indifference to human life which created a grave risk of death, but rather they argue that it was just as likely that Stafford would be miraculously rescued by a good samaritan. We cannot accept such an argument. There can be little doubt but that Stafford would have frozen to death in his state of undress had he remained on the shoulder of the road. The only alternative left to him was the highway, which in his condition, for one reason or another, clearly foreboded the probability of resulting death. Affirmed.

CASE DISCUSSION

Was the defendants' conduct the factual and legal cause of the victim's death? Was it the substantial cause? Had the consequences of the defendants' action come to rest in a position of apparent safety? Was the college student's driving a supervening cause? What facts do you use to support your conclusion?

A final causation problem arises when the result differs from what actors intend in purposeful and knowing conduct, expect in recklessness, and should expect in negligence. Chapter 7 discusses crimes where the result is *less* than actors *intend*, such as in attempt. Here, the discussion analyzes cases in which the actual harm *exceeds* what actors intend, expect, or should expect. Generally, criminal law does *not* hold defendants liable for these greater harms unless the harms are close in degree and kind to those intended. For example, a defendant who intends to beat a victim within an inch of her life, but does not want to kill her, has committed criminal homicide if the victim dies (see chapter 8). More difficult are cases where actual harm greatly exceeds intended harm. *Hyam v. Director of Public Prosecutions* addresses this problem.

CASE

What if You Kill when You Intend Only to Frighten?

Hyam v. Director of Public Prosecutions

2 All E.R. 43 (1974)

[Mrs. Hyam was convicted of murder. She appealed.]

FACTS

The facts are simple, and not in dispute. In the early hours of Saturday, 15th July 1972, the appellant set fire to a dwelling-house in Coventry by deliberately pouring about a half gallon of petrol through the letterbox and igniting it by means of a newspaper and a match. The house contained four persons, presumably alseep. They were a Mrs. Booth and her three children, a boy and the two young girls who were the subjects of the charges. Mrs. Booth and the boy escaped alive through a window. The two girls died as the result of asphyxia by the fumes generated by the fire. The appellant's motive (in the sense in which I shall use the word "motive") was jealousy of Mrs. Booth whom the appellant believed was likely to marry a Mr. Jones of whom the appellant herself was the discarded, or partly discarded, mistress. Her account of her actions, and her defence, was that she had started the fire only with the intention of frightening Mrs. Booth into leaving the neighbourhood, and that she did not intend to cause death or grievous bodily harm. The judge directed the jury:

> The prosecution must prove, beyond all reasonable doubt, that the accused intended to do serious bodily harm to Mrs. Booth, the mother of the deceased girls. If you are satisfied that when the accused set fire

to the house she knew that it was highly probable that this would cause serious bodily harm then the prosecution will have established the necessary intent. It matters not if her motive was, as she says, to frighten Mrs. Booth.

OPINION

The judge explained that he had put brackets round the words "kill or" and "death or" in which it seems to be said that a rational man must be taken to intend the consequences of his acts. It is not a revival of the doctrine of constructive malice or the substitution of an objective for a subjective test of knowledge or intention. It is the man's actual state of knowledge and intent which, as in all other cases, determines his criminal responsibility.

It simply proclaims the moral truth that if a man, in full knowledge of the danger involved, and without lawful excuse, deliberately does that which exposes a victim to the risk of the probable grievous bodily harm (in the sense explained) or death, and the victim dies, the perpetrator of the crime is guilty of murder and not manslaughter to the same extent as if he had actually intended the consequence to follow, and irrespective of whether he wishes it. That is because the two types of intention are morally indistinguishable, although factually and logically distinct, and because it is therefore just that they should bear the same consequences to the perpetrator as they have the same consequences for the victim if death ensues.

This is not very far from the situation in this case. The jury appear to have taken this as a carefully premeditated case and that this was so can hardly be disputed, and, though it was disputed, the jury clearly rejected this view. The appellant had made her way to the house in a van in the early hours of the morning. She took with her a jerry can containing at least half a gallon of petrol. As she passed Mr. Jones's house she carefully made sure that he was in his own home and not with Mrs. Booth, because, as she said, she did not want to do Mr. Jones any harm. She parked the van at a distance from Mrs. Booth's house, and when she got to the front door she carefully removed a milk bottle from the step in case she might knock it over and arouse somebody by the noise. And when she had started the fire she crept back to her van and made off home without arousing anyone or giving the alarm. Once it is conceded that she was actually and subjectively aware of the danger to the sleeping occupants of the house in what she did, and that was the point which the judge brought to the jury's attention, it must surely follow naturally that she did what she did with the intention of exposing them to the danger of death or really serious injury regardless of whether such consequences actually ensued or not.

CASE DISCUSSION

No problem arises about Mrs. Hyam's *mens rea*. She intended to frighten her victim. This intention was joined to an *actus reus*—setting the house on fire—to accomplish her purpose. The problem is that Mrs. Hyam intended only to frighten her victims, not to kill them. Therefore, she caused a harm greater than what she intended or expected. The court concluded that she can be held accountable for the greater harm, even though she did not intend it. The reasoning is that she acted purposely to create a risk that her victims might die or be seriously injured. Precisely, Mrs. Hyam's state of mind was purposeful in relation to the act of setting the house on fire and reckless with respect to her victims' deaths. She is therefore held accountable for the harmful consequences of the risk she recklessly created. Do you feel comfortable with making Mrs. Hyam a murderer when she meant only to frighten? Would you give her a punishment as severe as that given to someone like Godfrey in an earlier case, who wanted to kill his wife, said he had wanted to do it for eight years, and would do it again if he had the chance?

The established law in most jurisdictions is that conscious risk creators are accountable for the "natural and probable consequences" of their actions. Natural and probable consequences include killing a person other than the intended victim—as, for example, if I shoot at Jim, intending to kill him, but instead hit his friend Moira standing next to him. It does not include consequences that are accidental—as, for example, if I shoot at my wife, intending to kill her, but miss, and she is so distraught that she runs off to California, goes horseback riding to forget the horrible incident, is thrown off her horse, and dies when her head strikes a rock. In such cases, the harms are too remote to "justly" impose criminal liability. Note that the proximate cause standard also applies to the last example—striking the rock was the direct or efficient cause of death. (See Model Penal Code Section 2.03, Appendix.)

GRADING OFFENSES ACCORDING TO *MENS REA*

The seriousness of an offense rests on numerous considerations. First, and perhaps most serious, is the harm done. Harms to persons are generally considered most serious, followed by harms to habitation, property, public order, and public morals. Incomplete harms are less serious than completed ones (see chapter 5). Second, sometimes the act affects seriousness, such as in torture murder. Third, *mens rea* influences grading by suggesting justifying, excusing, and mitigating circumstances. For example, if I kill in self-defense, my intention to kill is justified; if I kill upon adequate provocation, I am guilty of manslaughter, a less serious criminal homicide than murder (see chapter 8). Finally, the level of *mens rea*—purposeful, knowing, reckless, and negligent—bears upon the determination of an offense's seriousness. Purpose or specific intent is the most blameworthy, or "evil," mental state. Knowledge is next, followed in order by negligence and strict liability. Purposeful wrongdoing deserves more punishment than reckless harm because reckless wrongdoers do not intent to harm their victims. Still less blameworthy are negligent wrongdoers who do not consciously create risks that expose others to serious harm. Least blameworthy of all are those who harm others accidentally—that is, without regard to fault. Penalties account for these degrees of blameworthiness.

≡ SUMMARY

Every criminal code reflects the general principles of criminal liability: *actus reus, mens rea,* concurrence, causation, and resulting harm. The *actus reus* includes not only voluntary physical acts but also omissions and possession. The *mens rea* includes purpose, knowledge, recklessness, and negligence. Some crimes do not require a *mens rea;* they constitute criminal liability without fault, or strict liability. Criminal conduct means that a *mens rea* prompted an *actus reus.* This is expressed in the principle that there is no criminal conduct without concurrence of *actus reus* and *mens rea.*

Criminal conduct sometimes constitutes a crime by itself—the harm is the conduct. In other crimes, conduct must cause a separate harm. The causal relation in crime is expressed both in the idea of but-for or *sine qua non* causation, and in proximate cause. Problems arise when the resulting harm exceeds what actors contemplated, expected, or should have expected. In those cases, actors are generally criminally liable for harms that exceed only slightly those contemplated; they are held accountable for harms that exceed in considerable degree those contemplated if punishment is "just." They are not criminally liable for harms distinct both in kind and degree from those intended or expected.

≡ QUESTIONS FOR REVIEW AND DISCUSSION

1. Define *actus reus.* Should status ever be a ground of criminal liability? possession? failure to act? Explain why or why not.
2. Define the levels of culpability in criminal law. What is a proper standard for culpability in criminal law? Should negligent persons be punished? Should persons who accidentally harm be punished?
3. Explain the principle of concurrence. How does it relate to the term *criminal conduct?*
4. Define but-for and proximate cause. Why are they important in criminal law?
5. Under what circumstances should people be punished for harms that exceed what they intend, expect, or should expect?
6. To what extent should *mens rea* determine the seriousness of an offense?

≡ SUGGESTED READINGS

1. George Fletcher, *Rethinking Criminal Law* (Boston: Little, Brown, 1978), pt. II, is a thorough and thought-provoking discussion of the principles of criminal liability. Although difficult in places, it is well worth the effort to read.

2. Jerome Hall, *General Principles of Criminal Law,* 2d ed. (Indianapolis: Bobbs-Merrill, 1960), chap. 3–6, treats *mens rea.* This material is difficult but rewarding reading, and provides much that is worth the effort.

3. Hyman Gross, *A Theory of Criminal Justice* (New York: Oxford University Press, 1979), chap. 2, untangles knotty questions surrounding *actus reus.*

4. American Law Institute, *Model Penal Code and Commentaries* (Philadelphia: American Law Institute, 1985), pt. I, is probably still the best overall treatment of the general principles of criminal liability.

5. Rollin M. Perkins and Ronald N. Boyce, *Criminal Law,* 3d ed. (Mineola, N.Y.: Foundation Press, 1982), chap. 6 and 7, is a good, straightforward treatment of act, *mens rea,* and causation.

≡ NOTES

1. Brian Forst et al., *What Happens after Arrest?* (Washington, D.C.: National Institute of Law Enforcement and Criminal Justice, May 1978), chap. 5; Kathleen B. Brosi, *A Cross-City Comparison of Felony Processing* (Washington, D.C.: Institute for Law and Social Research, April 1979), chap. 3.

2. Rollin M. Perkins and Ronald N. Boyce, *Criminal Law,* 3d ed. (Mineola, N.Y.: Foundation Press, 1982), chap. 6 and 7; Jerome Hall, *General Principles of Criminal Law,* 2d ed. (Indianapolis: Bobbs-Merrill, 1960), especially chap. 3–8.

3. *Papachristou v. City of Jacksonville,* 405 U.S. 156, 92 S.Ct. 839, 31 L.Ed.2d 110 (1972).

4. Herbert Morris, *On Guilt and Innocence* (Los Angeles: University of California Press, 1976), chap. 1, "Punishing Thoughts," thoroughly and provocatively discusses the law and punishing intention.

5. Glanville Williams, *Criminal Law,* 2d ed. rev. (London: Stevens and Sons, 1961), pp. 1–2.

6. Norval Morris, "Somnambulistic Homicide: Ghosts, Spiders, and North Koreans," *Res Judicata* 5 (1951), p. 29.

7. See Leo Katz, *Bad Acts and Guilty Minds* (Chicago: University of Chicago Press, 1987), chap. 2, for a provocative discussion of this and other cases like it.

8. Joseph Goldstein et al., *Criminal Law: Theory and Process* (New York: Free Press, 1974), p. 766.

9. *A Copy of the Penal Code Prepared by the Indian Law Commissioners* (London: S. Austin, 1851), pp. 158–60.

10. George Fletcher further develops these points in an interesting discussion in *Rethinking Criminal Law* (Boston: Little, Brown, 1978), pp. 421–26 and 581–633.

11. Bibb Latane and John Darley, *The Unresponsive Bystander: Why Doesn't He Help?* (New York: Appleton-Century-Crofts, 1970), pp. 1–2.

12. American Law Institute, *Model Penal Code and Commentaries*, vol. 1 (Philadelphia: American Law Institute, 1985), p. 24. See *Jenkins v. State*, 215 Md. 70, 137 A.2d 115 (1957), for the mere possession rule.

13. See *Robinson v. California*, 370 U.S. 660 (1962), and Fletcher, *Rethinking Criminal Law*, pp. 202–5.

14. Oliver Wendell Holmes, Jr., *The Common Law* (Boston: Little, Brown 1963), p. 7; American Law Institute, *Model Penal Code*, tentative draft no. 11 (1955).

15. Williams, *Criminal Law*, p. 1; quoted in Hall, *General Principles of Criminal Law*, p. 153.

16. Quoted in Goldstein et al., *Criminal Law: Theory and Process*.

17. Wayne R. LaFave and Austin W. Scott, Jr., *Handbook on Criminal Law*, 2d ed. (St. Paul: West Publishing Co., 1972), pp. 201–2; Hall, *General Principles of Criminal Law*, pp. 142–44.

18. American Law Institute, *Model Penal Code and Commentaries*, pt I, p. 229.

19. *Haupt v. United States*, 330 U.S. 631, 67 S.Ct. 874, 91 L.Ed. 1145 (1947) (treason).

20. West's Revised Code Wash. Ann. 9A.08010(1)(b).

21. Michigan Statute 82 § 305(a) and (b).

22. *New York Times* (September 14, 1985).

23. For a thorough discussion, see Perkins and Boyce, *Criminal Law*, pp. 896–907.

24. The Penal Code of California, § 20, *West's California Penal Codes*, 1988 compact ed. (St. Paul: West Publishing Company, 1988), p. 7.

25. Hall, *General Principles of Criminal Law*, pp. 185–90.

26. *Regina v. Cunningham*, 41 Crim.App.R. 155 (1957) (ripping out gas meter); *Regina v. Pembletonn*, 12 Cox Crim.Cas. 607 (1874)(throwing a rock); *Regina v. Faulkner*, 13 Cox Crim.Cas. 550 (1877).

27. LaFave and Scott, *Handbook on Criminal Law*, pp. 243–46.

28. Katz, *Bad Acts and Guilty Minds*, chap. 4.

29. Perkins and Boyce, *Criminal Law*, pp. 776–77.

30. *State v. Preslar*, 48 N.C. 421 (1856).

Chapter Four

Parties to Crime: The Doctrine of Complicity

CHAPTER OUTLINE

CHAPTER MAIN POINTS

1. The doctrine of complicity defines when one person may be criminally liable for another's conduct.

2. Parties before and during crime are liable for the principal crime; parties following crime are guilty of separate, lesser offenses.

3. The liability of accomplices and accessories depends on *participation;* vicarious liability depends on *relationships*.

4. Business relationships most often give rise to vicarious liability.

5. Vicarious liability may be either strict liability or based on culpable conduct.

6. Attributing responsibility to corporate officers is often difficult and sometimes impossible.

7. Businesses might be criminally responsible for harms they condoned or at least recklessly tolerated.

CHAPTER KEY TERMS

accessory a party following crime who is liable for separate, lesser offenses.

accomplices parties before and during crime who are liable as principals.

alter ego **doctrine** the doctrine that high corporate officers are the corporation's brain.

doctrine of complicity parties to crime

respondeat superior the doctrine that employers are responsible for their employees' actions.

superior officer rule the precept that only the highest officers in the corporate structure can make a corporation criminally liable.

vicarious liability the doctrine that one party is criminally liable for a third party's conduct.

≡ INTRODUCTION

Much crime involves teamwork. The **doctrine of complicity**, or parties to crime, responds to that fact (see also conspiracy and solicitation discussed in chapter 5). This doctrine establishes the conditions under which more than one person incurs liability before, during, and after committing crimes. Complicity predicates criminal liability on conduct—the concurrence of *actus reus* and *mens rea*—but addresses the problem of when *another's* conduct constitutes that liability. When one person is accountable for another's conduct, it is immaterial whether the defendant's own conduct, the conduct of another or others, or both together establish the elements of the crime charged. Hence, those who join with others to commit crime are equally guilty.

Three problems arise in complicity: (1) What conduct does the doctrine include? (2) Whose conduct does the doctrine include? (3) What *mens rea* brings about the conduct of the others? Culpability depends both on the defendants' *mens rea* and conduct, and on the others' conduct brought about by defendants.[1]

Parties to Crime

The common law recognized four parties to crime: (1) principals in the first degree—the actual perpetrators; (2) principals in the second degree—aiders and abettors present when crimes are committed, such as lookouts, getaway drivers, and coconspirators; (3) accessories before the fact—aiders and abettors *not* present when crimes are committed, such as one who provides the gun that a third person uses in a murder; and (4) accessories after the fact—individuals who give aid and comfort to persons known to have committed crimes, such as those who harbor fugitives. The significance of these distinctions lay largely in the doctrine that only after principals were convicted could the government try accomplices. Hence, if principals were not convicted before the government brought accomplices to trial, common-law complicity shielded accomplices even in the face of certain proof of their guilt. The doctrine arose during a period in history when all felonies were capital offenses; it provided a means to ameliorate that harsh penalty. When the number of capital crimes diminished, the need to distinguish between principals and accessories dissipated.

Statutes in virtually all jurisdictions have removed the common-law distinction by making **accomplices**—accessories before and during crime—principals. Most jurisdictions retain the common-law **accessory** after the fact for complicity following crime. Several states have adopted statutes similar to the Model Penal Code, Section 2.06, set out in Appendix.

Complicity requires that defendants

> in some sort associate [themselves] with the venture, that [t]he[y] participate in it as in something that [t]he[y] wish . . . to bring about, that [t]he[y] seek by . . . their action to make it succeed.[2]

The law of complicity, as represented in the statutes and case law, requires (1) an act contributing to the commission of a crime, (2) the *mens rea* to aid in the crime's execution, and (3) that someone actually commit the crime. Chapter 5 deals with teamwork that does not result in completed crimes—conspiracy and solicitation.[3]

Actus Reus *of Parties before and during Crime*

Although statutes have substantially altered complicity categories, they have retained largely intact the words used to describe the common-law acts required to establish liability. Aid and abet appear frequently; others include counsel, procure, hire, command, induce, advise, and willfully cause. A widely accepted doctrine is that "aiding and abetting contemplates some positive act in aid of the commission of the offense"; the "mere presence of a defendant at the scene of a crime is insufficient to establish guilt." Determining just how much action qualifies is difficult, however. The most common acts are supplying guns, supplies, or other instrumentalities of crime, serving as a lookout, driving a getaway car, sending the victim to the principal, or preventing warnings from reaching the victim.[4]

Where there is a duty to act, mere presence may suffice to satisfy the complicity *actus reus*. In *State v. Walden*, for example, a jury found Walden guilty as an accomplice to assault. Walden stood by and did nothing while her boyfriend beat her young son. On appeal, the court said that

> the trial court properly allowed the jury . . . to consider a verdict of guilty of assault . . . upon a theory of aiding and abetting, solely on the ground that the defendant was present when her child was brutally beaten. . . . A person who so aids or abets another in the commission of a crime is equally guilty with that other person as a principal.[5]

CASE

Did He Rape DM?

State v. Pierson

610 S.W.2d 86 (Mo. App. 1980)

[Pierson was convicted of forcibly raping DM, a minor, and was sentenced to five years in prison. He appealed. Justice Shangler delivered the opinion.]

FACTS

[T]he female DM went to the residence of her male companion, Boyett, on the afternoon of July 25, 1978. She brought a change of clothes in anticipation of a social event with him. Boyett shared the premises with one Coates. Boyett left for a brief employment with a friend, Christopherson. DM remained with Coates and with one Tack, who came by after the departure of the other two. In that interim, five males—the defendant Pierson, Mercer, Hadley, Riley and Miller—came into the house. The defendant Pierson was an acquaintance of the resident Coates and . . . suggested Coates as a source for marihuana, which the men then fancied. On arrival, Mercer ordered Tack [whom he disliked from an earlier encounter] to "hit it," and Tack left promptly. Coates left minutes later and DM was left in the company of the fives males. [DM was not acquainted with any of them but had seen the defendant Pierson once before at that house.] DM started out the door also but was told by Mercer: "Set down, you're not going anywhere. You are going to go out partying with us." DM sat down but refused the invitation. Mercer grabbed her by the hair, slapped her, and repeated: "You're going with us." Mercer clenched her arm, twisted it behind the back and said: "Let's go." They all went into a white automobile parked outside where DM was placed in the back seat between Mercer and Miller. The defendant Pierson owned the vehicle and assumed the position behind the wheel.

At that time, Boyett and Christopherson returned from work. DM ran to Boyett through a door of the car, still open, and the three returned into the house. DM tearfully told Boyett the men were going to take her out and rape her. The five men followed them into the premises. Mercer again told DM she was going "to party with them." DM again refused. Mercer asked Boyett: "Do you mind if we take her partying with us?" and Boyett answered: "She can go if she wants to." The five left after a few minutes. DM changed her garments in preparation of an evening out with Boyett. As they started to leave, the five men returned in the same vehicle as before. Mercer asked if

Boyett was there, but then he recognized Christopherson and, prompted by an old enmity, struck him in the face. Then another of the five, Hadley, took up the attack upon Christopherson, struck him and was about to use a knife, but was restrained by Mercer. The defendant Pierson, and another, on the orders of Mercer, guarded the doors to the house during this episode. Christopherson was rendered bloody. Mercer told Boyett and DM: "Come here, I want you to see this; that's mild to what is going to happen if I catch any heat behind this from the police or anybody." Mercer continued to vaunt his toughness with the remark: "I'm not afraid of anybody; I will whip the police or anybody."

The five men then left with DM. Mercer grabbed her arm and with a twist ordered her to come or he would break her arm. They entered the Pierson car once again and drove to a liquor store where the defendant and Mercer returned with a case of beer and some wine. There the defendant Pierson encountered a man, engaged him in a brawl, and inflicted knife wounds on him. They resumed the car journey, during which Mercer told DM she was going to get "a good lesson tonight" in the performance of the oral sex act. The defendant Pierson drove them to an open field and everyone got out of the car. Mercer ordered DM to remove all her clothing and jewelry. She complied, in tears all the while, and he told her to "let [his] bros do whatever they wanted." The defendant Pierson was the first of them to engage DM. He performed the act of sexual intercourse; his phallus penetrated her generative orifice.

DM begged him to stop and repeated: "Please take me home," but to no avail. Miller next performed the same act; then Riley attempted a sexual act. Mercer then ordered the others to leave, and defendant Pierson drove away. DM was left with Mercer in the open field. Mercer attempted anal sodomy upon DM. She resisted, so he engaged in the normal act of conjugation. Miller returned with a van and he drove them to his residence. Mercer again ravished DM, continuously throughout that journey. At the Miller residence, the assault continued—first by Miller and then by Mercer. DM was then allowed to dress and, at about 2:00 A.M. on July 26, was returned to the Boyett residence.

OPINION

[The judge instructed the jury in part that:] . . .

> If you find and believe from the evidence beyond a reasonable doubt:
>   First, that on or about July 26, 1978, that defendant inserted his sexual organ into the sexual organ of DM, and
>   Second, that he did so against her will and after George Mercer caused her to submit by threats which caused her to fear physical violence to herself, and
>   Third, that the defendant acted either alone or knowingly and with common purpose together with George Mercer in the conduct referred to in the above paragraphs, then you will find the defendant guilty of rape. . . .

All persons are guilty who knowingly act together with the common purpose of committing an offense, or who knowingly and intentionally aid or encourage another in committing it, and whatever one does in furtherance of the offense is the act of each of them.

The presence of a person at or near the scene of an offense at the time it was committed is alone not sufficient to make him responsible therefore, although his presence may be considered together with all of the evidence in determining his guilt or innocence.

Our law allows a determination of guilt for rape where the victim submits through fear of physical violence, even where one other than the defendant causes the fear, if at the time of the sexual act the defendant has knowledge that the victim succumbs through that fear. That is to say, a rape may be the result of a concert of action aided and abetted between perpetrators. Thus, where persons act with common purpose for a criminal enterprise, the prosecution need not prove that the defendant personally committed all of the acts essential to the offense. The participation in crime may be shown by such circumstances as presence, companionship and conduct attendant to the offense.

The actual presence of the defendant Pierson from the first intrusion by the five into the Boyett residence where DM, Coates and Tack alone were there until his own carnal act upon DM in the open field was continuous and coincident with that of Mercer. The evidence of the prosecution, which we assume as true, that during that interim Pierson was present when

Mercer announced purpose to take DM against her will for sexual gratification,

Mercer used physical force to wrest her compliance and compel her into the car on two occasions,

DM refused to submit by words and by physical resistance,

DM wept continuously from the first insistence by Mercer that she submit,

DM fled the car when Boyett returned home,

DM was warned by Mercer after Christopherson was beaten bloody that "that's mild to what is going to happen if I catch the heat behind this from the police or anybody," the order by Mercer to DM, when once in the open field, in front of the other four men to remove all her clothing and to "let [his] bros do whatever they wanted," her tearful compliance, allows clear inference that Pierson knew when he then engaged DM in the sexual act that she submitted from fear of Mercer. The willing use by Pierson of his automobile for the enterprise, his ready acquiescence to every Mercer direction, and his eagerness to be the first to ravish DM—notwithstanding her plea to stop and let her return home—all show that he exploited the fear engendered by Mercer for his own criminal purpose. That no word was spoken between Pierson and Mercer does not allay the participation between them; the actions were surrogates as conclusive as words. Thus, the jury could have found that at the time Pierson took carnal advantage of DM, he knew she was instilled with fear of rape by threats and acts of violence upon her by Mercer and that she submitted on that account.

The defendant argues that the departure from the field by Pierson shows that the criminal enterprise between Mercer and Pierson "terminated by mutual consent at that point." Thus, the sexual assaults upon DM thereafter were irrelevant to the crime alleged against Pierson. An aider and abetter or participant in a crime may detach from the enterprise before consummation in a time and fashion and by words or deeds which show the accomplices that he disapproves of the scheme, so that the crime results from agency other than his own.

The removal by Pierson from the open field was not to withdraw from any common purpose with Mercer but merely obedience to order—and was not a detachment from the criminal activity, but to allow Mercer to have DM to himself. That episode was typical of the servile acquiescence Pierson and the others gave every direction by Mercer. The evidence of the continued sexual assault by Mercer and Miller upon DM after Pierson departed, rather, was one aspect of the continuous criminal transaction and thus part of the res gestae.

Affirmed.

CASE DISCUSSION

According to Missouri law, Pierson was guilty if he acted either alone or together with Mercer in raping DM. Since Mercer terrorized DM, do you agree that he raped her forcibly? Do you think Pierson is as guilty as Mercer, even though he was a more "passive" participant? Wasn't Mercer clearly the pack leader and Pierson only an obedient underling? Do you think everyone present was equally guilty? Would you give them all equal punishment? Should Pierson get less punishment because he did not lead the group or terrorize DM but only followed along? Should he be accountable for what happened *after* he left the scene? Explain why or why not.

Mens Rea *of Parties before and during Crime*

As a general rule, complicity requires intent or purpose to aid or abet third persons to commit crimes. Recklessness and negligence suffice when participants commit crimes reasonably foreseeable during commission of the main crime. In *People v. Poplar,* for example, Poplar acted as a lookout for a breaking and entering. Poplar and the other participants were convicted of assault with intent to murder, on the ground that death during breaking and entering is reasonably foreseeable. In ruling so, the court reduced the *mens rea* to recklessness or even negligence in a crime of purpose—assault with *intent* to commit murder.[6]

CASE

Did He Possess Cocaine with Intent to Deliver?

State v. Hecht

116 Wis.2d 605, 342 N.W.2d 721 (1984)

[Justice Ceci delivered the opinion.]

FACTS

. . . In September of 1973, undercover agent John Heidecker contacted defendant Hecht and Donald Grove. At the meeting, Heidecker asked Hecht if he had any drugs to sell. The defendant subsequently sold him twenty-five dollars worth of cocaine. The following day, Heidecker returned, attempting to make an additional purchase. . . . Heidecker told the defendant that he had a friend who wanted to make a substantial cocaine purchase. The friend was William Malone, also an undercover agent. The defendant testified that Heidecker offered him $1,700 for contacting a supplier who could sell him this large quantity of the drug. . . .

Hecht . . . called Virgil Vollmer to ask Vollmer if Vollmer knew a source who could supply a large quantity of cocaine. . . .

On October 2, 1978, agent Heidecker telephoned Hecht. The defendant told Heidecker that Vollmer had indicated a price of $2,000 for the drug . . . Heidecker arranged to meet Hecht at the garage where the defendant worked that same evening. Heidecker and agent Malone met with the defendant and Grove briefly at the garage and agreed to follow the defendant's car to the Vollmer residence. . . . After reaching the residence, Grove and Malone remained in the cars while Hecht and Heidecker entered the home. The defendant introduced Heidecker to Vollmer, and the three men went into the basement. There, Vollmer and Heidecker discussed the particulars of the cocaine deal in the defendant's presence. Vollmer told Heidecker that he expected a phone call from his supplier. Hecht testified that he did not know who the caller would be. Subsequently, the phone call came, and Vollmer told Heidecker that there could be no exchange that evening. . . .

On October 3, 1978 Heidecker again called the garage and spoke with both Hecht and Grove. Heidecker testified that both men stated that "they had put the deal together" and that Hecht related prices for five ounces of cocaine: $2,000 an ounce from one source and $2,200 an ounce from another. Heidecker and Malone later met Hecht at a tavern . . . Grove had been left out of the meeting because he appeared to Heidecker to be extremely nervous.

Once again, Heidecker and Malone followed the defendant to Vollmer's home. Again, Heidecker accompanied Hecht into the house while Malone remained behind him in the car. Vollmer received a phone call at approximately 9:30 P.M. and told Heidecker that the cocaine was on the way. Vollmer and Heidecker went out to the car to speak with Malone, who showed them $10,000 in cash. The defendant remained inside the house during this discussion.

Vollmer and Heidecker then returned to the house, where a second phone call was received, confirming the fact that the exchange would indeed take place. The defendant was present during the phone conversation, but did not participate in the negotiations. Heidecker made arrangements through Vollmer with Vollmer's source. The price was set at $2,000 per ounce of cocaine. The defendant again testified that he did not know who the caller was. . . .

At midnight, Heidecker and Malone drove to a prearranged location in Whitewater. At the parking lot adjacent to the lot where the exchange was to take place, the agents met in a car driven by Vollmer. Hecht was a passenger in Vollmer's car. As Heidecker approached Vollmer's car, Hecht got out and left the area. Heidecker testified that while at Vollmer's house, Vollmer had stated that his source did not want to see anyone other than Heidecker when the exchange was made. It was agreed, then, that Hecht would not be present when the sale was made.

Heidecker then entered Vollmer's car, and the two of them drove to the adjacent parking lot, followed by agent Malone. They were there approximately three to four minutes when Daniel Kohls approached Vollmer's car, and produced two clear plastic bags containing cocaine. Heidecker left the bags on the car console, stating that he was going to get the money. He then left the car, entered Malone's car, and Malone gave the signal for the arrest. Agent Frank Wingert arrested Hecht a short time later at a nearby bar.

A jury trial was commenced on December 21, 1981. On December 22, the jury found the defendant guilty of being a party to the crime of possession of a controlled substance with the intent to deliver. . . .

OPINION

Section 939.05, Stats., provides:

> (1) Whoever is concerned in the commission of a crime is a principal and may be charged with and convicted of the commission of the crime although he did not directly commit it and although the person who directly committed has not been convicted or has been convicted of some other crime based on the same act.
> (2) A person is concerned in the commission of the crime if he:
>   (a) Directly commits the crime; or
>   (b) Intentionally aids and abets the commission of it . . .

The elements of complicity, or aiding and abetting are that a person (1) undertakes conduct (either verbal or overt action) which as a matter of objective facts aids another person in the execution of a crime, and further (2) he consciously desires or intends that his conduct will yield such assistance. . . .

Under the second of the two elements, namely, that Hecht intended that his actions yield such assistance, we believe that such intent may be inferred from the defendant's conduct itself. Although Hecht claims that he was merely a passive observer and that his only participation was to introduce Vollmer to Heidecker, we believe that his conduct proceeded much beyond this point. Once again, we are struck by glaring fact that Hecht appeared to do all within his power to ensure that Vollmer and the agents continued their contact in order to reach the point of making the exchange, short of being present at the actual transfer. . . . In this case, we believe that Hecht's continued pattern of conduct was inconsistent with any reasonable hypothesis of innocence, namely, his claim of passive observation. . . .

This court has also held that aider and abettor liability extends to the natural and probable consequences of the intended acts, as well as any other crime which, under the circumstances, was a natural and probable consequence of the intended crime. . . . In this case, the jury could reasonably find that the defendant put into motion the wheels of a mechanism that would ultimately lead to a sale of cocaine to the agents. By his acts of keeping Vollmer and the agents in close contact, he kept those wheels turning in a fluid motion. Under these circumstances, the jury could also reasonably find that the natural and probable consequence of this chain of events was the sale of cocaine and that the defendant is, therefore, liable for the possession of a controlled substance with the intent to deliver, under the theory of aiding and abetting the commission of a crime. . . .

The decision of the court of appeals is affirmed; the judgment of the circuit court is affirmed.

CASE DISCUSSION

Complicity aims at teamwork in committing crimes. Did Hecht participate in the crime, or was he merely present when it took place? What facts point to his participation? Do you think he was "dangerous" enough to warrant punishment as a cocaine dealer? Was he sufficiently involved to make him part of a team? What definition would you formulate for complicity?

Complicity following Crime

The common law included accessories after the fact—complicity following the commission of crimes—within the scope of liability for the main offense. For example, one who gave a burglar a place to hide was an accessory after the fact, and, as such, also guilty of burglary. Modern statutes impose liability for complicity following commission of the main crime, but the liability is for separate, less serious offenses, such as obstructing justice, interfering with prosecution, and aiding in escape.

Most statutes follow the common-law requirements for accessories after the fact: (1) that a third person had actually committed a felony; (2) that the accessory knew the other person had committed the felony; and (3) that the accessory personally aided the third person to hinder prosecution. Some statutes even preserve the term accessory after the fact in their classification scheme. The Supreme Court of Louisiana dealt with that state's accessory-after-the-fact statute in *State v. Chism.*

CASE

Was He an Accessory After the Fact?

State v. Chism

436 So.2d 464 (La. 1983)

[The defendant, Brian Chism, was convicted by a judge of being an accessory after the fact, and sentenced to three years in the parish prison, with two and one-half years suspended. The defendant was placed on supervised probation for two years. We affirm his conviction. Justice Dennis gave the opinion. Chief Justice Dixon gave a dissenting opinion.]

FACTS

On the evening of August 26, 1981 in Shreveport, Tony Duke gave the defendant Brian Chism, a ride in his automobile. Brian Chism was impersonating a female, and Duke was apparently unaware of Chism's disguise. After a brief visit at a friend's house the two stopped to pick up some beer at the residence of Chism's grandmother. Chism's one-legged uncle, Ira Lloyd, joined them, and the three continued on their way, drinking as Duke drove the automobile. When Duke expressed a desire to have sexual relations with Chism, Lloyd announced that he wanted to find his ex-wife Gloria for the same purpose. Shortly after midnight, the trio arrived at the St. Vincent Avenue Church of Christ and persuaded Gloria Lloyd to come outside. As Ira Lloyd stood outside the car attempting to persuade Gloria to come with them, Chism and Duke hugged and kissed on the front seat as Duke sat behind the steering wheel.

Gloria and Ira Lloyd got into an argument, and Ira stabbed Gloria with a knife several times in the stomach and once in the neck. Gloria's shouts attracted the attention of two neighbors, who unsuccessfully tried to prevent Ira from pushing Gloria into the front seat of the car alongside Chism and Duke. Ira Lloyd climbed into the front seat also, and Duke drove off. One of the bystanders testified that she could not be sure but she thought she saw Brian's foot on the accelerator as the car left.

Lloyd ordered Duke to drive to Willow Point, near Cross Lake. When they arrived Chism and Duke, under Lloyd's direction, removed Gloria from the vehicle and placed her on some high grass on the roadway, near a wood line. Ira was unable to help the two because his wooden leg had come off. Afterwards, as Lloyd requested, the two drove off, leaving Gloria with him.

There was no evidence that Chism or Duke protested, resisted or attempted to avoid the actions which Lloyd ordered them to take. Although Lloyd was armed with a knife, there was no evidence that he threatened either of his companions with harm.

Duke proceeded to drop Chism off at a friend's house, where he changed to male clothing. He placed the blood-stained women's clothes in a trash bin. Afterward, Chism went with his mother to the police station at 1:15 A.M. He gave the police a complete statement, and took the officers to the place where Gloria had been left with Ira Lloyd. The police found Gloria's body in some tall grass several feet from the spot. An autopsy indicated that stab wounds had caused her death. Chism's discarded clothing disappeared before the police arrived at the trash bin.

OPINION

An accessory after the fact is any person, who, after the commission of a felony, shall harbor, conceal, or aid the offender, knowing or having reasonable ground to believe that he has committed the felony, and with the intent that he may avoid or escape from arrest, trial, conviction, or punishment. La. R.S. 14:25. . . .

[A] person may be punished as an accessory after the fact if he aids an offender personally, knowing or having reasonable ground to believe that he has committed the felony, and has a specific or general intent that the offender will avoid or escape from arrest, trial, conviction, or punishment. . . .

An accessory after the fact may be tried and convicted, notwithstanding the fact that the principal felon may not have been arrested, tried, convicted, or amenable to justice. . . . [I]t is essential to prove that a felony was committed and completed prior to the time the assistance was rendered the felon, although it is not also necessary that the felon already have been charged with the crime. . . .

[W]e must determine whether, after viewing the evidence in the light most favorable to the prosecution, any rational trier of fact could have found beyond a reasonable doubt that (a) a completed felony had been committed by Ira Lloyd before Brian Chism rendered him the assistance described below; (b) Chism knew or had reasonable grounds to know of the commission of the felony by Lloyd, and (c) Chism gave aid to Lloyd personally under circumstances that indicate either that he actively desired that the felon avoid or escape arrest, trial, conviction, or punishment or that he believed that one of these consequences was substantially certain to result from his assistance.

There was clearly enough evidence to justify the finding that a felony had been completed before any assistance was rendered to Lloyd by the defendant. The record vividly demonstrates that Lloyd fatally stabbed his ex-wife before she was transported to Willow Point and left in the high grass near the wood line. Thus, Lloyd committed the felonies of attempted murder, aggravated battery, and simple kidnapping, before Chism aided him in any way. . . .

The evidence overwhelmingly indicates that Chism had reasonable grounds to believe that Lloyd had committed a felony before any assistance was rendered. In his confessions and his testimony Chism indicates that the victim was bleeding profusely when Lloyd pushed her into the vehicle, that she was limp and moaned as they drove to Willow Point, and that he knew Lloyd had inflicted her wounds with a knife. . . .

The closest question presented is whether any reasonable trier of fact could have found beyond a reasonable doubt that Chism assisted Lloyd under circumstances that indicate that either Chism actively desired that Lloyd would avoid or escape arrest, trial, conviction, or punishment, or that Chism believed that one of these consequences was substantially certain to result from his assistance. After carefully reviewing the record, we conclude that the prosecution satisfied its burden of producing the required quantity of evidence. . . .

(1) Chism did not protest or attempt to leave the car when his uncle, Lloyd shoved the mortally wounded victim inside; (2) he did not attempt to persuade Duke, his would-be lover, exit [sic] out the driver's side of the car and flee from his uncle, whom he knew to be one-legged and armed only with a knife; (3) he did not take any of these actions at any point during the considerable ride to Willow Point; (4) at their destination, he docilely complied with Lloyd's direction to remove the victim from the car and leave Lloyd with her, despite the fact that Lloyd made no threats and that his wooden leg had become detached; (5) after leaving Lloyd with the dying victim, he made no immediate effort to report the victim's whereabouts or to obtain emergency medical treatment for her; (6) before going home or reporting the victim's dire condition he went to a friend's house, changed clothing and discarded his own in a trash bin from which the police where unable to recover them as evidence; (7) he went home without reporting the victim's condition or location; (8) and he went to the police station to report the crime only after arriving home and discussing the matter with his mother. . . .

Therefore, we affirm the defendant's conviction. We note, however, that the sentence imposed by the trial judge was illegal. The judge imposed a sentence of three years. He suspended two and one half of years [sic] of the term. The trial judge has no authority to suspend *part* of a sentence in a felony case. The correct sentence would have been a suspension of all three years of the term, with a six-month term as a condition of two years of probation. . . .

DISSENT

I respectfully dissent from what appears to be a finding of guilt by association. The majority lists five instances of *inaction,* or failure to act, by defendant: (1) did not protest or leave the car; (2) did not attempt to persuade Duke to leave the car; (3) did neither (1) nor (2) on ride to Willow Point; (5) [*sic*] made no immediate effort to report crime or get aid for the victim; (7) failed to report victim's condition or location after changing clothes. The three instances of defendant's *actions* relied on by the majority for conviction were stated to be: (4) complying with Lloyd's direction to remove the victim from the car and leave the victim and Lloyd at Willow Point; (6) changing clothes and discarding bloody garments; and (8) discussing the matter with the defendant's mother before going to the police station to report the crime.

None of these actions or failures to act tended to prove defendant's intent, specifically or generally, to aid defendant avoid arrest, trial, conviction or punishment.

CASE DISCUSSION

Was the crime completed at the time Chism aided Lloyd? What facts show this? Do you agree that Chism intended to help Lloyd avoid arrest, trial, conviction, or punishment? What does the dissent mean in saying that the ruling makes a person guilty of crime by association? Do you agree? In Louisiana, according to this ruling, is the *mens rea* for accessory after the fact purpose, knowledge, recklessness, or negligence? Explain.

≡ VICARIOUS LIABILITY

The doctrine of complicity applies to accomplices and accessories because they *participate* in crime. Complicity also encompasses vicarious liability. **Vicarious liability** does not require that the defendant participate by action; it is created by the *relationship* between the party who commits the crime and another party. Vicarious liability applies mainly to business relationships: employer-employee, manager-corporation, buyer-seller, producer-consumer, service provider–recipient.

Until recently, to most people criminal law meant "street crimes," or the crimes ordinary people commit for personal or individual private revenge, gratification, and gain. The common assumption was that street crimes predominate and that most harms stem from them. Because of growing attention, however, the public now knows more about the extent of corporate and other business crime.[7]

Business Crime

Business crime, as discussed in this chapter, is not equivalent to white-collar crime. Corporate and other business crimes further a business enterprise's interests, such as by increasing its profits or enhancing its competitive position and power. White-collar crime secures private gain. Hence, a bank officer who bilks customers to build up the bank's profits commits a business crime, but a bank teller who embezzles money to buy a new car is a white-collar criminal. Corporate and other business crime victimizes government, business, and the general public. Corporate crime extends beyond financial crimes, such as price fixing, stock misrepresentation, and fraud; it causes bodily injury, disease, and even death (see chapter 5). Finally, corporate crime breeds cynicism and disrespect for law because its perpetrators frequently escape punishment or receive lenient treatment.[8]

Losses from corporate crime are difficult to measure exactly, but estimates are staggering—probably totaling at least $44 billion. This does not include costs arising from product safety; from environmental, chemical, and antitrust violations, such as price fixing; and from fraud against government programs. The $44 billion figure outstrips by eleven times the $4 billion estimated loss from street crimes against property. Physical injuries, disease, and death due to corporate and other business crime are not known and are difficult to assess because so often they are considered accidents and do not enter the criminal justice system. But experts maintain that corporate violence is more serious than street violence. Despite its seriousness, the Uniform Crime Reports, the most widely known and publicized crime statistics, do not report corporate crime.[9]

Business Crime and the Law

Corporate crime is not only a serious social problem, it also creates problems in criminal law. Pinpointing responsibility for corporate crime is difficult. Often, not one person but many participate in decisions that cause harm. This problem increases as corporate structures become more complex. The larger and more dispersed the corporation or business, the harder it is to attribute responsibility. Furthermore, and related, it is difficult to establish *mens rea* in corporate crimes. A corporation cannot have a *mens rea* because it cannot think. To overcome this, the criminal law makes corporations criminals by two methods: (1) strict liability eliminates the material element of *mens rea*, and (2) vicarious liability attributes the intent of managers and agents to the corporation. Although vicarious and strict liability work together to impose criminal liability, they are distinct doctrines: strict liability eliminates the *mens rea*; vicarious liability dispenses with the *actus reus*.[10]

Punishing corporate crime is also problematic. Most corporate crimes never enter the criminal justice system. Out-of-court arrangements lead to consent decrees, or agreements to settle matters between corporations and those complaining against them. When the government tries corporate crimes and obtains convictions, sentences often appear lenient and inadequate compared with penalties for street crimes. Courts can only impose fines because corporations cannot go to jail. Furthermore, sending employers and managers to jail for the conduct of others raises constitutional problems. Some courts have ruled that imprisonment for vicarious liability violates the due process clause.

Even fines violate the due process clause when a noncriminal response to regulating business conduct suffices. Fines fall ultimately on stockholders, "most of whom, ordinarily had nothing to do with the offense and were powerless to prevent it." In addition, fines are ineffective if corporations consider them just another business expense. Finally, fines rarely deter officers or other agents who do not have to pay them; officers suffer no stigma if their organizations violate "mere regulations," not "real criminal laws." Quite the contrary. Some authorities believe officers risk prosecution and conviction for minor offenses in order to bring gains to their companies. By doing so, they receive their colleagues' approbation for "shrewd business."[11]

Little research about corporate crime exists. After reviewing what was available on the subject, sociologist Stanton Wheeler made the following conclusion:

> A two-volume criminology index, reviewing theoretical and empirical work in criminology lists nearly 3700 books or articles. Of that total, only some 92 (2.5%) deal with white-collar or corporate criminality even when we include studies of organized crime as part of the total.[12]

Criminal law's general principles apply to all crime, including corporate crime. However, corporate crime deserves special note for two reasons. First, some crimes are peculiar to business. Unlike with street and white-collar crimes, the gains sought are neither individual nor personal. For example, corporate executives do not fix prices for their personal profit but rather to enhance the company's business position. Second, corporations do not ordinarily injure or cause disease or death because of personal vendettas and anger. They do so while their officers pursue company interests. Hence, corporate executives may not mean to injure workers or customers, but to make the company competitive they may cut safety corners that lead to employee and customer deaths. Robbers do not usually desire to injure their victims either, but they are prepared to risk doing so in order to get the money they seek.[13]

> we are talking about . . . economic crime. We have tended in the past to call it property crime as distinguished from violent crime. And even there it is not easy to draw the line. If a surgeon knowingly commits unneeded surgery on a human being because he wants money, is that a less violent physical assault on an individual than to be mugged in the streets? I have to tell you that at a purely moral level I find it far more reprehensible.[14]

Vicarious Liability and Business Crime

Vicarious liability arises out of business relationships in some combination of the following circumstances: (1) where strict liability statutes or misdemeanors are involved; (2) where it is difficult to prove an employer's or corporate official's *legal* involvement; (3) where difficult burdens are put of that gang, shall be punished by imprisonment in the county jail for a period not to exceed one year, or by imprisonment in the state prison for 1, 2, or 3 years.

This bill would also prescribe the punishment applicable to any person who is convicted of a felony or misdemeanor which is committed or attempted to be committed for the benefit of, at the direction of, or in association with any criminal street gang, with the specific intent to promote, further, or assist in any criminal conduct by gang members, including the minimum term of imprisonment in the county jail and the state prison for 1, 2, or 3 years for these offenses and a 1-, 2-, or 3-year sentence enhancement applicable to the commission or attempted commission of a felony in furtherance of these objectives. This bill would thus impose a state-mandated local program by creating new crimes.

This bill would provide that every building or place, other than buildings in which there are 3 or fewer dwelling units, used by members of a criminal street gang for the purpose of committing specified offenses, and every building or place, other than buildings in which there are 3 or fewer dwelling units, where that criminal gang conduct takes place, is a nuisance. The bill would provide that the district attorney in any county, in the name of the people, and the city attorney of any incorporated city, may, and any citizen of the state residing in the county where the building, place, or residence is located, in his or her own name, may, bring an action to abate as a nuisance any building, place, or residence used for that purpose or enjoin the person so conducting the activity or maintaining the building in accordance with the proceedings governing the abatement of nuisances and injunction of persons involved in unlawful controlled substances offenses, except as specified.

This bill would provide that these provisions are not applicable to employees engaged in concerted activities for their mutual aid and protection, or to labor organization activities or the activities of their members or agents.

(2) Existing Law Provides That Every Person Who Commits Any Act or Omits the Performance of a Duty Which Causes or Tends to Cause or Encourage a Minor to Engage in Specified Prohibited Conduct, Is Guilty of a Misdemeanor. This bill would state that for purposes of the above provision, a parent or legal guardian of any person under the age of 18 years shall have the duty to exercise reasonable care, supervision, protection, and control over their minor child. . . .

(4) Existing Law Prescribes the Penalties for Criminal Assault. This bill would prohibit any person from willfully threatening to commit a crime which will result in death or great bodily injury to another person, with the specific intent that the statement is to be

Criminal Law Close-Up

MOTHER CHARGED BECAUSE SON IS STREET GANG RAPE SUSPECT

[A California prosecutor charged Gloria Williams with "failure to exercise reasonable care, supervision, protection and control" of her son. Free on $20,000 bail, she faced a penalty of up to one year in jail and a $2,500 fine. Gloria Williams's prosecution under California's Street Terrorism Enforcement and Prevention Act provides an excellent example of how policymakers and legislators draw upon the well-established principles of criminal law to meet new problems and challenges. In this case, the California legislature has drawn upon a blend of complicity and vicarious liability doctrine in an effort to respond to street gang violence in Los Angeles and other California cities.[1]]

From the Legislative Counsel's Digest

. . . The Legislature . . . finds that the State of California is in a state of crisis which has been caused by violent street gangs whose members threaten, terrorize, and commit a multitude of crimes against the peaceful citizens of their neighborhoods. These activities, both individually and collectively, present a clear and present danger to public order and safety and are not constitutionally protected. The Legislature finds that there are nearly 600 criminal street gangs operating in California, and that the number of gang-related murders is increasing. The Legislature also finds that in Los Angeles County alone there were 328 gang-related murders in 1986, and that gang homicides in 1987 have increased 80 percent over 1986. It is the intent of the Legislature in enacting this chapter to seek the eradication of criminal activity by street gangs by focusing upon patterns of criminal gang activity and upon the organized nature of street gangs, which together, are the chief source of terror created by street gangs. The Legislature further finds that an effective means of punishing and deterring the criminal activities of street gangs is through forfeiture of the profits, proceeds, and instrumentalities acquired, accumulated, or used by street gangs. . . .

(1) Under Existing Law, There Are No Special Provisions for the Punishment of Crimes Committed by Members of Street Gangs. This bill would provide that any person who actively participates in any criminal street gang with knowledge that its members engage in or have engaged in a pattern of criminal gang activity, and who willfully furthers, or assists in, any criminal conduct by members

taken as a threat, even if there is no intent to actually carry it out, which, on its face and under the circumstances in which it is made is so unequivocal, unconditional, immediate, and specific as to convey to the person threatened a gravity of purpose and an immediate prospect of execution. This bill would make this offense either a misdemeanor or a felony punishable either by imprisonment in the county jail not to exceed one year, or by imprisonment in the state prison, thereby imposing a state-mandated local program.

CA PENAL § 186.22

186.22. (a) Any person who actively participates in any criminal street gang with knowledge that its members engage in or have engaged in a pattern of criminal gang activity, and who willfully promotes, furthers, or assists in any felonious criminal conduct by members of that gang, shall be punished by imprisonment in the county jail for a period not to exceed one year, or by imprisonment in the state prison for one, two, or three years.

(b) Any person who is convicted of a felony or a misdemeanor which is committed for the benefit of, at the direction of, or in association with any criminal street gang, with the specific intent to promote, further, or assist in any criminal conduct by gang members, shall be punished in the following manner:

(1) Any person who violates this subdivision in the commission of a misdemeanor, shall be punished by imprisonment in the county jail not to exceed one year, or by imprisonment in the state prison for one, two, or three years, provided that any person sentenced to imprisonment in the county jail pursuant to subdivision (b) of Section 17, shall be imprisoned for a period not to exceed one year, but not less than 180 days, and shall not be eligible for release upon completion of sentence, parole, or any other basis, until he or she has served 180 days. If the court grants probation or suspends the execution of sentence imposed upon the defendant, it shall require as a condition thereof that the defendant serve 180 days in the county jail.

CA PENAL § 272

SEC. 2. Section 272 of the Penal Code is amended to read: 272. Every person who commits any act or omits the performance of any duty, which act or omission causes or tends to cause or encourage any person under the age of 18 years to come within the provisions of SECTION 300, 601, or 602 [truancy, habitual disobedience, delinquency, or curfew violation] of the Welfare and Institutions Code or which act or omission contributes thereto, or any person who, by any act or omission, or by threats, commands, or persuasion, induces or endeavors to induce any person under the age of 18 years or any ward or dependent child of the juvenile court to fail or refuse to conform to a lawful order of the juvenile court, or to do or to perform any act or to follow any course of conduct or to so live as would cause or manifestly tend to cause any such person to become or to remain a person within the provisions of SECTION 300, 601, or 602 of the Welfare and Institutions Code, is guilty of a misdemeanor and upon conviction thereof shall be punished by a fine not exceeding two thousand five hundred dollars ($2,500), or by imprisonment in the county jail for not more than one year, or by both such fine and imprisonment in a county jail, or may be released on probation for a period not exceeding five years. FOR PURPOSES OF THIS SECTION, A PARENT OR LEGAL GUARDIAN TO ANY PERSON UNDER THE AGE OF 18 YEARS SHALL HAVE THE DUTY TO EXERCISE REASONABLE CARE, SUPERVISION, PROTECTION, AND CONTROL OVER THEIR MINOR CHILD.

[1]"Mother Is Charged Because Son Is California Street Gang Suspect," *New York Times* (May 4, 1989), p. 8.
SOURCE: California Legislative Service 1987–1988, Regular Session (1988 Laws).

on prosecutors to obtain evidence to convict; (4) where widespread public harm is threatened by the prohibited conduct. Vicarious liability offends the notion of individual and personal guilt. The common law punished participants in crime. Corporate officers in high positions who either participated in, approved of, or consented to criminal conduct fall within the scope of common-law complicity. Corporations were not criminally liable under the common law; they could not form a *mens rea* because only "natural persons" think. The **alter ego doctrine**—that management was the corporation's "brain"—provided an exception to the common-law principle.[15]

The Wisconsin Supreme Court dealt with vicarious liability in *State v. Beaudry.*

CASE

Was She a Criminal Without Act or Mens Rea?

State v. Beaudry
123 Wis.2d 40, 365 N.W.2d 593 (1985)

[The jury found the defendant, Janet Beaudry, the agent designated by the corporation pursuant to . . . the alcoholic beverage laws, guilty of the misdemeanor of unlawfully remaining open for business after

1:00 A.M. in violation of Sec. 125.68(4)(c), which prohibits premises from . . . remaining open between the hours of 1:00 A.M. and 8:00 A.M. . . . . On the basis of the judgment the defendant was ordered to pay a fine in the amount of $200.00. . . . Justice Abrahamson delivered the opinion. Justice Ceci gave a dissenting opinion.]

FACTS

The defendant, Janet Beaudry, and her husband, Wallace Beaudry, are the sole shareholders of Sohn Manufacturing Company, a corporation which has a license to sell alcoholic beverages at the Village Green Tavern in the village of Elkhart Lake, Sheboygan county. Janet Beaudry is the designated agent for the corporation. . . .

At approximately 3:45 A.M., a deputy sheriff . . . drove past the Village Green Tavern. He stopped to investigate. . . . As he approached the tavern, he heard music, saw an individual standing behind the bar, and saw glasses on the bar. . . . The tavern manager [Mark Witkowski] and two men were the only persons inside the bar. All three were drinking. . . .

The case was tried before a jury . . . Janet Beaudry testified that she was not present at the tavern on the morning of February 9. Wallace Beaudry testified that Janet Beaudry had delegated to him . . . the responsibilities of business administration . . . ; that he hired Mark Witkowski . . . ; that he had informed Witkowski that it was his duty to abide by the liquor laws; and that he never authorized Witkowski to throw a private party for his friends, or to give away liquor to his friends.

Witkowski testified that he had served drinks after hours to two men. During cross-examination Witkowski confirmed that Wallace Beaudry had never authorized him to stay open after hours . . . ; that he knew it was illegal to serve liquor after 1:00 A.M. to anyone, including friends; that his two friends drank at the bar before 1:00 A.M. and had paid for those drinks; that he was having a good time with his friends before closing hours and wanted to continue partying and conversing with them after 1 A.M.; that after closing hours he was simply using the tavern to have a private party for two friends; that he did not charge his friends for any of the liquor they drank after 1:00 A.M.; and that by staying open he was trying to benefit not Wallace Beaudry but himself. . . .

OPINION

. . . The state's prosecution of the defendant under the criminal laws rests on a theory of vicarious liability, that is *respondeat superior* [emphasis added]. Under this theory of liability, the master (here the designated agent) is liable for the illegal conduct of the servant (here the tavern manager). . . .

While the focus in this case is on the defendant's vicarious liability, it is helpful to an understanding of vicarious liability to compare it with the doctrine of strict liability. Strict liability allows for criminal liability absent the element of *mens rea* found in the definition of most crimes. . . . Thus under strict liability the accused has engaged in the act of omission; the requirement of mental fault, *mens rea,* is eliminated. . . .

Vicarious liability, in contrast to strict liability, dispenses with the requirement of the *actus reus* and imputes the criminal act of one person to another. . . .

The state has not cited a statute expressly making the natural person licensee vicariously criminally liable for the conduct of an employee who illegally sells alcoholic beverages, and we have found none. Nevertheless, as the state correctly points out, over a long period the court has interpreted several statutes regulating the sale of alcoholic beverages as imposing on the natural person licensee vicarious criminal liability for the illegal conduct of an employee. . . .

Several factors influence this court to conclude that the purpose of the statute is promoted by the imposition of vicarious liability. First, the state has imposed numerous restrictions on the sale of alcoholic beverages to protect the public health and safety. . . . Statutes regulating the sale of alcoholic beverages have been recognized as creating strict liability "public welfare offenses." . . . Second, violation of closing hours law is a misdemeanor; the penalty is a monetary fine and a relatively short term of imprisonment. Third, in many cases it may be difficult for the state to prove that the natural person licensee or corporate agent was negligent in hiring or supervising the employee, or knew about or authorized the employee's violation of the statute. Lastly, the number of prosecutions may be large so that the legislature would want to relieve the prosecution of the task of proving the employer knew of or authorized the violation or was negligent. . . .

[T]he defendant's final argument is that due process requires blameworthy conduct on the part of the defendant as a prerequisite to criminal liability. Although the imposition of criminal liability for faultless conduct does not comport with the generally accepted premise of Anglo-American criminal justice that criminal liability is based on personal fault, this court and the United States Supreme Court have upheld statutes imposing criminal liability for some types of offenses without proof that the conduct was knowing or wilful or negligent.

The defendant's chief challenge to the constitutionality of the statute in issue in this case appears to be that the defendant could have received a jail sentence of up to 90 days for the violation. As the state points out, the defendant was fined $200, and the due process issue the defendant raises . . . is not presented by . . . this case. . . .

We now turn to the question of whether the evidence supports the verdict that the tavern manager was acting within the scope of his employment. As we stated previously, the jury was instructed that the defendant is liable only for the acts of the tavern manager that were within the scope of his employment. Thus the defendant is not liable for all the acts of the tavern manager, only for those acts within the scope of employment . . .

The application of the standard of scope of employment limits liability to illegal conduct which occurred while the offending employee was engaged in some job-related activity and thus limits the accused's vicarious liability to conduct with which the accused has a factual connection and with which the accused has some responsible relation to the public danger envisaged by the legislature. . . .

Considering that the conduct occurred on the employer's premises and began immediately after "closing time"; that the employee had access to the tavern after hours only by virtue of his role as an employee of the corporate licensee, which role vested him with the means to keep the tavern open; and that the defendant may anticipate that employees may be tempted to engage in such conduct; the jury could conclude that the tavern manager's conduct was sufficiently similar to the conduct authorized as to be within the scope of employment. . . .

Decision of the court of appeals is affirmed.

DISSENT

. . . I conclude that Mark Witkowski was not within the scope of employment when he kept the tavern open after 1:00 A.M. . . .

Witkowski stated that one of his duties as a manager included closing the tavern at one o'clock. He testified that Wallace Beaudry never authorized him to stay open after closing time. In fact, he was specifically instructed to close promptly at the legal closing time. Additionally, Witkowski testified, "I knew that Wally would not want me to stay open after hours but I decided to do it anyway." . . .

I conclude that Witkowski was not within the scope of his employment, because his act of keeping the tavern open until 3:45 A.M. was not authorized by Mr. or Mrs. Beaudry. . . .

Witkowski did not expect to get paid for these two hours when he was sitting at the bar and drinking with his friends. It is clear that Witkowski was no longer working at 3:45 A.M. and that his acts were far beyond the time limit authorized by Janet or Wally Beaudry. . . .

Witkowski's acts were in no way intended to further the defendant's business, but were motivated solely for his own enjoyment and convenience. . . . Witkowski stated, "I was not trying to benefit Wallace Beaudry by staying open after hours. I was simply using Wally's tavern to have a *private party* for my two friends." . . .

I conclude that Witkowski was not acting within the scope of his authority, because his acts were in no way intended to serve the defendant. . . .

CASE DISCUSSION

What circumstances does the court conclude justify imposing vicarious liability on Janet Beaudry? How do you justify criminal liability when there is neither *actus reus* nor *mens rea?* Do you believe that punishing Janet Beaudry violates the due process clause? If she were put in jail would you answer differently? Was the majority or dissent correct in its conclusion regarding Witkowski's acting within the scope of his employment? Explain.

Vicarious Corporate Liability for Real Crime

Vicarious corporate liability most often arises in connection with strict liability for misdemeanors, but is by no means limited to minor offenses. The criminal law also imposes vicarious criminal liability on corporations for real, or true, crimes. Several states have adopted corporate criminal liability statutes.

These statutes have several features in common. (1) They impose liability for all crimes, although the most commonly prosecuted crimes are involuntary manslaughter and property offenses. (2) Officials or agents high in the corporate structure must authorize, commit, request, or "recklessly tolerate" the conduct that constitutes the crime. This is called the **superior officer rule.** (3) Officers or agents must act for the corporation's benefit, not for their own personal gain. (4) Officers must act within the scope of their authority. Corporations can commit any crimes under these conditions. (See Model Penal Code Section 2.07 in Appendix.)

Most statutes restrict corporate liability to the conduct of officers and agents who are sufficiently high in the corporate hierarchy that their actions reflect corporate policy. This limitation originated in the *alter ego* **doctrine.** Only leading officers, such as (but not only) presidents, who constitute the corporation's brain can impose vicarious corporate criminal liability. The *alter ego* doctrine stems from the common-law rule that corporations cannot commit crimes because they do not possess minds. The doctrine also accords with *mens rea,* culpability, and personal and individual responsibility; corporations are blameworthy when the officers' mental states and the corporate structure correspond. Therefore, statutes adopting the *alter ego* doctrine impose corporate vicarious liability for the actions of a firm's president and general manager, but not for the actions of either a large plant's supervisor or a small branch's manager.[16]

Vicarious Individual Liability for Corporate Crime

Under most modern statutes, individuals who act for the corporation's benefit are as liable for that conduct as they would be if they were acting in their own behalf for their own private gain.

CASE

Did the Corporation President Commit the Crime?

United States v. Park

421 U.S. 658, 95 S.Ct. 1903, 44 L.Ed.2d 489 (1975)

[The president of Acme Markets, Inc., was charged with and convicted of five counts of violating the Federal Food, Drug, and

Cosmetic Act[a] because food in the corporation's warehouses was exposed to rodent contamination. The act provides for up to a $1,000 fine or not more than one year of imprisonment or both. Park was fined $250, $50 on each count. He appealed. Chief Justice Burger delivered the opinion, in which justices Douglas, Brennan, White, Blackmun, and Rehnquist joined. Justice Stewart filed a dissenting opinion in which justices Marshall and Powell joined.]

FACTS

In April 1970 the Food and Drug Administration (FDA) advised respondent by letter of insanitary conditions in Acme's Philadelphia warehouse. In 1971 the FDA found that similar conditions existed in the firm's Baltimore warehouse. An FDA consumer safety officer testified concerning evidence of rodent infestation and other insanitary conditions discovered during a 12-day inspection of the Baltimore warehouse in November and December 1971.[b] He also related that a second inspection of the warehouse had been conducted in March 1972. On that occasion the inspectors found that there had been improvement in the sanitary conditions, but that "there was still evidence of rodent activity in the building and in the warehouses and we found some rodent-contaminated lots of food items."

The Government also presented testimony by the Chief of Compliance of the FDA's Baltimore office, who informed respondent by letter of the conditions at the Baltimore warehouse after the first inspection.[c] There was testimony by Acme's Baltimore division vice president, who had responded to the letter on behalf of Acme and respondent and who described the steps taken to remedy the insanitary conditions discovered by both inspections. The Government's final witness, Acme's vice president for legal affairs and assistant secretary, identified respondent as the president and chief executive officer of the company and read a bylaw prescribing the duties of the chief executive officer.[d] He testified that respondent functioned by delegating "normal operating duties," including sanitation, but that he retained "certain things, which are the big, broad, principles of the operation of the company," and had "the responsibility of seeing that they all work together."

At the close of the Government's case in chief, respondent moved for a judgment of acquittal on the ground that "the evidence in chief has shown that Mr. Park is not personally concerned in this Food and Drug violation." The trial judge denied the motion. Respondent was the only defense witness. He testified that, although all of Acme's employees were in a sense under his general direction, the company had an "organizational structure for responsibilities for certain functions" according to which different phases of its operation were "assigned to individuals who, in turn, have staff and departments under them." He identified those individuals responsible for sanitation, and related that upon receipt of the January 1972 FDA letter, he had conferred with the vice president for legal affairs, who informed him that the Baltimore division vice president "was investigating the situation immediately and would be taking corrective action and would be preparing a summary of the corrective action to reply to the letter." Respondent stated that he did not "believe there was anything [he] could have done more constructively than what [he] found was being done."

On cross-examination, respondent conceded that providing sanitary conditions for food offered for sale to the public was something that he was "responsible for in the entire operation of the company," and he stated that it was one of many phases of the company that he assigned to "dependable subordinates." Respondent was asked about and, over the objections of his counsel, admitted receiving, the April 1970 letter addressed to him from the FDA regarding insanitary conditions at Acme's Philadelphia warehouse.[e] He acknowledged that, with the exception of the division vice president, the same individuals had responsibility for sanitation in both Baltimore and Philadelphia. Finally, in response to questions concerning the Philadelphia and Baltimore incidents, respondent admitted that the Baltimore problem indicated the system for handling sanitation "wasn't working perfectly" and that as Acme's chief executive officer he was responsible for "any result which occurs in our company."

At the close of the evidence, respondent's renewed motion for a judgment of acquittal was denied. The relevant portion of the trial judge's instructions to the jury challenged by respondent is set out [below].[f] Respondent's counsel objected to the instructions on the ground that they failed . . . to define "responsible relationship." The trial judge overruled the objection. The jury found respondent guilty on all counts of the information, and he was subsequently sentenced to pay a fine of $50 on each count.[g]

The Court of Appeals reversed the conviction and remanded for a new trial. That court viewed the Government as arguing "that the conviction may be predicated solely upon a showing that [respondent] was the President of the offending corporation," and it stated that as "a general proposition, some act of commission or omission is an essential element of every crime." . . . The Court of Appeals concluded that the trial judge's instructions "might well have left the jury with the erroneous impression that Park could be found guilty in the absence of 'wrongful action' on his part," and that proof of this element was required by due process.

OPINION

. . . [T]hose corporate agents vested with the responsibility, and power commensurate with that responsibility, to devise whatever measures are necessary to ensure compliance with the [Federal Food, Drug, and Cosmetic] Act [of 1938] bear a "responsible relationship" to, or have a "responsible share" in, violations.

[I]n providing sanctions which reach and touch the individuals who execute the corporate mission the Act imposes not only a positive duty to seek out and remedy violations when they occur but also, and primarily, a duty to implement measures that will insure that violations will not occur. The requirements of foresight and vigilance imposed on responsible corporate agents are beyond question demanding, and perhaps onerous, but they are no more stringent than the public has a right to expect of those who voluntarily assume positions of authority in business enterprises whose services and products affect the health and well-being of the public that supports them.

Cases under the Federal Food and Drugs Act reflected the view both that knowledge or intent were not required to be proved in prosecutions under its criminal provisions, and that responsible corporate agents could be subjected to the liability thereby imposed. Moreover, the principle had been recognized that a corporate agent, through whose act, default, or omission the corporation committed a crime, was himself guilty individually of that crime. The principle had been applied whether or not the crime required "consciousness of wrongdoing," and it had been applied not only to those corporate agents who themselves committed the criminal act, but also to those who by virtue of their managerial positions or other similar relation to the actor could be deemed responsible for its commission.

In the latter class of cases, the liability of managerial officers did not depend on their knowledge of, or personal participation in, the act made criminal by the statute. Rather, where the statute under which they were prosecuted dispensed with "consciousness of wrongdoing," an omission or failure to act was deemed a sufficient basis for a responsible corporate agent's liability. It was enough in such cases that, by virtue of the relationship he bore to the corporation, the agent had the power to prevent the act complained of.

Thus, the Court has reaffirmed the proposition that "the public interest in the purity of its food is so great as to warrant the imposition of the highest standard of care on distributors." In order to make "distributors of food the strictest censors of their merchandise," the Act punishes "neglect where the law requires care, or inaction where it imposes a duty." "The accused, if he does not will the violation, usually is in a position to prevent it with no more care than society might reasonably expect and no more exertion than it might reasonably exact from one who assumed his responsibilities."

Turning to the jury charge in this case, it is of course arguable that isolated parts can be read as intimating that a finding of guilt could be predicated solely on respondent's corporate position. But this is not the way we review jury instructions, because "a single instruction to a jury may not be judged in artificial isolation, but must be viewed in the context of the overall charge."

Reading the entire charge satisfies us that the jury's attention was adequately focused on the issue of respondent's authority with respect to the conditions that formed the basis of the alleged violations. Viewed as a whole, the charge did not permit the jury to find guilt solely on the basis of respondent's position in the corporation; rather, it fairly advised the jury that to find guilt it must find respondent "had a responsible relation to the situation," and "by virtue of his position had authority and responsibility" to deal with the situation. The situation referred to could only be "food held in unsanitary conditions in a warehouse with the result that it consisted, in part, of filth or may have been contaminated with filth."

[The evidence showed that] respondent was on notice that he could not rely on his system of delegation to subordinates to prevent or correct insanitary conditions at Acme's warehouses, and that he must have been aware of the deficiencies of this system before the Baltimore violations were discovered. The evidence was therefore relevant since it served to rebut respondent's defense that he had justifiably relied upon subordinates to handle sanitation matters.

Affirmed.

CASE DISCUSSION

The Park case tries to resolve the very difficult issue of just how far individual vicarious liability for corporate crime extends, particularly when the officer does not intend to commit crimes and did not act directly to violate the law. Park was the corporation president and was generally responsible for the corporation's operation. But was he responsible for keeping rats out of the corporation's warehouses? Did the court base Park's individual liability merely on his position in the company or on something he did or failed to do? In other words, is this a status offense, or is it liability based on conduct? If liability is based on conduct and not on status, was Park reckless or negligent with respect to the rats in the warehouse? Or was he strictly liable for the contamination? If keeping foods pure is so important, why did the trial court fine Park only $250? And why did he appeal his case all the way to the United States Supreme Court? Why was so much made of a $250 fine?

---

[a]Section 402 of the Act, 21 U.S.C. § 342, provides in pertinent part:

A food shall be deemed to be adulterated

(a) (3) if it consists in whole or in part of any filthy, putrid, or decomposed substance, or if it is otherwise unfit for food; or

(4) if it has been prepared, packed, or held under insanitary conditions whereby it may have become contaminated with filth, or whereby it may have been rendered injurious to health

Section 301 of the Act, 21 U.S.C. § 331, provides in pertinent part:

The following acts and the causing thereof are prohibited:

(k) The alteration, mutilation, destruction, obliteration, or removal of the whole or any part of the labeling of, or the doing of any other act with respect to, a food, drug, device, or cosmetic, if such act is done while such article is held for sale (whether or not the first sale) after shipment in interstate commerce and results in such article being adulterated or misbranded.

[b]The witness testified with respect to the inspection of the basement of the "old building" in the warehouse complex:

We found extensive evidence of rodent infestation in the form of rat and mouse pellets throughout the entire perimeter area and along the wall.

We also found that the doors leading to the basement area from the rail siding had openings at the bottom or openings beneath part of the door that came down at the bottom large enough to admit rodent entry. There were also roden[t] pellets found on a number of different packages of boxes of various items stored in the basement, and looking at this document, I see there were also broken windows along the rail siding.

On the first floor of the "old building," the inspectors found:

Thirty mouse pellets on the floor along walls and on the ledge in the hanging meat room. There were at least twenty mouse pellets beside bales of lime Jello and one of the bales had a chewed rodent hole in the product.
[c]The letter, dated January 27, 1972, included the following:

We note with much concern that the old and new warehouse areas used for food storage were actively and extensively inhabited by live rodents. Of even more concern was the observation that such reprehensible conditions obviously existed for a prolonged period of time without any detection, or were completely ignored.

We trust this letter will serve to direct your attention to the seriousness of the problem and formally advise you of the urgent need to initiate whatever measures are necessary to prevent recurrence and ensure compliance with the law.
[d]The bylaw provided in pertinent part:

The Chairman of the board of directors or the president shall be the chief executive officer of the company as the board of directors may from time to time determine. He shall, subject to the board of directors, have general and active supervision of the affairs, business, offices and employees of the company.

He shall, from time to time, in his discretion or at the order of the board, report the operations and affairs of the company. He shall also perform such other duties and have such other powers as may be assigned to him from time to time by the board of directors.
[e]The April 1970 letter informed respondent of the following "objectionable conditions" in Acme's Philadelphia warehouse:

1. Potential rodent entry ways were noted via ill fitting doors and door in irrepair at Southwest corner of warehouse; at dock at old salvage room and at receiving and shipping doors which were observed to be open most of the time.

2. Rodent nesting, rodent excreta pellets, rodent stained bale bagging and rodent gnawed holes were noted among bales of flour stored in warehouse.

3. Potential rodent harborage was noted in discarded paper, rope, sawdust and other debris piled in corner of shipping and receiving dock near bakery and warehouse doors. Rodent excreta pellets were observed among bags of sawdust (or wood shavings).
[f]In order to find the Defendant guilty on any count of the Information, you must find beyond a reasonable doubt on each count

Thirdly, that John R. Park held a position of authority in the operation of the business of Acme Markets, Incorporated.

However, you need not concern yourselves with the first two elements of the case. The main issue for your determination is only with the third element, whether the Defendant held a position of authority and responsibility in the business of Acme Markets.

The statute makes individuals, as well as corporations, liable for violations. An individual is liable if it is clear, beyond a reasonable doubt, that the elements of the adulteration of the food as to travel in interstate commerce are present. As I have instructed you in this case, they are, and that the individual had a responsible relation to the situation, even though he may not have participated personally.

The individual is or could be liable under the statute, even if he did not consciously do wrong. However, the fact that the Defendant is pres[id]ent and is a chief executive officer of the Acme Markets does not require a finding of guilt. Though, he need not have personally participated in the situation, he must have had a responsible relationship to the issue. The issue is, in this case, whether the Defendant, John R. Park, by virtue of his position in the company, had a position of authority and responsibility in the situation out of which these charges arose.

[g]Sections 303(a) and (b) of the Act, 21 U.S.C. §§ 333(a) and (b), provide:

(a) Any person who violates a provision of section 331 of this title shall be imprisoned for not more than one year or fined not more than $1,000, or both.

(b) Notwithstanding the provisions of subsection (a) of this section, if any person commits such a violation after a conviction of him under this section has become final, or commits such a violation with the intent to defraud or mislead, such person shall be imprisoned for not more than three years or fined not more than $10,000, or both.

≡ SUMMARY

Several persons may participate before, during, and after committing crimes. The doctrine of complicity defines the extent to which criminal liability attaches to these parties to crime. The common-law doctrine of complicity recognized four categories of participants: (1) principals in the first degree, (2) principals in the second degree, (3) accessories before the fact, and (4) accessories after the fact. Modern statutes have merged complicity before and during crime into one category—accomplices—while retaining the category of accessory after the fact. Accomplices are equally liable for the principal crime; accessories after the fact are liable for separate, lesser offenses.

Accomplice and accessory liability rest upon *participation*. The doctrine of complicity also includes liability based on *relationships* without participation. Vicarious liability applies to those who have not participated but whose relationship with actors justifies criminal sanction. Business relationships—employer-employee, principal-agent, corporation-management—most commonly give rise to vicarious criminal liability. Vicarious liability may be strict, in which case the vicariously liable party lacks both *actus reus* and *mens rea*. Penalties for vicarious strict liability are limited to fines.

Vicarious liability also extends to crimes requiring a *mens rea*, in which case the actor's conduct is imputed to the vicariously liable party. In real crimes, the law requires culpability. To convict, the prosecution must prove several elements, including the following: (1) the acts are done for the company's benefit, not for personal profit; (2) the acts are within the scope of the actor's authority; and (3) the acts are attributable to officers high in the organization. Culpability might vary from purposefulness to recklessness and even negligence, covering everything from participation, approval, and encouragement to "recklessly tolerating." Once these conditions are satisfied, business enterprises may—at least in theory—be prosecuted for any crime, including murder. Hence, high officers can be criminally liable for—and can make their corporations criminally liable for—criminal conduct that benefits the business enterprises they head.

≡ QUESTIONS FOR REVIEW AND DISCUSSION

1. Define complicity. Distinguish between common-law and statutory complicity.
2. Distinguish accomplices from accessories under modern law. Should accomplices receive harsher punishment than accessories? Defend your answer.
3. What are the differences among accomplices, accessories, and vicariously liable parties?
4. What is vicarious strict liability? Give the arguments in favor of and against it.
5. Is "suite" crime more dangerous than "street" crime? Explain your answer.
6. In what sense are corporate officers a corporation's brain?
7. Who in the corporate structure should be punished for corporate crimes?
8. What *mens rea* should business crime require? Should it be the same for all crimes committed for the company's benefit?

≡ SUGGESTED READINGS

1. George P. Fletcher, *Rethinking Criminal Law* (Boston: Little, Brown, 1978), pp. 131–205, 218–32, contains provocative discussions about complicity. Professor Fletcher clearly defines the terms in considerable detail. He also assesses participation in crime in ways that provoke considerable thought about the role of those terms in criminal law.
2. American Law Institute, *Model Penal Code and Commentaries*, vol. 1 (Philadelphia: American Law Institute, 1985), pt. 1, pp. 295–348, contains a detailed analysis of all elements in complicity and vicarious liability, especially of corporations, as well as arguments why these should be included in criminal law and to what extent participants should be criminally liable. It is an advanced discussion written for experts in the field but is well worth the effort to read and consider its points.
3. Rollin M. Perkins and Ronald N. Boyce, *Criminal Law,* 3d ed. (Mineola, N.Y.: Foundation Press, 1982), pp. 718–20, 911–22, discusses vicarious liability and corporate crime in some detail. It also provides a brief history of how these arose.
4. John Monahan, Raymond W. Novaco, and Gilbert Geis, "Corporate Violence: Research Strategies for Community Psychology," in *Challenges to the Criminal Justice System*, ed. Theodore R. Sarbin and Daniel Adelson (New York: Human Sciences Press, 1979), pp. 117–41, is an

excellent, clearly written, and easy-to-understand discussion of corporate violence. It defines and describes corporate violence, and includes a thorough bibliography for those who wish to read further.

═══ NOTES

1. American Law Institute, *Model Penal Code and Commentaries* (Philadelphia: American Law Institute, 1985), pp. 299–301.

2. *United States v. Peoni*, 100 F.2d 401 (2d. Cir. 1938).

3. *United States v. Greer*, 467 F.2d 1064 (7th Cir. 1972).

4. *Model Penal Code*, tentative draft no. 1, p. 43 (1953); *State v. Spillman*, 105 Ariz. 523, 468 P.2d 376 (1970); Wayne LaFave and Arthur Scott, *Criminal Law* (St. Paul: West Publishing Co., 1972), p. 504.

5. 306 N.C. 466, 293 S.E.2d 780 (1982).

6. 20 Mich. App. 132, 173 N.W.2d 732 (1969).

7. The corporate crime issue is discussed fully in a special symposium published in *American Criminal Law Review*, no. 17 (1980); see also Russell Mokhiber, *Corporate Crime and Violence* (San Francisco: Sierra Club Books, 1988).

8. John Conyers, "Corporate and White Collar Crime: A View by the Chairman of the House Subcommittee on Crime," and William Glaberson, "States Are Toppling Workplace-Injury Convictions," *New York Times* (September 19, 1988), pp. 1, 26; Philip Shenon, "Deaver Gets Fine of $100,000 and a Suspended Sentence," *New York Times* (September 24, 1988), p. 1.

9. Conyers, "Corporate and White Collar Crime"; Paul Jesilow, Henry Pontell, and Gilbert Geis, "Physician Immunity from Prosecution and Punishment for Medical Fraud," in W. Bryon Groves and Graeme Newman, *Punishment and Privilege* (New York: Harrow and Heston, 1986), pp. 7–22.

10. Brian Fisse, "Sanctions against Corporations: Economic Efficiency or Legal Efficacy?" in Groves and Newman, *Punishment and Privilege*, pp. 23–54.

11. *Commonwealth v. Koczwara*, 397 Pa. 575, 155 A.2d 825 (1959); *Davis v. Peachtree*, 251 Ga. 219, 304 S.E.2d 701 (1983).

12. *American Criminal Law Review*, no. 17 (1980), p. 291 at note 21.

13. Marshall B. Clinard and Richard Quinney, *Criminal Behavior Systems*, 2d ed. (Cincinnati: Anderson, 1986), chap. 7–8.

14. U.S. Congress, House Subcommittee on the Judiciary, *Hearings before the Subcommittee on White Collar Crime*, 95th Cong., 2d sess., June 21, July 12, and December 1, 1978 (Washington, D.C.: U.S. Government Printing Office, 1979).

15. *Commonwealth v. Koczwara*, 397 Pa. 575, 155 A.2d 825, 827 (1959).

16. American Law Institute, *Model Penal Code and Commentaries*, vol. 1, pt. 1, pp. 335–41.

Chapter Five

Uncompleted Crimes: Attempt, Solicitation, and Conspiracy

CHAPTER OUTLINE

CHAPTER MAIN POINTS

1. The doctrine of inchoate offenses imposes criminal liability on those who intend to commit crimes and take some steps toward completing the crimes.

2. Attempt, conspiracy, and solicitation are the crimes included within the doctrine of inchoate offenses.

3. The inchoate offenses require the highest culpability—purpose—to offset the corresponding absence of harm.

4. Those bent on criminal harm should not benefit from a fortuity that interrupts their criminal purpose.

5. Voluntary renunciation of criminal conduct before completing the crime removes criminal liability.

6. As crimes approach completion, the penalties increase.

CHAPTER KEY TERMS

extraneous factor a condition that is beyond the attempter's control and that makes it impossible to complete a crime.

factual impossibility the situation in which facts make it impossible to complete a crime; this is not a defense to criminal attempt liability.

inchoate crimes crimes not yet completed, such as attempt, conspiracy, and solicitation.

legal impossibility the situation in which legal conditions make it impossible to complete a crime; this is a good defense to attempt liability.

Wharton rule the principle that more than two parties must be involved in conspiracies to commit crimes that naturally involve at least two parties, such as rape.

INTRODUCTION

Criminal law punishes not only completed crimes but also conduct that requires further action to result in crime. Reckless endangerment (such as reckless driving), possession (see chapter 3), and burglary (see chapter 10) are crimes even though further action is required for them to culminate in intended harm. Reckless driving, for example, is a crime even if the driver injures no one; possessing a bomb may be a crime even though it does not harm until the bomb explodes; and burglary consists of breaking and entering with the *intent* to commit a crime. The doctrine of **inchoate crimes** applies specifically to three crimes: attempt, conspiracy, and solicitation. According to the doctrine, it is a crime to attempt, conspire to commit, or solicit a crime. Each inchoate offense has its own features, but they share in common a criminal purpose combined with some action short of fulfilling that purpose. Incompleted criminal conduct poses a dilemma: whether to punish someone who has harmed no one or to set free someone determined to commit a crime. The criminal law resolves the dilemma by imposing lesser penalties for inchoate offenses than for completed harms that have been attempted, conspired, or solicited.[1]

ATTEMPT

The place of attempt in criminal law has plagued lawmakers, judges, and philosophers for centuries. In *Laws*, Plato wrote that one who

has a purpose and intention to slay another and he [merely] wounds him should be regarded as a murderer.[2]

But, he added, the law should punish such wounding less than it would murder. In the thirteenth century, the great English jurist Bracton disagreed: "For what harm did the attempt cause, since the injury took no effect?" By the next century, English judges were applying what became a famous common-law maxim: "The will shall be taken for the deed." In one case, Justice Shardlowe said:

> One who is taken in the act of robbery or burglary, even though he does not carry it out, will be hanged.[3]

Common-law attempt meant more than the mere intention to harm: "The thoughts of man shall not be tried, for the devil himself knoweth not the thought of man." The early cases required that both substantial acts and harm accompany the intent. The two leading cases involved a servant who, after cutting his master's throat, fled with the latter's goods, and a wife's lover who attacked and seriously injured her husband, leaving him for dead. The servant and the lover were punished for attempted murder; both had taken substantial steps toward completing the crime and had substantially harmed their victims.[4]

By the sixteenth century, criminal attempt resembled its modern counterpart. Responding to dangers threatening peace and safety in a society known for its hot, short tempers and its violent, quarrelsome tendencies, the English Court of Star Chamber punished wide-ranging potential harms, hoping to nip violence in the bud. Typical cases included "lying in wait," threats, challenges, and even "words tending to challenge." Local records are replete with efforts to punish incipient violence.

By the early seventeenth century, an attempt doctrine was emerging. Stressing a need to prevent serious harms in dueling, Francis Bacon maintained that "all the acts of preparation should be punished." He then went on to argue for adopting the following criminal attempt principle:[5]

> I take it to be a ground infallible: that wheresoever an offense is capital, or matter of felony, though it be not acted, there the combination or acting tending to the offense is punishable. . . . Nay, inceptions and preparations in inferior crimes, that are not capital have likewise been condemned. . . .

As this brief historical sketch shows, the law has punished incomplete crimes since the sixteenth century. Since the seventeenth century, a formal attempt doctrine has governed attempt cases. Not until the late eighteenth century, however, did the English courts adopt a general inchoate offense doctrine. In *Rex v. Scofield*, a servant put a lighted candle in his master's house, intending to burn the house down. The house did not burn, but the attempt was punished nevertheless. The court ruled as follows:

> The intent may make an act, innocent in itself, criminal; nor is the completion of an act, criminal in itself, necessary to constitute criminality.[6]

By the nineteenth century, common-law attempt was well-defined:

> [A]ll attempts whatever to commit indictable offenses, whether felonies or misdemeanors, and whether, if misdemeanors they are so by statute or at common law, are misdemeanors, unless by some special statutory enactment they are subjected to special punishment.[7]

CASE

Is Common-Law Attempt Still a Crime?

Gray v. State

403 A.2d 853 (Md. 1979)

[Justice Moylan delivered the opinion.]

FACTS

[Gray] was convicted by a Prince George's County jury, . . . of attempted second degree rape. . . . He received a sentence for the attempt. . . . He now argues that there is no such crime as attempted second degree rape.

OPINION

. . . [T]he common law is still alive and well in Maryland. More particularly, that portion of the common law, which we today hold still prospers upon these shores is common law misdemeanor of criminal attempt. . . . [A]n attempt to commit any felony or misdemeanor of common law origin or created by statute, was itself a misdemeanor. . . . The common law misdemeanor of criminal attempt . . . has always been recognized as part of the common law of Maryland. . . .

For inchoate, not fully-consummated crime, society has long had available in its arsenal both the statutory offense of "assault with intent to . . ." and the common law offense of criminal attempt. . . .

[T]he common law of England is constitutionally guaranteed to the citizens of Maryland—that in enacting our very charter of liberty we provided "That the Inhabitants of Maryland are entitled to the Common Law of England . . ." The protection of our citizens against inchoate crime is part of that original entitlement, embedded in our very charter of statehood, and we do not lightly—by mere implication—dissolve so venerable a guarantee. . . .
Judgment affirmed.

CASE DISCUSSION

What exactly is the court's reason for adhering to the common law of attempt? Is it because the law is old and venerable? or that the law still makes sense in twentieth-century America? or that the Maryland Constitution requires adherence to the law? Are these good reasons?

Rationale of Attempt Law

Two rationales justify criminal attempt doctrine: (1) controlling dangerous *conduct* and (2) controlling dangerous *persons.* Jurisdictions adopting the dangerous conduct rationale focus on how close the actor came to completing the crime. The dangerous person rationale aims to curb persons determined to commit crimes. It concentrates not on how close actors came to completing their designs but rather on how fully actors developed their designs. Both rationales measure dangerousness according to actions: the dangerous conduct rationale does so to determine proximity to completion, the dangerous person rationale to gauge developed design.

Common-law attempt consisted of (1) an intent to carry out an act or bring about certain consequences that would in law amount to a crime, and (2) an act in furtherance of that intent that went beyond mere preparation.[8]

Material Elements in Attempt

The material elements of attempt include (1) an *intent* (or purpose) to commit a crime, (2) some overt *act* or *acts* in pursuance of the intention, and (3) a *failure* to consummate the crime. The basic notion in attempt law is that actors have done all they intended to do but still have not realized their criminal objective, either to engage in criminal conduct or to cause a result the law defines as a crime. Some jurisdictions make criminal an actor's attempts to commit *any* crime; others restrict the crimes that actors can criminally attempt to commit, either by eliminating specific categories or by listing specific crimes.[9]

MENS REA. Attempt is a crime of purpose. No jurisdictions include knowing, reckless, or negligent attempted homicides, for example, and the purpose requirement also eliminates attempted strict liability offenses. However, knowledge, recklessness, or negligence concerning material surrounding circumstances can support attempt. For example, if I try to kill another whom I should know is an FBI agent, I have attempted to kill a law enforcement officer, even though I have been only negligent concerning the material circumstance that the intended victim was an FBI agent.

CASE

Did He Intend to Rob the Bank?

Young v. State

303 Md. 298, 493 A.2d 352 (1985)

[Young was convicted of attempted armed robbery. He appealed. Justice Orth delivered the opinion.]

FACTS

. . . Several banks . . . had been held up. . . . In the early afternoon of 26 November 1982 the police . . . observed Young driving an automobile in such a manner as to give rise to a reasonable belief that he was casing several banks. They followed him in his reconnoitering. At one point when he left his car to enter a store, he was seen to clip a scanner onto his belt. The scanner later proved to contain an operable crystal number frequency that would receive Prince George's County uniform patrol transmissions. At that time Young was dressed in a brown waist-length jacket and wore sunglasses.

Around 2:00 P.M. Young came to rest at the rear of the Fort Washington branch of the First National Bank of Southern Maryland. Shortly before, he had driven past the front of the Bank and had parked in the rear of it for a brief time. He got out of his car and walked hurriedly beside the Bank toward the front door. He was still wearing the brown waist-length jacket and sunglasses, but he had added a blue knit stocking cap pulled down to the top of the sunglasses, white gloves and a black eye-patch. His jacket collar was turned up. His right hand was in his jacket pocket and his left hand was in front of his face. As one of the police officers observing him put it, he was sort of "duck[ing] his head."

It was shortly after 2:00 P.M. and the Bank had just closed. Through the windows of his office the Bank Manager saw Young walking on the "landscape" by the side of the Bank toward the front door. Young had his right hand in his jacket pocket and tried to open the front door with his left hand. When he realized that the door was locked and the Bank was closed, he retraced his steps, running past the windows with his left hand covering his face. The Bank Manager had an employee call the police.

Young ran back to his car, yanked open the door, got in, and put the car in drive "all in one movement almost," and drove away. The police stopped the car and ordered Young to get out. Young was in the process of removing his jacket. . . . The butt of what proved to be a loaded .22 caliber revolver was sticking out of the right pocket of his jacket. On the front seat of the car were a pair of white surgical gloves, a black eye-patch, a blue knit stocking cap, and a pair of sunglasses. Young told the police that his name was Morris P. Cunningham. As Young was being taken from the scene, he asked "how much time you could get for attempted robbery."

OPINION

A criminal attempt requires specific intent; the specific intent must be to commit some other crime. The requisite intent need not be proved by direct evidence. It may be inferred as a matter of fact from the actor's conduct and the attendant circumstances. Young concedes that "evidence is present . . . from which it is possible to infer that [he] may have intended to commit a crime inside the bank. . . ." He suggests, however, that this evidence is not "compelling. . . ." We believe that it is more than legally sufficient to establish beyond a reasonable doubt that Young had the specific intent to commit an armed robbery as charged. . . .

CASE DISCUSSION

What facts prove that young intended to rob the bank? The court did not feel the need to refer to them. Identify all the facts that prove his intent, and explain how these facts lead to proof beyond a reasonable doubt of what Young intended.

ACTUS REUS—THE DISTINCTION BETWEEN PREPARATION AND ATTEMPT. Criminal attempt does not require completed crime, but most agree that mere preparation does not constitute criminal attempt. Hence, if I sit in my armchair at home, plotting how I am going to buy a gun and kill my enemy, but before leaving my chair I decide against it, I have committed no crime. A major problem in attempt law is determining at what point on the spectrum between mere intention and ultimate harm a crime has taken place. States answer this question variously.[10]

The law requires action or steps beyond preparation to constitute attempt, but the distinction between preparation and attempt is difficult to draw in actual cases. Some states require "some steps." At the other extreme, a few states demand "all but the last act." Most states, along with the Model Penal Code, require "substantial steps" toward completing the crime. Under all three tests, if I stood over my enemy on the verge of pulling the trigger, I have attempted murder. Most jurisdictions require considerably less. But how much less? If I left my house only to buy a handgun to do the job, I have merely prepared to murder my enemy. Three means to distinguish mere preparation from full attempt are the **physical proximity doctrine**, the **dangerous proximity doctrine**, and the **Model Penal Code standard**.

Physical proximity emphasizes time, space, and the number of necessary acts—the *actus reus* remaining to complete the crime. In *People v. Rizzo*, Rizzo and his cohorts were driving through Boston looking for a payroll clerk they intended to rob. During their search, they were arrested. They were tried for attempted robbery but were acquitted because "they had not found or reached the presence of the person they intended to rob." Physical proximity looks to dangerous conduct, not dangerous actors; according to the **physical proximity doctrine**, the criminal law should punish conduct when it reaches a "dangerous proximity to success." Great importance, therefore, attaches to how closely the actor's conduct approached the intended crime. The physical proximity doctrine does not answer "how close is close enough for attempt liability."[11]

The **dangerous proximity doctrine** incorporates physical proximity but adds to it. It considers the following in determining whether acts have gone beyond preparation: (1) the *seriousness* of the intended offense, (2) the crime's *proximity* to completion, and (3) the *probability* that the conduct will result in the intended crime. The greater an intended crime's gravity, proximity, and probability, the more likely it is that the actor has proceeded beyond preparation. Like the physical proximity doctrine, the dangerous proximity doctrine assumes that the purpose of punishing attempts is to deter dangerous *conduct;* until an actor's conduct becomes sufficiently dangerous, the criminal law should not punish it.[12]

The **Model Penal Code approach** requires "substantial steps" to corroborate intent. (See 5.01 Model Penal Code in Appendix.) In contrast to the proximity doctrines, the Code focuses on neutralizing dangerous persons. In the Code, the key phrases regarding attempt *actus reus* are "substantial step in a course of conduct planned to culminate in his [the actor's] commission of the crime" and "strongly corroborative of the actor's criminal purpose." Substantial steps corroborate the *mens rea*. In other words, the Code requires sufficient steps toward completing the crime, not because such steps show that harms are about to occur but rather to prove that attempters are determined to commit crimes. Just what constitutes "substantial steps" is vague.

The drafters of the Code argue that the provision definitely improves the proximity doctrines in the following respects: (1) It emphasizes already completed conduct, not what remains to be done in order to complete the crime. (2) It reduces *mens rea* difficulties. (3) It removes "very remote preparatory acts" from criminal liability. (4) It brings persons whose behavior manifests dangerousness within the criminal law's ambit. (5) It illustrates actions that amount to substantial steps, such as lying in wait, searching and following, enticing, reconnoitering, entering unlawfully, possessing incriminating materials, and soliciting innocent agents.[13]

According to the Code's drafters, lying in wait and searching and following satisfy *actus reus*. In many jurisdictions, such actions are considered mere preparation. In *Rizzo*, for example, the court ruled that searching for a robbery victim was preparation. Some states, such as Louisiana, consider lying in wait or searching and following to be attempts only if they are performed while armed.

Borrowing from indecent liberties statutes, which make it a crime to lure minors into cars or houses for sex, the Model Penal Code makes enticement an *actus reus*. In defending their position, the drafters note that enticement demonstrates a firm purpose to commit a crime; hence, enticers are sufficiently dangerous to deserve punishment.[14]

The Code includes reconnoitering—popularly called casing a joint—within the scope of attempted *actus reus*, because "scouting the scene of a contemplated crime" sufficiently demonstrates a firm criminal purpose.

Unlawful intruders demonstrate their criminal purpose. Including unlawful entry within attempt relieves burglary from pressures to cover more than it rationally ought to include (see chapter 10). The unlawful entry provision particularly helps two types of cases: entries to commit sexual abuse (attempted rapes) and entries to commit larceny. In one case, two defendants entered a car intending to steal it, but they got out when the owner returned. The court ruled that the defendants had not attempted to steal the car. Under the Model Penal Code provision, however, they committed unlawful entry for a criminal purpose.[15]

Under existing law, collecting, possessing, or preparing materials used to commit crimes is preparation, not attempt. Hence, courts have found that buying a gun to murder someone, making a bomb to blow up a house, and collecting tools for a burglary are preparations, not attempts. Many jurisdictions, however, make it a crime to possess designated items and substances such as burglary tools, illegal drugs, drug paraphernalia, and concealed weapons. The Model Penal Code provision makes such possessions criminal only if they strongly corroborate a purpose to commit a crime. The Code's drafters concluded that people who carry weapons and burglary tools with the clear intent to commit crimes are dangerous enough to punish.[16]

The Model Penal Code also includes bringing weapons, equipment, and other materials to the scene of a crime, and intending to commit crimes with them. Examples are bringing guns to a robbery, explosives to an arson, a ladder to a burglary. The Code takes the position that such "bringing" constitutes a substantial step, not mere preparation, in commiting a crime. The drafters contend that actors demonstrate a firm purpose to commit crimes if materials are so plainly instrumentalities that their possession constitutes a sufficient substantial step toward completing the crime. A potential robber who takes a gun to a bank falls clearly within its scope; a would-be forger who takes a fountain pen into a bank does not. Acquiring these items alone does not suffice; attempters who must bring them to the contemplated crime scene are sufficiently dangerous to punish.[17]

Preparation is not attempt, but some jurisdictions make specified preparations separate, less serious, inchoate offenses. In Nevada, for example, preparing to commit arson is a crime. In some jurisdictions it is a crime to prepare to manufacture illegal liquor. These statutes balance the degree of threatening behavior and the dangerousness of persons against the remoteness in time and place of the intended harm.[18]

CASE

Did He Take Substantial Steps toward Escape?

Commonwealth v. Gilliam

273 Pa. Super. 586, 417 A.2d 1203 (1980)

[Gilliam was convicted of attempt to escape and possession of implements for escape. He appealed. Justice Wieand delivered the opinion.]

FACTS

On September 21, 1976, while appellant was incarcerated at Dallas State Correctional Institution, a guard discovered that the bars of the window in appellant's cell had been cut and were being held in place by sticks and paper. The condition of the bars was such that they could be removed manually at will. The same guard observed that a shelf hook was missing from its place in the cell. A subsequent search revealed visegrips concealed inside appellant's mattress and two knotted extension cords attached to a hook were found in a box of clothing. Appellant was arrested and charged with the offenses for which he has now been convicted.

At trial, evidence showed that the hook had been fashioned from the missing shelf hook. The visegrips were capable of cutting barbed wire of the type located along the top of the fence which was the sole barrier between appellant's cell window and the perimeter of the prison compound. Inspection of the cell immediately prior to the time when it was assigned to appellant as its sole occupant had disclosed bars intact and the shelf hooks in place.

OPINION

Prior to enactment of the Crimes Code, a criminal attempt was defined as "an overt act done in pursuance of an intent to do a specific thing, tending to the end by falling short of complete accomplishment of it. So long as the acts are confined to preparation only, and can be abandoned before any transgression of the law or others' rights, they are within the sphere of intent and do not amount to attempts."

With the adoption of the Crimes Code, however, the legislature devised a new test for attempt. Thus, in Section 901(a), an attempt is defined as follows:

> A person commits an attempt when, with intent to commit a specific crime, he does any act which constitutes a substantial step toward the commission of that crime.

The substantial step test broadens the scope of attempt liability be concentrating on the acts the defendant has done and does not any longer focus on the acts remaining to be done before actual commission of the crime.

Instantly, a jury could readily have found that appellant had taken a substantial step toward committing an escape. Not only did appellant manufacture and assemble the paraphernalia necessary to effectuate his escape, but he also sawed through the bars in his cell window. These acts, taken as a whole, constituted a substantial and necessary step toward escape. Under the standard established by the Crimes Code, it is of no consequence that appellant was not actually in the process of elopement when arrested. This evidence, coupled with evidence from which a jury could have found that appellant possessed the specific intent to escape, was sufficient to sustain the conviction of criminal attempt.

Affirmed.

CASE DISCUSSION

The Pennsylvania legislature changed its definition of the attempt act from an overt act to a substantial act, changing the focus from what has yet to be done to what has already been done. Using this test, do you think that Gilliam attempted escape? Which is the better rule? How important is it that Gilliam really never got his escape under way? Do you call his conduct preparation or attempt?

Legal and Factual Impossibility

Suppose a man sneaks an old book past customs, believing the law requires him to pay a duty. The law, however, exempts antiques from custom duty. Has he *attempted* to evade customs? Suppose a woman stabs her enemy while she believes he is asleep. In fact, the victim died of a heart attack two hours before. Has she *attempted* to murder her enemy?

The man in the first hypothetical case represents an example of legal impossibility. **Legal impossibility** means that actors have done all they intend to do, and yet the law does not prohibit what they did. The man intended to commit a crime and did everything he believed constituted that crime. Yet his act could not amount to a crime because the jurisdiction did not make such conduct criminal.

The woman in the second hypothetical case represents an example of factual impossibility. **Factual impossibility** exists when the actor intends to commit a crime but some fact—**extraneous factor**—prevents its completion. The woman in the example intended to commit murder. She did all she could to commit it; if the facts were different (if her victim had been alive), she would have committed murder.

Legal impossibility requires a different law to make the conduct criminal; factual impossibility requires different facts to complete the crime. In most jurisdictions, legal impossibility is a defense to criminal attempt; factual impossibility is not. The principal reason for the difference is that to convict for conduct that the law does not prohibit, no matter what the actor's intentions, violates the principle of legality—no crime without a law, no punishment without a law. Factual impossibility, on the other hand, would permit luck to determine criminal liability. A person who is determined to engage in conduct or cause harm prohibited by the criminal law, and who acts on that determination, should not escape liability and punishment because of luck.[19]

CASE

Was the Unloaded Gun a "Stroke of Luck"?

State v. Damms

9 Wis. 2d 183, 100 N.W.2d 592 (1960)

[Ralph Damms was convicted of attempted first-degree murder and was sentenced to up to ten years in prison. He appealed. Justice Currie delivered the opinion.]

FACTS

The alleged crime occurred on April 6, 1959, near Menomonee Falls in Waukesha county. Prior to that date Marjory Damms, wife of the defendant, had instituted an action for divorce against him and the parties lived apart. She was thirty-nine years and he thirty-three years of age. Marjory Damms was also estranged from her mother, Mrs. Laura Grant. That morning, a little before eight o'clock, Damms drove his automobile to the vicinity in Milwaukee where he knew Mrs. Damms would take the bus to go to work. He saw her walking along the sidewalk, stopped, and induced her to enter the car by falsely stating that Mrs. Grant was ill and dying. They drove to Mrs. Grant's home. Mrs. Damms then discovered that her mother was up and about and not seriously ill. Nevertheless, the two Damms remained there nearly two hours conversing and drinking coffee. Apparently it was the intention of Damms to induce a reconciliation between mother and daughter, hoping it would result in one between himself and his wife, but not much progress was achieved in such direction.

At the conclusion of the conversation Mrs. Damms expressed the wish to phone for a taxi-cab to take her to work. Damms insisted on her getting into his car, and said he would drive her to work. They again entered his car but instead of driving south towards her place of employment, he drove in the opposite direction. Some conversation was had in which he stated that it was possible for a person to die quickly and not be able to make amends for anything done in the past, and referred to the possibility of "judgment day" occurring suddenly. Mrs. Damms' testimony as to what then took place is as follows: "When he was telling me about this being judgment day, he pulled a cardboard box from under the seat of the car and brought it up to the seat and opened it up and took a gun out of a paper bag. [He] aimed it at my side and he said, 'This is to show you I'm not kidding.' I tried to quiet him down. He said he wasn't fooling. I said if it was just a matter of my saying to my mother that everything was all right, we could go back and I would tell her that."

They did return to Mrs. Grant's home and Mrs. Damms went inside and Damms stayed outside. In a few minutes he went inside and asked Mrs. Damms to leave with him. Mrs. Grant requested that they leave quietly so as not to attract the attention of the neighbors. They again got into the car and this time drove out on Highway 41 towards Menomonee Falls. Damms stated to Mrs. Damms that he was taking her "up North" for a few days, the apparent purpose of which was to effect a reconciliation between them. As they approached a roadside restaurant, he asked her if she would like something to eat. She replied that she wasn't hungry but would drink some coffee. Damms then drove the car off the highway beside the restaurant and parked it with the front facing, and in close proximity to, the restaurant wall.

Damms then asked Mrs. Damms how much money she had with her and she said "a couple of dollars." He then requested to see her checkbook and she refused to give it to him. A quarrel ensued between them. Mrs. Damms opened the car door and started to run around the restaurant building screaming, "Help!" Damms pursued her with the pistol in his hand. Mrs. Damms' cries for help attracted the attention of the persons inside the restaurant, including two officers of the State Traffic Patrol who were eating their lunch. One officer rushed out of the front door and the other the rear door. In the meantime, Mrs. Damms had run nearly around three sides of the building. In seeking to avoid colliding with a child, who was in her path, she turned, slipped and fell. Damms crouched down, held the pistol at her head, and pulled the trigger, but nothing happened. He then exclaimed, "It won't fire. It won't fire."

OPINION

Sec. 993.32(2), Stats., provides as follows:

> An attempt to commit a crime requires that the actor have an intent to perform acts and attain a result which, if accomplished, would constitute such crime and that he does acts toward the commission of the crime which demonstrate unequivocally, under all the circumstances, that he formed that intent and would commit the crime except for the intervention of another person or some other extraneous factor.

The issue boils down to whether the impossibility of accomplishment due to the gun being unloaded falls within the statutory words, "except for the intervention of some other extraneous factor." We conclude that it does.

Prior to the adoption of the new criminal code by the 1955 legislature the criminal statutes of this state had separate sections making it an offense to assault with intent to do great bodily harm, to murder, to rob, and to rape, etc. The new code did away with these separate sections by creating sec. 939.32, Stats., covering all attempts to commit a battery or felony, and making the maximum penalty not

to exceed one-half the penalty imposed for the completed crime,
except that, if the penalty for a completed crime is life imprisonment,
the maximum penalty for the attempt is thirty years imprisonment.

> Emphasis upon the dangerous propensities of the actor as shown by
> his conduct, rather than upon how close he came to succeeding, is
> more appropriate to the purposes of the criminal law to protect society
> and reform offenders or render then temporarily harmless.

Sound public policy would seem to support the majority view that
impossibility not apparent to the actor should not absolve him from
the offense of attempt to commit the crime he intended. An unequivocal act accompanied by intent should be sufficient to constitute a
criminal attempt. Insofar as the actor knows, he has done everything
necessary to insure the commission of the crime intended, and he
should not escape punishment because of the fortuitous circumstance
that by reason of some fact unknown to him it was impossible to
effectuate the intended result.

It is our considered judgment that the fact, that the gun was
unloaded when Damms pointed it at his wife's head and pulled the
trigger, did not absolve him of the offense charged, if he actually
thought at the time that it was loaded.
Affirmed.

CASE DISCUSSION

Does it matter whether or not the gun was loaded? Hasn't Damms
done everything possible to commit the terrible crime of murdering
his wife? What if Damms subconsciously "forgot" to load the gun
because he meant only to frighten his wife? Such speculation depends
on a belief in Freudian psychology. But assuming it to be so, was the
unloaded gun then an extraneous factor, or within Damms's control?
Is the Wisconsin rule punishing attempts at about half the amount for
completed crimes a good idea?

Renunciation

If an extraneous factor interrupts an attempt to commit a crime, the law
does not permit the interruption to benefit the attempter. If the attempter
decides not to complete the crime, the renunciation *sometimes* benefits the
actor. If I am about to steal a watch from a department store and a house
detective stops me just as I am reaching for the watch, the detective's
appearance is an extraneous factor, a preventive force outside myself that
the law does not allow to benefit me. If, on the other hand, just as I am
about to pick up the watch, I am overcome with pangs of conscience and
put it back, my voluntary actions constitute the force that interrupts the
crime. Such purity does not prompt all renunciations. Suppose a woman
spits out a pill to cause abortion because it tastes awful, or a robber does

not go through with a robbery because the amount of money is too small to bother with. Both are renunciations but not *morally* inspired.

Some argue that the law should encourage renunciation by rewarding those who renounce their criminal plans in progress, no matter what their motives. Others contend that only those who abandon attempts for *moral* reasons should benefit from renunciation. They argue that individuals who are motivated to renounce by *material* considerations are dangerous and need "neutralizing." Still others maintain that renunciation ought *never* to excuse attempts.[20]

CASE

Did He Voluntarily Renounce His Intent to Rape?

Le Barron v. State

32 Wis.2d 294, 145 N.W.2d 79 (1966)

[Le Barron was convicted of attempted rape and sentenced to not more than fifteen years in prison. He appealed. Chief Justice Currie delivered the opinion.]

FACTS

On March 3, 1965 at 6:55 P.M., the complaining witness, Jodean Randen, a housewife, was walking home across a fairly well-traveled railroad bridge in Eau Claire. She is a slight woman whose normal weight is 95 to 100 pounds. As she approached the opposite side of the bridge she passed a man who was walking in the opposite direction. The man turned and followed her, grabbed her arm and demanded her purse. She surrendered her purse and at the command of the man began walking away as fast as she could. Upon discovering that the purse was empty, he caught up with her again, grabbed her arm and told her that if she did not scream he would not hurt her. He then led her—willingly, she testified, so as to avoid being hurt by him—to the end of the bridge. While walking he shoved her head down and warned her not to look up or do anything and he would not hurt her.

On the other side of the bridge along the railroad tracks there is a coal shack. As they approached the coal shack he grabbed her, put one hand over her mouth, and an arm around her shoulder and told her not to scream or he would kill her. At this time Mrs. Randen thought he had a knife in his hand. He then forced her into the shack and up against the wall. As she struggled for her breath he said, "You

know what else I want," unzipped his pants and started pulling up her skirt. She finally succeeded in removing his hand from her mouth, and after reassuring him that she would not scream, told him she was pregnant and pleaded with him to desist or he would hurt her baby. He then felt her stomach and took her over to the door of the shack, where in the better light he was able to ascertain that, under her coat, she was wearing maternity clothes. He thereafter let her alone and left after warning her not to scream or call the police, or he would kill her.

OPINION

The material portions of the controlling statutes provide:

> Sec. 944.01(1), Stats. "Any male who has sexual intercourse with a female he knows is not his wife, by force and against her will, may be imprisoned not more than 30 years."
> Sec. 939.32(2), Stats. "An attempt to commit a crime requires that the actor have an intent to perform acts and attain a result which, if accomplished, would constitute such crime and that he does acts toward the commission of the crime which demonstrate unequivocally, under all the circumstances, that he formed that intent and would commit the crime except for the intervention of another person or some other extraneous factor."

The two statutory requirements of intent and overt acts which must concur in order to have attempt to rape are as follows:

> (1)The male must have the intent to act so as to have intercourse with the female by overcoming or preventing her utmost resistance by physical violence, or overcoming her will to resist by the use of threats of imminent physical violence likely to cause great bodily harm; (2) the male must act toward the commission of the rape by overt acts which demonstrate unequivocally, under all the circumstances, that he formed the intent to rape and would have committed the rape except for the intervention of another person or some other extraneous factor.

The thrust of defendant's argument, that the evidence was not sufficient to convict him of the crime of attempted rape, is two-fold: first, defendant desisted from his endeavor to have sexual intercourse with complainant before he had an opportunity to form an intent to accomplish such intercourse by force and against her will; and, second, the factor which caused him to desist, viz., the pregnancy of complainant, was intrinsic and not an "extraneous factor" within the meaning of sec. 939.32(2), Stats.

It is difficult to consider the factor of intent apart from that of overt acts since the sole evidence of intent in attempted rape cases is almost always confined to the overt acts of the accused, and intent must be inferred therefrom. In fact, the express wording of sec. 939.32(2), Stats. recognizes that this is so.

We consider defendant's overt acts, which support a reasonable inference that he intended to have sexual intercourse with complainant by force and against her will, to be these: (1) He threatened

complainant that he would kill her if she refused to cooperate with him; (2) he forced complainant into the shack and against the wall; and (3) he stated, "You know what else I want," unzipped his pants, and started pulling up her skirt. The jury had the right to assume that defendant had the requisite physical strength and weapon (the supposed knife) to carry out the threat over any resistance of complainant.

We conclude that a jury could infer beyond a reasonable doubt from these overt acts of defendant that he intended to have sexual intercourse with defendant by force and against her will. The fact, that he desisted from his attempt to have sexual intercourse as a result of the plea of complainant that she was pregnant, would permit of the opposite inference. However, such desistance did not compel the drawing of such inference nor compel, as a matter of law, the raising of a reasonable doubt to a finding that defendant had previously intended to carry through with having intercourse by force and against complainant's will.

Defendant relies strongly on *Oakley v. State* where this court held that defendant Oakley's acts were so equivocal as to prevent a finding of intent beyond a reasonable doubt to have sexual intercourse by force and against the will of the complainant. The evidence in the case disclosed neither physical violence nor threat of physical violence up to the time Oakley desisted from his attempt to have sexual intercourse with the complainant. He did put his arm around her and attempted to kiss her while entreating her to have intercourse, and also attempted to put his hand in her blouse and to lift up her skirt but did not attempt to renew this endeavor when she brushed his hand away. Thus the facts in Oakley are readily distinguishable from those of the case at bar. To argue that the two cases are analogous because, in the one instance the accused desisted because the complainant was menstruating and in the other because of pregnancy, is an oversimplification. Such an argument overlooks the radical difference in the nature of the overt acts relied upon to prove intent.

The argument, that the pregnancy of the instant complainant which caused defendant's desistance does not qualify as an "extraneous factor" within the meaning of sec. 939.32, Stats., is in conflict with our holding in *State v. Damms.* There we upheld a conviction of attempt to commit murder where the accused pulled the trigger of an unloaded pistol intending to kill his enstranged wife thinking the pistol was loaded. It was held that the impossibility of accomplishment due to the gun being unloaded fell within the statutory words, "except for the intervention of some other extraneous factor." Particularly significant is this statement in the opinion:

> An unequivocal act accompanied by intent should be sufficient to constitute a criminal attempt. Insofar as the actor knows, he has done everything necessary to insure the commission of the crime intended, and he should not escape punishment because of the fortuitous circumstance that by reason of some fact unknown to him it was impossible to effectuate the intended result.

Affirmed.

CASE DISCUSSION

Le Barron demonstrates how difficult it can be to apply the renunciation doctrine. Did Le Barron desist because he believed it was morally wrong to rape a pregnant woman, or did the pregnancy simply repel him sexually? Should his reason make a difference? Is Le Barron equally dangerous, whichever reason led to interrupting the rape?

Do you agree that Le Barron's victim's pregnancy was an extraneous factor? The court said a jury could conclude either that it was or that Le Barron voluntarily renounced his intention to rape because the victim was pregnant. If you were a juror, how would you have voted on the pregnancy question?

Summary

Attempt requires a purpose to commit a crime combined with some steps toward completing that crime. Several difficult issues surround attempt law. First, conflicting rationales support criminal attempt. Some justify it on the ground that it controls dangerous persons; others maintain that it aims to prevent crime. Second, dispute arises over how many acts toward completion constitute attempt. Generally, this requires distinguishing between preparation and attempt. Third, difficulties surround legal and factual impossibility. Is it attempt if it was impossible to complete the crime? Most jurisdictions say no to legal impossibility but yes to factual impossibility. Factual impossibilities are generally referred to as extraneous factors. Finally, renunciation creates problems: Should it matter if a person bent on criminal conduct has a change of heart and desists from committing the crime? If the answer is yes, does it matter whether moral or nonmoral considerations prompted the change?

═══ CONSPIRACY

The inchoate offenses force lawmakers and enforcers to decide the vexing problem of how close to completion conduct must be to constitute a crime. That is, at what point is it proper to punish people for what they might do, as opposed to what they have already done? As a general rule, the more remote a crime is from completion, the less justifiable criminal punishment is. In this respect, attempt and preparation (where criminal at all), conspiracy, and solicitation stand on a continuum, with attempt closest to and solicitation most remote from actual harm. The inchoate offense of conspiracy

> strikes against the special danger incident to group activity, facilitating prosecution of the group, and yielding a basis for imposing added penalties when combination is involved.[21]

Material Elements in Conspiracy

At common law, conspiracy is a combination between two or more persons formed for the purpose of doing either an unlawful act or a lawful act by an unlawful means. In words famous in conspiracy law, Justice Oliver Wendell Holmes defined conspiracy as "a partnership in criminal purpose." Holmes's broad definition needs some refinement, but it captures conspiracy's basic idea. A conspiracy is (1) an agreement or combination (Holmes's "partnership") (2) for the purpose of attaining (3) an unlawful (Holmes's "criminal") objective, or a lawful objective by unlawful means.

ACTUS REUS—THE AGREEMENT. One vague area in conspiracy law is what constitutes a conspiratorial agreement. The law does not require a written agreement; tacit understandings suffice. That makes sense since conspirators rarely put their agreement in writing. Some courts hold that agreement includes "aid," even when given without another party's consent. In one case, a judge learned that someone planned to kill one of the judge's enemies. The judge wanted the plan to succeed, so he intercepted a letter warning the intended victim of the plan. The judge committed conspiracy to commit murder because he aided the other conspirators, even though he had nothing to do with them.

Defining agreement imprecisely can lead to abuses. In a highly publicized trial during the 1960s, the government tried Dr. Benjamin Spock for conspiracy to avoid the draft law. Videotapes showed several hundred spectators clapping while Dr. Spock tried to get young men to resist the draft during the Vietnam War. According to the prosecutor, any person seen clapping on videotape was a coconspirator. By virtue of their encouragement, according to the prosecutor, these people were aiding Dr. Spock, hence agreeing to violate the draft law.[22]

In most jurisdictions, the agreement alone constitutes the conspiracy *actus reus.* Some jurisdictions, however, require action beyond the agreement. They differ as to how much action in addition to the agreement the criminal design requires. Some specify "some act," in others "any act" suffices. One jurisdiction demands that conspirators "go forth for the purpose of committing" the prohibited act.[23]

CASE

Did They Agree to Distribute Heroin?

United States v. Brown

776 F.2d 397 (2d.Cir.1985)

[A jury convicted Brown and Valentine (a fugitive) of conspiring to distribute heroin. Circuit judge Friendly delivered the opinion.]

FACTS

[William Grimball, a New York City undercover police officer, purchased a "joint" of "D" ($40 worth of heroin) in Harlem.] Officer Grimball was the government's principal witness. He testified that in the evening of October 9, 1984, he approached Gregory Valentine on the corner of 115th Street and Eighth Avenue and asked him for a joint of "D." Valentine asked Grimball whom he knew around the street. Grimball asked if Valentine knew Scott. He did not. Brown "came up" and Valentine said, "He wants to buy a joint, but I don't know him." Brown looked at Grimball and said, "He looks okay to me." Valentine then said, "Okay. But I am going to leave it somewhere and you [Grimball] can pick it up." Brown interjected, "You don't have to do that. Just go and get it for him. He looks all right to me." After looking at Grimball, Brown said, "He looks all right to me" and "I will wait right here."

Valentine then said, "Okay. Come on with me around to the hotel." Grimball followed him to 300 West 116th Street, where Valentine instructed him, "Sit on the black car and give me a few minutes to go up and get it." Valentine requested and received $40, which had been prerecorded, and then said, "You are going to take care of me for doing this for you, throw some dollars my way?" to which Grimball responded, "Yeah."

Valentine then entered the hotel and shortly returned. The two went back to 115th Street and Eighth Avenue, where Valentine placed a cigarette box on the hood of a blue car. Grimball picked up the cigarette box and found a glassine envelope containing white powder, stipulated to be heroin. Grimball placed $5 of the prerecorded buy money in the cigarette box, which he replaced on the hood. Valentine picked up the box and removed the $5. Grimball returned to his car and made a radio transmission to the backup field team that "the buy had went down" and informed them of the locations of the persons involved. Brown and Valentine were arrested. Valentine was found to possess two glassine envelopes of heroin and the $5 of prerecorded money. Brown was in possession of $31 of his own money; no drugs or contraband were found on him. The $40 of marked buy money was not recovered, and no arrests were made at the hotel.

[At the trial Grimball testified that] the typical drug buy in the Harlem area involved two to five people. As a result of frequent police sweeps, Harlem drug dealers were becoming so cautious that they employed

> people who act as steerers and the steerer's responsibility is basically to determine whether or not you are actually an addict or a user of heroin and they are also used to screen you to see if there is any possibility of you being a cop looking for a bulge or some indication that would give them that you are not actually an addict. And a lot of the responsibility relies [sic] on them to determine whether or not the drug buy is going to go down or not.

Officer Grimball . . . then . . . testif[ied] that based on his experience as an undercover agent he would describe the role that Ronald Brown played in the transaction as that of a steerer. When asked why, he testified . . . "Because I believe that if it wasn't for his approval, the buy would not have gone down."

OPINION

. . . Since the jury convicted on . . . conspiracy . . . the evidence must permit a reasonable juror to be convinced beyond a reasonable doubt not simply that Brown had aided and abetted the drug sale but that he had agreed to do so. . . .

A review of the evidence convinces us that it was sufficient. . . . Although Brown's mere presence at the scene of the crime and his knowledge that a crime was being committed would not have been sufficient to establish Brown's knowing participation in the conspiracy, the proof went considerably beyond that. Brown was not simply standing around while the exchanges between Officer Grimball and Valentine occurred. He came on the scene shortly after these began and Valentine immediately explained the situation to him. Brown then conferred his seal of approval on Grimball, a most unlikely event unless there was an established relationship between Brown and Valentine. Finally, Brown took upon himself the serious responsibility of telling Valentine to desist from his plan to reduce the risks by not handing the heroin directly to Grimball. A rational mind could take this as bespeaking the existence of an agreement whereby Brown was to have the authority to command, or at least to persuade. Brown's remark, "Just go ahead and get it for him," permits inferences that Brown knew where the heroin was to be gotten, that he knew that Valentine knew this, and that Brown and Valentine had engaged in such a transaction before. . . .

When we add to the inferences that can be reasonably drawn from the facts to which Grimball testified . . . his testimony about the use of steerers in street sales of narcotics . . . we conclude that the Government offered sufficient evidence . . . for a reasonable juror to be satisfied beyond a reasonable doubt not only that Brown had acted as a steerer but that he had agreed to do so.
Affirmed.

DISSENT

While it is true that this is another $40 narcotics case, it is also a conspiracy case. . . . An agreement—a "continuous and conscious union of wills upon a common undertaking . . . [was not proved here] unless an inference that Brown agreed to act as a "steerer" can be drawn from the fact that he said to Valentine (three times) that Grimball "looks okay [all right] to me," as well as "[j]ust go and get it for him." . . . It could not be drawn from Brown's possession, constructive or otherwise, of narcotics or narcotics paraphernalia, his sharing in the proceeds of the street sale, his conversations with others, or even some hearsay evidence as to his "prior arrangements" with Valentine or an "established working relationship" with Brown and Valentine. . . . [I]ndeed, Brown was apprehended after leaving the area of the crime with only thirty-one of his own dollars in his pocket, and no drugs or other contraband. He did not even stay around for another Valentine sale. . .

I cannot believe there is proof of *conspiracy*, or Brown's membership in it, beyond a reasonable doubt. . . .

This case may be unique. It . . . supports Justice Jackson's reference to the history of the law of conspiracy as exemplifying, in Cardozo's phrase, the "tendency of a principle to expand itself to the limits of its logic. . . ." If today we uphold a conspiracy to sell narcotics on the street, on this kind of evidence, what conspiracies might we approve tomorrow. The majority opinion will come back to haunt us, I fear. . . .

Accordingly, I dissent.

CASE DISCUSSION

What specific facts point to an agreement in the case? Do they convince you beyond a reasonable doubt that Brown and Valentine had a "continuous and conscious union of wills upon a common undertaking?" Is the dissent right that this case pushes conspiracy law to "the limits of its logic"? Why do you think the prosecution chose to charge Brown with conspiracy instead of with aiding and abetting? (Review relevant sections in chapter 4.) If the police had found evidence of possession (see chapter 3) or the marked money, would they have charged Brown with conspiracy? Should they have done so?

MENS REA. Statutes and courts frequently define conspiracy *means rea* vaguely. Common-law and modern statutes traditionally have not mentioned conspiracy *mens rea,* leaving courts to define it. The courts in turn have taken imprecise, widely divergent, and often inconsistent approaches to the *mens rea* problem. According to former Supreme Court justice Robert Jackson, "The modern crime of conspiracy is so vague that it almost defies definition."[24]

Authorities frequently call conspiracy a specific intent crime. But what does that mean? Does it mean that conspiracy involves intent to enter a criminal agreement or combination? Or must conspiracy also include an intent to attain a particular criminal objective, or at least to use a specific criminal means to attain the objective? For example, if two men agree to burn down a building, they have conspired to commit arson. However, if they do not intend to hurt anyone, do they also conspire to commit murder? Surely not, if the conspiracy *mens rea* requires an intent to attain a particular criminal objective. The example demonstrates the importance of distinguishing between the intent to make *agreements* or combinations and the intent to attain a particular criminal *objective*. If the objective is to commit a specific crime, it must satisfy that crime's *mens rea*. Hence, conspiring to take another's property is not conspiring to commit larceny unless the conspirators intended to permanently deprive the owner of possession (see larceny in chapter 11).

Courts further complicate *mens rea* by not clarifying whether they require purpose. Consider cases involving suppliers of goods and services, such as doctors who order from drug supply companies in order to use or sell drugs illegally. At what point do suppliers become coconspirators, even though they have not agreed specifically to supply drugs for illegal distribution? Must prosecutors prove that suppliers entered an agreement or combination intending specifically to further buyers' criminal purposes? Most courts require such proof, even though it is difficult to obtain, because conspirators rarely subject their purposes to written contracts. Purpose must, therefore, be inferred from circumstances surrounding the combination, such as sales quantities, the continuity of the supplier-recipient relationship, the seller's initiative, a failure to keep records, and the relationship's clandestine nature.[25]

Some argue that knowing, or conscious, wrongdoing ought to satisfy the conspiracy *mens rea*. However, in *People v. Lauria*, the court refused to substitute knowledge for purpose. Lauria owned a telephone answering service and knew that three prostitutes were using it to solicit and serve their customers. Lauria was not, however, making any profit from their work; neither was he referring customers nor doing anything else except supplying an answering service for what he knew was an illegal business. Lauria was acquitted of conspiracy to commit prostitution because, although he knew he was supplying the telephone service, he did not do it for the purpose of furthering prostitution but to make a profit on his telephone service.[26]

THE AGREEMENT'S OBJECTIVE. Another problem in conspiracy is disagreement over what objectives constitute conspiratorial agreements and combinations. In some states—Texas and Arkansas, for example—only combinations or agreements to commit felonies constitute conspiracies. Several other states—such as Colorado, Arizona, and Hawaii—include both felonies and misdemeanors. Still other states follow the broad, common-law definition, making it a crime to enter into any conspiracies, agreements, or combinations to "accomplish any unlawful object by lawful means," or "any lawful object by unlawful means," or any "unlawful object by unlawful means." Courts have even extended "unlawful" beyond criminal conduct to embrace civil wrongs. For example, an agreement to interfere unfairly with trade is not a crime in most states, but it may be against the law. An agreement to engage in unfair trade practices has an unlawful, if not criminal, objective and is considered a conspiracy.

Some conspiracy statutes reach still further. In Alabama, for instance, conspiracy not only applies to agreements and combinations to accomplish criminal and other unlawful objectives, it also encompasses "any act injurious to public health, morals, trade, and commerce." Agreements and combinations falling within this sweeping phrase are almost limitless in number. Examples include combinations to commit fornication, to interfere with social intercourse at a picnic, and to use another person's car without permission.[27]

Reformers have worked to get courts to declare the most sweeping statutes unconstitutional on the ground that they are too vague to satisfy the due process clauses in the United States and state constitutions. In *State v. Musser* (a case in which the state prosecuted Mormons for urging the practice of polygamy), the Utah Supreme Court ruled that the "public morals" provision in Utah's conspiracy statute was unconstitutionally vague. Most efforts have failed, however. Courts have actually expanded the federal conspiracy-to-defraud provision in the United States Code to encompass "virtually any impairment of the Government's operating efficiency." The United States Supreme Court remarked that these broad statutes

> would seem to be warrant for conviction for agreement to do almost any act which a judge and jury might find at the moment contrary to his or its notions of what was good for health, morals, trade, commerce, justice or order.[28]

Another path toward reform is to draft narrower conspiracy statutes. The Model Penal Code, for example, provides that only agreements or combinations with "criminal objectives" are subject to prosecution for conspiracy. (See Section 5.03 in Appendix.) Several states have followed suit. Connecticut, Georgia, Illinois, and others now include only agreements or combinations made to pursue criminal objectives.

PARTIES TO CONSPIRACY. At common law and in most jurisdictions today, a conspiracy requires two or more parties. The criminal law punishes conspiracies in part because group offenses are more dangerous than individual offenses. Thus, some have argued that when unlawful combinations do not have an element of *added* danger they are not conspiracies unless they involve more than the number of parties required to commit the completed crime. According to **Wharton's rule** (named after a nineteenth-century criminal law commentator), in a crime that requires two or more persons to commit such as bigamy, bribery, incest, and gambling—the state must prove that *more* than two persons agreed to commit the offense. For example, a police officer who agreed not to arrest a person in exchange for money did not conspire to obstruct justice because bribery requires two persons—the offerer and receiver. Had two police officers agreed to take the money, then conspiracy would have occurred.[29]

Some jurisdictions have abolished the Wharton rule on the ground that whether or not the object offense required more than one party, the actor's danger justifies making the effort criminal. Hence, the Model Penal Code adopts a unilateral approach to liability for conspiracy. (See Section 5.03 in the Appendix.)

Sometimes a person only pretends to intend to commit a crime. In a New Jersey case, a defendant was convicted of assault and battery on a police officer, even though his "coconspirator" was an undercover police officer who clearly did not intend to attack a fellow officer.[30]

Another problem arises when one party to the agreement cannot be convicted. Should that relieve the defendant from liability? Most modern statutes provide for liability whether or not the other party could be convicted. The Illinois Criminal Code provides as follows:

It shall not be a defense to conspiracy that the person or persons with whom the accused is alleged to have conspired
1. Has not been prosecuted or convicted, or
2. Has been convicted of a different offense, or
3. Is not amenable to justice, or
4. Has been acquitted, or
5. Lacked the capacity to commit an offense.[31]

CASE

Were They Partners in Crime?

Williams v. State

274 Ind. 94, 409 N.E.2d 571 (1980)

[Carl and Diane Williams were convicted of conspiracy to commit murder. Carl Williams was sentenced to thirty years in prison. Diane Williams was sentenced to twenty years in prison. She appealed. Justice Pivarnik delivered the opinion.]

FACTS

[The Indiana Criminal Code] codifies the offense of conspiracy. That section provides:]

> Conspiracy.—(a) A person conspires to commit a felony when, with intent to commit the felony, he agrees with another person to commit the felony. A conspiracy to commit a felony is a felony of the same class as the underlying felony. However, a conspiracy to commit murder is a class A felony. (b) The state must allege and prove that either the person or the person with whom he agreed performed an overt act in furtherance of the agreement.

In early January, 1978, Hammond police officer James Lawson was working as an undercover agent for the Drug Enforcement Administration branch of the United States Department of Justice. During the course of his work for the federal government, he came in contact with Dr. Carl N. Williams and Diane Kendrick Williams, the defendants in this case. On January 5, Lawson was in the Williams' home in Gary, Indiana, discussing certain other matters not related to the present case. Dr. Williams and appellant both engaged in conversation with Lawson. Late in the afternoon, appellant began reading that day's edition of the Gary Post-Tribune. The January 5 edition of the Post-Tribune carried an article on page one under the by-line of Alan Doyle. This article related how the Williams had been charged in connection with an automobile theft. Appellant Diane Williams brought the story to the attention of Dr. Williams and Officer Lawson.

Dr. and Mrs. Williams became very angry over the contents of the article. Appellant explained the general content of the story to Lawson, and he remarked, "It sounds like they are really trying to get you." Dr. Williams explained that his family had been involved in politics and that Gary was a "dog town."

When Diane Williams asked what they were going to do about the article, Dr. Williams stated that he wanted "something" done about it. Lawson's suggestion that they talk to their attorneys and pursue legal remedies was rejected out of hand by both Dr. Williams and appellant. Diane Williams stated that lawyers were of no help, and Dr. Williams said he was tired of dealing with lawyers. Both remained very angry over the article, and appellant again asked what they were going to do about Doyle and his article. Dr. Williams then stated that he wanted Doyle "shut up."

Dr. Williams then asked Lawson if he could "undertake an extra service." Lawson asked what he was referring to, and Dr. Williams repeated that he wanted Doyle "shut up." When Lawson asked him exactly what he meant by "shutting someone up," the doctor said he wanted to stop what he called "this malicious slander." Lawson remarked that breaking somebody's legs and arms wouldn't necessarily shut them up, and appellant Diane Williams agreed. Dr. Williams asked Lawson again if he would "perform an extra service." He stated that he wanted Alan Doyle killed, and he asked Lawson if he knew someone who would do the job. Lawson said he could put them in touch with someone who would, but that whoever he contacted would want to know "specifics" about the intended victim, such as his appearance, his place of employment, and what kind of car he drove. Dr. Williams said he would go to the newspaper office to learn this information, but appellant Diane Williams counselled against such an idea, saying it would connect Dr. Williams too closely with what was going to happen.

Lawson and Dr. Williams left the room to pick up a two-way police radio Williams possessed, because he thought it would be helpful in their plans. A short time later, they returned to the room where Diane was sitting. Lawson reiterated his feeling that the people he contacted to perform the killing would need to know who Doyle is, where he worked, and the kind of car he drove. Appellant Diane Williams volunteered to obtain this information.

The next day, Lawson returned to the Williams home with Michael Bolin, another undercover police officer. Lawson identified Bolin to Dr. Williams as the person who would perform the killing for them. Bolin demanded one thousand dollars for his services, half to be paid at that time, and the remainder after the job was completed. Dr. Williams then paid five hundred dollars to Bolin. Appellant Diane Williams was not present during this conversation.

On January 12, 1978, Lawson and Bolin went back to the Williams residence. After a brief conversation, Lawson, Bolin and Dr. Williams went for a drive in the agents' car. At their request, Dr. Williams directed them to the location of the Post-Tribune offices in Gary. During the course of the conversation in the car,

Dr. Williams stated on two occasions that appellant Diane Williams knew of and concurred in their plan to kill Alan Doyle.

OPINION

Thus, in this case, the prosecution must have proved that Diane Williams had the intent to commit murder; that she agreed with another person to commit murder; and that some overt act was performed in furtherance of that agreement. The requisite intent, of course, may be inferred from the acts committed and the circumstances surrounding the case.

We think there was substantial evidence from which the jury could have found beyond a reasonable doubt that Diane Williams had the intent to kill Alan Doyle, and that she had an intelligent understanding with Dr. Williams and Lawson that the killing would be done. Clearly, Dr. Williams committed several overt acts in pursuance of this agreement and plan. Thus, the evidence is sufficient to support the jury's finding that appellant Diane Williams conspired to commit murder.

CASE DISCUSSION

Considering the previous discussion, has Diane Williams conspired to commit murder? What was the agreement? the act in furthering it? the criminal purpose? Do you think the penalty is excessive? Is Diane Williams as guilty as her husband, Dr. Williams? Why is he punished more severely?

Summary

Conspiracy is further removed from completed crimes than are both attempt and preparation. Conspiracy law is based on the rationale that it not only prevents dangerous persons from finishing their evil plans but also strikes at a second evil, combinations for wrongful purposes, which is considered a serious social problem in itself. Conspiracy's material elements are simply stated—conspiracy is an agreement or combination intended to achieve an illegal objective—but are applied according to widely varied interpretation and meaning.

The often vague definitions of the material elements in conspiracy offer considerable opportunity for prosecutorial and judicial discretion. At times, this discretion borders on abuse, leading to charges that conspiracy law is unjust. First, a general criticism is that conspiracy law punishes conduct far remote from actual crime. Second, labor organizations, civil liberties groups, and large corporations charge that conspiracy is a weapon against their legitimate interests of collective bargaining and strikes, dissent from accepted points of view and public policies, and profit making.

Critics say that when prosecutors do not have enough evidence to convict for the crime itself, they turn as a last hope to conspiracy. Conspiracy's vague definitions greatly enhance the chance for a guilty verdict.

Not often mentioned, but extremely important, is the issue that intense media attention to conspiracy trials can lead to abuse. This happened in the conspiracy trials of Dr. Benjamin Spock and the Chicago Eight, and in other conspiracy trials involving radical politics during the 1960s. It also occured in the Watergate conspiracy trials involving President Nixon's associates during the 1970s, and in the alleged conspiracies surrounding the sale of arms to Iran for hostages and the subsequent alleged diversion of funds during the 1980s.

Several states have made efforts to overcome these criticisms by defining conspiracy elements more narrowly. Agreement or combination are no longer so vague as they once were. The Model Penal Code requires acts in furtherance of agreement, and several states are following the Code's lead. Those states have refined *mens rea* to include only purposeful conduct—that is, a specific intent to carry out the agreement's or combination's objective. Knowledge, recklessness, and negligence are increasingly being attacked as insufficient culpability for an offense that is as remote from completion as conspiracy. Furthermore, most recent legislation restricts conspiratorial objectives to criminal ends. Phrases like "unlawful objects," "lawful objects by unlawful means," and "objectives harmful to public health, morals, trade, and commerce" are increasingly regarded as too broad and, therefore, unacceptable.

On the other hand, the Racketeer Influenced and Corrupt Organizations Act (RICO) demonstrates conspiracy law's continued vitality. RICO is based on the need for effective means to meet the threat posed by organized crime. It imposes enhanced penalties for

> all types of organized criminal behavior, that is, enterprise criminality— from simple political to sophisticated white collar schemes to traditional Mafia-type endeavors.[32]

Racketeering activity includes any act chargeable under state and federal law, including murder, kidnapping, bribery, drug dealing, gambling, theft, extortion, and securities fraud. Among other things, the statute prohibits using income from a "pattern of racketeering activity" to acquire an interest in or establish an enterprise affecting interstate commerce; conducting an enterprise through a pattern of racketeering; or *conspiring* to violate these provisions.[33]

RICO's drafters intended the statute to "break the back of organized crime." The racketeers they had in mind were

> loansharks, drug kingpins, prostitution overlords, and casino operators who hired murderers and arsonists to enforce and extort—you know, the designated bad guys who presumably did not deserve the rights of due process that should protect all of us.

Now however, aggressive prosecutors use RICO against white-collar crime. Rudolf Giuliani, for example, caused Drexel Burnham Lambert to plead guilty to several counts of securities violations in order to avoid

RICO prosecution, which would not only result in harsher legal penalties but also attach the label racketeer to white-collar criminals.[34]

SOLICITATION

Most remote from its underlying substantive crime is solicitation. At common law—and under most modern statutes—solicitation is a command, urging, or request to a third person to commit a crime. Suppose I want to murder my wife but am afraid to do it. If I ask a friend and he kills her, then we are both murderers. If he tries to kill her and fails because his gun is defective, then he has committed attempted murder. If he agrees to kill her and buys the gun but gets no further, then we have conspired to commit murder. But simply soliciting or urging another to commit murder is also a crime. Hence, if I ask my friend to commit murder and offer him money to do it, even if he rejects the offer, I have committed the crime called solicitation to commit murder.

Opinion differs as to whether solicitation to commit a crime presents a sufficient social danger to constitute a crime. On one side, it is argued that solicitation is not dangerous because an independent moral agent (the person solicited) stands between solicitors and their criminal objectives. Furthermore, by soliciting others to commit crimes, solicitors demonstrate their reluctance to commit crimes themselves. On the other side, advocates argue that solicitation creates the special danger inherent in group participation in crime; in this sense, solicitation is an attempt to conspire. In addition, solicitors manifest masterful and intelligent manipulation of their underlings. According to the commentary of the Model Penal Code,

> [t]here should be no doubt on this issue. Purposeful solicitation presents dangers calling for preventive intervention and is sufficiently indicative of a disposition towards criminal activity to call for liability.[35]

Material Elements in Solicitation

ACTUS REUS. Words constitute the act in solicitation, but the law imprecisely prescribes what words qualify. Courts generally agree that statements simply favoring or approving crime do not constitute solicitation. Hence, someone who merely says "I think it would be great if someone killed that terrorist" has not solicited murder. Courts demand some sort of inducement. Statutes or judicial decisions have deemed to be sufficient a statement that does any of the following: advises, commands, counsels, encourages, entices, entreats, importunes, incites, induces, instigates, procures, requests, solicits, and urges. Uttering the proper inducement accompanied by the required *mens rea* constitutes solicitation. In other words, criminal solicitation consists of the effort to engage another in crime, whether or not the inducement ever ripens into a completed crime. The law considers that those who urge others to commit crimes are sufficiently dangerous to punish.[36]

Must the solicitor address the words to particular individuals? Some say yes, but courts have ruled that public exhortations to audiences suffice. One speaker who was convicted urged his audience from a public platform to commit murder and robbery. It is also solicitation to put an inducement in writing and send it through the mail, even if the party solicited never receives the letter. Soliciting is a crime even if the solicitor does not personally communicate the inducement, and despite the inducement's failure to reach its object. Hence, if I send a letter to my hoped-for collaborator, offering her $30,000 to kill my enemy, I have solicited murder even if the letter gets lost in the mail. A criminal solicitor's danger does not depend on the inducement's reaching its object; a solicitor bent on engaging another in crime will simply try again.[37]

OBJECTIVE. Some statutes restrict the objective in solicitation to felonies, in some cases to violent felonies. In other jurisdictions, it is a crime to solicit another to commit *any* crime, whether felony, misdemeanor, or violation. Furthermore, solicitation need not include an inducement to commit a crime. For example, suppose a robber urges a friend to borrow money and lend it to the robber for a plane ticket to escape from the jurisdiction. The robber has solicited escape, or aiding and abetting a robbery. Although borrowing money is not a crime, and lending money to a robber is not by itself a crime, both escape and aiding and abetting robbers are crimes. One who urges another to commit those crimes has committed the crime of solicitation.

MENS REA. The *actus reus* in solicitation makes it clear that criminal solicitation requires specific intent. The words in a solicitation must convey the author's intention to induce another to commit the substantive offense. If I urge my friend who works in an expensive jewelry shop to take a gold chain for me, I have solicited larceny. If, on the other hand, I ask another friend who works in a clothing shop to get a coat for me to use for the evening, and I plan to return the coat the next morning before anyone knows it is missing, I have not solicited larceny because I do not intend to steal the coat, only to use it for the night (see larceny in chapter 11).

Solicitation by Law Enforcement Officers

A problem arises when law enforcement officers solicit in order to determine whether someone is disposed to commit a crime. For example, police decoys who try to get suspected prostitutes to offer sex for money have not solicited criminally under present law because the decoys' motive is not dangerous. It is maintained (not without objection) that the decoys' motives are nobly addressed to upholding the law, hardly a dangerous propensity. Similarly, narcotics police or street decoys hoping to catch muggers are working to prevent and control crime, not to foster crime, according to supporters. Others argue that decoys encourage innocent people to commit crimes. Although law enforcement officers acting properly in the course of their duties may not be guilty of solicitation, their too-energetic encouragement may constitute entrapment (see chapter 7).

CASE

Did He Solicit His Wife's Murder?

State v. Furr

292 N.C. 711, 235 S.E.2d 193 (1977)

[Furr was convicted of three counts of soliciting to commit his wife's murder. He was sentenced to three consecutive eight- to ten-year prison terms for each murder. He appealed. Justice Exum gave the opinion.]

FACTS

The defendant and his wife had been married about 21 years and had four children when they separated in 1973. After the separation, Furr moved his real estate office from their home to a nearby location near the square in Locust, North Carolina. His wife, Earlene, continued to live at the house on Willow Drive and Furr moved into Western Hills Mobile Home Park. The couple's relationship was apparently quite volatile and Furr exhibited increasing hostility towards Earlene after the separation.

In April, 1973, Earlene filed a civil action against defendant resulting in a judgment against him in October, 1973. A year later, on his wife's motion, defendant was adjudged to be in contempt and was committed to jail. While in Stanly County jail, Furr met Raymond Clontz and Donald Owens, and related his marital problems to them, especially his concern over the property dispute. He was released from jail on December 6, 1974, upon payment of $13,623.00. After his release, Furr approached Clontz and Owens, drove them by Earlene's home and explained how to get into the house. He offered Owens $3,000.00 to kill Earlene and offered to give Clontz a lot which the latter wanted to store cars on if Clontz would do the job. Neither man accepted the offer.

In October, 1974, defendant asked "Buck" Baker if he knew a "hit man." At the time Furr was angry because Earlene had disposed of some racing equipment. Furr also approached Donald Eugene Huneycutt on several occasions to ask whether Huneycutt knew a "hit man." In the initial encounters, Furr wanted Johny Jhue Laney killed because Laney had murdered his own wife, Doris, who was defendant's girl friend. By early 1975, however, Furr's plans extended as well to Earlene and her attorney, Charles Brown. Huneycutt told him killing women and lawyers would create "too much heat," but defendant responded that he could stand the heat and had his mother for an alibi.

Defendant also asked George Arnold Black, Jr., to kill Earlene, and drove him by the house in the fall of 1974. Like the others, Black declined the offer.

OPINION

Solicitation of another to commit a felony is a crime in North Carolina, even though the solicitation is of no effect and the crime solicited is never committed. The gravamen of the offense of soliciting lies in counseling, enticing or inducing another to commit a crime.

Defendant argues that the evidence shows only that defendant requested that Huneycutt find someone else to murder each of the three intended victims, and not that Huneycutt himself commit the crime. "Under no authority," says defendant, "is that a criminal offense." Accepting for the moment defendant's argument that defendant solicited Huneycutt only to find another "hit man," we hold that such a request constitutes the crime of solicitation to commit a felony in North Carolina. In W. LaFave and A. Scott, *Criminal Law*, 419 (1972) it is observed that "[i]n the usual solicitation case, it is the solicitor's intention that the criminal result be directly brought about by the person he has solicited; that is, it is his intention that the crime be committed and that the other commit it as a principal in the first degree, as where A asks B to kill C. However, it would seem sufficient that A requested B to get involved in the scheme to kill C in any way which would establish B's complicity in the killing of C were that to occur. Thus it would be criminal for one person to solicit another to in turn solicit a third party, to solicit another to join a conspiracy, or to solicit another to aid and abet the commission of a crime."

Defendant further contends that there was no evidence to support three indictments alleging solicitation of Raymond Clontz to murder Earlene Furr. There is no merit to these contentions in two of the counts. Indictment Number 76–CR–700 alleges that Clontz was solicited in January to murder Furr's wife. The evidence is that during that month, shortly after both men were released from jail where defendant had been quite talkative about his marital problems, Clontz and Furr met to discuss a lot which Clontz wished to purchase. Furr said he wanted $3,000.00 for the lot and Clontz agreed to take it. Then, as Clontz related at trial Furr told him not to be so hasty, that "he would make some arrangements about the payment for the lot in another way; that he wanted me to do a job for him." Clontz told Furr that he "knew what he was talking about, but that [he] wasn't interested in it." Defendant then told him he had to go to court with

his wife in a few weeks and "that he had to have something done before court time or he was going to be in serious trouble. He said his wife was already getting $250.00 a week from him, and she had possession of the house, and had his property tied up and that he had to have something done." In the context, we find no other reasonable interpretation of defendant's words on this occasion than that he was requesting Clontz to kill his wife.
Affirmed.

CASE DISCUSSION

Can you identify Furr's *means rea*, his act, and the resulting harm? Do you think the prosecution proved them beyond a reasonable doubt? Solicitation is aimed at controlling dangerous persons. Is Furr a dangerous social problem who should be punished whether or not his inducements ever came to fruition? Do you think eight to ten years' imprisonment is too little, too much, or just about enough punishment for what he did? Why or why not?

≡ SUMMARY

Attempt, conspiracy, and solicitation aim primarily to prevent crime and control dangerous persons. Clear commitment to crime, measured by intent and conduct, sufficiently indicates a person's dangerousness. Persons who demonstrate their determination to commit crimes deserve punishment and justify making even some incomplete crimes punishable. If extraneous factors interrupt or frustrate completion—such as when police officers or others arrive at the scene—that fortuity should not permit would-be criminals to escape punishment. However, if perpetrators voluntarily renounce their efforts because their consciences compel them, some argue that the law should excuse them because they are no longer dangerous. Since the actor's dangerousness, not harm's actuality, justifies making inchoate harms criminal, most agree that it does not matter whether it was impossible to complete the harm intended. It is enough that the crime could have been committed if circumstances were as the perpetrator reasonably believed they would be.

The justification for imposing criminal liability in inchoate crimes rests, therefore, not only on the danger of potential *conduct* but also on the danger of *individuals*. When dangerousness (and not harmful result) is the criterion for punishment, it is always possible to erroneously predict who is dangerous. Available research strongly suggests that high risks of error attend any such predictions, especially when those predictions are directed toward violent behavior. This has led some to argue that criminal law should never punish potential harm, only past conduct.

≡ QUESTIONS FOR REVIEW AND DISCUSSION

1. What is the difference between preparation and attempt?
2. What kinds of agreement should conspiracy encompass?
3. What two reasons support making conspiracies crimes?
4. Should renunciation of criminal intent be a defense to inchoate offenses? Explain.
5. Why are inchoate offenses crimes? Should they be?
6. What is the act in attempt? in conspiracy? in solicitation?
7. What is the *mens rea* in attempt? in conspiracy? in solicitation?
8. What is the objective in attempt? in conspiracy? in solicitation?
9. Should it be a crime to attempt to commit any offense, or only felonies? to conspire to commit any crime, or only felonies? to solicit any crime, or only felonies?

≡ SUGGESTED READINGS

1. Jerome Hall, *General Principles of Criminal Law*, 2d ed. (Indianapolis: Bobbs-Merrill, 1960), chap. 15, is an excellent survey of attempt law. It includes a good history of attempt and the theoretical justifications for it, and discusses some proper limits to be placed on it.
2. George P. Fletcher, *Rethinking Criminal Law* (Boston: Little, Brown, 1978), pp. 131–205, 218–32, contains provocative discussions about the inchoate offenses. Professor Fletcher only clearly defines the terms in considerable detail. He also assesses the inchoate crimes and participation in crime in ways that provoke considerable thought about the roles of those terms in criminal law.
3. Jessica Mitford, *The Trial of Dr. Spock* (New York: Knopf, 1969), is an excellent narrative, written for the general public. It reveals much about conspiracy within the context of a real case that attracted enormous publicity.
4. American Law Institute, *Model Penal Code and Commentaries*, vol. 1 (Philadelphia: American Law Institute, 1985), pt. 1, pp. 295–328, contains a detailed analysis of all elements in complicity as well as arguments for why complicity should be included in criminal law and to what extent participants should be criminally liable. This is an advanced discussion written for experts in the field but is well worth the effort to read and consider its points. In vol. 2, pt. 1 the inchoate offenses are treated similarly.

≡ NOTES

1. Rollin M. Perkins and Ronald N. Boyce, *Criminal Law*, 3d ed. (Mineola, N.Y.: Foundation Press, 1982), pp. 611–58, 700–714; American Law Institute, *Model*

Penal Code and Commentaries, vol. 2 (Philadelphia: American Law Institute, 1985), pp. 293–98.

2. Plato, *The Laws*, trans. Trevor J. Saunders (Middlesex, England: Penguin Books, 1975), pp. 397–98; Jerome Hall, *General Principles of Criminal Law*, 2d ed. (Indianapolis: Bobbs-Merrill, 1960), pp. 560–64.

3. Quoted in Hall, *General Principles of Criminal Law*, p. 560.

4. Ibid.

5. Joel Samaha, *Law and Order in Historical Perspective* (New York: Academic Press, 1974); Joel Samaha, "The Recognizance in Elizabethan Law Enforcement, "*American Journal of Legal History*, 25 (1981), pp. 189–204.

6. Cald. 397 (1784).

7. Sir James F. Stephen, *A History of the Criminal Law of England*, reprint (New York: Burt Franklin, 1973), p. 224.

8. Wayne R. LaFave and Austin W. Scott, Jr., *Criminal Law* (St. Paul: West Publishing Co., 1972), p. 423.

9. *United States v. Mandujano*, 499 F.2d 370, 374 (5th Cir. 1974).

10. *United States v. Mandujano*, 499 F.2d 370, 375–376 (5th Cir. 1974) (more than intention required).

11. American Law Institute, *Model Penal Code and Commentaries*, vol. 2 pp. 321–22; *People v. Rizzo*, 246 N.Y. 334, 158 N.E. 888 (1927).

12. American Law Institute, *Model Penal Code and Commentaries*, vol. 2, pp. 322–23.

13. American Law Institute, *Model Penal Code and Commentaries*, vol. 2, pt. 1, pp. 329–31.

14. Ibid.

15. *Bradley v. Ward*, N.Z.L.R. 471 (1955).

16. American Law Institute, *Model Penal Code and Commentaries*, vol. 2, pp. 337–46.

17. Ibid.

18. Nev.Rev.Stat. sec. 205.055; American Law Institute, *Model Penal Code and Commentaries*, vol. 2, pp. 354–55.

19. Fernand N. Dutile and Harold F. Moore, "Mistake and Impossibility: Arranging a Marriage between Two Difficult Partners," *Northwestern University Law Review*, 74 (1979), pp. 166. 181 ff.

20. American Law Institute, *Model Penal Code and Commentaries*, vol. 2, pp. 356–62.

21. Ibid., p. 387.

22. Jessica Mitford, *The Trial of Dr. Spock* (New York: Knopf, 1969), pp. 70–71.

23. Kentucky Rev. Stat. 427.110 (1958).

24. Concurring in *Krulewich v. United States*, 336 U.S. 440, 445–46, 69 S.Ct. 716, 719–20, 93 L.Ed. 790 (1949).

25. *Direct Sales Co. v. United States*, 319 U.S. 703, 63 S. Ct. 1265, 87 L.Ed. 1674 (1943).

26. 251 Cal. App. 2d 471, 59 Cal.Rptr. 628 (1967).

27. Ala.Gen.tat. 54–197 (1958); *Baker v. Commonwealth*, 204 Ky. 420, 264 S.W. 1069 (1924); *State v. Ameker*, 53 S.E. 484 (1906); *State v. Davis*, 229 S.E. 811 (1911).

28. 118 Utah 537, 223 P.2d 193 (1950); 18 U.S.C.A. § 371 (1976); *Musser v. Utah*, 333 U.S. 95, 97, 68 S.Ct. 397, 92 L.Ed.562 (1948).

29. *People v. Davis*, 408 Mich. 255, 290 N.W.2d 366 (1980).

30. *State v. Lavary,*152 N.J. Super. 413, 377 A.2d 1255 (1977).

31. *Illinois Criminal Law and Procedure* (St. Paul: West Publishing Co., 1988), chap. 38, § 8–4.

32. Blakely and Gettings, "Racketeer Influenced and Corrupt Organizations (RICO): Basic Concepts—Criminal and Civil Remedies," *Temple Law Quarterly,* 53 (1980), pp. 1013–14.

33. 18 U.S.C.A. § 1961 et seq.

34. William Safire, "The End of RICO," *The New York Times* (January 30, 1989), p. 19.

35. American Law Institute, *Model Penal Code and Commentaries,* vol. 2, pp. 365–66.

36. LaFave and Scott, *Criminal Law,* p. 419.

37. *State v. Schleifer,* 99 Conn. 432 121 A. 805 (1923).

Chapter Six

Defenses to Criminal Liability: Justifications

CHAPTER OUTLINE

CHAPTER MAIN POINTS

1. Defenses to criminal liability are either justifications or excuses.

2. Justifications make otherwise criminal conduct right under special conditions.

3. The law needs defenses, or justifications, to soften its harshness in particular situations.

4. Self-defense justifies using force or threats of force to ward off attacks against individuals and sometimes third persons under certain special conditions.

5. Necessity justifies what otherwise is criminal if it requires one to choose a lesser evil to avoid a greater evil.

6. Consent justifies what otherwise is criminal in crimes where it is a material element.

CHAPTER KEY TERMS

affirmative defenses defenses that the prosecution need not disprove unless defendants first present some evidence.

defenses evidence that defendants bring to raise reasonable doubts concerning prosecutions' proof.

excuses defenses in which defendants admit wrongdoing but claim that, under the circumstances, they were not responsible for what they did.

justifications defenses in which defendants admit responsibility for harm but argue that, under the circumstances, what they did was right.

mitigating circumstances facts that reduce defendants' culpability but do not completely justify or excuse wrongdoing.

motive the reason a defendant commits a crime.

perfect defense defense that leads to acquittal.

═ INTRODUCTION

The criminal law requires the government to prove all the material elements of crimes beyond a reasonable doubt. **Defenses** permit the accused to avoid criminal liability. Defenses arise in three main ways. In one, defendants have not committed the crime, in which case alibi constitutes a defense. In another, a material element may be missing, in which case failure to establish the element provides the defense. For example, suppose a defendant shows that a partner consented to sexual intercourse in a charge of rape. The case lacks a material element in rape: sexual penetration *without consent* (see chapter 9). Finally, the general defenses of justification and excuse can lead to acquittal. In **justifications,** the subject of this chapter, defendants admit responsibility for crimes but argue that, under the circumstances, what they did was right. In **excuses,** the subject of chapter 7, defendants admit that what they did was wrong but argue that, under the circumstances, they were not responsible for what they did.[1]

Justification permits certain circumstances to justify (make right) otherwise criminal conduct and the causing of criminal harms. Justified behavior precludes punishment because the conduct lacks blameworthiness. For example, it is wrong to blame—hence, punish—one who kills another in self-defense. Similarly, it is unjust to punish those not responsible for their conduct or its results. If I am so mentally diseased that I think I am squeezing a lemon when, in fact, I am choking my wife, my conduct is wrong but my insanity excuses my responsibility for the wrong.[2] (See chapter 7.)

The government must prove all the material elements of criminal liability beyond a reasonable doubt. In technical terms, the government has the burden of proof. However, in the **affirmative defenses,** including self-defense, necessity, insanity, intoxication, and duress, the burden falls on defendants. This burden varies. Sometimes the defense need only present initial evidence; that is, it must bear the burden of production. For example, in a jurisdiction that requires defendants to bear the burden of production in insanity, once initial evidence of insanity is produced, the burden shifts to the government to prove sanity beyond a reasonable doubt. Sometimes the defense has the burden to prove an affirmative defense by a preponderance of the evidence—by evidence that carries more weight than that in opposition to it. These complicated matters of burdens and quantities of proof vary from jurisdiction to jurisdiction, but can affect the outcome of cases.[3]

Perfect defenses, such as self-defense successfully pleaded, lead to outright acquittal. On the other hand, even if successfully pleaded, insanity ordinarily does not set defendants free, at least not automatically. Frequently, special insanity hearings following insanity verdicts result in defendants being sent to maximum-security hospitals until they regain their sanity. Often, defendants never regain their sanity; they remain committed for life to maximum-security hospitals.

Sometimes evidence that does not lead to a perfect defense results in conviction for a lesser charge, such as when provocation reduces murder to manslaughter. This can mean the difference between death or life imprisonment for murder, and ten to twenty years for manslaughter (see chapter 8).

Even when defenses do not lead to acquittal or to conviction for lesser crimes, they may still influence punishment. Evidence that does not amount to a perfect defense might still demonstrate **mitigating circumstances,** or facts that convince judges or juries that defendants do not deserve the maximum penalty for the crimes they committed. For example, if a state authorized the death penalty for first-degree murder, a murderer who killed without legal provocation might still get life imprisonment instead of the death penalty. Although words, however provocative, do not amount to legal provocation that reduces murder to manslaughter, they are a mitigating circumstance that might reduce capital punishment to life imprisonment. Hence, if a black person killed someone in an outburst of rage brought about by the victim's relentless taunting with the racist epithet "nigger," the taunting might mitigate the death penalty. (See chapter 8.)

Motive also influences punishment, or even conviction itself in some cases. **Motive** refers to the reason actors do what they do, and is distinguished from *mens rea*. *Mens rea* refers to whether defendants acted or caused a result purposely, knowingly, recklessly, and negligently. Motive refers to the reason defendants acted or caused particular results. Suppose a burglar purposely breaks into and enters a house with the intent to steal food because she is hungry. Hunger is the motive; breaking and entering with the intent to steal food is the *mens rea*. Mercy killing also illustrates both *mens rea* and motive: the mercy killer kills on purpose in order to ease the victim's suffering. The law does not require proof of motive to convict; *mens rea* suffices. However, motive might aid in proving *mens rea:* knowing the defendant killed to end the victim's suffering helps prove purpose and knowledge.

The motive of mercy might also affect conviction and punishment.[4] A jury might refuse to convict a mercy killer even though the *mens rea* clearly exists—the premeditated, purposeful causing of another's death. Or, a judge might reduce the sentence to a minimum, and corrections officials might parole the mercy killer at the earliest possible date. For example, seventy-eight-year-old Oscar Carlson, who could no longer endure his wife's suffering from advanced Alzheimer's disease, shot and killed his wife. On his first day in prison, Carlson said,

> I know it's better for me to sit here in prison than for Agnes to sit up there in the home like she was.

A barrage of negative publicity surrounded his sentence to prison, generating considerable sympathy for the elderly "murderer." Mitigating circumstances are extraordinarily important in criminal law, especially because American judges have wide sentencing discretion.[5]

═══ SELF-DEFENSE

Several justifications—self-defense, defense of others, law enforcement, and sometimes defense of home and property—deal with when actors may use force and under what circumstances that force may be deadly. Self-defense refers to using or threatening to use force against another in order to repel an unprovoked attack. At common law, self-defense was defined as follows:

> A man may repel force by force in the defense of his person, habitation, or property, against one or many who manifestly intend and endeavor, by violence or surprise, to commit a known felony on either. In such a case he is not obliged to retreat, but may pursue his adversary until he find himself out of danger; and if, in a conflict between them, he happen to kill, such killing is justifiable. The right of self-defense in cases of this kind is founded on the law of nature; and is not, nor can be, superseded by any law of society. . . . To make homicide excusable on the ground of self-defense, the danger must be actual and urgent.[6]

Self-defense rests on the notion that those subjected to unprovoked attacks may use force to do for themselves what the law cannot, at the moment, do for them. Self-defense does not include preemptive strikes, or attacks based on the prediction that an assailant will use force sometime in the future. Nor does it include retaliation, or the use of force to "pay back" an assailant for an attack. The law allows private citizens to use force only for *protection* when *necessary* against *imminent* attack. Citizens must use other means to protect against future attacks, and only the state can punish past attacks.[7]

CASE

Can You Shoot Muggers when They Approach?

People v. Goetz

68 N.Y.2d 96, 506 N.Y.S.2d 18, 497 N.E.2d 41 (1986)

[Chief Justice Watchler delivered the opinion.]
A Grand Jury has indicted defendant on attempted murder, assault, and other charges for having shot and wounded four youths on a New York City subway train after one or two of the youths approached him and asked for $5. The lower courts, concluding that the prosecutor's charge to the Grand Jury on the defense of justification was erroneous, have dismissed the attempted murder, assault, and weapons possessions charges. We now reverse and reinstate all counts of the indictment.

FACTS

The precise circumstances of the incident giving rise to the charges against defendant are disputed, and ultimately it will be for a trial jury to determine what occurred. We feel it necessary, however, to provide some factual background to properly frame legal issues before us. . . .

On Saturday afternoon, December 22, 1984, Troy Canty, Darryl Cabey, James Ramseur, and Barry Allen boarded an IRT express subway train in The Bronx and headed south toward lower Manhattan. The four youths rode together in the rear portion of the seventh car of the train. Two of the four, Ramseur and Cabey, had screwdrivers inside their coats, which they said were to be used to break into the coin boxes of video machines.

Defendant Bernhard Goetz boarded this subway train at 14th Street in Manhattan and sat down on a bench towards the rear section of the same car occupied by the four youths. Goetz was carrying an unlicensed .38 caliber pistol loaded with five rounds of ammunition in a waistband holster. The train left the 14th Street station and headed towards Chambers Street.

It appears from the evidence before the Grand Jury that Canty approached Goetz, possibly with Allen beside him, and stated "give me five dollars." Neither Canty nor any of the other youths displayed a weapon. Goetz responded by standing up, pulling out his handgun and firing four shots in rapid succession. The first shot hit Canty in the chest; the second struck Allen in the back; the third went through Ramseur's arm and into his left side; the fourth was fired at Cabey, who apparently was then standing in the corner of the car, but missed, deflecting instead off of a wall of the conductor's cab. After

Goetz briefly surveyed the scene around him, he fired another shot at Cabey, who then was sitting on the end bench of the car. The bullet entered the rear of Cabey's side and severed his spinal cord.

All but two of the passengers fled the car when, or immediately after, the shots were fired. The conductor, who had been in the next car, heard the shots and instructed the motorman to radio for emergency assistance. The conductor then went into the car where the shooting occurred and saw Goetz sitting on a bench, the injured youths lying on the floor or slumped against a seat, and two women who had apparently taken cover, also lying on the floor. Goetz told the conductor that the four youths had tried to rob him.

While the conductor was aiding the youths, Goetz headed towards the front of the car. The train had stopped just before the Chambers Street station and Goetz went between two of the cars, jumped onto the tracks, and fled. Police and ambulance crews arrived at the scene shortly thereafter. Ramseur and Canty, initially listed in critical condition, have fully recovered. Cabey remains paralyzed, and has suffered some degree of brain damage.

On December 31, 1984, Goetz surrendered to police in Concord, New Hampshire. . . . Later that day, after receiving *Miranda* warnings, he made two lengthy statements, both of which were tape recorded with his permission. In his statements, which are substantially similar, Goetz admitted that he had been illegally carrying a handgun in New York City for three years. He stated that he had first purchased a gun in 1981 after he had been injured in a mugging. Goetz also revealed that twice between 1981 and 1984 he had successfully warded off assailants simply by displaying the pistol.

According to Goetz's statement, the first contact he had with the four youths came when Canty, sitting or lying on the bench across from him, asked "how are you," to which he replied "fine." Shortly thereafter, Canty, followed by one of the other youths, walked over to the defendant and stood to his left, while the other two youths remained to his right, in the corner of the subway car. Canty then said "give me five dollars." Goetz stated that he knew from the smile on Canty's face that they wanted to "play with me." Although he was certain that none of the youths had a gun, he had a fear, based on prior experiences, of being "maimed."

Goetz then established "a pattern of fire," deciding specifically to fire from left to right. His stated intention at that point was to "murder [the four youths], to hurt them, to make them suffer as much as possible." When Canty again requested money, Goetz stood up, drew his weapon, and began firing, aiming for the center of the body of each of the four. Goetz recalled that the first two he shot "tried to run through the crowd [but] they had nowhere to run." Goetz then turned to his right to "go after the other two." One of these two "tried to run through the wall of the train, but . . . he had nowhere to go." The other youth (Cabey) "tried pretending that he wasn't with [the others]" by standing still, holding on to one of the subway hand straps, and not looking at Goetz. Goetz nonetheless fired his fourth shot at him. He then ran back to the first two youths to make sure they had been "taken care of." Seeing that they had both been shot, he spun back to check on the other two. Goetz noticed that the youth who had been standing still was now sitting on a bench and seemed unhurt. As Goetz told the police, "I said '[y]ou seem to be all right, here's another,'" and he fired the shot which severed Cabey's spinal cord. Goetz added that "if I was a little more under self-control . . . I would have put the barrel against his forehead and fired." He also admitted that "if I had had more [bullets], I would have shot them again, and again, and again."

After waiving extradition, Goetz was brought back to New York and arraigned on a felony complaint charging him with attempted murder and criminal possession of a weapon. The matter was presented to a Grand Jury in January 1985, with the prosecutor seeking an indictment for attempted murder, assault, reckless endangerment, and criminal possession of a weapon. . . . [T]he Grand Jury indicted defendant on one count of criminal possession of a weapon in the third degree for possessing the gun used in the subway shootings, and two counts of criminal possession of a weapon in the fourth degree. . . . It dismissed, however, the attempted murder and other charges stemming from the shootings themselves.

Several weeks after the Grand Jury's action, the People, asserting that they had newly available evidence, moved for an order authorizing them to resubmit the dismissed charges to a second Grand Jury . . .

. . . [T]he second Grand Jury filed a 10-count indictment, containing four charges of attempted murder, four charges of assault in the first degree, one charge of reckless endangerment in the first degree, and one charge of criminal possession of a weapon in the second degree. . . .

On October 14, 1985, Goetz moved to dismiss the charges contained in the second indictment alleging, among other things, that the evidence before the second Grand Jury was not legally sufficient to establish the offenses charged and that the prosecutor's instructions to that Grand Jury on the defense of justification were erroneous and prejudicial to the defendant so as to render its proceedings defective.

On November 25, 1985, while the motion to dismiss was pending before Criminal Term, a column appeared in the *New York Daily News* containing an interview which the columnist had conducted with Darryl Cabey the previous day in Cabey's hospital room. The columnist had told him in this interview that the other three youths had all approached Goetz with the intention of robbing him. . . .

. . . The court, after inspection of the Grand Jury minutes, . . . held . . . that the prosecutor, in a supplemental charge elaborating upon the justification defense, had erroneously introduced an objective element into this defense by instructing the grand jurors to consider whether Goetz's conduct was that of a "reasonable man in [Goetz's] situation." The court . . . concluded that the statutory test for whether the use of deadly force is justified to protect a person should be wholly subjective, focusing entirely on the defendant's state of mind when he used such force. It concluded that dismissal was required for this error because the justification issue was at the heart of the case. . . .

On appeal by the People, a divided Appellate Division affirmed Criminal Term's dismissal of the charges. . . .

Justice Asch, in a dissenting opinion in which Justice Wallach concurred, disagreed with both bases for dismissal relied upon by Criminal Term. On the justification question, he opined that the statute requires consideration of both the defendant's subjective beliefs and whether a reasonable person in defendant's situation would have had such beliefs. . . . Justice Wallach stressed that the plurality's adoption of a purely subjective test effectively eliminated any reasonableness requirement contained in the statute.

Justice Asch granted the People leave to appeal to this court. We agree with the dissenters that neither the prosecutor's charge to the Grand Jury on justification nor the information which came to light. . . .

OPINION

Penal Law article 35 recognizes the defense of justification, which "permits the use of force under certain circumstances." . . . Penal Law § 35.15 (1) sets forth the general principles governing all such uses of force: "[a] person may . . . use physical force upon another person when and to the extent he *reasonably believes* such to be necessary to defend himself or a third person from what he *reasonably believes* to be the use or imminent use of unlawful physical force by such other person." [Emphasis added.]

Section 35.15 (2) . . . "A person may not use deadly physical force upon another person under circumstances specified in subdivision one unless (a) He *reasonably believes* that such other person is using or about to use deadly physical force . . . or (b) He *reasonably believes* that such other person is committing or attempting to commit a kidnapping, forcible rape, forcible sodomy or robbery." [Emphasis added.]

Thus, consistent with most justification provisions, Penal Law § 35.15 permits the use of deadly physical force only where requirements as to triggering conditions and the necessity of a particular response are met. As to the triggering of conditions, the statute requires that the actor "reasonably believes" that another person either is using or about to use deadly physical force or is committing or attempting to commit one of certain enumerated felonies, including robbery. As to the need for the use of deadly physical forces as a response, the statute requires that the actor "reasonably believes" that such force is necessary to avert the perceived threat.

Because the evidence before the second Grand Jury included statements by Goetz that he acted to protect himself from being maimed or to avert robbery, the prosecutor correctly chose to charge the justification defense . . . The prosecutor properly instructed the grand jurors to consider whether the use of deadly physical force was justified to prevent, either serious physical injury or a robbery, and, in doing so, to separately analyze the defense with respect to each of the charges. . . .

When the prosecutor had completed his charge, one of the grand jurors asked for clarification of the term "reasonably believes." The prosecutor responded by instructing the grand jurors that they were to consider the circumstances of the incident and determine "whether the defendant's conduct was that of a reasonable man in the defendant's situation." It is this response by the prosecutor—and specifically his use of "a reasonable man"—which is the basis for the dismissal of the charges by the lower courts. As expressed repeatedly in the Appellate Division's plurality opinion, because section 35.15 uses the term "*he* reasonably believes," the appropriate test, according to that court, is whether a defendant's beliefs and reactions were "reasonable to *him.*" Under that reading of the statute, a jury which believed a defendant's testimony that he felt that his own actions were warranted and were reasonable would have to acquit him, regardless of what anyone else in defendant's situation might have concluded. Such an interpretation defies the ordinary meaning and significance of the term "reasonably" in a statute, and misconstrues the clear intent of the Legislature, in enacting section 35.15, to retain an objective element as part of any provision authorizing the use of deadly physical force. . . .

We cannot lightly impute to the Legislature an intent to fundamentally alter the principles of justification to allow the perpetrator of a serious crime to go free simply because that person believed his actions were reasonable and necessary to prevent some perceived harm. To completely exonerate such an individual, no matter how aberrational or bizarre his thought patterns, would allow citizens to set their own standards for the permissible use of force. It would also allow a legally competent defendant suffering from delusions to kill or perform acts of violence with impunity, contrary to fundamental principles of justice and criminal law.

We can only conclude that the Legislature retained a reasonableness requirement to avoid giving a license for such actions. The plurality's interpretation, as the dissenters . . . recognized, excises the impact of the word "reasonably." . . .

Accordingly, the order of the Appellate Division should be reversed, and the dismissed counts of the indictment reinstated.

CASE DISCUSSION

New York tried Goetz for attempted murder and assault. The jury acquitted him of both charges. The jury said Goetz "was justified in shooting the four men with a silver-plated .38-caliber revolver he purchased in Florida." They did convict him of illegal possession of a firearm, for which the court sentenced Goetz to one year in jail. Following the sentencing, Goetz told the court that

> [t]his case is really more about the deterioration of society than it is about me. . . . Well, I don't believe that's the case. . . . I believe society needs to be protected from criminals.[1]

Criminal law professor George Fletcher followed the trial closely. Following the acquittal, he commented that

> [t]he facts of the Goetz case were relatively clear, but the primary fight was over the moral interpretation of the facts. . . . I am not in the slightest bit convinced that the four young men were about to mug Goetz. If he had said, "Listen buddy, I wish I had $5, but I don't," and walked to the other side of the car the chances are 60–40 nothing would have happened. Street-wise kids like that are more attuned to the costs of their behavior than Goetz was.[2]

If Professor Fletcher is right, was Goetz justified in shooting? Were Goetz's shots a preemptive strike? retaliation? necessary for self-protection? Explain.

---

[1]*New York Times* (January 14, 1989), p. 9.
[2]Quoted in *New York Times* (January 23, 1989), p. 14; see also Professor Fletcher's book on the Goetz trial, *A Crime of Self-Defense: Bernhard Goetz and the Law on Trial* (New York: Free Press, 1988).

Elements

Using force for self-protection does not always qualify as self-defense under the law. Highly technical and complicated limits surround the law of self-defense. Self-defense justifies the use of force only (1) against *unprovoked* attacks (ones that the defender did not encourage, invite, or cause); (2) when it is *necessary* and there is no alternative (such as retreat); (3) against an *imminent* attack (one that is going to happen immediately); (4) with the *intent to defend*, not to prevent a future attack or retaliate against a past one; and (5) when the force used is *proportional* to the need, such as when one only points a gun instead of shooting it if the threat will repel the attack. Generally, those who are free from blame may threaten to use force, or may use enough actual force, to repel unwarranted attacks.

UNPROVOKED ATTACKS. Those who provoke attacks cannot later claim they were defending themselves. However, if attackers completely withdraw from fights they start, they can forcibly defend themselves against a subsequent attack by their initial victims. Thus, a man who attacked another with a knife was acquitted on self-defense even though he provoked the attack. After attacking a much larger man with the knife, he realized he had taken on too much. He retreated in an effort to escape, but to no avail. The larger man, now thoroughly aroused, pursued him relentlessly. Unable to escape, the smaller man finally stood his ground and, in the process, stabbed his attacker to death. He was acquitted on self-defense because the jury was satisfied that he "withdrew in good faith," and had not merely retreated in order to regain enough strength to resume the attack.[8]

NECESSITY. Self-defense includes more than killing an assailant who threatens to kill. Less-than-deadly attacks authorize repelling the same with less-than-deadly responses. Thus, self-defense applies in all crimes against persons: homicide, rape, other assaults, and battery. Threats to persons constitute the common element in all these crimes. Self-defense also applies to defending property, but with limits.

IMMINENT DANGER. Only attacks in progress, or on the verge of taking place, justify the use of force. Thus, after a street gang member threw a brick at a cabdriver from the far side of an intersection, the driver justifiably shot into the gang because, despite their distance, they could have killed the driver at any moment.[9]

Some maintain that present danger suffices and that self-defense does not require immediate or imminent danger. For example, if an assailant leaves a scene to get reinforcements in order to continue an attack with a better advantage, the victim is not in immediate danger because the attack is not on the verge of happening. Nevertheless, some argue, the present danger justifies using force. The Model Penal Code permits using force to repel present-but-not-imminent danger. A few states, such as Delaware, Hawaii, New Jersey, Nebraska, and Pennsylvania, have followed the Model Penal Code, substituting present for imminent danger. Most states, however, retain the immediate or imminent danger requirement.[10]

HONEST AND/OR REASONABLE BELIEF IN DANGER. How does the law determine whether immediate or present danger of attack exists so that actors may use force to repel it? Must defenders face actual danger? Or is it enough that there are reasonable grounds to believe danger exists? Or is the honest belief that danger exists enough, even if in fact no danger exists and believing so is not reasonable?

Most jurisdictions adopt an objective test; they permit force only if under the circumstances actors reasonably believed the use of force was necessary. In some states, such as Illinois, Connecticut, and Wisconsin, statutes spell this out specifically. In states where statutes do not prescribe a test—subjective (honest belief), objective (reasonable belief), or combination (honest and reasonable belief)—courts imply a reasonableness test. Before Illinois legislated an objective test, for example, the Illinois Supreme Court ruled that a man who turned and immediately shot an unknown attacker who struck him in the head from behind "was not under a reasonable apprehension of death or great bodily harm."[11]

Occasionally, courts adopt a combined objective-subjective test. In *Beard v. United States*, Beard killed an attacker who threatened to assault him. The court ruled that Beard must have had "reasonable grounds to believe, and in good faith believed" he had to use force to protect against great bodily harm.

The reasonableness test and the objective-subjective test create *mens rea* problems. Defendants who, like Beard, make honest but unreasonable mistakes about danger—that is, reckless or negligent mistakes—cannot claim self-defense.[12]

Glanville Williams, a criminal law scholar, strongly objects to the reasonableness test:

> The criminal law of negligence works best when it gives effect to the large number of rules of prudence which are commonly observed though not directly incorporated into the law. Such rules include the rule against pulling out on a blind corner, the rule against carrying a gun in such a way that it is pointing at another person, the rule against deliberately pointing a gun at another person, even in play, and so on. These rules are not part either of enacted or of common law, but as customary standards of behavior they become binding via the law of negligence. Are there any similar rules of behavior applicable when a person acts in self-defense or in making an arrest? It must be recollected that the injury he inflicts on the other is, in itself intentional, so that the usual rules of prudence in respect to the handling of weapons are not in question. The only question is whether the defendant was negligent in arriving at the conclusion that the use of the force in question was called for. It is hard to imagine what rules of prudence could normally serve in this situation. Either the defendant is capable of drawing the inferences that a reasonable man would draw or he is not. If he is not, and he is a peace officer, his tendency to make miscalculations would certainly justify his dismissal from the police force. But there is no obvious case for the intervention of the criminal courts.[13]

Despite opposition, few states have removed the reasonableness requirement. Tennessee is one that has. In *Frazier v. State*, a hemophiliac assaulted Frazier. Frazier struck a moderate blow to defend himself. The hemophiliac bled to death from Frazier's moderate blow. The court stated the self-defense requirement as follows:

> If the defendant honestly fears himself to be in danger of life or great bodily harm from the circumstances as they appear to him, and he acts under that fear to kill his assailant, it is justifiable homicide.[14]

PROPORTIONALITY OR REASONABLE FORCE. Defenders may use only reasonable force under the particular circumstances. If someone slaps my face, I cannot shoot my assailant to death. Defenders may use only nondeadly force to repel a nondeadly attack; they may use deadly force only to prevent death or grievous bodily harm. It is always reasonable to use nondeadly force to repel deadly force. Threatened force is justified to stave off threatened physical injury and is reasonable to stop attacks in progress, whether deadly or not. However ominous, threats by themselves do not justify using force. For example, a prisoner threatened another prisoner with sodomy if the prisoner did not immediately pay back a loan. The prisoner stabbed his would-be sodomizer. The court held that mere threats do not justify preventive assaults.[15]

CASE

Was it Reasonable to Kill Her Wife-beating Husband?

State v. Gallegos

104 N.M. 247, 719 P.2d 1268 (App. 1986)

[Mrs. Gallegos was convicted of voluntary manslaughter for killing her husband George. The trial court refused to give her requested instruction on self-defense. She appealed. Justice Bivins delivered the opinion.]

FACTS

Defendant testified that George was a heavy drinker, and she displayed to the jury scars near her eye, on her forehead, and on her nose, resulting from beatings she claimed George administered to her. George's knife was introduced into evidence. Defendant testified that George threatened to cut off her breasts with the knife if her breasts grew any larger. When she was pregnant with their second child, defendant testified that George picked her up and threw her against a wall, causing the premature birth of the child. George's gun also was put into evidence. Defendant claimed that George would place the loaded gun at her head and threaten to shoot her if she ever left him. On numerous occasions, defendant testified, George would tie her hands behind her back and sodomize her to the point of inducing rectal bleeding. He would also force her to engage in fellatio. On one occasion, according to defendant's testimony, the Gallegos' neighbors, aware that George was abusing defendant, summoned the police. The police, however, apparently failed to take action because they had not witnessed the brutality.

On the day defendant killed George, she had taken her older children to school. She testified that when she returned home, George sodomized her against her will, making her cry and bleed. During the course of the day, George apparently drank beer. At one point in the day, defendant said that she told George she was tired of being hurt and that she threatened to leave him. George pulled out his gun and threatened to kill her if she left. Also, on that same day, George had struck one of their sons in the face with a belt buckle.

That evening, after the children went to bed, George asked the victim why she was not a virgin when they married. Defendant answered that she was not a virgin because of her brother. Defendant testified that George became angry, called her a profane name, and said "you probably liked it." At that moment, defendant testified, when she looked at George she saw her father, her brother, and George, all coming toward her.

George then called her into the bedroom. He added something to the effect that if she did not come, he would find someone else. Defendant testified that she feared for her life. She did not know whether George intended to kill her, rape her, or to beat her. Defendant picked up a loaded rifle which George kept in the living room. While George was lying on the bed, defendant testified that she cocked the rifle and shot him. After shooting him, defendant stabbed George numerous times.

OPINION

In order to assert a valid self-defense claim, a defendant must satisfy the three elements of the defense. First, there must have been the appearance to the defendant of immediate danger of death or great bodily harm. Second, the defendant, in fact, must have been put in fear by the apparent danger of death or great bodily harm, and must have killed the victim because of that fear. Finally, the defendant must have acted as a reasonable person would have acted in the same circumstances.

With this in mind, we now analyze the evidence which the defendant presented to determine whether it merited the giving of the self-defense instruction. . . .

We believe that defendant presented evidence sufficient to allow reasonable minds to differ as to whether defendant believed that she was in imminent danger of death or great bodily harm. Defendant was a victim of recurrent violence. On the day of George's death, he had been drinking. Already that day he had sexually abused defendant; he had struck a child in the face with a belt buckle; he had threatened to kill defendant; and, finally, he was angry and calling her into the bedroom. Based upon that evidence, reasonable minds could believe that defendant was afraid. While one inference from George's statement that if defendant did not come into the bedroom he would find someone else, might be that George only desired sex, another equally permissible inference could be that he was using that as a ploy to catch defendant off guard so he could harm her.

She stated she was put in fear. Dr. Cave, a clinical psychologist who regularly treats battered wife cases, testified at the trial. According to Dr. Cave's opinion, the above facts, coupled with a history of prior physical, sexual and verbal abuse and her testing of defendant, the appearance of "great bodily harm, even death," was present. Dr. Cave testified that the history of abuse in this case, as extensive as any she had ever seen, combined with the events of the day, created "great fear" which was real to defendant.

The fear present in this case also was prompted by more than a history of abuse. Based on the brutality which defendant testified she had experienced that day, George's anger, and her knowledge of what had happened to her in similar circumstances, George's calling her into the bedroom could provide the requisite immediacy of danger. . . .

Having found that defendant introduced substantial evidence of imminent danger upon which reasonable minds could differ, we also conclude that defendant has satisfied the remaining two elements of the self-defense instruction. Defendant introduced sufficient evidence of George's past brutality and the ominous events of his final day upon which reasonable minds could disagree as to whether she, in fact, feared for safety and killed George as a result of that fear. Finally, we rule that sufficient evidence was presented to enable reasonable minds to disagree as to whether a reasonably prudent person, in defendant's circumstances, also would have acted in self-defense. To deny the defense of self-defense under the facts of this case would ignore reality.

We, therefore, hold that the trial court erred in rejecting defendant's tendered self-defense instruction. . . .

We reverse and remand this case for a new trial, consistent with this opinion.

CASE DISCUSSION

Assume you are now on the jury at the new trial. How would you apply the three elements of the self-defense rule, as outlined by the court, to this case? Did Mrs. Gallegos kill her husband in self-defense? Precisely what facts lead you to your conclusion? Is it important that she stabbed her husband after shooting him? Why? Was she in imminent or present danger of death or great bodily harm? Did she use force that was reasonable under the circumstances? Explain. What self-defense rule would you write for a criminal code? One commentator notes that

> retaliation, as opposed to defense, is a common problem in cases arising from wife battering and domestic violence. The injured wife waits for the first possibility of striking against a distracted or unarmed husband. The man may even be asleep when the wife finally reacts. Retaliation is the standard case of "taking the law into your own hands." There is no way, under the law, to justify killing a wife batterer or a rapist in retaliation or revenge, however much sympathy there may be for the wife wreaking retaliation. Private citizens cannot act as judge and jury toward each other. They have no authority to pass judgment and to punish each other for past wrongs.

Was Gallegos retaliating? making a preemptive strike? protecting herself? Is it easy to distinguish?

The Retreat Doctrine

What if escape is open to those who are attacked? Must they retreat? Or can they stand their ground? Different values underlie each of these alternatives. The retreat rule places a premium on human life, and discourages inflicting bodily injury and death except as a last resort. A different rule permitting victims to stand their ground against unwarranted attacks rests on the idea that retreat forces innocent people to take a cowardly or humiliating position. This idea is captured by the phrase used to describe the rule: the true man doctrine. Most jurisdictions require retreat if retreat does not unreasonably risk the retreater's life.[16]

Jurisdictions requiring retreat have carved out a major exception to the retreat doctrine: when attacked in their homes, defenders may stand their ground and use deadly force to repel an unprovoked attack, if the unprovoked attack reasonably threatens life or serious bodily injury. A problem arises over just what "home" means. Does it include the entryway? the sidewalk in front of the house? Does it extend to the property line? What if a person lives in a car? a hotel room? or under a bridge? Similarly, does it include businesses?

≡ DEFENSE OF OTHERS

Historically, self-defense meant protecting both the individuals attacked and their immediate families. Although several jurisdictions still require a special relationship, the trend is definitely away from such a prescription. Several states that retain it have relaxed its meaning to include lovers and friends. Many states have abandoned the special relationship requirement altogether. They either write a special provision for defending others, which is the same as that for defending oneself, or they modify their self-defense statutes to read "himself or third persons."[17]

≡ GENERAL PRINCIPLE OF NECESSITY

Some argue that creating special defenses for every situation prevents designing a rational criminal code. They maintain that a defense governed by a principle of necessity makes more sense. The general principle of necessity includes self-defense, as well as other justifications, because it encompasses not only crimes against persons—homicide, rape, and assault—but also most other crimes. Correctly choosing a lesser of two evils constitutes the essence of the necessity principle. The Model Penal Code has adopted a necessity provision that takes these elements into account. When actors believe conduct is necessary to avoid a greater evil, they are justified in causing a lesser evil. (See Appendix, Section 3.02.) Some states, such as Illinois, New York, and Texas, have enacted necessity defense statutes that follow to some extent the Model Penal Code provision.[18]

Self-defense illustrates how the necessity principle works. Self-defense involves a series of discrete, if not always articulated, analytical steps. First, the law identifies two conflicting values and their opposite "evils": the values sanctioning the crime that would be committed if self-defense were not available (the assailant's life), and the value protected by violating the law (the defender's life). The law ranks the defender's life higher than the assailant's. If defenders must choose between protecting their own lives and their assailants', the necessity principle guarantees that those who defend themselves will not suffer criminal punishment for choosing correctly. In other words, self-defense protects those who, out of necessity, choose to cause a lesser evil (injuring or killing their assailants) rather than submit to a greater one (losing their own lives or suffering injury themselves).

The analytical steps in self-defense permit the necessity principle's straightforward application. Other justifications, however, give rise to greater complexity. Until recently, most jurisdictions did not formulate a general necessity principle. Since the Model Penal Code articulated a general principle of necessity, twenty-one states have done so. The Model Penal Code's provision extends the necessity principle beyond self-defense to include (1) destroying property to prevent spreading fire; (2) violating a speed limit to get a dying person to a hospital; (3) throwing cargo overboard to save a sinking vessel and its crew; (4) dispensing drugs without a prescription in an emergency; and (5) breaking and entering a mountain cabin to avoid freezing to death. In all these instances, life, safety, and health are values superior to the strict property interests that actors violate to protect these superior interests.[19]

CASE

Was Trespass Necessary to Save Fetuses' Lives?

Gaetano v. United States

406 A.2d 1291 (D.C. App. 1979)

[The trial court convicted David Gaetano and Amy Donohoo of violating a trespass statute because of a sit-in at a private abortion facility. They appealed. Associate Justice Kelley delivered the opinion.]

FACTS

. . . [A]ppellants and several others staged a protest "sit in" at the Preterm Clinic, a private abortion facility. The protest was a well-orchestrated scenario, which began with two protestors presenting themselves to the receptionist. While these two occupied the receptionist, appellants and others proceeded to the "medical area" behind the desk. Appellants blocked the entrances to the "procedure rooms." They were advised that they were trespassing and would be subject to arrest if they did not leave. Meanwhile, two co-actors had chained themselves to treatment tables; they were not personally informed that they were trespassing. The police arrived shortly thereafter and informed appellants that they would be arrested for unlawful entry if they did not leave the premises. Appellants remained and were placed under arrest and carried, by the police, from the clinic. . . .

Appellants were each found guilty of one count of unlawful entry . . . and sentenced to pay a fine of $50.00. . . .

OPINION

The statute under which appellants were convicted states:

> Any person who, without lawful authority, shall enter, or attempt to enter, any public or private dwelling, building or other property, or part of such dwelling, building or other property, against the will of the lawful occupant or of the person lawfully in charge thereof, or being therein or thereon, without lawful authority to remain therein or thereon shall refuse to quit the same on demand of the lawful occupant, or of the person lawfully in charge thereof, shall be deemed guilty of a misdemeanor, and on conviction thereof shall be punished by a fine not exceeding $100 or imprisonment in jail for not more than six months, or both, in the discretion of the court.

The elements of the crime are clear; they are not at issue here . . . [The defendants argue that they acted out of necessity—they trespassed to save fetal lives.] Appellants' argument concerning necessity is . . . misdirected. . . . [A]ppellants can rely only on their own evidence that abortion terminates the life of the fetus. While correct, such evidence does not support an immediate call to action in violation of the law of the land.

Indeed, when stripped from its rhetoric, the [appellants'] necessity argument . . . is that "public policy" favors the commission of a lesser harm (the commission of what would otherwise be a crime) when this would avoid a greater harm. This argument is what the defendants intended to provide for the jury had their evidence been admitted.

It is important to note that the defendants certainly have moral beliefs which motivate them and permit them to recognize the horror of destroying unborn human life. But, the defendants do not ask to be judged on their moral beliefs. What they asked the trial court was to permit them to produce extrinsic evidence which would establish reasonable and objective, not a moral, basis for their beliefs. They ask to establish that they have been faced with the pressure of circumstances and it is in the public interest to select the lesser of two evils. . . .

The rights to free speech, to assembly, and to petition the government for grievances are a cornerstone of the American system. So, too, is the right to be free from criminal interference. These appellants trespassed on the rights of others and did so without excuse. Therefore . . . the convictions are affirmed.

CASE DISCUSSION

How do you rank the evils here? Does the court say that fetal lives are not as important as property rights? Or does the court say that fetal life did not require trespass to preserve it? Did these defendants honestly believe that it was necessary to commit trespass to protect fetal lives? Was their belief reasonable?

Historically, the defense of necessity appears periodically in English and American cases. The great thirteenth-century jurist Bracton declared that what "is not otherwise lawful, necessity makes lawful." Other famous commentators, such as Sir Francis Bacon, Sir Edward Coke, and Sir Matthew Hale in the sixteenth and seventeenth centuries, concurred with Bracton's judgment. The influential seventeenth-century judge Hobart expressed the argument this way:

> All laws admit certain cases of just excuse, when they are offended in letter, and where the offender is under necessity, either of compulsion or inconvenience.[20]

Early cases record defendants successfully pleading necessity. The most common example in older cases is destroying a house to stop fires from spreading. As early as 1499, jurors could leave a trial without a judge's permission for good cause—to avoid injury from a melee that broke out. In 1500, a prisoner successfully defended against a prison break because he was trying to avoid a fire that burned down the jail. In 1912, a man was acquitted who burned a strip of heather to prevent a fire from spreading.[21]

As a practical matter, the necessity defense creates problems. Most legislatures write statutes—and most lawyers and judges think—in terms of specific defenses for particular crimes. For example, they regard self-defense as a particular defense against homicide, not as a subdivision of the necessity principle. Furthermore, the necessity principle has strong critics. Nineteenth-century historian and judge Sir James F. Stephen believed the necessity defense to be so vague that judges could interpret it to mean anything they wanted. In the same vein, Glanville Williams, a modern criminal law professor, writes:

> It is just possible to imagine cases in which the expediency of breaking the law is so overwhelmingly great that people may be justified in breaking it, but these cases cannot be defined beforehand.[22]

Defining necessity is a major problem and therefore an obstacle to stating clearly how to apply it in real cases. The Model Penal Code provision attempts to deal with this problem by the choice-of-evils concept. The Code does not leave the ranking decision to individuals who claim its protection; legislatures, or judges and juries at trial, must rank the evils in advance. Once actors have made the "right" choice, the Code either frees them entirely from criminal liability or considers the right choice a mitigating circumstance.

CASE

Can You Break and Enter to Avoid Freezing?

State v. Celli

263 N.W.2d 145 (S.D. 1978)

[Defendants were convicted of fourth-degree burglary. They appealed. Justice Porter delivered the opinion.]

FACTS

On Sunday, January 30, 1977, defendants left Deadwood, South Dakota, to go to Newcastle, Wyoming, a distance of approximately seventy-five miles, to secure employment. It was necessary for them to hitchhike, because they had no car. Defendant Brooks had been employed there previously and knew they could both obtain work upon arrival. The sun was shining when they started out, but the day was chilly. They dressed as warmly as they could and began hitchhiking in the morning. Because they received no rides, they were forced to walk all afternoon. At approximately 3:00 P.M. they passed the Cheyenne Crossing store, which is about ten miles from Deadwood. They continued walking for two miles west of the Crossing, when defendant Celli slipped into the snow on the embankment along the road. As he fell he grabbed defendant Brooks, and they tumbled down to the bottom of the embankment. Both defendants tried unsuccessfully to climb up the embankment, but the snow was too deep. They then attempted to cross a small partially frozen creek at the bottom of the embankment, to get to a point where they thought they could get back up on the road. As they crossed the creek both defendants broke through the ice, soaking their footwear, and pants halfway up their legs. After about fifteen minutes of effort, they made it back onto the highway. By that time their outer clothing was damp and covered with snow. The temperature was below freezing.

They decided that they would try to hitchhike back to Deadwood, but were unable to get a ride. The sun was beginning to set and they were numb from the cold. They had traveled about one-half mile back from the point where they slipped off the road when they noticed the cabin in question. The stiffness of their feet from the cold was making it difficult for them to walk, so they entered the cabin, breaking the lock on the front door. Defendant Celli immediately crawled into a bed to warm up, and defendant Brooks attempted to light a fire in the fireplace. They rummaged through drawers to look for matches, which they finally located and started a fire. Finally defendant Celli emerged from the bedroom, took off his wet moccasins, socks and coat, placed them near the fire, and sat down to warm himself. After warming up somewhat they checked the kitchen for edible food. That morning they had shared a can of beans, but had not eaten since. All they found was dry macaroni, which they could not cook because there was no water.

A neighbor noticed the smoke from the fireplace and notified the police. When the police entered the cabin, both defendants were warming themselves in front of the fireplace. The defendants were searched, but nothing belonging to the cabin owners was found. They were taken to the Lawrence County jail, where they remained incarcerated until February 25, 1977, the day of the trial. They were tried and convicted of fourth-degree burglary. They appeal from their convictions.

OPINION

Defendants briefed and argued several other issues on appeal, one being that under the facts here they were entitled to raise the common law defense of necessity, and that their proposed instruction submitting that defense to the jury should have been given. Reversed on other grounds.

CASE DISCUSSION

The great French novel *Les Miserables* dealt with a compelling problem: whether it was right for a father to steal a loaf of bread to feed his starving children. That problem is not always fiction, as *State v. Celli* makes clear. Because it requires balancing values, the necessity defense creates both ethical and social dilemmas. In *Celli*, the conflict was between life and property, between breaking and entering or freezing to death. The natural thing to do in the situation is just what the defendants did. How, then, should the law view their conduct? How would you balance the values? Did Celli make the right decision when he broke and entered to avert freezing? Should the law support his choice?

Sharp disagreement has always existed over stealing to avert hunger. The classic case is Jean Valjean in *Les Miserables*, who stole a loaf of bread to feed his starving children. Conflicting comments abound throughout Anglo-American law regarding "economic necessity." In *Maxims*, Francis Bacon asserted that stealing food to satisfy present hunger was not larceny. In *Leviathan*, written later in the seventeenth century, Thomas Hobbes was more cautious, asserting that hungry people could take food during great famine if they could not get it either with money or through charity. In *Pleas of the Crown*, Hawkins claimed that necessity was not a defense if hunger was due to defendants' own unthriftiness. Late in the seventeenth century, Sir Matthew Hale stated the law as it is today; he rejected the defense altogether, because (1) the poor are already adequately cared for, (2) "[m]en's properties would be under a strange insecurity, being laid open to other men's necessities, whereof no man can possibly judge, but the party himself," and (3) pardons can resolve economic necessity cases. Blackstone adopted the same rule and reasoning in the eighteenth century, and American law imported it from him. The doctrine has prevailed since then in both America and England.[23]

Blackstone and Hale have not persuaded everyone. Professor Glanville Williams assesses it this way:

> Although Hale and Blackstone settled the rule that economic necessity is no defense, their arguments were not impressive. The Crown's power of pardon really means the discretion of a politician who happens to be Home Secretary, and its existence is hardly a valid justification for what may otherwise be thought to be imperfect law. It is not a sincere argument to say that no one can judge the extremity of want, especially when the argument goes on to say that the Home Secretary can judge it. In fact, Blackstone's opinion would have the logical result of ruling out the whole defense of necessity in criminal law, including the defenses of self-defense and duress; yet Blackstone himself admitted them. The argument based upon the existence of the poor law has a much stronger foundation; but English social history does not suggest that the scale occurred after Blackstone's day, in the troubled years following the Napoleonic wars, when public assistance was kept at only just above starvation level, notwithstanding the desperate straits of the working classes and the growing wealth of farmers and landlords. It became clear at that time that no trust could be placed in the executive to look with sympathetic eye upon the defense of economic necessity. On the contrary, the hunger riots and machine breaking that inevitably followed from the mass misery were vindictively suppressed. If the judges of this period had had the courage to recognize famine as an excuse for stealing, they might have helped to bring the Government to a realization of the need for adequate public relief.
>
> Whatever the defects of the poor law in the past, it can hardly be doubted that the only satisfactory solution of the problem of economic necessity is through the provision of social services that prevent the question arising. Otherwise an impossible conflict is created between humanitarianism and social exigencies. No society, capitalist or communist, can tolerate a state of affairs in which the poorest are allowed to help themselves. The law must set its face against anarchy, but it can morally do so only on condition of itself making provision for the relief of extreme need.[24]

≡ THE USE OF FORCE IN EXECUTING PUBLIC DUTIES

Public executioners throw switches to electrocute condemned murderers; soldiers shoot and kill wartime enemies; police officers use force to make arrests or to take citizens' property pursuant to search warrants. In all these examples, individuals' lives, liberty, and property are intentionally taken away. Yet, none of these examples is a crime. Why? Because all the actors were doing their jobs, and the deprivations they caused were justified because they were carried out as public duties.

These examples illustrate the justification called execution of public duty. The defense is at least as old as the sixteenth century, as its common-law definition illustrates:

> A public officer is justified in using reasonable force against the person of another, or in taking his property, when he acts pursuant to a valid law, court order, or process, requiring or authorizing him so to act.[25]

The values that underlie the execution-of-public-duty defense are clear: Once the state legitimately formulates laws, citizens must obey them; the law takes precedence over citizens' property, their liberty, and even their lives. Therefore, the value in enforcing the law ranks higher than individual property, liberty, and life.

The public duty defense arouses most controversy over the power of the police to kill suspects. A furious debate has raged over whether, and under what circumstances, the police may lawfully kill fleeing suspects. Some say the defense should cover officers who "need" to kill in order to make arrests. Others insist that only protecting officers' or other innocent people's lives justifies killing—that police have only the defense of self-defense belonging to private citizens. Still others believe that officers cannot shoot at fleeing suspects if doing so endangers innocent lives.

At one time, state laws authorized police officers to kill when necessary to effect felony arrests, including property crimes. Recently, however, the Supreme Court has restricted the constitutionality of police use of deadly force under the Fourth Amendment search and seizure clause (see *Tennessee v. Garner*, excerpted later in this section). Furthermore, police departments have established rules that prescribe in detail when officers can use force, including deadly force, in arresting suspects.[26]

The argument favoring the police power to kill in order to arrest fleeing suspects is based not only on protecting lives but also on maintaining respect for law enforcement authority. One commentator said:

> I am convinced that only through truly effective power of arrest can law be satisfactorily enforced. Obviously until violators are brought before the courts the law's sanctions cannot be applied to them. But effectiveness in making arrests requires more than merely pitting the footwork of policemen against that of suspected criminals. An English director of public prosecutions once explained to me that the English police had no need to carry pistols because (1) no English criminal would think of killing a police officer, and (2) even if a suspected offender should outrun an officer in the labyrinth of London he could be found eventually in Liverpool or Birmingham. As the director put it, if a man offends in his own district everyone knows him, if he goes somewhere else everyone notices him.
>
> [Without such power, he continued] we say to the criminal, "You are foolish. No matter what you have done you are foolish if you submit to arrest. The officer dare not take the risk of shooting at you. If you can outrun him, if you are faster than he is, you are free, and God bless you. I feel entirely unwilling to give that benediction to the modern criminal.[27]

The value of general obedience to the law rests on the reasonable assumption that life, liberty, and property mean little without order. The power to kill in order to make an arrest is therefore grounded not only on the value of life but also on the need for law observance in general. On the other hand, critics contend that the police power to kill creates social problems. More than twenty years ago, during the troubled 1960s, the United States attorney general, Ramsey Clarke, commented:

> In these dog days of 1968, we have heard much loose talk of shooting looters. This talk must stop. The need is to train adequate numbers of police to prevent riots and looting altogether. Where prevention fails, looters must be arrested not shot. The first need in a civil disorder is to restore order. To say that when the looting starts, the shooting starts means either that shooting is preferable to arrest, or that there are [sic] not enough police protection, or the unpredictable nature of a disorder makes arrest impossible. Other techniques—including the use of tear gas—may be necessary. The use of deadly force is neither necessary, effective nor tolerable.
>
> Far from being effective, shooting looters divides, angers, embitters, drives to violence. It creates the very problems its advocates claim is their purpose to avoid. Persons under the influence of alcohol killed 25,000 Americans in automobile accidents in 1967. Fewer than 250 people have died in all riots since 1964. Looters, as such, killed no one. Why not shoot drunken drivers? What is it that causes some to call for shooting looters when no one is heard to suggest the same treatment for a far deadlier and less controllable crime?
>
> Is the purpose to protect property? Bank embezzlers steal ten times more money each year than bank robbers. Should we shoot embezzlers? What do the police themselves believe? It is the police to whom some would say, pull the trigger when looters are fleeing—perhaps dozens of looters fleeing toward a crowd; women, children; some making trouble, some committing crime, some trying to talk sense to a mob, to cool it.[28]

CASE

Did Hymon Violate the Constitution When He Shot Garner?

Tennessee v. Garner

471 U.S. 1, 105 S.Ct. 1694, 85 L.Ed.2d 1 (1985)

[Justice White delivered the opinion, joined by Justices Brennan, Marshall, Blackmun, Powell, and Stevens. Justice O'Connor filed a dissenting opinion, joined by Chief Justice Burger and Justice Rehnquist.]

FACTS

At about 10:45 P.M. on October 3, 1974, Memphis Police Officers Elton Hymon and Leslie Wright were dispatched to answer a "prowler inside call." Upon arriving at the scene they saw a woman standing on her porch gesturing toward the adjacent house. She told them she had heard glass breaking and that "they" or "someone" was breaking in next door. While Wright radioed the dispatcher to say that they were on the scene, Hymon went behind the house. He heard a door slam and saw someone run across the back yard. The fleeing suspect, who was appellee-respondent's descendent, Edward Garner, stopped at a 6-feet-high chain link fence at the edge of the yard. With the aid of a flashlight, Hymon was able to see Garner's face and hands. He saw no sign of a weapon, and, though not certain, was "reasonable sure" and "figured" that Garner was unarmed. He thought Garner was 17 or 18 years old and about 5'5" or 5'7" tall. While Garner was crouched at the base of the fence, Hymon called out "police, halt" and took a few steps toward him. Garner began to climb over the fence. Convinced that if Garner made it over the fence he would elude capture, Hymon shot him. The bullet hit Garner in the back of the head. Garner was taken by ambulance to a hospital, where he died on the operating table. Ten dollars and a purse taken from the house were found on his body.

In using deadly force to prevent escape, Hymon was acting under the authority of a Tennessee statute and pursuant to Police Department policy. The statute provides that "[i]f, after notice of the intention to arrest the defendant, he either flee or forcibly resist, the officer may use all the necessary means to effect the arrest." Tenn. Code Ann. § 40–7–108 (1982). The Department policy was slightly more restrictive than the statute, but still allowed the use of deadly force in cases of burglary. The incident was reviewed by the Memphis Police Firearm's Review Board and presented to a grand jury. Neither took any action.

Garner's father then brought this action in the Federal District Court for the Western District of Tennessee, seeking damages under 42 U.S.C. § 1983 for asserted violations of Garner's constitutional rights. The complaint alleged that the shooting violated the Fourth, Fifth, Sixth, Eighth, and Fourteenth Amendments of the United States Constitution. It named as defendants Officer Hymon, the Police Department, its Director, and the Mayor and city of Memphis. After a 3-day bench trial, the District Court entered judgement for all defendants. It dismissed the claims against the Mayor and the Director for lack of evidence. It then concluded that Hymon's actions were authorized by the Tennessee statute, which in turn was constitutional. Hymon had employed the only reasonable and practicable means of preventing Garner's escape. Garner had "recklessly and heedlessly attempted to vault over the fence to escape, thereby assuming the risk of being fired upon."

The District Court . . . found that the statute, and Hymon's actions, were constitutional. The Court of Appeals reversed and remanded. . . .

OPINION

. . . Whenever an officer restrains the freedom of a person to walk away, he has seized that person. . . . [T]here can be no question that apprehension by the use of deadly force is a seizure subject to the reasonableness requirement of the Fourth Amendment.

A police officer may arrest a person if he has probable cause to believe that person committed a crime. Petitioners and appellant argue that if this requirement is satisfied the Fourth Amendment has nothing to say about *how* that seizure is made. This submission ignores the many cases in which this Court, by balancing the extent of the intrusion against the need for it, has examined the reasonableness of the manner in which a search or seizure is conducted. . . .

The use of deadly force to prevent the escape of all felony suspects, whatever the circumstances, is constitutionally unreasonable. It is not better that all felony suspects die than that they escape. Where the suspect poses no immediate threat to the officer and no threat to others, the harm resulting from failing to apprehend him does not justify the use of deadly force to do so. It is no doubt unfortunate when a suspect who is in sight escapes, but the fact the police arrive a little late or are a little slower afoot does not always justify killing the suspect. A police officer may not seize an unarmed, nondangerous suspect by shooting him dead. The Tennessee statute is unconstitutional insofar as it authorizes the use of deadly force against such fleeing suspects. . . .

Officer Hymon could not reasonably have believed that Garner—young, slight, and unarmed—posed any threat. Indeed, Hymon never attempted to justify his actions on any basis other than the need to prevent escape. . . . [T]he fact that Garner was a suspected burglar could not, without regard to the other circumstances, automatically justify the use of deadly force. Hymon did not have probable cause to believe that Garner, whom he correctly believed to be unarmed, posed any physical danger to himself or to others.

DISSENT

For purposes of Fourth Amendment analysis, I agree with the Court that Officer Hymon "seized" Garner by shooting him. Whether that seizure was reasonable and therefore permitted by the Fourth Amendment requires a careful balancing of the important public interest in crime prevention and detection and the nature and quality of the intrusion upon legitimate interests of the individual. In striking this balance here, it is crucial to acknowledge that police use of deadly force to apprehend a fleeing criminal suspect falls within the "rubric of police conduct . . . necessarily [involving] swift action predicated upon the on-the-spot observations of the officer on the beat." . . .

The public interest involved in the use of deadly force as a last resort to apprehend a fleeing burglary suspect relates primarily to the serious nature of the crime. Household burglaries represent not only the illegal entry into a person's home, but also "pos[e] a real risk of serious harm to others." According to recent Department of Justice statistics, "[t]hree-fifths of all rapes in the home, three-fifths of all home robberies, and about a third of home aggravated and simple assaults are committed by burglars." . . .

Against the strong public interests justifying the conduct at issue here must be weighed the individual interests implicated in the use of deadly force by police officers. The majority declares that "[t]he suspect's fundamental interest in his own life need not be elaborated upon." This blithe assertion hardly provides an adequate substitute for the majority's failure to acknowledge the distinctive manner in which the suspect's interest in his life is even exposed to risk. For purposes of this case, we must recall that the police officer, in the course of investigating a nighttime burglary, had reasonable cause to arrest the suspect and ordered him to halt. The officer's use of force resulted because the suspected burglar refused to heed this command and the officer reasonably believed that there was no means short of firing his weapon to apprehend the suspect. . . . "[T]he policeman's hands should not be tied merely because of the possibility that the suspect will fail to cooperate with legitimate actions by law enforcement personnel." . . .

CASE DISCUSSION

Should the Fourth Amendment prohibit the use of deadly force to arrest property felons? Is residential burglary simply a property crime? Do you agree with the majority or dissent? Explain. Will this rule embolden criminals? Defend your answer.

≡ RESISTING UNLAWFUL ARREST

A problem related to the execution of public duty arises when citizens use force to resist arrests. Jurisdictions differ over how much force citizens may use to resist unlawful arrests. They range across this spectrum:

1. Citizens cannot use force against even a plainclothes officer whom they know or believe is an officer.
2. Citizens can never use force against a known police officer.
3. Citizens can use nondeadly force against police officers.
4. If citizens use deadly force against officers, resisting unlawful arrest may reduce the charge from criminal homicide to a lesser degree of homicide.

Two policies underlie restricting citizens' use of force against police officers. These are (1) to encourage obedience to police, and (2) to encourage preferable remedies to force, such as civil lawsuits against the police, their departments, or the governmental units they serve.

Arguments favoring citizens' use of force to resist unlawful arrests are based on two major premises. First, citizens in a free society need not submit passively to detention when the government unlawfully deprives them of liberty. Under such circumstances, the use of force is crucial to a free society. Second, illegal arrests cause even the most otherwise restrained people to lose control, at least to the extent that they feel outraged at the arrest. Realistically therefore, citizens will resist arrests they believe are unlawful. Legislatures and courts have never accepted these arguments. The Maine Supreme Court addressed a citizen's use of force to resist arrest in *Maine v. Austin*.

CASE

Can You Use Force to Resist an Unlawful Arrest?

Maine v. Austin

381 A.2d 652 (Me. 1978)

[Chief Justice McKusick delivered the opinion.]

FACTS

At approximately 1 A.M. on July 11, 1976, Officer John Bernard, Jr., police chief of the Town of Mexico, and Officer Gregory Gallant of the Mexico Police Department, stationed themselves in a marked police cruiser opposite the MGM lounge on Main Street in Mexico, for the purpose of investigating repeated citizen complaints of loud noises from persons leaving the MGM around closing time. The officers observed several patrons come out of the MGM, some congregating in small groups on the sidewalk. Although some persons in the crowd were using loud language, the officers took no action until Chief Bernard heard someone shout an obscene name. As the same person repeated the phrase twice more, Chief Bernard singled out the defendant as the speaker and observed that he appeared to be directing his speech to a group of some five persons who were standing in an area between the MGM and an adjacent restaurant. As Chief Bernard watched, Austin crossed the street and started a conversation with one John Porello, who was seated in his parked car about 50 feet from the passenger side of the police cruiser. Chief Bernard, who was sitting in the seat with the window down, then heard Austin repeat the obscenity. Austin then put his arm up over the top of Porello's vehicle and, pointing his hand directly at the cruiser, called out another obscene name. Chief Bernard immediately got out of the cruiser and went over to Austin. When asked whether "he would clean up his mouth" and told by Chief Bernard that he did not appreciate Austin's name-calling, Austin replied that he had not called the Chief the obscene name. Chief Bernard, at that moment, advised Austin that he was under arrest for disorderly conduct.

Officer Gallant, who by that time had joined the others at the Porello car, assisted Chief Bernard, who was unsuccessfully attempting to put Austin in handcuffs, by picking Austin up around his waist from the rear and physically carrying him to the cruiser. There, the officers succeeded in handcuffing him, but in the process of placing him in the back seat of the cruiser, Austin kicked out at Officer Gallant, striking him in the thigh. On the ride to the police station, Austin continued to be unruly, positioning himself over the back of the front seat "screaming obscenities and threats." At one point, when Chief Bernard attempted to push him back down into the rear seat, Austin fell back and with his foot struck Chief Bernard in the area of his left ear, neck, and jaw. At the station, Austin was charged with disorderly conduct and two counts of assault [and was convicted. He appealed.]

OPINION

The thrust of the defendant's arguments on appeal concerns his asserted right to resist an illegal arrest with force. Prior to the effective date of the Criminal Code, May 1, 1976, Maine followed the prevailing common law rule that

> [a]n illegal arrest is an assault and battery. The person so attempted to be restrained of his liberty has the same right, and only the same right, to use force in defending himself as he would have in repelling any other assault and battery. *State v. Robinson,* 72 A.2d 260, 262 (1950).

Reading the provisions of the Criminal Code as a whole shows, however, that Robinson no longer states the law of Maine.

We thus read the Criminal Code as an integrated whole declaring the entire law relating to criminal responsibility for violence during an attempted arrest. In general, under [Section 107 of] the code a person being arrested must not respond violently. On the other hand, a police officer is given by the code substantial leeway in using nondeadly force in making an arrest—namely, that amount he reasonably believes necessary to make the arrest—provided he does not know the arrest is illegal. Section 108 gives the arrested person a right of self-defense against unlawful or excessive force used by the police officer; but if he reacts violently to nondeadly force applied by the police, he takes his chances on being able later to show the officer was not justified under section 107.

The legislature has thus cast the advantage on the side of law enforcement officers, leaving the person arrested in most cases to pursue his rights, not through violent self-help, but through prompt hearing before a magistrate with prompt consideration for release on bail or personal recognizance. At the same time, the police should exercise their code-granted prerogatives with restraint, with police departments using administrative discipline to assure that individual officers in fact use no more force than necessary to effect arrests. Violence breeds violence, whoever starts it.

The defendant has assigned as error the presiding justice's refusal to grant the following jury instruction:

> That when a person is illegally arrested, he is privileged to use such force as is reasonably necessary and calculated, in view of the totality of the circumstances, to resist and deter the unlawful apprehension and detention by the party effecting the arrest.

The requested instruction was obviously derived from the rule of State v. Robinson, which no longer is the law. The requested instruction was properly denied. The presiding justice's charge correctly stated the principles of law relevant to the defendant's defense of justification.

We have examined the defendant's remaining claims of error, and finding none with merit, the entry must be: Appeal denied.

Judgments affirmed.

CASE DISCUSSION

Self-defense does not mean defense only against death or bodily injury. It also includes defending personal liberty. Resisting unlawful arrests is a good, but controversial, example. Can citizens ever use force against the police, and if so, how much force can they use? *Maine v. Austin* answers these questions, at least as far as concerns Maine's law on the matter. Note the competing interests present in permitting citizens to use force against unlawful arrests.

DEFENSE OF HOMES AND PROPERTY

Ranking values is a complicated business, as shown by the foregoing discussion concerning executing the public duty to make arrests. Similarly complex values lie under the justification to defend property. From the early days of the common law, force, including deadly force, was justified in protecting homes:

> If any person attempts . . . to break open a house in the nighttime (which extends also to an attempt to burn it) and shall be killed in such attempt, the slayer shall be acquitted and discharged. This reaches not to . . . the breaking open of any house in the daytime, unless it carries with it an attempt of robbery.[29]

Nearly all states authorize the use of force to protect homes; some states go further and adopt provisions authorizing the use of force to protect property. Texas, for example, has enacted the following statute:

§ 9.42 Deadly Force to Protect Property
   A person is justified in using deadly force against another to protect land or tangible, movable property:
    (1) if he would be justified in using force against the other under Section 9.41 of this code; and

(2) when and to the degree he reasonably believes the deadly force is immediately necessary:
  (A) to prevent the other's imminent commission of arson, burglary, robbery, aggravated robbery, theft during the nighttime, or criminal mischief during the nighttime; or
  (B) to prevent the other who is fleeing immediately after committing burglary, robbery, aggravated robbery, or theft during the nighttime from escaping with the property; and
(3) he reasonably believes that:
  (A) the land or property cannot be protected or recovered by any other means; or
  (B) the use of force other than deadly force to protect or recover the land or property would expose the actor or another to a substantial risk of death or serious bodily injury.

CASE

Can You Use Deadly Force to Protect Your Home?

People v. Guenther

740 P.2d 971 (Colo. 1987)

[The people appealed from a judgment dismissing the charges of second-degree murder, first-degree assault, and the commission of a crime of violence filed against the defendant, David Alan Guenther. The judgment of dismissal was reversed and the case was remanded to the district court for further proceedings. Chief Justice Quinn delivered the opinion.]

FACTS

During the evening of April 19 and the early morning hours of April 20, 1986, a small group of people were drinking and playing pool at the home of Michael and Josslyn Volosin, which was located across the street and two houses to the north of David and Pam Guenther's home. Late in the evening three of the men left the party and went to the Guenther's. One of the men began banging on the Guenther's car, shouting obscenities, and challenging David Guenther to come out of the house. The men left after Pam Guenther told them her husband was not at home and she was going to call the police. The police arrived, discussed the incident with Pam Guenther, went to Volosins' home and talked to Josslyn Volosin, and then left.

The events that followed constitute the basis for the criminal charges against the defendant and for the district court's subsequent dismissal of those charges. The witnesses' versions of these events, however, are in substantial conflict with one another. Michael Volosin stated that shortly after the police left he heard a loud noise at his front door. When he saw no one at his door, he ran to the Guenthers' house and knocked on the front door, whereupon Pam Guenther opened the door, grabbed him, threw him onto the grass, and had him on the ground when her husband came out of the house shooting. Volosin's version was corroborated by Bonnie Smith, a neighbor who observed the incident from her window. . . .

In contrast to the account given by Michael Volosin and Bonnie Smith, Pam Guenther testified that when she went to the front door and opened it, Michael Volosin grabbed her, pulled her out the door, threw her against the wall, and began to beat her up. Pam Guenther stated that as she and Michael began struggling, she screamed for her husband to get the gun. It was her further testimony that Josslyn Volosin had appeared and was trying to break up the fight when the sound of gunshots was heard. After Pam Guenther screamed for help, the defendant came to the front door of his house and, from the doorway, fired four shots from a Smith and Wesson .357 Magnum six-inch revolver. The defendant's account was substantially the same as his wife's.

One shot hit and wounded Michael Volosin, who was lying on the ground next to the Guenther's porch. Robbie Alan Wardwell, a guest of the Volosins, was wounded by a second shot as he was walking across the Guenther's front yard to help Josslyn Volosin break up the fight. A third shot killed Josslyn Volosin. There was conflicting testimony as to whether she was hit while standing near the Guenthers' front porch or in the street as she was running away.

OPINION

The issues raised on appeal center on section 18–1–704.5, 8B, C.R.S. (1986). . . .

(1) The general assembly hereby recognizes that the citizens of Colorado have a right to expect absolute safety within their own homes.
(2) . . . [A]ny occupant of a dwelling is justified in using any degree of physical force, including deadly physical force, against another person when that other person has made an unlawful entry into the dwelling, and when the occupant has a reasonable belief that such other person has committed a crime in the dwelling in addition to the uninvited entry, or is committing or intends to commit a crime against a person or property in addition to the uninvited entry, and when the occupant reasonably believes that such other person might use any physical force, however slight, against any occupant.
(3) Any occupant of a dwelling using physical force, including deadly force, in accordance with the provisions in subsection (2) of this section shall be immune from criminal prosecution for the use of such force.
(4) Any occupant of a dwelling using physical force, including deadly physical force, in accordance with the provisions of subsection (2) of this section shall be immune from any civil liability for injuries or death resulting from the use of such force. . . .

In accordance with the explicit terms of the statute, we hold that section 18–1–704.5 provides the home occupant with immunity from prosecution only for force used against one who has made an unlawful entry into the dwelling, and that this immunity does not extend to force used against non-entrants. . . .

The district court . . . erred in concluding that section 18–1–704.5(3) immunizes from criminal prosecution an occupant of a dwelling who uses force against persons who did not actually enter the dwelling. . . . The defendant . . . [is] entitled to immunity from prosecution for any force used against any person or persons who actually entered his dwelling, but [is] . . . not immune from prosecution for any force used against non-entrants.

We reverse the district court's order of dismissal, and we remand the case for further proceedings not inconsistent with the views herein expressed.

CASE DISCUSSION

Do you think the court interpreted the statute correctly? Should the law known as the "make my day law" apply to intruders onto the Guenthers' front lawn? their porch? If you were writing the law, how would you write it? How would you interpret it? Should the law cover any intrusions, or only those that threaten life? Does the court make clear just what the statute means? Does it mean that citizens may use deadly force to protect their property even if such intrusions do not threaten life? How should it read?

═══ CONSENT

The consent defense constitutes a special defense to some crimes. In theft, for example, taking property without the owner's consent is central to the crime. In rape, too, consent eliminates the *mens rea*—the intent is to have sexual penetration without consent. Furthermore, the same act may be criminal in one situation and appropriate in another. Grabbing another forcibly around the ankles and bringing him or her abruptly to the ground is assault if it happens between strangers on the street, but it generates thunderous approval from fans supporting the defensive team if it takes place on the playing field during the Super Bowl. A surgeon commits neither assault and battery by cutting into a patient's body nor murder if the patient dies. Furthermore, consent constitutes either the general defense of justification or excuse. Consent justifies conduct or results when they were right under the circumstances.[30]

Consent gives rise to two critical issues: (1) To what crimes can victims consent? For example, can you consent to your own murder? (2) What constitutes legal consent? For example, can a four-year-old child legally consent to sexual penetration? In all jurisdictions, consent constitutes a defense to crime if it negates a material element (such as consent to sexual penetration). In most jurisdictions, consent constitutes a justification or excuse only when conduct causes only minor injuries, such as in some assault and battery. Courts tend to recognize the defense only when (1) no serious injury results, such as with a slap in the face that requires no medical treatment; (2) society widely accepts the risk of injury, such as in ice hockey, football, soccer, and boxing; and (3) the defendant's conduct has a beneficial result, such as with a doctor who performs surgery.[31]

"Victims" must *legally* consent to the conduct or its result for their consent to constitute a defense. Parties must consent voluntarily; that is, consent must result from their own free will without compulsion or duress. The person consenting must be competent to do so; youth, intoxication, or mental abnormality might disable the consent. Consent by fraud or deceit renders the consent ineffective. Finally, forgiveness *after* defendants have committed crimes does not constitute consent. (See chapter 9 for consent in sex offenses.)

CASE

Can You Consent to an Assault?

State v. Brown

143 N.J. Super. 571, 364 A.2d 27 (1976)

[Brown was convicted of atrocious assault and battery. He appealed. Supreme Court justice Bachman delivered the opinion.]

FACTS

[Reginald] and Mrs. Brown, the victim, had an understanding to the effect that if she consumed any alcoholic beverages (and/or became intoxicated), he would punish her by physically assaulting her. The testimony revealed that the victim was an alcoholic. On the day of the alleged crime she indulged in some spirits, apparently to Mr. Brown's dissatisfaction. As per their agreement, defendant sought to punish Mrs. Brown by severely beating her with his hands and other objects.

OPINION

There are a few situations in which the consent of the victim (actual or implied) is a defense. These situations usually involve ordinary physical contact or blows incident to sports such as football, boxing, or wrestling. But this is expected and understood by the participants.

The state cannot later be heard to charge a participant with criminal assault upon another participant if the injury complained of resulted from activity that is reasonably within the rules and purview of the sports activity.

However this is not to be confused with sports activities that are not sanctioned by the state. Thus, street fighting which is disorderly and mischievous on many obvious grounds (even if for a purse and consented to), and encounters of that kind which tend to and have the specific objective of causing bodily harm, serve no useful purpose, but rather tend to breach the peace and thus are unlawful. No one is justified in striking another, except it be in self defense, and similarly whenever two persons go out to strike each other and do so, each is guilty of an assault. It is no matter who strikes the first blow, for the law proscribes such striking.

[I]t is a matter of common knowledge that a normal person in full possession of his or her mental faculties does not freely and seriously consent to the use upon his or herself of force likely to produce great bodily harm. Those persons that do freely consent to such force and bodily injury no doubt require the enforcement of the very laws that were enacted to protect them and other humans. A general principle of law is that a person cannot contract out of protective legislation passed for his other benefit. "If an act be prohibited, it cannot be the subject of a valid contract. The laws of this State and others that have dealt with the question are simply and unequivocally clear that the defense of consent cannot be available to a defendant charged with any type of physical assault that causes appreciable injury. If the law were otherwise, it would not be conducive to a peaceful, orderly and healthy society.

This court concludes that, as a matter of law, no one has the right to beat another even though that person may ask for it. Assault and battery cannot be consented to by a victim, for the State makes it unlawful and is not a party to any such agreement between the victim and perpetrator. To allow an otherwise criminal act to go unpunished because of the victim's consent would not only threaten the security of our society but also might tend to detract from the force of the moral principles underlying the criminal law. A major dissent to the view that the victim's consent may be a valid defense to a charge of assault has been voiced by the noted English jurist, Sir Patrick Devlin, who stated,

> It is not a defense to any form of criminal assault that the victim thought his punishment well deserved and consented to it. To make a good defense the accused must prove that the law gave him the right to chastise and that he exercised it reasonably. There are certain standards of behavior or moral principles which society requires to be observed; and the breach of them is an offense not merely against the person who is injured, but against society as a whole.[32]

Thus, for the reasons given, the State has an interest in protecting those persons who invite, consent to and permit others to assault and batter them. Not to enforce these laws which are geared to protect such people would seriously threaten the dignity, peace, health and security of our society. Affirmed.

CASE DISCUSSION

The court ruled that consent to assault is no defense because victims cannot contract away their interests, especially when it involves a state interest as well. Do you agree? Doesn't the state also have an interest in curing drunkenness? Why should the law intervene where citizens agree to what otherwise would be crimes? Is Mrs. Brown really an assault victim? What rule would you make for this case?

SUMMARY

This chapter confronted defendants who denied criminal liability because they were justified. They assumed full responsibility for their actions but maintained that special circumstances justified their conduct or its result. They were confronted with a dilemma: choosing between two evils. They killed or injured persons, or violated property, to avoid an imminent or present greater evil.

Theoretically, these evils—and the greater ones defended against—apply the general principle of necessity to specific crimes. Practically, however, neither codes, courts, nor lawyers for that matter think in such broad, theoretical terms. Rather they look at specific defenses to particular crimes. Hence, self-defense means defending against homicide charges or, less frequently, rape and assault. Other defenses, such as executing public duties and protecting property, also occur in this light. Necessity appears as a special defense, not a general principle, applying to cases such as where freezing people break into deserted cabins to keep warm.

Viewed in this practical light, the distinction between justification (responsible action that is right under the circumstances) and excuse (wrongful action for which perpetrators are not responsible) is not important. Nevertheless, justification does differ from excuse, even though both bring about the same practical result: acquittal, reduced charges, or punishments. The distinction makes sense of the "laundry list" of offenses usually presented in cases and criminal codes.

Finally, distinguishing between justification and excuse is not always easy. In consent, defendants may have meant to do what they did, but since their "victims" consented, what they did was right under the circumstances. Or, even if what defendants did was wrong, their "victims" are responsible because they consented to it.[33]

QUESTIONS FOR DISCUSSION AND REVIEW

1. Is an honest belief in danger enough to justify using force, or must the belief in danger be reasonable?

2. Does the retreat doctrine belong in the defense of self-defense? Why or why not?

3. Should there be a general principle of necessity? How should it be formulated? Explain.

4. To what extent may force be used to protect property?

5. Should there be a defense of economic necessity? How should it be formulated?

6. When is it justifiable for public officers to use force?

7. Should consent of the victim ever be a defense to crime?

═══ SUGGESTED READINGS

1. George Fletcher, "Justification," in *Encyclopedia of Crime and Justice*, vol. 3, ed. Sanford H. Kadish (New York: Free Press, 1983), pp. 941–46, is an excellent introduction to the theory of justification in criminal law. Professor Fletcher describes and assesses the scope and criteria for justification, balancing evils and the imminent risk requirement.

2. American Law Institute, *Model Penal Code and Commentaries*, vol. 2 (Philadelphia: American Law Institute, 1985), pp. 8–22, is the fullest discussion of the principle of necessity by the foremost authorities on the subject. Although written primarily for lawyers, it is worth the serious student's effort.

3. George F. Dix, "Self Defense," in *Encyclopedia of Crime and Justice*, vol. 3, pp. 946–53, is a good general discussion of self-defense. Professor Dix covers the main elements in the defense, the defense by battered wives who attack their husbands, the retreat doctrine, the defense of others, and the use of force to resist arrest.

4. Rollin M. Perkins and Ronald N. Boyce, *Criminal Law*, 3d ed. (Mineola, N.Y.: Foundation Press, 1982), pp. 1074–92, treats thoroughly the consent defense in criminal law. Both the legal effect of consent and the crimes to which consent is a defense are described, and arguments both for and against consent are appraised, as is the law as it stands in several jurisdictions.

═══ NOTES

1. Rollin M. Perkins and Ronald N. Boyce, *Criminal Law*, 3d ed. (Mineola, N.Y.: Foundation Press, 1982), chap. 8–10.

2. American Law Institute, *Model Penal Code and Commentaries*, vol. 2 (Philadelphia: American Law Institute, 1985), pt. I, page 3.

3. See Arnold H. Loewy, *Criminal Law* (St. Paul: West Publishing Co., 1987), pp. 192–204, for a brief introduction to the topics of burdens and amount of proof.

4. Perkins and Boyce, *Criminal Law*, pp. 926–32; Jerome Hall, *General Principles of Criminal Law*, 2d ed. (Indianapolis: Bobbs-Merrill, 1960), pp. 86–88.

5. Hall, *General Principles of Criminal Law*, pp. 97–102; Carol Byrne, "Was Mercy in This Killing?" *Minneapolis Star and Tribune* (May 1, 1988), p. 1A; Carol Byrne, "An Old Man Starts a New Life—In Prison," *Minneapolis Star and Tribune* (June 5, 1988), p. 1A.

6. Francis Wharton, *A Treatise on the Criminal Law of the United States* (Philadelphia: Kay and Brother, 1861), § 1020.

7. American Law Institute, *Model Penal Code and Commentaries*, vol. 2, pt. I, pp. 30–61; George P. Fletcher, *A Crime of Self-Defense: Bernhard Goetz and the Law on Trial* (New York: Free Press, 1988), pp. 18–27.

8. *State v. Goode*, 195 S.W. 1006 (Mo. 1917); Perkins and Boyce, *Criminal Law*, pp. 1128–29.

9. *People v. Williams*, 56 Ill.App.2d 159, 205 N.E.2d 749 (1965).

10. American Law Institute, *Model Penal Code and Commentaries*, art. 3.04.

11. *People v. Johnson*, 2 Ill.2d 165, 117 N.E.2d 91 (1954).

12. 158 U.S. 550, 15 S.Ct. 962, 39 L.Ed. 1086 (1894); American Law Institute, *Model Penal Code and Commentaries*, vol. 3, pt. I, pp. 35–37.

13. Quoted in *Model Penal Code*, tentative draft no. 8 (Philadelphia: American Law Institute, 1958), pp. 79–80.

14. 117 Tenn. 430 (1907).

15. *State v. Schroeder*, 199 Neb. 822, 261 N.W.2d 759 (1978).

16. *State v. Kennamore*, 604 S.W.2d 856 (Tenn. 1980).

17. Ibid.

18. For a general introduction to the topic, see Edward Arnolds and Norman Garland, "The Defense of Necessity in Criminal Law: Right to Choose the Lesser Evil," *Journal of Criminal Law and Criminology*, 65 (1974), pp. 291–93; see American Law Institute, *Model Penal Code and Commentaries*, vol. 2, pt. I, pp. 8–22, for a summary of this position.

19. American Law Institute, *Model Penal Code and Commentaries*, vol. 1, pt. I, p. 18.

20. Quoted in Glanville Williams, *Criminal Law*, 2d ed. rev. (London: Stevens and Sons, 1961), p. 725.

21. Hall, *General Principles of Criminal Law*, pp. 425 ff.

22. American Law Institute, *Model Penal Code and Commentaries*, vol. 3, pt. I, p. 18; Williams, *Criminal Law*, p. 724.

23. *The Queen v. Dudley and Stephens*, 14 Q.B.D. 273 (1884).

24. Williams, *Criminal Law*, pp. 735–36.

25. Wayne R. LaFave and Arthur Scott, *Criminal Law* (St. Paul: West Publishing Co., 1972), p. 389.

26. *Mattis v. Schnarr*, 547 F.2d 1007 (8th Cir. 1976); Catherine H. Milton et al., *Police Use of Deadly Force* (Washington, D.C.: The Police Foundation, 1977), contains a detailed discussion. See also Lawrence O'Donnell, Jr., *Deadly Force* (New York: Morrow, 1983), for a spirited attack on deadly force.

27. Quoted in American Law Institute, *Model Penal Code*, tentative draft no. 8, pp. 60–62.

28. Address delivered to National College of State Trial Judges, Chapel Hill, North Carolina, August 15, 1968. Quoted in Sanford Kadish and Manfred Paulson, *Criminal Law and Its Processes*, 3d ed. rev. (Boston: Little, Brown, 1975), pp. 541–42.

29. Sir William Blackstone, *Commentaries on the Laws of England* (New York: Garland, 1978), pt. IV, p. 180.

30. Perkins and Boyce, *Criminal Law,* pp. 1154–60.

31. Richard L. Binder, "The Consent Defense: Sports, Violence, and the Criminal Law," *The American Criminal Law Review,* 13 (1975), pp. 235–48.

32. Sir Patrick Devlin, *The Enforcement of Morals* (London: 1965), p. 6.

33. American Law Institute, *Model Penal Code and Commentaries,* vol. 2, pt. I, pp. 1–5.

Chapter Seven

Defenses to Criminal Liability: Excuses

CHAPTER OUTLINE

CHAPTER MAIN POINTS

1. Excuses relieve defendants of criminal liability because, although defendants did something that was wrong, they were not responsible.

2. The main excuses are duress, intoxication, mistake, age, entrapment, insanity, diminished capacity, and syndromes.

3. Insanity is not the same as mental illness.

4. A mental disease or defect is relevant to criminal law only to determine whether defendants formed *mens rea*.

5. Diminished capacity is a partial defense based on the idea that defendants can suffer from a disease or defect that impairs their responsibility but does not remove it.

CHAPTER KEY TERMS

diminished capacity mental capacity is a condition in which less than "normal" but more than insane.

Durham **rule,** or **product test** an insanity test that measures capacity by determining whether crime was a product of mental disease or defect.

irresistible impulse a supplement to the *M'Naghten* rule that permits an insanity defense when defendants know the difference between right and wrong but cannot sufficiently control their behavior to do what is right.

M'Naghten **rule,** or **right-wrong test** an insanity defense based on a mental disease or defect that removes defendants' capacity to know the difference between right and wrong.

substantial capacity test a test in which insanity is determined by whether a mental disease or defect has impaired defendants' substantial capacity to either appreciate their conduct's wrongfulness or conform their behavior to what the law requires.

═ INTRODUCTION

For defendants, excuse and justification provide the same opportunity: to escape criminal liability. Theoretically, however, the two defenses differ. Defendants who plead excuse accept that what they did was wrong, bad, and immoral, but they ask the law not to call them criminals because they were not responsible, blameworthy, or culpable. They offer numerous specific excuses, or impairments from which they suffered at the time they caused harm. The most common are duress, intoxication, mistake, age, entrapment, insanity, diminished capacity and responsibility, and various syndromes.

═ DURESS

Duress, or the excuse that defendants were coerced into committing crimes, resembles necessity in that defendants choose between evils. However, defendants acting under duress choose to commit crimes against *innocent* people, while defendants acting in necessity commit crimes against *wrongdoers*. Duress gives rise to four major problems: (1) What crimes does duress excuse? (2) What constitutes duress? (3) How close to committing the crime must coercion take place? (4) Is an honest belief in threat sufficient, or must the belief be reasonable?

At common law, duress consisted of

threats or menaces, which induce a fear of death or other bodily harm, and which take away for that reason the guilt of many crimes and misdemeanors; at least before a human tribunal. But then that fear, which compels a man to do an unwarrantable action, ought to be just and well grounded. . . . [However,] though a man be violently assaulted, and hath no other possible means of escaping death, but by killing an innocent person; this fear and force shall not acquit him of murder; for he ought rather to die himself, than escape by the murder of an innocent.[1]

Under present law, wide variations exist. In some states, duress excuses all crimes except murder; in others, duress excuses only minor crimes. Some jurisdictions require that only the fear of instant death amounts to sufficient coercion; others accept an imminent fear of death or serious bodily harm.[2]

Theorists and scholars disagree over what ought to constitute duress. English jurist Sir James F. Stephen argued that duress should never be a defense to criminal liability because "it is at the moment when temptation is strongest that the law should speak most clearly and emphatically to the contrary." Stephen conceded that judges might mitigate sentences if offenders committed crimes under duress. Borrowing from necessity, American theorist Jerome Hall maintained that coercion should excuse only minor crimes committed under the threat of death. Professor Glanville Williams argued that duress should excuse because the law has no effect on defendants' choices when defendants are "in thrall to some power," such as duress.[3]

As for the kind of threat required to invoke the defense, states differ. Some permit only threats to kill: With a loaded gun at another's head, a robber says, "If you do not take that purse from her, I'll pull this trigger!" Other states accept threats to do serious bodily harm: "If you don't steal that car for me, I'll break your arms!" Threats to property—such as a threat to smash a car if another does not steal a stereo—do not constitute duress. Neither do threats to reputation: "If you don't smoke this marijuana, I'll tell your boss you have AIDS." Nor, in some states do threats to harm others, such as to kill a mother, son, or lover, constitute duress.[4]

The threat's immediacy is important in most jurisdictions, but the degree varies from state to state. In Minnesota, for example, only threats of "instant death" qualify. Most states are somewhat less restrictive, accepting immediate *or* imminent threats. Disagreement arises over what constitutes an immediate threat. For example, a man threatened to stab a woman if she did not lie in court to give him an alibi. The man who threatened her sat in the courtroom while she committed the perjury. The trial court ruled that he did not threaten her with an immediate threat because he could not stab her at that moment. The appellate court disagreed:

> In the present case the threats of Farrell were likely to be no less compelling, because their execution could not be effected in the court room, if they could be carried out in the streets of Salford the same night. Insofar, therefore, as the [trial judge] ruled the threats were not sufficiently present and immediate to support the duress we think that he was in error.[5]

Jurisdictions also differ over whether to measure threats objectively or subjectively. Some states accept the subjective honest belief, others demand reasonable belief and honest belief. A few states speak of actual compulsion.

The Kansas Supreme Court dealt with the excuse of duress in *State v. Myers*.

CASE

Did He Attempt to Rob under Duress?

Armand v. State

474 N.E.2d 1002 (Ind. 1985)

[The trial court convicted Ray Armand of attempted robbery. He appealed. Justice Prentice delivered the opinion.]

FACTS

. . . [A]t approximately 1:00 P.M. on October 20, 1982, Laura Sheridan, holding her three year old daughter in her arms, had just got out of her automobile in the Venture store parking lot in Merrillville, Indiana. As she walked toward the back of her automobile, the Defendant grabbed her and hit her on the top of her head. He then demanded her purse; but Mrs. Sheridan did not release it, fearing that she would drop her daughter. The Defendant then hit her at least half a dozen times, and she and her daughter fell to the ground. She looked at the Defendant who was standing over her and saw in his hands what appeared to be the butt of a gun. All that she could see was a brown handle. She then pushed and kicked the defendant and was able to stand, still holding her daughter. She screamed, and the Defendant hit her again and she ran. She observed the Defendant leave the parking lot in an automobile being driven by another man.

Mrs. Sheridan suffered a one and one-half inch gash wound to the top of her head and a cut on her forehead. She also suffered from headaches for several days.

The Defendant testified that . . . he was driving toward a friend's house when he encountered Robert Shorts, a man he had known in school, who asked him if he would give him a ride to Crown Point where he had a scheduled court appearance. During the trip to Crown Point, the two men stopped to use some drugs provided by Shorts. The Defendant stated that the drugs, "tees and blues," made him shaky and nervous. On the return trip, the Defendant stopped at a service station to buy gasoline. When he returned to his car, Shorts, who had moved into the driver's seat, pointed a gun at him and told him to get in on the passenger side. Shorts then told him that he wanted money for the drugs that the Defendant had used and drove into the Venture store's parking lot. Shorts parked his car, threatened to hurt the Defendant and his family if he did not get him some money, gave him a gun, and told him to "get her."

OPINION

. . . [T]he trial court informed the jury that duress is not a defense to the crime of attempted robbery. . . . Ind[iana] § 35–41–3–8 . . . provides:

> (a) It is a defense that the person who engaged in the prohibited conduct was compelled to do so by threat of imminent serious bodily injury to himself or another person. With respect to offenses other than felonies, it is a defense that the person who engaged in the prohibited conduct was compelled to do so by force or threat of force. Compulsion . . . exists only if the force, threat, or circumstances are such as would render a person of reasonable firmness incapable of resisting the pressure. . . .
> (b) This section does not apply to . . . offense[s] against the person . . .

Defendant argues that the defense of duress is available to one accused of attempted robbery, that evidence of duress existed, and that, consequently, the trial court erred. . . . His argument is without merit. . . .

[W]e hold that *attempted* robbery is an offense against the person . . . and that the trial court properly instructed the jury that the defense of duress was not applicable in the case at bar. . . . [A]ffirmed . . .

CASE DISCUSSION

If Armand is telling the truth, was he under duress? What facts are relevant? Do you agree that duress is not available in attempted robbery? Why? Was Armand's belief honest? reasonable? both? Was he in fact in danger? Was the danger instant? immediate? imminent? Was he in danger of death? serious bodily injury? What are the relevant facts to answer these questions? How would you define duress?

One variation, or extension, to duress is superior orders. Two cases that received public attention illustrate this extension; the first is *United States v. Calley.*

CASE

Do Superior Orders Constitute Duress?

United States v. Calley

46 C.M.R. 1131 (1975)

[Calley was convicted of murder. He appealed.]

FACTS

[D]uring midmorning on 16 March 1968 a large number of unresisting Vietnamese were placed in a ditch on the eastern side of My Lai and summarily executed by American soldiers.

[PFC] Meadlo gave the most graphic and damning evidence. He had wandered back into the village alone after the trail incident. Eventually, he met his fire team leader, Specialist Four Grzesik. They took seven or eight Vietnamese to what he labeled a "ravine," where Lieutenant Calley, Sledge, and Dursi and a few other Americans were located with what he estimated as seventy-five to a hundred Vietnamese. Meadlo remembered also that Lieutenant Calley told him, "We got another job to do, Meadlo," and that the appellant started shoving people into the ravine and shooting them. Meadlo, in contrast to Dursi, followed the directions of his leader and himself fired into the people at the bottom of the "ravine." Meadlo then drifted away from the area but he doesn't remember where.

Specialist Four Grzesik found PFC Meadlo, crying and distraught, sitting on a small dike on the eastern edge of the village. He and Meadlo moved through the village, and came to the ditch, in which Grzesik thought were thirty-five to fifty dead bodies. Lieutenant Calley walked past and ordered Grzesik to take his fire team back into the village and help the following platoon in their search. He also remembered that Calley asked him to "finish them off," but he refused.

Specialist Four Turner saw Lieutenant Calley for the first time that day as Turner walked out of the village near the ditch. Meadlo and a few other soldiers were also present. Turner passed within fifteen feet of the area, looked into the ditch and saw a pile of approximately twenty bodies covered with blood. He also saw Lieutenant Calley and Meadlo firing from a distance of five feet into another group of people who were kneeling and squatting in the ditch. Turner recalled he then went north of the ditch about seventy yards, where he joined with Conti at a perimeter position. He remained there for over an hour, watching the ditch. Several more groups of Vietnamese were brought to it, never to get beyond or out of it. In all he thought he observed about ninety or a hundred people brought to the ditch and slaughtered there by Lieutenant Calley and his subordinates.

OPINION

There is no dispute as to the fact of killings by and at the instance of appellant at a ditch on the eastern edge of My Lai.

Of the several bases for his argument that he committed no murder at My Lai because he was void of mens rea, appellant emphasized most of all that he acted in obedience to orders. . . .

An order of the type appellant says he received is illegal. Its illegality is apparent upon even cursory evaluation by a man of ordinary sense and understanding.

[Calley argues] essentially that obedience to orders is a defense which strikes at mens rea; therefore in logic an obedient subordinate should be acquitted so long as he did not personally know of the order's illegality. [We] [do] not agree with the argument. Heed must be given not only to subjective innocence-through-ignorance in the soldier, but to the consequences for his victims. Also, barbarism tends to invite reprisal to the detriment of our own force or disrepute which interferes with the achievement of war aims, even though the barbaric acts were preceded by orders for their commission. Casting the defense of obedience to orders solely in subjective terms of mens rea would operate practically to abrogate those objective restraints which are essential to functioning rules of war. The court members, after being given correct standards, properly rejected any defense of obedience to orders.

We find no impediment to the findings that appellant acted with murderous mens rea, including premeditation. The aggregate of all his contentions against the existence of murderous mens rea is no more absolving than a bare claim that he did not suspect he did any wrong act until after the operation, and indeed is not convinced of it yet. This is no excuse in law.

Affirmed.

CASE DISCUSSION

Lieutenant Calley's defense was that he was obeying the orders of his superior officer, Captain Medina. Because he was not free to disobey the orders, Calley maintained, he was not responsible for the My Lai massacre. He was therefore coerced into killing. Rejecting Calley's defense, the court ruled that every person must accept responsibility for killing. No one who obeys the order to kill can transfer that responsibility. Despite the need for military discipline, which is admittedly great, the court held that officers must disobey clearly illegal orders, particularly when they lead to death.

The Nazi war criminals tried to use the same defense after World War II. In the famous Nuremberg trials, German officers attempted to defend Nazi atrocities against the Jews, claiming they were merely

> obeying their commanders' orders and were not criminally responsible for the people they killed. Their defenses were rejected for reasons similar to those in Calley.

The second superior orders case is that of Oliver North. In the name of the United States government, the independent counsel charged North with numerous offenses against the United States. The government had sold arms to Iran, and $14 million of the profits were illegally diverted to finance the Nicaraguan contras' war against the Sandanistas. The special prosecutor dropped two major charges—conspiracy to defraud the government and theft related to the funds—when the Reagan administration refused to turn over evidence on the ground that it would endanger national security. The remaining charges included (1) lying to congressional committees under oath, (2) lying to the attorney general, (3) lying to the Tower Commission investigating the Iran-contra affair, (4) shredding and altering National Security Council records of North's activities, (5) accepting a private security system as an illegal gift, (6) converting to personal use traveler's checks North received in his White House job, and (7) conspiring to defraud the Internal Revenue Service.

After long delays, the North trial opened in the Federal District Court for the District of Columbia on February 21, 1989, Justice Gerhard Gesell presiding. The following excerpts from the opening statements of the prosecutor and defense attorney make it clear that Oliver North intended to rely heavily on the defense of superior orders.

John W. Keker, associate independent counsel, outlined the government's case against North in his opening statement:

> The evidence will show that when the time came for Oliver North to tell the truth, he lied. When the time came for Oliver North to come clean, he shredded, he erased, he altered. When the time came for Oliver North to let the light shine, he covered up. . . . The evidence will show that these are crimes, and the reason was the Lieutenant Colonel North was covering up crimes he had already committed. You will hear he considers himself a patriotic person. But there is no higher patriotic purpose than to protect our system of government. To lie to Congress because you mistrust it then is a crime not a defense.

Brenden Sullivan, Oliver North's lawyer, revealed the defense strategy in his opening statement, portraying a very different picture of North and his activities. Sullivan described North as a mid-level policy mechanic who acted out of patriotic ideals and whose actions to preserve secrets were taken under orders from the highest officials in the government. Sullivan said,

> You should know early on that the defense says to you absolutely not guilty on all charges. . . . [Oliver North] was doing his job as he understood it. He was doing his duty as he understood it, and that if he did otherwise there could be death resulting to people that he worked with, and dangers resulting to the United States.

Sullivan argued that North was acting under orders from superiors to keep material secret from Congress, which

> leaked like a sieve. The evidence will show that Mr. North had no criminal intent and he was acting to protect information as it had to be protected. He lived with that Marine Corps motto. He was always faithful to country, to commander in chief, to his family, to those whose lives depended on him.

As he described the administration's efforts to aid the contras at a time when such assistance was prohibited, Sullivan quoted Reagan as saying, "If this leaks out, we'll all be hanging by our thumbs outside the White House until we find out who did it."[6]

Another extension to duress is brainwashing, which came to public view in heiress Patty Hearst's trial. A self-styled revolutionary group, the Symbionese Liberation Army (SLA), kidnapped Hearst and confined her for months. During that time, she and her abductors robbed a bank. Hearst's defense against the bank robbery charge was that her captors pressured her for months, breaking down and overcoming her will. She had no mind of her own left, their beliefs became her beliefs, and thus her actions were their actions. Therefore, she was not responsible for what she did.

The court denied the defense, but its logic is clear. The Model Penal Code reporters say that the Code's duress provision includes brainwashing by implication because it includes coercion, which means breaking down a person's will.[7] Puerto Rico provides specifically for brainwashing:

> Whoever acts compelled by intimidation or violence shall not be held liable [and] [t]he concept of violence also includes the use of hypnotic means, narcotic substances, depressant or stimulant drugs, or other means or substances.[8]

Three reasons support the duress defense. First, those forced to commit a crime did not act voluntarily; hence, there is no *actus reus* unless actors intentionally, recklessly, or negligently put themselves in a position where others could coerce them. Second, subjection to another's will removes *mens rea*. Third, as a practical matter, the criminal law cannot force people to do other than their common sense dictates. Under enough pressure, people will save their own lives even if it means hurting someone else. The limits to duress, on the other hand, are supposed to encourage resistance to pressure to commit crimes.

≡ INTOXICATION

At common law, voluntary intoxication had the following effect on criminal liability:

> As to artificial, voluntarily contracted madness, by drunkenness or intoxication, which, depriving men of their reason, puts them in a temporary frenzy; our law looks upon this as an aggravation of the offense, rather than as an excuse for any criminal misbehavior.[9]

The effect of intoxication on criminal liability differs according to whether the intoxication was voluntary or involuntary. Involuntary intoxication excuses criminal liability. Modern law follows the common law with respect to voluntary intoxication: it never constitutes a total defense. However, it sometimes negatives *mens rea*. Jurisdictions define voluntary and involuntary intoxication differently, as the common law and representative statutes demonstrate.

Involuntary intoxication includes cases where defendants do not know they are taking intoxicants, or know but do so under duress. In one case, a man took what his friend told him were "breath perfumer" pills; in fact, they were cocaine tablets. While under their influence, he killed someone. The court allowed the defense of intoxication.[10]

Only extreme duress qualifies as involuntary intoxication. One author concluded that

> a person would need to be bound hand and foot and the liquor literally poured down his throat, or . . . would have to be threatened with immediate serious injury.[11]

For example, an eighteen-year-old youth was traveling with an older man across the desert. The man insisted that the youth drink some whisky with him. When the youth declined, the man became abusive. The youth, fearing the man would put him out of the car in the middle of the desert without any money, drank the whisky, became intoxicated, and killed the man. The court rejected the involuntary intoxication by duress excuse because the man had not compelled the youth "to drink against his will and consent."[12]

Involuntary intoxication might also arise out of some physiological abnormality. Owing to these abnormalities, intoxicating substances cause defendants to act in ways they cannot control. For example:

> A twenty year old man, living alone with his mother stabbed her to death with a kitchen knife, inflicting many wounds on her body. In the five days preceding the murder he had worked hard and had had but irregular meals. Also, there had been some quarreling with his mother over money. On the morning of the day of the murder he struck her, a very unusual act, for which he apologized. He ate poorly on that day. He had his last carbohydrate meal at noon. Between 9 and 10:30 P.M. he drank four pints of mild ale. At 11 P.M. there was again a quarrel with his mother over money and she pushed him out of her room. At this moment he suddenly felt thirsty, went to the kitchen to get a bottle opener, saw a knife, and then "something came over" him: "I was like a homicidal maniac." He stabbed his mother to death. . . . There is a gap in his memory for seven hours following the crime. The next day, he gave himself up to the police. . . .
>
> After the patient's arrest, his family physician notified the defense that two years prior to the crime a sugar tolerance curve had shown a tendency to hypoglycemia. . . . [A] number of tests . . . showed that the prisoner was definitely suffering from hypoglycemia. . . . [H]is blood at the time of the crime must have been below 100 mgm and . . . his brain at that time was functioning abnormally; . . . his judgment was impaired at the time.[13]

Some maintain that denying the excuse of intoxication—whether involuntary or voluntary—results in punishing involuntary acts. Others say that those who are intoxicated cannot form the requisite *mens rea*. Supporters argue that those who voluntarily get intoxicated to a point where they are likely to reduce or eliminate normal control should and must take the consequences stemming from their lost control. Those who voluntarily induced their intoxicated state should not then escape criminal liability simply because they either acted involuntarily or could not form the requisite intent.[14]

Voluntary intoxication, although not a defense, may negative a material element in the crime. It may impair the capacity to form either the purpose or the knowledge required to prove particular crimes. Hence, in crimes requiring purpose and knowledge, sufficient intoxication might negative *mens rea*. For example, a heavily intoxicated person may not have the capacity to premeditate a homicide, or intoxication may have prevented premeditation in fact. Both cases lack a material element in first-degree murder: premeditation. However, intoxication may not have impaired the capacity to form, or to have in fact formed, the *mens rea* for manslaughter. Generally, intoxication may disprove purpose or knowledge, but not recklessness or negligence.[15]

Intoxication might also prove that defendants were unable to commit the requisite act in the crime charged. Hence, a man so intoxicated he could not get an erection could not commit rape, because performing the requisite act was impossible. This should not be taken to mean that defendants who voluntarily induce intoxication act involuntarily. Their voluntary act in drinking establishes voluntariness, even though when committing the crime charged they were "overwhelmed or overpowered by alcohol to the point of losing [their] . . . faculties or sensibilities."[16]

CASE

Does Intoxication Excuse Criminal Liability?

State v. Stasio

78 N.J. 467, 396 A.2d 1129 (1979)

[Stasio appealed from conviction for assault with intent to rob and assault while armed with a dangerous knife, for which he was sentenced to three to five years and one to two years, respectively. Justice Schreiber delivered the opinion.]

FACTS

Robert Colburn had frequented the Silver Moon Tavern not only for its alcoholic wares but also to engage in pool. On October 7, Colburn arrived at the Tavern about 11:00 A.M. and started to play pool.

Sometime before noon the defendant joined him. They stayed together until about 3:00 P.M. when the defendant left the bar. Though the defendant had been drinking during this period, in Colburn's opinion the defendant was not intoxicated upon his departure. Neither the defendant's speech nor his mannerisms indicated drunkenness.

Peter Klimek arrived at the Tavern shortly before 5:00 P.M. and assumed his shift at tending bar. There were about eight customers present when, at approximately 5:40 P.M., the defendant entered and walked in a normal manner to the bathroom. Shortly thereafter he returned to the front door, looked around outside and approached the bar. He demanded that Klimek give him some money. Upon refusal, he threatened Klimek. The defendant went behind the bar toward Klimek and insisted that Klimek give him $80 from the cash register. When Klimek persisted in his refusal, the defendant pulled out a knife. Klimek grabbed the defendant's right hand and Colburn, who had jumped on top of the bar, seized the defendant's hair and pushed his head toward the bar. The defendant then dropped the knife.

Almost immediately thereafter Police Officer Rowan arrived and placed the defendant in custody.

[Stasio's defense was that he "was so intoxicated he could not form intent to rob."]

OPINION

It is generally agreed that a defendant will not be relieved of criminal responsibility because he was under the influence of intoxicants or drugs voluntarily taken. This principle rests upon public policy, demanding that he who seeks the influence of liquor or narcotics should not be insulated from criminal liability because that influence impaired his judgment or his control. The required element of badness can be found in the intentional use of the stimulant or depressant.

> [I]f a person casts off the restraints of reason and consciousness by a voluntary act, no wrong is done to him if he is held accountable for any crime which he may commit in that condition. Society is entitled to this protection.

Purpose or knowledge has been made a component of many offenses so that voluntary intoxication will be an available defense in those situations. Thus, voluntary intoxication may be a defense to aggravated assaults consisting of attempts to cause bodily injury to another with a deadly weapon. Intoxication could exonerate those otherwise guilty of burglaries and criminal trespass. It would be an available defense to arson. . . .

Our holding today does not mean that voluntary intoxication is always irrelevant in criminal proceedings. Evidence of intoxication may be introduced to demonstrate that premeditation and deliberation have not been proven so that a second degree murder cannot be raised to first degree murder or to show that the intoxication led to a fixed state of insanity. Intoxication may be shown to prove that a defendant never participated in a crime. Thus it might be proven that a defendant was in such a drunken stupor and unconscious state that he was not a part of a robbery. His mental faculties may be so prostrated as to preclude the commission of the criminal act. Under some circumstances intoxication may be relevant to demonstrate mistake. However, in the absence of any basis for the defense, a trial court should not in its charge introduce that element. A trial court, of course, may consider intoxication as a mitigating circumstance when sentencing a defendant.

Affirmed.

DISSENT

Today's holding by the majority stands logic on its head. This Court and the Legislature have long adhered to the view that criminal sanctions will not be imposed upon a defendant unless there exists a "concurrence of an evil-meaning mind with an evil-doing hand." The policies underlying this proposition are clear. A person who intentionally commits a bad act is more culpable than one who engages in the same conduct without any evil design. The intentional wrongdoer is also more likely to repeat his offense, and hence constitutes a greater threat to societal repose. A sufficiently intoxicated defendant is thus subject to less severe sanctions not because the law "excuses" his conduct but because the circumstances surrounding his acts have been deemed by the Legislature to be less deserving of punishment.

It strains reason to hold that a defendant may be found guilty of a crime whose definition includes a requisite mental state when the defendant actually failed to possess that state of mind. Indeed, this is the precise teaching of cases allowing the intoxication defense in first-degree murder prosecutions. To sustain a first-degree murder conviction, the State must prove that the homicide was premeditated, willful, and deliberate. If the accused, due to intoxication, did not in fact possess these mental attributes, he can be convicted of at most second-degree murder.

That offense, however, can be sustained on a mere showing of recklessness, and the necessary recklessness can be found in the act of becoming intoxicated.

Just as the lack of premeditation, willfulness, or deliberation precludes a conviction for first-degree murder, so should the lack of intent to rob or steal be a defense to assault and battery with intent to rob, or breaking and entering with intent to steal. The principle is the same in both situations. If voluntary intoxication negates an element of the offense, the defendant has not engaged in the conduct proscribed by the criminal statute, and hence should not be subject to the sanctions imposed by that statute.

CASE DISCUSSION

Stasio points up the disagreement over whether intoxication ought to excuse criminal liability. The majority follows most jurisdictions, ruling that ordinarily it does not. However, as the court notes, if intoxication impairs the capacity to form specific intent in crimes such as first-degree murder, which requires premeditation, then raising a reasonable doubt concerning *mens rea* is relevant. The dissent makes this latter point even more strongly, arguing that Stasio may well have been so drunk he could not form the intent to rob. The jury should have been allowed to decide that, according to the dissent. Furthermore, the excuse is not related to the harm caused by intoxicated persons. It has only to do with their culpability. They cannot form the intent to commit the crime with which they are charged. In this case, Stasio could not be guilty of an assault with intent to rob, because he was too drunk to form that intent. Do you agree with the majority or with the dissent? Does your answer depend on the harm Stasio caused or on his capacity to form the intent to rob?

A major problem is that intoxication might result from chronic alcoholism, increasingly regarded as a disease among experts. If alcoholism is a disease and intoxication a symptom, then punishing an intoxicated alcoholic is in effect punishing an illness, a status, or a condition, which, according to *Robinson v. California* is cruel and unusual punishment. (See excerpt in Chapter 3.) In *Powell v. Texas*, the United States Supreme Court rejected Powell's defense that his alcoholism excused him from liability for "being drunk in public." The Court ruled that Powell's conviction for appearing on the street drunk was not for his alcoholism, but rather for his voluntary act—going outdoors while he was drunk—and offending public decency while he was out there. Even if alcoholism is a disease and Powell suffered from it, the Court reasoned, he could refrain from exhibiting its offensive symptom, drunkenness, in public. His failure to do so was a proper ground for criminal liability, and, therefore, punishing him did not violate the Eighth Amendment prohibition against cruel and unusual punishment.[17]

Alcohol is the most widely used intoxicant, but it is not the only one qualifying defendants to claim the intoxication excuse. The Model Penal Code and most states define intoxication to include disturbing mental and physical capacities by introducing "substances" into the body. *State v. Hall* illustrates this point. Hall's friend gave him a pill containing LSD (lyserigic acid diethylamide). Hall did not know this; he knew only that, as his friend assured him, it was only a "little sunshine" to make him feel "groovy." A car picked up the hitchhiking Hall. At that time, the drug caused Hall to hallucinate that the driver was a rabid dog. Under this sad delusion, he shot and killed the driver. The court recognized no legal distinction between the voluntary use of alcohol and the voluntary use of other intoxicants in determining criminal responsibility.[18]

══ MISTAKE

"Ignorance of the law is no excuse," nearly everyone knows; most do not know that this doctrine is no longer hard and fast, if it ever was. Ignorance of fact, on the other hand, has always excused criminal responsibility under some circumstances.

Mistake of fact excuses criminal liability when it negates a material element in the crime. For example, if I take from a restaurant coatroom a coat that I believe is mine, I have not stolen the coat because I do not have the requisite *mens rea:* to deprive the owner of her property. The actor's mistake must be "honest," and "reasonable"; hence, the proper way to state the defense is that an honest and reasonable mistake of fact excuses criminal responsibility. For example, if I take the coat because it is where I left mine an hour ago, it is the same color and size as mine, and no other coat hanging there resembles it, I have honestly and reasonably mistaken the coat for mine. (For a full discussion of mistake of fact in statutory rape, see chapter 9.)

Mistake of law does not ordinarily excuse criminal responsibility for several reasons grounded in public policy. First, the state must determine what constitutes crime; individuals cannot define crimes for themselves. Second, the doctrine supposedly encourages citizens to know the law. Finally, nearly everyone could shield themselves behind the claim, since most people do not know the specifics of criminal statutes and court decisions interpreting them. Hence, the law presumes that everyone knows the law.[19]

Ignorance of the law, following reasonable efforts to learn it, sometimes excuses criminal liability. For example, a defendant carried on a lottery, relying on a statute that a state supreme court later ruled unconstitutional. The defendant's honest and reasonable belief that the lottery was lawful was an excuse, even though the supreme court later ruled that the lottery was unconstitutional. Furthermore, relying on an attorney's advice does not constitute an excuse to criminal liability. Hence, if I ask my lawyer if it is lawful to put a sign in my front yard and she tells me yes, and later the government prosecutes me for violating an ordinance prohibiting signs in residential areas, I have no defense of mistake. If I had instead asked the prosecutor, I might have an excuse; some states permit reliance on such officials, others do not.[20]

The distinction between law and fact, although important legally, is not easy to draw in practice. In *United States v. Merkt*, the court addresses the defense of mistake, and the problem in determining whether the defendant mistook the law or a fact.

CASE

Did Her Mistake Excuse Her?

United States v. Merkt

764 F.2d 266 (5th Cir. 1985)

[A jury convicted Stacey Merkt of conspiring to transport and move, and transporting and moving, two illegal aliens within the United

States. The judge suspended execution of her sentence and placed her on supervised probation for two years. She appealed. Circuit Justices Williams and Davis delivered the opinion. Circuit Justice Rubin delivered a dissenting opinion.]

FACTS

. . . Stacey Merkt worked at the Casa Oscar Romero in San Benito, Texas, The Casa, which is supported by the Diocese of Brownsville and other church groups in the Rio Grande Valley, offers food and housing to Central American refugees regardless of the manner in which they entered the United States. Merkt taught English, helped refugees to communicate with their families, and ran errands.

In February, 1984, Merkt drove Brenda Elizabeth Sanchez-Galan and Mauricio Valle, two illegal aliens from El Salvador, in her car from the Casa to a farmhouse near McAllen, Texas so that they could meet with a newspaper reporter. Merkt testified that she had agreed to act as an interpreter for the interview. She also testified that the aliens planned to leave for San Antonio, Texas, with the reporter after the interview in a different car driven by a nun who worked in the Casa, Sister Diane Muhlenkamp. When the interview was not completed after several hours, however, Merkt testified that she agreed to accompany the others to San Antonio. . . . Merkt testified that Sanchez-Galan and Valle wanted to go to San Antonio in order to file claims for political asylum at the district office of INS [Immigration and Naturalization Service] located in that city. . . .

The car left the farmhouse at 3:00 A.M. heading north on Highway 649. . . . Border Patrol agents observed the car. . . . The agents noticed that the license plates on the car indicated that it was not from the immediate area and that the five people in the car did not appear to be either a family or a group of oil workers travelling to work, such as riggers, the type of worker in this area who usually worked unusual hours. When the agents stopped the car, they noticed that all of the occupants appeared to be nervous, and that Merkt was talking and gesturing to others. After an identification check, the agents determined that both Sanchez-Galan and Valle were illegal aliens. . . .

[The agents took all of the people in the car, including Merkt, to a border patrol station, arrested them, advised them of their rights, and questioned them. Merkt was charged and convicted for violating U.S.C. § 1324(a)(2)., which provides in part that whoever knowing that aliens are illegally in the United States, or having reasonable grounds to believe that the last entry occurred less than three years prior thereto, transports or moves any alien within the United States is guilty of a felony, punishable by a fine not exceeding $2,000 or imprisonment for not more than 5 years, or both.]

OPINION

To establish a violation of 8 U.S.C. § 1324(a)(2), the government must prove that: (1) the defendant transported or moved an alien within the United States; (2) the alien was in the United States in violation of the law; (3) the defendant knew this fact; (4) the defendant knew or had reasonable grounds to believe that the alien's last entry into the United States was within the last three years; and (5) the defendant acted willfully in the furtherance of the alien's violation of the law. . . .

One of Merkt's defenses at trial is that she did not know Sanchez-Galan and Valle were in the United States in violation of the law because she believed them to be bona fide political refugees and, as such, entitled to reside in this country under the terms of the 1980 Refugee Act. Merkt and others testified as to the sincerity of this belief, and the defense requested an instruction that she be acquitted unless the jury found that she knew that the Act did not entitle the aliens lawfully to reside in the United States. The trial court refused, and instead . . . instructed the jury that Merkt's belief that the alien's genuine qualifications for political asylum entitled them to "legal status" prior to such filing was based on a mistake of law, and could not constitute a defense of the charged crime.

A majority of this panel agrees that the district court correctly instructed the jury on this point. We hold that the district court properly based its instruction on the well-established rule that a citizen is presumed to know the law, and that "ignorance of the law will not excuse." Moreover, although a mistake of fact may constitute a valid defense, the error that Merkt alleges she made is purely a mistake of law, and cannot be stretched into a mistake of fact in order to take advantage of that defense. . . . [Reversed on other grounds.]

DISSENT

. . . I disagree with the view of the majority concerning . . . [the defense of mistake]. . . . The aphorism that imputes knowledge of the law to all is not applicable if a mistaken belief concerning how the law would treat a situation negatives the existence of the *mens rea* essential to the crime charged. If "an apparent 'mistake of law' was actually a 'mistake of fact' in that the mistake pertained to a question of legal status which was determined by a law other than the one under which the defendant was prosecuted," such a mistake constitutes a valid defense. . . .

The statute does not penalize the transportation of any alien who has not lawfully been admitted to the United States by a person who is not aware of the alien's illegal status. The defendant's knowledge of the alien's illegal status is an essential element of the offense, which the government is required to prove. This status, in turn, can be determined only by reference to a law separate from the one defining the crime Merkt allegedly committed. If Merkt could establish that she was ignorant of the true legal status of the two aliens, therefore, she should be allowed to assert this state of mind, however mistaken it was, as a defense to her prosecution under § 1324(a)(2).

CASE DISCUSSION

Merkt admitted she helped the aliens but she argues that she has a defense—the excuse of mistake. The Court refers to mistake of law and fact. What exactly was Merkt mistaken about? Is the court right that her mistake was a mistake of law? Can you distinguish between Merkt's mistake of fact and law? Explain.

═══ AGE

A four-year-old boy stabs his two-year-old sister in a murderous rage. Is this a criminal assault? What if the boy is eight? or twelve? or sixteen? or eighteen? At the other end of the age spectrum, what if he is eighty-five? At how early an age are people liable for criminal conduct? And when, if ever, has someone become too old for criminal responsibility? Age—both old and young—does affect criminal liability, sometimes to excuse it, sometimes to mitigate it, and sometimes even to aggravate it.

Ever since the days of the early English common law, immaturity has excused criminal liability. A rigid but sensible scheme for administering the defense was developed at least by the sixteenth century. The irrebuttable presumption was that no one under age seven had the mental capacity to commit crimes. That meant juries had to conclude that children under seven could not form *mens rea*, no matter what the evidence in particular cases might show to the contrary. Everyone over fourteen was presumed conclusively to have the mental capacity to form *mens rea*. For those between the ages of seven and fourteen, the law presumed incapacity. The presumption, however, was rebuttable, meaning evidence that capacity in fact existed could set aside the presumption. The presumption was strong at age seven but gradually weakened until it disappeared at age fourteen.

About half the states initially adopted the common-law approach, but altered the specific ages within it. Some excluded the juvenile court from proceeding when juveniles committed serious crimes, such as those carrying the death penalty or life imprisonment. Recently, guided by the Model Penal Code, states have increasingly integrated the age of criminal responsibility with the jurisdiction of the juvenile courts. Some grant the juvenile court exclusive jurisdiction up to a particular age, usually between fifteen and sixteen. Then, from sixteen to eighteen (although occasionally up to twenty-one), juvenile court judges can transfer, or certify, cases to adult criminal courts. The number of cases certified has increased with the public recognition that youths commit serious felonies.[21]

CASE

Too Young to Murder?

People v. Wolff

61 Cal.2d 795, 40 Cal. Rptr. 271, 394 P.2d 959 (1964)

[Wolff was convicted of first-degree murder for killing his mother. He was sentenced to life imprisonment. Wolff was fifteen years old when the crime occurred. Justice Schauer delivered the opinion.]

FACTS

In the year preceding the commission of the crime defendant "spent a lot of time thinking about sex." He made a list of the names and addresses of seven girls in his community whom he did not know personally but whom he planned to anesthetize by ether and then either rape or photograph nude. One night about three weeks before the murder he took a container of ether and attempted to enter the home of one of these girls through the chimney, but he became wedged in and had to be rescued. In the ensuing weeks defendant apparently deliberated on ways and means of accomplishing his objective and decided that he would have to bring the girls to his house to achieve his sexual purposes, and that it would therefore be necessary to get his mother (and possibly his brother) out of the way first.

The attack on defendant's mother took place on Monday, May 15, 1961. On the preceding Friday or Saturday defendant obtained an axe handle from the family garage and hid it under the mattress of his bed. At about 10 P.M. on Sunday he took the axe handle from its hiding place and approached his mother from behind, raising the weapon to strike her. She sensed his presence and asked him what he was doing; he answered that it was "nothing," and returned to his room and hid the handle under his mattress again. The following morning defendant arose and put the customary signal (a magazine) in the front window to inform his father that he had not overslept. Defendant ate the breakfast that his mother prepared, then went to his room and obtained the axe handle from under the mattress. He returned to the kitchen, approached his mother from behind and struck her on the back of the head. She turned around screaming and he struck her several more blows. They fell to the floor, fighting. She called out her neighbor's name and defendant began choking her. She bit him on the hand and crawled away. He got up to turn off the water running in the sink, and she fled through the dining room. He gave chase, caught her in the front room, and choked her to death with his hands. Defendant then took off his shirt and hung it by the fire, washed the blood off his face and hands, read a few lines from a Bible or prayer book lying upon the dining room table, and walked down to the police station to turn himself in. Defendant told the desk officer, "I have something I wish to report. I just killed my mother with an axe handle." The officer testified that defendant spoke in a quiet voice and that "His conversation was quite coherent in what he was saying and he answered everything I asked him right to a T."

OPINION

Defendant's counsel repeatedly characterizes as "bizarre" defendant's plan to rape or photograph nude the seven girls on his list. Certainly in common parlance it may be termed "bizarre"; likewise to a mature person of good morals, it would appear highly unreasonable. But many a youth has committed—or planned—acts which were bizarre and unreasonable. This defendant was immature and lacked experience and judgment in sexual matters.

[D]efendant was questioned by Officers Stenberg and Hamilton shortly after he came to the police station and voluntarily announced that he had just killed his mother. The interrogation was transcribed and shown to defendant; he changed the wording of a few of his answers, then affixed his signature and the date on each page. When asked by Officer Hamilton why he had turned himself in, defendant replied, "Well, for the act I had just committed." Defendant then related the events leading up to and culminating in the murder, describing his conduct in the detail set forth hereinabove. With respect to the issue of his state of mind at the time of the crime, the following language is both relevant and material: When asked how long he had thought of killing his mother, defendant replied, "I can't be clear on that. About a week ago, I would suppose, the very beginning of the thoughts. First I thought of giving her the ether. Then Thursday and Friday I thought of it again. Q. Of killing your mother? A. Not of killing. Well, yes, I think so. Then Saturday and Sunday the same." After stating that he struck her the first blow on the back of the head, defendant was asked:

Q. Did you consider at the time that this one blow would render her unconscious, or kill her?

A. I wasn't sure. I was hoping it would render her unconscious.

Q. Was it your thought at this time to kill her?

A. I am not sure of that. Probably kill her, I think.

Defendant described the struggle in which he and his mother fell to the floor, and was asked:

Q. Then what happened.

A. She moved over by the stove, and she just laid still. She was breathing, breathing heavily. I said "I shouldn't be doing this"—not those exact words, but something to that effect, and laid down beside her, because we were on the floor.

Q. Were you tired?

A. Yes.

After defendant had choked her to death he said, "God loves you, He loves me, He loves my dad, and I love you and my dad. It is a circle, sort of, and it is horrible you have done all that good and then I come along and destroy it."

Detective Stenberg thereafter interrupted Officer Hamiliton's interrogation, and asked the following questions:

Q. (Det. W.R. Stenberg) You knew the wrongfulness of killing your mother?

A. I did. I was thinking of it. I was aware of it.

Q. You were aware of the wrongfulness. Also had you thought what might happen to you?

A. That is a question. No.

A. Your thought has been in your mind for three weeks of killing her?

A. Yes, or of just knocking her out.

Q. Well, didn't you feel you would be prosecuted for the wrongfulness of this act?

A. I was aware of it, but not thinking of it.

Officer Hamilton asked:

Q. Can you give a reason or purpose for this act of killing your mother? Have you thought out why you wanted to hurt her?

A. There is a reason why we didn't get along. There is also the reason of sexual intercourse with one of these other girls, and I had to ger her out of the way.

Q. Did you think you had to get her out of the way permanently?

A. I sort of figured it would have to be that way, but I am not quite sure.

Thus, contrary to the misunderstanding of counsel and amicus curiae, Officer Stenberg's question ("You knew the wrongfulness of killing your mother?") related unequivocally to defendant's knowledge at the time of the commission of the murder; and defendant's equally unequivocal answer ("I did. I was thinking of it. I was aware of it.") related to the same period of time. This admission, coupled with defendant's uncontradicted course of conduct and other statements set forth hereinabove, constitutes substantial evidence from which the jury could find defendant legally sane at the time of the matricide.

Certainly in the case now at bench the defendant had ample time for any normal person to maturely and appreciatively reflect upon his contemplated act and to arrive at a cold, deliberated and premeditated conclusion. He did this in a sense—and apparently to the full extent of which he was capable. But, indisputably on the record, this defendant was not and is not a fully normal or mature, mentally well person. He knew the difference between right and wrong; he knew that the intended act was wrong and nevertheless carried it out. But the extent of his understanding, reflection upon it and its consequences, with realization of the enormity of the evil, appears to have been materially—as relevant to appraising the quantum of his moral turpitude and depravity—vague and detached.

Reduced to second degree murder.

CASE DISCUSSION

Do you agree that Wolff was too immature to premeditate his mother's murder? Would you treat him just as you would an adult? Would you sentence him to death if capital punishment was legal for adults? Would you remove him altogether from the adult criminal justice system? Would you convict him but send him to a juvenile institution? Or would you do what the court did: convict him, but of the lesser crime, second-degree murder?

Youth does not always excuse criminal responsibility, or mitigate the punishment; sometimes it aggravates conduct. For example, seventeen-year-old Munoz was convicted of possessing a switchblade under a New York City ordinance that prohibited youths under twenty-one from carrying such knives. Had Munoz been over twenty-one, what he did would not have been a crime.[22]

CASE

Too Old to Commit Crimes?

Old Age as Criminal Defense

Fred Cohen, *Criminal Law Bulletin*, 21 (1985), p. 9

[A prosecutor related the following tragedy.]

You have this married couple, married for over 50 years, living in a retirement home. The guy sends his wife out for bagels and while the wife can still get around she forgets and brings back onion rolls. Not a capital offense, right? Anyway, the guy goes berserk and he axes his wife; he kills the poor woman with a Boy Scout–type axe!

What do we do now? Set a high bail? Prosecute? Get a conviction and send the fellow to prison? You tell me! We did nothing. The media dropped it quickly and, I hope, that's it.

CASE DISCUSSION

Which alternatives available to the prosecutor would you choose? What about an old-age defense? In *Regina v. Kemp*, a respectable old man, who had never been in trouble, beat his wife. The old man, Kemp, suffered from arteriosclerosis, or hardening of the arteries, a disease that affects mental capacity. The condition caused him to assault his wife. Although the court did not permit his old age to excuse him, the judges did permit his arteriosclerosis to prove he was insane. The jury found Kemp not guilty but insane.[23]

ENTRAPMENT

Law enforcement officers who lead citizens to commit crimes provide those citizens with the excuse called entrapment. Entrapment does not justify crime; it excuses crime because the law enforcement officer "manufactured" the crime. Entrapment also excuses criminal liability in order to deter police from encouraging crime; it allows the "criminal" to go free because the police abused their power. Police encouragement of crime breeds public resentment toward law and undermines the law's effectiveness. The verdict acquitting John DeLorean of drug charges illustrates this. Jurors said the FBI went too far in trying to prove DeLorean guilty. Although DeLorean was, in their estimation, clearly guilty, the jurors acquitted him to show the FBI that it should use less offensive methods to catch criminals.[24]

Entrapment does not excuse the most serious crimes, such as murder and rape. Until recently, the government used decoys and other undercover tactics mainly against consensual crimes, such as narcotics, prostitution, and gambling. Increasingly, the government has come to rely on similar tactics against street muggers and white-collar criminals, such as in the ABSCAM cases involving members of Congress and "greylord," involving Chicago judges. Furthermore, not everybody can legally entrap. Paid, full-time law enforcement officers can entrap. So can paid informants, private detectives, and other "civilians" working for the government. Private persons who induce others to commit crime cannot entrap.[25]

Some state courts prohibit defendants from taking inconsistent positions by denying that they committed the crime charged and pleading the defense of entrapment. For example, a defendant cannot deny buying crack by claiming that she was in another city when an undercover agent testified she bought the heroin from him, and then claim that the officer entrapped her by pressuring her into buying it. The United States Supreme Court, however, has ruled that defendants can deny guilt and then plead entrapment under federal criminal law. The reason for the rule prohibiting inconsistent positions rests in part on the logic that without crime there can be no entrapment.[26]

Jurisdictions vary as to what constitutes entrapment. According to the traditional, or subjective, entrapment test, entrapment required the officer to instigate the crime—that is, to create or manufacture the intent to commit a crime in the mind of one who was not otherwise disposed to commit it. Entrapment, therefore, depends on what stimulated the specific defendant to commit the crime; if the stimulus came from the government, then the law excuses the defendant. The subjective standard assumes that the legislature did not intend to make criminals out of people whom the police (or other government agents) induced to commit crimes.

The subjective test requires more than the government merely providing the defendant with the opportunity to commit a crime. For example, if I am walking down the street looking for a drunk to roll and I find a decoy with $100 sticking out of her pocket and take it, the decoy did not entrap me. I was predisposed to commit the crime; the decoy only provided me with the opportunity to commit it. On the other hand, suppose I am in a drug treatment center where for months I have tried to control my addiction to heroin. An undercover agent begs me to get him some heroin. At first I refuse, but after repeated pressure in which he appeals to my sympathy for his desperate need for it, I finally get some for him. The agent entrapped me because I did not want to deal in heroin; he instigated the crime.[27]

Some courts have adopted an objective test to determine entrapment. The objective test finds entrapment whenever law enforcement activity would cause a reasonable person who is not so predisposed to commit a crime. The objective standard focuses on the government's actions, not the defendant's. The test asks: Would a reasonable person have responded to the officer's action by committing the crime? The objective standard's primary objective is to discourage government misconduct, not to protect "innocent" defendants.[28]

CASE

Are Police Decoys Illegal Traps?

Cruz v. State

465 So.2d 516 (Fla.1985)

[Cruz was convicted of grand theft. He appealed. Justice Ehrlich delivered the opinion.]

FACTS

Tampa police undertook a decoy operation in a high-crime area. An officer posed as an inebriated indigent, smelling of alcohol and pretending to drink wine from a bottle. The officer leaned against a building near an alleyway, his face to the wall. Plainly displayed from a rear pants pocket was $150 in currency, paper-clipped together. Defendant Cruz and a woman happened upon the scene as passersby sometime after 10 P.M. Cruz approached the decoy officer, may have attempted to say something to him, then continued on his way. Ten to fifteen minutes later, the defendant and his companion returned to the scene and Cruz took the money from the decoy's pocket without harming him in any way. Officers then arrested Cruz as he walked from the scene. The decoy situation did not involve the same modus operandi as any of the unsolved crimes which had occurred in the area. Police were not seeking a particular individual, nor were they aware of any prior criminal acts by the defendant.

OPINION

The entrapment defense arises from a recognition that sometimes police activity will induce an otherwise innocent individual to commit the criminal act the police activity seeks to produce.

In articulating [the entrapment doctrine], our Court has adopted two standards respecting entrapment. The traditional or subjective standard defines entrapment as law enforcement conduct which implants in the mind of an innocent person the disposition to commit the alleged crime, and hence induces its commission. Under this traditional formulation, the defense of entrapment is limited to those defendants who were not predisposed to commit the crime induced by government actions.

In recent years, however, this Court has fashioned a second, independent standard for assessing entrapment. It recognizes that when official conduct inducing crime is so egregious as to impugn the integrity of a court that permits a conviction, the predisposition of the defendant becomes irrelevant.

[A]s the part played by the State in the criminal activity increases, the importance of the factor of defendant's criminal intent decreases, until finally a point may be reached where the methods [employed] by the state to obtain a conviction cannot be countenanced, even though a defendant's predisposition is shown. Whether the police activity has overstepped the bounds of permissible conduct is a question to be decided by the trial court rather than the jury.

To guide the trial courts, we propound the following threshold test of an entrapment defense: Entrapment has not occurred as a matter of law where police activity (1) has as its end the interruption of a specific ongoing criminal activity; and (2) utilizes means reasonably tailored to apprehend those involved in the ongoing criminal activity.

The first prong of this test addresses the problem of police "virtue testing," that is, police activity seeking to prosecute crime where no such crime exists but for the police activity engendering the crime. "Society is at war with the criminal classes." Police must fight this war, not engage in the manufacture of new hostilities.

The second prong of the threshold test addresses the problem of inappropriate techniques. Considerations in deciding whether police activity is permissible under this prong include whether a government agent "includes or encourages another person to engage in conduct constituting such offense by either: (a) making knowingly false representations designed to induce the belief that such conduct is not prohibited; or (b) employing methods of persuasion or inducement which create a substantial risk that such an offense will be committed by persons other than those who are ready to commit it." Model Penal Code § 2.13 (1962).

Applying this test to the case before us, we find that the drunken bum decoy operation fails. In Cruz's motion to dismiss, one of the undisputed facts was that "none of the unsolved crimes occuring [*sic*] near this location involved the same modus operandi as the simulated situation created by the officers." The record thus implies police were apparently attempting to interrupt some kind of ongoing criminal activity. However, the record does not show what specific activity was targeted. This lack of focus is sufficient for the scenario to fail the first prong of the test. However, even if the police were seeking to catch persons who had been "rolling" drunks in the area, the criminal scenario here, with $150 (paper-clipped to ensure more than $100 was taken, making the offense a felony) enticingly protruding from the back pocket of a person seemingly incapable of noticing its removal, carries with it the "substantial risk that such an offense will be committed by persons other than those who are ready to commit it." Model Penal Code § 2.13. This sufficiently addresses the proper recognition that entrapment has occurred where "the decoy simply provided the opportunity to commit a crime to anyone who succumbed to the lure of the bait." This test also recognizes, that the considerations inherent in our threshold test are not properly addressed in the context of the predisposition element of the second, subjective test.

For reasons discussed, we hold that the police activity in the instant case constituted entrapment as a matter of law under the threshold test adopted here. Accordingly, we quash the district court decision. It is so ordered.

CASE DISCUSSION

Notice that the court adopts both the objective test (whether reasonable persons would be enticed by the police decoy tactic used) and the subjective test (whether Cruz himself was enticed into doing something he would otherwise not do). Most courts do not use both tests; they use one or the other. States are divided on the question. Some use the subjective test; others use the objective test. Which do you prefer? Or would you do as this court did: adopt a threshold objective test, which, if passed, then goes to a subjective test?

═══ INSANITY

The insanity defense commands great public and scholarly attention. However, defendants rarely plead insanity because they have too much to lose and too little to gain if they succeed. Contrary to widely held beliefs, and unlike all other defenses discussed up to this point, a successful insanity plea does not lead to automatic freedom. The verdict is not guilty by reason of insanity. Since defendants were insane when they committed the crime, they are not released immediately. Instead, special proceedings take place in which the court decides whether they still require custody for their own and society's safety. Courts nearly always commit them to maximum-security hospitals, institutions that are virtually indistinguishable from prisons. Successful insanity pleas thus merely bestow upon the government the authority to incarcerate without conviction. Persons found not guilty by reason of insanity rarely, if ever, go free immediately, and some never do. Not surprisingly, then, only a few defendants resort to the insanity plea. The few who do plead insanity—nearly all charged with capital crimes or ones subject to life imprisonment—rarely succeed. [29]

Insanity excuses because it impairs the *mens rea*. The rationale of the insanity defense is that punishing insane persons does not serve criminal law's objectives. If defendants were so mentally diseased that they could not form *mens rea*, then both retribution and general deterrence are inappropriate. The state can invoke its civil commitment authority to incapacitate and treat mentally ill persons without calling upon the criminal law.

Insanity is a legal concept, not a medical term. What psychiatry calls mental illness may or may not conform to the law's definition of insanity. Hence, mental disease sufficient to prove insanity may not mean mental illness, which psychiatrists treat in various ways. Legal insanity is the test that excuses criminal responsibility. Psychiatrists testify in courts only to aid in determining whether defendants are legally insane, not to prove they are mentally ill. The verdict "guilty but mentally ill" makes this point clear. In that verdict, used in some jurisdictions, the jury can find that defendants were not insane but were mentally ill when they committed crimes. These defendants receive criminal sentences and go to prison, but they may require and are supposed to receive treatment for their mental illness while in prison.[30]

Jurisdictions determine insanity according to two primary tests: (1) the right-wrong test and (2) the substantial capacity test. Both require looking at defendants' mental capacity, but they differ in what they emphasize about that capacity. The right-wrong test focuses on the intellect, or *cognition*—what defendants know. The substantial capacity test focuses not only on knowledge, but also on the emotional dimension to understanding—defendants' appreciation of what they did. Freud expressed this distinction in his phrase, "there is knowing, and there is *knowing!*" A child knows intellectually that stealing is wrong but does not fully appreciate—or feel—its significance. The substantial capacity test also stresses *volition*, or defendants' will to control their actions. Defendants may know that what they are doing is wrong but lack the will to control what they do.

M'Naghten Rule, or Right-Wrong Test

The **M'Naghten rule,** or **right-wrong test,** focuses narrowly on defendants' intellectual capacity to know what they are doing and to distinguish right from wrong. In *Rex v. Porter,* the judge explains the right-wrong test in these instructions to the jury:

> I wish to draw your attention to some general considerations affecting the question of insanity in the criminal law in the hope that by so doing you may be helped to grasp what the law prescribes. The purpose of the law in punishing people is to prevent others from committing a like crime or crimes. Its prime purpose is to deter people from committing offences. It may be that there is an element of retribution in the criminal law, so that when people have committed offences the law considers that they merit punishment, but its prime purpose is to preserve society from the depredations of dangerous and vicious people. Now, it is perfectly useless for the law to attempt, by threatening punishment, to deter people from committing crimes if their mental condition is such that they cannot be in the least influenced by the possibility or probability of subsequent punishment; if they cannot understand what they are doing or cannot understand the ground upon which the law proceeds. The law is not directed, as medical science is, to curing mental infirmities. The criminal law is not directed, as the civil law of lunacy is, to the care and custody of people of weak mind whose personal property may be in jeopardy through someone else taking a hand in the conduct of their affairs and their lives. This is quite a different thing from the question, what utility there is in the punishment of people who, at a moment, would commit acts which, if done when they were in sane minds, would be crimes. What is the utility of punishing people if they be beyond the control of the law for reasons of mental health? In considering that, it will not perhaps, if you have ever reflected upon the matter, have escaped your attention that a great number of people who come into a Criminal Court are abnormal. They would not be there if they were the normal type of average everyday people. Many of them are very peculiar in their dispositions and peculiarly tempered. That is markedly the case in sexual offences. Nevertheless, they are mentally quite able to appreciate what they are doing and quite able to appreciate the threatened punishment of the law and the wrongness of their acts, and they are held in check by the prospect of punishment. It would be very absurd if the law were to withdraw that check on the ground that they were somewhat different from their fellow creatures in mental make-up or texture at the very moment when the check is most needed. You will therefore see that the law, in laying down a standard of mental disorder sufficient to justify a jury in finding a prisoner not guilty on the ground of insanity at the moment of offence, is addressing itself to a somewhat difficult task. It is attempting to define what are the classes of people who should not be punished although they have done actual things which in others would amount to crime. It is quite a different object to that which the medical profession has in view or other departments of the law have in view of defining insanity for the purpose of the custody of a person's property, capacity to make a will, and the like.[31]

The right-wrong test, although it has deep historical antecedents, derived its present form from the famous English *M'Naghten* case. In 1843,

Daniel M'Naghten suffered the paranoid delusion that the prime minister, Sir Robert Peel, had masterminded a conspiracy to kill M'Naghten. M'Naghten shot at Peel in delusional self-defense, but killed Peel's secretary, Edward Drummond, by mistake. Following his trial for murder, the jury returned a verdict of not guilty by reason of insanity. On appeal, England's highest court, the House of Lords, formulated the right-wrong test, or M'Naghten rule. According to the rule, the court designed a two-pronged insanity test: (1) the defendant must suffer from a *disease* or *defect* of the mind, and (2) the disease or defect must *cause* the defendant to not know either the nature and quality of the criminal act or that the act was wrong.[32]

The right-wrong test, as the House of Lords formulated it, creates several difficulties. First, what mental diseases or defects does the "disease of the mind" include? All formulations include severe psychoses, such as the paranoia from which M'Naghten himself suffered, and schizophrenia. Virtually all also include severe mental retardation affecting cognition. They exclude neuroses and/or personality disorders, particularly psychopathic and sociopathic personalities—those who engage in repeated criminal or antisocial conduct.[33]

The word *knowing* also creates problems. Most statutes and decisions say it means pure intellectual awareness: cognition. Others include more than intellectual awareness, which nearly everyone possesses. They bring within the compass of knowing the ability to understand or appreciate, meaning to grasp an act's true significance. Hence, some courts add to cognition or intellectual awareness an emotional, affective, or feeling dimension. Some jurisdictions do not define the term, leaving it to juries to define it by applying it to the facts of specific cases.

The following example captures the meaning of not knowing the "nature and quality of the act," as *M'Naghten* defined that phrase: If a man believes he is squeezing lemons when in fact he is strangling his wife, he clearly does not know the nature and quality of his act. Some hold that the phrase means knowing right from wrong. A few go further, contending that it refers to more than knowing the nature of the physical act. One court, for example, required "true insight" into the act's consequences. This does not mean that defendants must believe the act is wrong. M'Naghten himself knew that he was killing, but he thought the killing was justified.

The word *wrong* itself has created problems in the definition of the right-wrong test. Some jurisdictions require that defendants did not know their conduct was *legally* wrong; others interpret wrong to mean that defendants did not know their conduct was *morally* wrong. Consider the madman who kills another person under the insane delusion that his subsequent conviction and execution for the murder will save the human race. The madman knew that killing was legally, but not morally, wrong. If wrong means legal, the madman is guilty; if it means moral, he is insane. Some jurisdictions adopt an objective test to determine moral wrongfulness: Do defendants lack the capacity to know that their conduct violated the prevailing moral standard of the community? Others adopt a subjective test: Do defendants know the conduct was wrong by their own moral standards?[34]

CASE

Too Insane to Be Guilty?

State v. Crenshaw

98 Wn.2d 789, 659 P.2d 488 (1983)

[Crenshaw was convicted of first-degree murder. He appealed. Justice Brachtenbach delivered the opinion.]

FACTS

While defendant and his wife were on their honeymoon in Canada, petitioner was deported as a result of his participation in a brawl. He secured a motel room in Blaine, Washington and waited for his wife to join him. When she arrived 2 days later, he immediately thought she had been unfaithful—he sensed "it wasn't the same Karen she'd been with someone else."

Petitioner did not mention his suspicions to his wife, instead he took her to the motel room and beat her unconscious. He then went to a nearby store, stole a knife, and returned to stab his wife 24 times, inflicting a fatal wound. He left again, drove to a nearby farm where he had been employed and borrowed an ax. Upon returning to the motel room, he decapitated his wife with such force that the ax marks cut into the concrete floor under the carpet and splattered blood throughout the room.

Petitioner then proceeded to conceal his actions. He placed the body in a blanket, the head in a pillowcase and put both in his wife's car. Next, he went to a service station, borrowed a bucket and sponge, and cleaned the room of blood and fingerprints. Before leaving, petitioner also spoke with the motel manager about a phone bill, then chatted with him for awhile over a beer.

When Crenshaw left the motel he drove to a remote area 25 miles away where he hid the two parts of the body in thick brush. He then fled, driving to the Hoquiam area, about 200 miles from the scene of the crime. There he picked up two hitchhikers, told them of his crime, and enlisted their aid in disposing of his wife's car in a river. The hitchhikers contacted the police and Crenshaw was apprehended shortly thereafter. He voluntarily confessed to the crime.

The defense of not guilty by reason of insanity was a major issue at trial. Crenshaw testified that he followed the Moscovite religious faith, and that it would be improper for a Moscovite not to kill his wife if she committed adultery. Crenshaw also has a history of mental problems, for which he has been hospitalized in the past. The jury, however, rejected petitioner's insanity defense, and found him guilty of murder in the first degree.

OPINION

The insanity defense is not available to all who are mentally deficient or deranged; legal insanity has a different meaning and a different purpose than the concept of medical insanity. A verdict of not guilty by reason of insanity completely absolves a defendant of any criminal responsibility. Therefore, "the defense is available only to those persons who have lost contact with reality so completely that they are beyond any of the influences of the criminal law."

Petitioner assigned error to insanity defense instruction 10 which reads:

> Insanity existing at the time of the commission of the act charged is a defense.
>
> For a defendant to be found not guilty by reason of insanity you must find that, as a result of mental disease or defect, the defendant's mind was affected to such an extent that the defendant was unable to perceive the nature and quality of the acts with which the defendant is charged or was unable to tell right from wrong with reference to the particular acts with which defendant is charged.
>
> What is meant by the terms "right and wrong" refers to knowledge of a person at the time of committing an act that he was acting contrary to the law.

Petitioner contends . . . that the trial court erred in defining "right and wrong" as legal right and wrong rather than in the moral sense.

First, in discussing the term "moral" wrong, it is important to note that it is society's morals, and not the individual's morals, that are the standard for judging moral wrong under M'Naghten. If wrong meant moral wrong judged by the individual's own conscience, this would seriously undermine the criminal law, for it would allow one who violated the law to be excused from criminal responsibility solely because, in his own conscience, his act was not morally wrong.

This principle was emphasized by Justice Cardozo:

> The anarchist is not at liberty to break the law because he reasons that all government is wrong. The devotee of a religious cult that enjoins polygamy or human sacrifice as a duty is not thereby relieved from responsibility before the law.

There is evidence on the record that Crenshaw knew his actions were wrong according to society's standards, as well as legally wrong. Dr. Belden testified:

> I think Mr. Crenshaw is quite aware on one level that he is in conflict with the law *and with people*. However, this is not something that he personally invests his emotions in. (Italics ours.)

We conclude that Crehshaw knew his acts were morally wrong from society's viewpoint and also knew his acts were illegal. His personal belief that it was his duty to kill his wife for her alleged infidelity cannot serve to exculpate him from legal responsibility for his acts.

We also find that, under any definition of wrong, Crenshaw did not qualify for the insanity defense under M'Naghten; therefore, any alleged error in that definition must be viewed as harmless.

Here, any error is harmless for two alternate reasons. First, Crenshaw failed to prove an essential element of the defense because he did not prove his alleged delusions stemmed from a mental defect; second, he did not prove by a preponderance of the evidence that he was legally insane at the time of the crime.

In addition to an incapacity to know right from wrong, M'Naghten requires that such incapacity stem from a mental disease or defect. RCW 9A.12.010. Assuming, arguendo, that Crenshaw did not know right from wrong, he failed to prove that a mental defect was the cause of this inability.

Petitioner's insanity argument is premised on the following facts: (1) he is a Moscovite and Moscovites believe it is their duty to assassinate an unfaithful spouse; (2) he "knew," without asking, that his wife had been unfaithful when he met her in Blaine and this was equivalent to an insane delusion; and (3) at other times in his life, he had been diagnosed as a paranoid personality and had been committed to mental institutions. A conscientious application of the M'Naghten rule demonstrates, however, that these factors do not afford petitioner the sanctuary of the insanity defense.

To begin, petitioner's Moscovite beliefs are irrelevant to the insanity defense, because they are not insane delusions. Some notion of morality, unrelated to a mental illness, which disagrees with the law and mores of our society is not an insane delusion.

Nor was petitioner's belief that his wife was unfaithful an insane delusion. Dr. Trowbridge, a psychiatrist, explained:

> A man suspects his wife of being unfaithful. Certainly such suspicions are not necessarily delusional, even if they're ill based. Just because he suspected his wife of being unfaithful doesn't mean that he was crazy.

Certainly when a man kills his wife he doesn't do it in a rational way. No one ever does that rationally. But that is not to suggest that every time a man kills his wife he was [sic] insane.

Finally, evidence of prior commitments to mental institutions is not proof that one was legally insane at the time the criminal act was committed.

Those who are commonly regarded as "odd" or "unsound" or even "deranged" would not normally qualify [for the insanity defense]. Many, if not most, mentally ill persons presently being treated in the mental institutions of this state who are there under the test of "likelihood of serious harm to the person detained or to others," would not meet the M'Naghten test, if charged with a crime.

Thus, petitioner does not establish the necessary connection between his criminal acts and his psychological problems to qualify for the insanity defense.

In addition, the preponderance of the evidence weighs against finding Crenshaw legally insane. All of the psychological experts, save one, testified that defendant was not insane at the time of the murder. The only doctor who concluded defendant (petitioner) was legally insane, Dr. Hunger, was a psychologist who had not examined petitioner for a year and a half.

Given the various qualifications of the experts, the time they spent with the petitioner, and the proximity in time of their examinations to the murder, the testimony does not establish by a preponderance of the evidence that petitioner was legally insane at the time of the murder.

Furthermore, in addition to the expert testimony, there was lay testimony that petitioner appeared rational at the time of the killing. After cleaning the motel room, Crenshaw resolved a phone bill dispute with the manager, then shared a beer with him without arousing any suspicion in the manager's mind. Also, the woman who gave him the ax testified as to his behavior the day before the murder:

> Well, he seemed very normal or I certainly wouldn't have handed him an ax or a hoe. He was polite, he done his work. He didn't, I wasn't afraid of him or anything. I mean we were just out there working and I certainly wouldn't have handed him an ax or anything like that if I would have thought that there was anything even remotely peculiar about him.

And, with specific reference to the time when petitioner borrowed the ax to decapitate his wife:

> Q. Did he seem rational to you?
> A. Oh, yes, he was very nice.
> Q. Did he seem coherent when he spoke to you?
> A. Oh, yes.
> Q. Did he appear to be sane to you then?
> A. Yes.

Thus, at the same time that he was embroiled in the act of murdering his wife, he was rational, coherent, and sane in his dealings with others.

Finally, evidence of petitioner's calculated execution of the crime and his sophisticated attempts to avert discovery support a finding of sanity. Crenshaw performed the murder methodically, leaving the motel room twice to acquire the knife and ax necessary to perform the deed. Then, after the killing he scrubbed the motel room to clean up the blood and remove his fingerprints. Next, he drove 25 miles to hide the body in thick brush in a remote area. Finally, he drove several hundred miles and ditched the car in a river.

Such attempts to hide evidence of a crime manifest an awareness that the act was legally wrong. Moreover, petitioner testified that he did these things because he "didn't want to get caught."

To summarize thus far, we find no error in instruction 10 for the following reasons: (1) As we interpret the M'Naghten case, it was not improper for the trial court to instruct with reference to the law of the land, under the facts of this case; (2) because the concept of moral wrong refers to the mores of society and not to the individual's morals, "moral" wrong is synonymous with "legal" wrong with a serious crime such as this one, therefore, instructing in terms of legal wrong did not alter the meaning of the M'Naghten rule; (3) any error was harmless because (a) Crenshaw did not show that at the time of

the crime his mind was affected as a result of a mental disease or defect and without this essential element the insanity defense was not available to him, and (b) an overwhelming preponderance of the evidence supports the finding that Crenshaw was not legally insane when he killed his wife. We thus conclude that the additional statement in instruction 10 was not improper, or, at the very least, that it was harmless error.

Affirmed.

CASE DISCUSSION

Do you agree that moral wrong and legal wrong are the same? Should the test be whether Crenshaw knew he was breaking the law or that he knew it was wrong in the general sense? What would you do with Crenshaw? Do you think it is possible to be objective about Crenshaw's insanity? Or does the brutal way he killed his wife make you want to call him a criminal? Do you see how this can create serious problems with the insanity defense?

CRITICISMS AND DEFENSE. The right-wrong test has generated protracted argument. Critics mainly contend that modern developments in both law and psychiatry have rendered the test obsolete. This criticism loomed large during the 1950s when many social reformers relied on Freudian psychology to cure a wide spectrum of individual and social ills. *Durham v. United States* reflects psychiatry's influence on criminal law generally and on the insanity defense particularly. With regard to the right-wrong test, the court said:

> The science of psychiatry now recognizes that a man is an integrated personality and that reason, which is only one element in that personality, is not the sole determinant of his conduct. The right-wrong test, which considers knowledge or reason alone, is therefore an inadequate guide to mental responsibility for criminal behavior.[35]

Borrowing from a New Hampshire rule formulated in 1871 and still in effect in that state, the *Durham* court formulated a broad insanity definition reflecting the influence of psychiatry. According to the **Durham rule, or product test,** acts that are the product of mental disease or defect excuse criminal liability. The court aimed to broaden the concept of insanity beyond the purely intellectual knowledge in the right-wrong test to deeper areas of cognition and will. Only New Hampshire (where the test orginated), the federal court of appeals for the District of Columbia (which decided *Durham*), and Maine ever adopted the product test. The federal court and Maine have since abandoned the test, leaving it in effect only in New Hampshire.[36]

M'Naghten's defenders contend that the product test misses the point of legal insanity. They maintain that the right-wrong test should not

substitute mental illness for insanity. Rather, it is an instrument to determine which mental states ought to relieve persons of criminal responsibility. Two articulate defenders put it this way:

> It is always necessary to start any discussion of M'Naghten by stressing that the case does not state a test of psychosis or mental illness. Rather, it lists conditions under which those who are mentally diseased will be relieved from criminal responsibility. Thus, criticism of M'Naghten based on the proposition that the case is premised on an outdated view of mental disease is inappropriate. The case can only be criticized justly if it is based on an outdated view of the mental conditions that ought to preclude application of criminal sanction.[37]

Other critics contend that the M'Naghten rule focuses too narrowly on intellectual knowledge of right and wrong in cognition, neglecting the deeper emotional components necessary to full appreciation of conduct. Furthermore, considering only cognition excludes volition—whether defendants can control their behavior even though they fully appreciate, both intellectually and emotionally, that they are acting wrongfully. These critics say that criminal law acts inappropriately if it excuses only those who do not know or appreciate what they are doing while punishing those who cannot stop themselves from doing what they know is wrong. We can neither blame nor deter those who cannot conform their conduct to what the law requires. The law of civil commitment can protect society from them and treat them without resorting to criminal sanctions.

M'Naghten's supporters contend that the law should presume everyone has some control because operating on that assumption deters more potential offenders. Therefore, the insanity defense ought to include only those who (1) did not know what they were doing or (2) did know what they were doing but did not know it was wrong, assuming that the second group can choose right if they know what right is.

IRRESISTIBLE IMPULSE. Several jurisdictions have supplemented the right-wrong test with the irresistible impulse test in an effort to deal with the volition problem. **Irresistible impulse** requires

> a verdict of not guilty by reason of insanity if it is found that the defendant has a mental disease which kept him from controlling his conduct. Such a verdict is called for even if the defendant knew what he was doing and that it was wrong.[38]

Although the irresistible impulse test predates M'Naghten (it goes back to at least 1834), the leading case occurred in 1877. In *Parsons v. State,* the court ruled that whenever defendants plead insanity, juries should determine the following:

1. At the time of the crime was the defendant afflicted with "a disease of the mind"?
2. If so, did the defendant know right from wrong with respect to the act charged? If not, the law excuses the defendant.
3. If the defendant did have such knowledge the law will still excuse the defendant if two conditions concur:

(a) if mental disease caused the defendant to so far lose the power to choose between right and wrong and to avoid doing the alleged act that the disease destroyed the defendant's free will, and

(b) if the mental disease was the sole cause of the act.[39]

Despite broadening the right-wrong defense, critics maintain that the irresistible impulse supplement still restricts the insanity defense too much. It includes only impulsive acts, ignoring mental disease "characterized by brooding and reflection." Defenders deny this. Courts do not tell juries that they must limit their findings to sudden and unplanned impulses; juries can consider any evidence showing that defendants lack control owing to mental disease. Critics also claim that the irresistible requirement implies that defendants must lack control totally. In practice, however, juries do acquit defendants who have some control—rarely, if ever, demanding an utter lack of control.

Other critics claim that irresistible impulse includes too much. By permitting people who lack control to escape criminal liability, it unduly curtails criminal law's deterrent purposes. For example, the jury acquitted John Hinckley, Jr., on the grounds that Hinckley was insane when he attempted to assassinate former president Ronald Reagan in order to gain the attention of actress Jodie Foster. Shortly after Hinckley's trial, Harvard criminal law professor Charles Nesson wrote:

> [T]o many Mr. Hinckley seems like a kid who had a rough life and who lacked the moral fiber to deal with it. This is not to deny that Mr. Hinckley is crazy but to recognize that there is a capacity for craziness in all of us. Lots of people have tough lives, many tougher than Mr. Hinckley's, and manage to cope. The Hinckley verdict let those people down. For anyone who experiences life as a struggle to act responsibly in the face of various temptations to let go, the Hinckley verdict is demoralizing, an example of someone who let himself go and who has been exonerated because of it.[40]

Defenders claim that empirical research has not demonstrated the effectiveness of deterrence; hence, the law should not base the insanity defense on it. Finally, opponents who are disillusioned with the rehabilitative ideal argue that the state should not engage in hopeless efforts to treat and cure the mentally diseased. (See chapter 2 for a discussion of deterrence.)

Despite its defenders, several jurisdictions have recently rejected irresistible impulse on the ground that juries cannot accurately distinguish between irresistible and merely unresisted impulses. Unresisted impulses should not excuse criminal conduct.[41] The federal statute abolishing irresistible impulse in federal cases provides as follows:

> It is an affirmative defense to a prosecution under any Federal statute that, at the time of the commission of the acts constituting the offense, the defendant, as a result of a severe mental disease or defect, was unable to appreciate the nature and quality or the wrongfulness of his acts. Mental disease or defect does not otherwise constitute a defense.[42]

Substantial Capacity or Model Penal Code Test

The right-wrong test, either supplemented by the irresistible impulse or not, was the rule in most states until the 1960s, after which the Model

Penal Code's **substantial capacity test** became the majority rule. During the 1970s, and in the 1980s following John Hinckley's trial, the pure right-wrong test (unencumbered by either the emotional component of understanding or irresistible impulse, or both) has enjoyed a resurgence.[43]

The Model Penal Code provision resulted from efforts to remove objections to both the M'Naghten rule and the irresistible impulse test while preserving both tests' legal nature. It emphasizes the qualities in insanity that affect culpability: the intellectual (cognitive) and emotional (affective) components of understanding, and will (volition).

The Model Penal Code requires that defendants lack "substantial," not total, mental capacity. Both the right-wrong and irresistible impulse tests are ambiguous on this point, leading some to maintain that both require total lack of knowledge and control. Hence, persons who know right and wrong minimally and whose will to resist is slightly intact are insane according to the Code provision. (See Appendix, Section 4.01.)

The use of the word *appreciate* instead of *know* makes clear that mere intellectual awareness does not constitute culpability. The Code includes affective or emotional components of understanding. The phrase "conform conduct" removes the requirement of a "sudden" lack of control. In other words, the Code provision eliminates the suggestion that losing control means losing it on the spur of the moment, as the irresistible impulse test unfortunately implies. The Code's definition of "mental disease or defect" excludes psychopathic personalities, habitual criminals, and antisocial personalities from the defense.

Until the recent return to right-wrong, the substantial capacity test had replaced right-wrong as the majority rule. The history of the insanity defense in California illustrates the original adoption of the M'Naghten rule, then the Model Penal Code substantial capacity test, and then a return to right-wrong by an initiative that the electorate approved in 1982. *People v. Skinner* raised the issue of whether the insanity test approved by the electorate reverted to an even stricter test of insanity—the wild beast test in effect before 1850. According to the wild beast test, defendants must lack total knowledge both of the nature of what they did and that what they did was wrong.

CASE

Was He Insane?

People v. Skinner

39 Cal.3d 765, 217 Cal. Rptr. 685, 704 P.2d 752 (1985)

[Skinner was convicted of second-degree murder, being determined legally sane, and he appealed. The California Supreme Court reversed, finding Skinner not guilty by reason of insanity, without further hearing on the sanity issue. Justice Groddin delivered the opinion. Chief Justice Byrd delivered a dissenting opinion.]

FACTS

. . . Defendant strangled his wife while he was on a day pass from the Camarillo State Hospital at which he was a patient. [Psychiatric testimony included] the opinion . . . that defendant suffered from either classical paranoic schizophrenia, or schizo-affective illness with significant paranoid features. A delusional product of this illness was a belief held by the defendant that the marriage vow "till death do us part" bestows on a marital partner a God-given right to kill the other partner who has violated or was inclined to violate the marital vows, and that because the vows reflect the direct wishes of God, the killing is with complete moral and criminal impunity. The act is not wrongful because it is sanctified by the will and desire of God. . . .

OPINION

For over a century prior to the decision in *People v. Drew,* (1978), California courts framed this state's definition of insanity, as a defense in criminal cases, upon the two-pronged test adopted by the House of Lords in *M'Naghten's Case* . . . [owing to mental disease or defect, defendant (1) did not know the nature and quality of the act he was doing or (2) if he did know it, he did not know that it was wrong]. Over the years the *M'Naghten* test became subject to considerable criticism and was abandoned in a number of jursidictions. In *Drew* this court followed suit, adopting the test for mental incapacity proposed by the American Law Institute . . .

In June 1982 the California electorate adopted an initiative measure . . . which . . . for the first time established a statutory definition of insanity . . . It is apparent from the language of section 25(b) that it was designed to eliminate the *Drew* test and to reinstate the prongs of the *M'Naghten* test. However, the section uses the conjunctive "and" instead of the disjunctive "or" to connect the two prongs. Read literally, therefore, section 25(b) would do more than reinstate the *M'Naghten* test. It would strip the insanity defense from an accused who, by reason of mental disease, is incapable of knowing that the act he was doing was wrong. That is, in fact, the interpretation adopted by the trial court in this case. . . .

The judge stated that under the *Drew* test of legal insanity defendant would qualify as insane, and also found that "under the right-wrong prong of section 25(b), the defendant would qualify as legally insane; but under the other prong, he clearly does not." Concluding that by the use of the conjunctive "and" in section 25(b), the electorate demonstrated an intent to establish a stricter test of insanity than the *M'Naghten* test, and to "virtually eliminate" insanity as a defense, the judge found that defendant had not established that he was legally insane. . . .

In this context we must determine whether the trial court's conclusion . . . was correct, and if not, whether the court's finding that defendant met the "right-wrong" aspect of the test requires reversal. . . .

For more than a century after . . . the *M'Naghten* test [was adopted in this state], although sometimes stated in the conjunctive, [it] was in fact applied so as to permit a finding of insanity if either prong of the test was satisfied. . . . [T]he insanity defense reflects a fundamental legal principle common to the jurisprudence of this country and to the common law of England that criminal sanctions are imposed only on persons who act with wrongful intent in the commission of a *malum in se* offense. Since 1850 the disjunctive *M'Naghten* test of insanity has been accepted as the rule by which the minimum cognitive function which constitutes wrongful intent will be measured in this state. As such it is itself among the fundamental principles of our criminal law. Had it been the intent of the drafters . . . or of the electorate which adopted it both to abrogate the more expansive ALI-*Drew* test and to abandon that prior fundamental principle of culpability for crime, we would anticipate that this intent would be expressed in some more obvious manner than the substitution of a single conjunctive in a lengthy initiative provision. . . .

Applying section 25(b) as a conjunctive test of insanity would erase that fundamental principle. It would return the law to that which preceded *M'Naghten*, a test known variously as the "wild beast test" and as the "good and evil" test under which an accused could be found insane only if he was "totally deprived of his understanding and memory, and doth not know what he is doing, no more than an infant, than a brute, or a wild beast. . . . "We find nothing in the language . . . [of the initiative], or in any other source from which the intent of the electorate may be divined which indicates that such a fundamental, far-reaching change in the law of insanity as that was intended. . . .

We conclude . . . that section 25(b) reinstated the *M'Naghten* test as it was applied in California prior to *Drew* as the test of legal insanity in criminal prosecutions in this state. . . .

The judgment is reversed and the superior court is directed to enter a judgment of not guilty by reason of insanity. . . .

DISSENT

In June of 1982, the voters adopted a ballot measure which radically altered the test for criminal insanity in this state. . . . I cannot ignore the fact that they adopted language which unambiguously requires the accused to demonstrate that "he or she was incapable of knowing or understanding the nature and quality of his or her act *and* of distinguishing right from wrong at the time of the commission of the offense." (Emphasis added.) There is nothing in the statute . . . or in the ballot arguments that implies that the electorate intended "and" to be "or." However unwise that choice, it is not within this court's power to ignore the expression of popular will and rewrite the statute.

Since appellant failed to establish his insanity under the test enunciated in Penal Code section 25, subdivision (b), I cannot join the decision of my brethren.

CASE DISCUSSION

Did the electorate make its position clear by using "and" and not "or" as Chief Justice Byrd argued in her dissent? Or is the majority right in arguing that they would have made it clearer? How could they make it any more clear? Do you think the court violated the electorate's intent by interpreting the provision to mean "or"? Now that you have had the chance to consider right-wrong, irresistible impulse, substantial capacity, and the California statutory initiative, what definition do you favor? Explain.

Burden of Proof

Insanity not only poses definition problems but also gives rise to difficulties in applications. Authorities disagree and critics hotly debate who must prove insanity, and how convincingly. The burden-of-proof question received public attention, and generated hostility among both the public and criminal justice professionals when the jury acquitted John Hinckley, Jr. Federal law required that the government prove Hinckley's sanity beyond a reasonable doubt. Thus, if Hinckley's lawyers could raise a doubt in jurors' minds about his sanity, the jury had to acquit. That means that even though the jury thought Hinckley was insane, if they were not convinced beyond a reasonable doubt that he was, then they had to acquit. That is what happened. They thought he was insane but had their doubts, so they acquitted.

The result was not only criticism but also swift legislative action. In the Comprehensive Crime Control Act of 1984, the burden of proof was shifted from the government proving sanity beyond a reasonable doubt to defendants having to prove they were insane by clear and convincing evidence.[44]

The Model Penal Code rejects this standard, and so do most states. The Model Penal Code adopts the standard of affirmative defenses. Sanity and responsibility are presumed unless the defense offers some evidence to show that defendants are insane. Once the sanity presumption is overcome by some evidence, then under the Model Penal Code provision, prosecutors must prove the defendants sane beyond a reasonable doubt. Prosecutors need not prove sanity, however, unless defendants raise the issue. Insanity is also an affirmative defense under the new federal rule.

Some jurisdictions require proof beyond a reasonable doubt. Others accept proof by a preponderance of the evidence. There is a trend in favor of shifting the burden to defendants and making that burden heavier. This is both because Hinckley's trial generated antagonism toward the insanity defense and owing to growing hostility toward rules that the public believes coddle criminals.[45]

The insanity defense has one primary purpose in criminal law. No matter how advanced psychiatry becomes, no matter who must prove it and by how much, the insanity defense is primarily a legal, not a medical, question: Has a mental disease or defect, however defined, sufficiently altered defendants' mental states to excuse their crimes?

═══ DIMINISHED CAPACITY AND RESPONSIBILITY

Some defendants suffer from mental diseases or defects that do not affect their mental capacity sufficiently to constitute insanity according to the tests outlined earlier. They may still have a defense, if the mental disease or defect impairs their capacity to form the *mens rea* of the crimes with which the government charged them. Theoretically, this defense ought to apply to all crimes requiring *mens rea*, if impaired mental capacity raises a reasonable doubt about defendants' *mens rea.* In practice, however, jurisdictions severely restrict the use of **diminished capacity.**

Some jurisdictions prohibit all evidence short of insanity; defendants are either sane or insane without gradation. California once allowed the diminished capacity defense, but in the wake of hostility to mental impairment excuses it recently enacted the following provision:

> The defense of diminished capacity is hereby abolished. In a criminal action . . . evidence concerning an accused person's intoxication, mental illness, disease, or defect shall not be admissible to show or negate capacity to form the particular purpose, intent, motive, malice aforethought, knowledge, or other mental state required for the commission of the crime charged. . . . Notwithstanding the foregoing, evidence of diminished capacity or of a mental disorder may be considered by the court at the time of sentencing or other disposition or commitment.[46]

At the other extreme, under the Model Penal Code, relevant evidence showing impaired capacity is uniformly admissible to negative a particular *mens rea.* For example, if some mental disease or defect not sufficient to constitute insanity causes a defendant to steal property she believed belonged to her, such evidence would negative the specific intent to take "another's property" that larceny *mens rea* requires.

The jurisdictions that permit evidence of diminished capacity take a middle ground. They restrict its use to crimes of more than one degree that require specific intent—usually murder. A defendant in these jurisdictions can introduce evidence that a mental disease or defect negatives the capacity to form the specific intent to premeditate a homicide, but not the general intent to kill. Hence, the defendant could not commit first-degree murder requiring premeditation, but could commit second-degree murder requiring the general intent to kill. Some states go further, permitting mental impairment to reduce murder to manslaughter if a mental disease or defect generated the required heat of passion in manslaughter.[47] (See chapter 8 on homicide.)

CASE

Does Diminished Capacity Constitute a Defense?

State v. Gallegos

628 P.2d 999 (Colo. 1981)

[Gallegos was convicted of second-degree murder. He appealed. Justice Quinn delivered the opinion.]

FACTS

The defendant, Leroy Joe Gallegos, was charged with murder in the first degree after deliberation. The charge arose out of the shooting death of the defendant's wife on December 19, 1977. The prosecution's evidence established that the defendant and his wife were living apart and on the night of the homicide he visited her about a possible reconciliation. After a prolonged argument during which she accused him of incompetence and sexual inadequacy he shot her five times with a pistol.

The defense presented opinion evidence from two psychiatrists and a psychologist that the defendant was afflicted with minimal brain dysfunction and an associated explosive personality disorder with paranoid features. Minimal brain dysfunction was described as a biochemical imbalance in the brain that prevents a person from maintaining control over his bodily functions and emotional impulses, especially in situations of stress. The expert witnesses expressed the opinion that the defendant's condition rendered him incapable of forming the specific intent to kill at the time of the shooting of his wife. The defendant offered no testimony specifically addressing his capacity to act "knowingly" at the time of the homicide, although some of the expert testimony described the shooting as beyond the defendant's control. The trial court submitted the case to the jury on the charge of first degree murder after deliberation and on the lesser offenses of murder in the second degree and manslaughter upon sudden heat of passion. The jury was instructed that the requisite culpability for first degree murder and manslaughter was the specific intent to cause the death of another, and that the culpable mental state for second degree murder was knowingly causing the death of another. The instructions on the affirmative defense of impaired mental condition were as follows:

Instruction No. 13

The evidence presented in this case has raised the issue of the affirmative defense of impaired mental condition. The prosecution, therefore, has the burden of proving to your satisfaction beyond a reasonable doubt the guilt of the defendant as to that issue as well as all of the elements of the crime charged. If, after consideration of the evidence concerning the affirmative defense, along with all the other evidence, you are not convinced beyond a reasonable doubt of the guilt of the defendant then you must return a verdict of not guilty.

Instruction No. 14

It is an affirmative defense to the crime of murder in the first degree and manslaughter that the defendant, due to an impaired mental condition, did not have the capacity to form the specific intent required by the offense.

OPINION

Under the Colorado Criminal Code issues relating to lack of responsibility are affirmative defenses. One may be relieved of criminal responsibility on grounds of insufficient age, insanity, impaired mental condition, or intoxication.

The statutory categorization of a matter as an affirmative defense has consequences for the prosecution's burden of proof. Under the Colorado Criminal Code once the issue of an affirmative defense is raised, the prosecution must prove the guilt of the defendant beyond a reasonable doubt as to that issue as well as all other elements of the offense.

Second degree murder is defined as causing "the death of a person knowingly." By statute, offenses with the culpability requirement of "knowingly" are deemed to be general, rather than specific, intent crimes. Section 18–3–102(2), C.R.S. 1973 (1978 Repl. Vol. 8) states that "[d]iminished responsibility due to lack of mental capacity is not a defense to murder in the second degree." A diminished responsibility attributable to a lack of mental capacity is the statutory equivalent of the affirmative defense of impaired mental condition in section 18–1–803, C.R.S.1973 (1978 Repl. Vol. 8), which provides:

Evidence of an impaired mental condition though not legal insanity may be offered in a proper case as bearing upon the capacity of the accused to form the specific intent if such an intent is an element of the offense charged.

Thus, section 18–3–103(2) merely makes explicit with respect to second degree murder what already is implicit in section 18–1–803: the affirmative defense of diminished responsibility due to impaired mental condition is not an affirmative defense to the general intent crime of second degree murder.

The record before us establishes that the defendant's psychiatric and psychological experts testified without restriction to the defendant's mental status. Each witness expressed the opinion that at the time of the shooting the defendant was incapable not only of forming an intent to kill but also of exercising any control over his actions. One psychiatrist described the shooting as "an act based on a chemical brain disorder" rather than "a wilful, voluntary act." When this opinion evidence was admitted, the trial court did not caution the jury to consider it in relation to the specific intent crimes of first degree murder and manslaughter only. One must conclude, therefore, that it was admitted and considered as to all offenses, including second degree murder.

Jury's guilty verdict reinstated.

CASE DISCUSSION

Should Gallegos's brain dysfunction and the chemical imbalance resulting from it reduce his liability? If so, is it right only to reduce it to second-degree murder? Do you agree that it is possible to intend something but not as much when you are somewhat incapacitated? Or do you believe the rule should be that either you intended to kill or you did not? In other words, do you believe that "sort of" intending something is not possible? The difficulty in applying the rule and the objections raised to deciding who is "sort of" responsible have led California to abolish its diminished capacity defense.

═══ SYNDROMES

Recently, a range of "syndromes" affecting mental states have led to novel defenses in criminal law. The most bizarre of these include the policeman's, love fear, chronic brain, and holocaust syndromes.

When former San Francisco city official Dan White was tried for killing fellow official Harvey Milk and Mayor George Moscone, the defense introduced the junk foods syndrome, popularly called the Twinkie defense. White's lawyer argued that junk foods diminished White's mental faculties. One psychiatrist testified as follows concerning White's frequent depressions:

> During these spells he'd become quite withdrawn, quite lethargic. He would retreat to his room. Wouldn't come to the door. Wouldn't answer the phone. And during these periods he found that he could not cope with people. Any confrontations would cause him to kind of become argumentative. Whenever he felt things were not going right he would abandon his usual program of exercise and good nutrition and start gorging himself on junk foods. Twinkies, Coca Cola.
>
> Mr. White had always been something of an athlete, priding himself on being physically fit. But when something would go wrong he'd hit the high sugar stuff. He'd hit the chocolate and the more he consumed the worse he'd feel, and he'd respond to his ever-growing depression by consuming even more junk food. The more junk food he consumed, the worse he'd feel. The worse he'd feel, the more he'd gorge himself. . . .

The defense argued that these depressions, which junk food aggravated, sufficiently diminished White's capacity to reduce his responsibility. The jury returned a verdict of manslaughter, and White was sentenced to a relatively short prison term. Recently, he was released from prison and committed suicide. No one has ventured to blame his suicide on junk food.

During the *White* case, much public comment—most of it negative—was directed at the Twinkie defense. Despite that derision, substantial evidence exists to suggest that white sugar does indeed diminish capacity. Whether or not it does so to sufficiently reduce responsibility is a highly controversial and far-from-settled question.[48]

Three additional syndromes suggest more widespread and serious use to excuse criminal conduct. The battered spouse syndrome has appeared in self-defense (see chapter 6). The premenstrual syndrome and posttraumatic stress syndrome are discussed here.

Premenstrual Syndrome

A New York case raised the possibility that premenstrual syndrome (PMS) excuses criminal liability. Shirley Santos called the police, telling them, "My little girl is sick." The medical team in the hospital emergency room diagnosed the welts on the girl's legs and blood in her urine as the results of child abuse. The police arrested Santos, who explained, "I don't remember what happened. . . . I would never hurt my baby . . . I just got my period." At a preliminary hearing, Santos asserted PMS as a complete defense to assault and endangering the welfare of a child, both felonies. She admitted beating her child but argued that she had blacked out owing to PMS, hence could not have formed the intent to assault or endanger her child's welfare. After lengthy plea bargaining, the prosecutor dropped the felony charges and Santos pleaded guilty to the misdemeanor of harrassment. Santos received no sentence, not even probation or a fine, even though her daughter spent two weeks in the hospital from the injuries. The plea bargaining prevented a legal test of the PMS defense in this case. Nevertheless, the judge's leniency suggests that PMS affected the outcome informally.

Three difficulties stand in the way of proving the PMS defense: (1) Defendants must prove that PMS is a disease; little medical research exists to demonstrate that it is. (2) The defendant must suffer from PMS; rarely do medical records document the disease. (3) The PMS must cause the mental impairment that excuses the conduct; too much skepticism still surrounds PMS to expect ready acceptance that it excuses criminal conduct.[49]

Posttraumatic Stress Syndrome—the Vietnam Vet Defense

The years since the Vietnam War have revealed that combat soldiers suffered more lasting and serious casualties than physical injury. The war took a heavy emotional and mental toll on the veterans. The effects have created what some call a "mental health crisis which has had a dramatic impact on the incidence of major crime." Medical research has established a complex relationship between the stress of the combat tour in guerilla-type, as opposed to conventional, warfare and later antisocial conduct. At the same time, lawyers have begun to consider the effect the Vietnam Vet syndrome has on criminal responsibility.[50]

CASE

Did Vietnam Vet Syndrome Excuse His Crime?

In Defense of the Defenders: The Vietnam Vet Syndrome

John R. Ford, *Criminal Law Bulletin*, 19 (1983), pp. 434–43.

A man had been charged with assaulting a group of police officers who had been summoned to investigate a call that a man (the defendant) was wandering about in a park late at night. The police reports indicated that when the officers arrived in the park they could hear someone thrashing about in the wooded area. While attempting to follow the sounds they were suddenly confronted by the defendant who was carrying a large log as if it were a rifle. The officers reported that the man did not respond to their orders and seemed to be in a drunken and incoherent rage. The man charged toward the officers, wounded two of them, and was finally subdued and arrested.

A series of discussions with the defendant revealed that he was a Vietnam combat veteran who had a post-military history of job-related difficulties and marital discord. His wife related that he had begun within the last few years to suffer from periods of depression which were usually punctuated by episodes of excessive drinking, explosive violence, and recurrent nightmares. He had apparently been in the midst of such a period on the date of the incident and had spent a few hours drinking in a bar just prior to stopping in the park on his way home. When asked why he had stopped in the park, he responded that he was unsure but thought that he had needed some fresh air to "clear his head." He professed to have no recollection of the attack on the police and attributed it to his drunken condition.

The extensive medical investigation disclosed that the defendant was, at the time of the incident, engulfed in a delusional flashback in which he genuinely believed he was once again in the jungles of Vietnam and perceived the police officers to be enemy soldiers who were experiencing an incident in which his patrol had been ambushed and a friend killed. As a result of this information, the medical experts were able to testify that although it was clear that he "knew the nature and quality of his acts" in the sense that he knew he was attacking someone, it was equally clear that he "did not know that those acts were wrong" since, in his mind, he was not attacking police officers but was attacking enemy soldiers. The defendant was accordingly found to be not guilty by reason of insanity. [The defendant was hospitalized shortly after his arrest for two months, then was released but continued out-patient therapy until the trial.]

On the basis of his response to this treatment, the court . . . conclude[d] that the defendant no longer constituted a danger and could therefore be placed on probation, with a condition that he continue his therapy.

SUMMARY

The general defenses to criminal liability rest on two rationales. First are justifications. Defendants commit what are ordinarily crimes but which, under particular circumstances, are right. These circumstances are called justifications. Self-defense is the primary justification, but a general defense called necessity also exists in most jurisdictions. Second are the excuses. Defendants do what is admittedly wrong but which, under special circumstances, they are not responsible for doing. The main excuses are duress, intoxication, mistake, age, entrapment, insanity, diminished capacity, and syndromes.

General defenses sometimes, but not always, lead to outright acquittal. Defenses can also work to reduce the degree of an offense or to reduce the offense to a lesser, related offense. In some cases, defenses offer an opportunity to lighten a penalty attached to a particular crime because of mitigating circumstances. Finally, the insanity defense can lead to confinement in a mental hospital rather than incarceration. Whatever their specific consequences, the general defenses to criminal liability are based on the idea that the criminal law's harshness ought to be softened where defendants' culpability is weakened by special circumstances. In this sense, the defenses are companions to the general principles of criminal liability outlined in chapter 3. They work together to ensure that criminal law works fairly and according to well-defined principles so that persons are not punished if circumstances surrounding otherwise criminal conduct justify or excuse that conduct.

QUESTIONS FOR DISCUSSION AND REVIEW

1. Should superior orders ever be a defense to crime? brainwashing? duress? Why or why not?
2. When, if ever, should intoxication be a defense to crime?
3. When, if ever, should age be an excuse for criminal liability?
4. What is a proper limit to the defense of entrapment?
5. What is a proper scope for the defense of insanity? Is it the right-wrong test? the Durham rule? The substantial capacity requirement?
6. If you were writing a criminal code, would you include a partial defense called diminished capacity? If so, how would you justify such a defense? If you would not permit it, what reasons would you give for denying it?

▆▆▆ SUGGESTED READINGS

1. Telford Taylor, *Nuremberg and Vietnam: An American Tragedy* (New York: Quadrangle, 1970), discusses the superior orders defense as Taylor tells the stories of the Nuremberg trials and the Calley case. This is an interesting topic written for the general public.

2. David G. Bromley and James T. Richardson, *The Brainwashing/Deprogramming Controversy: Sociological, Psychological, Legal, and Historical Perspectives* (New York: Edwin Mellen Press, 1983), discusses brainwashing from a multidisciplinary perspective. It covers many topics relevant to the defense of brainwashing.

3. Peter Meyer, *The Yale Murder* (New York: Empire Books, 1982), is a compelling narrative relating the "fatal romance" of Yale student Richard Herrin and Bonnie Garland. It gives a detailed account of the trial, the insanity plea, the jury deliberations, and the verdict. This is an excellent journalistic account revealing much about the insanity plea and written for the general reader.

4. Joseph Livermore and Paul Meehl, "The Virtues of M'Naghten," *Minnesota Law Review*, 51 (1967), p. 800, is a well-argued, articulate defense of the right-wrong test. Although intended for specialists, it is well worth the novice's efforts.

5. Mike Weiss, *Double Play: The San Francisco City Hall Killings* (Reading, Mass.: Addison-Wesley, 1984), is a detailed account of former San Francisco city supervisor Dan White's shooting of Mayor George Moscone and fellow supervisor Harvey Milk in San Francisco City Hall, and of the trial that followed. It gives an excellent description of the diminished capacity defense, which came to be called the Twinkie defense because it was based on the argument that White's excessive use of junk foods, particularly those containing white sugar, led to his erratic behavior.

▆▆▆ NOTES

1. William Blackstone, *Commentaries on the Laws of England* (New York: Garland Publishing, 1978), pt. IV, p. 30.

2. American Law Institute, *Model Penal Code and Commentaries*, vol. 1 (Philadelphia: American Law Institute, 1985), pt. I, pp. 368–80.

3. Jerome Hall, *General Principles of Criminal Law*, 2d ed. (Indianapolis: Bobbs-Merrill, 1960), pp. 437–44; Glanville Williams, *Criminal Law: The General Part*, 2d ed. rev. (London: Stevens and Sons, 1961), pp. 765–66; American Law Institute, *Model Penal Code and Commentaries*, vol. 1, pt. I, pp. 372–73.

4. American Law Institute, *Model Penal Code and Commentaries*, vol. 1, pt. I, pp. 380–81.

5. Regina v. Hudson, 2 All E.R. 244 (1971).

6. Quotes taken from *New York Times* (February 20, 1989).

7. American Law Institute, *Model Penal Code and Commentaries*, vol. 1, pt. I, p. 376.

8. P. R. tit. 33, 3098.

9. Blackstone, *Commentaries,* pt. IV, pp. 25–26.

10. People v. Penman, 271 Ill. 82, 110 N.E. 894 (1915).

11. Hall, *General Principles of Criminal Law,* p. 540.

12. Burrows v. State, 38 Ariz. 99, 297 P. 1029 (1931).

13. Podolsky, "The Chemical Brew of Criminal Behavior," *Journal of Criminal Law, Criminology, and Police Science,* 45 (1955), pp. 676–77.

14. American Law Institute, *Model Penal Code and Commentaries,* vol. 1, pt. I, pp. 350–66, surveys most of these arguments.

15. State v. Hall, 214 N.W.2d 205 (Iowa 1974).

16. Powell v. Texas, 392 U.S. 514, 88 S.Ct. 2145, 20 L. Ed. 2d 1254 (1968); American Law Institute, *Model Penal Code and Commentaries,* vol. 1, pt. I, p. 353. Commonwealth v. Reiff, 489 Pa. 12, 413 A.2d 672 (1980).

17. 392 U.S. 514, 88 S. Ct. 2145, 20 L.Ed. 2d 1254 (1968).

18. 214 N.W. 2d 205 (Iowa 1974).

19. Rollin M. Perkins and Ronald N. Boyce, *Criminal Law,* 3d ed. (Mineola, N.Y.: Foundation Press, 1982), p. 1030.

20. Brent v. State, 43 Ala. 297 (1869) (lottery); Ostrosky v. State, 704 P.2d 786 (Alaska App. 1985) (game laws); Hopkins v. State, 193 Md. 489, 69 A.2d 456 (1949) (sign).

21. American Law Institute, *Model Penal Code and Commentaries,* vol. 1, pt. I, pp. 273–79.

22. People v. Munoz, 22 Misc. 2d 1078, 200 N.Y.S.2d 957 (1960).

23. Regina v. Kemp, 3 All E.R. 249 (1956).

24. "Feds Run into an Entrapment Backlash," *New York Times* (August 19, 1984), p. 2.

25. See American Law Institute, *Model Penal Code and Commentaries,* vol. 1, pt. I, pp. 406–20, for a full discussion of entrapment and its status in today's criminal law.

26. State v. Nilsen, 134 Ariz. 433, 657 P.2d 419 (1983) (defendant cannot deny guilt and plead entrapment); Mathews v. United States, _____U.S._____109 S. Ct. 162, 102 L.Ed.2d 132 (1988).

27. Sherman v. United States, 356 U.S. 369, 78 S.Ct. 819, 2 L.Ed.2d 848 (1958).

28. People v. Barraza, 23 Cal. 3d 675, 153 Cal. Rptr. 459, 591 P.2d 947 (1979).

29. American Law Institute, *Model Penal Code and Commentaries,* vol. 1, pt. I, pp. 182–83.

30. Mich. Stat. Ann. § 28.1059(1).

31. 55 Comm. L.R. 182, 186–188 (1933).

32. M'Naghten's Case, 8 Eng. Rep. 718 (1843).

33. Herbert M. Fingarette, *The Meaning of Criminal Insanity* (Berkeley: University of California, 1972), contains a full treatment of the subject. A good introduction is Abraham S. Goldstein, "Insanity," in *Encyclopedia of Crime and Justice,* ed. Sanford Kadish (New York: Free Press, 1983), pp. 735–42; American Law Institute, *Model Penal Code and Commentaries,* vol. 1, pt. I, pp. 174–76.

34. People v. Schmidt, 110 N.E. 949 (1915).

35. 214 F.2d 862 (D.C. Cir. 1954).

36. 18 U.S.C. A § 17 adopted the right-wrong test; United States v. Brawner, 471 F.2d 969 (D.C. Cir. 1972) rejected the Durham rule for that circuit; adopted by Maine Rev. Stat. Ann. tit. 15, § 102 (1964), superseded by Marne Rev. Stat. Ann. tit. 17–A, § 58 adopting the substantial capacity test.

37. Joseph Livermore and Paul Meehl, "The Virtues of M'Naghten," *Minnesota Law Review,* 51 (1967), p. 800.

38. Wayne R. LaFave and Arthur Scott, *Criminal Law,* (St. Paul: West Publishing Co., 1972), p. 283.

39. 2 So. 854 (Ala. 1877).

40. "A Needed Verdict: Guilty but Insane," *New York Times* (July 1, 1982), p. 29.

41. See Slovenko, "The Insanity Defense in the Wake of the Hinckley Trial," *Rutgers Law Journal*, 14 (1983), p. 373.

42. 18 U.S.C. A § 17.

43. Robert F. Schopp, "Returning to M'Naghten to Avoid Moral Mistakes: One Step Forward, or Two Steps Backward for the Insanity Defense?" *Arizona Law Review*, 30 (1988), p. 135.

44. *Federal Criminal Code and Rules* (St. Paul: West Publishing Co., 1988), § 17(b).

45. American Law Institute, *Model Penal Code and Commentaries*, vol. 2, pt. I, p. 226.

46. *California Penal Code* (St. Paul: West Publishing Co., 1988) § 25 (b); (c).

47. People v. Colavecchio, 11 A.D. 2d 161, 202 N.Y.S.2d 119 (1960) (mental disease negatives the specific intent to take another's property).

48. Mike Weiss, *Double Play: The San Francisco City Hall Killings* (Reading, Mass.: Addison-Wesley, 1984), pp. 349–50.

49. "Not Guilty Because of PMS?" *Newsweek* (November 8, 1982), p. 111; "Premenstrual Syndrome: A Criminal Defense," *Notre Dame Law Review*, 59 (1983), pp. 263–69.

50. John R. Ford, "In Defense of the Defenders: The Vietnam Vet Syndrome," *Criminal Law Bulletin*, 19 (1983), pp. 434–43.

Chapter Eight

Crimes against Persons I: Criminal Homicide

CHAPTER OUTLINE

CHAPTER MAIN POINTS

1. For criminal homicide's purposes, the meaning of life is difficult to determine, especially when life begins and when it ends.

2. Criminal homicide is divided into two main categories: murder and manslaughter.

3. Murder is commonly divided into first and second degrees; capital murder constitutes one form of first-degree murder.

4. The murder *mens rea* includes not only the intent to kill but also the intent to seriously injure, to commit certain felonies, and to resist lawful arrests.

5. Voluntary manslaughter is an intentional killing that takes human frailty into account when provocation leads to killing in the sudden heat of passion.

6. Vehicular homicide is a separate offense called negligent in some jurisdictions.

CHAPTER KEY TERMS

deliberate done with a cool, reflecting mind.

felony murder death occurring during a serious felony.

malice aforethought the old common definition of the murder *mens rea*.

paramour rule the principle that adequate provocation is provided by discovering a spouse in an adulterous act.

premeditated planned in advance.

≡ INTRODUCTION

Homicide—one human being killing another—took three forms at common law: (1) justifiable homicides, such as self-defense and police use of deadly force; (2) excusable homicides, such as those caused by accident or insanity; and (3) criminal homicides, or all homicides that were neither justified nor excused—murder and manslaughter. Criminal homicides must include an *actus reus* and a *mens rea*, concurring to produce a harmful result—in this case, death. In other words, they require applying the general principles of criminal liability, as well as the excuses and justifications that eliminate or reduce that liability. Since the excuses are general to most crimes and the principal justification relating to homicide (self-defense) was discussed fully in chapter 6, they are not repeated here.

Criminal homicide embodies difficult problems. The criminal homicide *actus reus*—taking another's life—requires deciding the thorny moral questions of when life begins and ends, and whether particularly atrocious acts aggravate the offense. Criminal homicide refines *mens rea* to its highest point in criminal law; it encompasses purposeful, knowing, reckless, and negligent killings. Furthermore, purposeful criminal homicide is aggravated by premeditation and deliberation, and is mitigated by the sudden heat of passion upon adequate provocation. Capital murder takes into account a range of circumstances in addition to *mens rea* that can aggravate first-degree murder into a crime mandating either the death penalty or life imprisonment.[1]

Criminal homicides constitute the most serious, but by no means the only, crimes against persons. Other crimes against the person include criminal sexual conduct; a wide range of other attacks on the person, such as nonsexual assaults and batteries; and crimes against free movement, such as kidnapping and false imprisonment. These other crimes, which far outnumber criminal homicide, are discussed in chapter 9.

TABLE 3   12 Million Uniform Crime Reports Index Crimes Were Reported to Police in 1985

Violent Crimes	1,327,440
Murder	18,980
Forcible rape	87,340
Robbery	497,870
Aggravated Assault	723,250
Property Crimes	**11,102,600**
Burglary	3,073,300
Larceny-theft	6,926,400
Motor vehicle theft	1,102,900
Total	12,430,000

NOTE: Offenses may not add to totals because of rounding.

SOURCE: FBI *Crime in the United States, 1985*, Federal Bureau of Investigation.

THE *ACTUS REUS* OF CRIMINAL HOMICIDE

Criminal homicide requires causing death, or "taking another's life." A major problem concerns what life and death mean for purposes of the law of criminal homicide, particularly the extreme ends of life's spectrum— when life begins and ends. Increasingly, courts have begun to interpret life to include fetuses, and legislatures have specifically defined life to include fetuses. Some statutes say that life begins at conception; others include only "viable fetuses," such as those twenty-eight weeks past conception. Still other jurisdictions construe life to mean "born alive."[2]

The Beginning of Life

Fetal death statutes have generated heated debate over whether abortion is criminal homicide. Fetal death and abortion differ fundamentally. Whatever personal values concern abortion, the procedure involves terminating pregnancies with the mother's consent. Fetal death statutes address killing fetuses without the mother's consent outside normal medical means. Many who oppose making abortion murder support fetal death statutes directed toward third persons who, without the mothers' consent, injure or kill fetuses. Furthermore, after *Roe v. Wade*, in which the Supreme Court upheld mothers' right to terminate pregnancies under some conditions, equating abortion with criminal homicide violated the constitution.[3]

In Minnesota, two groups in the legislature worked to enact different statutes. One group hoped to make fetal death equivalent to homicide. Another, trying to separate fetal death from abortion, drafted a bill to punish people who injure or kill fetuses while committing other crimes. The impetus for passing this version stems from two types of cases: where fetuses are injured or killed when pregnant women are either (1) assaulted

or (2) in automobile crashes owing to criminal recklessness or negligence.
In the end, Minnesota made it criminal homicide to kill "the unborn
offspring of a human being conceived but not yet born," except in the case
of legal abortions. A test case in Minnesota challenges the constitutionality of the law, as it applies to a man who shot his girlfriend in the chest
and killed her. Unknown to him, she was between three and four weeks
pregnant when he killed her. The fetus died, and the state charged him
with murdering both his girlfriend and the fetus.[4]

Applying homicide law to fetuses is not strictly a legal question—or, for
that matter, strictly a medical question. Defining life for purposes of the
law of criminal homicide ought to rely more on religious, moral, and
ethical values than on technical legal rules and medical science. It is not
easy to say what wise public policy on the matter ought to be. But
whatever highly charged emotions surround the debate over abortion,
neither legal principles nor medical knowledge mandate any specific
definition. Abortion is, rather, a value question, resting on when life in its
earliest stages is considered sufficiently valuable that to take it constitutes
murder. This in turn depends on the value placed on conceived-but-
not-yet-born or just-born human beings. One art student captured the
dilemma in a poster. Under a drawing of a just-fertilized egg in a happy,
laughing fourteen-year-old girl is a caption that reads: "Which life is
worth more?"[5]

CASE

Did He Murder a Fetus?

Hollis v. Commonwealth

652 S.W.2d 61 (Ky.1983)

[The trial court dismissed a murder indictment against Hollis for
murder of a fetus. The court of appeals reversed. The Supreme Court
affirmed the trial court's dismissal of the indictment. Justice Leibson
delivered the opinion. Justice Wintersheimer delivered a dissenting
opinion.]

FACTS

. . . Hollis went to the home of his wife's parents, where she was
staying, took her from that home out to the barn, told her he did not
want a baby, and then forced his hand up her vagina intending to
destroy the child and deliver the fetus. The medical evidence in the
record of the deposition is that the fetus was killed and the mother's
uterus and vagina substantially damaged. The doctor delivered the
dead fetus by abdominal incision. In separate indictments Hollis was

charged with murder for causing the death of the fetus. But we are also confronted with the question of whether Hollis can be charged with two offenses, one in connection with the fetus and a separate one in connection with the mother.

The trial court dismissed the murder indictment, reasoning that destroying the life of a viable fetus was not considered murdering a person at common law and that the statutory definition of murder did not enlarge the scope of the word "person." The Kentucky Court of Appeals reversed the decision of the trial court, reasoning that Kentucky now permits recovery for damages in civil cases for the wrongful death of a viable fetus and that it "cannot perceive any sound reason why it should have any less status when it becomes an alleged murder victim."

OPINION

The Commonwealth concedes that historically, at common law, "a conviction of homicide was not possible . . . unless the infant had been born alive." . . .

The position of the Commonwealth is that, by the process of evolution, the status of the fetus has so changed in the eyes of society, and of the law as expressed by the United States Supreme Court, that a viable fetus is a "person" for purposes of criminal homicide. While this argument may appeal to us instinctively, it cannot stand up to the rule of law which both guides and restrains our hand. . . .

When we turn to the Kentucky Penal Code, we find that although "person" is not defined in the chapter related to "Criminal Homicide" the Commentary refers repeatedly to the *Model Penal Code:* . . .

> The effect of this language is to continue the common-law rule limiting criminal homicide to the killing of one who has been born alive. . . .

This Court cannot presume that the legislature intended to license us to expand the class of persons who could be treated as victims of criminal homicide as we should deem appropriate in our own discretion. . . .

There are other problems which arise if this Court is to include the unborn persons who can be considered victims of criminal homicide. Although it is well recognized medically that a normal, healthy fetus in the third trimester of pregnancy has a potential of sustaining life outside the body of the mother, it is quite another matter to say that a particular fetus was viable at the time it was terminated or that a particular defendant knew, or should have known beyond a reasonable doubt, that he was killing a viable fetus. . . .

DISSENT

I must respectfully dissent from the majority opinion because the trial court was in error in dismissing the murder indictment when the only medical evidence indicated that the unborn child was alive.

The deposition of Dr. Nunemaker shows that he definitely considered the child to be alive. He was asked:

Q. In your opinion was this 28 to 30 week old fetus a viable living being?
A. Yes.

He repeated and explained his opinion but never changed it, nor deviated from it. Under aggressive cross-examination, the doctor said he called the seven-month-old infant a baby, and stated "it was a living person." . . .

Stripped of its rhetoric, this matter is simply a brutal murder committed on an innocent, defenseless victim. It is directly connected to a savage criminal assault on the mother and on the child.

There is no need to speculate as to when life begins. A baby human is biologically little different from a fish, frog, or horse. For each life begins at the moment of conception. Here, the child was seven months along in development in the womb; clearly, his individual life had begun. The doctor testified he was a living person. Even *Roe v. Wade* tacitly recognizes the viability of the child at 28 weeks.

Consequently it is not really necessary to enter an extended discussion on the legal, moral, theological, medical, or philosophical questions in the pro-life/pro-abortion debate. This is a clear case of an unlawful killing of a human, living person as confirmed by the uncontradicted medical evidence in the record. . . .

It is hypertechnical judicial hairsplitting to abstractly theorize on the meaning of "person," "human being," or "being born alive." It is semantical sophistry of the worst order to deny the equal protection of the criminal law to an unborn living human being.

Those who would do so can find no real refuge in the United States Constitution because that sacred but living document also once was erroneously interpreted to refuse to recognize women and blacks as "legal persons." . . .

CASE DISCUSSION

The *Hollis* court majority adopted the common-law rule that for homicide purposes, human life does not begin until babies are "born alive." Using "born" as the standard is not without difficulties. It can mean anything from when the baby's umbilical cord is severed, to when the baby is outside its mother, to when the baby gives its first cry, to when the baby's circulation works independently. If life is pushed back to before birth, as the dissent strongly urges, then it is difficult to decide just how far back: to conception? to when life is felt? to when the fetus can live independently?

If you were writing a homicide statute, at what point at or after conception does life begin for criminal homicide purposes? Is medical science relevant? old legal precedent? present morals? Do you agree with the dissent that it is "overtechnical judicial hairsplitting" to get into discussions of person, human being, or being born alive? In *Keeler v. Superior Court*, the California Supreme Court reached a result similar to that in *Hollis*, when a man kicked his wife's stomach to cause an abortion. Shortly after the decision, the California legislature changed its criminal homicide statute to read "unlawful killing of a human being or a fetus."[6]

The End of Life

At the age spectrum's other extreme is the question, When does life end for homicide purposes? This is a growing problem as advancing medical technology brings organ transplants and sophisticated artificial life-support mechanisms into common use. To kill a dying person, to accelerate a person's death, or to kill a "worthless" person are clearly homicide under current law. Under these general rules, a doctor who—with requisite *mens rea*—causes death by removing a vital organ too soon has committed criminal homicide. Anyone who causes death by purposely disconnecting a respirator has also committed criminal homicide.

Historically, *alive* meant breathing and having a heartbeat. Recently, the new concept of *brain death* is gaining prominence, with implications not only for medicine and morals but also for criminal law. If only artificial supports maintain breathing and heartbeat while brain waves remain minimal or flat, brain death has occurred. The Uniform Brain Death Act provides that an individual who has suffered irreversible cessation of all brain functions, including those of the brain stem, is dead.[7]

More difficult cases involve individuals with brain functions sufficient to sustain breathing and heartbeat but nothing more: patients in a *deep coma* who have suffered serious injury. They may breathe and their hearts may beat—even without artificial support—but they are not really alive for criminal law purposes. Troubling cases arise where medical specialists have described deep-coma patients as "vegetables," but the patients regain consciousness and live for considerable time afterwards. A Minneapolis police officer was shot and written off for dead after more than a year of deep coma, but then regained consciousness and lived several years. Reports of other such cases appear from time to time.[8]

CASE

Is Causing Brain Death Murder?

Commonwealth v. Golston

373 Mass. 249, 366 N.E.2d 744 (1977)

[Golston was convicted of first-degree murder. Justice Braucher delivered the opinion.]

FACTS

About 2 P.M. on Sunday, August 24, 1975, the victim, a white man thirty-four years old, came out of a store in Dorchester and walked toward his car. The defendant, a black man of eighteen, tiptoed behind him and hit him on the head with a baseball bat. The defendant then went into a building, changed his clothes, and crossed the street to the store, where he worked. When asked why he had hit the man, he said "For kicks." The victim was taken to a hospital. There a large portion of the front of his skull was removed to relieve pressure on his brain, and he breathed with the aid of an artificial respirator. On August 26, his blood pressure, heartbeat and pulse were not observable, he failed to breathe when taken off the respirator for two minutes, and an electroencephalogram failed to reveal any cerebral electrical activity. On August 28, he again made no attempt to breathe when taken off the respirator, there were no reflex actions or responses to painful stimulation, and a second electroencephalogram showed no evidence of brain wave activity. After consultation with the victim's family, the respirator was removed on August 31, and his heart stopped.

1. The proof of "brain death." There was medical testimony that on August 25 only the part of the victim's brain responsible for the most primitive responses, the brain stem, was still to some degree working. On August 26 the remaining brain stem functions, such as responding to painful stimuli and gasping for air, had disappeared; the victim never again exhibited any signs that his brain stem or cortex was functioning. In the opinion of the responsible physician, the victim was then dead, having reached the stage of irreversible "brain death." This opinion was confirmed by an electroencephalogram on August 26 and by another on August 28. The removal of the respirator on August 31 was in accordance with good medical practice. An autopsy the next day revealed a brain without architecture, a decomposed, jelly-like mass, consistent with a brain dead for substantially more than two days. The medical examiner concluded that the victim had been dead since August 28.

According to the testimony, a definition of "brain death" was developed by the Harvard Ad Hoc Committee in 1968. The traditional definition of death as the cessation of the heartbeat is erroneous; death does not occur until the heart has stopped long enough so that there is complete loss of brain function. When the heart is maintained artificially, the brain function must be examined directly. The Harvard Committee developed basic clinical criteria, which are generally accepted by the medical community. Subsequent studies resulted in the establishment by an inter-agency committee of slightly less rigorous criteria, but the physicians attending the victim applied the original Harvard Committee criteria.

The three basic criteria were (1) unresponsiveness to normally painful stimuli, (2) absence of spontaneous movements or breathing, and (3) absence of reflexes. The diagnosis of "brain death" was to be confirmed by an electroencephalogram, and was to be observed over a twenty-four-hour period. No reported individual has ever survived when these criteria were met. In accordance with these criteria, several doctors testified that the victim was dead by August 28.

2. The judge's instructions on "brain death." The judge instructed the jury that "as a matter of law, the occurrence of a brain death, if you find it, satisfies the essential element of the crime of murder requiring proof beyond a reasonable doubt of the death of the victim. Brain death occurs when, in the opinion of a licensed physician, based on ordinary and accepted standards of medical practice, there has been a total and irreversible cessation of spontaneous brain functions and further attempts at resuscitation or continued supportive maintenance would not be successful in restoring such functions." The judge also submitted two questions to the jury, to be answered if they found the defendant guilty of murder in either the first or the second degree: (1) whether they found that the element of death in the crime of murder was satisfied by the proof of a brain death; (2) if so, whether the brain death occurred before or after the artificial life support was disconnected. The jury answered the first question, "Yes," and the second, "Before."

OPINION

So far as we can ascertain, this court has never before decided the question when death occurs for the purposes of the law of homicide. The judge recognized the significant technological advances in the area of artificial life support and applied traditional principles, we think correctly, to the novel case presented. "The rules and principles of the common law are broad and expansive enough to embrace all new cases as they arise." The judge made an "evolutionary restatement" of the rule rather than a substantively new rule. Proof of the same facts would permit conviction under either the old or the new formulation. . . .
Affirmed.

CASE DISCUSSION

The *Golston* court decided, essentially, that putting another in a deep coma is first-degree murder. The underlying idea in brain death is that insufficient activity exists to appreciate life. Do you agree? What about killing other people in somewhat similar circumstances? What about persons who are born so retarded or so seriously brain damaged that they cannot ever hope to perform life's most basic tasks? Are they "live" human beings? What about psychotics so deep in paranoia that they have no lucid intervals? Are such tragic persons "alive" in a meaningful sense? How would you define death for homicide purposes?

As was true for defining when life begins, defining death need not be fastened to traditional legal doctrine or medical practice. Definitions that satisfy criminal law's purposes should rather depend on the underlying values that homicide statutes are meant to preserve. Resolving definition problems, therefore, requires policymakers and legislators to grapple with how to determine what worth they will ultimately attribute to continuing life for the critically and hopelessly injured, the gravely mentally ill, and other tragic victims of advanced disease and life's vicissitudes. This is bound to become a more pressing, but never an easy or pleasant, task that lawmakers and ultimately society must perform in the immediate future.

☰ CAUSING ANOTHER'S DEATH

The material element—causing another's death—occasionally creates difficulties. Some killers never touch their victims but still cause their deaths. For example, if I invite my blind enemy to step over a precipice he cannot see, and he dies, I have caused his death. If I expose my helpless wife or child to freezing temperatures, I have killed him or her. Such bizarre examples rarely occur.[9]

More commonly, death stems from several causes. In some cases, victims do not die immediately after brutal attacks. One man beaten almost to death was taken to a hospital where, in a delirious state, he pulled life-support plugs, and died. Another victim was so stunned from a beating that he stumbled in front of a speeding car and was killed. Factual cause exists in these killings because the assailants set in motion chains of events that ended in the victims' deaths. Whether the assailants legally caused their victims' deaths depends on whether it is fair, just, and expedient to impose liability for criminal homicide. (See chapter 3). In *Commonwealth v. Golston*, the court ruled that even if a doctor's negligence contributed to the victim's death, Golston's brutal attack with a baseball bat constituted sufficient evidence for the jury to find Golston's actions the legal cause of death.

The ancient **year-and-a-day rule,** still followed in some states today, mandates that no act occurring more than one year and one day before death constitutes the legal cause of death for purposes of the law of criminal homicide. According to the year-and-a-day rule, the law conclusively presumes that death was due to "natural causes," not the defendant's acts. The rigid common-law formulation of this rule does not conform to modern medical realities.

One recent case illustrates this. On July 8, 1982, Larry Minster shot his girlfriend Cheryl in the neck. As a result, she became a quadriplegic. Owing to modern medical techniques, Cheryl lingered until October 3, 1983, when she finally died—one year and eighty-seven days following the shooting. In prosecuting Minster for murder, the state maintained that modern lifesaving devices rendered the year-and-a-day rule obsolete. The court saw merit in the argument, but decided that the legislature should change the rule. The court also noted some trend toward either abrogating the rule, or extending the time period it encompasses. Nevertheless, twenty-six states still retained the rule.[10]

THE *MENS REA* IN CRIMINAL HOMICIDE

To a large extent, *mens rea* accounts for the grading of criminal homicides. In fact, criminal homicide refines the concept of *mens rea* more than does any other crime. Therefore, the same culpability levels that make up the general principal *mens rea*—purposeful, knowing, reckless, and negligent—apply with particular reference to criminal homicide. Most of the time, but not always, purposeful killings are graded most serious and negligent killings least serious.

Criminal homicide divides intentional killings into several categories. The law treats premeditated murder (first-degree murder) more seriously than purposeful killing without deliberation (second-degree murder), which it treats more seriously than sudden killing with adequate provocation (voluntary manslaughter). Furthermore, some surrounding circumstances can aggravate, and others mitigate, purposeful, reckless, and negligent homicides. Deaths that occur in the course of committing other felonies, such as armed robbery, constitute first-degree murder in some states even when the killer's *mens rea* may have been reckless or even negligent with respect to the death. The mental element combined with special material surrounding circumstances provides the basis for grading criminal homicide.

TYPES AND DEGREES OF CRIMINAL HOMICIDE

Criminal law divides homicide into two major kinds: murder and manslaughter. These in turn are subdivided into several categories. Nearly all distinctions among these categories depend on the killer's mental state. The discussion that follows treats homicide as an organized whole, but one that is much simplified compared with actual homicide law, which is filled with many special homicide statutes enacted over time to meet special situations arising as society became more complex. Special statutes govern deaths resulting from operating machinery in a negligent manner, leaving vicious animals at large, overloading passenger vessels, and driving or practicing as a doctor while drunk.[11]

Murder

At common law, murder meant

> [w]hen a man of sound memory and of the age of discretion unlawfully kills any reasonable creature in being, and under the King's peace, with malice aforethought, either express or implied by the law, the death taking place within a year and a day.[12]

In the sixteenth century when Lord Coke defined murder, malice afore-thought may have referred to purposeful killings planned well in advance, such as when someone lay in wait to kill, or poisoned an enemy. By modern times, it had come to include several states of mind, as well as causing death during the course of some specified felonies whether or not the felon premeditated the killing.

Malice aforethought includes the intent to do all the following:

1. Kill
2. Do serious bodily harm
3. Commit specified serious felonies
4. Create a greater-than-reckless risk of death or serious bodily harm, acting with such disregard for human life that the action evidences an "abandoned and depraved heart," such as by shooting into a crowd of people
5. Resist arrest by force

This broad scope has rendered the term malice aforethought almost meaningless; hence, most statutes and cases have refined the murder *mens rea* to make it more practical to apply to the situations outlined above.

FIRST-DEGREE MURDER. The common law did not recognize degrees of murder; all criminal homicides were capital felonies. Pennsylvania departed from the common law in 1794, enacting the first statute that divided murder into degrees. The Pennsylvania statute provided that

> all murder, which shall be perpetrated by means of poison, lying in wait, or by any other kind of wilful, deliberate or premeditated killing, or which shall be committed in the perpetration, or attempt to perpetrate any arson, rape, robbery or burglary shall be deemed murder in the first degree; and all other kinds of murder shall be deemed murder in the second degree.[13]

Pennsylvania created first-degree murder in order to confine the death penalty (at the time prescribed for all common-law murders) to particularly heinous murders. Most states followed the practice of calling first-degree murder capital murder. As states abolished the death penalty, first-degree murder became a life imprisonment felony.

Capital murder has recently come to attention again in view of the constitutionality of the death penalty. The Supreme Court has ruled that states with a mandatory death penalty are not constitutional unless courts take into account specified aggravating and mitigating circumstances, adjudicated and decided according to strict procedural safeguards. As a result, most states that prescribe the death penalty for murder now have statutes outlining the aggravating and mitigating circumstances that qualify convicted murderers for the death penalty.[14]

The most common first-degree murders are premeditated, purposeful, and deliberate killings. **Premeditated** means "planned in advance." **Deliberate** means done with a cool, reflecting mind. A person who kills in a towering rage is not a deliberate killer; neither, in some cases, is an intoxicated person too drunk to act with cool reflection. Two other

first-degree murders—felony murder and heinous murder—do not require proof of purpose, deliberation, and premeditation.[15]

Premeditated Courts variously define premeditation. Some require substantial time to formulate a well-laid plan to kill.

> A verdict of murder in the first degree . . . [on a theory of willful, deliberate, and premeditated killing] is proper only if the slayer killed "as a result of careful thought and weighing of considerations; as a *deliberate* judgment or plan; carried on cooly and steadily, according to a *preconceived design.*"[16]

Others virtually eliminate the element of advanced planning by holding that premeditation includes killing instantly after forming the intent. One judge said that a defendant premeditated when the intent to kill arose "at the very moment the fatal shot was fired." Some require sufficient maturity or mental health (or both) to appreciate fully what it means to plan to kill in advance of doing so. The Idaho Supreme Court dealt with deliberate, premeditated murder in the capital murder case of *State v. Snowden.*[17]

CASE

A Premeditated Killing?

State v. Snowden

79 Idaho 266, 313 P.2d 706 (1957)

[Snowden was found guilty of first-degree murder and sentenced to death. He appealed. Justice McQuade delivered the opinion.]

FACTS

Defendant Snowden had been playing pool and drinking in a Boise pool room early in the evening. With a companion, one Carrier, he visited a club near Boise, then went to nearby Garden City. There the two men visited a number of bars, and defendant had several drinks. Their last stop was the HiHo Club.

Witnesses related that while defendant was in the HiHo Club he met and talked to Cora Lucyle Dean. The defendant himself said he hadn't been acquainted with Mrs. Dean prior to that time, but he had "seen her in a couple of the joints up town." He danced with Mrs. Dean while at the HiHo Club. Upon departing from the tavern, the two left together.

In statements to police officers, that were admitted in evidence, defendant Snowden said after they left the club Mrs. Dean wanted him to find a cab and take her back to Boise, and he refused because he didn't feel he should pay her fare. After some words, he related:

[S]he got mad at me so I got pretty hot and I don't know whether I back handed her there or not. And, we got calmed down and decided to walk across to the gas station and call a cab.

They crossed the street, and began arguing again. Defendant said: "She swung and at the same time she kneed me again. I blew my top."

Defendant said he pushed the woman over beside a pickup truck which was standing near a business building. There he pulled his knife—a pocket knife with a two-inch blade—and cut her throat.

The body, which was found the next morning, was viciously and sadistically cut and mutilated. An autopsy surgeon testified the voice box had been cut, and that this would have prevented the victim from making any intelligible outcry. There were other wounds inflicted while she was still alive—one in her neck, one in her abdomen, two in the face, and two on the back of the neck. The second neck wound severed the spinal cord and caused death. There were other wounds all over her body, and her clothing had been cut away. The nipple of the right breast was missing. There was no evidence of a sexual attack on the victim; however, some of the lacerations were around the breasts and vagina of the deceased. A blood test showed Mrs. Dean was intoxicated at the time of her death.

Defendant took the dead woman's wallet. He hailed a passing motorist and rode back to Boise with him. There he went to a bowling alley and changed clothes. He dropped his knife into a sewer, and threw the wallet away. Then he went to his hotel and cleaned up again. He put the clothes he had worn that evening into a trash barrel.

OPINION

By statute, murder is defined as the unlawful killing of a human being with malice aforethought. Degrees of murder are defined by statute as follows:

All murder which is perpetrated by means of poison, or lying in wait, torture, or by any other kind of wilful, deliberate and premeditated killing, or which is committed in the perpetration of, or attempt to perpetrate arson, rape, robbery, burglary, kidnaping or mayhem, is murder of the first degree. All other murders are of the second degree.

The defendant admitted taking the life of the deceased.

The principal argument of the defendant pertaining to . . . [premeditation] is that the defendant did not have sufficient time to develop a desire to take the life of the deceased, but rather his action was instantaneous and a normal reaction to the physical injury which she had dealt him.

There need be no appreciable space of time between the intention to kill and the act of killing. They may be as instantaneous as successive thoughts of the mind. It is only necessary that the act of killing be preceded by a concurrence of will, deliberation, and premeditation on the part of the slayer, and, if such is the case, the killing is murder in the first degree.

In the present case, the trial court had no other alternative than to find the defendant guilty of willful, deliberate, and premeditated killing with malice aforethought in view of the defendant's acts in deliberately opening up a pocket knife, next cutting the victim's throat, and then hacking and cutting until he had killed Cora Lucyle Dean and expended himself. The full purpose and design of defendant's conduct was to take the life of the deceased. . . .

[Snowden objected to the imposition of the death penalty. Idaho provides the following punishment for murder:]

> Every person guilty of murder in the first degree shall suffer death or be punished by imprisonment in the state prison for life, and the jury may decide which punishment shall be inflicted. . . .

The trial court could have imposed life imprisonment, or, as in the instant case, sentenced the defendant to death. It is abuse of discretion we are dealing with, and in particular the alleged abuse of discretion in prescribing the punishment for murder in the first degree as committed by the defendant. To choose between the punishments of life imprisonment and death there must be some distinction between one homicide and another. This case exemplifies an abandoned and malignant heart and sadistic mind, bent upon taking human life. It is our considered conclusion, from all the facts and circumstances, the imposition of the death sentence was not an abuse of discretion by the trial court.

The judgment is affirmed.

CASE DISCUSSION

The *Snowden* court had no difficulty finding that Snowden premeditated Dean's death. In fact, in a part of the opinion not included here, the court approved the trial judge's death sentence over life imprisonment because Snowden clearly premeditated Dean's murder. Do you agree? If you were defining premeditation in a criminal statute, would you say it is sufficient that the deed followed instantly upon the intention? What practical meaning does premeditation have according to that definition? Do you think the court used premeditation as an "excuse" to make it possible to sentence Snowden to death for the especially brutal way he murdered Dean? (When you read about second-degree murder, rethink how you defined premeditation in first-degree murder.) As for the sentence, do you find any mitigating circumstances, such as Snowden's intoxication, Dean's provocation, and Snowden's quick response to Dean's provocation?

Not everyone agrees that premeditated killings constitute the worst murders. According to James F. Stephen, a nineteenth-century English judge and criminal law reformer:

As much cruelty, as much indifference to the life of others, a disposition at least as dangerous to society, probably even more dangerous, is shown by sudden as by premeditated murders. The following cases appear to me to set this in a clear light. A, passing along the road, sees a boy sitting on a bridge over a deep river and, out of mere wanton barbarity, pushes him into it and so drowns him. A man makes advances to a girl who repels him. He deliberately but instantly cuts her throat. A man civilly asked to pay a just debt pretends to get the money, loads a rifle and blows out his creditor's brains. In none of these cases is there premeditation unless the word is used in a sense as unnatural as "aforethought" in "malice aforethought," but each represents even more diabolical cruelty and ferocity than that which is involved in murders premeditated in the natural sense of the word.[18]

The British Home Office's remarks to the Royal Commission on Capital Punishment observed that

[a]mong the worst murders are some which are not premeditated, such as murders committed in connection with rape, or murders committed by criminals who are interrupted in some felonious enterprise and use violence without premeditation, but with a reckless disregard of the consequences to human life. There are also many murders where the killing is clearly intentional, unlawful and unaccompanied by any mitigating circumstances, but where there is no evidence to show whether there was or was not premeditation. For the foregoing reasons, we deem ourselves constrained to reject the determinants of first degree murder suggested by existing law. The question then is whether it is possible to construct a more satisfactory delineation of the class of murders to which the capital sanction ought to be confined insofar as it is used at all.[19]

Atrocious Atrocious murder constitutes another kind of first-degree murder in some jurisdictions. In atrocious murder, the killer not only means to kill but also does it in an especially brutal manner. In *Commonwealth v. Golston*, Golston beat his victim with a baseball bat; he was found guilty of first-degree murder "by reason of extreme atrocity or cruelty." According to the court,

[t]here was evidence of great and unusual violence in the blow, which caused a four-inch cut on the side of the skull. [T]here was also evidence that after he was struck the victim fell to the street, and that five minutes later he tried to get up, staggered to his feet and fell again to the ground. He was breathing very hard and a neighbor wiped vomit from his nose and mouth. Later, according to the testimony, the defendant said he did it, "For kicks."

There is no requirement that the defendant know that his act was extremely atrocious or cruel, and no requirement of deliberate premeditation. A murder may be committed with extreme atrocity or cruelty even though death results from a single blow. Indifference to the victim's pain, as well as actual knowledge of it and taking pleasure in it, is cruelty; and extreme cruelty is only a higher degree of cruelty.[20]

Extremely atrocious or cruel murder frequently lacks premeditation or deliberation; the brutality substitutes for these elements to raise the crime to first-degree murder. Therefore, although Golston did not premeditate the murder, he took pleasure in his victim's pain, which Golston brought on by the particularly brutal attack with a baseball bat.

Felony In most jurisdictions, deaths that occur during the commission, or attempted commission, of enumerated felonies constitute **felony murder,** sometimes first-degree murder. The felonies underlying first-degree felony murder include arson, rape, robbery, burglary, kidnapping, mayhem, and sexual molestation of a child. Deaths during felonies that are not enumerated can constitute second-degree murder in most states.

First-degree felony murder does not require premeditation. In fact, most felony murderers do not intend to kill their victims. Frequently, they recklessly or negligently kill their victims. The underlying felonies constitute the reckless or negligent state of mind. For example, if a robber's gun fires during the robbery and kills a 7-Eleven clerk, even if the robber does not intend to kill, the robbery constitutes sufficient recklessness (or negligence) to constitute first-degree felony murder. Similarly, if a man forcibly rapes a child, not intending to kill, but the child dies, the rape amounts to recklessness sufficient to constitute first-degree felony murder. Some felony murder statutes impose strict liability for deaths occurring during the commission of some felonies. In other words, even accidental killings during felonies constitute felony murder.

The felony murder doctrine aims to accomplish several policy goals. First, the rule might deter would-be felons from committing crimes because of the added threat of a murder conviction, perhaps even first-degree capital murder. Second, the rule might curtail the use of violence during the commission of felonies. Research has not demonstrated that the rule accomplishes either of these goals. Finally, the rule also embodies the idea that people who commit felonies, creating high risks, should take the most serious possible consequences for their actions.

Owing to skepticism about the effectiveness of the policy goals the doctrine is supposed to achieve, four states—Ohio, Hawaii, Michigan, and Kentucky—have abolished felony murder. Other states have placed restrictions on felony murder. Some courts require that death resulting from the underlying felony was foreseeable. Some courts readily find foreseeability in the facts of a particular case. In *State v. Noren*, for example, Noren struck a drunken man three times in the head in the course of robbing him. The blows rendered the victim unconscious, and he died from asphyxiation. The court found that striking an intoxicated victim involves a foreseeable risk of causing death. Similarly, in *State v. McKeiver*, McKeiver robbed a bar. During the robbery, a woman suffered a fatal heart attack. The court upheld McKeiver's conviction for felony murder, finding that the woman died "as a result of fear and apprehension during defendant's commission of a robbery."[21]

Problems arise when someone other than the felon causes a death. The third person who actually kills might be the victim, police officers, or even a co-felon. Some states exclude from the felony murder rule deaths caused by third persons. For example, a resisting victim who shot and killed one of two burglars relieved the other burglar from felony murder liability. Similarly, it was not felony murder when a cab driver and police officer shot at two men attempting to rob the driver, killing one of the would-be robbers. Other states include within the scope of felony murder deaths caused by resisting victims. Where a victim of felonious assault returned fire and killed one assailant, a co-felon of the deceased was convicted of felony murder.[22] Increasingly, only deaths occurring during "dangerous" felonies constitute felony murder. For example, the California Supreme Court held that a chiropractor was not guilty of felony murder when he fraudulently treated cancer with chiropractic and the patient died. The court ruled that fraud was not a "dangerous" felony.[23] The Minnesota Supreme Court dealt with the meaning of felonies endangering life in *State v. Aarsveld*.

CASE

Did He Commit a "Life-Endangering" Felony?

State v. Aarsveld

376 N.W.2d 518 (Minn. App. 1975)

[Judge Leslie delivered the opinion. Judge Parker delivered a dissenting opinion.]

FACTS

During the late evening of September 2, 1984, and the early morning of September 3, respondent was at a party with several people, including Craig Schweiger. At the request of Schweiger, respondent obtained and sold Schweiger a quantity of cocaine. Schweiger, respondent, and others administered to themselves a portion of the cocaine by injection. There was conflicting testimony during the grand jury proceedings as to whether respondent had assisted Schweiger with an injection. Soon after the injection, Schweiger collapsed and was taken to a nearby hospital where he was pronounced dead.

The amended indictment charges respondent with felonious sale of cocaine, felonious distribution of cocaine by injection, second-degree felony murder with distribution by injection as the predicate felony, and second-degree felony murder with sale of cocaine as the predicate felony.

Respondent moved to dismiss the charge of felony murder predicated on sale of cocaine. The trial court granted the motion. . . .

OPINION

Minn. Stat. § 609.19 (1984) reads in pertinent part as follows:

> Whoever does either of the following is guilty of murder in the second degree and may be sentenced to imprisonment for not more than 40 years: . . .

(2) Causes the death of a human being, without intent to effect the death of any person, while committing or attempting to commit a felony offense other than criminal sexual conduct in the first or second degree with force or violence.

Although the language of this felony-murder statute appears on its face to apply to all felonies, this does not prohibit the use of common law rules to aid in statutory construction and interpretation.

Broadly construed, the common law felony-murder rule holds that any death occurring during the commission of a felony is chargeable against the felon as murder. The common law felonies included homicide, mayhem, rape, arson, robbery, burglary, larceny, prison breach, and rescue of a felon. The basic premise underlying the rule and its various modifications have long been debated by scholars, judges, and legislators. Its critics have protested the absolute liability that results from labeling accidental deaths as murder, and proponents of the rule have argued that its harshness is a deterrent for the use of violence in the commission of crimes. . . .

Although Hawaii, Kentucky, and Ohio have . . . abolish[ed] the felony-murder rule, many legislatures and courts have attempted to limit the application of the common law doctrine in a variety of ways. Many states require that the underlying felony be inherently dangerous to life. Some courts have required that the felony be a common law felony or that the felony be malum in se rather than malum prohibitum. Other courts impose an additional requirement that the homicide be proximately caused by the felonious act. Still other courts impose an additional requirement that the time period during which the underlying felony is considered to have taken place.

The Minnesota Supreme Court has held that the purpose of the felony-murder rule is "to isolate for special treatment those felonies that involve some special danger to human life." . . . The supreme court has . . . stated that a "typical felony-murder . . . probably is an unintentional killing that occurs in the course of a robbery or some other crime against the person."

It is an established rule of common law that penal statutes are to be construed strictly, with any reasonable doubt to be interpreted in the favor of the defendant. It is with this principle in mind that we seek to determine whether the sole act of selling cocaine is a felony that involves some special danger to human life. . . .

We conclude that the sole act of selling cocaine does not fall within the scope of the felony-murder statute. The legislature did not create the felony of sale of cocaine because of any inherent life-threatening qualities. Rather, it was created by the legislature because cocaine has a high potential for abuse and may lead to psychological dependence. Thus, although cocaine is admittedly a substance with an adverse effect on a person's health, use of cocaine, even when injected, does not generally cause death. Because the sale of cocaine alone does not justify the assumption that the purchaser is incurring a substantial and unjustified risk of death, we hold that sale alone is not a proper felony upon which to predicate a charge of felony murder. To hold otherwise would give the felony-murder statute a broader scope than this court will impute in the absence of clear legislative intent to effectuate that meaning.

Furthermore, the State has failed to show a direct causal relationship between the sale of cocaine and the subsequent death of the buyer. . . . [O]nce the exchange of money was complete, the collateral felony of selling cocaine had terminated. Because the death of Craig Schweiger did not occur "while committing or attempting to commit a felony offense," Minn. Stat. § 609.19(2) does not apply. . . .

DISSENT

In adopting an absolute rule that sale of a controlled substance cannot be an appropriate felony upon which to predicate a charge of felony murder, the majority opinion ignores the facts offered to be proved in this case, and misreads the language and intent of our felony murder statute. Accordingly, I respectfully dissent. . . .

The majority determines that no sale of cocaine could ever involve special danger to human life asserting, without any evidence whatsoever, that "use of cocaine, even when injected, does not generally cause death." As authority for its position, the majority cites a case which is inapposite, a case holding of which is directly contrary to Minnesota law, a case where the actual holding is that felonious sale of chloral hydrate with presence of seller during the consumption by buyer of a lethal dose is a proper predicate for felony murder. . . .

Minnesota law already considers some sales of cocaine to be felonies involving "special danger to human life." . . . [In another case] the supreme court examined evidence relevant to the physiological effect of cocaine and found that cocaine "can be fatal when taken with narcotics, or *injected into the blood,* or ingested orally in large quantities." . . .

The majority has fallen into the trap of "determin[ing] from the elements of each felony *in the abstract* whether it inherently involved some special danger to human life," instead of examining the facts of the particular case and the circumstances under which this sale was committed. The facts of this particular case and the circumstances under which the sale was committed compel the conclusion that this sale, where there was knowledge that the cocaine was to be taken by injection, involved special danger to human life. This sale of cocaine, therefore, should be held to be a proper predicate felony to prosecute a charge under Minn. Stat. § 609.19(2).

Finally, the majority misreads the felony murder statute and holds that if a felony "terminates" before the death of the victim the offense cannot be a predicate felony. No Minnesota decision is cited for this proposition. Our felony murder statute requires the actor only to *cause* the death while committing the crime, not that the death has to occur while the actor is committing the offense. . . .

Here, the predicate felony offered to be proved was sale of cocaine with the defendant allegedly knowing that the drug was to be taken in a potentially fatal manner, i.e. by injection. The injection took place with respondent's presence, presumably within a few minutes of the sale. The sale and the injection, therefore, are part of one continuous transaction, and if it can be shown that Schweiger died as a result of the cocaine injection, there would exist a strong causal connection between the felonious act and the death.

CASE DISCUSSION

How did the majority come to the conclusion that selling cocaine is not a felony dangerous to human life? Do you agree? Should it matter what the felony was, so long as death occurs during its commission? Do you think the dissent has a better argument for how the court *should* decide this case? Do you favor the felony murder rule? What reasons support it? What reasons support limiting it to certain felonies? Should felony murder ever be first-degree murder? Explain your answer. What penalty do you think Aarsveld deserves?

SECOND-DEGREE MURDER. Second-degree murder—a catchall—includes all criminal homicides that constitute neither first-degree murder nor manslaughter. A good way to think of murder is to consider the "ordinary" murder second degree. Some circumstances—those outlined under first-degree murder—aggravate murder to first degree. Other circumstances—outlined later in this chapter—reduce murder to manslaughter.

CASE

Did He Intend to Kill?

People v. Thomas

85 Mich. App. 618, 272 N.W.2d 157 (1978)

[Thomas was convicted of second-degree murder. He appealed. Presiding judge D. E. Holbrook, Jr., delivered the opinion.]

FACTS

The victim, a 19 year old male "catatonic schizophrenic," was at the time of his death a resident of Oak Haven, a religious practical training school. When it appeared he was not properly responding to ordinary treatment, defendant, the work coordinator at Oak Haven, obtained permission from the victim's parents to discipline him if such seemed necessary. Thereafter defendant, together with another supervisor at Oak Haven, took decedent to the edge of the campus, whereupon decedent's pants were taken down, following which he was spanked with a rubber hose. Such disciplinary session lasted approximately 15 to 30 minutes. During a portion thereof decedent's hands were tied behind his back for failure to cooperate.

Following the disciplinary session aforesaid, defendant testified that the young man improved for awhile but then commenced to backslide. Defendant again received permission from decedent's parents to subject him to further discipline. On September 30, 1976, defendant again took decedent to the approximate same location, removed his pants, bound his hands behind him with a rope looped over a tree limb and proceeded to beat him with a doubled-over rubber hose. This beating lasted approximately 45 minutes to an hour. While the evidence conflicted, it appears that the victim was struck between 30 to 100 times. The beating resulted in severe bruises ranging from the victim's waist to his feet. Decedent's roommate testified that decedent had open bleeding sores on his thighs. On the date of death, which was nine days after the beating, decedent's legs were immobile. At no time did defendant obtain medical attention for the victim.

Defendant admitted he had exercised poor judgment, after seeing the bruises, in continuing the discipline. He further testified that in the two days following the discipline, decedent seemed to be suffering from the flu, but by Sunday was up and walking and was in apparent good health until one week following the beating, when decedent became sick with nausea and an upset stomach. These symptoms continued for two days, when decedent died.

As a result of the autopsy, one Dr. Clark testified that the bruises were the result of a trauma and that decedent was in a state of continuous traumatization because he was trying to walk on his injured legs. Dr. Clark testified that decedent's legs were swollen to possibly twice their normal size. He further testified that the actual cause of death was acute pulmonary edema, resulting from the aspiration of stomach contents. Said aspiration caused a laryngeal spasm, causing decedent to suffocate on his own vomit. Although pulmonary edema was the direct cause of death, Dr. Clark testified that said condition usually had some underlying cause and that, while there were literally hundreds of potential underlying causes, it was his opinion that in the instant case the underlying cause was the trauma to decedent's legs. In explaining how the trauma ultimately led to the pulmonary edema, Dr. Clark testified that the trauma to the legs produced "crush syndrome" or "blast trauma," also known as "tubular necrosis." "Crush syndrome" is a condition caused when a part of the body has been compressed for a long period of time and then released. In such cases, there is a tremendous amount of tissue damage to the body part that has been crushed. When the compression is relieved, the tissues begin to return to their normal position, but due to the compression, gaps appear between the layers of tissues, and these areas fill up with blood and other body fluids, causing swelling. In the present case, Dr. Clark estimated that about 10–15% of decedent's entire body fluids were contained in the legs, adding an additional ten pounds in weight to the normal weight of the legs and swelling them to twice their normal size. This extra blood and body fluid decreased the amount of blood available for circulation in the rest of the body and would cause the person to become weak, faint and pass out if he attempted to sit up or do other activities. Decedent was sitting up when he died. It was Dr. Clark's opinion that the causal connection between the trauma and death was more than medically probable and that it was "medically likely." He further testified he could say with a reasonable degree of medical certainty that the trauma to the legs was the cause of death.

OPINION

Appellant claims that the prosecution failed to establish the malice element of second-degree murder. We disagree. Malice or intent to kill may be inferred from the acts of the defendant. In People v. Morrin, then Judge, now Justice Levin, stated that the intent to kill may be implied where the actor actually intends to inflict great bodily harm or the natural tendency of his behavior is to cause death or great bodily harm. In the instant case defendant's savage and brutal beating of the decedent is amply sufficient to establish malice. He clearly intended to beat the victim and the natural tendency of defendant's behavior was to cause great bodily harm.

Death was medically likely to have been caused by the beating through a chain of natural effects and causes unchanged by human action. Pulmonary edema resulted and the victim choked to death on his own vomit. Sufficient evidence of causal relationship was established by the prosecution. No reversible error occurred.
Affirmed.

CASE DISCUSSION

The court in *Thomas* ruled that Thomas had the requisite *mens rea* for second-degree murder because he intended to "inflict great bodily harm" on the deceased. The reason it is murder even though Thomas did not intend to kill is plain: Intending to beat someone within an inch of his or her life is not different enough from intending to beat someone to death to grade the two crimes differently. Do you agree that it is murder if Thomas intended only to beat the deceased severely? What is Thomas's *mens rea* with respect to the death: purposeful, reckless, negligent? Does this case mean that reckless homicide is murder?

What if a man, intending merely to unload his gun, shoots into the air, and bullets penetrate an airplane passing overhead, killing a passenger? Here, an intent neither to kill nor even to harm accompanied the death. Can this be murder? According to what used to be called depraved-heart murder and what is now called reckless murder, the answer is yes. Defendants who create high risks that people will either die or suffer serious injury and know they are creating those risks are considered sufficiently culpable to be punished for criminal homicide. Suppose the man shooting the gun had said aloud: "I know I might hit this plane and kill someone. Of course, I don't want to hurt or kill anyone. I hope I don't, but I'm going to clear the gun anyway." He thus created the risk of death purposely or at least consciously or knowingly. If death results from such a conscious risk creation, holding the risk creator criminally liable is considered reasonable. Whether the crime is murder, however, is open to debate.

To some analysts, careful adherence to *mens rea* suggests that too great a distance separates purposely or knowingly creating a risk to life from actually intending to kill. Intent to kill, they contend, is the only proper murder *mens rea*. Despite these objections, depraved-heart killing constitutes murder in most jurisdictions, although only in the second degree.

In addition to murders that result from intent to do serious bodily harm and depraved-heart murders, some felony murders constitute second-degree murders. Several jurisdictions distinguish between two types of felony murders. First degree is reserved for murders committed during the most dangerous felonies: rape, armed robbery, and arson. Killings resulting from some abortions and from felonies that are considered less life threatening—including aggravated assault and felonious drunken driving—are made second-degree murder. Courts have rejected the notion that an accidental death during a forcibly resisted lawful arrest constitutes second-degree murder.[24]

CORPORATE MURDER. Owing to several recent cases, the question of whether corporations can commit murder has taken a dramatic turn. Prosecutors have charged several corporations with criminal homicide, even murder in a few cases.

Three young women were killed on an Indiana highway when their Ford Pinto exploded after being struck from behind. The explosion followed several other similar incidents that led to grisly deaths. Evidence was published revealing that perhaps Ford knew the Pinto gas tanks were not safe but took the risk that they would not explode and injure or kill anyone. Following the three young women's deaths, Indiana indicted Ford Motor Company for reckless homicide, charging that Ford had recklessly authorized, approved, designed, and manufactured the Pinto and allowed the car to remain in use with defectively designed fuel tanks. These tanks, the indictment charged, killed the three young women in Indiana. For a number of reasons not related directly to whether corporations can commit murder, the case was later dismissed.[25]

In 1986, Autumn Hills Convalescent Centers, a corporation that operates nursing homes, went on trial under charges that it had murdered an eighty-seven-year-old woman by neglect. David Marks, a Texas assistant attorney general, said, "From the first day until her last breath, she was unattended to and allowed to lie day and night in her own urine and waste." The case attracted attention because charges were made that as many as sixty elderly people had died from substandard care at the Autumn Hills nursing home near Galveston, Texas. The indictment charged that the company had failed to provide nutrients, fluids, and incontinent care for Mrs. Breed and neglected to turn and reposition her regularly to combat bedsores. One prosecution witness testified that Mrs. Breed's bed was wet constantly and the staff seldom cleaned her. The corporation defended against the charges, claiming that Mrs. Breed had died from colon cancer, not improper care.[26]

The Model Penal Code and most comparable state criminal codes apply to criminal homicide as they do to other crimes committed for the corporation's benefit. Specifically, both corporations and high corporate officers acting within the scope of their authority for a corporation's benefit can commit murder. Practically speaking, however, prosecutors rarely charge corporations or their officers with criminal homicide, and convictions rarely, if ever, follow when they do.

The reluctance to prosecute corporations for murder or for any homicide requiring intent has to do with the hesitation to view corporations as persons. Although theoretically the law clearly makes that possible, in practice prosecutors and courts have drawn the line at involuntary manslaughter, a crime whose *mens rea* is negligence and occasionally recklessness. As for corporate executives, the reluctance to prosecute stems from vicarious liability and the questions it raises about culpability. (See Chapter 4.) It has been difficult to attribute deaths linked with corporate benefit to corporate officers who were in charge generally but did not order or authorize a killing, did not know about it, or even did not want it to happen.

A third, and practical, reason why so few corporations or their officers face murder charges is that prosecutors cannot link particular officers with the deaths. Therefore, they cannot prove guilt beyond a reasonable doubt—the standard required in criminal cases. This is particularly true where organizations are complex and authority is diffused among so many officers and their subordinates that blaming any one or a few might not be feasible. Although signs indicate that this is changing, the cases brought to date are noteworthy mainly because they are exceptions to the general rule that corporations and their officers are rarely, if ever, charged with or found guilty of any criminal homicide except involuntary manslaughter.

Only in particularly egregious cases that receive strong public attention, such as the Pinto and nursing home cases mentioned earlier, will prosecutors risk acquittal by trying corporations and their officers for criminal homicide. In these cases, prosecutors do not hope to win the case in traditional terms, meaning to secure convictions. Business law professor William J. Maakestad says:

> At this point, success of this type of corporate criminal prosecution is defined by establishing the legitimacy of the case. If you can get the case to trial, you have really achieved success.[27]

CASE

Did They "Murder" Their Employee?

Three Executives Convicted of Murder for Unsafe Workplace Conditions

New York Times (June 14, 1985), pp. 1, 9

FACTS

On 14 June 1985, Steven J. O'Neill, former president of Film Recovery Systems, Charles Kirschbaum, the plant supervisor, and Daniel Rodriguez, the plant foreman, were convicted of murder. They face prison sentences ranging from twenty to forty years.

The prosecution arose when Stefan Golab, a fifty-nine-year-old Polish immigrant, died from what the coroner declared was cyanide poisoning. Golab worked at the Film Recovery Systems plant, which used cyanide to extract silver from old films. The poisoning occurred from breathing hydrogen cyanide fumes present in the plant. The prosecution argued that the defendants knew about the fumes and did nothing about them. Workers testified that the stench from the fumes was often so bad they had to rush outside the plant to vomit.

The prosecution argued further that many employees did not speak or read English, so they could not read warnings and were not told the bubbling vats from which the cyanide fumes emanated were dangerous.

The defense argued that after federal and state regulatory agencies had inspected the plant, they never told the defendants that they were doing anything wrong. Their case was built mainly on the argument that the defendants were not aware they had created the risk that led to Golab's death. "There has been nobody who ever came forward to say, 'Fellas, this plant is not being operated acceptably,'" said one defense attorney. Ronald J. P. Banks, Cook County Circuit Court judge, ruled:

> The conditions under which workers performed their duties "were totally unsafe" and the executives "were totally knowledgeable" of the plant's hazardous conditions.

In a trial without a jury, Judge Banks found all three defendants guilty.

CASE DISCUSSION

According to Judge Banks's ruling, the defendants consciously created a risk that Golab might die from cyanide poisoning but did nothing about it. Is this murder or manslaughter? If you were deciding the case, what crime would you call it if the defendants are telling the truth? if the prosecution's version is the truth? Do you see why vicarious liability is a difficult ground upon which to rest a criminal homicide conviction?

Following the conviction, Attorney Richard M. Daley said the verdicts meant that employers who knowingly expose their workers to dangerous conditions leading to injury or even death can be held criminally responsible for the results of their actions.

Ralph Nader, consumer advocate lawyer, said:

> The public is pretty upset with dangerously defective products, bribery, toxic waste, and job hazards. The polls all show it. The verdict today will encourage other prosecutors and judges to take more seriously the need to have the criminal law catch up with corporate crime.

Professor John Coffee, Columbia University Law School, said, "When you threaten the principal adequately, he will monitor the behavior of his agent."

A California deputy district attorney put it more bluntly: "A person facing a jail sentence is the best deterrent against wrongdoing."

Joseph E. Hadley, Jr., a corporate lawyer who specializes in health and safety issues, said the decision would not send shock waves through the corporate community:

> I don't think corporate America should be viewed as in the ballpark with these folks. This was a highly unusual situation, but now people see that where the egregious situation occurs, there could be a criminal remedy.

Robert Stephenson, a lawyer defending another corporation, said, "I don't believe these statutes [murder and aggravated battery] were ever meant to be used in this way."

Utah's governor Scott M. Matheson refused to extradite Michael T. McKay, a former Film Recovery vice-president then living in Utah, because he was an "exemplary citizen who should not be subjected to the sensational charges in Illinois."

Which of the preceding statements best describes what you think is proper policy regarding corporate executive murder prosecutions?

SUMMARY. Murder includes all killings committed with malice. Legal malice does not mean hate or spite as those terms are commonly used. Rather, it embraces several mental states, including a purpose to kill, an intent to do serious bodily harm, a depraved heart, and the intent to commit a serious felony.

Murder is divided into degrees. First-degree murder includes (1) purposeful, premeditated, and deliberate killing; (2) atrocious or cruel murder; and (3) felony murder. Second-degree murder is a catchall category including all criminal homicides that constitute neither first-degree murder nor manslaughter. The principal second-degree murders include (1) murders not premeditated or deliberate; (2) killings resulting from the intent to inflict great bodily injury; (3) some felony murders; and, according to a few courts, (4) murders that occur while resisting lawful arrest.

Manslaughter

Manslaughter, another catchall, includes all homicides that are neither justified or excused at one extreme, nor murder at the other. The criminal law divides manslaughter into two categories: voluntary and involuntary. A third type of manslaughter—**negligent homicide**—applies mainly to fatal auto accidents. Negligent homicide, sometimes called vehicular homicide, requires less than criminal negligence to sustain a conviction. At common law, manslaughter meant

> the unlawful killing of another, without malice either express or implied . . . either voluntarily, upon a sudden heat; or involuntarily, but in the commission of some unlawful act.[28]

VOLUNTARY MANSLAUGHTER. Voluntary manslaughter, another catchall, includes all homicides that are not murder, involuntary manslaughter, negligent homicide, justifiable, or excusable. Several circumstances reduce murder to voluntary manslaughter. An intentional killing in the *un*reasonable belief that self-defense required use of deadly force can reduce murder to voluntary manslaughter even if it is not justified enough to constitute self-defense.

> A person is guilty of voluntary manslaughter, if, in taking another's life, he believes that he is in danger of losing his own life or suffering great bodily harm but his belief is unreasonable.[29]

Most voluntary manslaughters involve provocation. While the criminal law aims to bridle passions and build self-control, it does not ignore the frailty of human nature. Hence, an intentional killing is still a crime, but it might fall into a lower grade than murder. In other words, the law does not reward individuals who give in to their rages by freeing those individuals; it reduces murder to manslaughter under carefully defined conditions, making up the **provocation rule.** The rule of provocation requires that killing occur

1. with adequate provocation;
2. in a "heat of passion";
3. with "sudden" passion—that is, without time for passions to cool; and
4. where a causal connection links the provocation, the passion, and the fatal act.[30]

Adequate Provocation Not all provocations constitute adequate provocations. All individuals who fly into a rage and suddenly kill someone have not necessarily committed voluntary manslaughter instead of murder. Adequate provocation includes mutual combat or quarrel, battery, assault, gestures, trespass, certain *informational* words, and adultery.

Mutual fights are provocations sufficient to reduce murder to man-slaughter only if they meet the requirements mentioned earlier. That is, the fight must be serious, not just a scuffle; the fight must result from passion without time to cool off; and the fight, passion, and death must have causal links.

Battery, or offensive touching, is considered adequate provocation, but not all touchings are legally sufficient provocation. Pistol-whipping on the head, striking hard with fists in the face, and "staggering" body blows constitute adequate provocation. Slight slaps do not qualify.

Assault, where the assailant establishes no body contact, can constitute adequate provocation. In one case, a man shot at the defendant and missed him. The defendant was so enraged that as the assailant ran away, he shot him in the back. The initial assault, although not enough to qualify the defendant's action as self-defense, was regarded sufficiently provocative to reduce murder to manslaughter.[31]

Insulting gestures are not considered adequate provocation, at least not on their own. If, however, they indicate an intent to attack with deadly force, they constitute adequate provocation. Thus, using a well-known obscene gesture is not adequate provocation, but waving a gun around in a threatening manner might well be.

Some trespasses are sufficient provocation to reduce murder to man-slaughter. A common statement is that trespasses are adequate provocation only if trespassers invade slayers' home and put them in danger.[32]

The case of *State v. Watson* examined whether certain informational words provided adequate provocation.

CASE

Are Words Adequate Provocation?

State v. Watson

287 N.C. 147, 214 S.E.2d 85 (1975)

[Watson was convicted of second-degree murder and was sentenced to life imprisonment. He appealed, arguing that he was legally provoked. Justice Copeland delivered the opinion.]

FACTS

At the time of this incident, defendant, a black, was twenty-years-old. He was serving a twenty-five year prison sentence on judgment imposed at the October, 1972, Session of Rockingham County Superior Court upon his plea of guilty to second-degree murder. The decedent Samples, was white. Neither Samples' age nor the basis for his incarceration appears from the record.

The defendant was called "Duck" by his fellow prisoners in I-Dorm. Samples, the decedent, was known as "Pee Wee." Although Samples was referred to as "Pee Wee," there appeared to be no relation between this nickname and his physical size. In fact, he was a strong man who worked out daily with weights.

The "hearsay" among the residents of I-Dorm was to the effect that Watson and Samples were "swapping-out." "Swapping-out" is a prison term that means two inmates are engaging in homosexual practices. Generally, prisoners that are "swapping-out" try to hide the practice from their fellow inmates. In particular, they try to hide it from any "home-boys" that may be in their particular unit. A "home-boy," in the prison vernacular, is a fellow inmate from one's own hometown or community. One of the State's witnesses, Johnny Lee Wilson, a resident of I-Dorm on the date of the offense, was Samples' "home-boy."

It appears that Watson and Samples had been "swapping-out" for several months. Approximately a month or so prior to the date of the killing, Watson and Samples had engaged in a "scuffle" while working in the prison kitchen. This appears to have been nothing more than a fist-fight. Samples was the winner. Although it is by no means clear from the record, it appears that this "scuffle" arose out of Samples' suspicion that Watson had been "swapping-out" with another prisoner.

At approximately 4:30 P.M. on the afternoon of the killing, Johnny Lee Wilson, Samples' "home-boy," saw Watson and Samples sitting together on a bunk in the back of I-Dorm. At this time, "they were close talking, they were close." Apparently, assuming that they were about to "swap-out," and not wanting to embarrass Samples, Wilson quickly turned around and left the dorm.

Shortly before the lights were to be dimmed (10:00 P.M.), Watson and Samples began to argue. After several minutes, Watson got up and walked across the aisle, a distance of approximately seven feet, to his bunk. Samples subsequently followed him and renewed the dispute. At this time, both parties were seated on Watson's bottom bunk. During the course of the renewed argument, Samples was verbally abusing Watson and challenging him to fight. At one point, he said: "Nigger, nigger, you're just like the rest of them." He also told Watson that he was too scared to fight him and that all he was going to do was tremble and stay in his bunk. Finally, Samples made several derogatory and obscene references to Watson's mother. The prisoners refer to this as "shooting the dove." Generally, when a prisoner "shoots the dove," he expects the other party to fight. At this point, Watson told Johnny Lee Wilson, whose bunk was nearby on Watson's side of the room: "You better get your home-boy straightened out before I f—— him up." Responding to this statement, Samples said: "Why don't you f—— me up if that's what you want to do. All you're gonna do is tremble, nigger."

As Samples was making the above quoted statement, he was walking over to Wilson's bunk. Samples borrowed a cigarette from Wilson and then proceeded to his own bed. He got up in his bunk (top) and was more or less half sitting up with his back propped up against the wall. At this point, he renewed the argument with Watson, who was still in his bottom bunk on the opposite side of the room. He called Watson a "nigger" and "a black mother f———." While this was going on, Watson, without saying a word, either walked or ran across the aisle between the two rows of bunks and violently and repeatedly stabbed Samples with a kitchen-type paring knife. According to the State's witnesses, this occurred approximately two (2) to ten (10) minutes after Samples had left Watson's bed.

(1) After summarizing the evidence, and prior to fully instructing on first-degree murder, the court stated: "[L]et me say here, that mere words will not form a justification or excuse for a crime of this sort."

(2) In instructing the jury on voluntary manslaughter, the court stated: "[T]he defendant must satisfy you that this passion was produced by acts of Samples which the law regards as adequate provocation. This may consist of anything which has a natural tendency to produce such passion in a person of average mind and disposition. However, words and gestures alone, where no assault is made or threatened, regardless of how insulting or inflammatory those words or gestures may be, does not constitute adequate provocation for the taking of a human life."

OPINION

[After reviewing several other decisions, the court wrote:]

These decisions establish the following rules as to the legal effect of abusive language: (1) Mere words, however abusive, are never sufficient legal provocation to mitigate a homicide to a lesser degree; and (2) A defendant, prosecuted for a homicide in a difficulty that he has provoked by the use of language "calculated and intended" to bring on the encounter, cannot maintain the position of perfect self-defense unless, at a time prior to the killing, he withdrew from the encounter within the meaning of the law. These two rules are logically consistent and demonstrate that abusive language will not serve as a legally sufficient provocation for a homicide in this State.

These well-settled rules are clearly controlling in the instant case. Hence, if defendant had provoked an assault by the deceased through the use of abusive language and had thereafter killed the deceased, then it would have been for the jury to determine if the language used by defendant, given the relationship of the parties, the circumstances surrounding the verbal assertions, etc., was "calculated and intended" to bring on the assault. If the jury had found this to be the case, then defendant would not have had the benefit of the doctrine of perfect self-defense, even though the deceased instigated the actual physical attack. But, here there was no evidence that defendant killed the deceased in self-defense. In fact, all of the evidence tends to show that the fatal attack was brought on by the continued verbal abuses directed toward defendant by the deceased. Under these circumstances, there was no basis for a jury determination of whether any of the words were "calculated and intended" to bring on the difficulty.

At this point, we note that in those few jurisdictions that permit abusive language to mitigate the degree of homicide, the majority hold that the words are only deemed sufficient to negate premeditation, thereby reducing the degree of homicide from first to second. Most of these courts reason that since the deceased had made no attempt to endanger the life of the accused, the action of the latter in meeting the insulting remarks with sufficient force (deadly or otherwise) to cause the death of the former, was beyond the bounds of sufficient retaliation to constitute sufficient provocation to reduce the homicide to manslaughter. See Annot., 2 A.L.R.3d 1292, 1308–10 (1965). Although we expressly decline to adopt this minority view, we note that the jury in the instant case apparently applied the same reasoning and found defendant guilty of second-degree murder. Thus, even if the minority rule applied in this State, defendant would not be entitled to a new trial as a result of the instructions here given.

Defendant contends that the trial court committed prejudicial error in charging the jury as follows:

> Now, ladies and gentlemen of the jury, this case is to be tried by you under the laws of the State of North Carolina, and not upon the rules and regulations and customs and unwritten code that exists within the walls of the North Carolina Department of Correction. I can't charge you on that law because I don't know that law. I think I know this one, and this is the law that you are trying this case under.

Defendant argues that this instruction "tends to discount as a matter of law all of the factual information" that the jury was "entitled to consider, not as law, but as a part of the factual background situation within which the incident took place." We find nothing in the charge to support such an inference. During the course of the trial, several of the State's witnesses (either present or former prison inmates) testified about a "prison code," i.e., a set of unwritten rules developed by the prisoners themselves. For example, one of the State's witnesses made the following statements on cross-examination:

> In the prison system, if Watson had not fought after Samples had called him nigger, nigger, and talked about his mother, I guess, you know, everybody else probably would be jugging at him. What I mean by "jugging at him," I mean, messing with him, you know. Taking advantage of the fact that he won't stand up for himself. It is important that you stand up for yourself in the system because if you don't, somebody might get you down in the shower, you know. You might get dead-ended. It means if you don't take up for yourself, everybody picks on you.

Apparently, standing up for oneself was a vital part of this so-called "prison code." In this context, the import of the above instruction was clearly to inform the jurors that the case—like all other criminal cases tried in the North Carolina General Courts of Justice—had to be tried under the laws of this State and not upon any unwritten prisoners' code that existed within the walls of North Carolina's prisons. It is certainly not error for a trial judge to so instruct a jury. Furthermore, it appears that defendant's conduct even constituted a violation of the prisoners' code. We refer to the following redirect testimony of the same witness previously quoted above: "Stand up for yourself in the prison system would not necessarily include using a knife. He could have run over there and fought with bare fists, that would have been standing up for himself."

Defendant's contention under this assignment is without merit. Therefore, it is overruled. Affirmed.

CASE DISCUSSION

The *Watson* court states flatly that words are never adequate provocation to reduce murder to manslaughter, although they may be adequate to reduce murder from first to second degree. Do you think this is a good rule for this case? Especially, is it good when the prison code called on Watson to stand up for himself or be mistreated in the future? In fact, if the unwritten prison code does call for him to stand up for himself, was it the words or fears for his personal safety that provoked him? If you were the judge, would you have interpreted the provocation rule differently? Why or why not?

According to the common law, a man who caught his wife in the act of adultery had adequate provocation to kill: "there could be no greater provocation than this." Many cases have held that it is voluntary manslaughter for a husband to kill his wife, her paramour, or both in the first heat of passion following the sight of adultery. For a short time, statutes went beyond the common-law rule, and called paramour killings justified homicide. Historically, the **paramour rule** did not apply to both spouses; the common law made it available only to husbands. Furthermore the common law and statutes have restricted the rule to cases where spouses are caught in adulterous acts; the rule has not covered spouses who reacted upon learning about adultery after it occurred.[33]

CASE

Is Admitting to Adultery Adequate Provocation?

Commonwealth v. Schnopps

383 Mass. 178, 417 N.E.2d 1213 (1981)

[Schnopps was convicted of first-degree murder. He appealed. Justice Abrams delivered the opinion.]

FACTS

On October 13, 1979, Marilyn R. Schnopps was fatally shot by her estranged husband, George A. Schnopps. A jury convicted Schnopps of murder in the first degree, and he was sentenced to the mandatory term of life imprisonment. Schnopps claims that the trial judge erred by refusing to instruct the jury on voluntary manslaughter. We agree. We reverse and order a new trial.

Schnopps testified that this wife had left him three weeks prior to the slaying. He claims that he first became aware of problems in his fourteen-year marriage at a point about six months before the slaying. According to the defendant, on that occasion he took his wife to a club to dance, and she spent the evening dancing with a coworker. On arriving home, the defendant and his wife argued over her conduct. She told him that she no longer loved him and that she wanted a divorce. Schnopps became very upset. He admitted that he took out his shotgun during the course of this argument, but he denied that he intended to use it.

During the next few months, Schnopps argued frequently with his wife. The defendant accused her of seeing another man, but she steadfastly denied the accusations. On more than one occasion Schnopps threatened his wife with physical harm. He testified he never intended to hurt his wife but only wanted to scare her so that she would end the relationship with her coworker.

One day in September, 1979, the defendant became aware that the suspected boy friend used a "signal" in telephoning Schnopps' wife. Schnopps used the signal, and his wife answered the phone with "Hi, Lover." She hung up immediately when she recognized Schnopps' voice. That afternoon she did not return home. Later that evening, she informed Schnopps by telephone that she had moved to her mother's house and that she had the children with her. She told Schnopps she would not return to their home. Thereafter she "froze [him] out," and would not talk to him. During this period, the defendant spoke with a lawyer about a divorce and was told that he had a good chance of getting custody of the children, due to his wife's "desertion and adultery."

On the day of the killing, Schnopps had asked his wife to come to their home and talk over their marital difficulties. Schnopps told his wife that he wanted his children at home, and that he wanted the family to remain intact. Schnopps cried during the conversation, and begged his wife to let the children live with him and to keep their family together. His wife replied, "No, I am going to court, you are going to give me all the furniture, you are going to have to get the Hell out of here, you won't have nothing." Then, pointing to her crotch, she said, "You will never touch this again, because I have got something bigger and better for it."

On hearing those words, Schnopps claims that his mind went blank, and that he went "berserk." He went to a cabinet and got out a pistol he had bought and loaded the day before, and he shot his wife and himself. When he "started coming to" as a result of the pain she asked him to summon help. The victim was pronounced dead at the scene, and the defendant was arrested and taken to the hospital for treatment of his wound.

OPINION

The issue raised by Schnopps' appeal is whether in these circumstances the judge was required to instruct the jury on voluntary manslaughter. Instructions on voluntary manslaughter must be given if there is evidence of provocation deemed adequate in law to cause the accused to lose his self control in the heat of passion, and if the killing followed the provocation before sufficient time had elapsed for the accused's temper to cool. A verdict of voluntary manslaughter requires the trier of fact to conclude that there is a causal connection between the provocation, the heat of passion, and the killing.

Schnopps argues that "[t]he existence of sufficient provocation is not foreclosed absolutely because a defendant learns of a fact from oral statements rather than from personal observation," and that a sudden admission of adultery is equivalent to a discovery of the act itself, and is sufficient evidence of provocation.

Schnopps asserts that his wife's statements constituted a "peculiarly immediate and intense offense to a spouse's sensitivities." He concedes that the words at issue are indicative of past as well as present adultery. Schnopps claims, however, that his wife's admission of adultery was made for the first time on the day of the killing, and hence the evidence of provocation was sufficient to trigger jury consideration of voluntary manslaughter as a possible verdict.

Reversed and remanded for new trial on manslaughter issue.

CASE DISCUSSION

The paramour rule was adopted to cover cases where husbands found their wives in bed with other men. The provocation was the sight itself. Thus, the passion was immediately connected to the adulterous act. If you were a juror, could you in good conscience say that Schnopps was adequately provoked? If so, was it the adultery that provoked him or the provocative words his wife used to describe her adulterous relationship? Do you think the prohibition against provocative words makes sense? If you were writing a manslaughter law, how would you treat cases like *Schnopps?*

Voluntary manslaughter requires not only adequate but also actual provocation. The provocation must, in fact, provoke the defendant. The provocation rule contains both objective and subjective dimensions. The provocations that the law recognizes as adequate constitute the objective side of provocation; that these provocations in fact provoke the defendant constitute the subjective side.

Sudden Passion At common law, and in most modern statutes, voluntary manslaughter requires killing in the "sudden heat of passion" with no "cooling off" period. The actual time between provocation and killing—whether seconds, hours, or even days—depends upon the facts of the individual case. Courts usually apply an objective test: Would a reasonable person under the same circumstances have had time to cool off? If defendants had reasonable time for their murderous rages to subside, the law views their killings as murders even if the provocations were adequate to reduce those killings to manslaughter had they taken place immediately following the provocations.

Using the objective test, the time for cooling off may be considerable. In one case, a man's wife told him her father had raped her. The court ruled that the husband's passion had not reasonably cooled even after he walked all night to his father-in-law's house and killed him the next day! The court said the heinous combination of incest and rape was sufficient to keep a reasonable person in a murderous rage for at least several days.[34]

Causal Link between Provocation, Passion, and Death To prove voluntary manslaughter, the prosecution must prove a causal link between the provocation, passion, and killing. It is not voluntary manslaughter if I intend to kill an enemy, and, just as I am about to execute my intent, I find him in bed with my wife and use that as my excuse to kill. The provocation must cause the passion that leads to the killing.

Voluntary manslaughter, then, consists of the following material elements: (1) intentional or purposeful killing that (2) occurs in a sudden heat of passion (3) without time to cool off and that is (4) caused by (5) reasonable and actual provocation.

INVOLUNTARY MANSLAUGHTER. Involuntary manslaughter is a criminal homicide in which the killer did not intend to cause death. In involuntary manslaughters, deaths result from either reckless or negligent legal acts, or during illegal conduct. The last case, called the **misdemeanor manslaughter rule,** is the counterpart to the felony murder doctrine. According to this rule, if death occurs during the commission of a misdemeanor, the misdemeanant has committed involuntary manslaughter. Courts vary as to the kinds of unlawful acts that qualify under the misdemeanor manslaughter doctrine. Most include breaches of public order, injuries to persons or property, and outrages against public decency and morals. Examples include nonfelonious assault, carrying a concealed weapon, driving illegally, and dispensing drugs.

CASE

Was Dr. Youngkin a Reckless Killer?

Commonwealth v. Youngkin

285 Pa. Super. 417, 427 A.2d 1356 (1981)

[Dr. Youngkin was convicted of involuntary manslaughter. He was fined $5,000 and sentenced to between one and three years' imprisonment. He appealed. Judge Price delivered the opinion.]

FACTS

Barbara Fedder, a seventeen-year old patient of appellant, lapsed into a state of unconsciousness while attending a party on the night of July 23, 1976. Attempts at cardiopulmonary resuscitation proved unsuccessful, and Ms. Fedder was pronounced dead during the early morning hours of July 24. The cause of death was determined to be asphyxiation from aspiration of the contents of her stomach due to depression of her gag reflex. Simply stated, Ms. Fedder suffocated when the contents of her stomach entered her lungs. Normally, one's gag reflex would expel the regurgitated material. However, in Ms. Fedder's case, her gag reflex was depressed. Postmortem laboratory analyses performed on the decedent revealed the presence of the drugs amobarbital and secobarbital, components of a chemical compound known as Tuinal, a barbiturate prescribed as a hypnotic or sleeping pill. Medical and toxicological experts for the Commonwealth testified that the depression of Ms. Fedder's gag reflex was caused by ingestion of the barbiturate. Further Commonwealth evidence revealed that in the seven weeks preceding Ms. Fedder's death appellant prescribed numerous drugs for her, including seven prescriptions for Tuinal, the last of which was written July 23, 1976.

The Commonwealth charged appellant with involuntary manslaughter, alleging that, as a direct result of the reckless and grossly negligent manner in which he prescribed the drug Tuinal he caused the death of Ms. Fedder. Involuntary manslaughter is defined in the Crimes Code as follows:

> A person is guilty of involuntary manslaughter when as a direct result of the doing of an unlawful act in a reckless or grossly negligent manner, or the doing of a lawful act in a reckless or grossly negligent manner, he causes the death of another person. 18 Pa. C.S. § 2504.

OPINION

In the instant case, death was caused by aspiration of the regurgitated contents of the stomach due to a depressed gag reflex. The jury found that the depression of the gag reflex was caused by ingestion of the drug Tuinal, prescribed to the decedent by appellant. Our review of the record supports the jury's finding that the drug Tuinal caused Ms. Fedder's demise.

However, the mere finding that the decedent died from ingestion of a drug prescribed to her by appellant is insufficient, in itself, to support a conviction for involuntary manslaughter. Prescription of a controlled drug by a licensed physician does not constitute an unlawful act. Therefore, under the Crimes Code, the Commonwealth must prove that appellant executed this lawful act, i.e. prescription, in a reckless or grossly negligent manner and that his conduct was the legal cause of Ms. Fedder's death.

The recklessness or criminal negligence required to sustain an involuntary manslaughter conviction may be found if the accused consciously disregarded or, in gross departure from a standard of reasonable care, failed to perceive a substantial and unjustifiable risk that his action might cause death or serious bodily harm.

Evidence produced at trial indicated that during the months of June and July, 1976, appellant issued to the decedent seven separate prescriptions for the compound Tuinal, the latest of which was issued on July 23, 1976. Testimony adduced at trial indicated that Ms. Fedder had in her possession on the night of the party a bottle containing the July 23 prescription.

The Coroner of Columbia County, Dr. D. Ernest Witt, testified that the size of the Tuinal pills prescribed by appellant (3 grains) was double the normal pill size and that it was questionable practice to prescribe Tuinal to an out-patient. Regarding the instant fact situation, the coroner stated that prescribing Tuinal to a seventeen year old girl in the amounts and frequencies evidenced by appellant's prescriptions was "over-prescribing," "considerably irresponsible and reckless" and "totally wrong." The Deputy Coroner of Columbia County, Dr. Frederick B. Clemens, concurred in Dr. Witt's assessment and termed the practice dangerous, with fatal results a possibility.

The Commonwealth also produced testimony from nine pharmacists who described the dozens of prescriptions for controlled substances which appellant had issued to Ms. Fedder in the months preceding her death. One of the pharmacists testified that the decedent came into his store on one occasion, about a month before her death, in such a dazed and stuporous condition that she had to hold onto the cash register to maintain her balance. Leery of selling the decedent a prescription that would enhance her stuporous state, the pharmacist telephoned appellant, described to him Ms. Fedder's condition, and queried whether it was advisable to fill the prescription in those circumstances. Appellant's response to the pharmacist was "fill the damn thing."

Our review of the evidence leads us to the conclusion that there was sufficient evidence to prove each element of involuntary manslaughter. The evidence indicates that appellant prescribed Tuinal to the decedent in quantities and frequencies termed irresponsible and totally inappropriate in the circumstances. The frequency with which the prescriptions were written should have suggested that the decedent was abusing Tuinal. Moreover, this fact was specifically brought to appellant's attention by a pharmacist who called appellant alarmed over the decedent's physical condition. However, appellant chose to ignore these indications of abuse and continued to prescribe the drug to decedent. In these circumstances the record supports and justifies the jury's conclusion that appellant consciously disregarded a substantial and unjustifiable risk, which disregard involved a gross deviation from the standard of conduct a reasonable person would have observed.

The record also supports the jury's finding that appellant's acts were a direct and substantial factor in producing Ms. Fedder's death. Appellant recklessly overprescribed Tuinal to decedent over the course of several months, he was aware of her abuse of the drug yet took no remedial measures, and her death was attributed to asphyxiation due to a depressed gag reflex caused by ingestion of Tuinal. Appellant contends that the sentencing court abused its discretion by imposing a sentence that was manifestly excessive.

In sentencing appellant, the sentencing judge considered, inter alia, a presentence report, the character and reputation of appellant, the gravity of the offense, and the particular circumstances of the crime. The record discloses that the sentencing judge was particularly concerned with the seriousness of appellant's actions, since they resulted in the loss of a life. Furthermore, the judge noted appellant's apparent lack of remorse, as evidenced by certain responses given by appellant during the presentence investigation. Noting that appellant's counsel's arguments for probation were persuasive, the judge nevertheless concluded that the seriousness of the offense dictated the term of imprisonment imposed. Our review of the record supports the conclusion of the sentencing judge, and we find that he did not impose a manifestly excessive sentence.

Accordingly, the judgment of sentence is affirmed.

CASE DISCUSSION

The Pennsylvania statute makes it involuntary manslaughter to cause death by recklessly or with gross negligence performing either legal or illegal acts. The court in *Youngkin* found Dr. Youngkin reckless and further decided that his reckless prescribing practices caused Barbara Fedder's death. Do you agree that Dr. Youngkin was reckless? Do you also agree that he deserved a harsh sentence because he was a doctor who had a special responsibility for his patients' welfare? During the trial, the prosecutor mentioned that Dr. Youngkin was especially dangerous because he threatened everyone in the state with his recklessness. Do you agree?

NEGLIGENT HOMICIDE. Involuntary manslaughter also includes *criminally* negligent homicides—that is, unintentional killings where actors should have known they were creating substantial and unjustified risks of death by conduct that *grossly* deviated from ordinary care. The common law did not recognize these involuntary manslaughters. However, statutes have brought within the criminal law's scope a variety of deaths caused by criminal negligence, including negligently using firearms, handling explosives, allowing vicious animals to run free, practicing medicine, and operating trains, planes, and ships.

The most common negligent homicide involves negligent driving. Most states require gross negligence to convict drivers in fatal accidents. However, a few states have reduced the culpability to something less than gross negligence in special vehicular homicide statutes. One court held that

> [b]y the enactment of this [vehicular homicide] statute, the Legislature obviously intended to create a lesser offense than involuntary manslaughter . . . where the negligent killing was caused by the operation of a vehicle. . . . Therefore, this statute was intended to apply only to cases where the negligence is of a lesser degree than gross negligence.[35]

Under this scheme, if drivers' reckless or grossly negligent driving causes death, they have committed involuntary manslaughter. If the death resulted from less-than-gross negligence, the driver has committed negligent, or vehicular, homicide.

In effect, then, three degrees of negligence govern liability: (1) gross negligence for involuntary homicide; (2) something less than gross negligence for vehicular homicide; and (3) ordinary carelessness for civil liability in wrongful death actions. The line between gross negligence and recklessness is often fine. Yet, courts and numerous statutes use the distinction. Fact finders, whether juries or judges, apply the definition or standard to particular facts before them. Hence, although criminal recklessness, gross and lesser criminal negligence, and ordinary negligence are difficult to quantify, they nonetheless determine how to grade conduct resulting in death.

The reason for this complex grading in vehicular homicide has to do with the reluctance of juries to convict drivers in fatal car accidents of manslaughter. They do so more willingly in vehicular homicide, with its milder penalties and reduced stigma. In line with this thinking, some states have included vehicular homicide in their motor vehicle or traffic codes, rather than placing it in the criminal code sections.[36]

Neither legislatures, courts, or juries extend the same leniency to fatal accidents involving drunken drivers. In fact, some drunken drivers who cause death face murder charges, as *Essex v. Commonwealth* illustrates.

CASE

Was the D.W.I. Death a Murder?

Essex v. Commonwealth

228 Va. 273, 322 S.E.2d 216 (1984)

[Defendant was convicted of driving while under the influence of alcohol and convicted on three counts of second-degree murder for deaths resulting from injuries sustained in an automobile collision. He appealed. Justice Russell delivered the opinion, which reversed and remanded the initial judgment. Justice Poff dissented in part.]

FACTS

A jury convicted Warren Wesley Essex of one count of driving under the influence of alcohol (defined as a misdemeanor) and three counts of second-degree murder for deaths resulting from injuries sustained in an automobile collision. . . . The collision occurred about 10:45 P.M. on November 20, 1981, at a point on State Route 28 south of its intersection with State Route 17. Essex, driving a Plymouth Duster automobile, entered Route 23, a two-lane, hard surfaced highway, north of the intersection and headed south. Linda Bates, who was traveling south on Route 28, testified that the Duster entered the highway behind her, passed her across a solid center line, almost struck her car as it returned to the right lane, and ran onto the shoulder of the road, nearly striking a mailbox before it reentered the southbound lane. She said that the Duster passed another vehicle across a solid line and returned to the right lane just in time to avoid a northbound pickup truck. Later, it crossed double solid lines on a curve to pass yet another vehicle. For a distance of six miles, Mrs. Bates watched the car as it swerved from one lane to the other and off the edge of the hard surface.

Although there were "speed bumps" in the pavement north of the intersection, the Duster ran through a red traffic signal at a speed Mrs. Bates estimated at 55 m.p.h. A tractor-trailer truck moving through the intersection on Route 17 "nearly hit the back end of the Plymouth." A mile and a half south of the intersection, the Duster collided with a northbound pickup truck driven by John Gouldthorpe.

Gouldthorpe testified that "[t]he last thing I remember was seeing four headlights, one set in one lane and one in the other." State Trooper Donald Johnson, the investigating officer, testified that when he asked Essex what had happened, the defendant replied, "I was in his lane because my steering had gone. . . . I had been having trouble with it all night." An expert mechanic who inspected the Duster at the officer's request testified that "there was nothing loose" and "no failures" in any part of the steering linkage, and that the only damage he found was a break in the steering column which he said was "due to the impact where the front end had been shoved back about a foot."

Debra Gouldthrope and Nora Neale, passengers in the pickup, and James Carter, a passenger in the defendant's car, died from injuries sustained in the collision. Essex was treated at Fauquier Hospital for "a large laceration on his knee" and "a small laceration of the tongue." Dr. Steven Von Elten, the attending physician in the emergency room who examined Essex about 12:30 A.M., testified that Essex was in a "stuporous condition" and that although "the lady next to him was screaming very intensely . . . he was totally unaware of that." Because he could "very easily . . . smell the odor of alcohol . . . at that bedside," Dr. Elton ordered a blood alcohol content test. The test, conducted about two and a half hours after the collision, disclosed an alcohol content of .144 percent. . . .

OPINION

Where death proximately results from the want of ordinary care as practiced by a reasonably prudent person, the causative negligence is actionable as a tort. If the negligence is so gross, wanton, and culpable as to show a reckless disregard of human life, a killing resulting therefrom, although unintentional, is both a tort and a crime, punishable as involuntary manslaughter.

Criminal homicides in Virginia are classified as follows:

1. Capital murder,
2. First-degree murder,
3. Second-degree murder,
4. Voluntary manslaughter, and
5. Involuntary manslaughter.

Malice, a requisite element for murder of any kind, is unnecessary in manslaughter cases and is the touchstone by which murder and manslaughter cases are distinguished. Malice may be either express or implied by conduct. . . . "Express malice is evidenced when 'one person kills another with a sedate, deliberate mind, and formed design.' . . . Implied malice exists when any *purposeful, cruel act* is committed by one individual against another without any, or without great provocation; . . . "

The authorities are replete with definitions of malice, but a common theme running through them is a requirement that a wrongful act be done "willfully or purposefully." This requirement of volitional action is inconsistent with inadvertence. Thus, if a killing results from negligence, however gross or culpable, and the killing is contrary to the defendant's intention, malice cannot be implied. In order to elevate the crime to second-degree murder, the defendant must be shown to have willfully or purposefully, rather than negligently, embarked upon a course of wrongful conduct likely to cause death or great bodily harm. . . .

We have not, heretofore, had occasion to review a second-degree murder conviction based upon the use of an automobile, but the governing principles are the same as those which apply to any other kind of second-degee murder: the victim must be shown to have died as a result of the defendant's conduct, and the defendant's conduct must be shown to be malicious. In the absence of express malice, this element may only be implied from conduct likely to cause death or great bodily harm, wilfully or purposefully undertaken. Thus, for example, one who deliberately drives a car into a crowd of people at a high speed, not intending to kill or injury [sic] any particular person, but rather seeking the perverse thrill of terrifying them and causing them to scatter, might be convicted of second-degree murder if death results. One who accomplishes the same result inadvertently, because of grossly negligent driving, causing him to lose control of his car, could be convicted only of voluntary manslaughter. In the first case the act was volitional; in the second it was inadvertent, however reckless and irresponsible.

What effect has the defendant's degree of intoxication, if any, upon the fact-finder's determination? The defendant may negate the specific intent requisite for capital or first-degree murder by showing that he was so greatly intoxicated as to be incapable of deliberation or premeditation, but voluntary intoxication is no defense to the lesser degrees of homicide, or to any other crime. . . .

Drunken driving is not only unlawful in itself, but it tends to make the defendant's dangerous conduct more dangerous. A sober but reckless driver may rely on his skill and prompt reflexes to extricate himself from any emergency created by his reckless driving. A drunken driver has dulled his perceptions, blunted his skill, and slowed his reflexes in advance. The same reckless driving is more dangerous at his hands than it would be if he were sober, and his conduct is therefore more culpable. Intoxication, therefore, is relevant as an aggravating factor, increasing with its degree, bearing upon the relative culpability of the defendant's conduct, even though it is irrelevant to the determination of malice. . . . It may serve to elevate the defendant's conduct to the level of "negligence so gross, wanton, and culpable as to show a reckless disregard for human life," a requisite element for a conviction of involuntary manslaughter.

. . . [W]e find the evidence, viewed in the light most favorable to the Commonwealth, insufficient to support a finding of implied malice. The defendant was intoxicated and guilty of an appalling degree of reckless driving. His multiple tortious acts conjoined as proximate causes of three tragic deaths . . . The Commonwealth, however, has the burden of proving malice beyond a reasonable doubt. The jury could only speculate, upon this evidence, whether the defendant embarked upon his ill-fated course of conduct wilfully and with malicious purpose. . . .

DISSENT

. . . Negligence in an accidental death may be a tort or a crime, or both. The character of such negligence is the determinative factor. Ordinary negligence, *i.e.*, the want of ordinary care as practiced by a reasonably prudent person, is actionable tort. Negligence so gross as to manifest depravity of mind and a callous disregard for human safety is criminal negligence, and if death results, constitutes criminal homicide. Unlike violations of some statutory rules of the road, the offense of driving under the influence of intoxicants constitutes criminal negligence. . . .

The level of culpability of criminal negligence determines the grade of the offense. Between the class of deliberate deeds committed with premeditated intent to kill, which is the essence of murder of the first degree, and the type of negligence inherent in the definition of involuntary manslaughter there is a species of reckless behavior so willful and wanton, so heedless of foreseeable consequences, and so indifferent to the value of human life that it supplies the element of malice which distinguishes murder of the second degree from manslaughter. . . .

. . . The great weight of authority holds that a motorist's negligence may be so gross and culpable as to imply a malicious intent to kill and that, in determining whether the homicide is manslaughter or murder, intoxication is an aggravating factor. The vehicular homicide statutes adopted by some states abandon the definitional differences the common law makes between manslaughter and murder and define homicide resulting from the criminal negligence of the driver of a motor vehicle as a unique offense, graded according to the nature and extent of the driver's negligence. Virginia has no such statute, and as defined by the majority opinion, vehicular homicide is hereafter relegated to the lowest grade of criminal homicide. The degree of culpability is immaterial.

. . . I would hold that where the evidence is sufficient to show that the driver of a motor vehicle, whether drunk or sober, is guilty of criminal negligence which is the sole proximate cause of a homicide, such evidence raises a question of fact whether the offense is manslaughter or murder of the second degree. . . .

I am of the opinion that the evidence of record in this case is fully sufficient to justify the jury's finding that the defendant's negligence was the sole proximate cause of three deaths and that such negligence was so willful and wanton, so heedless of foreseeable consequences, and so indifferent to the value of human life as to imply the element of malice charged in the homicide counts of the indictment.

CASE DISCUSSION

What facts indicate Essex's culpability? Was it recklessness? gross negligence? less-than-gross negligence but still criminal negligence? ordinary negligence? How do you decide which level of culpability caused the death? Do you agree that this evidence supports a conviction for murder?

≡ SUMMARY

The following outline summarizes the complicated and intricate elements in criminal homicide.

I. Criminal homicide is divided into two main categories: murder and manslaughter.

II. Murder requires taking another's life with malice aforethought.
   A. The precise points at which life begins and ends for purposes of criminal homicide are difficult to determine.
   B. Malice aforethought includes five distinct mental states—the specific intent or purpose to do one of the following:
      1. Kill another person
      2. Seriously injure another person
      3. Forcibly resist a lawful arrest
      4. Commit specified dangerous felonies
      5. Create a higher than criminally reckless risk of death or serious bodily injury
   C. Murder is divided into two primary degrees.
      1. First-degree murder
         a) Premeditated, deliberate killings
         b) Killings that take place while committing some dangerous felonies
         c) Particularly brutal or cruel murders
      2. Second-degree murder
         a) Killings resulting from the intent to do serious bodily injury
         b) Killings resulting from the resisting of lawful arrest
         c) Killings taking place during the commission of less serious felonies

III. Manslaughter is either voluntary or involuntary.
   A. Voluntary manslaughter is the intentional killing of another in the following circumstances.
      1. Under provocation, where such provocation
         a) is actual and adequate
         b) occurs in the heat of passion
         c) occurs before an adequate cooling off period
      2. Where defendants believed they acted in self-defense but where it was unreasonable to do so
   B. Involuntary manslaughter is the killing of another person unintentionally, either
      1. recklessly or
      2. with gross criminal negligence
      3. while committing certain misdemeanors.

C. Negligent homicide is causing death by negligence that is less than gross but more than careless and sufficient to sustain civil tort liability. It is ordinarily limited to fatal car accidents.

QUESTIONS FOR REVIEW AND DISCUSSION

1. For purposes of the law of criminal homicide, when does life begin and end?
2. Why is *mens rea* so important in the law of criminal homicide?
3. Should there be such a thing as felony murder? Why?
4. What is the difference between murder and manslaughter?
5. Should involuntary manslaughter be a crime? Why?

SUGGESTED READINGS

1. Rollin M. Perkins and Ronald N. Boyce, *Criminal Law,* 3d ed. (Mineola, N.Y.: Foundation Press, 1982), pp. 46–151, thoroughly covers criminal homicide. Many cases and examples are used to illustrate the complicated elements in criminal homicide. In addition, new developments in the law are discussed, including the Model Penal Code approach to negligent homicide.
2. George Fletcher, *Rethinking Criminal Law* (Boston: Little, Brown, 1978), chap. 4 and 5, takes a critical look at criminal homicide. Professor Fletcher stresses homicide's uniqueness as a crime because of its irreversibility. He goes into the philosophical underpinnings of homicide law. These chapters enhance much of what is said in this text about various homicides, including the *mens rea* and circumstances surrounding them.
3. American Law Institute, *Model Penal Code and Commentaries*, vol. 1 (Philadelphia: American Law Institute, 1980), pt. II, pp. 1–90, develops the Model Penal Code's effort to restructure homicide law, getting rid of degrees and replacing them with three classifications: murder, manslaughter, and negligent homicide. It is a thorough, thought-provoking discussion, well worth the serious student's efforts.

NOTES

1. Rollin M. Perkins and Ronald N. Boyce, *Criminal Law,* 3d ed. (Mineola, N.Y.: Foundation Press, 1982), pp. 46–150.
2. Ibid., pp. 49–53.
3. 410 U.S. 113, 93 S.Ct. 705, 35 L.Ed.2d 147 (1973); American Law Institute, *Model Penal Code and Commentaries*, vol. 1 (Philadelphia: American Law Institute, 1980), pt. II, pp.11–13, maintains that abortion and fetal death statutes should be kept distinct.

4. Minnesota Criminal Code of 1963, as amended through 1987, Section 609.266–2665; *Minneapolis Star and Tribune* (February 18, 1989).

5. I am grateful to Randall Rogers, the poster's creator, for this idea.

6. 2 Cal. 3d 619, 87 Cal. Rptr. 481, 470 P.2d 617 (1970).

7. Quoted in State v. Fierro, 124 Ariz. 182, 603 P.2d 74, 77-78 (1979); Perkins and Boyce, *Criminal Law*, pp. 48–49, discusses the case.

8. American Law Institute, *Model Penal Code and Commentaries*, vol. 1, pt. II, pp. 10–11, discusses this and summarizes recent legislation on the subject.

9. Perkins and Boyce, *Criminal Law*, pp. 822–24.

10. State v. Minster, 302 Md. 240, 486 A.2d 1197 (1985).

11. American Law Institute, *Model Penal Code and Commentaries*, vol. 1, pt. II, pp.6–7.

12. Quoted in American Law Institute, *Model Penal Code and Commentaries*, vol. 1, pt. II, p. 14.

13. Pa. Laws of 1794, ch. 257, § § 1,2 (1794); Herbert Wechsler and Jerome Michael discuss this development thoroughly in "A Rationale of the Law of Homicide I," *Columbia Law Review*, 37(1937), pp. 703–17.

14. Gregg v. Georgia, 428 U.S. 153, 96 S.Ct. 2909, 49 L.Ed.2d 859 (1976); Proffitt v. Florida, 428 U.S. 242, 96 S.Ct. 2960, 49 L.Ed.2d 913 (1976); Woodson v. North Carolina, 428 U.S. 280, 96 S.Ct. 2978, 49 L.Ed.2d 944 (1976).

15. Goodman v. State, 573 P.2d 400 (Wyo. 1977); Perkins and Boyce, *Criminal Law*, pp. 131–34.

16. Quoted in People v. Anderson, 70 Cal. 2d 15, 73 Cal. Rptr. 550, 447 P.2d 942 (1968).

17. State v. Hall, 54 Nev. 213, 13 P.2d 624 (1932) (intent formed when shot fired); People v. Wolff, 61 Cal. 2d 795, 40 Cal. Rptr. 271, 394 P.2d 959 (1964) (immaturity).

18. Sir James F. Stephens, *History of the Criminal Law* (New York: Burt Franklin, 1973), p. 94.

19. "Minutes of Evidence," *Report*, 12, pp. 174–75.

20. 373 Mass. 249, 366 N.E.2d 744 (1977).

21. 125 Wis. 2d 204, 371 N.W.2d 381 (1985); 89 N.J. Super. 52, 213 A.2d 320 (1965).

22. State v. Crane, 247 Ga. 779, 279 S.E.2d 695 (1981) (victim shooting burglar); Campbell v. State, 293 Md. 438, 444 A.2d 1034 (1982) (victim cab driver and police officer); State v. O'Dell, 684 S.W.2d 453 (Mo.App.1984) (victim of felonious assault).

23. People v. Phillips, 64 Cal.2d 574, 51 Cal. Rptr. 225, 414 P.2d 353 (1966).

24. State v. Weisengoff, 85 W.Va. 271, 101 S.E. 450 (1919) (accidental death); Jerome Hall, "The Substantive Law of Crimes—1187–1936," *Harvard Law Review*, 50 (1937), pp. 616, 642.

25. Francis T. Cullen, William J. Maakestad, and Gray Cavender, *Corporate Crime under Attack: The Ford Pinto Case and Beyond* (Cincinnati: Anderson Publishing Company, 1987).

26. "Texas Nursing Home on Trial in Death," *New York Times* (October 1, 1985) and (March 18, 1986), p. 11.

27. "Business and the Law," *New York Times* (March 5, 1985), p. 30, and (May 19, 1985).

28. Sir William Blackstone, *Commentaries* (University of Chicago Press, 1979), IV, p. 191.

29. People v. Davis, 33 Ill. App. 3d 105, 337 N.E.2d 256 (1975); also State v. Grant, 418 A.2d 154 (Me. 1980); but to the contrary see State v. Tuzon, 118 Ariz. 205, 575 P.2d 1231 (1978).

30. Perkins and Boyce, *Criminal Law,* p. 85.

31. Beasley v. State, 64 Miss. 518, 8 So. 234 (1886).

32. Perkins and Boyce, *Criminal Law,* pp. 95–96.

33. Manning's Case, 83 Eng. Rep. 112 (1793); Palmore v. State, 283 Ala. 501, 218 So.2d 830 (1969) (husband killed wife); Dabney v. State, 21 So. 211 (Ala. 1897) (husband killed both wife and paramour).

34. State v. Flory, 40 Wyo. 184, 276 P. 458 (1929).

35. People v. Campbell, 237 Mich. 424, 212 N.W. 97 (1927).

36. Perkins and Boyce, *Criminal Law,* pp. 116–18.

Chapter Nine

Crimes against Persons II: Criminal Sexual Conduct, and Others

CHAPTER OUTLINE

CHAPTER MAIN POINTS

1. Sex offenses cover a broad spectrum, including everything from violent assaults to nonviolent private sex between consenting adults.

2. Rape is both a violent crime and a sexual violation.

3. Criminal sexual conduct statutes have expanded traditional rape law, making sexual violations, no matter what their nature, sex-neutral crimes.

4. Violence is not always required in rape and related offenses; immaturity and other conditions sometimes substitute for it.

CHAPTER KEY TERMS

assault an attempt to injure or intent to frighten without actually injurying.

battery unjustified offensive touching.

carnal knowledge the sexual contact that qualifies an act for rape and related offenses.

constructive force a substitute for actual force, generally used in cases where the victim is unable to consent.

criminal sexual conduct a gender-neutral statute directed toward a wide range of sexual violations not covered in traditional rape statutes.

marital rape exception the rule that husbands cannot rape their wives.

reasonable resistance standard the principle that women must use the amount of force required by the totality of the circumstances surrounding sexual assault.

statutory rape carnal knowledge of a person under the age of consent whether or not accomplished by force.

utmost resistance standard the principle that female rape victims had to use all the physical strength they had to prevent penetration.

INTRODUCTION

Crimes against persons include more than conduct causing death; they also encompass a range of conduct that injures, invades personal sexual integrity, and frightens and exploits youth and children. Criminal conduct against persons might be acting violent, threatening, using deception, or taking advantage of positions of trust and authority. It includes both sexual and nonsexual dimensions. The law could treat sexual violations as circumstances that aggravate simple assault and battery. However, organizing sex offenses according to strict assault and battery law ignores social reality.

Sex offenses are considered special. Sexual violation is more than mere physical injury; it violates intimacy in a way that physical injury does not. This is true even of some lesser offensive sexual touchings, such as pinching buttocks and so on. Rape stands only slightly below murder in both public recognition and law as the most serious crime against a person. The public and the law regard offensive sexual contacts that are short of rapes as more serious than other offensive touchings found in the law of battery. An unwanted erotic caress can offend far more than an insulting spit in the face.[1]

CRIMINAL SEXUAL CONDUCT

Historically, the principal sex offenses were rape and sodomy. Modern statutes have added conduct that extends beyond the forced heterosexual penetration and consensual homosexual conduct included in common-law rape and sodomy. Modern **criminal sexual conduct** embraces a wide range of contacts and other abuses, not restricted to violence. Until recently, public attention and the criminal justice response focused on rape by strangers: the classic case of a man who jumps from the shadows and attacks a defenseless woman on a dark street at night. Another type of rape, long held in secret, has come to public attention and has brought changes in both the law of rape and the criminal justice response to it: cases of men who rape the women they know. The overwhelming number of rapes occur within relationships, involving men who rape their employees, their dates, their fellow workers, and their wives. According to women interviewed in one survey—not those who report rapes to the police—more than eighty percent were raped by men they knew! More striking, in three separate surveys of college women, one in five reported being "physically forced" to have sexual intercourse by their dates.[2]

History of Rape

Rape is an ancient crime, dating from at least the time of the Anglo-Saxons in England when it was punishable by death. At common law, a man who had sexual intercourse with (**carnal knowledge** of) a woman who was not his wife, forcibly and without her consent, committed rape, a capital felony. The common law, therefore, limited rape according to these conditions: (1) only men could rape, not minors or women; (2) rape included only vaginal intercourse, not anal intercourse or fellatio; (3) men could rape only females, not other men or boys; (4) men could rape only women who were not their wives—the **marital rape exception;** (5) rape required force—it was a crime of violence; and (6) rape had to occur against the woman's will, or without her consent, unless she was a minor, in which case consent did not remove criminal liability.[3]

The common law required high standards of proof because, as Lord Hale noted in the seventeenth century,

> it must be remembered, that it is an accusation to make, hard to be proved, and harder to be defended by the party accused, though innocent. . . . the heinousness of the offence many times transporting the judge and jury with so much indignation, that they are overhastily carried to the conviction of the person accused thereof, by the confident testimony of sometimes false and malicious witnesses.[4]

The common law allowed the victim to testify, leaving the jury to determine her credibility. Her credibility depended on several circumstances concerning which judges regularly instructed jurors. The victim's "good fame" (that is, her chastity) bore heavily on her credibility, although in the eighteenth century, according to Blackstone, men could rape prostitutes. Women who promptly reported rapes were considered more credible than those who did not. Finally, corroboration by other witnesses, although not absolutely required, bolstered credibility. On the other hand, Blackstone warned, if the victim

> be of evil fame, and stand unsupported by others; if she concealed the injury for any considerable time after she had opportunity to complain; if the place

where the fact was alleged to be committed, was where it was possible she might have been heard, and she made no outcry: these and the like circumstances carry a strong, but not conclusive, presumption that her testimony is false or feigned.[5]

From the seventeenth century to the 1970s, consent was the main issue in rape. Women had to show by resistance that they did *not* consent:

> [V]oluntary submission by the woman, while she has power to resist, no matter how reluctantly yielded, removes from the act an essential element of the crime of rape . . . if the carnal knowledge was with the consent of the women, no matter how tardily given, or how much force had theretofore been employed, it is not rape.[6]

The requirement that women show their *non*consent by resistance is peculiar to the law of rape. In other crimes, passive acceptance does not constitute consent. For example, robbery requires taking another's property by force or threat of force; the law of robbery does not require victims to resist in order to prove the material element of force. Furthermore, if I enter a house because the door was unlocked, it is still trespass; the owner does not have to prove she did *not* consent to my entry. Similarly, in criminal procedure, defendants' passive acceptance of violations of their rights does not constitute consent to violations. The law requires positive proof that the government obtained suspects' and defendants' consent, not that defendants merely acquiesced. For example, suspects do not waive their right to remain silent by failing to object to illegal questioning by the police; the police must warn suspects that they have a right to remain silent, and then suspects have to specifically waive the right.[7]

The degree of resistance women had to display to show that they did not consent changed over time. From the nineteenth century until the 1950s, the law adopted an **utmost resistance standard,** requiring that women use all the power at their command to physically resist in order to demonstrate nonconsent. In *Brown v. State*, the victim, a sixteen-year-old virgin, testified that her neighbor grabbed her, tripped her to the ground, and forced himself on her.

> I tried as hard as I could to get away. I was trying all the time to get away just as hard as I could. I was trying to get up; I pulled at the grass; I screamed as hard as I could, and he told me to shut up, and I didn't, and then he held his hand on my mouth until I was almost strangled.

The jury convicted the neighbor of rape. On appeal, the Supreme Court reversed because the victim had not adequately demonstrated she did not consent.

> Not only must there be entire absence of mental consent or assent, but there must be the most vehement exercise of every physical means or faculty within the woman's power to resist the penetration of her person, and this must be shown to persist until the offense is consummated.[8]

In another case, the Nebraska Supreme Court put the matter even more strongly:

> [T]he general rule is that a mentally competent woman must in good faith resist to the utmost with the most vehement exercise of every physical means or faculty naturally within her power to prevent carnal knowledge, and she must persist in such resistance as long as she has the power to do so until the offense is consummated.[9]

The law did not require physical resistance in all cases. Intercourse with women who were incapacitated by intoxication, mental deficiency, or insanity was rape regardless of force or consent. Sexual penetration obtained by fraud did not constitute rape. Only fraud as to the nature of the act constituted rape. For example, if a doctor told a woman he needed to insert an instrument into her vagina for treatment, but in fact was engaging in intercourse, the law did not recognize her consent. On the other hand, if a woman consented to sexual intercourse because a doctor convinced her that it was good for her health, the law recognized this consent because the woman was defrauded only as to the benefits, not as to the act of sexual intercourse. Finally, sexual intercourse with a minor who consented and did not resist constituted rape.[10]

By the 1950s, courts began replacing the utmost resistance test with a **reasonable resistance standard**, which measured resistance by the amount required by the totality of the circumstances in individual cases. For example, the Virginia Supreme Court ruled that a

> woman is not required to resist to the utmost of her physical strength if she reasonably believes that resistance would be useless and result in serious bodily injury.[11]

The Illinois Appeals Court dealt with the problem of consent and reasonable resistance in *People v. Borak.*

CASE

Did Dr. Borak Use Force against His Patient's Will?

People v. Borak

13 Ill. App. 3d 815, 301 N.E.2d 1 (1973)

[Dr. Borak was convicted of rape and sodomy and was sentenced to two concurrent eight-year prison terms. He appealed. Justice Seidenfeld delivered the opinion.]

FACTS

The prosecutrix, a married woman 18 years of age at the time of the acts in question, testified that defendant, a doctor, conducted gynecological examinations on her on two occasions. During the examinations, she laid on an examining table, unclothed from the waist down, with her hips at the end of the table and her feet in stirrups about a foot higher than the table and a foot out from it on either side. She had never before been examined internally.

She testified that during the first examination, conducted on September 22, 1970, defendant asked extremely personal questions about the details of her sexual relationship with her husband, and conducted intimate manipulations of her body for which he gave medical explanations. Defendant breathed heavily, but was not flushed. Defendant ceased his manipulations when she told him they were hurting her. After leaving, prosecutrix did not tell anyone what took place at this examination.

During the second examination, conducted two days after the first, defendant again asked personal questions and manipulated her body. Prosecutrix did not wear a brassiere to this examination. While manipulating his finger in her vagina, defendant asked, "Why don't you come?" "Why don't you come with your husband?" Prosecutrix noticed that he was breathing heavy and was flushed. She said she couldn't get off the table because he was standing right there, and she didn't ask him to let her up because she was scared and thought he was sexually stimulated. She closed her eyes, as instructed, and felt defendant's tongue on her vaginal area. She got up on her elbows, but laid back down and closed her eyes when defendant told her to in a voice that was not loud or soft, but "(k)ind of commanding." About thirty seconds later, she felt his organ enter hers, at which time she sat up quickly and got dressed. After a brief conversation about what she owed defendant, she left. On arriving home, she related the incident to her husband, and the police were called.

Prosecutrix testified that she was not tied down or restrained while on the examining table, and could remove her feet from the stirrups. She also stated that defendant had no weapon and never threatened her or used force against her, and that she never cried out for help or used force against defendant.

OPINION

The difficult questions before us are whether the act of intercourse was performed "by force and against her will," as required to sustain a rape conviction (Ill.Rev.Stat. 1969, ch. 38, par. 11–1(a)).

The general rules as to the degree of force required under our rape statute are [:] . . . that the degree of force exerted by the defendant and the amount of resistance on the part of the complaining witness are matters that depend on the facts of the particular case; that resistance is not necessary under circumstances where resistance would be futile and would endanger the life of the female as where the assailant is armed with a deadly weapon, and that proof of physical force is unnecessary if the prosecuting witness was paralyzed by fear or overcome by superior strength of her attacker; that it is, however, fundamental that there must be evidence to show that the act was committed by force and against the will of the female, and if she has the use of her faculties and physical powers, the evidence must show such resistance as will demonstrate that the act was against her will.

In the case before us, due to the nature of the examination being conducted, defendant was allegedly able to accomplish the acts by surprise, and the necessity for force, as the term is generally used in rape and deviate sexual assault cases, was negated. The question then becomes whether some theory of implied or statutory force can be employed.

It would indeed be a reproach upon our statute if a physician, under the pretense that it was necessary for a woman patient to submit to examination of her sexual organs in order to assist him in the diagnosis of her ailment, and under the pretense that it was necessary for her to expose her person and to assume a position which, at the same time, incidently afforded ready opportunity for sexual attack, could safely take advantage of her position and make an unexpected and uninvited sexual invasion of her person. If, under such circumstances, a physician takes such an unconscionable advantage of the woman's position, and, to her complete surprise, and without the slightest ground to assume that he has her consent, violates the trust and confidence imposed in him and perverts her position and his opportunity into an uninvited and cowardly attempt to gratify his lust, the force merely incident to penetration should be deemed sufficient force within the meaning of our rape statute.

In the case before us, even if the prosecutrix realized that defendant's questions were improper, this would not in itself indicate what was to follow. While defendant's appearance indicated to prosecutrix that he was sexually aroused, he had not performed any actions which she knew to be improper, and prosecutrix was not put on notice that defendant would perform an overt, deviate act upon her body. Defendant's act of deviate sexual conduct was, "through surprise," with prosecutrix being "utterly unaware of his intention in that regard." Prosecutrix was therefore incapable of consenting to the act, and "statutory" force was present.

However, the contrary is true as to the act of intercourse. When defendant put his mouth on prosecutrix's organ, she became aware of his intentions, and nothing he did thereafter could come as a surprise. It then became her duty, under the previously stated general rules of force applicable to rape cases to use resistance to prevent further acts. Yet she failed to object and followed defendant's instruction to lay back down and close her eyes. While prosecutrix points to her testimony that the instruction was given in a commanding voice, and that she was scared because of his appearance, the evidence does not show that she was restrained in any way, or that defendant used any actual force or threat of force upon her. We cannot conclude that prosecutrix was paralyzed by fear or overcome by defendant's superior strength. Her failure to resist when it was within her power to do so amounts to consent, and removes from the act an essential element of the crime of rape. We therefore reverse defendant's rape conviction.

CASE DISCUSSION

Unlike the night prowler rapist who violently attacks a young woman on a lonely street despite her utmost resistance, Dr. Borak approached his victim while she was in his office undergoing a gynecological examination. Dr. Borak did not use actual physical force to have sexual intercourse with his patient. Did he use force? Do you think his patient was "paralyzed with fear"? Even if she was not, do you think Dr. Borak's special relationship with her removed the need to resist? Do you agree with the court that his patient consented to sexual intercourse? If someone picked up my wallet from a restaurant table and I did not resist, does this mean the person who took the wallet did not steal it? What standard would you write for force in rape? Would you add patients who tend to do what doctors tell them to the list of conditions where victims effectively cannot consent?

During the 1970s and 1980s, major reforms took place in the formal law of rape and several changes took place in the procedural law of rape. Many states no longer required corroboration to prove rape. Most states had enacted **rape shield statutes,** which prohibited the wholesale exposure of women's sexual pasts. Many states have relaxed the requirement that prohibits prosecution unless women promptly report rapes. A few states have abolished the marital exception.

States have also made substantive changes. Recently enacted criminal sexual conduct statutes have shifted the emphasis from the victims' consent by failure to resist to the force rapists use to effect penetration. The Pennsylvania Superior Court found that the common-law emphasis on lack of consent had

> worked to the unfair disadvantage of the woman who, when threatened with violence, chose quite rationally to submit to her assailant's advances rather than risk death or serious bodily injury.[12]

The Model Penal Code eliminated consent as an element in rape because of its "disproportionate emphasis upon objective manifestations by the woman."[13]

These statutes have also expanded the definition of criminal sexual conduct to include all sexual penetrations: vaginal, anal, and oral. Sexual contact now constitutes a lesser degree of criminal sexual conduct. Statutes have also made criminal sexual conduct gender-neutral; men can rape men or women, and women can rape men or women. The trend seems definitely toward including a wide range of gender-neutral sexual penetrations and contacts within the scope of criminal sexual conduct.[14]

The Actus Reus of Rape and Criminal Sexual Conduct

Rape requires some force beyond that required to effect penetration. The amount of force required varies according to the circumstances of particular cases. According to the Model Penal Code commentaries, determining the degree of force

> necessitates the drawing of a line between forcible rape on the one hand and reluctant submission on the other, between the true aggression and desired intimacy. The difficulty of drawing this line is compounded by the fact that there often will be no witness to the event other than the participants and that their perceptions may change over time. The trial may turn as much on an assessment of the motives of the victim as of the actor.[15]

The *actus reus* in the Model Penal Code focuses on the "objective manifestations of aggression by the actor," at least in the most serious degrees of rape. The actor's use of force that "compels" the victim to "submit" constitutes the rape *actus reus*. Threats of "imminent death, serious bodily injury, extreme pain or kidnapping, to be inflicted on anyone" and the infliction of serious bodily harm aggravate the offense to first-degree rape.

The rape *actus reus* does not require actual force when threats secure the submission. Hence, **constructive force,** consisting of threats to kill, seriously injure, or kidnap either the victim or another, substitutes for the actual use of force. Finally, the *actus reus* requires neither force nor threat where actors obtain consent fraudulently, or when a minor, mentally deficient, or insane person consents. In these cases, the act of penetration itself suffices.

From the earliest days of the common law, rape did not require full sexual intercourse to emission. The common-law phrase "penetration however slight" describes the modern requirement. For example, the defendant "put[ting his] fingers between folds of skin over her vagina, but not insert[ing] his fingers . . ." constitutes penetration.[16]

CASE

Did He Forcibly Effect Penetration?

State v. Rusk

289 Md. 230, 424 A2d 720 (1981)

[Chief Judge Murphy delivered the opinion. Judge Cole delivered a dissenting opinion.]

FACTS

. . . At the trial, the 21 year-old prosecuting witness, Pat, testified that on the evening of September 21, 1977, she attended a high school alumnae meeting where she met a girl friend, Terry. After the meeting, Terry and Pat agreed to drive in their respective cars to Fells Point to have a few drinks. On the way, Pat stopped to telephone her mother, who was baby sitting for Pat's two year-old son; she told her mother that she was going with Terry to Fells Point and would not be late in arriving home.

The women arrived in Fells Point about 9:45 P.M. They went to a bar where each had one drink. After staying approximately one hour, Pat and Terry walked several blocks to a second bar, where each of them had another drink. After about thirty minutes, they walked two blocks to a third bar known as E.J. Buggs. The bar was crowded and a band was playing in the back. Pat ordered another drink and as she and Terry were leaning against the wall, Rusk approached and said "hello" to Terry. Terry, who was then conversing with another individual, momentarily interrupted her conversation and said "Hi, Eddie." Rusk then began talking with Pat and during their conversation both of them acknowledged being separated from their respective spouses and having a child. Pat told Rusk that she had to go home because it was a week-night and she had to wake up with her baby early in the morning.

Rusk asked Pat the direction in which she was driving and after she responded, Rusk requested a ride to his apartment. Although Pat did not know Rusk, she thought that Terry knew him. She thereafter agreed to give him a ride. Pat cautioned Rusk on the way to the car that "I'm just giving a ride home, you know, as a friend, not anything to be, you know, thought of other than a ride"; and he said, "Oh, okay." They left the bar between 12:00 and 12:20 A.M.

Pat testified that on the way to Rusk's apartment, they continued the general conversation that they had started in the bar. After a twenty-minute drive, they arrived at Rusk's apartment in the 3100 block of Guilford Avenue. Pat testified that she was totally unfamiliar with the neighborhood. She parked the car at the curb on the opposite side of the street from Rusk's apartment but left the engine running. Rusk asked Pat to come in, but she refused. He invited her again, and she declined. She told Rusk that she could not go into his apartment even if she wanted to because she was separated from her husband and a detective could be observing her movements. Pat said that Rusk was fully aware that she did not want to accompany him to his room. Notwithstanding her repeated refusals, Pat testified that Rusk reached over and turned off the ignition to her car and took her car keys. He got out of the car, walked over to her side, opened the door, and said, "Now, will you come up?" Pat explained her subsequent actions:

> At that point I was scared, because he had my car keys. I didn't know what to do. I was someplace I didn't even know where I was. It was in the city. I didn't know where to run. I really didn't think at that point, what to do.
>
> Now, I know that I should have blown the horn. I should have run. There were a million things I should have done. I was scared, at that point, and I didn't do any of them.

Pat testified that at this moment she feared that Rusk would rape her. She said: "[I]t was the way he looked at me, and said 'Come on up, come on up'; and when he took the keys, I knew that was wrong."

It was then about 1 A.M. Pat accompanied Rusk across the street to a totally dark house. She followed him up two flights of stairs. She neither saw nor heard anyone in the building. Once they ascended the stairs, Rusk unlocked the door to his one-room apartment, and turned on the light. According to Pat, he told her to sit down. She sat in a chair beside the bed. Rusk sat on the bed. After Rusk talked for a few minutes, he left the room for about one to five minutes. Pat remained seated in the chair. She made no noise and did not attempt to leave. She said that she did not notice a telephone in the room. When Rusk returned, he turned off the light and sat down on the bed. Pat asked if she could leave; she told him that she wanted to go home and "didn't want to come up." She said, "Now, [that] I came up, can I go?" Rusk, who was still in possession of her car keys, said that he wanted her to stay.

Rusk then asked Pat to get on the bed with him. He pulled her by the arms to the bed and began to undress her, removing her blouse and bra. He unzipped her slacks and she took them off after he told her to do so. Pat removed the rest of her clothing, and then removed Rusk's pants because "he asked me to do it." After they were both undressed Rusk started kissing Pat as he was lying on her back. Pat explained what happened next:

> I was still begging him to please let, you know, let me leave. I said, "you can get a lot of other girls down there, for what you want," and he just kept saying, "no"; and then I was really scared, because I can't describe, you know, what was said. It was more the look in his eyes; and I said, at that point—I didn't know what to say; and I said, "If I do what you want, will you let me go without killing me?" Because I didn't know, at that point, what he was going to do; and I started to cry; and when I did, he put his hands on my throat, and started lightly to choke me; and I said, "If I do what you want, will you let me go?" And he said, yes, and at the same time, I proceeded to do what he wanted me to.

Pat testified that Rusk made her perform oral sex and then vaginal intercourse.

Immediately after the intercourse, Pat asked if she could leave. She testified that Rusk said, "Yes," after which she got up and got dressed and Rusk returned her car keys. She said that Rusk then "walked me to my car, and asked me for my telephone number; and I said, 'No, I'll see you down Fells Point sometime,' just so I could leave." Pat testified that she "had no intention of meeting him again." She asked him for directions out of the neighborhood and left.

On her way home, Pat stopped at a gas station, went to the ladies room, and then drove "pretty much straight home and pulled up and parked the car." At first she was not going to say anything about the incident. She explained her initial reaction not to report the incident: "I didn't want to go through what I'm going through now [at the trial]." As she sat in her car reflecting on the incident, Pat said she began to "wonder what would happen if I hadn't of done what he wanted me to do. So I thought the right thing to do was to go report it, and I went from there to Hillendale to find a police car." She reported the incident to the police at about 3:15 A.M. Subsequently, Pat took the police to Rusk's apartment, which she located without any great difficulty. . . .

OPINION

. . . [T]he issue was whether . . . there was evidence before the jury legally sufficient to prove beyond a reasonable doubt that the intercourse was "[b]y force or threat of force against the will and without the consent" of the victim in violation of Art. 27, § 463(a)(1). Of course, due process requirements mandate that a criminal conviction not be obtained if the evidence does not reasonably support a finding of guilt beyond a reasonable doubt. . . .

The vaginal intercourse once being established, the remaining elements of rape in the second degree under § 463(a)(1) are, as in a prosecution for common law rape (1) force—actual or constructive, and (2) lack of consent. The terms in § 463(a)(1)—"force," "threat of force," "against the will" and "without the consent"—are not defined in the statute, but are to be afforded their "judicially determined meaning" as applied in cases involving common law rape. In this regard, it is well settled that the terms "against the will" and "without the consent" are synonymous in the law of rape. . . .

. . . [I]t is readily apparent to us that the trier of fact could rationally find that the elements of force and non-consent had been established and that Rusk was guilty of the offense beyond a reasonable doubt. Of course, it was for the jury to observe the witnesses and their demeanor, and to judge their credibility and weigh their testimony. Quite obviously, the jury . . . believed Pat's testimony. From her testimony, the jury could have reasonably concluded that the taking of her car keys was intended by Rusk to immobilize her alone, late at night, in a neighborhood with which she was not familiar; that after Pat had repeatedly refused to enter his apartment, Rusk commanded in firm tones that she do so; that Pat was badly frightened and feared that Rusk intended to rape her; that unable to think clearly and believing that she had no other choice in the circumstances, Pat entered Rusk's apartment; that once inside Pat asked permission to leave but Rusk told her to stay; that he then pulled Pat by the arms to the bed and undressed her; that Pat was afraid that Rusk would kill her unless she submitted; that she began to cry and Rusk then put his hands on her throat and began "lightly to choke" her; that Pat asked him if he would let her go without killing her if she complied with his demands; that Rusk gave an affirmative response, after which she finally submitted.

Just where persuasion ends and force begins in cases like the present is essentially a factual issue, to be resolved in light of the controlling legal precepts. That threats of force need not be made in any particular manner in order to put a person in fear of bodily harm is well established. Indeed, conduct, rather than words, may convey threat. . . .

Considering all of the evidence in the case, with particular focus upon the actual force applied by Rusk to Pat's neck, we conclude that the jury could rationally find that the essential elements of second degree rape had been established and that Rusk was guilty of that offense beyond a reasonable doubt.

DISSENT

. . . The conduct of the defendant, in and of itself, must clearly indicate force or the threat of force such as to overpower the prosecutrix's ability to resist or will to resist. In my view, there is no evidence to support the majority's conclusion that the prosecutrix was forced to submit to sexual intercourse, certainly not fellatio. . . .

The majority relies on the trial court's statement that the defendant responded affirmatively to her question "If I do what you want, will you let me go without killing me?" The majority further suggests that the jury could infer the defendant's affirmative response. The facts belie such inference since by the prosecutrix's own testimony the defendant made no responses. *He said nothing!*

She then testified that she started to cry and he "started lightly to choke" her, whatever that means. Obviously, the choking was not of any persuasive significance. During this "choking" she was able to talk. She said "If I do what you want will you let me go?" It was at this point that the defendant said yes.

I find it incredible for the majority to conclude that on these facts, without more, a woman was *forced* to commit oral sex upon the defendant and then to engage in vaginal intercourse. In the absence of any verbal threat to do her grievous bodily harm or the display of any weapon and threat to use it, I find it difficult to understand how a victim could participate in these sexual activities and not be willing. . . .

Once in the room she waited while he went to the bathroom where he stayed for about five minutes. In his absence, the room was lighted but she did not seek a means of escape. She did not even "try the door" to determine if it was locked. She waited. Upon his return, he turned off the lights and pulled her on the bed. There is no suggestion or inference to be drawn from her testimony that he yanked her on the bed or in any manner physically abused her by this conduct. . . .

He then proceeded to unbutton her blouse and her bra. He did not rip her clothes off or use any greater force than was necessary to unfasten her garments. He did not even complete this procedure but requested that she do it, which she did "because he asked me to." However, she not only removed her clothing but took his clothes off, too.

Then for a while they lay together on the bed kissing, though she says she did not return his kisses. However, without protest she then proceeded to perform oral sex and later submitted to vaginal intercourse. After these activities were completed, she asked to leave.

CASE DISCUSSION

What constituted the "force" in this case? Do you agree with the dissent that the victim's conduct indicates that Rusk did not use force? Did the victim consent? How do you distinguish facts that indicate force from those that demonstrate consent? Should consent ever be relevant in rape? Does this court essentially remove consent as an element in the crime despite its presence in the statute?

The Mens Rea of Rape

The *actus reus* in forcible rape implies that the defendant intends to effect sexual penetration by force or threat. In *Regina v. Morgan*, a widely publicized English case, four companions were drinking in a bar. When they failed to "find some women," Morgan invited the other three to come home with him to have sexual intercourse with his wife. Morgan told the others not to worry if she struggled because she was "kinky"; the struggle "turned [her] on." The trial court convicted the men and the intermediate appellate court upheld the conviction. The House of Lords, England's highest appeal court, overturned the conviction because the defendants lacked the *mens rea*. Rape requires the specific intent to have sexual intercourse by force *and* without consent. Since the men believed Morgan's wife wanted the struggle, they could not have formed that intent.[17]

Regina v. Morgan generated a storm of debate. Although England has adhered to the specific intent requirement, American statutes and decisions barely mention intent, except in attempted rape where intent is the essence of the crime. Where courts face the intent question, they vary in their response. The Maine Supreme Judicial Court ruled that forcible rape is a strict liability crime:

> The legislature, by carefully defining the sex offenses in the criminal code, and by making no reference to a culpable mental state for rape, clearly indicated that rape compelled by force or threat requires no culpable state of mind.[18]

Other courts have adopted a reckless or negligent standard with regard to the sexual penetration, saying that rapists must be either aware that they are risking coerced sexual intercourse or should know that their victims have not consented. Against the argument that rape constitutes a crime too serious with penalties too harsh for the law to impose liability for reckless or negligent rape, one law professor responds:

> If inaccuracy or indifference to consent is "the best that this man can do" because he lacks the capacity to act reasonably, then it might well be unjust and ineffective to punish him for it. . . . More common is the case of the man who could have done better but did not; heard her refusal or saw her tears, but decided to ignore them. The man who has the inherent capacity to act reasonably but fails to has, through that failure, made a blameworthy choice for which he can justly be punished. The law has long punished unreasonable action which leads to the loss of human life as manslaughter—a lesser crime than murder, but a crime nonetheless. . . . The injury of sexual violation is sufficiently great, the need to provide that additional incentive pressing enough, to justify negligence liability for rape as for killing.[19]

CASE

Did He Intend to Rape Her?

People v. Jansson

116 Mich. App. 674, 323 N.W.2d 508 (1982)

[Judge Tahvonen delivered the opinion.]

FACTS

Carolyn Lamoreaux, the complainant, testified that on January 7, 1979, she was introduced to the defendant by a mutual friend at a Dunkin' Donuts Restaurant. The complainant was asked by the defendant if she was looking for a job and she answered she was. The defendant suggested that she fill out an application that night for a full-time secretarial position at his place of employment. The two left the restaurant and drove to the Stedman Agency. The defendant explained the responsibilities of the job while showing the complainant around the building. The two then entered Frank Stedman's office and the defendant and the complainant sat down. During the ensuing conversation, the defendant told the complainant that he was interested in "someone to fuck." The complainant indicated to the defendant that she would not "do things like that." Defendant walked over and turned off the light. The complainant stood up and was grabbed by the defendant. The defendant pulled the complainant to the floor and removed her clothing. He then removed his own clothing and had sexual intercourse with the complainant.

The complainant testified that she did not engage in the act willingly but was forced by the defendant. She was frightened and panicked and did not know what action to take.

Following intercourse, defendant called John Stedman. Mr. Stedman came to the office building. Complainant testified that when Mr. Stedman arrived at the office, the defendant lifted her blouse and underclothing to expose her breasts.

Complainant then waited outside the building for the defendant to drive her home. The defendant drove the complainant to Dunkin' Donuts. He asked the complainant for her phone number and she complied.

Complainant called David Heyboer, a police officer and former boyfriend. They met and she told him what had transpired. He encouraged her to report the incident to the police. . . .

The jury returned a verdict of guilty of criminal sexual conduct in the third degree, M.C.L. § 750.520d(1)(b); M.S.A. § 28.788(4)(1)(b), and the defendant was later sentenced to a term of 10 to 15 years in prison. . . .

OPINION

. . . [T]he defendant asserts that, because there was no indication in the record that the complainant advised or communicated to the defendant that she did not wish to engage in sexual intercourse, the defendant did not know that the sexual relations were nonconsensual and, therefore, could not have intended to engage in those relations by force or coercion. Without some manifestation of the complainant's unwillingness to engage in sexual relations, defense counsel argues that defendant could not have intended to engage in sexual relations against the complainant's will but may rather have assumed that signs of physical resistance by the complainant were what defense counsel terms, "the final token manifestations of modesty."

Defendant in the case at bar was convicted of third-degree criminal sexual conduct. As alleged here, that offense required proof beyond a reasonable doubt that sexual penetration was accomplished by force or coercion. Force or coercion includes, but is not limited to, situations where the actor overcomes the victim through the actual application of physical force or physical violence or where the actor coerces the victim to submit by threatening to use force or violence on the victim, and the victim believes that the actor has the present ability to execute these threats.

The statute is silent on the defense of consent. However, this court has previously stated that the statute impliedly comprehends that a willing, noncoerced act of sexual intercourse between persons of sufficient age who are neither mentally defective, or incapacitated nor physically helpless is not criminal sexual misconduct. . . .

Defense counsel . . . would require that there be proved a specific intent to overcome the will of the victim and, as a necessary precondition, knowledge on the part of the actor that the victim was not engaging in the act consensually. In short, defense counsel would have us require some manifestation of nonconsent by the victim. In our judgement, this is simply a suggestion that we require proof that the victim resisted the actor or at least expressed an intent to resist. The express language of the statute precludes any such requirement.

We are satisfied that there was evidence adduced at trial which would justify a trier of fact in reasonably concluding that the defendant is guilty beyond a reasonable doubt of the offense with which he was charged and of which he was convicted. That being the case, the evidence is sufficient and the conviction does not contravene the due process requirement of the state and federal constitutions. . . .

CASE DISCUSSION

Can you tell from these facts what Jansson intended? What specific facts bear upon his intent? Can you characterize it as a specific intent to have sexual intercourse by force? Did he recklessly or negligently risk sexual intercourse against the victim's will? Do you think rape can be reckless or negligent? Would you make it a strict liability crime? Consider the arguments of the law professor presented earlier.

Statutory Rape

Statutory rape, or carnal knowledge of a woman under the age of consent, substitutes for force in all jurisdictions. States differ, however, over whether liability for statutory rape is strict (that is, without regard to fault). Some jurisdictions call for strict liability, but others accept a reasonable mistake about the victim's age as a defense. Hence, if a victim is seventeen years, nine months, and three days old, looks twenty-three but tells her partner she is twenty-one, and has well-faked identification to prove her age is twenty-one, the young man who has sexual intercourse with her has not raped her, even if eighteen is the age of legal consent. The young man made a reasonable mistake in believing the girl was over eighteen.

CASE

Was His State of Mind Irrelevant to Liability?

State v. Navarrete

221 Neb. 171, 376 N.W.2d 8 (1985)

[Chief Justice Krivosha delivered the opinion.]

FACTS

PER CURIAM by Krivosha, C. J.

The record shows that the offense occurred on April 15, 1984. On the evening of the 14th the defendant, the victim, and a third person had been drinking and driving around Ogallala, Nebraska. The defendant, who was 22 years of age, purchased the beer which was consumed by the defendant, the victim, and the third person. The victim was only 15 years of age, although he was within approximately 6 weeks of his 16th birthday.

At about midnight the defendant and the victim were at the defendant's home. The third person had gone home. The victim was feeling the effect of the beer and went into the defendant's bedroom so that he could lie down on the bed. He awakened sometime later and found the defendant on the bed beside him. The defendant spoke with the victim for a while and then placed his hand on the victim's penis. Later the defendant put his penis in the victim's mouth and then into the victim's anus. The victim again fell asleep. When he did awaken he returned to his home but did not enter the house. The victim sat in his father's pickup truck for about an hour and then decided to report the incident to the police.

At the police station a statement by the victim was recorded. He was then taken to a medical clinic, where he was examined by a physician. A complaint was filed and the defendant was arrested on April 16, 1984. . . .

OPINION

The defendant . . . contends that the statute under which he was prosecuted, § 28–319(1)(c), is unconstitutional because consent and reasonable mistake concerning the victim's age are not defenses. The statute in this respect is similar to ones on statutory rape in which consent is not a defense "[M]istake or lack of information as to the victim's chastity is no defense to the crime of statutory rape." We have expressly rejected the "California Rule." . . .

The majority of the cases hold that a defense of reasonable mistake is not constitutionally required.

> It is not violate of due process for the Legislature, in framing its criminal laws, to cast upon the public the duty of care or extreme caution. Nor is it unfair to require one who gets perilously close to an area of proscribed conduct to take the risk that he may cross over the line.

There being no error, the judgment is affirmed.
AFFIRMED.

CASE DISCUSSION

Do you agree that this victim was too young to consent, no matter what? In other words, would you make statutory rape a strict liability offense? What reasons do you give for making it strict liability? If you think reasonable mistake concerning age ought to be a defense, why do you think so?

Criminal Sexual Conduct with Children

In recent years, child sex abuse has drawn much attention. Several notorious cases came to public attention, leading researchers to conclude that people in trust positions with authority over children—parents, teachers, counselors, ministers, and others—were abusing their authority by sexually violating the children under their care. The law has long taken a strong stance against such activity, as made clear not only by statutory rape but also by statutes concerning deviate sex and corrupting minors.

Criminal Law Close-Up

PROSECUTION OF CHILD SEXUAL ABUSE: INNOVATIONS IN PRACTICE

Child sexual abuse occurs with alarming frequency. The National Center on Child Abuse and Neglect (a division of the U.S. Department of Health and Human Services) estimates that in 1983 nearly 72,000 children were reported as sexually maltreated by a parent or household member.[1] Local law enforcement agencies also receive a large and growing number of reports of child sexual abuse although the FBI's Uniform Crime Reports do not tabulate sexual assaults by age of victim.

Perhaps even more disturbing is that an unknown number of similar cases never reach the attention of authorities.

Very young children may lack the verbal capacity to report an incident or the knowledge that an incident is inappropriate or criminal; older children may be too embarrassed. Many child victims are threatened into silence. When they do confide in a trusted adult, their reports may be dismissed as fantasy or outright lies.

Even if the child's story is believed, parents and health and social services professionals have been reluctant to enlist the aid of enforcement agencies, largely for fear of the adverse effects of the criminal justice process on child victims and their families.

Even cases that are filed with police may not result in prosecution for a variety of reasons. These include inability to establish the crime, insufficient evidence, unwillingness to expose the child to additional trauma, and the belief that child victims are incompetent, unreliable, or not credible as witnesses. Yet, public sentiment increasingly favors criminal justice intervention in these cases.

---

[1]U.S. Department of Health and Human Services, National Center on Child Abuse and Neglect, *National Study on Child Neglect and Abuse Reporting* (Denver: American Humane Association, 1984).

SOURCE: Debra Whitcomb, *Prosecution of Child Sexual Abuse: Innovations in Practice*, Bureau of Justice Statistics, United States Justice Department, Washington, D.C., November 1985.

New developments are taking place, however, to strengthen existing law and even to create new authority to punish child sex abuse. In some cases, penalties are being made harsher for child sex abuse, and rules are being changed to make it easier for children to testify against perpetrators and to extend the law's reach beyond sexual intercourse to broad-ranging offensive touchings.

It is too soon either to tell how far these developments will go or to know just where to draw the line between appropriately demonstrating affection to children and making unwanted and otherwise harmful sexual advances. Harsh penalties and fear of prosecutions ought not to offset advances made over the past three or four decades in releasing repressed healthy desires to demonstrate affection toward children. The issue is sensitive but important. It will take time to learn how to encourage healthy, affectionate demonstrations while responding to damaging sexual advances with proper legislation, prosecution, and punishment. One encouraging development is programs that guide children to discover what touching they like and do not like and that teach them to say no to offensive touchings. For example, even if they are meant only to show affection and even when Mom or Dad thinks he ought to, Tommy need not accept Aunt Theresa's unwanted kisses.

Marital Rape

Until recently, a man could not rape his wife, according to the **marital rape exception.** The reasons for the exception include the following: (1) when a woman marries, she consents to sex at her husband's demand, (2) permitting rape within marriage encourages unhappy wives to make false charges against their husbands, and (3) criminal law's intervention into marital problems hinders reconciliation during marital difficulties.[20]

However warmly criminal policymakers embraced these arguments in the past, modern civil rights and feminist movements have attacked them savagely. In essence, the argument is that women are no longer possessions and that simply because women consent to marriage their husbands are not granted the right to "sex on demand." Marriage is increasingly coming to mean an equal partnership. Hence, sex practices must be negotiated and mutually agreed upon.

It is now a crime in twenty-five states for a husband to rape his wife while they are living together. New York excludes legally separated married couples from the marital exception rule. New Jersey and Oregon have gone further and abolished the marital exception completely. From 1978 to 1985, 118 husbands were prosecuted for raping their wives; 104 were convicted. Despite these efforts, it remains generally true that men cannot rape their wives.[21]

CASE

Did He Rape His Wife?

Kizer v. Commonwealth

228 Va. 256, 321 S.E.2d 291 (1984)

[The jury found Kizer guilty of rape. The judge sentenced him to twenty years in prison but suspended the last fifteen years and put Kizer on probation for life. He appealed. Justice Compton delivered the opinion.]

FACTS

Defendant and his wife, Jeri, were married in June of 1981 in Texas. The couple moved to Norfolk where defendant, age 20, was stationed aboard ship as an enlisted man in the Navy. They occupied rented quarters ashore that were leased in both names. Following the birth of a child, the couple began having marital difficulties. In September of 1982, about six months before the incident in question, the wife returned to Texas briefly. According to her testimony, the purpose of the trip was "to visit" her parents for two weeks; the visit was not "a separation" from her husband.

During the "middle of February" 1983, about three weeks before the alleged offense, the defendant "moved back to the ship." The wife continued to reside in the apartment with the child. According to the wife's testimony, the separation occurred because "[t]he marriage was over and I did not want the marriage to be any longer." The wife added that she "wanted to be separated and in the process to file for divorce after the legal separation in Virginia." The defendant testified that the parties were not "legally separated" and that he moved to the ship "to avoid any other arguing with my wife in front of our son because we did not want to subject him to arguing between me and my wife, Jeri."

The evidence showed that the parties did not engage in sexual intercourse during the period from September 1982, when she visited her parents in Texas, until the date of the incident in question. During a portion of this time, the defendant was aboard ship at sea.

Prior to the alleged offense, the defendant filed a petition in court seeking an award of custody of his child. In addition, the parties decided in February to consult a lawyer "about getting a legal separation." As the parties were en route to an attorney's office, the wife told defendant that she had changed her mind and that she did not want to separate "right now." He said, "Are you sure?" and she responded, "Yes." They returned to their apartment. The wife testified that she decided to discontinue the trip to the attorney because the defendant had just received notification that his father was very ill and she did not want to put more "pressure" on him at that time.

The evidence showed that before the day of the alleged offense, the defendant discussed "the rape laws of Virginia" with a friend. The defendant had said that "he [the defendant] was kind of hard up for sex" and that he thought he "ought to go over there and rip her clothes off of her and take it."

On the day in question, March 6, the defendant had been visiting friends in an apartment "across the hall" from the marital home. He knocked on the door to his apartment about 6:00 P.M. and asked his wife to allow him to use the shower. She refused because she was afraid to be in the premises alone with him. The defendant insisted on gaining entry and, as the wife tried to lock the front door to the apartment, he kicked the door twice. The door "came open and the frame came off the door," according to the wife's testimony. The defendant took the child from the mother's arms and placed him on the floor. The defendant picked up the wife, carried her to the bedroom, ripped off her clothing, and forcibly had sexual intercourse with her. During this time, she was screaming, scratching, kicking, and pulling defendant's hair. At one point during the 45-minute episode, the wife broke away from the defendant and rushed to the bedroom window, screaming for help. After the assault, the wife ran from the apartment and reported the incident to a police officer who was in the area.

OPINION

On appeal, the question presented is whether, under this evidence, the Commonwealth established beyond a reasonable doubt the elements necessary to sustain a conviction for marital rape. In such a case, the prosecution, in addition to establishing a violation of the general rape statute, Code § 18.2–61, must prove beyond a reasonable doubt that the wife unilaterally had revoked her implied consent to marital intercourse. The wife's revocation of consent must be demonstrated by a manifest intent "to terminate the marital relationship." The facts necessary to show this intention to terminate must reveal that the wife: has lived separate and apart from the husband; has refrained from voluntary sexual intercourse with her husband; and, "in light of all the circumstances," has conducted herself "in a manner that establishes a de facto end to the marriage."

In the present case, the evidence shows, first, a violation of the rape statute sufficient to sustain a conviction of the defendant for the rape of a female not his wife. Second, the evidence establishes that the parties lived separate and apart. Third, the proof shows that the wife refrained from voluntary sexual intercourse with the defendant. The evidence fails, however, to show beyond a reasonable doubt the wife conducted herself in a manner that established an actual end to the marriage, in light of all the circumstances.

Significantly, the wife's marital conduct during the six-month period before the assault was equivocal, ambivalent, and ambiguous. Prior to September 1982, the parties had been having domestic difficulties but apparently had been living together as husband and wife. She left Norfolk and went to Texas to "visit" her parents. But she testified that this was not a "separation" in the divorce sense. She returned from Texas and during part of the September-January period, the husband was on shipboard duty at sea. In January, the wife left again but returned after the parties "talked." She stated at the time that she wanted to make the marriage "work." In February, she terminated a planned trip with her husband to a divorce lawyer, advising the husband that she had changed her mind and did not wish to separate "right now." Finally, about three weeks before the alleged offense, the husband began living aboard ship in port. At the time, the wife considered the marriage to be "over."

Evaluating the foregoing circumstances in the light most favorable to the Commonwealth, we think it is apparent that the wife subjectively considered the marriage fractured beyond repair when the parties separated in February. Nevertheless, we cannot say that this subjective intent was manifested objectively to the husband, in view of the wife's vacillating conduct, so that he perceived, or reasonably should have perceived, that the marriage actually was ended. Reversed and dismissed.

CASE DISCUSSION

Why did the court reverse the jury's verdict and dismiss the rape charge against Kizer? Do you agree? What rule would you formulate for marital rape? Can you make an argument that marital rape is worse than nonmarital rape? the same as nonmarital rape? less serious? no crime at all?

Criminal Sexual Conduct Statutes

Civil rights and feminist forces, along with some criminal law reform sentiment, have combined to call for abolishing existing rape and other deviate sex legislation. In its place, they recommend that legislatures should create new, gender-neutral offenses. Some states have done this, enacting criminal sexual conduct laws. Michigan's 1974 statute provides, in summary, the following:

1st degree: This consists of "sexual penetration," defined as sexual intercourse, cunnilingus, fellatio, anal intercourse, "or any other intrusion, however slight, of any part of a person's body or of any object into the genital or anal openings of another person's body." In addition, one of the following must have occurred:
(1) the defendant must have been armed with a weapon;
(2) force or coercion was used and the defendant was aided by another person; or
(3) force or coercion was used and personal injury to the victim was caused.
2nd degree: This consists of "sexual contact," defined as the intentional touching of the victim's or actor's personal parts or the intentional touching of the clothing covering the immediate area of the victim's intimate parts, for purposes of sexual arousal or gratification. "Intimate parts" is defined as including the primary genital area, groin, inner thigh, buttock, or breast. In addition, one of the circumstances required for 1st degree criminal sexual conduct must have existed.
3rd degree: This consists of sexual penetration accomplished by force or coercion.
4th degree: This consists of sexual contact accomplished by force or coercion.[22]

As the Michigan statute indicates, the new legislation purports to cover all offensive and violent sexual penetration and contact without regard to victims' and perpetrators' gender. Under the Michigan statute, what crime did the women in the following true incident commit?

Police have received a complaint from a man stating he was raped by two women. According to the complaint the 24-year-old man was driving home when he stopped to help two women who appeared to be having car trouble. He said that as he approached them one of the women pointed a gun at him and told him to get into the back seat of their car. He said the women bound his hands with rope, pulled a ski mask over his head, and drove "about half an hour" to a house at an undetermined location. There, he said, they forced him into a bedroom and "used his body repeatedly" for "several hours." He told police he was driven back, unharmed, to his own car late that night. He gave police a sketchy description of the two women.[23]

Grading Rape

Most statutes divide rape into two degrees: simple or second-degree rape, and aggravated or first-degree rape. Aggravated rape involves at least one of the following:

1. The victim suffers serious bodily injury
2. A stranger commits the rape
3. The rape occurs in connection with another crime
4. The rapist is armed
5. The rapist has accomplices
6. The victim is a minor and the rapist is several years older

All other rapes are simple rapes for which the penalties are less severe. The criminal sexual conduct statutes have added more degrees, usually four, to accommodate the distinction between penetration and contact. Aggravated penetration constitutes first-degree criminal sexual conduct, aggravated contact second degree, simple criminal penetration third degree, and simple criminal contact fourth degree.

Summary

Rape is a special kind of assault, one that entails the specific purpose to have sexual intercourse by force and against the victim's will. Traditionally, and to a large extent even today, only men who try to force vaginal intercourse on women who are not their wives can commit rape. Because of changing moral, sexual, and social values, combined with civil rights and feminist pressures, some states have recently modified their rape laws. A few have gone far under this influence, making rape a gender-neutral crime in which a variety of sexual violations are brought together under general criminal sexual conduct statutes. Other states have made more modest changes, altering old evidence rules such as corroboration and the victim's prior sexual history. Some have abolished, or at least qualified, the marital rape exception. Taken together, these modifications indicate enhanced sensitivity in two important respects: (1) to the harms caused by a wide range of sexual assaults and (2) to the trauma suffered by victims who have the courage to bring these offensive assaults into public view. Despite these beneficial effects, however, rape laws are still more closely aligned with seventeenth-century notions than to recent reformist ideas.

Recent notorious child sex abuse cases have drawn attention to problems that arise when people in authority use their superior positions to sexually abuse children. Parents and teachers come readily to mind, but coaches, counselors, and religious leaders are also in such special positions. This area is a sensitive one, calling for careful attention. Proper policy requires that the public interest in encouraging healthy affection toward children not be thwarted. But at the same time, the equally strong public interest in preventing, discovering, and punishing damaging sexual advances toward children must also be served. It is too soon to tell how far policymakers will go toward achieving the latter without unduly impeding the former.

≡ BATTERY

Assault and battery, although frequently combined, have been distinct offenses for centuries. A **battery** is an unjustified offensive touching. Central to the offense, therefore, is actual bodily contact. An **assault** is an attempted or threatened battery. Assault, therefore, is different from battery because it does not require actual physical contact. An assault is complete before the offender touches the victim.

The Actus Reus *of Battery*

Unjustified offensive touching constitutes the battery *actus reus.* Corporal punishment that parents or other guardians inflict to "discipline" those under their legal authority, although offensive, does not constitute battery because the law justifies it. Within that limit, offensive touching covers a wide spectrum. Brutal attacks with baseball bats, kicking with heavy boots, staggering blows with fists obviously fall within its scope. But what about offensive touchings, particularly ones with sexual overtones, such as pinching buttocks, squeezing breasts, or even putting arms around another who does not want such contacts? Criminal sexual conduct statutes make most of these contacts crimes.

Other unwanted and unjustified touchings create problems, particularly when they cause no injury. For example, what about employers, or even companions, who tend to demonstrate their affections by throwing arms around shoulders, or grasping another's arm to make a point? Do these actions constitute battery if they have no sexual motivation but the person touched finds them offensive? Or, consider touching children at all, whether affectionately or sexually, who do not want to be touched. What about the child who "must" let Aunt Sylvia hug and kiss him because otherwise it will hurt the aunt's feelings? Is this a battery? It surely is offensive to the nephew who has to endure it. Just where to draw the line is difficult, but clearly battery encompasses more than blows that result in actual physical injury.

The Mens Rea *of Battery*

Existing law does not clearly specify the battery *mens rea.* At common law, battery was an injury inflicted "willfully or in anger." Modern courts and statutes extend battery *mens rea* to include reckless and negligent contacts. In *J.A.T. v. State*, a defendant who negligently urged his dog to attack another as a joke, without the intent to hurt the other, was convicted of battery because "even if the [defendant] was sicking the dog on the victim in sport, not necessarily intending to injure him, it could be found to be a battery if such action amounted to criminal negligence."[24]

Most jurisdictions either include reckless and negligent injuring within battery's scope or create a separate offense to that effect. Louisiana, for example, provides that "inflicting any injury upon the person of another by criminal negligence" constitutes "negligent injuring." The Model Penal Code removes the *mens rea* confusion by defining battery to include "purposely, recklessly, or negligently caus[ing] bodily injury," or "negligently caus[ing] bodily injury . . . with a deadly weapon."[25]

The Harm in Battery

The bodily injury provision in the Model Penal Code addresses another problem: What about the harm resulting from battery? The Code requires at least some bodily injury; offensive touching is not in itself sufficient to constitute a battery. This provision is a major departure from existing law. Its supporters believe that it removes criminal law's sanctions from trivial harms, leaving criminal law to deal with more serious harms. The Code's supporters admit that psychological and emotional sufferings from insulting touchings are real. But, they maintain, such harms are more appropriately left to tort law or to informal sanctions.

Some codes include provisions regarding specific harms. Recent injuries surrounding pit bulls prompted the Minnesota legislature to enact the following:

> 609.26 A person who causes great or substantial bodily harm to another by negligently or intentionally permitting any dog to run uncontrolled off the owner's premises, or negligently failing to keep it properly confined is guilty of a petty misdemeanor. . . .
>
> Subd. 3. If proven by a preponderance of the evidence, it shall be an affirmative defense to liability under this section that the victim provoked the dog to cause the victim's bodily harm.[26]

Injuries and deaths resulting from drug abuse have led the same legislature to enact the following provision:

> 609.228 Whoever proximately causes great bodily harm by, directly or indirectly, unlawfully selling, giving away, bartering, delivering, exchanging, distributing, or administering a controlled substance . . . may be sentenced to imprisonment for not more than ten years or to payment of a fine of not more than $20,000, or both.

The Model Penal Code grades bodily harm offenses as follows:

> Section 211.1
>   (2) Bodily injury is a felony when
>   (a) such injury is inflicted purposely or knowingly with a deadly weapon; or
>   (b) serious bodily injury is inflicted purposely, or knowingly or

recklessly under circumstances manifesting extreme indifference to the value of human life.

(c) except as provided in paragraph (2), bodily injury is a misdemeanor, unless it was caused in a fight or scuffle entered into by mutual consent, in which case it is a petty misdemeanor.

CASE

Is Spitting a Battery?

State v. Humphries

21 Wn. App. 405, 586 P.2d 130 (1978)

[Humphries was convicted of simple assault. He appealed. Notice that the charge and conviction were assault. The excerpt here concerns only the part dealing with battery. Judge Dore delivered the opinion.]

FACTS

On the evening of January 17, 1977, Seattle police officers responded to a radio call seeking to locate defendant Humphries concerning some traffic and robbery warrants. The officers went to an address they had been given, and upon arriving knocked on the door, and entered when a woman opened it. Officer Burtis testified that the woman opened the door quite wide and he walked in. The woman controverted the officer's statement and testified that the officers pushed the door open and elbowed their way in.

A birthday party was in progress and numerous people were present. When the officers asked for Humphries, an argument broke out concerning their presence and the apparent lack of a warrant. Humphries appeared and joined the argument. The officers testified that during the argument Humphries spat twice in Officer Burtis's face.

Humphries was convicted of simple assault, a lesser included offense of third-degree assault.[a]

OPINION

A battery is a consummated assault. Spitting may constitute a battery. In applying the statute governing assault on federal officers, 18 U.S.C. § 111, it was said:

> We do not think it could be ruled that spitting in the face is not a battery falling within the statutory description. Although minor, it is an

application of force to the body of the victim, a bodily contact intentionally highly offensive.

Under the facts and circumstances of this case, we find no error in the prosecutor characterizing "spitting" as an assault.

We hold there was substantial evidence in the subject case on which the jury could find the defendant Humphries guilty of simple assault.

CASE DISCUSSION

The court in *Humphries* calls the spitting a battery, based on its finding that spitting is so offensive that it qualifies as a battery. Do you agree? Why is spitting so offensive? If it is a criminal battery, what penalty would you give to Humphries? Why? What purpose of criminal law is served by making what he did a crime? Is this a case where the tort by the same name might be appropriate? In other words, does the police officer deserve money for what happened to him, or should the state get a fine? Or should Humphries go to jail for what he did?

a. RCW 9A.36.030 provides:
Assault in the third degree. (1) Every person who, under circumstances not amounting to assault in either the first or second degree, shall assault another with intent to prevent or resist the execution of any lawful process or mandate of any court officer, or the lawful apprehension or detention of himself or another person shall be guilty of assault in the third degree.
RCW 9A.36.040 provides:
Simple assault. (1) Every person who shall commit an assault or an assault and battery not amounting to assault in either the first, second, or third degree shall be guilty of simple assault.

≡ ASSAULT

Assault encompasses both attempted battery assaults and threatened battery assaults. In attempted battery assault, note two critical elements: (1) the intent to commit a battery and (2) taking substantial steps toward actually completing the battery. In threatened battery assault, the offense is to intentionally scare another person.

Threatened Battery Assault

Threatened battery assault requires only that actors intend to frighten their victims, thus expanding assault beyond attempted battery. Under this view, even if there is no intent to do physical harm, but instead a purpose to scare victims into believing they will be hurt and a resulting fear, threatened batteries or intentional scarings have occurred. For example, a person who approaches a victim with a gun he knows is unloaded, points the gun at the victim, and pulls the trigger, intending to frighten his victim, has committed assault under the threatened battery theory.

Criminal Law Close-Up

VIOLENT CRIME BY STRANGERS

Three of every five violent crimes are committed by persons who are strangers to their victims. This finding emerges from a study of National Crime Survey data for the crimes of rape, robbery, and assault from 1973 through 1979. An estimated 23.4 million of these crimes were committed during the 7-year period—an average of more than 3 million a year. (See Table 1.)

TABLE 1   Violent Crimes by Strangers, 1973–79 Averages

Type of Crime	
Total	3,356,851,100
Rape	1,053,083
Robbery	84,368,625
Aggravated assault	94,757,928

The fear of crime is, in general, the fear of a random unprovoked attack or robbery by a stranger. A 1967 Presidential commission on crime concluded that "the fear of crimes of violence is not a simple fear of injury or death or even of all crimes of violence, but, at bottom, a fear of strangers."

In recent years, Americans have become increasingly crime conscious. During the past year, the national media and public officials have focused much attention on the volume of crime, its costs, and its effects on people in the Nation. Recent polls have found that many of us are becoming increasingly afraid of crime and, as a result, are changing our lifestyles. Yet, the overall rate at which these violent crimes were committed by strangers over the 1973–79 period shows no upward trend.

The study of crimes committed by strangers was limited to rape, robbery, and assault (both simple and aggravated).[2]

Murder and kidnapping are not covered by the National Crime Survey, and comparable data for these two crimes from other sources do not exist.

Some data on the relationship of murderers to their victims are available from the FBI Uniform Crime Reports (UCR).[3] The proportion of murders by strangers remained relatively stable during 1976–79.[4] In 1979, the relationship between murderer and victim was unknown in more than a third of the cases, but in cases where the relationship was known, only 20% of the victims were killed by strangers. When only the murders committed along with another felony (such as rape or robbery) are considered, the proportion of crimes in which the victim-offender relationship is not known rises to more than 45%. In cases where the relationship is known, the proportion of murders by strangers rises to nearly 60%.

Who Is a Stranger?

In the National Crime Survey, victims identify their offender, when known, by one of a series of relationships ranging from that of stranger to specified relative. The study of the 1973–79 data on crimes committed by strangers included both persons identified by the victim as strangers and persons identified as "known by sight." A group of offenders committing a single crime was considered to be a group of strangers only when the victim identified them as strangers or as known by sight only. No data are available on how well the offenders knew the victims.

How Often Are People Victimized by Strangers?

Evidence and logic both suggest that a victim is more likely to report a crime to an interviewer if the offender is a total stranger and less likely to do so if the offender is a close relative. In the latter case, both embarrassment and fear of retaliation are inhibiting forces; there may even be failure to recognize that a crime has occurred. In view of this possible bias, the number of crimes committed by nonstrangers may be somewhat understated, and the proportion of crimes committed by strangers may be somewhat overstated.

Americans age 12 and over were victims of violent crimes by strangers at an average rate of 20 victimizations per 1,000 people over the 1973–79 period. This compares with a nonstranger victimization rate of 12 per 1,000 people. Robbery and rape were the two violent crimes most often committed by strangers. The average percent of violent crime committed by strangers during 1973–79 was:

All violent crime	59
Rape	65
Robbery	76
Aggravated assault	56
Simple assault	53

Robbery was committed by strangers so often that the victimization rates for robbery by strangers and aggravated assaults by strangers were about the same (roughly 5 per 1,000) even though the overall rate for aggravated assault (10.0 per 1,000) was 52% higher than that for robbery.

Trends in Crimes by Strangers

Because crimes by strangers account for 60% of all violent crimes, the pattern in their rates over time is virtually the same as for total

violent crimes—one of great stability. In contrast, the rate of
violent crimes committed by persons known to their victims
increased by 10% over the 1973–79 period.

[1]The Challenge of Crime in a Free Society, a report by the President's Commission on
Law Enforcement and the Administration of Justice, U.S. Government Printing Office,
Washington, D.C., 1967, p. 52.
[2]For a definition of these crimes and an explanation of the National Crime Survey, see
the BJS Bulletin, Measuring Crime, February 1981, NCJ–75710.
[3]For an explanation of the UCR and its relationship to the NCS, see Measuring Crime.
[4]UCR data on relationship between victim and offender are not available for homicides
before 1976.
SOURCE: *Violent Crime by Strangers*, Bureau of Justice Statistics, United States Justice
Department, Washington, D.C., April 1982.

Victims' awareness is critical in threatened battery assault. Specifically,
victims must fear an immediate battery, and that fear must be reasonable.
Under this requirement, words alone are not sufficient to constitute an
assault; threatening gestures must accompany them. This is not always
just. For example, what if an assailant approaches from behind a victim,
saying, "Don't move, or I'll shoot!" These words are certainly sufficient to
produce a reasonable fear that injury is imminent.

Two other points concerning threatened battery assault are worth
noting. First, conditional threats are not immediate. Hence, my conditional threat, "I'd punch you out if you weren't a kid," is not immediate
because it is conditioned on my victim's age. Therefore, no threatened
battery assault has taken place. Second, an apparent ability to carry out
threats must accompany those threats. Apparent need not mean real.
Hence, if I threaten my enemy with an unloaded gun, and if he does not
know or cannot reasonably be expected to know that the gun is not
loaded, I have put my enemy in apparent reasonable apprehension of
immediate harm.

The Harm in Assault

Threatened and attempted battery assaults address two somewhat distinct harms. Attempted battery assault deals with an incomplete or
inchoate physical injury. Threatened battery assault is directed at a
present psychological or emotional harm: the victim's fear. In attempted
battery assault, therefore, a victim's awareness is immaterial, while in
threatened battery assault, it is crucial.

The Model Penal Code deals with threatened and attempted battery
assaults as follows:

Section 211.1 Simple Assault.
A person is guilty of assault if he:
  (a) attempts to cause bodily injury to another; or
  (b) attempts by physical menace to put another in fear of imminent
      serious bodily harm.
  Simple assault is a misdemeanor unless committed in a fight or scuffle
entered into by mutual consent, in which case the assault is a petty
misdemeanor.

Historically, all assaults were misdemeanors. However, modern statutes have created several aggravated assaults that are felonies. Most common are assaults with the intent to commit violent felonies (murder, rape, and robbery, for example), assaults with deadly weapons (such as guns and knives), and assaults on police officers. Once again, the Model Penal Code has a comprehensive assault statute, integrating, rationalizing, and grading assault and battery. It takes into account *mens rea*, material surrounding circumstances, and intended harm. Note the careful attention paid to these critical elements:

Section 211.2
A person is guilty of aggravated assault if he:
  (a) attempts to cause serious bodily injury to another, or causes such injury purposely, knowingly or recklessly under circumstances manifesting extreme indifference to the value of human life; or
  (b) attempts to cause or purposely or knowingly causes bodily injury to another with a deadly weapon.
  Aggravated assault under paragraph (a) is a felony of the second degree; aggravated assault under paragraph (b) is a felony of the third degree.

Section 211.2
A person commits a misdemeanor if he recklessly engages in conduct which places or may place another person in danger of death or serious bodily injury. Recklessness and danger shall be presumed where a person knowingly points a firearm at or in the direction of another, whether or not the actor believed the firearm to be loaded.

CASE

Did He Attempt to Stab the Police Officer?

Stoutmire v. State

358 So.2d 508 (Ala. Cr. App. 1978)

[Stoutmire was convicted of assaulting a police officer with a deadly weapon and was sentenced to two years in prison. He appealed. Judge Bowen delivered the opinion.]

FACTS

The state's evidence reveals that on the night of the 11th of September, 1977, officers of the Georgiana Police Department received information as to the whereabouts of the appellant who was being sought on charges of burglary and grand larceny in Butler and Montgomery County.

Inside the residence of Margaret Reese the officers attempted to arrest the appellant. When approached the appellant ran into the bedroom where he turned and pulled a pocket knife on the pursuing officers. Because the conviction must stand or fall on these events, they must be examined in detail.

Officer James Blackmon of the Georgiana Police Department testified that after the appellant was advised of the fact that he was under arrest, he "broke loose and ran." The appellant knocked two officers back and "slung them loose."

"Then, all three of us followed him back to the back room, and he went over to a window and had knocked the screen out, and had the window open. We told him not to go out the window, not to go any further, something in that order, and he started turning around, and as he turned around, he pulled that knife out of his pocket and opened the blade on it. At that time, all three of us drawed our guns on him at that time."

> A. Well, he was waving it in front of him (indicating) like that, warning us not to come any closer.
> Q. Did he threaten you with the knife?
> A. Well, he was just waving it around telling us and warning us to stay back.
> Q. And, telling you not to come any closer?
> A. That's correct.
> A. Well, when he was waving the knife, we pleaded with him to drop the knife, and several seconds, seems like maybe longer, but we pleaded with him several seconds. He wouldn't do it, and he started easing out the window, backing out.

After the appellant was out the window,

> [H]e run a short distance from us, and when he went outside, I could hear Joe telling how to throw the knife down. He didn't do it, and when I got out there, he had done started easing along a little sidewalk, · along in front of the house, and he ran a short distance, then he turned back on us.

And again on cross examination:

> [A]ll of us followed him into the bedroom.
> Yes, sir, that's when he turned around and pulled the knife.
> Oh, we was pretty doggone close to him, maybe five or six or seven or eight feet, something like that.
> Well, when he run in there, he turned around and he pulled the knife on us, he waved the knife around and warned us not to come any closer.
> Q. Did he charge you with the knife?
> A. No, sir, not exactly, not inside the house.
> Q. He just tried to hold you back with it?
> A. That's correct.

Once outside the house, the appellant

> went a little further to the corner of the building. He went on back towards like he was going towards the back yard, then he turned around, and then he took a few steps forward.
> A. He didn't say anything on the outside.

Q. Did he again charge the officers?

A. Like I said, he turned around and took several steps back towards us, at that time, I was about ten or fifteen feet away from him.

When the appellant turned around in the backyard and turned toward the officers he had the knife in his hand.

OPINION

"An assault is an attempt or offer, with force or violence, to do a corporal hurt to another, whether from malice or wantonness, with such circumstances as denote at the time an intention to do it, coupled with a present ability to carry it out." Every assault and battery includes an assault. To constitute an assault, there must be the commencement of an act which, if not prevented, would produce a battery. The term assault includes, of necessity, an attempt to do another personal violence.

An intent to injure is an essential element of the crime of assault. The intent to harm is the essence of an assault.

Assault has been defined as an intentional attempt to strike within striking distance, which fails of its intended effect, either by preventive interference or by misadventure. Because a criminal assault involves a present attempt to commit a battery, a mere menace or conditional offer of violence does not constitute an assault in this state. Though the defendant need not actually strike at his victim, a mere threat of violence is insufficient.

In this case when the offer of violence was conditioned, that is, when the officers were "warned" to stay away, it is our opinion that the jury was justified in finding that an assault had already been committed. The evidence is sufficient to support a finding that when the appellant turned toward the officers, drew a knife from his pocket and opened the blade, he had commenced an act which, if not prevented, would produce a battery.

The second act of the appellant in turning toward the officers with the knife in his hand after running some distance from them in the backyard does not constitute an assault because there was no evidence to support even an inference that he had a present ability to carry out any unlawful attempt—that he was in striking distance. Affirmed.

CASE DISCUSSION

Notice that according to attempted battery assault, Stoutmire had to intend to stab the police and take substantial steps toward carrying out the stabbing. Do you think Stoutmire intended to stab the police or only to keep them away from him? Do you think he took substantial steps toward carrying out his intention?

FALSE IMPRISONMENT

A few states have false imprisonment statutes. California makes it a misdemeanor carrying a one-year jail term. The California Penal Code defines false imprisonment as "the unlawful violation of the personal liberty of another."[27]

False imprisonment is a specific intent crime. Prosecutors must prove that defendants meant to take away their victims' liberty forcibly and unlawfully. The Model Penal Code provides that such restraint, if done knowingly, is sufficient to prove false imprisonment. Motive is ordinarily not material in such cases. For example, if police officers make unlawful arrests, they can be prosecuted for false imprisonment even if they believed the arrests were lawful. Whether the error concerning an arrest was reckless, negligent, or merely honest causes problems.

Most forcible detentions or confinements are considered false imprisonment under existing law. This does not include restraints authorized by law, however, as when police officers make lawful arrests, parents restrict their children's activities, or victims detain their victimizers. False imprisonment does not require long detentions, nor does it include all detentions. The standard for criminal false imprisonment is somewhat higher than the civil requirement, which is satisfied by any confinement, however short.

The Model Penal Code requires the restraint to "interfere substantially with the victim's liberty." Although physical force often accomplishes the detention, it is not essential; threatened force is enough. Hence, the threat, "If you don't come with me, I'll break your arm," suffices. Even nonthreatening words occasionally qualify, such as when a police officer who has no right to do so orders someone on the street into a squad car, asserting, "You're under arrest."

KIDNAPPING

Like false imprisonment, kidnapping is a crime that invades privacy and takes away citizens' liberty. Kidnapping is essentially aggravated false imprisonment. As such, all kidnappings are also false imprisonments. Originally, kidnapping was the "forcible abduction or stealing away of man, woman or child from their own country." Although kidnapping was only a misdemeanor, Blackstone called it a "heinous crime" because

> it robs the king of his subjects, banishes a man from his country, and may in its consequences be productive of the most cruel and disagreeable hardships.[28]

The Origins and Harshness of Kidnapping Statutes

Primarily for historical reasons, kidnapping is still a serious felony; until recently, it was a capital offense in some jurisdictions. During

Prohibition (1919 to 1933), kidnapping was prevalent in the organized crime world. One gang member might abduct a rival, "take him for a ride," and kill him. Much more frequently, rivals were captured and held hostage for ransom. Before long, law-abiding citizens were abducted, especially the spouses and children of wealthy and otherwise prominent citizens.

The most famous early case was the ransom kidnap and murder of Charles Lindbergh's son. Lindbergh was an aviator who captured Americans' hearts and imaginations when he flew solo across the Atlantic Ocean. Kidnapping was only a misdemeanor in New Jersey in 1932 when the crime occurred. The tremendous sympathy that Lindbergh's popular hero status generated and the public outrage toward what was perceived as a rampant increase in random kidnappings of America's "pillars of wealth and virtue" led legislatures to enact harsh new kidnapping statutes. These statutes are largely in force today, even though they were passed in an emotional overreaction to a few notorious cases.[29]

Another widely publicized case breathed new life into these harsh statutes. In 1974, Patricia Hearst, heiress to newspaper tycoon William Randolph Hearst, was kidnapped. Public outrage met the case, not only because of sympathy for the prominent Hearst family but also because of shock at the psychological and physical dimensions of the crime. The kidnappers were self-styled revolutionaries called the Symbionese Liberation Army. One of the SLA's first demands was that William Randolph Hearst distribute $1 million in food to the poor of California. Later on, much to her parents' and the public's horror, Patricia Hearst converted to the SLA, participating in bank robberies to raise money for the "revolution." This all happened during a time when radicalism and violence were much feared, when the Vietnam War protest and airline hijackings for terrorist political purposes were very much on the public's mind. Hence, the public saw not only Patty Hearst's capture and her family's deep trauma but also a threat to destroy American society.

The Hearst case brought kidnapping's heinous side into bold relief. It drew together in one story capture and detention, terror, violence, and political radicalism. The details were trumpeted sensationally every day in newspapers and on radio and television. Hope that existing harsh and sweeping kidnapping legislation would be reflectively reassessed vanished in this inflamed, emotional atmosphere. President Nixon expressed his hope—a hope that many others shared—that the Supreme Court would not declare capital punishment for kidnapping to be unconstitutional. California governor Reagan wished aloud that the kidnappers' demand for a free food program would set off a botulism epidemic among the poor.

The Material Elements of Kidnapping

Like false imprisonment, the offense from which it descended, kidnapping is a crime against personal liberty. Its main elements are (1) seizing, (2) confining, and (3) carrying away (asporting) (4) another person by (5) force, threat of force, fraud, or deception.

The critical difference between false imprisonment and kidnapping is the carrying away, or asportation of victims. Since at least the eighteenth century, as Blackstone makes clear, carrying a victim into a foreign country where no friends or family could give aid and comfort added a particularly terrifying dimension to kidnapping. In the early days, the victim had to be carried at least as far as another county and usually into a foreign country. Modern interpretations leave the asportation requirement virtually meaningless.

The famous *People v. Chessman* illustrates how broadly asportation is interpreted by courts faced with especially revolting cases. Caryl Chessman was a multiple rapist who, in one instance, forced a young woman to leave her car and get into his, which was only twenty-two feet away. The court held that asportation's mere fact, not its distance, determined kidnapping. They upheld Chessman's conviction for kidnapping, a capital crime in California. After many years of fighting the decision, Chessman eventually was executed.[30]

Grading Kidnapping

Kidnapping is usually divided into two degrees: simple and aggravated. In addition to rape, as in the *Chessman* case, several circumstances aggravate kidnapping. The most common are (1) to obtain a hostage, (2) for ransom, (3) for robbery, (4) for murder, (5) to blackmail, (6) to terrorize, and (7) for political aims. The penalty for aggravated kidnapping is usually life imprisonment and, until recently, occasionally even death.

CASE

Can You Kidnap Your Own Child?

State v. McLaughlin

125 Ariz. 505, 611 P.2d 92 (1980)

[McLaughlin was convicted of child abduction. He appealed. Justice Hays delivered the opinion.]

FACTS

On February 18, 1977, Dr. Stephen Zang, a physician and attorney admitted to practice in both Arizona and Nevada, obtained a default divorce from his spouse, Cheryl Zang, in Las Vegas, Nevada. Pursuant to the terms of the dissolution, Dr. Zang was awarded custody of the two minor children of the marriage, subject to a right of visitation; however, the decree provided for subsequent review of the custody issue upon termination of the school semester. On February 20, 1977, Dr. Zang and the children moved to Arizona and shortly thereafter he had the Nevada decree entered on the Arizona dockets. Although the record at this point is unclear, the transcripts do establish the existence of a written order of the Maricopa County Superior Court granting custody of the children to Dr. Zang and suspending the visitation rights of his former spouse.

Apparently dissatisfied with the custody decrees, Ms. Zang allegedly decided to covertly remove the children from Arizona and her husband's possession. In furtherance of this scheme, she contacted appellant, the owner and operator of the local security guard service, requesting protection from interference by Dr. Zang. Although again the record is not clear, it is apparent that appellant was shown at least the Nevada decree of dissolution and possibly the order of the Arizona court.

On the morning of October 12, 1977, appellant, along with two employee security guards, met with Ms. Zang and a male companion at a Phoenix restaurant in order to finalize plans to remove the Zang children from their Tempe school. Appellant outlined the proposed course of action on a napkin which was subsequently introduced into evidence. In essence, the strategy involved the blocking of Dr. Zang's driveway with a purportedly inoperative automobile and the removal of the children from the schoolyard at the first appropriate moment. Ms. Zang wore a blond wig, sunglasses and a security guard shirt supplied her by appellant as a method of concealing her identity from school officials.

Pursuant to the scheme, appellant, a guard and Ms. Zang proceeded to the school, arriving at approximately 10:30 A.M. Appellant approached the school's principal, informed her that he was seeking a younger cousin and inquired regarding the lunch hour of the second grade. Nothing more occurred until noon recess, when Ms. Zang, accompanied by one of appellant's guards, removed one of her children from the lunch line and directed him towards a waiting auto. It was only the immediate pursuit of the child's teacher and a nearby resident which prevented the successful completion of the plan and forced the parties to await the arrival of police.

OPINION

On appeal, appellant alleges that he has violated no law. He contends that jurisdiction in the Nevada divorce proceedings was fraudulently obtained and that any decree issued pursuant thereto was void and without effect. Based upon this premise, appellant would have us hold that there could thus have been no attempt at removing the youngster from a "person having lawful charge of the child" within the meaning A.R.S. § 13–841 (1956) of our previous Criminal Code. In our opinion, however, although the record before us is void of evidence other than defendant's testimony regarding the validity or invalidity of the Nevada decree, we find this contention of little significance.

A.R.S. § 13–841 provides in part: A person who

> maliciously, forcibly or fraudulently takes or entices away a child under the age of seventeen years *with intent to detain and conceal the child from its parent, guardian or other person having lawful charge of the child*, shall be punished by imprisonment. (Emphasis added.)

The underscored language establishes clearly the *mens rea* sufficient for conviction of child abduction. There must be an intent to detain and conceal the minor from a person in lawful control. In this regard, it must thus suffice if the accused knows that he is removing the child from the custody of one who appears to have lawful custody. [Conviction affirmed.]

CASE DISCUSSION

Recently, a new form of kidnapping has come into prominence. With increasing numbers of families separating and with the growing participation of both parents in child rearing, noncustodial parents are no longer willing to endure long periods without seeing their children. In fact, some cannot accept the noncustodial role. They take desperate measures to get their children, often illegally. Do you think McLaughlin was guilty of child abduction? Should Cheryl Zang be prosecuted, too? How serious a crime do you think child abduction is under these circumstances? Is it simple kidnapping, aggravated kidnapping, or a separate, less serious offense when parents kidnap their own children?

≡ SUMMARY

Although homicide is the most serious crime against persons, it is not the only one. In fact, measured in sheer numbers, assault and battery far outnumber homicides. Although often considered one crime, battery and assault are separate offenses. Batteries are offensive touchings, ranging from severe beatings to insulting contacts. Assaults are attempted batteries or threatened batteries, in which no physical contact is required to complete the crime.

Another harm to persons covered by criminal law is deprivation of liberty. Short detentions without asportations are misdemeanors called false imprisonment. More serious detentions accompanied by asportation are kidnappings, ancient offenses generally associated with carrying off important persons for ransom. Aggravated kidnapping generally involves some circumstance that generates public outrage, such as kidnappings accompanied by rape, murder, terror, and so on. Related to simple kidnapping is child abduction, a growing phenomenon as noncustodial parents are unwilling to accept separation from their children.

Restraints on liberty take three forms under existing criminal law. The misdemeanor of false imprisonment is a brief detention without asportation, the penalty for which is generally a fine or a short jail term. Simple kidnapping is a significant detention accompanied by asportation, however slight. The penalty for simple kidnapping is usually up to ten years' imprisonment. Aggravated kidnapping is reserved for cases touching off the most public outrage: kidnappings associated with murder, rape, ransom, blackmail, and terror. For aggravated kidnapping, the penalty is severe: usually life imprisonment and occasionally even death, at least until recently. A recent development, parents abducting or kidnapping their own children, has created new problems in false imprisonment and kidnapping law.

QUESTIONS FOR REVIEW AND DISCUSSION

1. What is the proper scope for a law of rape? Should it be limited to sexual intercourse by force with a woman not married to the assailant? Why or why not?
2. Should all rape be a strict liability offense? Should reasonable mistake regarding age and consent constitute a defense?
3. Should the marital rape exception be abolished? Why or why not?
4. What are the main elements in the criminal sexual conduct statutes?
5. Should criminal sexual penetration be more serious than criminal sexual contact?
6. What circumstances aggravate criminal sexual conduct? Explain.

SUGGESTED READINGS

1. Rollin M. Perkins and Ronald N. Boyce, *Criminal Law*, 3d ed. (Mineola, N.Y.: Foundation Press, 1982), pp. 197–224 and 453–77, discusses all matters in this chapter, including recent developments in the law.
2. American Law Institute, *Model Penal Code and Commentaries*, vol. 1 (Philadelphia: American Law Institute, 1980), pt. II, pp. 273–439, summarizes the legal points and the debate surrounding revision of rape laws. It is worth reading for the arguments raised for and against various definitions of the sex offenses.
3. Battelle Law and Justice Study Center, *Forcible Rape: A National Survey* (Washington, D.C.: National Institute of Law Enforcement and Criminal Justice, March 1977), is an excellent study of how rape is viewed by criminal justice professionals and how rape law is enforced. This work shows rape law in action as opposed to what the books say rape law should be. It develops some important points concerning prosecutors' attitudes toward rape victims.
4. Susan Estrich, *Real Rape* (Cambridge: Harvard University Press, 1987), is a stimulating history and critique of rape law in the United States with particular attention to rape by acquaintances. The author writes

forcefully and convincingly, stimulating readers to think about the definition and enforcement of rape laws.

≡ NOTES

1. For the feminist position regarding the special significance of the sexual component in rape, see Diana Russell, *The Politics of Rape: The Victim's Perspective* (New York: Stein and Day, 1975); Anra Medea and Kathleen Thompson, *Against Rape* (New York: Farrar, Straus and Giroux, 1974).

2. Linda S. Williams, "The Classic Rape: When Do Victims Report?" *Social Problems,* 31 (April 1984), p. 464; Diana E. H. Russell, *Sexual Exploitation* (Beverly Hills: Sage, 1984); Judy Foreman, "Most Rape Victims Know Assailant, Don't Report to Police, Police Report Says," *Boston Globe* (April 16, 1986), p. 27; *Parade Magazine* (September 22, 1985) p. 10.

3. Sir William Blackstone, *Commentaries* (University of Chicago Press, 1979), IV, p. 210.

4. Quoted in Blackstone, *Commentaries,* p. 215.

5. Ibid., pp. 213–14.

6. *Reynolds v. State,* 27 Neb. 90, 42 N.W. 903, 904 (Neb. 1879).

7. I owe this insight to Susan Estrich, *Real Rape* (Cambridge: Harvard University Press, 1987), pp. 40–41.

8. 127 Wis. 193, 106 N.W. 536, 538 (Wis. 1906).

9. *Casico v. State,* 147 Neb. 1075, 25 N.W.2d 897, 900 (1947).

10. *State v. Ely,* 114 Wash. 185, 194 P. 988 (1921) (fraud as to nature of the act); *Moran v. People,* 25 Mich. 356 (1872) (told intercourse beneficial).

11. *Satterwhite v. Commonwealth,* 201 Va. 478, 111 S.E.2d 820 (1960).

12. *Commonwealth v. Mlinarich,* 345 Pa. Super. 269, 498 A.2d 395, 397 (1985).

13. American Law Institute, *Model Penal Code and Commentaries,* vol. 1 (Philadelphia: American Law Institute, 1980), pt. II, pp. 279–80.

14. For example, see *Minnesota Statutes Annotated* § 609.341, subd. 12 (St. Paul: West, 1987).

15. American Law Institute, *Model Penal Code and Commentaries,* vol. 1, pt. II, p. 281.

16. *State v. Shamp,* 422 N.W.2d 520 (Minn.App. 1988).

17. *Regina v. Morgan,* [1975] 2. W.L.R. 923 (H.L.).

18. *State v. Reed,* 479 A.2d 1291, 1296 (Me. 1984).

19. Estrich, *Real Rape,* pp. 97–98.

20. American Law Institute, *Model Penal Code and Commentaries,* vol. 1, pt. II, pp. 42–44.

21. N.Y. Penal Law 130.00(4) (1975); New Jersey Stat.Ann. 2C:14–2 (1979); Oregon Rev. Code §§ 163.365, 163.375 (1977); statistics from J. C. Barden, "Marital Rape: Drive for Tougher Laws Is Pressed," *New York Times* (May 13, 1987), p. 10.

22. Mich.Stat.Ann. § 750(a) through (g).

23. Unidentified source.

24. 133 Ga. App. 922, 212 S.E.2d 879 (1975).

25. Louisiana Stat.Ann.—Rev. Stat. tit. 17–A, 14.39 (1974); American Law Institute, *Model Penal Code* (Philadelphia: American Law Institute, 1960), tentative draft no. 11.

26. *Minn.Stat.Ann.* § 609.26 (1987) (1989 Cumulative Supplement).

27. *California, West's Ann. Penal Code,* § 236 (St. Paul: West, 1988).

28. Blackstone, *Commentaries,* IV, p. 219.

29. *State v. Hauptmann,* 115 N.J.L. 412, 180 A. 809 (1935).

30. 38 Cal.2d 166, 238 P.2d 1001 (1951).

Chapter Ten

Crimes Against Habitation: Burglary and Arson

CHAPTER OUTLINE

CHAPTER MAIN POINTS

1. Burglary and arson protect both personal security and property.

2. The harm in burglary stems from intrusions to homes and other structures.

3. The harm in arson is damage and destruction to homes and other property.

4. The structures subject to burglary and arson cover a broad spectrum.

5. Burglary is a specific intent crime.

6. Arson is a general intent crime.

CHAPTER KEY TERMS

general intent intent that is purposeful with respect to the act and reckless with respect to the harm.

surreptitious remaining entering a structure with the intent to commit a crime inside.

unprivileged entry entry of a structure without right, license, or permission.

INTRODUCTION

The ancient saying "A home is a castle" is not merely a popular belief. Two common-law felonies—burglary and arson—were created to protect where people lived. Common-law burglary protected dwellings from intruders in the night. Arson guarded against someone "maliciously and wilfully" burning another person's home. Crimes against habitation are not merely property offenses, although to be sure homes have monetary value. Perhaps the best way to express a home's additional value is in the expression "A house is not a home." A house is the material thing worth money; a home is the haven of refuge where security and privacy from the outside world are possible.

In modern law, the ancient felonies of burglary and arson have grown far beyond their common-law origins. They have come to cover a broad spectrum and protect many interests beyond their original purposes. But they are still aimed primarily at two harms: intrusion and destruction or damage. These harms are considered serious according to most public opinion polls. Burglary, for example, is a much-feared crime. In a recent poll, nearly half the people answered that they were afraid they were going to be burglary victims, and a third believed burglars would hurt them at home during burglaries.

BURGLARY

A felon, that in the night breaketh and entereth into the mansion house of another, with intent to kill some reasonable creature, or to commit some other felony within the same, whether his felonious intent be executed or not.[1]

This was the common-law burglary definition given by the famous seventeenth-century English jurist Sir Edward Coke. Notice the principal elements in Lord Coke's definition: (1) breaking and entering, (2) dwellings, (3) in the nighttime, (4) with a purpose to commit a terrible crime inside. Based on the old English proverb "A man's home is his castle," the idea ran deep in English law that homes deserved the law's special

---

Criminal Law Close-Up

HOUSEHOLD BURGLARY

A substantial proportion of violent crimes that occur in the home are committed during household burglaries. Three-fifths of all rapes in the home, three-fifths of all home robberies, and about a third of home aggravated and simple assaults are committed by burglars. During the 10-year period 1973–82, 2.8 million such violent crimes occurred during the course of burglaries, even though the vast majority of burglaries occur when no household member is present.

Defining Burglary

Burglary, like many other crimes, has a precise legal definition that may vary among jurisdictions.

The definitions used in the National Crime Survey (NCS) differ somewhat from the definition used in the Uniform Crime Reporting program (UCR) of the Federal Bureau of Investigation.[1] The UCR bases its classification upon a determination of the offender's intent. Because this concept is often difficult or impossible to establish in a victimization survey, the NCS replaces the test of intent with a test of whether the offender had the right to enter the residence.

The NCS defines burglary as unlawful or forcible entry of a residence, usually, but not necessarily, attended by theft, including attempted forcible entry. The entry may be by force, such as picking a lock, breaking a window, or slashing a screen, or it may be through an unlocked door or an open window. As long as the person had no legal right to enter, a burglary has occurred.

Furthermore, the structure entered need not be the residence itself for a household burglary to have taken place. Illegal entry into a garage, shed, or any other structure on the premises also constitutes household burglary. In fact, burglary does not necessarily have to occur on the premises. If the breaking and entering occurred in a hotel or a vacation residence, it would still be classified as burglary for the household whose member or members were staying there at the time.

Three types of burglary can be distinguished:

- **Forcible entry**—in which force is used to gain entry (e.g., by breaking a window or slashing a screen).
- **Attempted forcible entry**—in which force is used in an attempt to gain entry.
- **Unlawful entry**—in which someone with no legal right to be on the premises gains entry even though force is not used.

During the 10-year period examined here, 73 million incidents of forcible entry, attempted forcible entry, and unlawful entry took place. Unlawful entry accounted for 45% of all burglaries, forcible entry made up 33%, and attempted forcible entry accounted for 22% of all burglaries (table 1). These and other data derived from the Bureau's National Crime Survey (NCS) provide a detailed description of the crime of household burglary.

TABLE 1   Household Burglaries, 1973–1982

Type of Burglary	Number	Percent	Average Annual Rate[a]
Total	73,308,000	100%	94.6
Forcible entry	24,251,000	33	31.3
Unlawful entry	32,956,000	45	42.5
Attempted forcible entry	16,100,000	22	20.8

NOTE: Detail may not sum to totals because of rounding.

a. Rate per 1,000 households.

Findings

Not every household burglary fits the common view of burglary: intrusion by a stranger, by force or stealth, with intent to steal property. In reality, a substantial percentage of household burglaries are committed by persons related to or known by the victims, and in a large number of burglaries the victims report that there was no theft or attempt to steal property.

Information about offenders was available for about 10 percent of all burglaries.[2] Slightly less than half of these burglaries were

TABLE 2   Relationship to Offenders in Household Burglaries, 1973–82

	Percent of Incidents			
Offender Characteristics	Burglary Total	Forcible Entry	Unlawful Entry	Attempted Forcible Entry
Total burglaries in which offender characteristics were obtained	100.0%	100.0%	100.0%	100.0%
Spouse/ex-spouse	7.5	7.5	10.0	1.8
Other relatives	3.9	5.6	3.9	2.2
Acquaintances	25.0	25.5	28.9	15.6
Known by sight only	5.6	5.8	5.8	4.9
Strangers	47.8	44.1	45.1	57.6
Offender identity uncertain	10.3	11.5	6.4	17.9
Percent of all burglaries in which offender characteristics were obtained	9.4	6.9	11.0	10.1

NOTE: Detail may not sum to totals because of rounding.

known to have been committed by strangers (table 2). Spouses or ex-spouses committed 7%; other relatives, 4%; and acquaintances, 25%. The percent distribution of offenders for completed forcible entry and for unlawful entry were quite similar. Attempted forcible entry had a far higher proportion of strangers and persons of unknown relationship than either of the other two burglary types.

Characteristics of Households Victimized by Burglary

Race of Household Head Black households were forcibly entered (including attempts) much more frequently than white households, but they were unlawfully entered at roughly the same rate (table 3). Households of other races (Native Americans, Asians, and Pacific Islanders) had burglary rates comparable to those of white households.[3]

Family Income Families with incomes under $7,500 a year had the highest overall burglary rates during the 10-year period. Among other income groups, there was little difference in the rate at which households were forcibly entered. For unlawful entry,

TABLE 3   Burglary Incident Rates, 1973–82 Average Yearly Rates, by Household Characteristics

| | Rate per 1,000 Households | | | |
Household Characteristics	Burglary Total	Forcible Entry	Unlawful Entry	Attempted Forcible Entry
All households	94.6	31.3	42.5	20.8
Race of household head				
White	89.6	27.9	42.4	19.2
Black	137.1	59.7	44.0	33.3
Other	96.3	32.0	40.8	23.4
Family income				
Less than $7,500	111.9	37.2	49.7	25.1
$7,500–$14,999	90.1	30.5	38.9	20.7
$15,000–$24,999	84.7	26.4	40.0	18.2
$25,000 or more	90.5	28.6	44.2	17.7
Tenure				
Owned or being bought	76.5	24.9	35.8	15.8
Rented	127.0	42.8	54.5	29.6
Number of units in structure				
1	86.0	28.5	39.8	17.8
2	108.0	37.9	45.1	24.9
3	112.9	42.9	44.5	25.6
4	128.1	42.9	50.0	35.1
5–9	133.3	47.0	51.3	35.0

however, households with incomes over $25,000 had a higher rate than any others except those with incomes under $7,500.

Tenure and Number of Units in Structure Households in owner-occupied residences had lower rates for each type of burglary than households in rented quarters. Households in single-family houses, whether owned or rented, had lower burglary rates than households in multi-unit dwellings. The households most susceptible to burglary (especially to forcible entry) were in buildings with three to nine dwelling units.

	Rate per 1,000 Households			
Household Characteristics	Burglary Total	Forcible Entry	Unlawful Entry	Attempted Forcible Entry
10 or more	105.6	33.6	45.2	26.8
Mobile homes	82.7	28.4	36.1	18.1
Other than housing units	170.1	22.3	133.6	14.2
Place of residence[a]				
Urban	113.5	43.7	41.7	28.1
Suburban	83.3	26.8	37.7	18.8
Rural	66.1	17.7	36.0	12.4

NOTE: Detail may not sum to totals because of rounding.

a. Based on only nonseries, nonescalating burglaries—see text.

Households in buildings with 10 or more units were forcibly entered at a rate closer to that for households in 2-unit buildings than to that for households in multi-unit buildings of intermediate size. It is possible that the larger number of neighbors and the greater traffic in buildings with 10 or more units, as well as the higher security measures offered in many such buildings, have a deterrent effect on forcible entry.

Persons living in group quarters, such as nontransient hotel rooms and dormitories, had unlawful entry rates that were 2½ to 3 times higher than the rates for households. On the other hand, their forcible entry rates were lower than those for other households.

Place of Residence[4] Urban, suburban, and rural households differ greatly in rates of forcible entry (either attempted or completed). Urban households had the highest rates; rural households, the lowest. There was much less difference among urban, suburban, and rural households in the rate at which they were unlawfully entered.

Ninety-five percent of both forcible entries and unlawful entries and 99% of all attempted entries took place at the respondent's residence. The rest occurred at a vacation home, hotel, or motel at which household members were staying at the time of the burglary.

1. The differences and similarities between the NCS and UCR are discussed in the first BJS bulletin, *Measuring Crime* (February 1981, NCJ–75710).

2. The National Crime Survey is designed to collect offender information only for incidents during which a household member was present.

3. The data are inadequate to examine each of the other races separately.

4. The comparison of burglary rates by place of residence is based on published NCS data rather than on the complete NCS file (including escalated and series burglaries) used for the rest of the report because of missing place-of-residence data on the complete file.

SOURCE: *Household Burglary*, Bureau of Justice Statistics, United States Justice Department, Washington, D.C., January 2, 1985.

protection. Not even the king with all his majesty and power had the right to enter the poorest subject's meanest hovel without just cause.

Reflecting that idea, debate over unreasonable searches and seizures in homes began long before the United States Constitution's Fourth Amendment guaranteed protection against them. In 1575, for example, an irate burgess from Colchester (an English town from which many American settlers originated) successfully challenged the right of Queen Elizabeth's officers to enter his home to search for seditious libels against a local public figure. When the officers tried to enter the burgess's front door without a warrant, he met them, armed with a sword. The burgess warned that officers who had earlier tried to come in without a warrant were heavily fined in the Queen's court for trespass. At this announcement, the officers disbanded, leaving the burgess alone for the time being.

Burglary's history reaches even further back than that sixteenth-century episode. Its definition has varied greatly over the centuries, reaching far back into medieval times. Unlike Lord Coke's seventeenth-century definition, which limited the crime to homes broken into and entered with the intention to commit felonies, medieval burglary protected any place likely to attract people (churches, houses, even walled towns) against intrusions, no matter what their purpose.

Some time in the sixteenth century, the offense started to resemble Lord Coke's narrower definition. The more general trespass from medieval times became nocturnally invading a home to commit a felony. Mere intrusions without further criminal purpose became misdemeanors called trespass, for which the penalty was a fine as opposed to capital punishment for burglary.

From Lord Coke's time to modern times, burglary gradually returned to its medieval origins. Both legislation and judicial decisions have broadened its sixteenth-century meaning. Consequently, burglary can mean entering, or even simply remaining in, any structure with four walls and a roof, and even most vehicles, with the intent to commit almost any crime. Hence, burglary, which began as a broad offense resembling criminal trespass, then narrowed to breaking into homes at night to commit felonies, gradually returned to its original broader meaning (see figure 4).

Material Elements of Burglary

Lord Coke's definition has seven specific elements: (1) breaking and (2) entering (3) the dwelling (4) of another (5) in the nighttime (6) with the intention of committing a felony (7) therein. The material acts in burglary are the breaking and entering, the time, and the place. The *mens rea* is the specific intent to commit some crime beyond the intrusion itself. The resulting harm is both the intrusion and the potential harm that might result if the burglar commits further crime once inside the unlawfully entered home.

The courts have liberally construed these elements, and legislatures have expanded further on these broad constructions to include intrusions across the widest possible spectrum. In other words, nocturnal intrusions into homes are only one of a very long list of crimes constituting burglary today.

FIGURE 4   Residence/Nonresidence Burglaries: Nighttime and Daytime 1979–1983

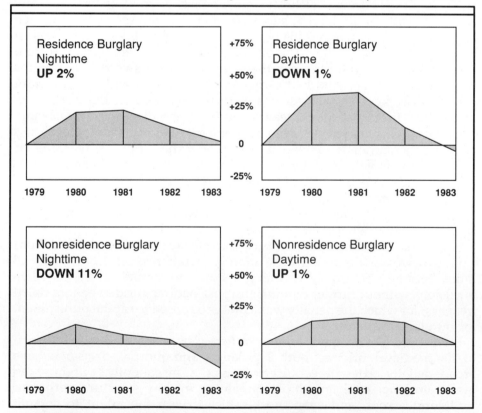

NOTE: Burglaries of unknown time of occurrence are not included.
SOURCE: Uniform Crime Reports, 1983 (Sept. 9, 1984).

Burglary Actus Reus

BREAKING. At one time, breaking may have meant a violent entry, but very early on it came to include much more than knocking down doors and smashing windows. Although it meant more than merely walking through an open door, breaking even under the common law was becoming a technicality. In the eighteenth century, Blackstone listed the following examples of breaking: "picking a lock, or opening it with a key; nay, by lifting up the latch of a door, or unloosing any other fastening which the owner has provided." Even if an outer door was left open and the felon entered through it, it was called breaking if an inner door had to be unloosened to get in.

Constructive breaking, a test often used, renders breaking's ordinary definition all but meaningless. Under certain circumstances, owners and employees who open their own doors are said to have broken in to support burglary convictions. In one case, burglars found a door locked and pretended they were there to visit the owner on official business. By this trick, they were able to get a servant to open a door. The act was considered a breaking.

It is also breaking to knock at a door and, when the owner opens it, to rush in intending to commit a felony, or to ask for a room to rent and then to enter with the intention to commit a felony. In addition to tricking owners, their employees, or other agents to secure entry, there are three other constructive breakings. They involve (1) owners or employees who open doors fearing violence, (2) employees who open doors to their accomplices, and (3) intruders who come down chimneys or enter buildings in other extraordinary ways.

The common-law requirement that the burglar break into a structure had, therefore, all but disappeared by the twentieth century. However, recent changes in the law reflect some retreat from totally eliminating breaking. Some states have introduced an **unprivileged entry** requirement. Under this innovation, anyone who enters a structure without a right, license, or permission to do so has fulfilled the burglary requirement that used to include breaking. The unprivileged entry standard creates a middle ground between requiring an actual breaking and eliminating all requirements surrounding the circumstances under which entry occurs.

The Model Penal Code burglary provision reflects this middle ground. It provides that

> [a] person is guilty of burglary if he enters a building or occupied structure, or separately secured or occupied portion thereof, with purpose to commit a crime therein, unless the premises are at the time open to the public or the actor is licensed to enter. It is an affirmative defense to prosecution for burglary that the building or structure was abandoned.[2]

ENTERING. Entering, like breaking, has a broad meaning in burglary law. From about 1650, partial entry was enough to satisfy the requirement. One burglar "entered" a house because his finger was inside the windowsill when he was caught. In another case, an intruder who

---

Criminal Law Close-Up

WHAT BURGLARY MEANS TODAY

The following brief burglary case summaries demonstrate how sweeping modern burglary law is. In every case, the defendant was convicted of burglary. What purposes does such an all-inclusive definition serve? What interests does it protect: persons, property, homes, or some other social interest?

State v. Hall[a]—Hall went into a tavern and had a few drinks at the bar. He later visited the men's room and took a latex vending machine off the wall. He was caught as he started to walk out with the machine under his coat.

People v. Miller[b]—Miller stole a few coins from a pay telephone in a booth.

People v. Sine[c]—Sine walked into a department store, intending to shoplift a few things from the counters.

Moss v. Commonwealth[d]—Moss drove up to a gasoline station and, finding no one about, pumped gasoline from the pumps at the station's front.

People v. Buyle[e]—Buyle tried to steal some goods his employer stored in a hillside cave.

People v. Burley[f]—Burley stole popcorn from a sidewalk stand.

People v. Chambers[g]—Chambers passed a parked car and took a few cases of cigarettes from the trunk.

---

assaulted an owner on the owner's threshold "entered" the house because his pistol crossed over the doorway. In Texas, a man who never got inside a building at all but who fired a gun into it intending to injure an occupant "entered" by means of the bullet.[3]

Some statutes remove the entering requirement entirely by providing that remaining in a structure satisfies the burglary act requirement. Hence, it is burglary to go into a department store during business hours and wait in a rest room until the store closes, with the intent to steal jewelry. If the remaining requirement is carried to its logical extreme, however, injustices result. For example, suppose I am invited into my friend's house, and after I am inside I notice that she has some valuable antiques. If I decide to put the antiques in my pocket when she leaves the room, I have satisfied the remaining requirement. Other states, such as North Carolina, do not even require that burglars get inside structures; it is enough that they tried. Hence, one man who got a door ajar but never set foot inside was convicted because burglary does not require entering or remaining, according to the North Carolina statute.[4]

The Model Penal Code and several jurisdictions take a middle ground between having strict entry requirements and eliminating entry requirements altogether. They have a standard called **surreptitious remaining,**

Commonwealth v. Wadley[h]—Wadley, a man of "low moral fibre," was on an elevated train platform one evening, watching a girl in the ticket booth who made change for commuters. When no one was around, he leered at the girl, threw a brick through the window, and climbed into the booth as the girl fled through the door. He chased and caught her, but ran away when other people appeared on the scene.

Today's criminal law reformers believe that the sweeping modern definition illustrated in these cases distorts burglary's core idea—nighttime intrusions into homes—far beyond what it ought to mean. Historically, burglary covered an even wider spectrum. That once upon a time burglary had a broad definition, however, is not a sufficient argument to retain burglary's definition in most modern statutes and court opinions. To determine burglary's proper scope, it is necessary to consider what interests burglary is supposed to protect and then define the crime according to those purposes.

a. 150 N.W. 97 (Iowa. 1914).
b. 213 P.2d 534 (1950).
c. 98 N.Y.S.2d 588 (1950).
d. 111 S.W.2d 628 (Ky. 1937).
e. 70 P.2d 955 (1937).
f. 79 P.2d 148 (1938).
g. 228 P.2d 93 (1951).
h. Philadelphia Quarter Sessions (January term, 1951).

which means entering lawfully but with the purpose to remain inside until it is not lawful to be there, in order to commit a crime. This reduces injustices that result from including invited guests who are clearly wanted and potential criminals who enter lawfully but stay in order to commit crimes.

CASE

Did He Enter the Office?

People v. Davis

54 Ill. App. 3d 517, 12 Ill. Dec. 362, 369 N.E.2d 1376 (1977)

[Davis was convicted of burglary and was sentenced to between six and two-thirds years and twenty years in prison. He appealed. Justice Mills delivered the opinion.]

FACTS

An information against Mr. Davis was filed charging him with the burglary of Consolidated Construction Co. in Champaign in that he knowingly and without authority "enter(ed) into part of" the building where its offices were located with the intent to commit a theft. At trial, Willie Gordon, Jr., owner and operator of Consolidated, stated that during the afternoon of May 4, 1976, he typed an estimate for a customer and left his offices at 3:20 P.M. to deliver it. The building had only one public entrance and he locked it when he left. He returned to his office at 4:05 P.M. and found the door open and his typewriter missing. Gordon left the building and, in a store two doors down, found John Lee Johnson. Johnson, who used part of the building for the Community Action Depot, was asked by Gordon if he took the typewriter. Johnson told Gordon he had unlocked the outside door about 3:55 P.M. and had left the building about ten minutes before Gordon's return. Gordon returned to the office, called the police and then went out to where 5 or 6 people were standing behind a nearby store. Gordon asked if any of them had seen anyone go into the office and get the typewriter or if any of them had taken it. Defendant was the only one of the group who replied, stating he "didn't know anything about the typewriter," and that he had not seen anyone go into the office and take the typewriter. Neither defendant nor the general public had authority to be in Consolidated's office or to take the typewriter.

The connecting doorway to the area occupied by Consolidated Construction is somewhere between 5 and 15 feet wide. There is no door. Johnson and Terry Townsend, both of whom work in the front part of the building, have free access to Gordon's office. Gordon has seen members of the public come into the front part of the building. He never saw defendant with the typewriter. The front door showed no signs of forced entry.

OPINION

At common law, burglary was a crime against habitation.

The elements of burglary were "the breaking and entering of the dwelling house of another in the nighttime with the intent to commit a felony therein." The rather strict interpretation by those courts of the individual elements resulted not only from normal rules of penal construction, but also from the terminal sentence waiting for those convicted. [The] Illinois legislature has shaped what is now called "burglary" into a form unrecognizable to our common law ancestors. Gone is the element of "breaking," from which word such fine distinctions sprang. Gone too are the elements of "nighttime" and "dwelling house"; burglary is now a 24-hour crime which may be practiced upon a number of designated man-made cubicles. Section 19–1(a) of the Criminal Code now states:

> A person commits burglary when without authority he knowingly enters or without authority remains within a building, housetrailer,

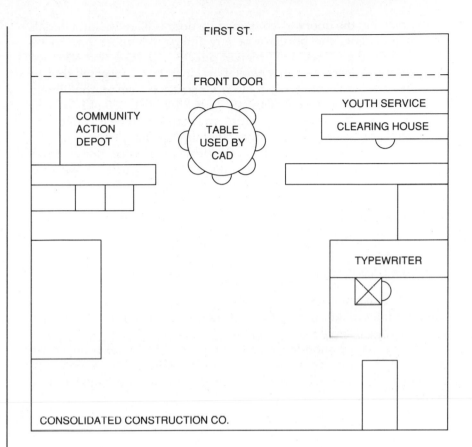

watercraft, aircraft, motor vehicle as defined in The Illinois Vehicle Code, railroad car, or any part thereof, with intent to commit therein a felony or theft. The offense shall not include the offenses set out in Section 4–102 of The Illinois Vehicle Code (Ill.Rev.Stat.1975, ch. 38, par. 19–1(a).)

The use of force in entry has not been a necessary element of burglary in Illinois for some time. The "close" broken in the instant case was not the front door of the building; the "entry" occurred by passing through the doorway inside the building into Gordon's office area. Historically, Illinois courts have recognized that entry into certain separate areas of a building with the requisite intent could support a burglary charge. The statute implements this logic by providing entry into certain structures "or any part thereof" as an element of burglary. The charge and the State's arguments at trial in this case were directed to proof of burglary into a part of the building, namely Gordon's office area. Any discussion by the State or the defense regarding the front door is therefore immaterial to proof of burglary. The fact that Johnson left the door open merely provided a means of quicker entry to the front portion of the building.

The fact that the doorway contained no door is likewise immaterial. At common law, the burglary of any interior chamber had to be pursuant to some "breaking" thereof directly requiring the existence of an interior barrier such as a hotel room door. Some recent authority indicates the requirement of an interior barrier. However, the Illinois Supreme Court in People v. Blair (1972), 52 Ill.2d 371, 288 N.E.2d 443, found a car wash with an open entry and exit-way to be a "building" susceptible of being entered under the burglary statute.

The key to the crime is entry into the prohibited space, not whether entry was made by turning a handle, cracking a lock, or walking through an open portal. In light of Blair and Shannon, logic demands that entry into a "part" of a building through an open doorway with the requisite intent is a prohibited act under our burglary statute. Affirmed.

CASE DISCUSSION

Illinois is one state that has abolished the entry requirement, replacing it with a remaining requirement. Is Davis really a burglar? What purpose does it serve to make him one? Does his crime have anything to do with the common-law idea that a home is a castle? If not, then how is his offense any worse than simply stealing the typewriter? Is he just "technically" a burglar? Is the surreptitious remaining requirement fairer?

DWELLING REQUIREMENT. A material surrounding circumstance in burglary concerns what broken-into, entered, or remained-in structures qualify as "dwellings." Clearly, modern law goes far beyond the common-law definition of dwelling. The structures included in burglary today stand somewhere between the sweeping medieval "any place where people are likely to congregate" and the very narrow sixteenth-century "dwelling." Even in the sixteenth-century, however, dwelling did not mean only fully constructed standard houses; it meant any place a person lived, no matter how poorly constructed or squalid. In one case, the dwelling was "a sheet stretched over poles and fastened to boards nailed to posts for sides, being closed at one end and having an old door at the other."[5]

In general, any structure meant for sleeping in regularly was a dwelling at common law. Houses under construction but not yet inhabited were not dwellings, but houses that were vacant while owners were away on vacation or were completed but not yet lived in were also dwellings. Furthermore, burglary did not require people's actual presence when committed, although actual occupancy then, as now, was an aggravating circumstance.

Dwelling included more than the house itself. Anything within what used to be called the curtilage, or courtyard, was also included. Therefore,

any outbuildings adjacent to a mansion or principal dwelling (such as butteries and storage areas) were included as dwellings even in the sixteenth century. Most such structures no longer exist in modern times, but they have important holdovers, such as garages.

Structures included in most modern burglary statutes cover a broad, sometimes almost limitless, spectrum. Many statutes include "any structure" or "any building." Many also include vehicles. One writer who surveyed the subject concluded that any structure with "four walls and a roof" was included.[6] This sweeping definition has led to bizarre results. In California, for example, a person who breaks into a car and steals something from the glove compartment has committed burglary, a crime punishable by up to fifteen years in prison. If, however, the person steals the entire car, including its contents, the crime is only grand larceny, for which the maximum penalty is ten years. Similarly, stealing a chicken at a hen house door is the misdemeanor of petty larceny, but entering a hen house intending to steal the chicken is the far more serious felony of burglary.

The Model Penal Code definition aims at limiting burglary to occupied structures. The reason for this definition, according to the Reporter, is that it covers "intrusions that are typically the most alarming and dangerous." According to Model Penal Code Section 221.0, "occupied structure" means any structure, vehicle, or place adapted for overnight accommodations of persons, or for carrying on business therein, whether or not a person is actually present.[7]

A few states follow the Model Penal Code approach and limit burglary to occupied structures, whether or not people are present when the burglary occurs.

CASE

Did He Burglarize the Garage?

People v. Jiminez

651 P.2d 395 (Colo.1982)

[The trial judge dismissed a burglary indictment against Jiminez. The prosecution appealed. Justice Lohr delivered the opinion.]

FACTS

At the defendant's request a preliminary hearing was held. The People presented evidence that the defendant had entered the open garage attached to the residence of Tom Tanguma, had taken Tanguma's bicycle valued at $275 from the garage, and had ridden off on the

bicycle, all without permission from Tanguma. The bicycle was not recovered. The court ruled that the proof did not establish that the garage was a dwelling within the meaning of section 18–4–203, so the burglary was only a class 4 felony.

OPINION

The pivotal question on this appeal is whether a garage attached to a residence is part of a dwelling within the meaning of section 18–4–203. We hold that it is. The burglary statute provides, in relevant part:

> A person commits second degree burglary, if he knowingly breaks an entrance into, or enters, or remains unlawfully in a building or occupied structure with intent to commit therein a crime against a person or property.

Second degree burglary is a class 4 felony, but if it is a burglary of a dwelling, it is a class 3 felony.

"Dwelling" means a building which is used, intended to be used, or usually used by a person for habitation.

Completing the relevant statutory definitions, "building" is defined in section 18–4–101(1), C.R.S.1973 (1978 Repl. Vol. 8) as follows:

> "Building" means a structure which has the capacity to contain, and is designed for the shelter of, man, animals, or property, and includes a ship, trailer, sleeping car, airplane, or other vehicle or place adapted for overnight accommodations of persons or animals, or for carrying on of business therein, whether or not a person or animal is actually present.

The statutory definition of dwelling comprehends an entire building. There is no room in the language of that clearly worded statute to exclude from the meaning of dwelling those parts of a residence that are not "usually used by a person for habitation." Moreover, at least some of the usual uses of a residential garage, including storage of household items, are incidental to and part of the habitation uses of the residence itself.

At the preliminary hearing the evidence was uncontroverted that the $275 bicycle was taken by the defendant without permission from the garage attached to the Tanguma residence. This established probable cause to believe that the defendant had committed the charged crimes of felony theft and burglary of a dwelling. The trial court erred, therefore, in dismissing those charges.

Reversed and remanded.

CASE DISCUSSION

The court says that the key question is whether or not an attached garage is a structure within the burglary statute's definition. It then goes on to say that garages are part of dwellings. Do you read the statute the same way? Is a garage really part of a dwelling or just a building? In Colorado, this is important because it is more serious to

burglarize a dwelling than to burglarize other buildings. Would you decide differently if this were not an attached garage? Why is this burglary and not just stealing?

MEANING OF ANOTHER. The common law required that burglars break and enter another's dwelling. As with breaking, entering, and dwelling, modern law has altered the meaning of another. It is now possible, for example, for landlords to burglarize their tenants' apartments. Some courts even say that owners can burglarize their own homes.

CASE

Did He Burglarize His Own Home?

People v. Gauze

15 Cal. 3d 709, 125 Cal. Rptr. 773, 512 P.2d 1365 (1975)

[Gauze was convicted of burglary. He appealed.]

FACTS

Defendant shared an apartment with Richard Miller and a third person and thus had the right to enter the premises at all times. While visiting a friend one afternoon, defendant and Miller engaged in a furious quarrel. Defendant directed Miller to "Get your gun because I am going to get mine." While Miller went to their mutual home, defendant borrowed a shotgun from a neighbor. He returned to his apartment, walked into the living room, pointed the gun at Miller and fired, hitting him in the side and arm. Defendant was convicted of assault with a deadly weapon and burglary; the latter charge was predicated on his entry into his own apartment with the intent to commit the assault.

OPINION

Common law burglary was generally defined as "the breaking and entering of the dwelling *of another* in the nighttime with intent to commit a felony." (Italics added.) The present burglary statute, Penal Code section 459, provides in relevant part that "Every person who enters *any* house, room, apartment with intent to commit grand or petit larceny or any felony is guilty of burglary." (Italics added.)

Facially the statute is susceptible of two rational interpretations. On the one hand, it could be argued that the Legislature deliberately revoked the common law rule that burglary requires entry into the building of another. On the other hand, the Legislature may have impliedly incorporated the common law requirement by failing to enumerate one's own home as a possible object of burglary.

Common law burglary was essentially an offense "against habitation and occupancy."

. . . [In] proscribing felonious nighttime entry into a dwelling house, the common law clearly sought to protect the right to peacefully enjoy one's own home free of invasion. In the law of burglary, in short, a person's home was truly his castle. It was clear under common law that one could not be convicted of burglary for entering his own home with felonious intent. This rule applied not only to sole owners of homes, but also to joint occupants. The important factor was occupancy, rather than ownership.

California codified the law of burglary in 1850. That statute and subsequent revisions and amendments preserved the spirit of the common law, while making two major changes. First, the statute greatly expanded the type of buildings protected by burglary sanctions. Not only is a person's home his castle under the statute, but so, inter alia, are his shop, tent, airplane, and outhouse. This evolution, combined with elimination of the requirement that the crime be committed at night, signifies that the law is no longer limited to safeguarding occupancy rights. However, by carefully delineating the type of structures encompassed under section 459, the Legislature has preserved the concept that burglary law is designed to protect a possessory right in property, rather than broadly to preserve any place from all crime.

The second major change effected by codification of the burglary law was the elimination of the requirement of a "breaking": under the statute, every person who enters with felonious intent is a burglar. This means, at a minimum, that it no longer matters whether a person entering a house with larcenous or felonious intent does so through a closed door, an open door or a window. The entry with the requisite intent constitutes the burglary.

The elimination of the breaking requirement was further interpreted in People v. Barry (1892) 94 Cal. 481, 29 P. 1026, to mean that trespassory entry was no longer a necessary element of burglary. In Barry, this court held a person could be convicted of burglary of a store even though he entered during regular business hours. A long line of cases has followed the Barry holding.

. . . [However,] the cases have preserved the common law principle that in order for burglary to occur, "The entry must be without consent." If the possessor actually invites the defendant, or actively assists in the entrance, e.g., by opening a door, there is no burglary.

Thus, section 459, while substantially changing common law burglary, has retained two important aspects of that crime. A burglary remains an entry which invades a possessory right in a building. And it still must be committed by a person who has no right to be in the building.

Applying the foregoing reasoning, we conclude that defendant cannot be guilty of burglarizing his own home. His entry into the apartment, even for a felonious purpose, invaded no possessory right of habitation; only the entry of an intruder could have done so. More importantly defendant had an absolute right to enter the apartment. This right did not derive from an implied invitation to the public to enter for legal purposes. It was a personal right that could not be conditioned on the consent of defendant's roommates. Defendant could not be "refused admission at the threshold" of his apartment, or be "ejected from the premises after the entry was accomplished." He could not, accordingly, commit a burglary in his own home.

In contrast to the usual burglary situation, no danger arises from the mere entry of a person into his own home, no matter what his intent is. He may cause a great deal of mischief once inside. But no emotional distress is suffered, no panic is engendered, and no violence necessarily erupts merely because he walks into his house. To impose sanctions for burglary would in effect punish him twice for the crime he committed while in the house. In such circumstances it serves no purpose to apply section 459.

It has been urged that the purpose of burglary laws is to protect persons inside buildings because indoor crime is more dangerous than outdoor crime. "We have often recognized that persons within dwellings are in greater peril from intruders bent on stealing or engaging in other felonious conduct." However, we have never categorized all indoor crimes to be more dangerous than all outdoor crimes. Nor would such a conclusion be relevant to the purposes of section 459. The statute protects against intruders into indoor areas, not persons committing crimes in their own homes.

To hold otherwise could lead to potentially absurd results. If a person can be convicted for burglarizing his own home, he could violate section 459 by calmly entering his house with intent to forge a check. A narcotics addict could be convicted of burglary for walking into his home with intent to administer a dose of heroin to himself. Since a burglary is committed upon entry, both could be convicted even if they changed their minds and did not commit the intended crimes.

In positing such hypotheticals, we indulge in no idle academic exercise. The differing consequences are significant, for the punishment for burglary is severe. First degree burglary is punishable by imprisonment for five years to life, while a second degree burglar is subject to imprisonment in the county jail for a one-year maximum or in state prison for one to fifteen years. (Pen.Code, § 461.) In contrast, the punishment for assault with a deadly weapon, the underlying crime committed in this case, is less severe: imprisonment in state prison for six months to life or in county jail for a maximum of one year, or a fine. (Pen.Code, § 245, subd. (a).)

For the foregoing reasons, we conclude defendant cannot be guilty of burglarizing his own home, and the judgment of conviction for burglary must therefore be reversed.

CASE DISCUSSION

The court ruled that burglary means entry without consent. Therefore, Gauze could not burglarize his own dwelling because he does
not need consent to enter it. According to the court, the California
legislature failed to mention "another" in the burglary statute because
the legislature meant to either eliminate or incorporate the common-
law requirement. If you were deciding this case, how might you find
out exactly what the legislature intended when it did not mention
"another"? What meaning would you give if you could not find out
what the legislature intended? Would you interpret the statute
broadly to include "another" or strictly to exclude it? If burglary aims
to protect against threatening people's security in their homes, what
meaning does that purpose require the statute to have?

NIGHTTIME REQUIREMENT. The common-law nighttime requirement was
based on three considerations. First, darkness facilitates committing
crimes. Second, darkness hampers identifying suspects. Finally, and
perhaps most important, nighttime intrusions alarm victims more than do
daytime intrusions. At least eighteen states retain the nighttime requirement specifically. Most recent statutory revisions have continued to
regard nighttime intrusions as an aggravating circumstance. Some proposals, however, eliminate the nighttime requirement entirely. According
to a recent survey, states with these proposals include Alaska, California,
Michigan, and Vermont. Although no hard statistics are available on the
point, a fair statement is that nighttime intruders are punished more
severely than daytime intruders.

BURGLARY *MENS REA.* Burglary is a specific intent crime. It requires not
only the intent to commit the *actus reus* but also the intent to commit a
crime once inside. That means breaking into, entering without privilege,
and remaining surreptitiously in structures, intending to commit crimes
beyond the trespass itself. Intrusions without the intention to commit
additional crimes are nonetheless criminal. They are, however, only
misdemeanors—criminal trespasses.

As in the other burglary elements, the list of crimes burglars must
intend to commit has expanded since the sixteenth century. In Lord
Coke's time, the intended crime had to be serious: murder or another
heinous felony. Although some law books emphasized violent felony, the
cases almost all entailed breaking and entering to steal something.

Modern statutes also concentrate on intrusions to commit theft. Many
include intruding with the intent to commit "a felony or any larceny." Under
these statutes, even petty theft is burglary. Hence, to enter a store intending
to steal a ball-point pen is burglary. Some jurisdictions extend the burglary
mens rea still further, making it burglary to intrude with the intent to commit
"any crime," "any public offense," and sometimes "any misdemeanor."[8]

It is not necessary to complete the intended crime in order to commit burglary. It is enough that an intent to commit crime is present at the moment entry takes place. Hence, if I break into my enemy's house intending to murder him, change my mind just inside the front door, and return home without hurting anyone, I have committed burglary. The *mens rea* of intending to commit murder is present. Burglary is complete at the moment the intrusion, however defined, occurs, so long as the intent to commit a further crime is present. Completing the intended crime, while not an element in burglary, constitutes evidence of *mens rea*. For example, if I am caught leaving a house, my arms loaded with valuable silver, jurors can infer that I entered the house in order to steal the silver.

CASE

Did He Enter Intending to Steal?

McIntosh v. State

559 S.W.2d 598 (Mo.App.1977)

[McIntosh was convicted of burglary and was sentenced to five years in prison. He appealed. Special Judge Welborn delivered the opinion.]

FACTS

The court advised the appellant that this case involved an incident of November 15, 1973 at 5228 East 40th Street in Kansas City and asked the appellant to tell what he did. The appellant responded:

> Well, I went into the place. I was going with my brother. He asked me to go with him, really.
> I was at home and my brother kept wanting me to go with him.
> And he had spotted a fellow that he thought took his coat. He told me. I didn't know. I went around, you know, to the house with him, you know, to get his coat back. I didn't know that it was going to be a burglary, but I know one thing, when he kicked the door in the officers arrived there and arrested us for the burglary, which I told them I had no idea it was anything about a burglary.
> I went with him in order to get his coat—get his coat back, but otherwise I had no intention of burglarizing it.

Interrogation by the court continued:

> Q. Now, you also understand, do you not, that even though you were going to get your brother's coat you didn't have any permission of the owner to break into that place, do you understand that?

A. Yes, sir.

Q. . . . [Y]ou understand that the act of burglary is the breaking in, do you understand that?

A. Yes, sir.

Q. And you understand that because of that set of facts you are guilty of the charge of Burglary, do you not?

A. Yes.

OPINION

The facts recited by appellant do not amount to an admission of facts constituting the offense with which he was charged. Burglary in the second degree requires a breaking "with intent to commit a felony or to steal" § 560.045, RSMo 1969. Apparently the trial court considered that appellant had admitted a breaking and entry with intent to steal, no other criminal intent having been suggested. However, the appellant said that he went with his brother to get his coat back from "a fellow that he thought took his coat." If such were the case, there was no intent to steal because the owner of the property was asserting his right to regain its possession.

Reversed and remanded.

CASE DISCUSSION

According to McIntosh's own admission, he illegally broke and entered someone else's house. But he did not do it in order to commit a crime. He went to help his brother get his coat back, or at least what he thought was his brother's coat. According to the court, this is not burglary because McIntosh did not intend to steal the coat. Do you agree that this breaking is less serious than if McIntosh intended to steal the coat? Why or why not?

Grading Burglary

Because burglary is so broadly defined in most jurisdictions, many states divide it into several degrees. In Minnesota, for example, first-degree burglary preserves the sixteenth-century emphasis on burglary of dwellings, if another is present, if the burglar possesses a weapon, or if the burglar assaults a person within the building. Burglary of a dwelling, a bank, or a pharmacy dealing in controlled substances constitutes second-degree burglary. Third-degree burglary includes burglary of any building with an intent to steal or commit any felony or gross misdemeanor. Fourth-degree burglary includes burglary of a building with an intent to commit a misdemeanor other than theft.[9]

Despite efforts to grade burglary into degrees that reflect the broad spectrum it covers, most burglary statutes do not eliminate possible injustices. This is true in large part because burglary punishes the intrusion and not the crime for which the intrusion took place. In many cases, the penalty for burglary is much harsher than the penalty for the intended crime. The difference between a five-year sentence and a twenty-year sentence sometimes depends upon the largely metaphysical question of whether a thief intended to steal before or after entering a building.

Rationale of Burglary Law

For several centuries following 1500, burglary protected primarily security in the home from nighttime intruders. Common law burglary did not protect other buildings considered mere real estate. Dwellings were guarded by the worst penalty—death—since burglary was a capital offense. Homes were almost sacred at common law. Invaders who threatened defenseless sleeping families and their treasured possessions at night were specters still feared in the 1980s.

Securing homes from nighttime intruders, however, far from explains burglary's rationale under present law. Two common features in modern burglary statutes indicate that burglary aims to protect additional interests. First, trespass statutes cover the intrusion itself. Burglary requires the *mens rea* of additional criminal purpose. Second, although first-degree burglary always includes dwellings, nearly all statutes require harm, threatened harm, or the victims' presence to accompany the intrusion. Furthermore, statutes usually require other aggravating circumstances for first-degree burglary, such as an intent to commit a violent crime or an actual assault upon a person. Modern burglary, therefore, protects more than people's homes. More accurately, burglary statutes are supposed to protect homes and people, or perhaps still more precisely, people's security in their homes.

Modern burglary statutes protect at least three basic interests in society: homes, persons, and property. But what do the statutes protect these interests from? Just as burglary law protects more than one interest, it protects against more than one harm. The paramount and most ancient is intrusion itself. The misdemeanor trespass protects intrusion without further criminal purpose, a social harm widely regarded as deserving at least minor punishment. Property owners who regularly file complaints against strangers, and even against their own neighbors, resemble in that respect their sixteenth-century and even medieval ancestors who prosecuted their neighbors for trespassing even without intending to commit further crimes.

Criminal trespass is not only very old but also appears to be worldwide. The Japanese criminal code, for example, condemns "intrusion upon a habitation," defined to include human habitations, structures, or vessels, or the refusal to leave on demand, punishable by a fine or up to three years' imprisonment. Nearly all countries similarly punish intruders even when they do not intend to commit additional crimes.

Burglary reaches beyond the trespass itself. It strikes at potential harms resulting from the intrusion, specifically those that could result if intruders accomplish further criminal purposes. This unfulfilled intention lies at the core of modern burglary statutes. In this sense, burglary is an inchoate

Criminal Law Close-Up

A POSSIBLE CRIMINAL TRESPASS STATUTE TO REPLACE CURRENT BURGLARY

1. Anyone who unlawfully enters the dwelling of another shall be subject to a fine and/or imprisonment of up to one year.
2. Anyone who, in the course of any crime punishable by one year's imprisonment or more.
   a. enters the dwelling of another in which there is a person at the time, or
   b. is armed with a deadly weapon, or so arms himself, or uses or attempts to use explosives, or
   c. commits assault or otherwise injures another, or
   d. is accompanied by confederates actually present, shall be subject to a penalty that shall not be more than double the penalty for the crime committed.

This example statute accomplishes several things. First, it separates security in homes from protecting life and property. It also takes into account elements usually included in present burglary statutes as aggravating circumstances, but it makes penalties dependent upon the crime committed rather than the trespass inherent in burglary. Attempt is removed entirely, leaving burglary's inchoate dimension to the specific attempted crime intruders intend to commit.

This solution, therefore, has many merits, but it is probably too radical. Burglary is an offense too deeply ingrained in English and American law to eradicate.

offense, an "attempt" to commit the crime the burglar intruded in order to commit.

Proposed Reforms to Burglary Law

Burglary's long history demonstrates efforts to protect several basic social values: homes, personal security, and property. Because its protection covers varied interests, logic does not explain its content. Burglary statutes are thus a hodgepodge of laws covering a diversity of conduct. A nighttime prowler who breaks into a family home to commit a sexual assault on a sleeping victim does not at all resemble a casual shoplifter who goes into a department store to steal a deck of cards.

Reformers recommend changes intended to remove injustices from present burglary law. Some recommend abolishing burglary as a separate offense for two reasons. First, attempt law can cover what is now burglary. Second, making burglary an aggravating circumstance to other crimes can deal adequately with trespassory or intrusive harms done to further other crimes. Under this scheme, criminal trespass would become the principal offense, and trespass would become a grading factor in other crimes.

An approach more likely to succeed is to not abolish burglary but modify its present condition. Such reforms accept burglary's historical roots and deal with its wide spectrum by grading according to the values and interests it protects. The Model Penal Code provision takes this approach. (See Appendix, Section 221.)[10]

Both the more radical abolition and the Model Penal Code's grading approach reduce or eliminate the most serious anomalies and injustices. Under both approaches, for example, the burglary cases used in the Close-up on pages 388-9 either are not crimes or, if they are crimes, are graded according to the interests they are intended to protect. This is so because, under both schemes, homes, personal security, and property are clearly ranked according to their seriousness, and burglary is defined strictly according to its seriousness.

═══ ARSON

In burglary and other criminal trespasses, the harm stems from intrusions that violate homes and other structures. Arson results from damage or destruction to these and similar buildings.

History and Rationale

> [I]f any person shall wittingly, and willing set on fire any dwelling house, meeting house, store house or any out house, barn, stable stack of hay, corn or wood, or any thing of like nature, whereby any dwelling house, meeting house or store house, cometh to be burnt shall be put to death, and to forfeit so much of his lands, goods, or chattels, as shall make full satisfaction, to the victim.[11]

This 1652 Massachusetts Bay Colony statute making arson a capital offense demonstrates clearly that the colonists considered arson a serious crime. Today, arson still poses a serious threat to life and property in America.

In 1977, arson killed over seven hundred persons in the United States and injured thousands of others. In 1977, arson caused an estimated $1.6 billion dollars in lost jobs and property taxes. Arson has also caused insurance rates throughout the United States to increase significantly.

The penalties usually prescribed for arson are harsh. In North Dakota and Hawaii, two states that recently reduced arson penalties, the maximum penalty is still ten years. In other states, such as Texas and Alabama, arson is punishable by life imprisonment.

Burning: The Arson Actus Reus

At common law, burning meant actually setting on fire. Merely setting a fire was not enough; the fire had to reach the structure and burn it. This did not mean the structure had to burn to the ground. Once it was ignited, then however slight the actual burning, arson was complete. Modern statutes generally adopt the common-law rule, and great efforts are devoted to determine if smoke merely blackened or discolored buildings, if fire scorched them, or if fire burned only the exterior material or the wood under it.

The Model Penal Code revises the common law, providing that "starting a fire," even if the fire never touches the structure aimed at, satisfies the burning requirement. The drafters justify expanding the common-law rule on the ground that no meaningful difference separates a fire that has already started but has not yet reached the basic structure and a fire that has reached the structure but has not yet done any real damage to it.[12]

Burning also includes explosions, even though the phrase "set on fire" does not generally mean "to explode." Many statutes state explicitly that explosions are burnings for the purposes of arson law. Including explosions is based on the idea that explosions threaten equally—perhaps more—the lives, property, and security that arson was designed to protect.

CASE

Did He Burn the House?

Lynch v. State

175 Ind. App. III, 370 N.E.2d 401 (1977)

[Lynch was convicted of first-degree arson. He appealed. Judge Buchanan delivered the opinion.]

FACTS

In the early morning hours of June 18, 1975, a man identified as Lynch was seen throwing a burning object at the residence of Mr. and Mrs. Estel Barnett (Barnett). Immediately after the object struck the house flames engulfed the side of the residence. The flames lasted for several minutes and then died out. The fire department was not called.

The Barnetts, who were awakened by a passing neighbor, investigated and discovered a bottle containing flammable liquid with a cotton or cloth wick protruding from the opening. A "burn trail" extended from the lawn approximately ten feet to the house. Damage to the building's aluminum siding consisted of blistering and discoloration of the paint. The amount of the damage was Ninety-one and 29/100 ($91.29) Dollars. No other part of the house was damaged.

OPINION

The phrase "sets fire to" in the First Degree Arson statute means something less than an actual burning and therefore is not synonymous with the word "burn."

The gist of Lynch's position is that he is not guilty of arson because "sets fire to" and "burns" as used in the First Degree Arson statute are synonymous, and no "burning" took place, i.e., the house was not consumed.

The statute, Ind.Code § 35–16–1–1 [10–801], provides:

> Arson in the First Degree.—Any person who willfully and maliciously sets fire to or burns, or causes the setting of fire to or the burning, or who aids, counsels or procures the setting of fire to or the burning of any dwelling house, rooming house, apartment house or hotel, finished or unfinished, occupied or unoccupied; or any kitchen, shop, barn, stable, garage or other outhouse, or other building that is part or parcel of any dwelling house, rooming house, apartment house or hotel, or belonging to or adjoining thereto, finished or unfinished, occupied or unoccupied, such being the property of another; or being insured against loss or damage by fire and such setting of fire to or burning, or such causing, aiding, counselling or procuring such setting of fire to or such burning, being with intent to prejudice or fraud the insuror; or such setting of fire to or burning or such causing, aiding, counselling or procuring such setting of fire to or such burning being with intent to defeat, prejudice or fraud the present or prospective property rights of his or her spouse, or coowner, shall be guilty of arson in the first degree, and, upon conviction thereof, shall be imprisoned in the state prison not less than five [5] years nor more than twenty [20] years, to which may be added a fine not to exceed two thousand dollars [$2,000].

Observe that the drafter used the disjunctive word "or" in separating the phrase "sets fire to" from the word "burns."

If we construe "or" in its "plain, or ordinary and usual, sense" as we are bound to do, it separates two different things. "Sets fire to" and "burns" are not synonymous in this context.

Traditionally the common law rigidly required an actual burning. The fire must be actually communicated to the object to such an extent as to have taken effect upon it.

Other jurisdictions have recognized the distinction between "sets fire to" and "burns" as two different concepts. To "set fire to" a structure is to "place fire upon," or "against" or to "put fire in connection with" it. It is possible to set fire to a structure which, by reason of the sudden extinction of the fire, will fail to change the characteristics of the structure. Nevertheless, it has been "set fire to."

Unlike Lynch, then, we cannot conclude that he is not guilty of first degree arson because there was no burning of the house. He set fire to the house by causing a flammable substance to burn thereon causing a scorching or blistering of the paint which was an integral part of the structure. The composition of the structure was changed. No more was necessary.

Thus the modern construction of statutory terms we are interpreting is that they are not synonymous, each having a separate, independent meaning, thereby eliminating any ambiguity.

The judgment is affirmed.

CASE DISCUSSION

The court ruled that "burn" and "set fire to" are two different concepts and that Lynch may not have burned the house but he did set fire to it. Does it make a difference, really, whether Lynch burned or set fire to the house? Does the Model Penal Code provision apply here? Which is the better rule, the court's or the Code's? How much destruction would you require if you were writing an arson statute?

Arson Mens Rea

Most arson statutes follow the common-law *mens rea* requirement that arsonists maliciously and willfully burn or set fire to buildings. Some courts call the arson *mens rea* **general intent.** Here is one example:

> Arson is a crime of general, rather than specific, criminal intent. The requirement that defendant act "willfully and maliciously" does not signify that defendant must have actual subjective purpose that the acts he does intentionally shall produce either (1) a setting afire or burning of any structure or (2) damage to or destruction of said structure. So long as defendant has actual subjective intention to do the act he does and does it in disregard of a conscious awareness that such conduct involves highly substantial risks that a structure will be set afire, burned or caused to be burned—notwithstanding that defendant does not "intend" such consequences in the sense that he has no actual subjective purpose that his conduct produce them—defendant acts "willfully and maliciously."[13]

Under modern decisions, such as that just quoted, defendants do not have to intend specifically to destroy buildings they set on fire or burn. It is generally considered enough if they intend to start a fire but do not intend, indeed do not even want, to burn a structure. In other words, the purpose requirement refers to the act in arson (burning or setting fire to buildings) and not to the harm (burning down or destroying buildings). Hence, a prisoner who burned a hole in his cell to escape was guilty of arson because he purposely started the fire. So, too, was a sailor who lit a match to find his way into a dark hold in a ship in order to steal rum. The criminal purpose in arson, then, is an intent or purpose to start a fire, even if there is no intent to burn a specific structure.

Burning property to defraud an insurer raises a special *mens rea* concern. The Model Penal Code divides arson into two degrees, according to defendants' culpability. Most culpable are defendants who intend to destroy buildings and not merely set fire to or burn them; these are first-degree arsonists. Second-degree arsonists are defendants who set buildings on fire for other purposes. For example, if I burn a wall with an

---

Criminal Law Close-Up

CALIFORNIA'S ARSON LAW

447a. Any person who willfully and maliciously sets fire to or burns or causes to be burned or who aids, counsels or procures the burning of any trailer coach, as defined in Section 635 of the Vehicle Code, or any dwelling house, or any kitchen, shop, barn, stable or other outhouse that is parcel thereof, or belonging to or adjoining thereto, whether the property of himself or of another, shall be guilty of arson, and upon conviction thereof, be sentenced to the penitentiary for not less than two or more than 20 years.[1]

448a. Private buildings other than dwelling; public buildings; punishment. Any person who willfully and maliciously sets fire to or burns or causes to be burned or who aids, counsels or procures the burning of any barn, stable, garage or other building, whether the property of himself or of another, not a parcel of a dwelling house; or any shop, storehouse, warehouse, factory, mill or other building, whether the property of himself or of another; or any church, meetinghouse, courthouse, workhouse, school, jail or other public building or any public bridge; shall, upon conviction thereof, be sentenced to the penitentiary for not less than 2 nor more than 20 years.[2]

Including so many structures in arson statutes has led to irrational penalties in some states. In California, prior to revising penalties in 1976, burning fresh produce was punishable by up to ten years' imprisonment, yet burning canned fruit and vegetables was punishable by only up to three years. In fact, California punished burning fresh fruits and vegetables the same as it did for burning a church, school, warehouse, or bridge.[3]

---

1. Calif.Penal Code, title 13 (1970).
2. Added by Stats. 1929, c. 25, p. 46, 2. Amended by Stats.1966, 1st Ex. Sess. c. 58, p. 442, 1.
3. American Law Institute, *Model Penal Code* (1985), sec. 220.1
SOURCE: Calif.Penal Code, title 13 (1970).

---

acetylene torch because I want to steal valuable fixtures attached to the wall, I am guilty of second-degree arson for "recklessly" exposing the building to destruction even though I meant only to steal fixtures.[14]

Property in Arson

Common-law arson, like common-law burglary, protected dwellings. Modern arson law, like modern burglary law, has vastly expanded the types of structures it protects. It almost always means more than homes and sometimes even includes personal property.

The trend in modern legislation is to divide arson into three degrees. Most serious (first-degree arson) is burning homes or other occupied structures (such as schools, offices, and churches) where there is possible danger to human life. Second-degree arson includes setting fire to, or burning, unoccupied structures and perhaps vehicles (such as boats and automobiles). Third-degree arson includes setting fire to or burning personal property.

Because arson originally aimed to protect security in dwellings, setting fire to one's own house was not arson. This is true in only a narrow sense today, since arson is a crime against possession and occupancy, not strictly against ownership. Hence, where owners are not in possession or do not occupy their own property, they can commit arson against it. For example, if I am a landlord and set fire to my house in order to hurt my enemy who leases it from me, I have committed arson because, although I own the house, I have transferred occupancy to my tenant enemy.

More important than this somewhat bizarre example is the significant number of owners who burn their property to collect insurance. Under common-law arson, such burnings were not arson if owners were in possession. The opportunities this provided to owners for defrauding insurance companies led to revision of the common-law rule. In most jurisdictions today, a specific provision makes it arson to burn property, whoever owns it, if done to defraud insurers.

Summary

Arson is a serious threat to at least three fundamental social interests: life, security, and property. It includes burning or setting fire to—however slightly—many structures, including houses, vehicles, and even personal property. First-degree arson includes burning homes and other occupied structures, second-degree includes burning unoccupied structures, and third-degree includes setting fire to personal property. The arson *mens rea* is general intent, meaning intent to burn but not necessarily to destroy. That is, arson requires purpose with respect to the act but generally recklessness with respect to destroying the building. Those who mean to destroy buildings are more culpable than those who recklessly destroy buildings.

One difficult problem with arson is that arsonists act for a variety of motives. There are those so consumed by rage that they burn down their enemies' homes. There are the pyromaniacs, whose neurotic or even psychotic compulsion drives them to set buildings on fire for thrill. Then there are the more rational, but equally deadly, defendants who burn down their own buildings or destroy their own property to collect insurance. Finally, the most deadly and difficult arsonist to catch is the professional torch who commits arson for hire.

Evidence indicates that professional arsonists are growing in numbers. Some even contend that arson rings are a multimillion dollar business. Statutory provisions may not grade arson according to motive, but motive probably ought to affect sentencing. The difference between an enraged enemy and a pyromaniac on the one hand, and a calculating property owner or professional arsonist on the other is clear.

SUMMARY

Burglary and arson are both aimed at protecting homes, other occupied structures, vehicles, and many other valuable properties. Their definitions have expanded since the sixteenth century, although signs are that statutes are limiting and grading both more stringently. Both felonies protect three basic social interests: personal security, homes, and property. Burglary's harm to these interests results from intrusion. Arson's harm is to damage and destroy them.

The act in burglary generally includes entering another's property without privilege. Whether done at night, to homes, or to occupied structures, violence or harm to occupants will aggravate the offense. The act in arson is setting fire to or burning various structures. In some cases, it means even throwing a lighted match at a structure. The *mens rea* in burglary is the specific intent to intrude in order to commit a crime. The *mens rea* in arson is the general intent to burn or set fire to various structures.

QUESTIONS FOR REVIEW AND DISCUSSION

1. Should burglary include only breaking and entering homes at night in order to commit serious felonies?
2. If your definition is broader than that proposed in question 1, how much broader would you make it?
3. What interests should burglary law protect? personal security? homes? property? all three?
4. What should constitute a burning in the law of arson?
5. Should arson be limited to intentionally burning a house?
6. How would you grade burglary? arson?

SUGGESTED READINGS

1. American Law Institute, *Model Penal Code and Commentaries*, vol. 2 (Philadelphia: American Law Institute, 1980), sec. II, pp. 3–94, is the most detailed, up-to-date survey of arson and burglary and all the offenses related to them. It compares various recent statutory developments, argues for reforms in the law, suggests grading the crimes, and includes model provisions for them. Meant for professionals, it is still worth the serious student's effort.
2. Rollin M. Perkins and Ronald N. Boyce, *Criminal Law*, 3d ed. (Mineola, N.Y.: Foundation Press, 1982), chap. 3, surveys arson and burglary very well. It includes a good history, thoroughly analyzes the material elements in both arson and burglary, and analyzes recent changes in the law.

3. Wayne R. LaFave and Austin W. Scott, Jr., *Handbook on Criminal Law* (St. Paul: West Publishing Co., 1972), is a good analysis of burglary's material elements.

4. Janet Rosenbaum, *Burglary Statistics* (Washington, D.C.: Bureau of Justice Statistics, 1985), is an excellent overview of burglary statistics—how many burglaries, reporting methods, demographic distribution, and many other interesting dimensions—that shows burglary as a social problem, not just a legal one.

5. James Inciardi, "The Adult Firesetter: A Typology," *Criminology*, 8 (August 1970), pp. 145–55, is a sociologist's effort to divide arsonists into types using considerably more detail than appears in this text. Professor Inciardi discusses not only the professional torch, the pyromaniac, and the businesspeople who burn down buildings to collect insurance, but also adolescent thrill seekers, revenge-seeking fire setters, political arsonists, and others. This is an excellent article that puts arson into a broader context than a strictly legal one.

═══ NOTES

1. Sir Edward Coke, *The Third Part of the Institutes of the Laws of England* (London: 1797), p. 63.

2. American Law Institute, *Model Penal Code and Commentaries* (Philadelphia: American Law Institute, 1985), sec. 221.1.

3. *Rex v. Bailey*, Crown Cases Reserved (1818); Hale, *Pleas of the Crown*, 553 (1670); *Nalls v. State*, 219 S.W. 473 (Tex.Cr.App.1920).

4. *State v. Myrick*, 306 N.C. 110, 291 S.E.2d 577 (1982).

5. Rollin M. Perkins and Ronald N. Boyce, *Criminal Law*, 3d ed. (Mineola, N.Y.: Foundation Press, 1982), p. 201.

6. Note, "Statutory Burglary: The Magic of Four Walls and a Roof," *University of Pennsylvania Law Review*, 100 (1951), p. 411.

7. American Law Institute, *Model Penal Code and Commentaries*, vol. 2, pt. II, pp. 72, 6.

8. Note, "Statutory Burglary," p. 420.

9. *Minn.Stat.Ann.*, § 609.52 (1987).

10. American Law Institute, *Model Penal Code*, tentative draft no. 11 (Philadelphia: American Law Institute, 1960).

11. William Whitmore, ed., *The Colonial Laws of Massachusetts* (Boston: 1887), p. 52.

12. American Law Institute, *Model Penal Code and Commentaries*, vol. 2, pt. II, p. 3.

13. *State v. O'Farrell*, 355 A.2d 396, 398 (Me. 1976).

14. *Crow v. State*, 189 S.W. 687 (Tenn.1916); *Regina v. Harris*, 15 Cox C.C. 75 (1882).

Chapter Eleven

Crimes against Property

CHAPTER OUTLINE

CHAPTER MAIN POINTS

1. Understanding property crimes depends more on history than on logic.

2. All property crimes originated in the ancient felony of larceny, which covered only wrongfully taking the property of others.

3. Consolidated theft statutes combine wrongful takings, conversion, and deceptions leading to property misappropriations.

4. Theft law aims to protect property possession and ownership.

5. Forgery and uttering statutes protect not only property but also confidence in the authenticity of documents, which fosters smoothly operating business transactions in modern society.

6. Robbery and extortion are crimes not only against property but also against persons.

CHAPTER KEY TERMS

asportation the carrying away of property.

claim of right the belief that property taken rightfully belongs to the taker; a defense to theft.

conversion the use of property for purposes other than what the owner intends.

misappropriation the act of getting possession of another's property.

theft an old word meaning larceny; it now includes the consolidated crimes of larceny, embezzlement, and false pretenses.

trespassory taking the wrongful taking required in larceny.

≡ INTRODUCTION

Crimes against property include damage, destruction, and misappropriation. The crimes of **misappropriation,** whether temporary or permanent, include many offenses with a long history. In fact, understanding **theft**—the general term used to describe the crimes of property misappropriation—depends more on history than on logic. Larceny, embezzlement, false pretense, receiving stolen property, robbery, and extortion constitute the main common-law crimes of property misappropriation. Whatever variations in their material elements, all aim at the same wrong: misappropriating property. For that reason, several states have consolidated some of these crimes into one general theft offense.

≡ HISTORY OF THEFT

Larceny is the oldest crime against property. All other property misappropriation crimes originated in it. Its history demonstrates that common lawyers developed larceny to protect the ancient Anglo-Saxons' most valuable possession: livestock. People on the American frontier placed a similar value on cattle and horses. The opprobrium with which offenders against these valuable possessions were regarded still lingers in the epithet "horse thief," used today to signify a dishonest or untrustworthy person.[1]

In the beginning, the threat to peace and order created by taking another's valuable possessions was regarded as at least equal to, and probably even more important than, the misappropriation involved. People who took other people's property by stealth or force were therefore considered evil. On the other hand, cheaters were considered clever; they did not deserve the law's condemnation. Owners foolish enough to put their property into the hands of untrustworthy others did not deserve the

law's support. Hence, larceny punished only those who got *possession* by
stealth or *force*. Early on, larceny by force grew into a separate offense
called robbery, a felony that violated both person and property.[2]

As society grew more complex, common-law larceny by stealth was too
crude and simple to protect the many personal possessions and other
valuable objects that clever people could get into their hands. Complex
urban, commercial, and industrial society with its banks, businesses,
services, and concentrated populations created a need to rely on others to
carry on transactions of daily life. Owners and possessors transferred
property to others voluntarily—for safekeeping, for shipping, for repair or
storage—trusting caretakers to carry out the purpose for which the
property was handed over (see figure 5).

Ordinary larceny did not cover abusing trust relationships in order to
acquire the property of others, because owners relinquished possession
voluntarily. This gap in the law led legislatures and judges to create

FIGURE 5   Property Crimes Outnumbered Violent Crimes by 9 to 1

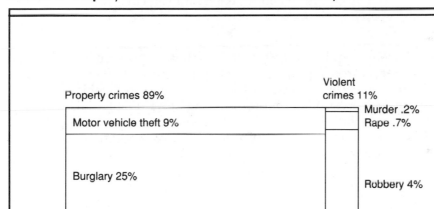
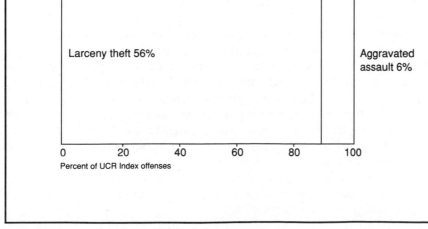

NOTE: Percents do not add to 100% because of rounding.

SOURCE: *Crime in the United States 1985,* Federal Bureau of Investigation.

additions to larceny and to new property offenses that would respond to the increased reliance on others in property transactions.[3]

═══ LARCENY

For at least five hundred years, larceny's material elements have included (1) wrongfully taking (2) and carrying away (3) another's (4) property (5) with the intent to permanently deprive the property's owner of its possession. Larceny is first and foremost a crime directed at possession, not necessarily ownership, and larceny law particularly aims at punishing those who take and carry away others' possessions intending to keep them permanently, not just temporarily.

Larceny Actus Reus

The larceny *actus reus* requires both taking and carrying away (asporting) another's property.

TAKING. Larceny requires actors to take—that is, to gain brief control over—another person's property. Taking is central to larceny, and it includes such direct actions as picking a pocket, lifting objects from a shop, or stealing a car. Some indirect takings also qualify. For example, suppose I see an unlocked bicycle that does not belong to me parked outside a shop. I offer to sell the bicycle to an unsuspecting passerby for forty dollars. He accepts my offer, pays me the money, and gets on the bike. In most states, as soon as the passerby gets on the bike, I have taken the bike, even though I never touched it. For another example, suppose I obtain money by threat. Even if I never actually touch the money, I have still taken it.

CARRYING AWAY. Larceny requires that misappropriators take and carry away other people's property. Also called **asportation,** carrying away in conjunction with taking completes the larceny *actus reus.* Carrying away essentially means that misappropriators are moving property from the place they took it. Carrying a short distance satisfies the asportation requirement; a few inches suffice. The word *carry* is not used in its ordinary sense; one can carry away that which one cannot carry literally. Hence, riding a horse away, driving a car off, leading a cow away, and pulling or pushing heavy objects away all constitute carrying away.

The property must actually move from its original place. A man who picked a pocket but got the money only partway out was not guilty because he did not carry the money away. Another man who tried to steal a barrel also was not guilty because he had only turned the barrel on its side so he could pick it up more easily.

WRONGFUL TAKING. Larceny violates possession, and it requires that actors wrongfully dispossess property—or, as the old law says, "There must be a trespass in the taking." Problems arise when a person who takes and carries away another person's property already lawfully possesses that property. Common examples are repair shop operators who have items in their possession, parking lot attendants who have their customers' car keys, and bank tellers who are authorized to handle money. In possession's ordinary sense, all these persons possess another's property. Therefore, they could not "take and carry away" the property wrongfully because they already have it.

The law does not define possession as simple possession alone. Instead, it looks to the nature of possession, drawing a distinction between mere custody for a particular purpose (such as when an employee possesses goods only to work on them) and legal possession (such as when someone leases a car, owns a television set, or rents a washing machine). Custodians for particular purposes can wrongfully take and carry away property they have in their possession, thereby committing larceny. Lawful possessors, however, cannot commit larceny if they take and carry away property in their possession. Possessors cannot larcenously take what they possess.

Possession is a technical concept, involving both complex history and property law questions. Distinguishing between mere custody and lawful possession is not simple, but a few rules elucidate what **trespassory taking** means. First, employees do not possess their employers' goods, they have custody. Second, those who hand over their personal property for repairs in their presence do not relinquish possession. Thus, money given to tellers or others for change does not transfer in possession, only in custody.

CASE

Did the Shoplifters Wrongfully Take the Property?

People v. Olivo

52 N.Y. 2d 309, 438 N.Y.S.2d 242, 420 N.E. 2d 40 (1981)

[Olivo and the other defendants were convicted of petit larceny. They appealed. Chief Judge Cooke delivered the opinion.]

FACTS

In *People v. Olivo*, defendant was observed by a security guard in the hardware area of a department store. Initially conversing with another person, defendant began to look around furtively when his acquaintance departed. The security agent continued to observe and saw defendant assume a crouching position, take a set of wrenches and secret it in his clothes. After again looking around, defendant began walking toward an exit, passing a number of cash registers en route. When defendant did not stop to pay for the merchandise, the officer accosted him a few feet from the exit. In response to the guard's inquiry, he denied having the wrenches, but as he proceeded to the security office, defendant removed the wrenches and placed them under his jacket. At trial, defendant testified that he had placed the tools under his arm and was on line at a cashier when apprehended. The jury returned a verdict of guilty on the charge of petit larceny. The conviction was affirmed by Appellate Term.

In *People v. Gasparik*, defendant was in a department store trying on a leather jacket. Two store detectives observed him tear off the price tag and remove a "sensormatic" device designed to set off an alarm if the jacket were carried through a detection machine. There was at least one such machine at the exit of each floor. Defendant placed the tag and the device in the pocket of another jacket on the merchandise rack. He took his own jacket, which he had been carrying with him, and placed it on a table. Leaving his own jacket, defendant put on the leather jacket and walked through the store, still on the same floor, by passing several cash registers. When he headed for the exit from that floor, in the direction of the main floor, he was apprehended by security personnel. At trial, defendant denied removing the price tag and the sensormatic device from the jacket, and testified that he was looking for a cashier without a long line when he was stopped. The court, sitting without a jury, convicted defendant of petit larceny. Appellate Term affirmed 102 Misc.2d 487, 425 N.Y.S.2d 936.

In *People v. Spatzier*, defendant entered a bookstore on Fulton Street in Hempstead carrying an attaché case. The two co-owners of the store observed the defendant in a ceiling mirror as he browsed through the store. They watched defendant remove a book from the shelf, look up and down the aisle, and place the book in his case. He then placed the case at his feet and continued to browse. One of the owners approached defendant and accused him of stealing the book. An altercation ensued and when defendant allegedly struck the owner with the attaché case, the case opened and the book fell out. At trial, defendant denied secreting the book in his case and claimed that the owner had suddenly and unjustifiably accused him of stealing. The jury found defendant guilty of petit larceny, and the conviction was affirmed by the Appellate Term.

OPINION

These cases present a recurring question in this era of the self-service store which has never been resolved by this court: may a person be convicted of larceny for shoplifting if the person is caught with goods while still inside the store? For reasons outlined below, it is concluded that a larceny conviction may be sustained, in certain situations, even though the shoplifter was apprehended before leaving the store.

The primary issue in each case is whether the evidence, viewed in the light most favorable to the prosecution, was sufficient to establish the elements of larceny as defined by the Penal Law. To resolve this common question, the development of the common-law crime of larceny and its evolution into modern statutory form must be briefly traced.

Larceny at common law was defined as a trespassory taking and carrying away of the property of another with intent to steal it. The early common-law courts apparently viewed larceny as defending society against breach of the peace, rather than protecting individual property rights, and therefore placed heavy emphasis upon the requirement of a trespassory taking.

As the reach of larceny expanded, the intent element of the crime became of increasing importance, while the requirement of a trespassory taking became less significant.

As a result, the bar against convicting a person who had initially obtained lawful possession of property faded. In King v. Pear, for instance, a defendant who had lied about his address and ultimate destination when renting a horse was found guilty of larceny for later converting the horse. Because of the fraudulent misrepresentation, the court reasoned, the defendant had never obtained legal possession. Thus, "larceny by trick" was born.

Later cases went even further, often ignoring the fact that a defendant had initially obtained possession lawfully, and instead focused upon his later intent. The crime of larceny then encompassed, not only situations where the defendant initially obtained property by a trespassory taking, but many situations where an individual, possessing the requisite intent, exercised control over property inconsistent with the continued rights of the owner. During this evolutionary process, the purpose served by the crime of larceny obviously shifted from protecting society's peace to general protection of property rights.

Modern penal statutes generally have incorporated these developments under a unified definition of larceny (see e.g., American Law Institute, Model Penal Code [Tent Draft No. 1], § 206.1 [theft is appropriation of property of another, which includes unauthorized exercise of control]). Case law, too, now tends to focus upon the actor's intent and the exercise of dominion and control over the property. Indeed, this court has recognized, in construing the New York Penal Law, that the "ancient common-law concepts of larceny" no longer strictly apply.

This evolution is particularly relevant to thefts occurring in modern self-service stores. In stores of that type, customers are impliedly invited to examine, try on, and carry about the merchandise on display. Thus in a sense, the owner has consented to the customer's possession of the goods for a limited purpose.

That the owner has consented to that possession does not, however, preclude a conviction for larceny. If the customer exercises dominion and control wholly inconsistent with the continued rights of the owner, and the other elements of the crime are present, a larceny has occurred. Such conduct on the part of a customer satisfies the "taking" element of the crime.

It is this element that forms the core of the controversy in these cases. The defendants argue, in essence, that the crime is not established, as a matter of law, unless there is evidence that the customer departed the shop without paying for the merchandise.

Although this court has not addressed the issue, case law from other jurisdictions seems unanimous in holding that a shoplifter need not leave the store to be guilty of larceny. This is because a shopper may treat merchandise in a manner inconsistent with the owner's continued rights—and in a manner not in accord with that of prospective purchaser—without actually walking out of the store.

Under these principles, there was ample evidence in each case to raise a factual question as to the defendants' guilt. In People v. Olivo, defendant not only concealed goods in his clothing, but he did so in a particularly suspicious manner. And, when defendant was stopped, he was moving towards the door, just three feet short of exiting the store.

In People v. Gasparik, defendant removed the price tag and sensor device from a jacket, abandoned his own garment, put the jacket on and ultimately headed for the main floor of the store. Removal of the price tag and sensor device, and careful concealment of those items, is highly unusual and suspicious conduct for a shopper. Coupled with defendant's abandonment of his own coat and his attempt to leave the floor, those factors were sufficient to make out a prima facie case of taking.

In People v. Spatzier, defendant concealed a book in an attaché case. Unaware that he was being observed in an overhead mirror, defendant looked furtively up and down the aisle before secreting the book. In these circumstances, given the manner in which defendant concealed the book and his suspicious behavior, the evidence was not insufficient as a matter of law.

In sum, in view of the modern definition of the crime of larceny, and its purpose of protecting individual property rights, a taking of property in the self-service store context can be established by evidence that a customer exercised control over merchandise wholly inconsistent with the store's continued rights. Quite simply, a customer who crosses the line between the limited right he or she has to deal with merchandise and the store owner's rights may be subject to prosecution for larceny. Such a rule should foster the legitimate interests and continued operation of self-service shops, a convenience which most members of the society enjoy.

Accordingly, in each case, the order of the Appellate Term should be affirmed.

CASE DISCUSSION

The court says that originally larceny stressed possession, but modern convenience shopping requires that the emphasis shift to intent. Do you see why the court says this? Under strict taking and carrying away requirements, do you think these defendants committed larceny? Is the court right in adopting a rule that does not require shoplifters to leave the store before they are guilty? What rule would you adopt?

In addition to temporary possessions, possessions secured by trick constitute wrongful takings—larceny by trick. If a possessor gives up possession because he or she believe another's lies, the law deems it a larcenous taking and carrying away even though the possessor voluntarily relinquished possession. Hence, if I lend a valuable watch to a friend who says he is only going to borrow it for the evening but who intends to sell it to a jeweler, I have retained legal possession of the watch; my "friend" has wrongfully taken possession from me. Larceny by trick should not be confused with acquiring property by false pretenses. False pretenses requires a transfer of ownership or title, not simply a shift in possession.

Larceny law does not follow the old rhyme "Finders keepers, losers weepers." Owners who lose their money or other property retain its possession for the purposes of larceny law. Hence, those who take and carry away lost money or other property commit larceny, assuming they do so with requisite intent.

Meaning of Property

Common-law larceny included only personal property, or "movables." Larceny was therefore limited to the misappropriation of goods and chattels. Real estate and anything attached to it—unharvested crops, uncut trees, unmined minerals, and attached fixtures—were not property within the meaning of common-law larceny. Thus, if I entered my neighbor's field, cut down growing wheat, and took and carried the wheat away, I did not commit larceny. Defining harvested crops, cut trees, and so on as movable property led to some odd results. For example, cutting down crops one day, leaving, and then returning the next day to take and carry the crops away was considered larceny.

Common-law larceny also excluded stocks, bonds, checks, and other negotiable paper. Such documents were intangible property or choses in action. This meant they were not actual property, except as paper and ink; they only represented property. Hence, they were not larcenable. Gas and electricity were also not property; nor were services and labor.

Modern statutes have drastically revised the common law larceny definition of property. In most American jurisdictions today, minerals, crops, fixtures, trees, utilities (gas and electricity), goods and services, and other intangible property can all be taken under the law of larceny. In short, virtually all property falls within the scope of modern larceny statutes. Texas, for example, defines property to include real property; tangible or intangible personal property including anything severed from the land; and a document, including money, that represents or embodies anything of value. The statute also includes theft of service, defined as (1) labor or professional services; (2) telecommunication, public utility, and transportation services; (3) lodging, restaurant services, and entertainment; and (4) the supply of a motor vehicle or other property for use.[4]

CASE

Did He "Steal" the Use of the Computer?

State of Indiana v. McGraw

480 N.E. 2d 552 (Ind. 1985)

[Justice Prentice delivered the opinion. Justice Pivarnik delivered a dissenting opinion.]

FACTS

Defendant was employed by the City of Indianapolis, as a computer operator. The City leased computer services on a fixed charge or flat rate basis, hence the expense to it was not varied by the extent to which it was used. Defendant was provided with a terminal at his desk and was assigned a portion of the computer's information storage capacity, called a "private library," for his utilization in performing his duties. No other employees were authorized to use his terminal or his library.

Defendant became involved in a private sales venture and began soliciting his co-workers and using a small portion of his assigned library to maintain records associated with the venture. He was reprimanded several times for selling his products in the office and on "office time," and he was eventually discharged for unsatisfactory job performance and for continuing his personal business activities during office hours.

Defendant, at the time of his being hired by the City, received a handbook, as do all new employees, which discloses the general prohibition against the unauthorized use of city property. Other city employees sometimes used the computer for personal convenience or entertainment; and although Defendant's supervisor knew or suspected that Defendant was using the computer for his business records, he never investigated the matter or reprimanded Defendant in this regard, and such use of the computer was not cited as a basis for his discharge.

Defendant, following his discharge, applied for and received unemployment compensation benefits, over the protest of the City. He requested a former fellow employee to obtain a "print-out" of his business data and then to erase it from what had been his library. Instead, the "print-out" was turned over to Defendant's former supervisor and became the basis for the criminal charges.

OPINION

Assuming that the Defendant's use of the computer was unauthorized and that such use is a "property" under the theft statute, there remains an element of the offense missing under the evidence. The act provides: "A person knowingly or intentionally exerts unauthorized control over property of another person with intent to deprive the other of any part of its value or use, commits theft, a class D felony." It is immediately apparent that the rest of the statute, the harm sought to be prevented, is a deprivation to one of his property or its use—not a benefit to one which, although a windfall to him, harmed nobody.

The Court of Appeals focused upon Defendant's unauthorized use of the computer for monetary gain and upon the definition of "property" as used in the statute . . . which we may assume, arguendo, includes the "use" of a computer, although we think that it would be more accurate to say that the information derived by use of a computer is property. Having determined that Defendant's use was property, was unauthorized and was for his monetary benefit, it concluded that he committed a theft. Our question is, "Who was deprived of what?" . . .

Defendant's unauthorized use cost the City nothing and did not interfere with its use by others. He extracted from the system only such information as he had previously put into it. He did not, for his own benefit, withdraw City data intended for its exclusive use or for sale. Thus, Defendant did not deprive the City of the "use of computers and computer services" as the information alleged that he intended to do. . . .

We have written innumerable times, that intent is a mental function and, absent an admission it must be determined by courts and juries from a consideration of the conduct and natural and usual consequences of such conduct. . . . It follows that when the natural and usual consequences of the conduct charged and proved are not such as would effect the wrong which the statute seeks to prevent, the intent to effect that wrong is so inferrable. No deprivation to the City resulted from Defendant's use of the computer, and a deprivation to it was not a result to be expected from such use, hence not a natural and usual consequence. There was no evidence presented from which the intent to deprive, an essential element of the crime, could be inferred. . . .

DISSENT

I must dissent from the majority opinion wherein the majority finds that Defendant did not take property of the City "with intent to deprive the owner of said property." In the first place, intent is clearly shown in that Defendant used the City computer system for his personal business, well knowing that he was doing so and well knowing that it was unauthorized. . . . Time and use are at the very core of the value of a computer system. To say that only the information stored in the computer plus the tapes and discs and perhaps the machinery involved in the computer system, are the only elements that can be measured as the value or property feature of that system, is incorrect. . . .

. . . Thus, when the defendant used the computer system, putting on data from his private business and taking it out on printouts, he was taking that which was property of the City and converting it to his own use, thereby depriving the City of its use and value. . . .

CASE DISCUSSION

Would you define the use of the computer as property? What facts would lead you to conclude that it was property? Do you think McGraw "stole" anything of value? Do you think the city lost anything of value? Should it matter? Does—or should—your definition of property depend on the purpose for which you are defining the term? Why should, or should not, that be the way to define property? Explain. Do you agree with the dissent or the majority? Was McGraw guilty of *anything*?

Value of Property

In all jurisdictions, grading depends on the value of the property taken: the higher the value of the misappropriated property, the more serious the larceny. The law determines the grade of larceny according to three criteria: (1) market value, (2) method of taking, (3) intrinsic value. Grand larceny, which is usually punishable by one year or more in prison, includes property exceeding a dollar amount, typically between $100 and $400. Property worth less than the designated amount for grand larceny is usually included in the misdemeanor of petty larceny, which is punishable by less than one year in jail or a fine, or both. The dividing line between grand and petty larceny differs from state to state. In South Carolina, for example, the critical amount is only $20; in Pennsylvania it is $2,000.

Determining property value is difficult, but generally market value governs, rather than price paid or misappropriators' evaluations. If several articles are taken from the same place at the same time, the value can be set at the aggregate value. If items are taken over an extended period from different people and different places, however, the aggregate value method cannot apply.

Market value does not always determine the gravity of theft. Pickpocketing, for example, is always a felony, and so is taking property from someone's home. These cases involve more interests than mere property; harms to both persons and habitation are present. Moreover, taking property from a person by force constitutes robbery, a serious felony. In most jurisdictions, taking and carrying away certain items is also a felony, no matter what the items' value. These items vary depending on the interests in particular jurisdictions. In Texas, for example, stealing natural oil, no matter what the value, constitutes grand larceny. California provides that grand larceny includes property valued in excess of $400, or avocados, olives, citrus or deciduous fruits, vegetables, artichokes, nuts, or other farm crops exceeding $100 in value.[5]

Criminal Law Close-Up

ELECTRONIC FUND TRANSFER FRAUD

The rapid increase in the use of computer-based systems for financial transactions has heightened public and private concern over the potential for electronic fund transfer (EFT) crime or fraud. Two principal types of crime highlighted by this report are incidents associated with automatic teller machines (ATMs) and with wire transfer, that is, the transfer of funds by electronic means between banks.

Data from a survey of 16 American banks, all but one with deposits in excess of one billion dollars, and related industry data sources reveal the following estimates of level of activity in electronic transfers and the extent of crime:

- In 1983, there were 2.7 billion transactions involving $262 billion processed through automatic teller machines (ATM).

- Of a sample of 2,707 ATM-related incidents (transactions resulting in accountholder complaints), 45% of all incidents were found to be potentially fraudulent, involving, for example, unauthorized use of lost or stolen cards, overdrafts, and "bad" deposits.

- Nationwide ATM bank loss from fraud during 1983 is estimated in the range between $70 and $100 million based on bank characteristics and a median bank loss of approximately $84 million calculated on the basis of 2.7 billion transactions.

- In 1980, roughly 60 million wire transfers were completed involving 117 trillion dollars.

- The average exposure to loss (i.e., loss potential) in 139 problem wire transfer incidents reported by 12 of the 16 banks was $833,279; actual losses occurred in 56% of these incidents.

- Anticipated losses from wire transfer fraud were estimated to increase approximately 70% over the next 5 years by a cross-section of bank managers and wire transfer experts.

SOURCE: *Electronic Fund Transfer Fraud*, Bureau of Justice Statistics, United States Justice Department, Washington, D.C., March 1985.

Larceny Mens Rea

To convict for larceny, the prosecution must prove that a defendant intended to permanently deprive the rightful possessor of the property taken and carried away. Therefore, larceny is a specific intent crime. For example, suppose I see a lawn mower on my neighbor's lawn, and I believe it is the one I loaned him last month but it is, in fact, his. If I take the mower and sell it, I have not committed larceny because I did not intend to keep *his* lawn mower.

Temporary misappropriations do not constitute common-law larceny. Modern statutes have filled that gap in common-law larceny by making some temporary misappropriations separate crimes. A typical case is joyriding, or taking a vehicle to drive for a short time only, fully intending to return it to its rightful possessor. The joyrider lacks the larceny *mens rea*—the intent to *permanently* deprive the owner of possession. Joyriding statutes make it a less serious offense than larceny to take and carry away another's vehicle with the intent to *temporarily* dispossess the vehicle's rightful possessor.[6]

Finally, taking property that actors believe is theirs is not larceny. Called the **claim of right,** this defense removes the *mens rea* requirement to intend to permanently dispossess rightful possessors. Most jurisdictions permit claim of right as a defense to larceny.[7]

Summary

Larceny, the ancient common-law felony, requires (1) a wrongful taking and (2) carrying away (3) of the property (4) of another (5) with the intent to permanently dispossess the property's rightful possessor. Some modern statutes have codified common law; in these jurisdictions, the old elements remain important. These jurisdictions have added a number of other misappropriations that follow the common-law development. Some jurisdictions have consolidated several misappropriations into general theft statutes. The principal misappropriations consolidated into theft include embezzlement and obtaining property by false pretenses.

▤ EMBEZZLEMENT

Historically, it was not a larcenous taking if a possessor voluntarily parted with property. For example, carriers, or persons hired to deliver owners' goods to third parties, could not "take" the goods while they were in the carriers' possession. Similarly, bank employees who removed money from an account could not "take" the money because the owner had voluntarily deposited it. That such clearly wrongful appropriations were originally not criminal shows that larceny is an ancient crime predating carriers, banks, and other modern institutions. Statutes have altered common-law larceny so that those who acquire property lawfully—parking lot attendants, dry cleaners, auto repair people, and bank tellers—and then convert it to their own use commit embezzlement.

Embezzlers do not "take" property because they already possess it lawfully. In other words, they cannot wrongfully take what they already lawfully possess. **Conversion** replaces taking in embezzlement. Conversion can occur only *after* someone acquires possession lawfully. Embezzlers acquire possession for a specific purpose—to repair a watch, to dry-clean clothes, and so on—and then turn (convert) the property to an unlawful purpose (their own use or profit). Embezzlers stand in a trust or fiduciary relationship with rightful possessors; they possess property only for the purpose for which the rightful permanent possessor transferred it. Conversion breaches this trust.

Embezzlers, or those who converted property temporarily in their possession for particular purposes, did not exist when larceny originated. They became important as society grew more complex. Larceny's trespassory taking requirement prevented the punishment of those who abused their trust and misappropriated property entrusted to them. Hence, the English Parliament created embezzlement during the period when temporary possessors, or bailees, were becoming common. With the onset of banking, industrialization, and modern society, many more embezzlement types were possible, and conversion became ever more important in misappropriation offenses. Under modern statutes, whether embezzlement and larceny or theft, either taking (larceny) or conversion (embezzlement) suffices.

FALSE PRETENSES

Larceny requires a trespassory taking, and embezzlement requires the conversion of property rightfully in the converter's possession. But what about owners who part with possession because they are deceived into giving up title or ownership? Embezzlement covers only those who temporarily have a lawful right to possess and then convert property to their own use. Those who obtain property by false pretenses have no right to possess it, and yet they do not take the property because owners willingly gave it to them. False pretenses fills the gap between larcenous takings and embezzlement that is created by deceitful misappropriation.

Material Elements in False Pretenses

The *actus reus* in false pretenses replaces taking in larceny. It requires first an actual false representation, such as a promise to deliver something one cannot or does not intend to ever deliver. The law often expresses this as falsely representing a material past or existing fact. The false pretenses *mens rea* requires the specific intent to obtain title or ownership by deceit and lies—the false pretenses. A material surrounding circumstance in false pretenses is that victims must part with the possession and ownership because they believe and rely on the false representation. Suppose someone promises me he is a financial wizard when in fact he is only saying so to get my money. If I rely on his promise and transfer my money to him for investment, then the fake financial wizard obtained my money by false pretenses. Finally, the victim must actually part with the property. Note the difference between obtaining property through false pretense and through larceny by trick. In larceny by trick, the possessor must part with possession. In false pretenses, the owner must part with title or ownership.

Rationale of False Pretenses Statutes

The law on obtaining property by false pretenses aims to protect owners from several harms inflicted by cheaters and con artists who misappropriate their wealth. From early on, English criminal law tried to protect against false weights and measures because they hindered trade. It was not until 1757, however, that individuals who privately cheated other individuals out of property were made criminals. In that year, the English Parliament made it a misdemeanor to "obtain [by false pretenses] from any person or persons, money, goods, wares, or merchandizes."[8]

The extension of criminal law to include cheating has not gone without criticism. Some critics base their attack on a general reluctance to use the criminal law in any but the most extreme situations. Others feel little sympathy with victims. Taking their cue from the ancient commercial doctrine of *caveat emptor* ("Let the buyer beware"), these critics believe that "fools and their money soon part." Such criticisms are especially effective against the view that duping the public is a crime even when no one loses property. This dimension to false pretenses—humiliating and making people fools without property loss—deserves serious attention that cannot be given here. Suffice it to say that despite objections, criminal law protects property from misappropriations based on lying, cheating, deception, and other forms of false pretenses, at least under some circumstances.

False Pretenses Distinguished from Larceny

Until the last twenty years, larceny, embezzlement, and obtaining property by false pretenses were distinct offenses in most criminal codes. Although all three involved misappropriation, the taking in larceny, the conversion in embezzlement, and the fraud in false pretenses were considered sufficiently different to require separate treatment under criminal codes. This view was largely due to the histories of these crimes, rather than to logic. Trespassory taking (first), conversion (later), and false pretense (last) created problems as society grew more complex during English and American history. The well-known Supreme Court justice Oliver Wendell Holmes, Jr., put it simply: "In law a page of history is worth a volume of logic."

CASE

Did He Intend to Deceive the Churches?

Hixson v. State

266 Ark. 778, 587 S.W.2d 70 (1979)

[Hixson was convicted of false pretenses misappropriation. He was sentenced to twelve years' imprisonment and fined $2,500. Judge Howard delivered the opinion. Judge Newbern dissented.]

FACTS

Mrs. Rita Sue Rogers, Secretary of Trinity Baptist Church, Fort Smith, Arkansas, testified that on January 16, 1977, appellant entered into an agreement with Trinity Baptist Church and its members to take pictures of the membership and in return for the sale of the pictures to the members, appellant would supply pictorial directories to the church free of charge. The number of church directories to be supplied was 125% of the number of members who had their pictures taken. In other words, the church would receive at the rate of 125 directories for every 100 members who purchased portraits. No money was to be paid by the church.

The evidence clearly shows that appellant received $1,700.00 from the membership of Trinity, but the church has never received any directories, although appellant promised to deliver the directories within 60 days after the pictures were taken. The photographing of the membership was completed on April 3, 1977.

Mrs. Rogers further testified that the project created such interest and enthusiasm among the members that a group of ladies volunteered to serve as a committee to inform the entire membership of the project and to solicit their support; that the committee scheduled the time for the individual and family sittings for the portraits; and that if shut-ins already had photographs, these photographs were to be placed in the directory for a fee of $5.00.

Mrs. Rogers also stated that appellant delivered a $500.00 personal check to the church, drawn on Sequoyah State Bank, Muldrow, Oklahoma, and made payable to Trinity Baptist Church to guarantee the delivery of the portraits to the membership; that when the pictures were not delivered, as scheduled, the check was deposited for collection, but was subsequently returned marked "account closed."

Dan Wilmoth, a representative of Photo World of Memphis, Tennessee, testified that his firm specialized in photographic processing for professional photographers; that appellant came to Memphis in April or May, 1977, to have a roll of film developed and that appellant advised him that appellant was just getting started in business for himself; that appellant discussed the prospects of Photo World printing church directories for appellant's firm and that while Photo World had never printed church directories, an agreement was made with appellant whereby Photo World would print the directories for $1.50 a copy with a minimum of 200 copies; that Photo World received the necessary materials for only one church directory and that was for Bethany Presbyterian Church. However, Mr. Wilmoth testified, the directory was never printed because appellant owed Photo World $1,200.00 for work previously done in which Photo World received an insufficient fund check that had not been made good; that appellant told Photo World that appellant could not pay the $1,200.00 at that time because appellant had paid $5,000.00 on a property note. Mr. Wilmoth further testified that Photo World printed its first directory, during its 11 years of existence, in 1978.

Testifying further, Mr. Wilmoth stated that when appellant requested Photo World to commence work on the materials supplied for
the one church directory, appellant was advised to "send me Three
Hundred Dollars ($300.00) Cashiers' Check and I'll get it printed for
him"; that a day or two later, appellant called and stated, "hey, I can't
get the money, you know, can you do it, please?" Wilmoth replied,
"I'll tell you what, you send me One Hundred Fifty Dollars ($150.00)
and I'll do it." Wilmoth testified he never heard anymore from
appellant.

OPINION

The relevant statutory provisions that appellant was accused of
violating are:

(1) A person commits theft of property if he:

> (b) knowingly obtains the property of another person, by decep-
> tion or by threat, with the purpose of depriving the owner
> thereof.

(2) (a) Theft of property is a class B felony if:
    (i) the value of the property is $2,500.00 or more.

We are persuaded that it was incumbent upon the State to establish
the following in order to convict the appellant-defendant of the
charge brought under the above provisions:

1. That appellant-defendant, at the time he received the monies
from the owners, did not intend to carry out his promise to deliver
church directories to the churches and the membership thereof in
return for the monies received by him.

2. That appellant-defendant knew, at the time he promised to
deliver church directories to the churches and the membership
thereof that the promise or representation was false and that the
promise was made for the purpose of depriving the owners of their
property.

Appellant argues essentially, for the reversal of his conviction, that
his promise to deliver church directories within 30 to 90 days after the
termination of the photographic work was "mere puffing" and,
moreover, the failure of appellant to perform a "promised future act"
is not criminal.

We are not persuaded by appellant's argument inasmuch as it is
plain from the evidence in this record that appellant's conduct
exceeded the conduct of a seller or a dealer in praising the virtues of
something that he has to offer for sale and which is not calculated to,
or is unlikely to deceive ordinary persons addressed. The evidence is
crystal clear that the representations and promises made by appellant
to deliver the church directories, which was an intricate part of the
entire project and was the sole motivating factor that induced the
churches and the membership to participate in the project, were false
as a matter of fact and as to the value of the articles that the churches
and members were to receive in return for delivering their monies to
the appellant. Moreover, it is plain from this record that appellant had

no experience or expertise either in photography or in the compilation of church directories; and that at the time that appellant made the promises to deliver the directories, appellant did not possess the facilities to print a directory, nor had he made arrangements with any other firm or source for the preparation of the directories.

The evidence establishes clearly that appellant made use of the funds received for purposes other than for what was promised by appellant. Consequently, the membership of the churches involved have been deprived of the use and benefit of their property; and it seems obvious that restitution is unlikely.

Affirmed.

DISSENT

The evidence of the intent of the Appellant to deceive was extremely weak. The record presented a picture of a person struggling to succeed in a business he thought would make a profit. It is true he lacked experience as a photographer, and he was an abysmal failure as a businessman, but his failure is not a crime. The majority opinion refers to instances in which he pleaded with a printer to get directories printed, and the record shows a great deal of effort expended in trying to get the directories together. The "substantial evidence" to which the majority refers is really nothing more than Appellant's failure to deliver the directories. The argument seems to be that Appellant must have intended to deceive with respect to the agreements he entered to produce directories after he had failed so miserably to produce in accordance with some of his prior agreements. In quoting the statutory definition of "deception," the majority opinion leaves out the part of subsection (3)(e) of the statute which is as follows:

> Deception as to a person's intention to perform a promise shall not be inferred solely from the fact that he did not subsequently perform the promise. Ark.Stat.Ann. § 41–2201(3) (e) (Repl. 1977).

CASE DISCUSSION

The critical issue in the case is determining whether Hixson intended to deceive the churches. In other words, did he use false pretenses to get their money? He argued he was only "puffing." Does the evidence presented convince you that he meant to deceive the churches in order to get their money? Or do you think the dissent has a point? Should the criminal law punish inept people who think they can do what they cannot legally do? Does Hixson deserve twelve years in prison?

a. This record is replete with testimony from the following named pastors and churches whose experiences with appellant parallel the experiences of Mrs. Rogers.
(1) Rev. Don Chandler, Pastor of Wakefield Baptist Church, Little Rock, Arkansas, whose members paid between $3,000.00 and $4,000.00; and,
(2) Rev. Jerry Highfill, Pastor of Sunset Baptist Church, Ponca City, Oklahoma, whose members paid $3,090.34; and
(3) First Christian Church, North Little Rock, Arkansas, whose members paid $2,000.00; and,

(4) Rev. Robert S. Jackson, Sr., Pastor of First Baptist Church, Poteau, Oklahoma, whose members paid approximately $2,509.23; and,

(5) Father Alan Loth, Pastor of Mother of Sorrows Church in Apache, Our Ladies in Sterling Church and St. Anna's Church in Elgin, Oklahoma, whose members paid approximately $1,400.00; and,

(6) First United Methodist Church of Harrison, whose members paid $1,375.24; and,

(7) First Church of the Nazarene, North Little Rock, Arkansas, whose members paid $1,825.00; and,

(8) Rev. William R. Edwards, Pastor of Elmdale Baptist Church, Springdale, Arkansas, whose members paid $2,010.00; and,

(9) First Baptist Church Arkoma, Oklahoma, whose members paid $1,100.00; and,

(10) Church of the Nazarene in Rogers, Arkansas, whose pastor paid $136.20, but had no knowledge of the amount of money paid by his membership; and,

(11) Church of Christ in Kingfisher, Oklahoma, whose members paid $656.35; and,

(12) Bethany Presbyterian Church of Muskogee, Oklahoma, whose members paid an undetermined amount of money; and,

(13) First Free Will Baptist Church of Ada, Oklahoma, whose members paid $2,299.00.

CONSOLIDATED THEFT STATUTES

Critics have long recommended reforming larceny, embezzlement, and false pretenses to conform more to logic than to history. They believe that misappropriating property, whether by stealth, conversion, or deception, represent different dimensions to one general harm. In 1962, the Model Penal Code included a consolidated theft provision, one that most state laws now follow. The most common statutes consolidate larceny, embezzlement, and false pretenses into one offense called theft.

Consolidated theft statutes eliminate the largely artificial need to decide whether property was "taken and carried away," "converted," or "swindled," as traditional larceny, embezzlement, and false pretense statutes require. Joining the offenses deals more realistically with the social problem in all three: criminal property misappropriations.

Some statutes are even more ambitious than those that simply consolidate larceny, embezzlement, and false pretenses. The Model Penal Code, for example, has a single theft article that covers not only larceny, embezzlement, and false pretense, but also extortion, blackmail, and receiving stolen property. Thus, the Code houses all nonviolent misappropriations. Only robbery—because it refers to imminent or actual physical harm—falls under a separate provision. Other consolidated theft statutes include some or all of the following thefts: taking, conversion, deception, extortion, lost property, receiving stolen property, services, failure to make required deposits, and unauthorized vehicle use.[9]

Consolidated theft statutes reflect only in part the criminal law's response to the rapidly developing opportunities to misappropriate property. Property itself has become too restrictive to describe what constitutes value subject to misappropriation in the late twentieth century. Electronics has created not only new value but also new methods to misappropriate it. This has led to legislation dealing with devices to misappropriate telephone long-distance services as well as information and services stored in electronic data banks, to mention only two.

Criminal Law Close-Up

CALIFORNIA'S CONSOLIDATED THEFT STATUTE

Penal Code section 484(a) says that "every person who shall feloniously steal the personal property of another, or who shall fraudulently appropriate property which has been entrusted to him, or who shall knowingly and designedly, by any false or fraudulent representation or pretense, defraud any other person of money, labor or real or personal property, shall be guilty of theft."[1]

Commenting on the provision, the California Supreme Court wrote:

> Included within section 484 is not only the offense of taking personal property (larceny), but also "embezzlement," theft by trick and device, and theft by false pretenses [of both personal and real property].[2]

1. Quoted in People v. Shirley, 144 Cal.Rptr. 282 at p. 289.
2. Ibid.

RECEIVING STOLEN PROPERTY

In some circumstances, it is a crime not only to take, convert, and acquire the property of others by deception but also to receive property after it has been criminally misappropriated. Called receiving stolen property, this offense aims to protect against those who stand to benefit from misappropriations even though they did not wrongfully acquire others' property. Benefit does not mean simply monetary profit; receiving stolen property includes not only fences (those who trade in stolen property), but also, for example, students who steal university equipment because they need calculators, typewriters, recorders, and other equipment. Large-scale fence operations, however, account for most traffic in stolen property.

Fences have the facilities to buy, store, and market property. They are as indispensable as go-betweens as their counterparts in legitimate operations are to farmers, manufacturers, and other producers. Large-city fences trade a remarkably large volume and variety in stolen property, ranging from narcotics and weapons to appliances and computers and even clothes. Receiving stolen property is aimed primarily at these large-scale operations.

The *actus reus* in receiving stolen property requires that property taken, converted, or acquired by deception come into the receiver's control for at least a short period. It does not mandate that the receiver personally possess the property. Hence, if I buy a stolen fur from a fence who hands it directly to my friend, I have received the fur. If my friend then gives the

Criminal Law Close-Up

MISAPPROPRIATIONS BY COMPUTER

§ 502. Definitions; computer system or network; intentional access to defraud or extort or to obtain money, property or services with false or fraudulent intent, representations or promises; malicious access, alteration, deletion, damage or disruption; violations; penalty; civil action

a. For purposes of this section:
1. "Access" means to instruct, communicate with, store data in, or retrieve data from, a computer system or computer network.
2. "Computer system" means a device or collection of devices, excluding pocket calculators which are not programmable and capable of being used in conjunction with external files, one or more of which contain computer programs and data, that performs functions, including, but not limited to, logic, arithmetic, data storage and retrieval, communication, and control.
3. "Computer network" means an interconnection of two or more computer systems.
4. "Computer program" means an ordered set of instructions or statements, and related data that, when automatically executed in actual or modified form in a computer system, causes it to perform specified functions.
5. "Data" means a representation of information, knowledge, facts, concepts, or instructions, which are being prepared or have been prepared, in a formalized manner, and are intended for use in a computer system or computer network.
6. "Financial instrument" includes, but is not limited to, any check, draft, warrant, money order, note, certificate of deposit, letter of credit, bill of exchange, credit or debit card, transaction authorization mechanism, marketable security, or any computer system representation thereof.
7. "Property" includes, but is not limited to, financial instruments, data, computer programs, documents associated with computer systems and computer programs, or copies thereof, whether tangible or intangible, including both human and computer system readable data, and data while in transit.
8. "Services" includes, but is not limited to, the use of the computer system, computer network, computer programs, or data prepared for computer use, or data contained within a computer system, or data contained within a computer network.

b. Any person who intentionally accesses or causes to be accessed any computer system or computer network for the purpose of (1) devising or executing any scheme or artifice to defraud or extort, or (2) obtaining money, property, or services with false or fraudulent intent, representations, or promises, is guilty of a public offense.

c. Any person who maliciously accesses, alters, deletes, damages, destroys or disrupts the operation of any computer system, computer network, computer program, or data is guilty of a public offense.

d. Any person who intentionally and without authorization accesses any computer system, computer network, computer program, or data, with knowledge that the access was not authorized, shall be guilty of a public offense. This subdivision shall not apply to any person who accesses his or her employer's computer system, computer network, computer program, or data when acting within the scope of his or her employment.

e. Any person who violates any provision of subdivision (b) or (c) unless specified otherwise, is punishable by a fine not exceeding ten thousand dollars ($10,000), or by imprisonment in the state prison for 16 months, or two or three years, or by both such fine and imprisonment, or by a fine not exceeding five thousand dollars ($5,000), or by imprisonment in the county jail not exceeding one year, or by both such fine and imprisonment.

f. (1) A first violation of subdivision (d) which does not result in injury is an infraction punishable by a fine not exceeding two hundred fifty dollars ($250).

2. A violation of subdivision (d) which results in an injury, or a second or subsequent violation of subdivision (d) with no injury, is a misdemeanor punishable by a fine not exceeding five thousand dollars ($5,000), or by imprisonment in the county jail not exceeding one year, or by both such fine and imprisonment.

3. As used in this subdivision, "injury" means any alteration, deletion, damage, or destruction of a computer system, computer network, computer program, or data caused by the access, or any expenditure reasonably and necessarily incurred by the owner or lessee to verify that a computer system, computer network, computer program, or data was not altered, deleted, damaged, or destroyed by the access.

g. In addition to any other civil remedy available, the owner or lessee of the computer system, computer network, computer program, or data may bring a civil action against any person convicted under this section for compensatory damages, including any expenditure reasonably and necessarily incurred by the owner or lessee to verify that a computer system, computer network, computer program, or data was not altered, damaged, or deleted by the access. For the purposes of actions authorized by this subdivision, the conduct of an unemancipated minor shall be imputed to the parent or legal guardian having control or custody of the minor, pursuant to the provisions of Section 1714.1 of the Civil Code.

In any action brought pursuant to this subdivision, the court may award attorney's fees to a prevailing plaintiff.

h. This section shall not be construed to preclude the applicability of any other provision of the criminal law of this state which applies or may apply to any transaction.

(Added by Stats. 1979, c. 858, p. 2968, § 1. Amended by Stats. 1981, c. 837, p. 3225, § 1; Stats. 1983, c. 1092, p. ----, § 292, urgency, eff. Sept. 27, 1983, operative Jan. 1, 1984; Stats. 1984, c. 949, p. ----, § 2; Stats. 1985, c. 571, p. ----, § 1.)

SOURCE: Calif. Penal Code, title 13, (1970).

fur to her friend, my friend has also received the stolen fur. Included in the definition of the *actus reus* are fences as well as friends who hide stolen goods temporarily for thieves.

A material element in receiving stolen property is that the property must in fact have been criminally misappropriated—that is, taken, converted, or acquired by deception. Hence, if I think I am hiding stolen weapons but in fact the weapons were not stolen, I have not received stolen weapons.

Mens rea is difficult to establish in receiving stolen property. The culpability required varies among the states. Some jurisdictions require actual knowledge that the goods are stolen. In other jurisdictions, an honest belief that the goods are stolen suffices. In all jurisdictions, this knowledge may be inferred from surrounding circumstances, as in receiving goods from a known thief or buying goods at a fraction of their real value (for example, buying a new twelve-speed bicycle for thirty-five dollars.) Some jurisdictions reduce the *mens rea* to recklessness or even negligence. This lowered culpability requirement is often directed at likely fences, usually junk dealers and pawn shop operators.

In addition to knowledge that property was stolen, *mens rea* requires that receivers intend to permanently dispossess rightful possessors. Hence, police officers who knowingly accept stolen property and secretly place it on suspected fences in order to catch them have not received stolen property because they intend to possess it only temporarily.

CASE

Did He Receive the Stolen Guns?

State v. Davis

607 S.W.2d 149 (Mo.1980)

[Davis was convicted of receiving stolen property, was sentenced to one year in county jail, and was fined $500. He appealed. Judge Seiler delivered the opinion.]

FACTS

Appellant was the elected city marshal and police chief of Mound City in Holt County, Missouri. He used his home as his office and headquarters. Prior to his becoming police chief, appellant had worked as a security guard; he had no formal training to be a law enforcement officer.

On July 11, 1977, Bobby Hall discovered that two rifles, a German-made eight millimeter Mauser and a .22 caliber Weatherby semi-automatic, had been stolen from the gun rack of his pickup truck parked outside his father's home in a rural area three miles south of Mound City. Hall and appellant were friends, had taken trips together and purchased guns together. Hall reported the theft to appellant, but was told that he should report the theft to the sheriff since the theft occurred outside appellant's jurisdiction.

Sometime prior to September 11, 1977, two informants, appellant's wife, Kate Davis, and her employer, John King, told Deputy Patterson that they had seen two rifles, a Mauser and a .22 caliber Weatherby, at the home of appellant. Deputy Patterson told informant John King that he needed the serial numbers from the guns and requested that he secure them. King provided two serial numbers, one which matched the number of Hall's stolen Mauser rifle and a second that did not match the serial number of the stolen Weatherby rifle.

On September 12, 1977, after Patterson received a telephone call from King informing him that the rifles were still in appellant's home, Sheriff Hayzlett and Deputy Patterson obtained a search warrant to search appellant's home for the guns. Deputy Patterson called appellant on a police radio and asked him to come to a local gas station restaurant. At approximately 9:30 in the evening appellant met Deputy Patterson and Sergeant Matthews of the Highway Patrol for coffee at the restaurant. The men sat and talked for a while. After they paid for their coffee and stepped outside the restaurant, Deputy Patterson told appellant that the sheriff's office had received information that appellant had two stolen guns at his house. Appellant denied that he had the guns and walked to his police car to drive away. Deputy Patterson went to Sergeant Matthews' patrol car and called Sheriff Hayzlett on the radio. The sheriff then heard appellant call his wife over a citizen's band radio. Within three or four minutes, Sheriff Hayzlett, Deputy Patterson, Sergeant Matthews and three other Highway Patrol officers, and the county prosecutor converged according to plan upon appellant's home to execute the search warrant.

Seriff Hayzlett and the six other law enforcement officers arrived at appellant's home and had entered it before appellant arrived on the scene. Appellant's son answered the door and said his mother was outside the building and appellant's wife subsequently entered the house through the back door. Appellant arrived moments after the arrival of the sheriff and other officers and the search of appellant's home, his bedroom in particular, commenced. No evidence of the guns was found in the house. The officers then went outside behind the house and decided to look into the cistern, where they eventually found the guns. Appellant, his wife, and one Barbara King, who evidently arrived at appellant's home after the search began, were then arrested. It was not until the trial that the "confidential informants" who supplied the information to support the issuance of the search warrant were identified for the first time as John King and appellant's wife.

When the two guns were found it was discovered that the original scopes of the rifles were missing. One of the scopes was found on one of appellant's rifles. It was later revealed that the other scope had been traded by appellant at a sporting goods store.

At trial, appellant testified that in July of 1977 he was investigating the unsolved homicide of Chester Leggins when Bobby Hall reported the theft of the rifles to him. Several days after learning of the theft of the guns, appellant was picking up some hay that he kept for his horses at Junior Yocum's barn in Mound City. After removing several bales, appellant saw the stocks of two guns in the hay. He removed the hay covering the guns and found them to be an eight millimeter Mauser and a .22 caliber Weatherby semi-automatic. Appellant took the guns to his office at home where he hid the guns without telling anyone, even his wife, of his discovery. He testified that he considered returning the guns to the barn and staking out the area to see if anyone would come to pick them up. He said he examined and test-fired the guns in an attempt to determine whether the guns could have been used in the unsolved Chester Leggins homicide.

He stated that he never doubted that the two guns were the ones that Bobby Hall had reported as having been stolen. He explained the removal of the scopes from the rifles as an attempt to test the scopes at the homicide scene without anyone becoming aware that he had found the rifles and or that he had suspected Bobby Hall could have been involved in the homicide. He explained that he owned many rifles and scopes and that he inadvertently traded Hall's scope during one of his many gun collection trading transactions.

Appellant also testified that he and Sheriff Hayzlett had had problems in their police relations and that in the past the sheriff had taken credit for appellant's successful police work while giving appellant credit only for assisting the efforts. Because of this previous competition between the Mound City police and the Holt County sheriff, appellant said he did not report the recovery of the rifles to Sheriff Hayzlett. Appellant explained his denial to Deputy Patterson of having the guns as an angry reaction to what he felt was an insinuation that he had stolen the guns or an implication that he was under an obligation to tell the sheriff whatever information he had uncovered. Appellant said he reconsidered his position after his denial and called his wife over his citizen's band radio and told her where the guns were and instructed her to put them on the back porch. He said he had decided to take the guns to the sheriff. He could not explain why his wife threw the guns into the cistern. When appellant arrived at his home and found the sheriff, deputy sheriff, four Highway Patrol officers and the county prosecutor inside, he became angry that they were conducting the search in front of his children and he did not assist the officers in finding the guns.

On November 28, 1977, the Holt County prosecuting attorney filed an information charging that "on or about the 18th of July, 1977, in Holt County, Missouri, defendant Larry Dale Davis willfully, unlawfully and feloniously received one German Mauser rifle and one .22 caliber automatic rifle, each rifle having a scope attached and the rifles having a combined value of at least $50.00 and both rifles having been stolen from Robert Hall on or about the 11th day of July, 1977, the said Larry Dale Davis knowing at the time he received said property that the property had been stolen and the said Larry Dale Davis received the rifles with the intent to defraud Robert Hall of his lawful interest therein, in violation of V.A.M.S. Section 560.270."

Accordingly, appellant was not charged with stealing the rifles on July 11th, but rather was charged with feloniously receiving them on July 18th, the day he said he found the rifles in a haystack at Junior Yocum's barn. As noted above, appellant was convicted of receiving stolen property under section 560.270, RSMo 1969 of the old criminal code.

OPINION

He [the defendant] also alleges error in the trial court's overruling his motion to quash the search warrant and the admitting into evidence of the items seized in the search.

The offense of receiving stolen property involves elements different from the offense of stealing: "a buying or receiving, from another, of property known to have been stolen, with intent to defraud." The first element has been stated variously as "the accused must receive the property in some way from another and not be the actual captor of the property" and "the property must be received in some way from another person." It is an essential element of receiving stolen property that there be at least two actors involved; the accused must receive the property from another, some person other than the owner.

In the case at bar, there is no claim that appellant stole the guns, nor evidence as to the identity of the thief, nor is there any evidence that appellant obtained the guns from another person. The only direct evidence as to appellant's coming into possession of the guns was his testimony that he recovered the guns from a haystack while acting in his official capacity as police chief of Mound City. The jury, of course, was not obligated to believe this explanation. However, the only other evidence about appellant's coming into possession of the guns is whatever follows from the facts that Mrs. Davis and her employer, King, told the deputy sheriff that they had seen two rifles at appellant's home and that when the house was searched the guns were found in the cistern, an unusual storage place. Even giving the state every legitimate inference favorable to the verdict, there is no evidence to account for the handling of the property from the time of its disappearance until it came into possession of appellant. Thus, there is no evidence of a thief or fence or anyone from whom appellant is alleged to have received the guns.

A conviction for receiving stolen property cannot stand where the evidence fails to show that defendant was the receiver rather than the taker of stolen property.

While an unexplained possession of recently stolen property can give rise to an inference that the possessor is the thief, possession of recently stolen property is no basis for an inference that the possessor received, rather than stole, the property.

The state has failed to make a case of receiving stolen property by neglecting to show that appellant received the stolen property from another with an intent to defraud.

Accordingly, the judgment must be reversed and the defendant discharged.

Under the new criminal code, the offense of receiving stolen property has been redefined and, unlike section 560.270, RSMo 1969, for which appellant was tried, now contemplates single-party transactions.

Section 560.270 was obviously intended to punish any "person who shall buy, or in any way receive any property that shall have been [previously] stolen from another." It is apparent that for there to be a "person who shall buy" previously stolen property, there must be a two-party transaction between a seller and a buyer. Likewise, in general context of the statute, any "person who shall in any way receive" from another person, denotes a two-party transfer of possession from a donor, giver, passer, etc., to a receiver, recipient, acceptor, etc. This problem appears to have been obviated by the enactment of § 570.080 RSMo 1978 (L.1977 S.B. 60, eff. 1–1–79) which provides: "1. A person commits the crime of receiving stolen property if for the purpose of depriving the owner of a lawful interest therein, he receives, retains or disposes of property of another knowing that it has been stolen, or believing that it has been stolen." The words "retains" and "disposes" can denote single-party transactions which the words in § 560.270 (now repealed) do not.

The judgment is reversed and defendant is ordered discharged.

CASE DISCUSSION

The court ruled that under the old Missouri statute that governed *Davis*, receiving stolen property required two parties. In other words, Davis had to receive the property from someone, not just get it into his possession. Since the prosecution did not prove that he got the property directly from some other individual, the court overturned his conviction. Did Davis escape on a technicality? Do you think Missouri improved its receiving stolen property law when it revised it as quoted in the court's opinion? Was Davis guilty under the new statute? How serious do you think Davis's crime was if he was convicted under the new statute? What sentence would you give him if you were the judge?

FORGERY AND UTTERING

Forgery includes making false legal documents or altering existing ones— such as checks, deeds, stocks, bonds, and credit cards; uttering means passing false documents on to others. Both misappropriate and destroy property. They harm not only the individuals directly involved but also society in general. Because day-to-day business in modern society relies on legal instruments for its smooth and efficient operation, impairing confidence in the authenticity of those instruments can lead to serious disruption in business, commercial, and financial transactions. It is this general harm, as much as individual losses, that forgery and uttering laws are designed to protect against.

Forgery

Forgery's subject matter is false writing. Documents subject to forgery make up a long list, since the law defines fraudulent or false writings broadly.

Many forgeries, such as forged checks, clearly and directly misappropriate property. These forgeries are obviously property offenses. Other forgeries are not so obviously harms to property. For example, a university might lose more reputation than property from forged diplomas. Injury to reputation and impairment of normal transactions make forgery more than a mere property offense.

The Model Penal Code drafters aimed the Code's forgery provision against three harms when they wrote a sweeping forgery definition: the harms of direct property loss, damage to reputation, and impaired business and commercial confidence. Except in grading forgery, the Code

Criminal Law Close-Up

CALIFORNIA'S FORGERY STATUTE

§ 470. Forgery, intent; documents of value; counterfeiting seal; uttering; falsification of records.

Every person who, with intent to defraud, signs the name of another person, or of a fictitious person, knowing that he has no authority so to do, to, or falsely makes, alters, forges, or counterfeits, any charter, letters patent, deed, lease, indenture, writing obligatory, will, testament, codicil, bond, covenant, bank bill or note, post note, check, draft, bill of exchange, contract, promissory note, due bill for the payment of money or property, receipt for money or property, passage ticket, trading stamp, power of attorney, or any certificate of any share, right, or interest in the stock of any corporation or association, or any controller's warrant for the payment of money at the treasury, county order or warrant, or request for the payment of money, or the delivery of goods or chattels of any kind, or for the delivery of any instrument of writing, or acquittance, release, or receipt for money or goods, or any acquittance, release, or discharge of any debt, account, suit, action, demand, or other thing, real or personal, or any transfer or assurance of money, certificates of shares of stock, goods, chattels, or other property whatever, or any letter of attorney, or other power to receive money, or to receive or transfer certificates of shares of stock or annuities, or to let, lease, dispose of, alien, or convey any goods, chattels, lands, or tenements, or other estate, real or personal, or any acceptance or indorsement of any bill of exchange, promissory note, draft, order, or any assignment of any bond, writing obligatory, promissory note, or other contract for money or other property; or counterfeits or forges the seal or handwriting of another; or utters, publishes, passes, or attempts to pass, as true and genuine, any of the abovenamed false, altered, forged, or counterfeited matters, as above specified and described, knowing the same to be false, altered, forged, or counterfeited, with intent to prejudice, damage, or defraud any person; or who, with intent to defraud, alters, corrupts, or falsifies any record of any will, codicil, conveyance, or other instrument, the record of which is by law evidence, or any record of any judgment of a court or the return of any officer to any process of any court, is guilty of forgery.[1]

California's is not the only approach to defining forgery. Other states do not list documents by name; instead, they use phrases such as "any writing," "any writing having legal efficacy or commonly relied on in business or commercial transactions," or

> "any written instrument to the prejudice of another's right."
> Either approach, however, indicates the legislatures' intention to
> cover written documents broadly.
>
> ------
>
> 1. California Penal Code (1970), enacted 1872, amended by Stats. 1905, c. 515, p. 673,
> 1; Stats. 1968, c. 713, p. 1414, 1.
> SOURCE: Calif. Penal Code, (1970).

abandons a significant traditional requirement: that a forged document
must have legal or evidentiary significance. Hence, it includes doctors'
prescriptions, identification cards, diaries, and letters, not just deeds,
wills, contracts, stocks, and bonds. Furthermore, documents are not
forgery's only subject matter. Coins, tokens, paintings, and antiques also
fall within its scope. In fact, says the commentary to this provision,
"Anything which could be falsified in respect of 'authenticity' can be the
subject of forgery."[10]

Defenders maintain that the grave harms caused by forgery and the
difficulty in drawing meaningful distinctions between forgery's various
forms justify the sweeping phrase "any writing or object." Even critics
admit that those who forge checks or fake antiques may respond more to
deterrence and rehabilitation than do other criminals. There is no clear
evidence that this is so, however, and some critics remain uneasy over
all-encompassing forgery provisions.

Making a false document or altering an authentic one constitutes the
forgery *actus reus*. Contrary to the Model Penal Code provision's apparent
logic, most jurisdictions limit forgery to the making of false writings that
have apparent legal significance. "Making" means making documents, in
whole or in part, or altering an authentic document in any material part.
Hence, if I make out and sign a check on someone else's account or a
nonexistent account, with no intent to back the check myself, I have
forged it because I falsified the whole check. Most existing forgery laws
require that either the whole document or some material part be falsified.

Merely presenting false information on an otherwise authentic document is not forgery. Hence, if I only change the amount on a check made
out and signed by the checking account's owner, I have not committed
forgery because the check itself is valid. Similarly, if a properly authorized
payroll clerk alters payrolls by adding hours, it is not forgery because the
payroll is still valid. However, both myself and the payroll clerk may have
obtained property under false pretenses. Furthermore, checks drawn on
insufficient funds are not forgeries for two reasons. First, they are not
false; second, unless the intention to back the checks is missing, they do
not have the requisite forgery *mens rea*.

Forgery is a specific intent crime. It requires the forger to falsely write,
intending to defraud others with the writing. It is not necessary to intend
to defraud specific individuals; a general purpose to fraudulently use the
falsified document suffices. Furthermore, forgery does not require the
falsifier to intend to obtain money fraudulently. Intending to secure any
advantage will do. Hence, a letter of recommendation intended to gain

membership in a desirable professional organization satisfies the forgery *mens rea*.

Once documents are falsified or altered with proper fraudulent intent, forgery is complete. Forgers need not actually gain from their falsifications and fraudulent intent. The reason is that forgery's harm lies in undermining confidence in documents' authenticity and the consequent disruption created by such undermined confidence.

Uttering

Uttering does not require making false writings or materially altering authentic ones. Rather, it means knowingly or consciously passing or using forged documents with the specific intent to defraud.

Forgery means the making of false documents in order to defraud, even if the forger never defrauds anyone. Uttering, on the other hand, means passing or using documents that someone else may have falsified—even if the utterer never altered anything on the documents—and intending to defraud others with those instruments. Forgery and uttering are thus two distinct offenses. Forgery is directed at making and altering documents in order to defraud. Uttering is directed at passing and using forged documents in order to defraud.

ROBBERY AND EXTORTION

Robbery and extortion are more than property crimes; they are also crimes against persons, and as such they constitute aggravated property crimes. In fact, they are violent or threatened violent thefts. Hence, they are more serious than ordinary thefts and usually carry much heavier penalties.

Robbery

Robbery's principal elements include (1) taking and (2) carrying away (3) others' (4) property (5) from their person or in their presence (6) by immediate force or threatened immediate force (7) with the intent to permanently dispossess the rightful possessor. Hence, robbery is essentially forcible larceny from the person—an aggravated larceny because actual threatened physical harm accompanies the misappropriation of property.

Any force beyond that needed to take and carry away property satisfies the force requirement. Picking a pocket is ordinary, although aggravated, larceny and not robbery because picking pockets requires only enough force to remove the pocket's contents. But even a slight mishandling of the victim (such as shoving) makes the crime robbery, if the mishandling secures the property. Determining just how much force satisfies the requirement is a problem in robbery, because the amount of force distinguishes between robbery and the less serious larcenies from the person, of which picking pockets is most common.

Some jurisdictions require no force. Under the Arkansas Criminal Code, for example, robbery is committed "if with the purpose of committing a theft or resisting apprehension immediately thereafter . . . [the criminal] employs or threatens to immediately employ physical force upon another." Under that statute, a defendant who stole a roast in a grocery store and, when caught just beyond the checkout stand, injured the apprehending officer was found guilty of robbery, not larceny.[11]

THREATENED FORCE. Robbery does not require actual force; threatened force ordinarily suffices. In addition, robbers need not threaten victims themselves; threats to family members qualify as well. However, robbers must threaten to kill, or at least to do great bodily injury. Threats to property, except perhaps to a dwelling house, do not satisfy the threatened force requirement.

Most jurisdictions require that robbers threaten to use force immediately, not at some time in the future. Furthermore, victims must relinquish their property because they honestly and reasonably fear robbers' threats. Critics maintain that honest fear ought to suffice. Whether robbery requires real, honest, or reasonable fear (or a combination) bears directly on the extent to which criminal law ought to punish potential harm.

CASE

Is Purse Snatching Robbery?

Commonwealth v. Jones

362 Mass. 83, 283 N.E.2d 840 (1972)

[Jones was convicted of unarmed robbery. He appealed. Chief Justice Tavro delivered the opinion.]

FACTS

On the evening of December 14, 1970, at approximately 6:30 P.M., Mrs. Florence Spring and her daughter, Miss Madeline Spring, left their apartment in Dorchester to go shopping by automobile. Each lady was carrying a pocketbook. Florence Spring opened both front and rear doors on the passenger's side in search of a snow scraper with which to remove snow from the car. She was unable to find it. Madeline Spring then knelt down on the front seat with feet extended outside the car and, leaning across the seat, she felt with her hand on the floor for the scraper. Meanwhile, Florence Spring opened the trunk of the car, took out a stick, and started to clean the rear window from the driver's side.

Madeline Spring testified that, while feeling along the floor of the front seat, she realized she "couldn't move [her] foot," "[f]or a minute" she was "stunned," but that then she turned back and saw "a black face with eyes" in the window and she "knew somebody was holding the door on [her] foot." Miss Spring stated that she became "petrified" and screamed; that she looked up and put her hand on the horn; and that while in this position, she observed a "shadow [go] by the driver's side towards the back of the car." The door was then released and she got out of the car. In answer to the question, "At that time, did you observe your pocketbook?" she indicated, "No."

Mrs. Spring testified that she saw a young man on the passenger's side by the headlight; that this young man started across the street but turned and approached her; and that he "grabbed [her] pocketbook." She indicated that the pocketbook was on her arm at the time. She described the taking as follows: "I really couldn't tell you what he did. All I knew he was standing there. Next thing I knew, I felt something off my arm. I realized my bag was gone." In answer to the question, "[H]ow did you feel?" Mrs. Spring said: "Petrified. I was scared to death." She also testified that, after the pocketbook was taken, "I said it belonged to me, and I wanted it, and he started towards the sidewalk and I started after him with the stick in my hand."

OPINION

1. We begin with a general discussion of the elements which distinguish robbery from larceny.

Under our statutes, as at common law, in order to sustain a charge of robbery, there must be proof of a larceny (1) "from [the] person," and (2) "by force and violence, or by assault and putting in fear." In other words, although it carries a separate label, "robbery is but an aggravated form of larceny."

The common law came to regard robbery as a more serious offence than larceny because of the added element of personal violence or intimidation. The exertion of force, actual or constructive, remains the principal distinguishing characteristic of the offence. Because the requirement is stated in the disjunctive, if there is actual force, there need be no fear (constructive force), and vice versa. Whether actual or constructive force is employed, the degree of force is immaterial so long as it is sufficient to obtain the victim's property "against his will." Similarly, in every case there must be a causal connection between the defendant's use of violence or intimidation and his acquisition of the victim's property.

The element of "from the person" is the other distinctive aspect of robbery. Although some statutory definitions of the offence, including our own, speak of a taking "from [the] person" without adding "or in his presence," a larceny in the presence of the victim is sufficient to constitute robbery. "[The phrase 'or in his presence'] adds nothing other than emphasis because, as pointed out by Coke, where deprivation is accomplished by violence or intimidation, 'that which is taken in his presence is in law taken from his person.' " Perkins, Criminal Law (2d ed.) 282, quoting 3 Co. Inst. 69. An object is deemed to be within the presence of the victim if it is within his area of control.

The question whether the snatching or sudden taking of property constitutes robbery has arisen in other jurisdictions although not in Massachusetts. Cf. Commonwealth v. Ordway, 12 Cush. 270. In Kentucky, the rule is that snatching, without more, involves the requisite element of force to permit a jury verdict on a charge of robbery. See Jones v. Commonwealth, 112 Ky. 689, 692–695, 66 S.W. 633; Brown v. Commonwealth, 135 Ky. 635, 640, 117 S.W. 281. According to the rule prevailing in most jurisdictions, however, snatching does not involve sufficient force to constitute robbery, unless the victim resists the taking or sustains physical injury, or unless the article taken is so attached to the victim's clothing as to afford resistance.

We prefer the Kentucky rule on purse snatching. The majority jurisdiction rule, in looking to whether or not the victim resists, we think, wrongly emphasizes the victim's opportunity to defend himself over the willingness of the purse snatcher to use violence if necessary. See Note, 23 J.Cr.Law, 111, 115. Historically, however, the law has singled out the robber from other thieves because of his readiness to inflict bodily injury upon his victims.

In a snatching or sudden taking, so long as the victim is aware of the application of force which relieves him of his property, the crime is, at least to some degree, "against [the victim's] will." Clearly, more is involved than in a mere stealthy taking where the victim has no present realization of the theft. In the circumstances of a purse snatching, we believe the force applied is sufficient to make the crime a robbery, even though the application of force may, in practice, be so quick as to deny the victim any opportunity to resist.

3. We consider first the indictment arising from the taking of Florence Spring's pocketbook.

Snatching necessarily involves the exercise of some actual force. For the reasons stated, supra, we hold that, where, as here, the actual force used is sufficient to produce awareness, although the action may be so swift as to leave the victim momentarily in a dazed condition, the requisite degree of force is present to make the crime robbery. In any event, Mrs. Spring testified that she was "[p]etrified." And also: "I was scared to death." Whether her fear aided the defendant in effecting the taking, or merely arose afterwards as the defendant argues, was a question properly for the determination of the jury. There is no reason for upsetting their factual determination.

Although no testimony was offered as to the precise location of Miss Spring's pocketbook at the moment of the taking, we think the evidence presented was ample to permit an inference that the pocketbook was inside the car with the victim when taken. It was not necessary that the Commonwealth show that she was physically in possession. The closing of the car door on Miss Spring's foot was sufficient evidence, coupled with the disappearance of her purse at approximately the same time, to allow the jury to infer the requisite causal relationship between the force and the taking.

Affirmed.

CASE DISCUSSION

The court admits that most jurisdictions do not call purse snatching robbery. Why does Massachusetts adopt the minority view that it is? Do you agree with the reasoning? Did Jones use force or threatened force to rob Miss Spring and Mrs. Spring? Were the women "reasonably" frightened that Jones might kill or seriously injure them? Do you think robbery ought to require honest, reasonable belief?

DEGREES OF ROBBERY. Most states have divided robbery into degrees according to injury done and force or threat used. New York, for example, grades robbery into three degrees. Robbers commit first-degree robbery if they carry deadly weapons, seriously injure victims, threaten the immediate use of dangerous instruments, or display what "*appears* to be a pistol, revolver, shotgun, machine gun or other firearm." (Emphasis added.) In other words, play weapons suffice. Second-degree robbery occurs if robbers rob with accomplices, cause any injury, or display "what appears to be a pistol, revolver, rifle, shotgun, machine gun or firearm." Third-degree robbery is unarmed robbery or "forcible stealing"; that is, it occurs when the actor "uses or threatens the immediate use of force upon another person."[12]

Statutory Extortion: Blackmail

At common law, extortion applied only to public officials who used their influence illegally to collect fees. Most modern extortions were not known at common law, although unusually extreme threats to gain property (such as a threat to accuse another of sodomy) were considered robbery. Statutory extortion, or blackmail, resembles robbery in that it involves forcibly misappropriating property. It is distinguished from robbery by time. Generally, robbery is a threat to harm someone immediately. Extortion, on the other hand, involves threats to do future harm. The line between extortion and robbery is often very fine, making it difficult to distinguish between the two offenses.

Threats sufficient to constitute extortion include those (1) to inflict bodily harm in the future (remember that robbery requires an immediate threat), (2) to do damage to property, and (3) to expose victims to shame or ridicule. Extortion requires the specific intent to obtain property by threats such as those just described. Some jurisdictions require that actors actually acquire the desired property to complete extortion. Others call it extortion if actors make threats with a present intention to carry them out.

In these jurisdictions, victims must actually be put in fear. Under this definition, extortion is an inchoate offense. It is a completed crime against persons, however, since fear completes the harm.

CASE

Did He Extort the Mopeds?

State v. Barber

93 N.M. 782, 606 P.2d 192 (1979)

[Barber was convicted of extortion. He appealed. Judge Andrews delivered the opinion.]

FACTS

On October 17, 1977, the victim, William Harris, entered into a lease with the defendant, Dan O. Barber, for the rental of commercial space in an Albuquerque shopping center. Harris began his business, selling mopeds, during the first week of November, and, although he remained "current" in his monthly rental payments, by the following summer he recognized that the moped business was not doing well. Harris then decided to move to a different location which offered more favorable rental terms. The defendant first learned of the victim's intended move while on a trip out of town and when he returned to work several days later he summoned Harris to his office for a meeting.

When Harris entered the office, the defendant asked him to sit down in a "peaceful" tone of voice, but the defendant quickly became agitated and accused Harris of skipping out on the lease and cheating the defendant out of the rent. Harris protested but the defendant called the explanation a lie. Without any provocation, the defendant struck the victim on the right side of the forehead causing him to fall and sustain lacerations on the back of the head and on the chin. The victim fell within the opening of a nearby credenza and, when he attempted to crawl to the other side, he was crudely ordered to return to his chair by the defendant. He complied with this order, resumed his seat, felt the lump on his head and asked to be taken to the hospital. The defendant replied, "you are not going anywhere until you sign this piece of paper. You are going to sell me five mopeds."

The piece of paper referred to was a previously prepared agreement which released the victim from his rental obligation totalling $1,735, in exchange for five mopeds, with an approximate wholesale value of $2,000. Harris and Barber discussed the agreement and Harris again requested that he be taken or be allowed to leave to drive to the hospital. The defendant then stated, "sit down, you are going to be alright—I'll be right back." The defendant then left the room and returned shortly with an ice pack and several paper towels for the victim's injuries. During the defendant's absence, the victim stated that he was too scared to leave, and when the defendant returned he became very red in the face, very angry. He started "screaming," "yelling" and "ranting," and when Harris thought he would be hit again, he signed the agreement. Barber dictated a release which purported to absolve him of all liability for injuries resulting from the battery which Harris wrote out and signed. The defendant then ordered Harris to unlock his store and the defendant removed the five mopeds.

OPINION

The defendant claims that the evidence (1) fails to show that a threat was made to induce the release of the mopeds; (2) fails to show that the victim consented to the transfer; and (3) fails to establish that Barber made an oral or written threat, the evidence showing only that he made threatening actions. A review of the facts recited above establishes that Harris signed the agreement to sell the mopeds under the threat of further physical injury. Mr. Harris testified:

> I started to say let's talk about this (the agreement). He became very red in the face, very angry, he started screaming, yelling and was ranting. I had no idea what he was really saying. He was very close to me, grabbed my lapel and I thought he was going to hit me again. At that point, I said, I'll sign anything, I'll sign. I'll sign anything you want.

There was substantial evidence of threat to injure.

Next, the defendant contends that the consent of the victim is the element which distinguishes extortion from the crime of robbery. Further, the defendant states that the consent of the victim was lacking in this case. The focus is on Mr. Harris' testimony during cross-examination.

> Question: Mr. Harris, did you turn over the mopeds willingly?
> Answer: No, I did not.
> Question: Did you consent to Mr. Barber's taking the mopeds?
> Answer: No, I did not consent to it.

It seems clear that the language of the New Mexico extortion statute does not require a showing of a "consented to taking." Compare People v. Peck, 185 P. 881 (1917)—interpreting a statute defining extortion to be "the obtaining of property from another, with his consent, induced by a wrongful use of force or fear." The difference between the statute in People v. Peck, supra, and the New Mexico statute is obvious. Section 30–16–9, supra, does not require the victim's consent.

Finally, defendant asserts that the threat which gives rise to the extortion may be either written or oral but that there is "no authority that the threat may be by actions." The defendant concludes that when the threat is made by actions, the crime committed is robbery, not extortion.

This argument, which focuses on the type of threat to distinguish robbery vis-a-vis extortion, is unpersuasive. The short answer is that the New Mexico extortion statute is not so limited as he suggests. The statute embraces "communication or transmission of any threat to another by any means whatsoever." § 30–16–9, supra. This broad language includes both written and oral threats and also includes actions constituting threats. The type of threat made is not determinative of the crime committed. Extortion can be committed where the threat is by action.

As we have shown, defendant's arguments concerning the distinction between robbery and extortion have disregarded the statutory language in New Mexico. Robbery, as defined in § 30–16–2, N.M.S.A.1978, is an aggravated form of larceny. Robbery requires a taking. N.M.U.J.I.Crim. 16.10, N.M.S.A.1978. Extortion, as defined in § 30–16–9, supra, does not require a taking, but requires a "threat with intent thereby to wrongfully obtain anything of value or to wrongfully compel the person threatened to do or refrain from doing any act against his will." Defendant need not have actually taken the mopeds to have committed extortion. The victim need not have signed the agreement for defendant to have committed extortion. These items are evidence of defendant's intent to wrongfully obtain a thing of value; in themselves, they were not elements of the crime of extortion in New Mexico. The extortion was a completed crime when defendant's threat was communicated to the victim with the requisite statutory intent.

Affirmed.

CASE DISCUSSION

The court calls this extortion, not robbery. Do you agree that Barber threatened Harris with "future harm" in order to obtain the mopeds? Do you consider Barber's crime more or less serious than robbery? Was Harris reasonably put in fear that Barber would hurt him? The court rejects Barber's argument that consent distinguishes extortion from robbery. Does Barber have a point? Would you require consent in extortion? Why or why not? Does New Mexico regard extortion as a property offense? an offense against persons? both?

≡ SUMMARY

Property misappropriation crimes originated in the ancient felony of larceny, which protected against wrongfully taking other people's possessions. Separate offenses were created primarily to keep pace with society's increasing complexity, which presented new ways to misappropriate property. Over time, the law changed piecemeal to keep pace with social and economic realities. Embezzlement protected against the wrongful conversion of property; false pretenses against deceitful misappropriations; receiving stolen property against aiding in stolen goods traffic; forgery and uttering against creating, altering, and passing false documents; and extortion against acquiring property by threatening harm in the future. These crimes responded to new ways to misappropriate property, as well as the expanding list of larcenable items. Their creation testifies to the way criminal misappropriation law developed over the past four hundred years. History, not logic, explains the distinctions between various misappropriation offenses.

In the past twenty years, consolidated theft statutes have made criminal property misappropriation more rational. They join together what used to be larceny, embezzlement, and false pretenses into a new offense called theft. They are based on the idea that whether culprits take, convert, or use deception to acquire other people's property, misappropriation is still the core evil that the separate statutes aim to combat. Some even more ambitious statutes cover all misappropriations except robbery, using the same logic that misappropriation is the core evil behind taking, converting, deceiving, receiving, forging, uttering, and extorting. Only robbery, a crime involving imminent physical harm, stands apart.

Although larceny, embezzlement, false pretenses, and receiving stolen property protect property almost exclusively, forgery, uttering, extortion, and robbery protect other interests as well. Forgery and uttering are also aimed at protecting society in general from the disruptive effects created by impairing confidence in the authenticity of documents. Therefore, they protect not only property but also society's interest in smoothly operating business in modern, complex society. Robbery and extortion are crimes against persons as well as property because they involve violence or threatened violence. Sometimes called aggravated larceny, their laws punish violent property misappropriations. By punishing when victims suffer fear but sustain no property loss, they demonstrate a wider application than for misappropriated property offenses.

═══ QUESTIONS FOR REVIEW AND DISCUSSION

1. What are the differences among larceny, embezzlement, and false pretenses? Should these offenses be grouped together as one crime?
2. Why should receiving stolen property be a crime? Is it more serious than, equally as serious as, or less serious than theft?
3. What is the purpose of the law of forgery? Is forgery a more serious crime than theft? Why? Why not?
4. What interest does uttering protect?
5. Why are robbery and extortion aggravated misappropriations? Are they crimes against property or persons? What is the most important interest they protect?

☰ SUGGESTED READINGS

1. Jerome Hall, *Theft, Law, and Society,* 2d ed. (Indianapolis: Bobbs-Merrill, 1952), is an excellent demonstration of the relationship between law and society in historical development. Professor Hall convincingly shows that larceny and other misappropriation crimes gew out of English social history. This is an interesting and authoritative work written for the general reader as well as for specialists.

2. Rollin M. Perkins and Ronald N. Boyce, *Criminal Law,* 3d ed. (Mineola, N.Y.: Foundation Press, 1982), chap. 4, surveys in detail all the property crimes, analyzes their development, discusses new developments, and presents arguments concerning most reforms.

3. Wayne R. LaFave and Austin W. Scott, Jr., *Handbook on Criminal Law* (St. Paul: West Publishing Co., 1972), has a useful chapter on property crimes that is not quite as current as the Perkins and Boyce reading.

4. American Law Institute, *Model Penal Code and Commentaries,* vol. 2 (Philadelphia: American Law Institute, 1980), pt. II, deals with the property crimes. This is the most comprehensive treatment of the history, contents, and recent reforms of property crimes. The commentary treats extensively its recommended consolidated theft provision, compares that provision with the state consolidated theft statutes, and discusses the influence the Model Penal Code provision had on those statutes.

☰ NOTES

1. Rollin M. Perkins and Ronald N. Boyce, *Criminal Law,* 3d ed. (Mineola, N.Y.: Foundation Press, 1982), chap. 4; Wayne R. LaFave and Austin W. Scott, Jr., *Handbook on Criminal Law* (St. Paul: West Publishing Co., 1972), chap. 8.

2. Perkins and Boyce, *Criminal Law,* p. 289.

3. Jerome Hall, *Theft, Law, and Society,* 2d ed. (Indianapolis: Bobbs-Merrill, 1952).

4. *Texas Penal Code,* §§ 31.01, 31.02, 31.03. Seventh Edition (St. Paul: West Publishing Co., 1988).

5. *California, West's Ann. Penal Code,* § 487. 1988 Compact Edition (St. Paul: West Publishing Co., 1989).

6. American Law Institute, *Model Penal Code and Commentaries,* vol. 2 (Philadelphia: American Law Institute, 1980), pt. II, pp. 175–76.

7. Ibid., p. 151.

8. 30 Geo. II c. 24.

9. Arts., *Model Penal Code,* 223.0 to 223.9.

10. American Law Institute, *Model Penal Code,* tentative draft no. 11 (Philadelphia: American Law Institute, 1960).

11. Arkansas Crim.Code 41–2103 (1977); *Wilson v. State,* 262 Ark. 339, 556 S.W.2d 657 (1977).

12. *New York Penal Code,* §§ 160.00–160.15.

Chapter Twelve

Crimes against Public Order and Morals

CHAPTER OUTLINE

CHAPTER MAIN POINTS

1. Crimes against public order offend society generally and often do not have individual victims.

2. Crimes against public order are punished much less severely than are felonies, but they touch far more people.

3. Balancing individual liberty and social order is a major challenge in public order crimes.

4. More than most other crimes, public order offenses raise constitutional questions related to due process of law, and free speech and assembly.

5. Disorderly conduct covers a broad spectrum from public brawling to obscene phone calls.

6. Vagrancy is an old offense that often makes status rather than conduct a crime.

7. Vagrancy's constitutionality has been successfully challenged.

8. Suspicious loitering is an offense devised to meet objections to vagrancy, but it, too, has faced constitutional challenge.

9. Objections to public order offenses are made on three levels: constitutional, principles of criminal law, and criminal policy.

10. Public morals offenses are sexual contacts between consenting adults in private.

11. The public morals offenses, particularly prostitution and sodomy between consenting adults in private, have generated heated debate.

12. The arguments for and against criminal penalties for morals offenses are generally based on value considerations.

KEY TERMS

Fourteenth Amendment due process clause the provision that "no state shall deprive any citizen of life, liberty or property without due process of law."

balancing interests the act of securing social order while at the same time protecting individual liberty.

due process the constitutional requirement that statutes be clear enough to define in advance and notify citizens just what conduct is criminal.

void for overbreadth the standard by which statutes so broad that they include too much behavior are declared unconstitutional under the Fourteenth Amendment to the United States Constitution.

void for vagueness the standard by which certain statutes are said to violate the Fourteenth Amendment due process clause because they leave too much discretion to law enforcement officers.

☰ INTRODUCTION

Most crimes have specific, individual victims. Crimes against public order and morals do not. For the most part, to the extent that they harm at all, they injure society as a whole or the public generally. In a general sense, all crimes injure society as a whole. Forgery, for example, not only harms particular individuals who lost something of value but also injures society as a whole because it undermines confidence in the authenticity of documents.

In crimes where there exist specific harms to individuals—homicide, rape, assault, robbery, burglary, arson, and theft—the general harm to society rarely receives attention. This does not mean such crimes do not cause harm to society as a whole. Quite the contrary. Homicides, rapes, and other violent crimes produce personal insecurity that definitely injures society. Similarly, burglary erodes confidence that homes are safe havens from intruders. Theft and other property crimes create anger and frustration that others will lose hard-earned money. All these crimes erode the basic mutual trust required to make modern, complex society function. These general harms to society, subordinated in serious felonies, take precedence in crimes against public order and morals. Most public order offenses do not involve specific victims, nor are specific victims required in order to convict. To the extent that harm occurs, society as a whole is the victim.

Not everyone agrees that public order and morals offenses harm society as a whole, or if they do, that they warrant expending scarce public resources to bring the criminal law to bear on them. Critics say that only harms to specific individuals deserve criminal law's attention, not these "victimless crimes." Nevertheless, including public order and morals offenses in criminal law enjoys a long tradition. In fact, far more people face criminal prosecution for these crimes than for all the serious crimes receiving the most attention. In 1983, for example, the police made 2.4 million arrests for serious crime. They made about 5 million arrests for public-order-related offenses, or double the number of serious felony arrests.[1]

Public order and morals offenses include behavior that crosses a wide spectrum. So pervasive is the conduct these offenses cover that it is fair to say the offenses make "criminals of us all." They not only affect more people than the serious crimes but also raise serious constitutional questions. More broadly, they define the limits of individual freedom when it involves behavior that is offensive without being physically harmful. If society's value depends on how much autonomy its individual members possess, then the public order and morals offenses define society's value. The public order and morals offenses require special attention to **balancing interests**—that is, weighing individual liberty against social order. For these three reasons—their broad reach, the numbers they make criminal, and their relevance to individual freedom from government interference—the public order and morals offenses are important in criminal law.[2]

Public order and morals offenses have never received systematic attention by courts, legislatures, or even scholars for that matter. This lack is due to the relatively mild penalties prescribed for these offenses—mainly fines and ten- to ninety-day jail terms—and to the type of people usually prosecuted for them. Unfortunately, most who are prosecuted for public order and morals offenses are on the outer fringes of "respectable" society: the poor, the young, the minorities, and dissidents. Trials are rare, convictions are frequent, and appeals are virtually nonexistent. Since public order and morals offenders are not politically powerful, demands for reform and even claims for attention are largely ignored.[3]

The need to reform public order and morals law is, however, great. First, the law defines the offenses vaguely. What disorderly conduct, drunkenness, and vagrancy mean are not at all clear. They can cover almost any conduct that law enforcement officers consider a public nuisance or annoyance. Clearer definitions, better categories, and more guidance are all needed to improve public order criminal law.

Second, judges have virtually unlimited discretion to fine public order and morals offenders or send them to jail. More sensible grading according to better definitions can control and guide judicial discretion.

Third, civil liberties, especially the rights to assemble, to travel about freely, and to openly express diversity, even if it deviates from what respectable society deems proper public behavior, are all threatened under vaguely defined public order and morals crimes. Clearer definitions, proper categories, and controlled discretion give more force to constitutional rights in particular and to individual liberty in general.

Fourth, some public order and morals offenses are obsolete and probably unconstitutional. Most vagrancy statutes, for example, hark back to the sixteenth century. Many, in fact, copy exactly the Elizabethan vagrancy statutes. Such provisions lead to abuse.

Fifth, it is important to decide whether—and if so, to what extent—criminal law should include conduct that merely offends respectable people's sensibilities, as opposed to hurting such people physically.[4]

═══ Disorderly Conduct

For almost as long as English law has existed, it has prohibited and punished conduct that disturbed or threatened to disturb community tranquility. Present-day disorderly conduct statutes, which virtually every state and municipality have enacted, are the modern counterpart to this long-established common-law offense.

At common law, mere threats to public peace were crimes. Some jurisdictions have preserved this common-law rule in modern legislation. New York, California, and several other states, for example, make it a misdemeanor to willfully and wrongfully commit any act that seriously disturbs or endangers the public peace or health. Under these statutes, not only disturbing the peace but also endangering it is a crime. Thus, a man who solicited two young girls to commit sodomy was convicted under a New York statute because the court held that such an act threatened to disturb the public peace. Under a similar Kentucky statute, a man was convicted for calling another a "son-of-a-bitch" because his act tended to provoke a breach of the peace. In these jurisdictions, disorderly conduct encompasses both actual and potential breaches of public tranquility. It is, to that extent, an inchoate offense. Some modern legislation removes potential harms from coverage, including only conduct that itself disturbs the peace.[5]

Fighting, Threats, Violence, and Noisemaking

Behavior that is considered disorderly conduct covers a wide spectrum, including fighting, threats, profanity, and even noisemaking. Brawling in public and other violent behavior are relatively easy to define, but making noise is vague and can lead to abuse of discretion. In general, noises loud enough to disturb the public are considered criminal under existing laws. Hence, a sound truck that blares its loudspeakers in a quiet neighborhood at seven o'clock on Sunday morning falls clearly within disorderly conduct. But someone running through a neighborhood at the same time, calling out that a terrorist blew up a plane over the Atlantic Ocean, probably does not.

Besides brawling and making noise, nearly any mischief that imagination can create has fallen at one time or another under the disorderly conduct laws. This behavior includes making "stink bombs," lighting firecrackers on a highway, strewing garbage in an alley, and blinding motorists by shining searchlights into their windshields. (See the criminal law close-up entitled "Chicago City Ordinance.")

Many broadly and vaguely worded statutes prevent reasonable prediction of the conduct encompassed by disorderly conduct. This situation

Criminal Law Close-Up

CHICAGO CITY ORDINANCE

This ordinance has been called "the most charming grabbag of criminal prohibitions ever assembled."[1] Enacted in 1905, it was still in force in 1968.[2]

All persons who shall make, aid, countenance or assist in making any improper noise, riot, disturbance, breach of the peace or diversion tending to a breach of the peace, within the limits of the city; all persons who shall collect in bodies or crowds for unlawful purposes, or for any purpose, to the annoyance or disturbance of other persons; all persons who are idle or dissolute and go about begging; all persons who use or exercise any juggling or other unlawful games, all persons who are found in houses of ill-fame or gaming houses; all persons lodging in or found at any time in sheds, barns, stables, or unoccupied buildings, or lodging in the open air and not giving a good account of themselves; all persons who shall wilfully assault another in the city, or be engaged in, aid, abet in any fight, quarrel, or other disturbance in the city; all persons who stand, loiter, or stroll about in any place in the city, waiting or seeking to obtain money or other valuable things from others by trick or fraud, or to aid or assist therein; all persons that shall engage in any fraudulent scheme, device or trick to obtain money or other valuable thing in any place in the city, or who shall aid, abet, or in any manner be concerned therein; all touts, rapers, steerers, or cappers, so called, for any gambling room or house who shall ply or attempt to ply their calling on any public way in the city; all persons found loitering about any hotel, block barroom, dramshop, gambling house, or disorderly house, or wandering about the streets either by night or day without any known lawful means of support, or without being able to give a satisfactory account of themselves; all persons who shall have or carry any pistol, knife, dirk, knuckles, slingshot, or other dangerous weapon concealed on or about their persons; and all persons who are known to be narcotic addicts, thieves, burglars, pickpockets, robbers or confidence men, either by their own confession or otherwise, or by having been convicted of larceny, burglary, or other crime against the laws of the state, who are found lounging in, prowling, or loitering around any steamboat landing, railroad depot, banking institution, place of public amusement, auction room, hotel, store, shop, public way, public conveyance, public gathering, public assembly, court room, public building, private dwelling house, house of ill-fame, gambling house, or any public place, and who are unable to give

> a reasonable excuse for being so found, shall be deemed guilty of disorderly conduct, and upon conviction thereof, shall be severally fined not less than one dollar nor more than two hundred dollars for each offense.

1. *Laundry v. Daley,* 280 F.Supp. 968 (N.D.Ill., 1968).
2. Chicago, Illinois, *Municipal Code,* chap. 193, sec. 1 (1905).

permits police and judges too much discretion to define the behavior after the fact. Because of vagueness and breadth, people charged with disorderly conduct frequently challenge statutes' constitutionality. Most commonly, statutes are attacked on the ground that they violate the United States Constitution's **Fourteenth Amendment due process clause,** which provides that "no state shall deprive any citizen of life, liberty or property without due process of law." The courts interpret that clause to mean that statutes are void when they violate **due process** by being too vague (**void for vagueness**) or too broad (**void for overbreadth**) to convey in advance what conduct they aim to punish.

CASE

Was His Conduct Disorderly?

Thompson v. City of Louisville

362 U.S. 199 80 S.Ct. 624, 4 L.Ed.2d 654 (1960)

[Justice Black delivered the opinion.]

FACTS

Petitioner was found guilty in the Police Court of Louisville, Kentucky, of two offenses—loitering and disorderly conduct. The ultimate question presented to us is whether the charges against petitioner were so totally devoid of evidentiary support as to render his conviction unconstitutional under the Due Process Clause of the Fourteenth Amendment. Decision of this question turns not on the sufficiency of the evidence, but on whether this conviction rests upon any evidence at all.

The facts as shown by the record are short and simple. Petitioner, a long-time resident of the Louisville area, went into the Liberty End Cafe about 6:20 on Saturday evening, January 24, 1959. In addition to selling food the cafe was licensed to sell beer to the public and some

12 to 30 patrons were present during the time petitioner was there. When petitioner had been in the cafe about half an hour, two Louisville police officers came in on a "routine check." Upon seeing petitioner "out there on the floor dancing by himself," one of the officers, according to his testimony, went up to the manager who was sitting on a stool nearby and asked him how long petitioner had been in there and if he had bought anything. The officer testified that upon being told by the manager that petitioner had been there "a little over a half-hour and that he had not bought anything," he accosted Thompson and "asked him what was his reason for being in there and he said he was waiting on a bus." The officer then informed petitioner that he was under arrest and took him outside. This was the arrest for loitering. After going outside, the officer testified, petitioner "was very argumentative—he argued with us back and forth and so then we placed a disorderly conduct charge on him." Admittedly the disorderly conduct conviction rests solely on this one sentence description of petitioner's conduct after he left the cafe.

The foregoing evidence includes all that the city offered against him, except a record purportedly showing a total of 54 previous arrests of petitioner.

Petitioner then put in evidence on his own behalf, none of which in any way strengthened the city's case. He testified that he bought, and one of the cafe employees served him, a dish of macaroni and a glass of beer and that he remained in the cafe waiting for a bus to go home. Further evidence showed without dispute that at the time of his arrest petitioner gave the officers his home address; that he had money with him, and a bus schedule showing that a bus to his home would stop within half a block of the cafe at about 7:30; that he owned two unimproved lots of land; that in addition to work he had done for others, he had regularly worked one day or more a week for the same family for 30 years; that he paid no rent in the home where he lived and that his meager income was sufficient to meet his needs. The cafe manager testified that petitioner had frequently patronized the cafe, and that he had never told petitioner that he was unwelcome there. The manager further testified that on this very occasion he saw petitioner "standing there in the middle of the floor and patting his foot," and that he did not at any time during petitioner's stay there object to anything he was doing. There is no evidence that anyone else in the cafe objected to petitioner's shuffling his feet in rhythm with the music of the jukebox or that his conduct was boisterous or offensive to anyone present. At the close of his evidence, petitioner repeated his motion for dismissal of the charges on the ground that a conviction on the foregoing evidence would deprive him of liberty and property without due process under the Fourteenth Amendment. The court denied the motion, convicted him of both offenses, and fined him $10 on each charge. A motion for new trial, on the same grounds, also was denied, which exhausted petitioner's remedies in the police court.

OPINION

Our examination of the record presented in the petition for certiorari convinced us that although the fines here are small, the due process questions presented are substantial and we therefore granted certiorari to review the police court's judgments.

Petitioner's conviction for disorderly conduct was under § 85–8 of the city ordinance which, without definition, provides that "[w]hoever shall be found guilty of disorderly conduct in the City of Louisville shall be fined" etc. The only evidence of "disorderly conduct" was the single statement of the policeman that after petitioner was arrested and taken out of the cafe he was very argumentative. There is no testimony that petitioner raised his voice, used offensive language, resisted the officers or engaged in any conduct of any kind likely in any way to adversely affect the good order and tranquility of the City of Louisville. The only information the record contains on what the petitioner was "argumentative" about is his statement that he asked the officers "what they arrested me for." We assume, for we are justified in assuming, that merely "arguing" with a policeman is not, because it could not be, "disorderly conduct" as a matter of the substantive law of Kentucky. Moreover, Kentucky law itself seems to provide that if a man wrongfully arrested fails to object to the arresting officer, he waives any right to complain later that the arrest was unlawful.

Thus we find no evidence whatever in the record to support these convictions. Just as "Conviction upon a charge not made would be sheer denial of due process," so is it a violation of due process to convict and punish a man without evidence of his guilt.

The judgments are reversed and the cause is remanded to the Police Court of the City of Louisville for proceedings not inconsistent with this opinion.

Reversed and remanded.

CASE DISCUSSION

Thompson raises the common constitutional objection to disorderly conduct statutes—that they are too vague and broad to satisfy due process. Do you think this case bears out the fear that police and judges abuse their discretion in disorderly conduct statutes? If Thompson's conduct was disorderly, who sets the standard for what conduct qualifies as disorderly? Was the disorderly conduct arrest and charge an excuse? If so, for what was it an excuse? Was Thompson arrested for what he did or for who he was? Review chapter 3 on status, and compare Thompson with Papachristou later in this chapter. Why did Thompson appeal so minor an offense to the Supreme Court? Are cases like these wasting the Court's time?

Coarse and Indecent Language and Gestures

Fighting, violent behavior, and, to a lesser extent, making noise all can create physical discomfort among the general public. Disorderly conduct, however, includes not only actions causing physical discomfort but also actions that could offend public sensibilities—such as coarse and indecent language and gestures.

Statutes variously characterize language and gestures as disorderly when they are "abusive," "unnecessarily insulting," "vulgar," "unseemly," "offensive," "rude," or "obscene." In some jurisdictions, language tending to disturb suffices; other jurisdictions require that the language itself disturb. Even with the latter restriction, coarse and indecent language statutes cause problems. In the first place, vague words lead to abuse of discretion. Rarely do statutes clarify whether merely profane language qualifies or whether obscenity is also required. Equally important, most statutes raise serious speech questions, particularly in cases involving unpopular but not necessarily offensive language or gestures. For example, calling the president of the United States a "Baptist bullshit artist" may be offensive and rude, and such coarse language may indeed offend the public. Nevertheless, the right to state an opinion about a political leader outweighs the discomfort to the public that such an utterance creates.

Statutes that restrict offensive language to words that are disturbing in themselves do not eliminate vagueness, abuse, and possible free speech violations. Limiting the offense to clearly offensive sexual, scatological, or threatening words and excluding words that harbor unacceptable political or religious connotations does not satisfy critics. For example, music that arouses passions that might lead to violence—whether suicide or other— is clearly offensive. Nonetheless, critics maintain that restrictions on such music infringe on free speech. Therefore, they recommend excluding offensive language and gestures entirely from criminal law.

CASE

Was His Obscene Phone Call Constitutionally Protected?

State v. Hagen

27 Ariz. App. 722, 558 P.2d 750 (1976)

[Hagen was convicted of using obscene and lewd language on the telephone and was sentenced to one year of probation. He appealed. Judge Wren delivered the opinion.]

FACTS

A.R.S. § 13–895A provides:

> A. It shall be unlawful for any person, with intent to terrify, intimidate, threaten, harass, annoy or offend, to telephone another and use any obscene, lewd or profane language or suggest any lewd or lascivious act, or threaten to inflict injury or physical harm to the person or property of any person. It shall also be unlawful to attempt to extort money or other thing of value from any person, or to otherwise disturb by repeated anonymous telephone calls the peace, quiet or right of privacy of any person at the place where the telephone call or calls were received.

The facts disclose that on or about the 19th day of March, 1975, appellant telephoned a Phoenix police officer and used obscene, lewd and profane language. Specifically he expressed a desire to engage in an act of sodomy with the Phoenix Chief of Police.

OPINION

Appellant's assertion that the statute is unconstitutionally void for vagueness was disposed of by this court in *Baker v. State*, (1972), wherein the same contention was turned aside. One whose conduct is clearly proscribed by the terms of a statute may not successfully challenge it for vagueness. Here the crime and the elements comprising it are expressly set forth, and a reasonable person would not be left to speculate as to the type of activity prohibited.

Appellant also claims overbroadness because the wording of A.R.S. § 13–895A is equally applicable to constitutionally protected speech. Again we disagree.

The state has a legitimate interest in prohibiting obscene, threatening, or harassing phone calls, none of which are generally thought of as protected by the First Amendment.

> [T]he intrusion into the home by means of telecommunications of those individuals who intend to terrify, harass, annoy and abuse the listener by means of the language proscribed by the statute.
>
> A resort to epithets of personal abuse is not in any proper sense communication of information or opinion safeguarded by the Constitution, and its punishment as a criminal act raises no constitutional question.

By specifying the intent with which the call must be made and the nature of the language prohibited, the statute clearly demonstrates that the prohibited activities find no protection under the First Amendment.

Such activities [are] not "an exercise of rights but rather [were] an abuse of rights and [entailed] a gross lack of understanding—or calloused indifference—to the simple fact that the offended parties also [had] certain rights under the same Constitution." supra at 332, 475 P.2d at 946.

We cannot conceive that the State is abridging anyone's First Amendment freedom by prohibiting telephone calls that are "obscene, lewd or profane" or that threaten physical harm, provided such calls are made with the intent specified in the statute.

Judgment and sentence affirmed.

CASE DISCUSSION

The court makes clear that the Constitution does not protect all speech. Obscene phone calls are speech that the Constitution does not protect. In fact, the court goes further, concluding that Hagen's phone call violated his victim's rights. What reasons can you give for ruling that the Arizona statute on obscene telephone calls is constitutional? Are your reasons the same as the court's? What public interest does such a statute protect? Is it public order? personal privacy? In what sense does it protect both?

Fighting Words

The First Amendment does not protect fighting words because they provoke violence, or at least threaten to do so. Making fighting words a crime punishes potential harm, as opposed to actual harm, thereby violating the basic principle that criminal law punishes people for harms they have already perpetrated, not harms they might provoke. Moreover, fighting words raise constitutional questions. Balancing the need for public order with the constitutional right to free speech is the crucial issue in fighting words cases, just as balancing public peace and tranquility against individual liberty overall is the issue in public order offenses generally. Determining whether statutes that criminalize offensive speech are constitutional to the extent they refer to fighting words is a major problem that courts face.[6]

Altercations with Police

Cases that involve fighting words in altercations between citizens and police require balancing public order with individual freedom. In addition, police officers enjoy wide discretion; in altercations with citizens, judges tend to favor what police say happened during them. As a result, convictions can lead more from offending a particular officer's sensibilities than from actual or threatened public disorder. This situation breeds resentment toward law enforcement, a condition likely to cause public disorder.[7]

Furthermore, police officers, simply by virtue of carrying out their lawful duties, provoke at least annoyance, and even outrage. For example, despite its lawfulness, arresting an innocent person usually makes the arrested person angry. Should this "typical" citizen resentment constitute a crime because it offends a police officer? Rather than oppose such reactions and, by doing so, trench on personal liberty, some experts contend that the better solution is to teach officers to withstand some rudeness without making an arrest. In *Lewis v. City of New Orleans,* Justice Powell wrote the following concerning this matter:

> A properly trained officer may reasonably be expected to "exercise a higher degree of restraint" than the average citizen, and thus be less likely to respond belligerently to "fighting words."[8]

Others disagree, arguing that the police are entitled to protection against abusive language and that permitting citizens to verbally abuse police affronts public order and decency.[9]

CASE

Were They Fighting Words?

In the Matter of the Welfare of S.L.J.

263 N.W.2d 412 (Minn. 1978)

[The juvenile court found S.L.J. delinquent for disorderly conduct. The order was appealed. Justice Rogosheske delivered the opinion.]

FACTS

On August 13, 1975, at about 9:30 P.M., appellant, S.L.J., a 14-year-old girl, and her friend of the same age were questioned by two police officers who had just apprehended some teenage boys for paint sniffing. Based only on a hunch that the girls were somehow involved in either the original crime or the taking of the boys' bicycles, they were questioned about the whereabouts of the bicycles, the identities of the apprehended boys, and their own identities. According to appellant's testimony, Officer Anderson, one of the officers involved, also threatened to take them to the police station and then informed them that they had better hurry home because it was past their curfew.

After starting down the alley, appellant and her friend, at a point somewhere between 15 and 30 feet from the squad car in which the officers were sitting, turned and said to them "fuck you pigs." The officers conferred and then pursued the girls down the alley and arrested them for disorderly conduct under § 609.72, subd. 1, which reads as follows:

> Whoever does any of the following in a public or private place, knowing, or having reasonable grounds to know that it will, or will tend to, alarm, anger or disturb others or provoke an assault or breach of the peace, is guilty of disorderly conduct, which is a misdemeanor:
>
> (1) Engages in brawling or fighting; or

(2) Disturbs an assembly or meeting, not unlawful in its character; or

(3) Engages in offensive, obscene, or abusive language or in boisterous and noisy conduct tending reasonably to arouse alarm, anger, or resentment in others.

A petition was filed in juvenile court alleging that appellant was a delinquent person because she—

did wrongfully and unlawfully engage in offensive, obscene or abusive language at Greenbrier and Case Sts., a public place, knowing or having reasonable grounds to know that such conduct would or would tend to arouse resentment in others.

At the trial before a referee of juvenile court, Officer Anderson testified that he was "mad" and "upset" at the words used by the girls:

I was mad. I was upset. They didn't have any right to say that to me. One of the thoughts that went through my head, I have a daughter four years younger. Should my daughter say something like that to an officer or anybody I'd be upset and ashamed as a parent. It would bother me.

During cross-examination, Officer Anderson admitted that he had received some sensitivity training on how to respond to name calling, and that, although angry, he did not react violently in this case or even consider such behavior because of the speaker's age, sex, and relative size. Appellant testified that she was upset by the officers' questions, but that she had not expected them to react to her remark.

The matter was continued to permit the parties to submit briefs on the constitutionality of the statute. After a hearing, the referee found that appellant was a delinquent. The juvenile court, in confirming this finding of delinquency, credited the testimony of the police officer over that of the child and concluded that the officer had suffered "resentment," a conclusion that is binding on this court unless clearly erroneous.

OPINION

The issues presented for decision in this appeal are: (1) Whether § 609.72, subd. 1(3), is unconstitutionally overly broad or vague on its face under the First and Fourteenth Amendments of the United States Constitution; (2) whether the statute can be narrowly construed to sustain its constitutionality; and (3) whether the evidence supports appellant's conviction for disorderly conduct under the statute as narrowly construed.

Whenever offensive language is the basis of a criminal charge, the court must determine whether that language is protected speech under the First and Fourteenth Amendments of the United States Constitution.

The fact that the words used by appellant are vulgar, offensive, and insulting, and that their use is condemned by an overwhelming majority of citizens does not make them punishable under the criminal statutes of this state unless they fall outside the protection afforded to speech by the First Amendment.

To be a constitutional exercise of the police power of the state, a statute that punishes speech must be neither overly broad nor unduly vague. The United States Supreme Court has more vigilantly scrutinized statutes that regulate speech than those that control only conduct because vague and overly broad statutes threaten both to ensnare the unwary who are not provided with fair notice of what behavior is prohibited and to curtail protected speech by those fearful of violating the law. Thus, the court has required statutes proscribing speech alone to be more narrowly and specifically drawn.

In general, a statute can be said to be overly broad if it deters the exercise of First Amendment rights by unnecessarily punishing constitutionally protected along with unprotected activity.

Ever since *Chaplinsky v. New Hampshire*, 315 U.S. 568, (1942), in which the Supreme Court examined a First Amendment challenge to a New Hampshire statute which prohibited the use of "offensive, derisive or annoying" language in a public place, such offensive speech statutes have been found to be constitutional only if criminal prosecution is permitted solely for "fighting words."

"Fighting words" have been defined as those "personally abusive epithets which, when addressed to the ordinary citizen, are, as a matter of common knowledge, inherently likely to provoke violent reaction," or "[words] which by their very utterance inflict injury or tend to incite an immediate breach of the peace." Words that do not fit this definition, no matter how offensive they may be, are not subject to criminal sanctions; and, if the statute being scrutinized punishes more than "fighting words," it must either be struck down as facially overbroad or, if possible, construed narrowly to make it constitutional.

Turning to the language of the statute, it is clear that, as written, § 609.72, subd. 1(3), is both overly broad and vague. Since the statute punishes words alone—"offensive, obscene, or abusive language"—, it must be declared unconstitutional as a violation of the First and Fourteenth Amendments unless it only proscribes the use of "fighting words." Section 609.72, subd. 1(3), however, punishes words that merely tend to "arouse alarm, anger, or resentment in others" rather than only words "which by their very utterance inflict injury or tend to incite an immediate breach of the peace." Since the statute does not satisfy the definition of "fighting words," it is unconstitutional on its face.

Although § 609.72, subd. 1(3), clearly contemplates punishment for speech that is protected under the First and Fourteenth Amendments, we can uphold its constitutionality by construing it narrowly to refer only to "fighting words."

Having narrowly construed § 609.72, subd. 1(3), we must now determine whether the words "fuck you pigs" were "fighting words." The real test is whether, under the facts and circumstances of this case, appellant's mere utterance of these vulgar, offensive, insulting words would "tend to incite an immediate breach of the peace," are "inherently likely to provoke violent reaction," or "hav[e] an immediate tendency to provoke retaliatory violence or tumultuous conduct by those to whom such words are addressed." The specific facts of the case are also important because whether words are "fighting words" depends on the circumstances surrounding their utterance.

Under this test, appellant's conviction for disorderly conduct cannot stand. While it is true that no ordered society would condone the vulgar language used by this 14-year-old child, and as the court found, her words were intended to, and did, arouse resentment in the officers, the constitution requires more before a person can be convicted for mere speech. In this case, the words were directed at two police officers sitting in their squad car from a distance of 15 to 30 feet by a small, 14-year-old child who was on her way home when she turned to the officers and made her statement. With the words spoken in retreat from more than 15 feet away rather than eye-to-eye, there was no reasonable likelihood that they would tend to incite an immediate breach of the peace or to provoke violent reaction by an ordinary, reasonable person. Thus, the state has failed to prove that under these circumstances the words uttered by appellant were "fighting words," and both her conviction for disorderly conduct and the finding of delinquency based on the conviction must be reversed.

Reversed.

CASE DISCUSSION

The court ruled that the Constitution does not protect fighting words and interpreted the Minnesota statute narrowly to cover them. Does the court's interpretation fairly read the statute's true meaning? What did the legislature mean when it enacted section 609.72? Do you think S.L.J.'s comment was criminal? If so, why? And how would you punish her for her remark? What is the difference between what she said and fighting words? Is this case really any of the criminal law's business, or is there a more appropriate way to deal with this problem? If there is a better way, what is it?

In *City of Houston v. Hill,* the United States Supreme Court addressed a similar problem that arose over verbal abuse of a Houston police officer. The Court came to the opposite conclusion that the Minnesota court reached in *In the Matter of the Welfare of S.L.J.*

CASE

Did His Verbal Abuse Constitute Free Speech?

City of Houston v. Hill
482 U.S. 578 (1987)

[Justice Brennan delivered the opinion of the Court, in which Justices White, Marshall, Blackmun, and Stevens joined. Justice Blackmun filed a concurring opinion. Justice Scalia filed an opinion concurring in the judgment. Justice Powell filed an opinion concurring in the judgment in part and dissenting in part, in which Justice O'Connor joined. Chief Justice Rehnquist filed a dissenting opinion.]

FACTS

. . . Raymond Wayne Hill is a lifelong resident of Houston, Texas. At the time this lawsuit began, he worked as a paralegal and as executive director of the Houston Human Rights League. A member of the Board of the Gay Political Caucus, which he helped found in 1975, Hill was also affiliated with a Houston radio station, and had carried city and county passes since 1975. He lived in Montrose, a "diverse and eclectic neighborhood" that is the center of gay political and social life in Houston.

The incident that sparked this lawsuit occurred in the Montrose area on February 14, 1982. Hill observed a friend, Charles Hill, intentionally stopping traffic on a busy street, evidently to enable a vehicle to enter traffic. Two Houston police officers, one of whom was named Kelley, approached Charles and began speaking with him. According to the District Court, "shortly thereafter" Hill began shouting at the officers "in an admitted attempt to divert Kelley's attention from Charles Hill."[a] Hill first shouted, "Why don't you pick on somebody your own size?" "[A]re you interrupting me in my official capacity as a Houston police officer?" Hill then shouted, "Yes, why don't you pick on someone your own size?" Hill was arrested under Houston Municipal Code § 34–11(a), [which provides that it "shall be unlawful for any person to assault, strike, or in any manner oppose, molest, abuse or interrupt any policeman in the execution of his duty, or any person summoned to aid in making an arrest"]. Charles Hill was not arrested. Hill was then acquitted after a nonjury trial in Municipal Court. . . .

Following his acquittal in the Charles Hill incident, Hill brought suit in Federal District Court for the Southern District of Texas seeking (1) a declaratory judgment that § 34–11(a) was unconstitutional both on its face and as it had been applied to him. . . .

The District Court held . . . that the ordinance was [not] unconstitutionally vague or overbroad . . . because "the ordinance does not . . . proscribe speech or conduct which is protected by the First Amendment." A panel of the Court of Appeals reversed, [holding that while the ordinance was not vague because it "plainly encompassed mere verbal as well as physical conduct," it was overbroad because "a significant range of protected speech and expression is punishable and might be deterred by the literal wording of the statute"]. . . .

The City appealed, claiming that the Court of Appeals erred in holding the ordinance overbroad. . . . We noted probable jurisdiction, and now affirm.

OPINION

. . . The City's principal argument is that the ordinance does not inhibit the exposition of ideas, and that it bans "core criminal conduct" not protected by the First Amendment. In its view, the application of the ordinance to Hill illustrates that the police employ it only to prohibit such conduct, and not "as a subterfuge to control or dissuade free expression." Since the ordinance is "content-neutral," and since there is no evidence that the City has applied the ordinance to chill particular speakers or ideas, the City concludes that the ordinance is not substantially overbroad.

We disagree with the City's characterization for several reasons. First, the enforceable portion of the ordinance deals not with core criminal conduct, but with speech. . . . [T]he enforceable portion of the ordinance makes it "unlawful for any person to . . . in any manner oppose, molest, abuse or interrupt any policeman in the execution of his duty," and thereby prohibits verbal interruptions of police officers.

Second, contrary to the City's contention, the First Amendment protects a significant amount of verbal criticism and challenge directed at police officers. "Speech is often provocative and challenging. . . . But it is nevertheless protected against censorship or punishment, unless shown likely to produce a clear and present danger annoyance, or unrest." In *Lewis v. City of New Orleans*, the appellant was found to have yelled obscenities and threats at an officer who had asked appellant's husband to produce his driver's license. Appellant was convicted under a municipal ordinance that made it a crime "for any person wantonly to curse or revile or to use obscene or opprobrious language toward or with reference to any member of the city police while in the actual performance of his duty." We vacated the conviction and invalidated the ordinance as facially overbroad. . . .

The Houston ordinance is much more sweeping than the municipal ordinance struck down in *Lewis*. It is not limited to fighting words nor even to obscene or opprobrious language, but prohibits speech that "in any manner . . . interrupts" an officer. The Constitution does not allow such speech to be made a crime. The freedom of individuals to verbally oppose or challenge police action without thereby risking arrest is one of the principal characteristics by which we distinguish a free nation from a police state. . . .

The City argues, however, that even if the ordinance encompasses some protected speech, its sweeping nature is both inevitable and essential to maintain public order. . . . This Houston ordinance, however, is not narrowly tailored to prohibit only disorderly conduct or fighting words. . . . Although we appreciate the difficulties in drafting precise laws, we have repeatedly invalidated laws that provide the police with unfettered discretion to arrest individuals for words or conduct that annoy or offend them. . . .

Houston's ordinance criminalizes a substantial amount of constitutionally protected speech, and accords the police unconstitutional discretion in enforcement. The ordinance's plain language is admittedly violated scores of times daily, yet only some individuals—those chosen by the police in their unguided discretion—are arrested. . . . We conclude that the ordinance is substantially overbroad. . . .

Today's decision reflects the constitutional requirement that, in the face of verbal challenges to police action, officers and municipalities must respond to the restraint. We are mindful that the preservation of liberty depends in part upon the maintenance of public order. But the first amendment recognizes, wisely we think, that a certain amount of expressive disorder not only is inevitable in a society committed to individual freedom, but must itself be protected if that freedom would survive. We therefore affirm the judgment of the Court of Appeals.

It is so ordered.

CASE DISCUSSION

In what ways does this case differ from *In the Matter of the Welfare of S.L.J.*, the previous case? Why should the Constitution protect Hill's speech here, and not S.L.J.'s speech? Do you agree that police officers—and society—have to put up with "a certain amount of expressive disorder"? Both *In the Matter of the Welfare of S.L.J.* and *City of Houston v. Hill* demonstrate difficulty in writing disorderly conduct laws that maintain public order without unduly restricting individual free speech. Did Hill commit a more serious offense than S.L.J.?

---

a. Hill testified that his "motivation was to stop [the officers] from hitting Charles." He also explained that "I would rather that I get arrested than those whose careers can be damaged; I would rather that I get arrested than those whose families wouldn't understand; I would rather that I get arrested than those who couldn't spend a long time in jail. I am prepared to respond in any legal nonaggressive or nonviolent way, to any illegal police activity, at any time, under any circumstances."

Threats

Both verbal and physical threats that create public inconvenience, annoyance, or alarm constitute a crime in most jurisdictions. Threatening is akin to but broader than assault. Assault protects against individual fear of serious bodily injury; threatening, a misdemeanor, aims to keep public order.[10]

CASE

Was His Threat Constitutional?

Thomas v. Commonwealth

574 S.W.2d 903 (Ky. App. 1978)

[Thomas was convicted of terroristic threatening, a gross misdemeanor, and was sentenced to twelve months in the county jail. Judge Hayes delivered the opinion.]

FACTS

The case for the Commonwealth was based solely on the testimony of Gladys Thomas. Mrs. Thomas on direct examination stated that on the Friday before she went to swear out the warrant that she was in her front yard cutting weeds with a butcher knife when appellant came out of the house, hit her across the back with his hand, laughed and ran into a barber shop next door. Appellant then came back laughing and hit her across the back with a belt and then ran into a liquor store about three doors down from the house. Appellant continued to aggravate Mrs. Thomas until she asked him to go and get her a coke.

Mrs. Thomas then testified thusly:

> So, we went about an hour, an hour and a half after my mom left and he came in and said, "I told you to get ready to go," and I said, "I'm not going," and he grabbed me by the hair of the head and threw me against the refrigerator and said, "you are going or I will kill you and prove self-defense. This is one time everything is on my side. So, just get dressed and let's go somewhere and show everybody what a happy family we are."

Next, Mrs. Thomas gave testimony concerning the circumstances surrounding the threat which is the basis for the charge against appellant:

So, on Wednesday, he came in and he said, "I will come home. I'm coming home." I said, "you can't. You absolutely cannot. I went and applied for welfare," and he said, "I have to tell the man, Mr. Clark, that I'm here or I'll be in trouble." One thing led to another and he jumped up in the middle of the floor and said, "you and Brenda have got me against the wall. You're going to get me in trouble. I will cut both your heads off before I go back." Those are almost the exact words. And I looked around and the little girl was standing right in the screen door.

On cross-examination, Mrs. Thomas testified that this threat was made in the late afternoon and that on the next morning, on July 15, 1976, she went and got a warrant.

KRS 508.080 provides thusly:

(1) A person is guilty of terroristic threatening when:
(a) He threatens to commit any crime likely to result in death or serious physical injury to another person or likely to result in substantial property damage to another person; or
(b) He intentionally makes false statements for the purpose of causing evacuation of a building, place of assembly, or facility of public transportation.
(c) Terroristic threatening is a Class A misdemeanor. (Enact. Acts 1974, ch. 405, § 72.)

OPINION

This court believes that KRS 508.080(1)(a) is not unconstitutionally vague and overbroad since the conduct proscribed, "threaten[ing] to commit a crime likely to result in death or serious physical injury" is not protected under either the Kentucky or United States Constitutions. Further, the language of the statute is sufficiently explicit to put the average citizen on notice as to the nature of the conduct so proscribed.

This court is aware of the recent decision in U.S. v. Sturgill, 563 F.2d 307 (6th Cir. 1977), which invalidated KRS 525.070(1)(b) on the basis that it was unconstitutionally overbroad. KRS 525.070(1)(b) provides: "A person is guilty of harassment when with intent to harass, annoy or alarm another person he: (b) In a public place, makes an offensively coarse utterance, gesture or display, or addresses abusive language to any person present."

In Sturgill, the court, citing Gooding v. Wilson, 405 U.S. 518, 92 S.Ct. 1103, 31 L.Ed.2d 408 (1972), held that in order for a statute, which punishes spoken words only, to withstand an attack on its constitutionality; it must be first authoritatively interpreted by the state courts as not interfering with speech protected by the First Amendment.

This case can be distinguished from Sturgill, in that the language so proscribed under KRS 508.080(1)(a) is clearly without constitutional protection under the First Amendment.

. . . [A]ppellant's assertion that the statute is defective because it does not require the defendant's threat to be serious or that it does not require an intent to actually convey a serious threat is ludicrous.

When the unlawful threat is knowingly and wilfully made, the offense is complete, so that the existence of an intention to carry out the threat, or a subsequent abandonment of the bad intent with which the threat was made, is immaterial. Although idle talk or jesting will not constitute the crime, the accused cannot be regarded as having used his language only as a joke because of the fact that he may have had no intention to carry out his threat. The motive which prompts the utterance of a threat is immaterial. To bring a case within the statute no evil purpose or malice is requisite other than an intention to give utterance to words which to the accused's knowledge were in the form of, and would be naturally understood by the hearers, as being a threat.

Certainly, KRS 508.080(1)(a) does not apply in the case of idle talk or jesting. The defendant's intent to commit the crime of "terroristic threatening" can be plainly inferred from the defendant's own words and the circumstances surrounding them. All the statute requires is that the defendant threaten "to commit any crime likely to result in death or serious physical injury to another person or likely to result in substantial property damage to another person."

Affirmed.

CASE DISCUSSION

Notice that Thomas's threat constituted the offense, not his ability or willingness to carry it out. Therefore, it is not assault, a more serious crime, from which threatening should be distinguished. The court says that Thomas was not idly jesting but was serious when he threatened his wife. Do you agree? Thomas said, and some friends testified, that when he slapped his wife's back, he was only "horse-playing." The court admitted that a Kentucky harassment statute that made it a crime to use coarse or abusive language or gestures in order to harass, annoy, or alarm another person was unconstitutionally vague. It went on to say that the threatening statute was different. Do you agree that threatening and harassment are distinguishable? How serious an offense is threatening? Should harassment be a crime as well? How serious is it?

Rioting and Other Group Disorderly Conduct

From at least the mid-sixteenth century, English law punished three forms of group disorderly conduct: (1) unlawful assembly (three or more people gathered for an unlawful purpose); (2) rout (any movement toward completing the unlawful purpose); and (3) riot (the unlawful act in which unlawful assemblies and routs culminated). The famous Riot Act of 1714 made riot a felony if twelve or more persons rioted and failed to disperse within one hour following a warning to do so. The warning of "reading the riot act" has come down to modern times as an informal warning to calm down.

Today, all jurisdictions punish rioting and unlawful assembly. Most modern statutes follow the old practice, making unlawful assemblies, routs, and riots misdemeanors, with maximum penalties ranging from six months to a year in jail. Aggravated rioting provisions make it a felony to carry weapons or obstruct police officers during riots.

During the 1960s and early 1970s, critics charged that modern riot legislation violated the United States Constitution. Rout, unlawful assembly, and riot violated the due process clause because they were both vague and overbroad. Courts have not sustained these charges, however. In fact, several United States Supreme Court opinions have upheld such legislation despite Justice Hugo Black's observation that the Bill of Rights was intended specifically to prevent the encroachments on free expression inherent in English riot legislation. Some critics maintain that even if modern riot legislation is constitutional, the legislation furthers an unwise public policy. They say that inchoate offense and disorderly conduct laws deal adequately with riot, and riot needs no further special legislation. Anything more poses too great a threat to individual autonomy. Defenders maintain that our modern, pluralistic society requires special legislation to condemn and punish group disorderly conduct in order to preserve order.

The use of, and debate over, group disorderly conduct ebbs and flows according to the temper of the times. For example, riot, rout, and unlawful assembly provisions were frequently used and hotly debated during the 1960s, as they had been in earlier troubled times. When times are freer from openly expressed discontent, as were the more placid 1950s, both the use of those provisions and the debate surrounding them subside. The similarly placid 1980s have not called group conduct activity into question. However, controversies over abortion, CIA (Central Intelligence Agency) recruitment on college and university campuses, and the purveying of pornography in some cities indicate that group disorderly conduct law remains relevant.

Fomenting Group Hatred

Fomenting group hatred also ebbs and flows with currents in society. For a long time, both civil law and criminal law have used libel and slander laws to protect individuals from character defamation. Most of this legislation remains intact today. However, some law reformers believe that a more general harm to the community results when racial, religious, national, gender, or other groups are defamed. These reformers argue that criminal law ought to protect the social cohesion that a healthy, diverse society needs in order to function smoothly and that is damaged by fomenting group hatred.

Disorderly Conduct Mens Rea

Disorderly conduct *mens rea* ranges across a wide spectrum. Some statutes do not mention *mens rea*, reading merely "whoever disturbs the peace." Other statutes apply only to "foreseeable" disturbances, implying negligence. Still others require "knowing" or "intentional" disturbances. Legislation is confused on the point and often reflects no clear policy. The Model Penal Code covers only "purposeful" disorderly conduct. This provision reflects concern that disorderly conduct laws, especially broadly drawn ones, threaten to abuse civil liberties and equal protection. By restricting liability to only the most culpable, it implements a policy to protect individual rights in disorderly conduct statutes.

≡ VAGRANCY

Vagrancy is an old offense. In medieval times, feudal lords used vagrancy law to keep their serfs from wandering away. After the Black Death killed over a third of the English laborers in the 1300s, vagrancy laws were used to force surviving laborers to remain with their present employers. To enforce the law, wandering about without proof of employment was made a crime punishable summarily (that is, without a trial).

To give alms to "sturdy beggars" was also a crime. Early on, the "impotent poor" (those who could not work) were distinguished sharply from the "sturdy poor" (those who would not work). Poor persons who could, but would not, work were vagrants and, therefore, criminals. The impotent poor were publicly supported as long as they did not leave their own neighborhoods. The assumption was that most poor people were able to work but would not. Only a few were too impotent to work.

The 1714 English Vagrancy Act governed colonial America and was in force at the American Revolution. Most subsequent legislation followed it closely. The statute established three vagrant categories: idle and disorderly persons, rogues and vagabonds, and incorrigible rogues. In some form, those categories still exist in modern legislation.

Personal Condition—the Vagrancy Actus Reus

Most crimes are defined as acts or omissions, applying the general principle that criminal liability rest on conduct, not status. Vagrancy accords with this principle if it means "to wander about." However, many vagrancy offenses are not acts or omissions at all; they are conditions, or statuses. In other words, the crime does not require doing or failing to do something. Rather, being an undesirable (according to lawmakers) person becomes the crime. (See the criminal law close-up entitled "Vagrancy's Broad Reach.")

One judge summed up vagrancy this way:

> Vagrancy differs from most other offenses in the fact that it is chronic rather than acute; that it continues after it is complete, and thereby subjects the offender to arrest any time before he reforms.[11]

Criminal Law Close-Up

VAGRANCY'S BROAD REACH

The Model Penal Code Reporter compiled the following most common vagrancy types from legislation still in force in 1961.[1]

1. Living in idleness without employment or visible means of support
2. Common prostitute
3. Common drunkard
4. Common gambler
5. Keeper of house of prostitution
6. Keeper of house of gambling
7. Wanton, dissolute, or lascivious persons
8. Associate of known thieves
9. Roaming, wandering, and loitering
10. Begging
11. Failure to support a family
12. Sleeping outdoors

1. American Law Institute Model Penal Code, tentative draft no. 13 (1961), 61.

Purposes of Modern Vagrancy Law

Modern vagrancy laws are not directly or predominantly intended to force the idle in our society to work or the roamers and wanderers to settle down. Few question, however, that their subsidiary or ancillary purpose is to make "irresponsible" and "unrespectable" persons "responsible" and "respectable." In addition, vagrancy laws are supported to prevent crime. According to one judge,

> [t]he principle exemplified in vagrancy statutes presupposes a criminal status, not due to the perpetration of a specific offense, presently or in the past, but rather by reason of an intent, sufficiently manifested by overt acts, to commit offenses [in the future].[12]

Vagrancy arrests permit the police to move "undesirables" to another community. In a typical case, unwelcome "potential criminals" are warned to leave town within a short time or face vagrancy charges. Such harassment has a long tradition in Anglo-American law. In the sixteenth century, a famous justice of the peace regularly charged grand juries that they "nip the weed of crime in the bud by rounding up vagrants and harrying them out of the community, thereby leaving society a healthy garden."[13]

The United States Supreme Court addressed the constitutionality of vagrancy statutes in *Papachristou et al. v. City of Jacksonville.*

CASE

Were They Vagrants or Job Seekers?

Papachristou et al. v. City of Jacksonville

405 U.S. 156, 92 S.Ct. 839, 31 L.Ed.2d 110 (1972)

[This case involved eight defendants who were convicted under Jacksonville, Florida's, vagrancy ordinance. Only Jimmy Lee Smith and Milton Henry's appeal is included here. Papachristou was one of the other defendants. Justice Douglas delivered the opinion. All members joined except Justices Powell and Rehnquist, who took no part.]

FACTS

Jacksonville Ordinance Code § 26–57 provided at the time of these arrests and convictions as follows:

> Rogues and vagabonds, or dissolute persons who go about begging, common gamblers, persons who use juggling or unlawful games or plays, common drunkards, common night walkers, thieves, pilferers or pickpockets, traders in stolen property, lewd, wanton and lascivious persons, keepers of gambling places, common railers and brawlers, persons wandering or strolling around from place to place without any lawful purpose or object, habitual loafers, disorderly persons, persons neglecting all lawful business and habitually spending their time by frequenting houses of ill fame, gaming houses, or places where alcoholic beverages are sold or served, persons able to work but habitually living upon the earnings of their wives or minor children shall be deemed vagrants and, upon conviction in the Municipal Court shall be punished as provided for Class D offenses.

Class D offenses at the time of these arrests and convictions were punishable by 90 days' imprisonment, $500 fine, or both. Jacksonville Ordinance Code § 1–8 (1965).

Jimmy Lee Smith and Milton Henry (who is not a petitioner) were arrested between 9 and 10 A.M. on a weekday in downtown Jacksonville, while waiting for a friend who was to lend them a car so they could apply for a job at a produce company. Smith was a part-time produce worker and part-time organizer for a Negro political group. He had a common-law wife and three children supported by him and his wife. He had been arrested several times but convicted only once. Smith's companion, Henry, was an 18-year-old high school student with no previous record of arrest.

This morning it was cold, and Smith had no jacket, so they went briefly into a dry cleaning shop to wait, but left when requested to do so. They thereafter walked back and forth two or three times over a two-block stretch looking for their friend. The store owners, who apparently were wary of Smith and his companion, summoned two police officers who searched the men and found neither had a weapon. But they were arrested because the officers said they had no identification and because the officers did not believe their story.

OPINION

This ordinance is void for vagueness, both in the sense that it "fails to give a person of ordinary intelligence fair notice that his contemplated conduct is forbidden by the statute," and because it encourages arbitrary and erratic arrests and convictions.

Living under a rule of law entails various suppositions, one of these is that "[all persons] are entitled to be informed as to what the State commands or forbids."

The poor among us, the minorities, the average householder are not in business and not alerted to the regulatory schemes of vagrancy laws; and we assume they would have no understanding of their meaning and impact if they read them. Nor are they protected from being caught in the vagrancy net by the necessity of having a specific intent to commit an unlawful act.

The Jacksonville ordinance makes criminal activities which by modern standards are normally innocent. "Nightwalking" is one. Florida construes the ordinance not to make criminal one night's wandering, Johnson v. State, 202 So.2d, at 855, only the "habitual" wanderer or, as the ordinance describes it, "common night walkers." We know, however, from experience that sleepless people often walk at night, perhaps hopeful that sleep-inducing relaxation will result.

Luis Munoz-Marin, former Governor of Puerto Rico, commented once that "loafing" was a national virtue in his Commonwealth and that it should be encouraged. It is, however, a crime in Jacksonville.

. . . "[P]ersons able to work but habitually living upon the earnings of their wives or minor children"—like habitually living "without visible means of support"—might implicate unemployed pillars of the community who have married rich wives.

. . . "[P]ersons able to work but habitually living upon the earnings of their wives or minor children" may also embrace unemployed people out of the labor market, by reason of a recession or disemployed by reason of technological or so-called structural displacements.

Persons "wandering or strolling" from place to place have been extolled by Walt Whitman and Vachel Lindsay.[a] The qualification "without any lawful purpose or object" may be a trap for innocent acts. Persons "neglecting all lawful business and habitually spending their time by frequenting places where alcoholic beverages are sold or served" would literally embrace many members of golf clubs and city clubs.

Walkers and strollers and wanderers may be going to or coming from a burglary. Loafers or loiterers may be "casing" a place for a holdup. Letting one's wife support him is an intra-family matter, and normally of no concern to the police. Yet it may, of course, be the setting for numerous crimes.

The difficulty is that these activities are historically part of the amenities of life as we have known them. They are not mentioned in the Constitution or in the Bill of Rights. These unwritten amenities have been in part responsible for giving our people the feeling of independence and self-confidence, the feeling of creativity. These amenities have dignified the right of dissent and have honored the right to be nonconformists and the right to defy submissiveness. They have encouraged lives of high spirits rather than hushed, suffocating silence.

They are embedded in Walt Whitman's writings, especially in his "Song of the Open Road." They are reflected too, in the spirit of Vachel Lindsay's "I Want to Go Wandering," and by Henry D. Thoreau.[b]

This aspect of the vagrancy ordinance before us is suggested by what this Court said in 1876 about a broad criminal statute enacted by Congress: "It would certainly be dangerous if the legislature could set a net large enough to catch all possible offenders, and leave it to the courts to step inside and say who could be rightfully detained, and who should be set at large."

While that was a federal case, the due process implications are equally applicable to the States and to this vagrancy ordinance. Here the net cast is large, not to give the courts the power to pick and choose but to increase the arsenal of the police.

These statutes are in a class by themselves, in view of the familiar abuses to which they are put. Definiteness is designedly avoided so as to allow the net to be cast at large, to enable men to be caught who are vaguely undesirable in the eyes of police and prosecution, although not chargeable with any particular offense. In short, these "vagrancy statutes" and laws against "gangs" are not fenced in by the text of the statute or by the subject matter so as to give notice of conduct to be avoided.

Where the list of crimes is so all-inclusive and generalized as the one in this ordinance those convicted may be punished for no more than vindicating affronts to police authority:

> The common ground which brings such a motley assortment of human troubles before the magistrates in vagrancy-type proceedings is the procedural laxity which permits "conviction" for almost any kind of conduct and the existence of the House of Correction as an easy and convenient dumping-ground for problems that appear to have no other immediate solution.

Another aspect of the ordinance's vagueness appears when we focus, not on the lack of notice given a potential offender, but on the effect of the unfettered discretion it places in the hands of the Jacksonville police. Caleb Foote, an early student of this subject, has called the vagrancy-type law as offering "punishment by analogy." Id., at 609. Such crimes, though long common in Russia, are not compatible with our constitutional system. We allow our police to make arrests only on "probable cause," a Fourth and Fourteenth Amendment standard applicable to the States as well as to the Federal Government. Arresting a person on suspicion, like arresting a person for investigation, is foreign to our system, even when the arrest is for past criminality. Future criminality, however, is the common justification for the presence of vagrancy statutes. See Foote, supra, at 625. Florida has, indeed, construed her vagrancy statute "as necessary regulations," inter alia, "to deter vagabondage and prevent crimes."

A direction by a legislature to the police to arrest all "suspicious" persons would not pass constitutional muster. A vagrancy prosecution may be merely the cloak for a conviction which could not be obtained on the real but undisclosed grounds for the arrest.

> It would be in the highest degree unfortunate if in any part of the country those who are responsible for setting in motion the criminal law should entertain, connive at or coquette with the idea that in a case where there is not enough evidence to charge the prisoner with an attempt to commit a crime, the prosecution may, nevertheless, on such insufficient evidence, succeed in obtaining and upholding a conviction.

Those generally implicated by the imprecise terms of the ordinance—poor people, nonconformists, dissenters, idlers—may be required to comport themselves according to the life style deemed appropriate by the Jacksonville police and the courts. Where, as here, there are no standards governing the exercise of the discretion granted by the ordinance, the scheme permits and encourages an arbitrary and discriminatory enforcement of the law. It furnishes a convenient tool for "harsh and discriminatory enforcement by local prosecuting officials, against particular groups deemed to merit their displeasure." It results in a regime in which the poor and the unpopular are permitted to "stand on a public sidewalk only at the whim of any police officer."

Under this ordinance,

> if some carefree type of fellow is satisfied to work just so much, and no more, as will pay for one square meal, some wine, and a flophouse daily, but a court thinks this kind of living subhuman, the fellow can be forced to raise his sights or go to jail as a vagrant.

A presumption that people who might walk or loaf or loiter or stroll or frequent houses where liquor is sold, or who are supported by their wives or who look suspicious to the police are to become future criminals is too precarious for a rule of law. The implicit presumption in these generalized vagrancy standards—that crime is being nipped in the bud—is too extravagant to deserve extended treatment. Of course, vagrancy statutes are useful to the police. Of course, they are nets making easy the roundup of so-called undesirables. But the rule of law implies equality and justice in its application. Vagrancy laws of the Jacksonville type teach that the scales of justice are so tipped that even-handed administration of the law is not possible. The rule of law, evenly applied to minorities as well as majorities, to the poor as well as the rich, is the great mucilage that holds society together.

The Jacksonville ordinance cannot be squared with our constitutional standards and is plainly unconstitutional.

Reversed.

CASE DISCUSSION

The Supreme Court ruled the Jacksonville ordinance unconstitutional because it was too broad and vague. Does the ordinance give the police too much power? Should the police have the power to use vagrancy statutes to investigate more serious crimes? Does the Jacksonville ordinance unduly restrict personal freedom? Does it discriminate against the poor, the young, and the minorities and dissidents? Would you declare it unconstitutional?

a. And see Reich, Police Questioning of Law Abiding Citizens, 75 Yale L.J. 1161, 1172 (1966): "If I choose to take an evening walk to see if Andromeda has come up on schedule, I think I am entitled to look for the distant light of Almach and Mirach without finding myself staring into the blinding beam of a police flashlight."

b. "I have met with but one or two persons in the course of my life who understood the art of Walking, that is, of taking walks,—who had a genius, so to speak, for sauntering: which word is beautifully derived 'from idle people who roved about the country, in the Middle Ages, and asked charity, under pretence of going a la Sainte Terre,' to the Holy Land, till the children exclaimed, 'There goes a Sainte Terrer,' a Saunterer, a Holy-Lander."

Criminal Policy and Vagrancy

Vagrancy law's critics do not limit their attacks to its unconstitutionality. They maintain that vagrancy law does not accord with criminal law's basic principles. In the first place, they contend, vagrancy aims at controlling and preventing future harm. Vagrancy itself is not a harm, they say, so the purpose of arresting and convicting vagrants is to prevent some "undesirable" people from doing harm sometime in the future. Even if the harm is present, they argue further, the conduct that vagrancy encompasses is not criminal. At worst it is annoying, and to restrict some people's freedoms merely to remove other people's annoyance is not consistent with a free society's values, particularly when the annoying behavior has strong class overtones. A free society, they say, ought to promote diversity, not enforce conformity to one group's standard as to what is proper behavior. As Justice Douglas wrote in *Papachristou*, "Persons 'wandering or strolling' from place to place have been extolled by Walt Whitman and Vachel Lindsay." Hence, vagrancy wastes public resources to combat harms that are either potential or insubstantial or even positive goods.

Critics also fault vagrancy statutes because they do not require *mens rea*. In most vagrancy cases, the poor, the unemployed, the dissidents, and the young who are prosecuted have no purposeful, knowing, reckless, or even negligent conduct to blame. They are simply in places at times when and where they are not wanted. That, say critics, is not what *mens rea* means in criminal law.

Reform in Vagrancy Law: Suspicious Loitering and Aggressive Panhandling

Some reformers recommend that legislatures should rewrite vagrancy laws in order to remove, or at least reduce, constitutional and policy objections to them. The Model Penal Code's suspicious loitering provision demonstrates one effort to improve vagrancy law without abolishing it. (See Section 250.6 in Appendix.)

The suspicious loitering provision reflects the drafters' effort to meet objections to existing vagrancy statutes. First, suspicious loitering is not a status; it requires an act ("loiters or prowls"). Second, loitering does not mean merely being lazy or drifting, it requires being suspicious. Hence, a known pickpocket hanging around a Greyhound bus station and a stranger in a small town lurking in an alley near a jewelry store for two hours, peering up and down the adjoining street every few minutes, are suspiciously loitering. On the other hand, punkers standing around on a street corner, with no apparent reason other than to display their wild hairstyles and clothes, are not loitering suspiciously, however annoying their presence might be to respectable society. In the drafters' judgment, therefore, the suspicious requirement removes both the status and the *mens rea* objections to existing vagrancy laws. Because the Code provision includes only suspicious conduct, constitutional objections are at least reduced, if not removed entirely.

The suspicious loitering provision does give police the power to question suspicious persons. The state can prosecute people who refuse to answer reasonable questions when there was probable cause to arrest them for suspicious loitering. Some critics object to this last part, saying it protects people who tell plausible lies but not those who tell the implausible truth. In addition, the possibility for police abuse is too great, critics say, even in this truncated vagrancy provision.

CASE

Was He Suspiciously Loitering?

Kolender, Chief of Police of San Diego v. Lawson

461 U.S. 352 103 S.Ct. 1855, 75 L.Ed.2d 903 (1983)

[Justice O'Connor delivered the Court's opinion. Berger, Brennan, Marshall, Blackmun, Powell, and Stevens joined. Justice White, with Justice Rehnquist joining, dissented.]

Appellee Edward Lawson was detained or arrested on approximately 15 occasions between March 1976 and January 1977 pursuant to Cal. Penal Code Ann. § 647(e) (West 1970). Lawson was prosecuted only twice, and was convicted once. The second charge was dismissed.

Lawson then brought a civil action in the District Court for the Southern District of California seeking a declaratory judgment that § 647(e) is unconstitutional, a mandatory injunction to restrain enforcement of the statute, and compensatory and punitive damages against the various officers who detained him. The District Court found that § 647(e) was overbroad because "a person who is stopped on less than probable cause cannot be punished for failing to identify himself." The District Court enjoined enforcement of the statute, but held that Lawson could not recover damages because the officers involved acted in the good-faith belief that each detention or arrest was lawful. . . . The Court of Appeals affirmed the District Court determination as to the unconstitutionality of § 647(e). The appellate court determined that the statute was unconstitutional in that it violates the Fourth Amendment's proscription against unreasonable searches and seizures, it contains a vague enforcement statute that is susceptible to arbitrary enforcement, and it fails to give fair and adequate notice of the type of conduct prohibited. . . .

The officers appealed to this Court from that portion of the judgment of the Court of Appeals which declared § 647(e) unconstitutional and which enjoined its enforcement. . . .

. . . [T]he trial transcript contains numerous descriptions of the stops given both by Lawson and by the police officers who detained him. For example, one police officer testified that he stopped Lawson while walking on an otherwise vacant street because it was late at night, the area was isolated, and the area was located close to a high crime area. Another officer testified that he detained Lawson, who was walking at a late hour in a business area where some businesses were still open, and asked for identification because burglaries had been committed by unknown persons in the general area. . . .

OPINION

In the courts below, Lawson mounted an attack on the facial validity of § 647(e). . . . § 647(e) requires that an individual provide "credible and reliable" identification when requested by a police officer who has reasonable suspicion of criminal activity. . . .

"Credible and reliable" identification is defined by the State Court of Appeal as identification "carrying reasonable assurance that the identification is authentic and providing means for later getting in touch with the person who has identified himself." In addition, a suspect may be required to "account for his presence . . . to the extent that it assists in producing credible and reliable identification. . . ." Under the terms of the statute, failure of the individual to provide "credible and reliable" identification permits the arrest.

Our Constitution is designed to maximize individual freedoms within a framework of ordered liberty. Statutory limitations on those freedoms are examined for substantive authority and content as well as for definiteness or certainty of expression.

. . . Section 647(e), as presently drafted and as construed by the state courts, contains no standard for determining what a suspect has to do in order to satisfy the requirement to provide a "credible and reliable" identification. As such, the statute vests virtually complete discretion in the hands of the police to determine whether the suspect has satisfied the statute and must be permitted to go on his way in the absence of probable cause to arrest. An individual, whom police may think is suspicious but do not have probable cause to believe has committed a crime, is entitled to continue to walk the public streets "only at the whim of any police officer" who happens to stop that individual under § 647(e). . . .

Appellants stress the need for strengthened law enforcement tools to combat the epidemic of crime that plagues our Nation. The concern of our citizens with curbing criminal activity is certainly a matter requiring the attention of all branches of government. As weighty as this concern is, however, it cannot justify legislation that would otherwise fail to meet constitutional standards for definiteness and clarity. Section 647(e), as presently construed, requires that "suspicious" persons satisfy some undefined identification requirement, or face criminal punishment. Although due process does not require "impossible standards" of clarity, this is not a case where further precision in the statutory language is either impossible or impractical.

We conclude § 647(e) is unconstitutionally vague on its face because it encourages arbitrary enforcement by failing to describe with sufficient particularity what a suspect must do in order to satisfy the statute. Accordingly, the judgment of the Court of Appeals is affirmed, and the case is remanded for further proceedings consistent with this opinion.

It is so ordered.

DISSENT

The majority finds that the statute "contains no standard for determining what a suspect has to do in order to satisfy the requirement to provide a 'credible and reliable' identification." At the same time, the majority concedes that "credible and reliable" has been defined by the state court to remain identification that carries reasonable assurance that the identification is authentic and that provides means for later getting in touch with the person. The narrowing construction given this statute by the state court cannot be likened to the "standardless" statutes involved in a statute that made it a crime to be a "vagrant." The statute provided:

> Rogues and vagabonds, or dissolute persons who go about begging, common gamblers, . . . common drunkards, common night walkers, . . . lewd, wanton and lascivious persons, . . . common railers and brawlers, persons wandering or strolling around from place to place without any lawful purpose or object, habitual loafers, . . . shall be deemed vagrants.

. . . The present statute, as construed by the state courts, does not fall in the same category.

CASE DISCUSSION

Lawson is widely known as the California Walkman because he spends most of his free time walking, sometimes in odd places at unusual times. He is a large, imposing figure who wears his hair in dredlocks. Why did the police arrest Lawson? Were they preventing crime? investigating crime? or harassing Lawson? What foundation did they have? Do you agree with the majority, or with the dissent's opinion? Were the Model Penal Code's efforts to draft a narrow suspicious loitering provision wasted after *Lawson v. Kolender*, which the United States Supreme Court later upheld? Or does the Model Penal Code provision overcome the objections raised to California's loitering statute? What interest is the court protecting when it strikes down a statute like the one in this case? What interests does it endanger? If you were a judge, how would you balance the interests and how would you decide this case?

Recently, a number of jurisdictions have adopted aggressive panhandling ordinances to deal with the increasing numbers of homeless people, particularly on the streets of large cities.

CASE

What Constitutes Aggressive Panhandling?

The Seattle, Washington, Pedestrian Interference Ordinance

"Brief of Amicus Curiae American Civil Liberties Union of Washington," No. 88-1-02856-3, In the Superior Court of the State of Washington for King County City of Seattle[14]

The Seattle City Council adopted the Pedestrian Interference Ordinance in October 1987, with an effective date of November 18, 1987. Approximately 150 arrests have been made under the ordinance through September of 1988. . . .

The declared purpose of the City Council in promulgating the ordinance is set forth in its recitals:

WHEREAS, there have been numerous complaints from citizens, particularly the elderly, about aggressive behavior on Seattle's streets; and

WHEREAS, all citizens should have free and unhampered access to public areas of Seattle without fear of harassment or intimidation.

The City Council is required to effectuate its purpose, if at all, in a Constitutional manner. "[E]ven the most legitimate goal may not be advanced in a constitutionally impermissible manner." *Carey v. Brown*, 447 U.S. 455, 465 (1980). . . .

The Pedestrian Interference Ordinance is divided into three sections. First, it contains a definitional section; second, a liability section; and third, a punishment section. A person is guilty of violating the ordinance under either of two alternative prongs set forth in the ordinance: (1) obstructing pedestrian vehicular traffic, or (2) aggressive begging. The Ordinance, SMC 12A.12.015, provides in full:

The following definitions apply in this section:
1. "Aggressively beg" means to beg with intent to intimidate another person into giving money or goods.
2. "Beg" means to ask for money or goods as a charity, whether by words, bodily gestures, signs, or other means.
3. "Obstruct pedestrian or vehicular traffic" means to walk, stand, sit, lie, or place an object in such a manner as to block passage by another person or vehicle, or require another person or driver of a vehicle to take evasive action to avoid physical contact. Acts authorized as an exercise of one's constitutional right to picket or to legally protest . . . shall not constitute obstruction of pedestrian or vehicular traffic.
4. "Public place" means an area generally visible to public view and includes alleys, bridges, buildings, driveways, parking lots, parks, plazas, sidewalks and streets open to the general public, including those that serve food or drink or provide entertainment, and the doorways and entrances to buildings or dwellings and grounds enclosing them. . . .
   B. A person is guilty of pedestrian interference if, in a public place, he or she intentionally:
       1. Obstructs pedestrian or vehicular traffic; or
       2. Aggressively begs.
   C. Pedestrian interference may be punished by a fine not to exceed Five Hundred Dollars ($500.00) or by imprisonment in jail for a term not to exceed ninety (90) days or by both such fine and imprisonment.

. . . The ordinance is vague in that it prohibits everyday activities, and because it fails to provide adequate standards for adjudication. The ordinance is overbroad in that it infringes upon protected speech activities without being content neutral. Finally, the ordinance unfairly impacts the homeless and thus violates equal protection requirements. The ordinance sweeps away fundamental rights, fails to comport with basic due process requirements, and infringes on the right of an insular minority to exist. . . .

It is an axiom of Washington constitutional law that fundamental rights may not be denied on the basis of poverty. Within the general rubric of the poor is the subcategory of the homeless. With respect to the homeless, the ordinance interferes with the most basic of human rights—the right to subsistence. . . . The infringement of this human right rises to the invidious infringement of a fundamental right of the homeless under Article I, Section 12, of the Washington Constitution and the equal protection clause of the Fourteenth Amendment of the United States Constitution. The effect of the ordinance is to hound homeless citizens under the threat of arrest until they relocate to a place where they will not "contaminate" the sterility of store displays that seek to entice an affluent clientele.

The infringement upon this human right of subsistence is hardly a chimera. The ordinance prohibits the use of the streets and sidewalks wherever some "evasive action" may be required by another. Obstruction of the street, or the creation of a dangerous or even disorderly situation, is not required for conviction. A homeless person sitting against a building on a wide sidewalk is in violation of the ordinance, because the conduct is intended and another walking along the side of the building must take evasive action to avoid her.

Most homeless people have no alternative to the sidewalks and parks for a place to sit or to take a short nap. . . . People with no income must necessarily depend upon handouts to survive.

In its 1987 report on homelessness, the Church Council of Greater Seattle noted:

> The stereotype of the grizzled street alcoholic does not conform to the reality of homelessness today. There is not a typical homeless person. There is, instead, a wide range of people who are homeless whose most common characteristic is their lack of income. In fact, one of the alarming realities is how normal many homeless people seem. . . . [T]he five major reasons people requested shelter in 1986 were:
> *Unemployment, 29%; Family crisis/eviction, 22%; Alcoholism, 21%; Domestic abuse, 15%; Mental illness, 13%*

Most are thus homeless for reasons beyond their control. . . . The fortunate one-third of the homeless can find beds in emergency shelters, but the majority has no alternative but to live in the streets, to eat morsels of food over the fumes and noise of passing trucks, and to try to sleep in the rain under discarded plastic sacks as the headlights of cars race by. The Pedestrian Interference Ordinance on its face denies them even this desolate (and often involuntary) existence, and leaves the homeless with the option of migrating to another town (which, if this ordinance is upheld, will soon have one just like it) or going to jail. In the words of Justice Frankfurter,

> [T]o sanction such a ruthless consequence . . . would justify a latter-day Anatole France to add one more item to his ironic comments on the "majestic equality" of the law. "The law, in its majestic equality, forbids the rich as well as the poor to sleep under bridges, to beg in the streets, and to steal bread."

CASE DISCUSSION

Ordinances such as the Seattle Pedestrian Interference Ordinance address the problem of public begging that takes an aggressive tone.

Their gist is to permit mild requests but to rule out intimidating behavior, such as shouting or offensive language. A lower court has ruled the Seattle, Washington, aggressive panhandling ordinance unconstitutional, on the ground that it violates the Fourteenth Amendment—that it is both vague and overbroad.[15]

The Superior Court judge ruled the ordinance unconstitutional. It is now on appeal to the Washington Supreme Court. Review the discussion of legality and other constitutional limitations on criminal law in chapter 2. Do you agree that this ordinance violates the constitutional rights of the homeless? How would you balance the rights of the homeless and the needs of society in this case? Would a homeless person have a defense of necessity? Review the defense of necessity in chapter 7. Does this statute punish thoughts or intentions? Does it punish status? Review the principles of criminal liability in chapter 3.

PUBLIC MORALS OFFENSES

In medieval days when great rivalries between monarchs and churches were fought over who had jurisdiction to hold courts and rule upon illegality, the church claimed exclusive jurisdiction over nonviolent sexual behavior, marital relations, and some other matters not relevant here. As monarchs grew stronger, royal secular courts eventually absorbed family and sex offenses into their own jurisdictions. These offenses became the modern crimes against public morals. Some modern critics maintain they should now be returned to the church, although not in the literal sense nor in the same form. They advocate allowing sexual behavior between consenting adults to remain a matter for private conscience and general moral persuasion.[16]

Rape and the offenses related to it deal with both violent sexual attacks and the nonviolent sexual conduct of children or others who are incompetent to decide whether or not they want to engage in sexual relations with others. In almost all crimes discussed in the following pages, criminal law punishes behavior between consenting adults. In other words, there is no *victim* in the word's ordinary sense. Public morals offenses raise the question, How far beyond traditional sexual intercourse between married heterosexual couples ought the criminal law to at least tolerate if not encourage? Under existing law, "normal" sexual intercourse between a husband and wife is legal, but almost everything else, even sexual intercourse between a man and a woman not married to each other, is a crime.

Nonviolent sex offenses range across a broad spectrum. The primary statutory nonviolent sex crimes include fornication, adultery, incest, sodomy, indecent exposure, and prostitution. These crimes make it especially difficult to balance public good and individual privacy. Unlike homicide, rape, and related crimes, where broad consensus exists as to their "harmfulness," the public morals offenses enjoy no such consensus. In fact, there are two conflicting and tenaciously held positions over criminal law's role in public morals enforcement. Hard lines divide those who believe criminal law ought to enforce morals in order to "purify" society and those who argue against criminal law's interference in citizens' lives.[17]

Perhaps no issue in criminal policy has caused more acrimonious debate over a longer time than that of the role law should play in enforcing public morals. Two English Victorian scholars, the philosopher John Stuart Mill and the historian Sir James F. Stephen, started the debate that has raged for more than a century among theorists, lawmakers, and the public. Although the debate has many strands, it features two major positions that were well stated in the Wolfenden report, an English document recommending that sexual relations between male homosexuals and prostitution be decriminalized when they took place between two consenting adults in private. Briefly, the majority position was as follows:

> There remains one additional argument which we believe to be decisive, namely, the importance which society and the law ought to give to individual freedom of choice and action in matters of private morality. Unless a deliberate attempt is to be made by society, acting through the agency of the law, to equate the sphere of crime with that of sin, there must remain a realm of private morality and immorality which is, in brief and crude terms, not the law's business. To say this is not to condone or encourage private immorality. On the contrary, to emphasize the personal private nature of moral or immoral conduct is to emphasize the personal and private responsibility of the individual for his own actions, and that is a responsibility which a mature agent can properly be expected to carry for himself without the threat of punishment from the law.[18]

English jurist Sir Patrick Devlin rebutted the majority Wolfenden position:

> I think, therefore, that it is not possible to set theoretical limits to the power of the State to legislate against immorality. It is not possible to settle in advance exceptions to the general rule or to define inflexibly areas of morality into which the law is in no circumstances to be allowed to enter. Society is entitled by means of its laws to protect itself from dangers, whether from within or without. Here again I think that the political parallel is legitimate. The law of treason is directed against aiding the king's enemies and against sedition from within. The justification for this is that established government is necessary for the existence of society and therefore its safety against violent overthrow must be secured. But an established morality is as necessary as good government to the welfare of society. Societies disintegrate from within more frequently than they are broken up by external pressures. There is disintegration when no common morality is observed and history shows that the loosening of moral bonds is often the first state of disintegration, so that society is justified in taking the same steps to preserve its moral code as it does to preserve its government and other essential institutions. The suppression of vice is as much the law's business as the suppression of subversive activities; it is no more possible to define a sphere of private morality than it is to define one of private subversive activity.[19]

Fornication and Illicit Cohabitation

Although pertinent legislation is rarely (if ever) enforced, extramarital and premarital sexual intercourse are crimes in many jurisdictions. A typical statute on this subject reads: "Whoever has sexual intercourse with a person he knows is not his spouse may be fined not more than $200 or imprisoned not more than 6 months or both." Other states make these acts punishable only if they are "an open and notorious relationship." Indiana, for example, specifies that "whoever cohabits with another in a state of adultery or fornication shall be fined not exceeding $500 or imprisoned in the county jail not exceeding 6 months or both."[20]

Prostitution and Related Offenses

Prostitution has flourished throughout human history, surviving virtually unabated the condemnation of moralists in both church and state. Recent evidence suggests that about 70 percent of the male population has hired a prostitute at some time, because of physical deformity, psychological inadequacy, emotional unwillingness to make more than casual acquaintances, or other reasons that make it difficult to find suitable noncommercial sex partners. In this sense, some argue, prostitution fills a social need. Nevertheless, nearly every American state carries on the fight against prostitution.

Prostitution means to offer sex for hire. Some statutes limit criminal liability to females who offer sexual intercourse. Others extend liability to any person who offers to buy sex or who accepts such an offer. The Model Penal Code extends the meaning still further: "[A] person who engages, or offers or agrees to engage in sexual activity for hire commits a petty misdemeanor." Sexual activity, according to the Code, includes "carnal knowledge, deviate sexual intercourse, and sexual contact or any lewd act," meaning, in addition to vaginal intercourse, sodomy, fellatio, cunnilingus, male prostitution, masturbation, and even voyeurism. The prostitution *mens rea* requires the purpose to sell or buy whatever sexual activity the statute includes.[21]

These definitions create problems. They exclude both sexually promiscuous people who regularly and indiscriminately engage in sex for no charge, and nonpromiscuous people who sell sex to or buy sex from one person, developing close relationships with their providers—the classic mistress and gigolo. Existing prostitution statutes aim primarily to curb promiscuity for hire—that is, situations that combine promiscuity and commercialism.

CASE

Was Cherie's Massage Prostitution?

Commonwealth v. Walter

388 Mass. 460, 446 N.E.2d 707 (1983)

[Walter was convicted of prostitution, a crime carrying a penalty of up to six months' imprisonment. She was sentenced to thirty days in jail. She appealed. Chief Justice Hennessey delivered the opinion.]

FACTS

On January 28, 1981, Officer James Walsh of the Cambridge police department received a radio call. In response, Officer Walsh changed into civilian clothes and went to the detective bureau of the Cambridge police department. There, Detective Anthony Bombino showed him a copy of an advertisement appearing in the January 27, 1981, edition of the Boston Phoenix newspaper, which read: "Swedish & Shiatsu Massage in Harvard Square Chris 661–————." The newspaper advertisement was admitted in evidence over the defendant's objection.

Officer Walsh placed a telephone call to 661–————, and asked to speak to "Chris." The person who answered the telephone stated that she was "Chris." Officer Walsh told her that he was answering the advertisement in the Boston Phoenix and that he was interested in getting a massage. "Chris" asked him if he was really interested in getting a massage, and he said, "Yes." "Chris" told him an address on Massachusetts Avenue, apartment 24, and that the massage would cost $30. Detective Bombino saw Officer Walsh call 661–————, and heard his conversation.

Officer Walsh went to the address in an unmarked police car with Detective Bombino and two other policemen. He pressed the buzzer for apartment 24, and a woman, whom he later identified as the defendant, came to the door. He asked if she were the "Chris" with whom he had just spoken, and she said, "Yes. Why don't you come up?" He followed her to apartment 24, where he saw a man sitting in the bedroom clothed only in pants. After a brief conversation with the defendant, the man put on the rest of his clothing and left.

The defendant invited Officer Walsh into the bedroom, and told him to get undressed. She asked him for $30, which he gave her. She massaged his body generally, using her hands and some oil. During the course of the massage she removed her shirt and was naked from the waist up. She then massaged his genitals, in an act of masturbation, for about forty-five seconds. Officer Walsh then got off the bed and said he was a police officer, and that she was under arrest for prostitution. During the arrest Detective Bombino gained entry to the apartment and seized two telephones bearing the number 661–———— from the apartment.

OPINION

The defendant argues that a full body massage which includes the genitals, by use of the hands only, for a fee, is not prostitution within the meaning of the statute. In Commonwealth v. King, 374 Mass. 5, 12, 372 N.E.2d 196 (1977), we noted that the Legislature had not defined prostitution, and so turned to common understanding for definition of the term. We concluded that prostitution is "common indiscriminate sexual activity for hire." The defendant does not argue that her acts were not common, indiscriminate, or for hire, but rather that they were not "sexual activity." She argues that "sexual activity" is confined to coitus or oral-genital contact.

We conclude that prostitution includes performing masturbation upon a person's genitals by another's hands, for a fee. The term "sexual activity," resting as it does on the common understanding of the meaning of prostitution, and on Commonwealth v. Cook, supra, includes such acts. Accordingly, we reject the defendant's contention that the acts proved were not prostitution within the meaning of G.L. c. 272, § 53.

The defendant next argues that prohibition of her activities interferes with her constitutional right to privacy . . . [In] Commonwealth v. Balthazar, 366 Mass. 298, 302, 318 N.E.2d 478 (1974), we held that G.L. c. 272, § 35, which prohibits "unnatural and lascivious acts," does not apply to private consensual conduct of adults. The defendant's prostitution conviction is based on the massage she gave Officer Walsh in her apartment.

The scope of the right to privacy under the United States Constitution is not well defined. However, whatever protection it affords to the private, sexual activities of consenting adults, we conclude that the defendant's activities were not protected, because they were performed for a fee. We will not extend a constitutional right to privacy to one who indiscriminately performs sexual acts for hire. Commercial sex is performed for profit and the sexual contact involved is incidental to that profit. The impersonal nature of the performance of commercial sex, such as was involved here, is indicated by the fact that anyone willing to pay could enter the defendant's apartment and receive a genital massage. The decision to engage in the business of sex for money is not the type of intimate, personal decision which is protected by the right to privacy.

Affirmed.

CASE DISCUSSION

The court concluded that Cherie Walter did not have a constitutional right to offer massage in her apartment. Do you believe the prostitution statute violated her right to privacy? Do you think the law should reach into an apartment where two adults willingly engage in sexual massages? If you do, what reasons can you give and what penalty would you prescribe? Do you agree that masturbation ought to be included within prostitution's meaning? Or should prostitution include only sexual intercourse?

Solicitation and Promotion of Prostitution

Some argue that publicly soliciting sex for hire ought to be a crime, even though an agreement has not been made. Thus, prostitution and related offenses would constitute three crimes: engaging in sex for hire, offering to buy or sell sex, and publicly soliciting to buy or sell sex. In most jurisdictions, to procure, transport, or receive money for prostitution constitutes a separate offense. These jurisdictions permit multiple prosecutions for acts that are, in a sense, part of the same offense: promoting prostitution. Promoting prostitution embraces collaborating with or exploiting prostitutes. It includes transporting prostitutes, supporting houses of prostitution, living off prostitutes (pimping), and patronizing prostitution.

Several arguments support criminal penalties for prostitution. First, the following utilitarian considerations favor repressing it:

1. Prostitution spreads venereal disease.
2. When combined with drug trade, liquor, gambling, robbery, and extortion, prostitution provides a source of power and profit for organized crime.
3. Prostitution spawns corruption and improper influence in government because politicians and law enforcement officials become easy marks for the threat of exposure.
4. Prostitution encourages sexual maladjustment, undermines the home and family, and contributes to individual moral decay.

The most potent argument favoring criminal penalties is not utilitarian, however. Moralists and religious groups have opposed commercial sex for centuries. If there is one constant theme in Western history, it is thunderous denunciation of sex for hire.

Several arguments make up the case against criminal sanctions. Most who oppose criminal penalties for prostitution recommend regulating it in other ways. In other words, to oppose making prostitution a crime does not mean supporting prostitution as a practice, at least not without qualification. Proponents argue that government's inability to effectively prosecute prostitution laws fosters extortion and results in the selective prosecution of minorities and "undesirables." Furthermore, they argue, strict enforcement cuts off an important outlet for sexual expression that might lead to more violent sex crimes. In addition, registration and mandatory health inspections can control and reduce venereal disease. Regulation also lessens the opportunities for official corruption. Finally, if prostitution were confined to specific neighborhoods—as regulation and registration permit—it would lead to more effective community health and safety.

The Wolfendon report says the following:

> Prostitution is a social fact deplorable in the eyes of moralists, sociologists and, we believe, the great majority of ordinary people. But it has persisted in many civilizations throughout many centuries, and the failure of attempts to stamp it out by repressive legislation shows that it cannot be eradicated through the agency of the criminal law. It remains true that without a demand for her services the prostitute could not exist, and that there are enough men who avail themselves of prostitutes to keep the trade alive. It also remains true that there are women who, even when there is no economic need to do so, choose this form of livelihood. For so long as these propositions continue to be true there will be prostitution, and no amount of legislation directed towards its abolition will abolish it.

It follows that there are limits to the degree of discouragement which the criminal law can properly exercise towards a woman who has deliberately decided to live her life in this way, or a man who has deliberately chosen to use her services. The criminal law, as the Street Offenses Committee plainly pointed out, "is not concerned with private morals or with ethical sanctions." This does not mean that society itself can be indifferent to these matters, for prostitution is an evil of which any society which claims to be civilized should seek to rid itself; but this end could be achieved only through measures directed to a better understanding of the nature and obligation of sexual relationships and to a raising of the social and moral outlook of society as a whole. In these matters, the work of the churches and of organizations concerned with mental health, moral welfare, family welfare, child and marriage guidance and similar matters should be given all possible encouragement. But until education and the moral sense of the community bring about a change of attitude towards the fact of prostitution, the law by itself cannot do so. In the final analysis, however, the opponents of criminal penalties for prostitution rely on more than utilitarian arguments. They also adhere to the basic libertarian view that morals are not the business of the law. The choice about whether to do a moral or an immoral thing should be left entirely to the individual, his conscience, his religion, his friends, and his family—not to the criminal law.[22]

The Model Penal Code prostitution provision falls between two extremes. The Code provision keeps criminal repression but attempts to remove gross abuses in existing law. It also encompasses homosexual acts and other deviate sexual practices for hire. Penalties prescribed for prostitution are mild in contrast to those for promoting commercial sex, the latter being considered a more serious crime. Customers, called johns or tricks, as well as prostitutes are subject to prosecution under the Code, and the Code grades public solicitation, prostitution, and promotion.

Sodomy and Related Offenses

Large numbers of "normal" persons deviate from expressing themselves sexually through heterosexual vaginal intercourse. Heterosexual "gratification is sought and bestowed digitally, orally or by the anus." Some people even gratify their sexual desires without human contact. Some masturbate. Others turn to animals. Some only look at others or expose themselves, and still others turn to inanimate objects for gratification. Crimes such as arson and burglary provide sexual stimulation to some who commit them. Finally, substantial numbers obtain sexual gratification from members of their own gender.[23]

For centuries, all sexual gratification except heterosexual copulation within marriage has generated substantial revulsion, at least when expressed publicly. Most religions censure sex that deviates from heterosexual vaginal intercourse in marriage. Criminal law subjects such deviation to severe punishment, according to the law's letter, if not its actual operation. Statutes in nearly every state specify punishment for fellatio, cunnilingus, anal intercourse (sodomy), bestiality, and even masturbation.

And some punishments are very harsh: ten to twenty years' imprisonment in most jurisdictions, up to maximum life imprisonment in a few.

The utilitarian reasons most often cited for making sodomy and related offenses criminal include (1) that the acts are widely disapproved and (2) that minor deviations can lead to grosser deviations and, eventually, to violent sexual aggression. Underlying these reasons, proponents believe that the state should interfere in citizens' "immoral" conduct and that criminal law is a proper instrument to enforce morality. Proponents contend that retribution, deterrence, and rehabilitation all favor punishing intentional deviate sex practices.

Not everyone agrees that criminal law should subject sodomy and related offenses to criminal penalties. Opponents maintain that enforcing sodomy law is impractical. They claim that deviate sex is not deviate in the eyes of many people, particularly those who practice it. Despite vocal opposition to such acts, normal people in substantial numbers practice fellatio, cunnilingus, and sodomy. In addition, authorities are in hopeless disagreement over the causes and "cures" for this sexual conduct. Some say the conduct constitutes an illness, others label it a congenital or hereditary defect, and still others say it is normal. The law should not interfere in conduct that punishment, deterrence, or rehabilitation cannot alter. The evidence does not support the contention either that sex offenders tend to progress from one kind of offense to another or that criminal penalties beneficially affect sexual behavior.

Furthermore, sodomy laws are largely unenforced and unenforceable, opening the way to selective enforcement, bribery, and corruption. This wastes resources that could otherwise help respond to serious harms to persons and property, particularly since so many robberies and burglaries go unsolved. Finally, opponents assert that unenforceable laws breed contempt and resentment toward sodomy laws in particular and disrespect for law in general.

> Employment of tight-panted police officers to invite homosexual advances or to spy upon public toilets in the hope of detecting deviant behavior at a time when public solutions of serious crimes are steadily declining is a perversion of public policy both malefficient in itself and calculated to inspire contempt and ridicule.[24]

Like those who support statutes for sodomy and related offenses, opponents base their views on value-determined arguments. They are committed to the libertarian view that unless they involve violence, corrupting youth, and public nuisance, the sex lives of consenting are not the criminal law's business. In addition, they maintain that state interference in this area intrudes into privacy to an extent not tolerable in an enlightened free and diverse society.

Most states retain Draconian penalties for consensual sodomy, whether homosexual or heterosexual. Most even include sodomy within marriage. As most state statutes are written, any form of deviate consensual sex (that is, anything other than heterosexual vaginal intercourse) constitutes sodomy. Recently, the United States Court declared the Georgia sodomy statute constitutional in *Bowers v. Hardwick*.

CASE

Is Sodomy Constitutional?

Bowers v. Hardwick

478 U.S. 186, 106 S.Ct. 2841, 92 L.Ed.2d 140 (1986)

[Justice White delivered the opinion of the Court, in which Chief Justice Burger and Justices Powell, Rehnquist, and O'Connor joined. Chief Justice Burger and Justice Powell filed concurring opinions. Justice Blackmun filed a dissenting opinion, in which Justices Brennan, Marshall, and Stevens joined. Justice Stevens filed a dissenting opinion, in which Justices Brennan and Marshall joined.]

FACTS

In August 1982, respondent was charged with violating the Georgia statute criminalizing sodomy[1] by committing that act with another adult male in the bedroom of respondent's home. After a preliminary hearing, the District Attorney decided not to present the matter to the grand jury unless further evidence developed.

Respondent then brought suit in the Federal District Court, challenging the constitutionality of the statute insofar as it criminalized sodomy. He asserted that he was a practicing homosexual, that the Georgia sodomy statute, as administered by the defendants, placed him in imminent danger of arrest, and that the statute for several reasons violates the Federal Constitution. The District Court granted the defendants' motion to dismiss for failure to state a claim. . . .

OPINION

A divided panel of the Court of Appeals for the Eleventh Circuit reversed. . . . [T]he court [held] that the Georgia statute violated respondent's fundamental rights because his homosexual activity is a private and intimate association that is beyond the reach of state regulation by reason of the Ninth Amendment and the Due Process clause of the Fourteenth Amendment. The case was remanded for trial, at which, to prevail, the State would have to prove that the statute is supported by a compelling interest and is the most narrowly drawn means of achieving that end.

Because other Courts of Appeals have arrived at judgments contrary to that of the Eleventh Circuit in this case, we granted the State's petition for certiorari questioning the holding that its sodomy statute violates the fundamental rights of homosexuals. We agree with the State that the Court of Appeals erred, and hence reverse its judgement.

This case does not require a judgment on whether laws against sodomy between consenting adults in general, or between homosexuals in particular, are wise or desirable. It raises no question about the right or propriety of state legislative decisions to repeal their laws that criminalize homosexual sodomy, or of state court decisions invalidating those laws on state constitutional grounds. The issue presented is whether the Federal Constitution confers a fundamental right upon homosexuals to engage in sodomy and hence invalidates the laws of the many States that still make such conduct illegal and have done so for a very long time. The case also calls for some judgment about the limits of the Court's role in carrying out its constitutional mandate. . . .

. . . [R]espondent would have us announce, as the Court of Appeals did, a fundamental right to engage in homosexual sodomy. This we are quite unwilling to do. . . .

Striving to assure itself and the public that announcing rights not readily identifiable in the Constitution's text involves much more than the imposition of the Justices' own choice of values on the States and the Federal Government, the Court has sought to identify the nature of the rights qualifying for heightened judicial protection. In Palko v. Connecticut, 302 US 319, 325, 326, 92 L.Ed. (1937), it was said that this category includes those fundamental liberties that are "implicit in the concept of ordered liberty," such that "neither liberty nor justice would exist if [they] were sacrificed." A different description of fundamental liberties appeared in Moore v. East Cleveland, 431 US 494, (1977), where they are characterized as those liberties that are "deeply rooted in this Nation's history and tradition."

It is obvious to us that neither of these formulations would extend a fundamental right of homosexuals to engage in acts of consensual sodomy. Proscriptions against that conduct have ancient roots. . . . Sodomy was a criminal offense at common law and was forbidden by the laws of the original thirteen States when they ratified the Bill of Rights. . . . [U]ntil 1961, all 50 States outlawed sodomy, and today, 24 States and the District of Columbia continue to provide criminal penalties for sodomy performed in private and between consenting adults. Against this background, to claim that a right to engage in such conduct is "deeply rooted in this Nation's history and tradition" or "implicit in the concept of ordered liberty" is, at best, facetious.

. . . Respondent, however, asserts that the result should be different where the homosexual conduct occurs in the privacy of the home. He relies on Stanley v. Georgia, 394 US 557 (1969), where the Court held that the First Amendment prevents convicting for possessing and reading obscene material in the privacy of his home: "If the First Amendment means anything, it means that a State has no business telling a man, sitting alone at his house, what books he may read or what films he may watch."

Stanley did protect conduct that would not have been protected outside the home, and it partially prevented the enforcement of state obscenity laws; but the decision was firmly grounded in the First Amendment. The right pressed upon us here has no similar support in the text of the Constitution, and it does not qualify for recognition

under the prevailing principles for construing the Fourteenth Amendment. . . .

Even if the conduct at issue here is not a fundamental right,
respondent asserts that there must be a rational basis for the law and
that there is none in this case other than the presumed belief of a
majority of the electorate in Georgia that homosexual sodomy is
immoral and unacceptable. This is said to be an inadequate rationale
to support the law. The law, however, is constantly based on notions
of morality, and if all laws representing essentially moral choices are
to be invalidated under the Due Process Clause, the courts will be
very busy indeed. Even respondent makes no such claim, but insists
that majority sentiments about the morality of homosexuality should
be declared inadequate. We do not agree, and are unpersuaded that
the sodomy laws of some 25 States should be invalidated on this
basis.

Accordingly, the judgment of the Court of Appeals is reversed.
Chief Justice Burger, concurring.

> I join the Court's opinion, but I write separately to underscore my
> view that in constitutional terms there is no such thing as a fundamen-
> tal right to commit homosexual sodomy.
> . . . Decisions of individuals relating to homosexual conduct have
> been subject to state intervention throughout the history of Western
> Civilization. Condemnation of those practices is firmly rooted in
> Judeao-Christian moral and ethical standards. Homosexual sodomy
> was a capital crime under Roman law. . . . Blackstone described "the
> infamous crime against nature" as an offense of "deeper malignity"
> than rape, an heinous act "that very mention of which is a disgrace to
> human nature," and "a crime not fit to be named." . . .

DISSENT

This case is no more about "a fundamental right to engage in
homosexual sodomy," than Stanley v. Georgia, was about a fundamental right to watch obscene movies. . . . Rather, this case is about
"the most comprehensive of rights and the most valued by civilized
men," namely, "the right to be left alone." . . . Like Justice Holmes, I
believe that "[i]t is revolting to have no better reason for a rule of law
than that so it was laid down in the time of Henry IV. It is still more
revolting if the grounds upon which it was laid down have vanished
long since, and the rule simply persists from blind imitation of the
past." I believe we must analyze respondent's claim in the light of the
values that underlie the constitutional right to privacy. If that right
means anything, it means that, before Georgia can prosecute its
citizens for making choices about the most intimate aspects of their
lives, it must do more than assert that the choice they have made is
an "abominable crime not fit to be named among Christians." . . .

"Our cases long have recognized that the Constitution embodies a
promise that a certain private sphere of individual liberty will be kept
largely beyond the reach of the government." . . .

Only the most willful blindness could obscure the fact that sexual
intimacy is "a sensitive, key relationship of human existence, central

to family life, community welfare, and the development of human personality." The fact that individuals define themselves in a significant way through their intimate sexual relationships with others suggests, in a Nation as diverse as ours, that there may be many "right" ways of conducting those relationships, and that much of the richness of a relationship will come from the freedom an individual has to choose the form and nature of these intensely personal bonds.

In a variety of circumstances we have recognized that a necessary corollary of giving individuals freedom to choose how to conduct their lives is acceptable of the fact that different individuals will make different choices. . . . The Court claims that its decision today merely refuses to recognize a fundamental right to engage in homosexual sodomy; what the Court really has refused to recognize is the fundamental interest all individuals have in controlling the nature of their intimate associations with others.

The behavior for which Hardwick faces prosecution occurred in his own home, a place to which the Fourth Amendment attaches special significance. . . .

. . . [T]he right of an individual to conduct intimate relationships in the intimacy of his or her own home seems to me to be the heart of the Constitution's protection of privacy.

CASE DISCUSSION

What major reasons did the Supreme Court give for ruling that statutes making consensual sodomy a crime do not violate the United States Constitution? Do you agree with the arguments of the majority or the dissent? Would you favor a statute making consensual sodomy within marriage a crime? Would you limit the crime to homosexual sodomy? Or, despite its constitutionality, would you oppose such a statute? Give your reasons?

---

[1]Ga Code Ann § 16–6–2 (1984) provides, in pertinent part, as follows:

(a) A person commits the offense of sodomy when he performs or submits to any sexual act involving the sex organs of one person and the mouth or anus of another. . . .

(b) A person convicted of the offense of sodomy shall be punished by imprisonment for not less than one nor more than 20 years. . . .

≡ SUMMARY

Crimes against public order and morals form a large part of the criminal law. Although these crimes carry minor penalties compared with felonies, they are nevertheless important. First, they touch far more people than do felonies. Second, they lead to abuse and discrimination against undesirables. Third, they can violate both constitutional rights and basic criminal law principles. Finally, they are faulted because they curtail freedom and diversity in a complex, pluralistic society that prizes individuality.

Balancing social order with individual freedom underlies all crimes against public order. Those who favor more public order see these offenses differently from those whose priorities lie with personal freedom. Both groups enlist the Constitution for support and find arguments favoring what they consider criminal law's proper purposes, principles, and policies. In the end, however, value choices determine whether public order will take precedence over promoting individual freedom and autonomy. Furthermore, these categories are not neatly defined. In fact, most agree that society cannot exist without order but that a society without freedom is not much worth having. Drawing the line between freedom and order, and then balancing them in order to secure, promote, and protect both, are challenges to criminal law and its administration.

Fundamental questions arise concerning the place of morals offenses in criminal law. First, there are constitutional questions: Does a provision offend the due process requirement that statutes must define clearly and specifically every offense that states wish to prosecute? Does it meet the equal protection requirement prohibiting discriminatory enforcement? Does it violate the First Amendment prohibition against free expression, the Eighth Amendment strictures against cruel and unusual punishment, and the constitutional right to privacy?

Assuming that a particular statute passes the constitutional test, still the question of whether it is wise public policy must be asked and answered. The Constitution establishes only minimum standards; as one judge said, "It doesn't pay a statute much of a compliment to say that it is not unconstitutional." If answered affirmatively, the following public policy questions would complement morals offense statutes:

1. Does the conduct offend most people and is it not condoned by a significant number of them?
2. Does the conduct do substantial harm?
3. Can and should the harm be punished?
4. Are there no effective alternatives to the criminal sanction to deal with the problem?
5. Does the suppression of such conduct still allow enough individual autonomy?
6. Is the cost of enforcing the law reasonable in relation to the good that comes from enforcement?
7. Is fair and substantial enforcement possible?
8. Does enforcement breed respect for and acceptance of the statute in particular and the law in general?

Applied to homicide, rape, and other assaults and batteries, these questions can almost invariably be answered affirmatively. When morals offenses are considered, however, yes answers are fewer and more hesitant.

≡ QUESTIONS FOR REVIEW AND DISCUSSION

1. Do you think that threatening to breach the peace should be a crime? Explain.
2. When does free speech become fighting words?
3. Why should making threats be a crime if assault is already in the criminal law?
4. Should making obscene telephone calls be a crime? Why or why not? How serious a crime is it?
5. Do you think that engaging in altercations with the police should be a crime? Why or why not?
6. What constitutional, legal, and policy objections to vagrancy statutes can you raise? Should vagrancy be a crime? Why or why not?
7. Does suspicious loitering remove the objections raised to vagrancy?
8. What are the conflicting interests in crimes against public order? Do disorderly conduct, vagrancy, and loitering statutes effectively balance these interests?
9. What types of nonviolent private sexual conduct between consenting adults belong within criminal law's scope? Why?
10. What are the arguments for making prostitution a crime? What are the arguments against doing so? Should solicitation and promotion of prostitution be crimes? Why or why not?
11. How would you define sodomy for criminal law's purposes? What are the arguments in favor of having criminal penalties for sodomy? What are the arguments against doing so?

≡ SUGGESTED READINGS

1. American Law Institute, *Model Penal Code and Commentaries*, vol. 3 (Philadelphia: American Law Institute, 1980), pt. II, pp. 309–453, is a starting point for anyone interested in learning more about the crimes against public order. It summarizes existing law on the subject, criticizes it, and recommends alterations, explaining in great detail why the changes should be made.
2. Rollin M. Perkins and Ronald N. Boyce, *Criminal Law*, 3d ed. (Mineola, N.Y.: Foundation Press, 1982), pp. 477–98, discusses disorderly conduct and vagrancy. This is a good survey, including references to many more cases to read on the subject.
3. Anthony Amsterdam, "Federal Constitutional Restrictions on the Punishment of Crimes of Status, Crimes of General Obnoxiousness, Crimes of Displeasing Police Officers, and the Like," *Criminal Law Bulletin*, 3 (1967), p. 205, discusses all the crimes in this chapter in addition to others in light of their constitutionality. Although written for the professional, it repays the effort to read it.

4. William J. Chambliss, *Criminal Law in Action* (Santa Barbara, Calif.: Hamilton, 1975), pp. 9–16, is a brief, interesting, and excellent history of vagrancy laws. It provokes thought about vagrancy's purpose in criminal law as well as its development throughout the last several centuries.

5. Caleb Foote, "Vagrancy-Type Law and Its Administration," *University of Pennsylvania Law Review,* 104 (1956), pp. 603–50, is a firsthand account of how vagrancy is administered in a Philadelphia court. It is lively, incisive, and provocative, and clearly brings into focus not only how vagrancy laws are administered but also the underlying purposes and policies they serve.

6. Charles A. Reich, "Police Questioning of Law Abiding Citizens," *Yale Law Journal,* 75 (1966), pp. 116–72, describes one person's experience with police stops such as those associated with suspicious loitering and vagrancy. The author, a black law professor, offers his insights into his encounters with police while he walked at night to deal with his chronic insomnia.

7. Gilbert Geis, *Not the Law's Business: An Examination of Homosexuality, Abortion, Prostitution, Narcotics, and Gambling in the United States* (New York: Schocken Books, 1979), is a well-written book covering the morals offenses and why they should not be within criminal law's scope. It covers in depth many crimes from a social science point of view. Professor Geis is a senior sociologist whose ideas on the subject are well worth considering.

8. Edwin M. Schur and Hugo Adam Bedau, *Victimless Crimes: Two Sides of a Controversy* (Englewood Cliffs, N.J.: Prentice-Hall, 1974), is an excellent debate over whether victimless crimes are victimless and should be criminal. Professor Schur, a senior sociology professor, explains why attempts to legislate morality fail to stop the behavior they are designed to prevent. Professor Bedau, a well-known philosophy professor, challenges the basic concept of victimless crimes. The two authors discuss the human, social, and constitutional costs of criminalizing morals offenses. This is a stimulating discussion concerning the issues brought up in the discussion of morals offenses.

≡ NOTES

1. Norval Morris and Gordon Hawkins, *The Honest Politician's Guide to Crime Control* (Chicago: University of Chicago Press, 1970), chap. 1 and 8.

2. Packer, *The Limits of the Criminal Sanction,* chap. 15–17.

3. American Law Institute, *Model Penal Code and Commentaries,* vol. 3 (Philadelphia: American Law Institute, 1980), pt. II, p. 309.

4. Ibid., pp. 309–12.

5. *People v. Casey,* 188 Misc. 352, 67 N.Y.S.2d 9 (1946); *Jones v. Commonwealth,* 307 Ky. 286, 210 S.W.2d 956 (1948); Model Penal Code sec. 250.2 and American Law Institute, *Model Penal Code and Commentaries,* vol. 3, pt. II, pp. 348–49.

6. See Mark Rutzick, "Offensive Language and the Evolution of First Amendment Protection," *Harvard Civil Rights–Civil Liberties Law Review,* (1974), 9, p. 1.

7. American Law Institute, *Model Penal Code and Commentaries*, vol. 3, pt. II, pp. 349–53.

8. 415 U.S. 130, 94 S.Ct. 970, 39 L.Ed.2d 214 (1974).

9. James Q. Wilson, *Thinking about Crime*, rev. ed. (New York: Vintage Books, 1985), p. 112.

10. American Law Institute, *Model Penal Code and Commentaries*, vol. 3, pt. II, p. 331.

11. *People v. Craig*, 152 Cal. 42, 91 P. 997 (1907); Caleb Foote, "Vagrancy-Type Law and Its Administration," *University of Pennsylvania Law Review*, 104 (1956), pp. 603–50.

12. Ibid.

13. William Lambarde, *Eirenarcha* (London: 1588).

14. I am grateful to J. Mark Weiss, the attorney for the American Civil Liberties Union who supplied the brief.

15. Conversation with J. Mark Weiss, the attorney who wrote the brief for the American Civil Liberties Union attacking the ordinance's validity. The case is on appeal, as of this writing.

16. Morris and Hawkins, *The Honest Politician's Guide to Crime Control*.

17. Ibid.

18. Edwin M. Schur and Hugo Adam Bedau, *Victimless Crimes: Two Sides of a Controversy* (Englewood Cliffs, N.J.: Prentice-Hall, 1974).

19. Home Office, *Scottish Home Department Report of the Committee on Homosexual Offenses and Prostitution* (London: Her Majesty's Stationery Office, 1957), pp. 20–21.

20. Sir Patrick Devlin, *The Enforcement of Morals* (London: Oxford University Press, 1959), p. 48.

21. Wisconsin Stat.Ann. tit. 45, 344.15 (1958); Indiana Stat.Ann. 10–4207 (1977).

22. Article 251.2.

23. Home Office, *Scottish Home Department Report*, p. 247.

24. American Law Institute, "Commentary," *Model Penal Code*, tentative draft no. 4, (Philadelphia: American Law Institute, 1954), p. 276.

Appendix:
Model Penal Code Excerpts

PART I: GENERAL PROVISIONS

Article 1. Section 1.02.

Purposes; Principles of Construction.

(1) The general purposes of the provisions governing the definition of offenses are:

(a) to forbid and prevent conduct that unjustifiably and inexcusably inflicts or threatens substantial harm to individual or public interests;

(b) to subject to public control persons whose conduct indicates that they are disposed to commit crimes;

(c) to safeguard conduct that is without fault from condemnation as criminal;

(d) to give fair warning of the nature of the conduct declared to constitute an offense;

(e) to differentiate on reasonable grounds between serious and minor offenses.

(2) The general purposes of the provisions governing the sentencing and treatment of offenders are:

(a) to prevent the commission of offenses;

(b) to promote the correction and rehabilitation of offenders;

(c) to safeguard offenders against excessive, disproportionate or arbitrary punishment;

(d) to give fair warning of the nature of the sentences that may be imposed on conviction of an offense;

(e) to differentiate among offenders with a view to a just individualization in their treatment;

(f) to define, coordinate and harmonize the powers, duties and functions of the courts and of administrative officers and agencies responsible for dealing with offenders;

(g) to advance the use of generally accepted scientific methods and knowledge in the sentencing and treatment of offenders;

(h) to integrate responsibility for the administration of the correctional system in a State Department of Correction [or other single department or agency].

(3) The provisions of the Code shall be construed according to the fair import of their terms but when the language is susceptible of differing constructions it shall be interpreted to further the general purposes stated in this Section and the special purposes of the particular provision involved. The discretionary powers conferred by the Code shall be exercised in accordance with the criteria stated in the Code and, insofar as such criteria are not decisive, to further the general purposes stated in this Section.

Section 1.03. Territorial Applicability.

(1) Except as otherwise provided in this Section, a person may be convicted under the law of this State of an offense committed by his own conduct or the conduct of another for which he is legally accountable if:

(a) either the conduct that is an element of the offense or the result that is such an element occurs within this State; or

(b) conduct occurring outside the State is sufficient under the law of this State to constitute an attempt to commit an offense within the State; or

(c) conduct occurring outside the State is sufficient under the law of this State to constitute a conspiracy to commit an offense within the State and an overt act in furtherance of such conspiracy occurs within the State; or

(d) conduct occurring within the State establishes complicity in the commission of, or an attempt, solicitation or conspiracy to commit, an offense in another jurisdiction that also is an offense under the law of this State; or

(e) the offense consists of the omission to perform a legal duty imposed by the law of this State with respect to domicile, residence or a relationship to a person, thing or transaction in the State; or

(f) the offense is based on a statute of this State that expressly prohibits conduct outside the State, when the conduct bears a reasonable relation to a legitimate interest of this State and the actor knows or should know that his conduct is likely to affect that interest.

Section 1.04. Classes of Crimes; Violations.

(1) An offense defined by this Code or by any other statute of this State, for which a sentence of [death or of] imprisonment is authorized, constitutes a crime. Crimes are classified as felonies, misdemeanors or petty misdemeanors.

(2) A crime is a felony if it is so designated in this Code or if persons convicted thereof may be sentenced [to death or] to imprisonment for a term that, apart from an extended term, is in excess of one year.

(3) A crime is a misdemeanor if it is so designated in this Code or in a statute other than this Code enacted subsequent thereto.

(4) A crime is a petty misdemeanor if it is so designated in this Code or in a statute other than this Code enacted subsequent thereto or if it is defined by a statute other than this Code that now provides that persons convicted thereof may be sentenced to imprisonment for a term of which the maximum is less than one year.

(5) An offense defined by this Code or by any other statute of this State constitutes a violation if it is so designated in this Code or in the law defining the offense or if no other sentence than a fine, or fine and forfeiture or other civil penalty is authorized upon conviction or if it is defined by a statute other than this Code that now provides that the offense shall not constitute a crime. A violation does not constitute a crime and conviction of a violation shall not give rise to any disability or legal disadvantage based on conviction of a criminal offense.

(6) Any offense declared by law to constitute a crime, without specification of the grade thereof or of the sentence authorized upon conviction, is a misdemeanor.

(7) An offense defined by any statute of this State other than this Code shall be classified as provided in this Section and the sentence that may be imposed upon conviction thereof shall hereafter be governed by this Code.

Section 1.05. All Offenses Defined by Statute; Application of General Provisions of the Code.

(1) No conduct constitutes an offense unless it is a crime or violation under this Code or another statute of this State.

(2) The provisions of Part I of the Code are applicable to offenses defined by other statutes, unless the Code otherwise provides.

(3) This Section does not affect the power of a court to punish for contempt or to employ any sanction authorized by law for the enforcement of an order or a civil judgment or decree.

Section 1.06. Time Limitations.

(1) A prosecution for murder may be commenced at any time.

(2) Except as otherwise provided in this Section, prosecutions for other offenses are subject to the following periods of limitation:

(a) A prosecution for a felony of the first degree must be commenced within six years after it is committed;

(b) a prosecution for any other felony must be commenced within three years after it is committed;

(c) a prosecution for a misdemeanor must be commenced within two years after it is committed;

(d) a prosecution for a petty misdemeanor or a violation must be commenced within six months after it is committed.

(3) If the period prescribed in Subsection (2) has expired, a prosecution may nevertheless be commenced for:

(a) any offense a material element of which is either fraud or a breach of fiduciary obligation within one year after discovery of the offense by an aggrieved party or by a person who has legal duty to represent an aggrieved party and who is himself not a party to the offense, but in no case shall this provision extend the period of limitation otherwise applicable by more than three years; and

(b) any offense based upon misconduct in office by a public officer or employee at any time when the defendant is in public office or employment or within two years thereafter, but in no case shall this provision extend the period of limitation otherwise applicable by more than three years.

(4) An offense is committed either when every element occurs, or, if a legislative purpose to prohibit a continuing course of conduct plainly appears, at the time when the course of conduct or the defendant's complicity therein is terminated. Time starts to run on the day after the offense is committed.

(5) A prosecution is commenced either when an indictment is found [or an information filed] or when a warrant or other process is issued, provided that such warrant or process is executed without unreasonable delay.

(6) The period of limitation does not run:

(a) during any time when the accused is continuously absent from the State or has no reasonably ascertainable place of abode or work within the State, but in no case shall this provision extend the period of limitation otherwise applicable by more than three years; or

(b) during any time when a prosecution against the accused for the same conduct is pending in this State.

Section 1.12. Proof beyond a Reasonable Doubt; Affirmative Defenses; Burden of Proving Fact when Not an Element of an Offense; Presumptions.

(1) No person may be convicted of an offense unless each element of such offense is proved beyond a reasonable doubt. In the absence of such proof, the innocence of the defendant is assumed.

(2) Subsection (1) of this Section does not:

(a) require the disproof of an affirmative defense unless and until there is evidence supporting such defense; or

(b) apply to any defense that the Code or another statute plainly requires the defendant to prove by a preponderance of evidence.

(3) A ground of defense is affirmative, within the meaning of Subsection (2)(a) of this Section, when:

(a) it arises under a section of the Code that so provides; or

(b) it relates to an offense defined by a statute other than the Code and such statute so provides; or

(c) it involves a matter of excuse or justification peculiarly within the knowledge of the defendant on which he can fairly be required to adduce supporting evidence.

(4) When the application of the Code depends upon the finding of a fact that is not an element of an offense, unless the Code otherwise provides:

(a) the burden of proving the fact is on the prosecution or defendant, depending on whose interest or contention will be furthered if the finding should be made; and

(b) the fact must be proved to the satisfaction of the Court or jury, as the case may be.

(5) When the Code establishes a presumption with respect to any fact that is an element of an offense, it has the following consequences:

(a) when there is evidence of the facts that give rise to the presumption, the issue of the existence of the presumed fact must be submitted to the jury, unless the Court is satisfied that the evidence as a whole clearly negatives the presumed fact; and

(b) when the issue of the existence of the presumed fact is submitted to the jury, the Court shall charge that while the presumed fact must, on all the evidence, be proved beyond a reasonable doubt, the law declares that the jury may regard the facts giving rise to the presumption as sufficient evidence of the presumed fact.

(6) A presumption not established by the Code or inconsistent with it has the consequences otherwise accorded it by law.

Section 1.13. General Definitions.

In this Code, unless a different meaning plainly is required:

(1) "statute" includes the Constitution and a local law or ordinance of a political subdivision of the State;

(2) "act" or "action" means a bodily movement whether voluntary or involuntary;

(3) "voluntary" has the meaning specified in Section 2.01;

(4) "omission" means a failure to act;

(5) "conduct" means an action or omission and its accompanying state of mind, or, where relevant, a series of acts and omissions;

(6) "actor" includes, where relevant, a person guilty of an omission;

(7) "acted" includes, where relevant, "omitted to act";

(8) "person," "he" and "actor" include any natural person and, where relevant, a corporation or an unincorporated association;

(9) "element of an offense" means (i) such conduct or (ii) such attendant circumstances or (iii) such a result of conduct as

(a) is included in the description of the forbidden conduct in the definition of the offense; or

(b) establishes the required kind of culpability; or

(c) negatives an excuse or justification for such conduct; or

(d) negatives a defense under the statute of limitations; or

(e) establishes jurisdiction or venue;

(10) "material element of an offense" means an element that does not relate exclusively to the statute of limitations, jurisdiction, venue, or to any other matter similarly unconnected with (i) the harm or evil, incident to conduct, sought to be prevented by the law defining the offense, or (ii) the existence of a justification or excuse for such conduct;

(11) "purposely" has the meaning specified in Section 2.02 and equivalent terms such as "with purpose," "designed" or "with design" have the same meaning;

(12) "intentionally" or "with intent" means purposely;

(13) "knowingly" has the meaning specified in Section 2.02 and equivalent terms such as "knowing" or "with knowledge" have the same meaning;

(14) "recklessly" has the meaning specified in Section 2.02 and equivalent terms such as "recklessness" or "with recklessness" have the same meaning;

(15) "negligently" has the meaning specified in Section 2.02 and equivalent terms such as "negligence" or "with negligence" have the same meaning;

(16) "reasonably believes" or "reasonable belief" designates a belief that the actor is not reckless or negligent in holding.

Article 2. General Principles of Liability

Section 2.01. Requirement of Voluntary Act; Omission as Basis of Liability; Possession as an Act.

(1) A person is not guilty of an offense unless his liability is based on conduct that includes a voluntary act or the omission to perform an act of which he is physically capable.

(2) The following are not voluntary acts within the meaning of this Section:

　(a) a reflex or convulsion;

　(b) a bodily movement during unconsciousness or sleep;

　(c) conduct during hypnosis or resulting from hypnotic suggestion:

　(d) a bodily movement that otherwise is not a product of the effort or determination of the actor, either conscious or habitual.

(3) Liability for the commission of an offense may not be based on an omission unaccompanied by action unless:

　(a) the omission is expressly made sufficient by the law defining the offense; or

　(b) a duty to perform the omitted act is otherwise imposed by law.

(4) Possession is an act, within the meaning of this Section, if the possessor knowingly procured or received the thing possessed or was aware of his control thereof for a sufficient period to have been able to terminate his possession.

Section 2.02. General Requirements of Culpability.

(1) <u>Minimum Requirements of Culpability</u>. Except as provided in Section 2.05, a person is not guilty of an offense unless he acted purposely, knowingly, recklessly or negligently, as the law may require, with respect to each material element of the offense.

(2) <u>Kinds of Culpability Defined</u>.

(a) <u>Purposely</u>. A person acts purposely with respect to a material element of an offense when:

(i) if the element involves the nature of his conduct or a result thereof, it is his conscious object to engage in conduct of that nature or to cause such a result; and

(ii) if the element involves the attendant circumstances, he is aware of the existence of such circumstances or he believes or hopes that they exist.

(b) <u>Knowingly</u>. A person acts knowingly with respect to a material element of an offense when:

(i) if the element involves the nature of his conduct or the attendant circumstances, he is aware that his conduct is of that nature or that such circumstances exist; and

(ii) if the element involves a result of his conduct, he is aware that it is practically certain that his conduct will cause such a result.

(c) <u>Recklessly</u>. A person acts recklessly with respect to a material element of an offense when he consciously disregards a substantial and unjustifiable risk that the material element exists or will result from his conduct. The risk must be of such a nature and degree that, considering the nature and purpose of the actor's conduct and the circumstances known to him, its disregard involves a gross deviation from the standard of conduct that a law-abiding person would observe in the actor's situation.

(d) <u>Negligently</u>. A person acts negligently with respect to a material element of an offense when he should be aware of a substantial and unjustifiable risk that the material element exists or will result from his conduct. The risk must be of such a nature and degree that the actor's failure to perceive it, considering the nature and purpose of his conduct and the circumstances known to him, involves a gross deviation from the standard of care that a reasonable person would observe in the actor's situation.

(3) <u>Culpability Required Unless Otherwise Provided</u>. When the culpability sufficient to establish a material element of an offense is not prescribed by law, such element is established if a person acts purposely, knowingly or recklessly with respect thereto.

(4) <u>Prescribed Culpability Requirement Applies to All Material Elements</u>. When the law defining an offense prescribes the kind of culpability that is sufficient for the commission of an offense, without distinguishing among the material elements thereof, such provision shall apply to all the material elements of the offense, unless a contrary purpose plainly appears.

(5) <u>Substitutes for Negligence, Recklessness and Knowledge</u>. When the law provides that negligence suffices to establish an element of an offense, such element also is established if a person acts purposely, knowingly or recklessly. When recklessness suffices to establish an element, such element also is established if a person acts purposely or knowingly. When acting knowingly suffices to establish an element, such element also is established if a person acts purposely.

(6) <u>Requirement of Purpose Satisfied if Purpose Is Conditional</u>. When a particular purpose is an element of an offense, the element is established although such purpose is conditional, unless the condition negatives the harm or evil sought to be prevented by the law defining the offense.

(7) <u>Requirement of Knowledge Satisfied by Knowledge of High Probability</u>. When knowledge of the existence of a particular fact is an element of an offense, such knowledge is established if a person is aware of a high probability of its existence, unless he actually believes that it does not exist.

(8) <u>Requirement of Wilfulness Satisfied by Acting Knowingly</u>. A requirement that an offense be committed wilfully is satisfied if a person acts knowingly with respect to the material elements of the offense, unless a purpose to impose further requirements appears.

(9) <u>Culpability as to Illegality of Conduct</u>. Neither knowledge nor recklessness or negligence as to whether conduct constitutes an offense or as to the existence, meaning or application of the law determining the elements of an offense is an element of such offense, unless the definition of the offense or the Code so provides.

(10) <u>Culpability as Determinant of Grade of Offense</u>. When the grade or degree of an offense depends on whether the offense is committed purposely, knowingly, recklessly or negligently, its grade or degree shall be the lowest for which the determinative kind of culpability is established with respect to any material element of the offense.

Section 2.03.   Causal Relationship between Conduct and Result; Divergence between Result Designed or Contemplated and Actual Result or between Probable and Actual Result.

(1) Conduct is the cause of a result when:

   (a) it is an antecedent but for which the result in question would not have occurred; and

   (b) the relationship between the conduct and result satisfies any additional causal requirements imposed by the Code or by the law defining the offense.

(2) When purposely or knowingly causing a particular result is an element of an offense, the element is not established if the actual result is not within the purpose or the contemplation of the actor unless:

   (a) the actual result differs from that designed or contemplated, as the case may be, only in the respect that a different person or different property is injured or affected or that the injury or harm designed or contemplated would have been more serious or more extensive than that caused; or

(b) the actual result involves the same kind of injury or harm as that designed or contemplated and is not too remote or accidental in its occurrence to have a [just] bearing on the actor's liability or on the gravity of his offense.

(3) When recklessly or negligently causing a particular result is an element of an offense, the element is not established if the actual result is not within the risk of which the actor is aware or, in the case of negligence, of which he should be aware unless:

(a) the actual result differs from the probable result only in the respect that a different person or different property is injured or affected or that the probable injury or harm would have been more serious or more extensive than that caused; or

(b) the actual result involves the same kind of injury or harm as the probable result and is not too remote or accidental in its occurrence to have a [just] bearing on the actor's liability or on the gravity of his offense.

(4) When causing a particular result is a material element of an offense for which absolute liability is imposed by law, the element is not established unless the actual result is a probable consequence of the actor's conduct.

Section 2.04. Ignorance or Mistake.

(1) Ignorance or mistake as to a matter of fact or law is a defense if:

(a) the ignorance or mistake negatives the purpose, knowledge, belief, recklessness or negligence required to establish a material element of the offense; or

(b) the law provides that the state of mind established by such ignorance or mistake constitutes a defense.

(2) Although ignorance or mistake would otherwise afford a defense to the offense charged, the defense is not available if the defendant would be guilty of another offense had the situation been as he supposed. In such case, however, the ignorance or mistake of the defendant shall reduce the grade and degree of the offense of which he may be convicted to those of the offense of which he would be guilty had the situation been as he supposed.

(3) A belief that conduct does not legally constitute an offense is a defense to a prosecution for that offense based upon such conduct when:

(a) the statute or other enactment defining the offense is not known to the actor and has not been published or otherwise reasonably made available prior to the conduct alleged; or

(b) he acts in reasonable reliance upon an official statement of the law, afterward determined to be invalid or erroneous, contained in

(i) a statute or other enactment; (ii) a judicial decision, opinion or judgment; (iii) an administrative order or grant of permission; or (iv) an official interpretation of the public officer or body charged by law with responsibility for the interpretation, administration or enforcement of the law defining the offense.

(4) The defendant must prove a defense arising under Subsection (3) of this Section by a preponderance of evidence.

Section 2.05. When Culpability Requirements Are Inapplicable to Violations and to Offenses Defined by Other Statutes; Effect of Absolute Liability in Reducing Grade of Offense to Violation.

(1) The requirements of culpability prescribed by Sections 2.01 and 2.02 do not apply to:

(a) offenses that constitute violations, unless the requirement involved is included in the definition of the offense or the Court determines that its application is consistent with effective enforcement of the law defining the offense; or

(b) offenses defined by statutes other than the Code, insofar as a legislative purpose to impose absolute liability for such offenses or with respect to any material element thereof plainly appears.

(2) Notwithstanding any other provision of existing law and unless a subsequent statute otherwise provides:

(a) when absolute liability is imposed with respect to any material element of an offense defined by a statute other than the Code and a conviction is based upon such liability, the offense constitutes a violation; and

(b) although absolute liability is imposed by law with respect to one or more of the material elements of an offense defined by a statute other than the Code, the culpable commission of the offense may be charged and proved, in which event negligence with respect to such elements constitutes sufficient culpability and the classification of the offense and the sentence that may be imposed therefor upon conviction are determined by Section 1.04 and Article 6 of the Code.

Section 2.06. Liability for Conduct of Another; Complicity.

(1) A person is guilty of an offense if it is committed by his own conduct or by the conduct of another person for which he is legally accountable, or both.

(2) A person is legally accountable for the conduct of another person when:

(a) acting with the kind of culpability that is sufficient for the commission of the offense, he causes an innocent or irresponsible person to engage in such conduct; or

(b) he is made accountable for the conduct of such other person by the Code or by the law defining the offense; or

(c) he is an accomplice of such other person in the commission of the offense.

(3) A person is an accomplice of another person in the commission of an offense if:

(a) with the purpose of promoting or facilitating the commission of the offense, he

(i) solicits such other person to commit it, or

(ii) aids or agrees or attempts to aid such other person in planning or committing it, or

(iii) having a legal duty to prevent the commission of the offense, fails to make proper effort so to do; or

(b) his conduct is expressly declared by law to establish his complicity.

(4) When causing a particular result is an element of an offense, an accomplice in the conduct causing such result is an accomplice in the commission of that offense if he acts with the kind of culpability, if any, with respect to that result that is sufficient for the commission of the offense.

(5) A person who is legally incapable of committing a particular offense himself may be guilty thereof if it is committed by the conduct of another person for which he is legally accountable, unless such liability is inconsistent with the purpose of the provision establishing his incapacity.

(6) Unless otherwise provided by the Code or by the law defining the offense, a person is not an accomplice in an offense committed by another person if:

(a) he is a victim of that offense; or

(b) the offense is so defined that his conduct is inevitably incident to its commission; or

(c) he terminates his complicity prior to the commission of the offense and

(i) wholly deprives it of effectiveness in the commission of the offense; or

(ii) gives timely warning to the law enforcement authorities or otherwise makes proper effort to prevent the commission of the offense.

(7) An accomplice may be convicted on proof of the commission of the offense and of his complicity therein, though the person claimed to have committed the offense has not been prosecuted or convicted or has been convicted of a different offense or degree of offense or has an immunity to prosecution or conviction or has been convicted.

Section 2.07. Liability of Corporations, Unincorporated Associations and Persons Acting, or under a Duty to Act, in Their Behalf.

(1) A corporation may be convicted of the commission of an offense if:

(a) the offense is a violation or the offense is defined by a statute other than the Code in which a legislative purpose to impose liability on corporations plainly appears and the conduct is performed by an agent of the corporation acting in behalf of the corporation within the scope of his office or employment, except that if the law defining the offense designates the agents for whose conduct the corporation is accountable or the circumstances under which it is accountable, such provisions shall apply; or

(b) the offense consists of an omission to discharge a specific duty of affirmative performance imposed on corporations by law; or

(c) the commission of the offense was authorized, requested, commanded, performed or recklessly tolerated by the board of directors or by a high managerial agent acting in behalf of the corporation within the scope of his office or employment.

(2) When absolute liability is imposed for the commission of an offense, a legislative purpose to impose liability on a corporation shall be assumed, unless the contrary plainly appears.

(3) An unincorporated association may be convicted of the commission of an offense if:

(a) the offense is defined by a statute other than the Code that expressly provides for the liability of such an association and the conduct is performed by an agent of the association acting in behalf of the association within the scope of his office or employment, except that if the law defining the offense designates the agents for whose conduct the association is accountable or the circumstances under which it is accountable, such provisions shall apply; or

(b) the offense consists of an omission to discharge a specific duty of affirmative performance imposed on associations by law.

(4) As used in this Section:

(a) "corporation" does not include an entity organized as or by a governmental agency for the execution of a governmental program;

(b) "agent" means any director, officer, servant, employee or other person authorized to act in behalf of the corporation or association and, in the case of an unincorporated association, a member of such association;

(c) "high managerial agent" means an officer of a corporation or an unincorporated association, or, in the case of a partnership, a partner, or any other agent of a corporation or association having duties of such responsibility that his conduct may fairly be assumed to represent the policy of the corporation or association.

(5) In any prosecution of a corporation or an unincorporated association for the commission of an offense included within the terms of Subsection (1)(a) or Subsection (3)(a) of this Section, other than an offense for which absolute liability has been imposed, it shall be a defense if the defendant proves by a preponderance of evidence that the high managerial agent having supervisory responsibility over the subject matter of the offense employed due diligence to prevent its commission. This paragraph shall not apply if it is plainly inconsistent with the legislative purpose in defining the particular offense.

(6) (a) A person is legally accountable for any conduct he performs or causes to be performed in the name of the corporation or an

unincorporated association or in its behalf to the same extent as if it were performed in his own name or behalf.

(b) Whenever a duty to act is imposed by law upon a corporation or an unincorporated association, any agent of the corporation or association having primary responsibility for the discharge of the duty is legally accountable for a reckless omission to perform the required act to the same extent as if the duty were imposed by law directly upon himself.

(c) When a person is convicted of an offense by reason of his legal accountability for the conduct of a corporation or an unincorporated association, he is subject to the sentence authorized by law when a natural person is convicted of an offense of the grade and the degree involved.

Section 2.08. Intoxication.

(1) Except as provided in Subsection (4) of this Section, intoxication of the actor is not a defense unless it negatives an element of the offense.

(2) When recklessness establishes an element of the offense, if the actor, due to self-induced intoxication, is unaware of a risk of which he would have been aware had he been sober, such unawareness is immaterial.

(3) Intoxication does not, in itself, constitute mental disease within the meaning of Section 4.01.

(4) Intoxication that (a) is not self-induced or (b) is pathological is an affirmative defense if by reason of such intoxication the actor at the time of his conduct lacks substantial capacity either to appreciate its criminality [wrongfulness] or to conform his conduct to the requirements of law.

(5) Definitions. In this Section unless a different meaning plainly is required:

(a) "intoxication" means a disturbance of mental or physical capacities resulting from the introduction of substances into the body;

(b) "self-induced intoxication" means intoxication caused by substances that the actor knowingly introduces into his body, the tendency of which to cause intoxication he knows or ought to know, unless he introduces them pursuant to medical advice or under such circumstances as would afford a defense to a charge of crime;

(c) "pathological intoxication" means intoxication grossly excessive in degree, given the amount of the intoxicant, to which the actor does not know he is susceptible.

Section 2.09. Duress.

(1) It is an affirmative defense that the actor engaged in the conduct charged to constitute an offense because he was coerced to do so by the use of, or a threat to use, unlawful force against his person or the person of another, that a person of reasonable firmness in his situation would have been unable to resist.

(2) The defense provided by this Section is unavailable if the actor recklessly placed himself in a situation in which it was probable that he would be subjected to duress. The defense is also unavailable if he was negligent in placing himself in such a situation, whenever negligence suffices to establish culpability for the offense charged.

(3) It is not a defense that a woman acted on the command of her husband, unless she acted under such coercion as would establish a defense under this Section. [The presumption that a woman acting in the presence of her husband is coerced is abolished.]

(4) When the conduct of the actor would otherwise be justifiable under Section 3.02, this Section does not preclude such defense.

Section 2.10. Military Orders.

It is an affirmative defense that the actor, in engaging in the conduct charged to constitute an offense, does no more than execute an order of his superior in the armed services that he does not know to be unlawful.

Section 2.11. Consent.

(1) In General. The consent of the victim to conduct charged to constitute an offense or to the result thereof is a defense if such consent negatives an element of the offense or precludes the infliction of the harm or evil sought to be prevented by the law defining the offense.

(2) Consent to Bodily Injury. When conduct is charged to constitute an offense because it causes or threatens bodily injury, consent to such conduct or to the infliction of such injury is a defense if:

(a) the bodily injury consented to or threatened by the conduct consented to is not serious; or

(b) the conduct and the injury are reasonably foreseeable hazards of joint participation in a lawful athletic contest or competitive sport or other concerted activity not forbidden by law; or

(c) the consent establishes a justification for the conduct under Article 3 of the Code.

(3) Ineffective Consent. Unless otherwise provided by the Code or by the law defining the offense, assent does not constitute consent if:

(a) it is given by a person who is legally incompetent to authorize the conduct charged to constitute the offense; or

(b) it is given by a person who by reason of youth, mental disease or defect or intoxication is manifestly unable or known by the actor to be unable to make a reasonable judgment as to the nature or harmfulness of the conduct charged to constitute the offense; or

(c) it is given by a person whose improvident consent is sought to be prevented by the law defining the offense; or

(d) it is induced by force, duress or deception of a kind sought to be prevented by the law defining the offense.

Section 2.12. De Minimis Infractions.

The Court shall dismiss a prosecution if, having regard to the nature of the conduct charged to constitute an offense and the nature of the attendant circumstances, it finds that the defendant's conduct:

(1) was within a customary license or tolerance, neither expressly negatived by the person whose interest was infringed nor inconsistent with the purpose of the law defining the offense; or

(2) did not actually cause or threaten the harm or evil sought to be prevented by the law defining the offense or did so only to an extent too trivial to warrant the condemnation of conviction; or

(3) presents such other extenuations that it cannot reasonably be regarded as envisaged by the legislature in forbidding the offense.

The Court shall not dismiss a prosecution under Subsection (3) of this Section without filing a written statement of its reasons.

Section 2.13. Entrapment.

(1) A public law enforcement official or a person acting in cooperation with such an official perpetrates an entrapment if for the purpose of obtaining evidence of the commission of an offense, he induces or encourages another person to engage in conduct constituting such offense by either:

(a) making knowingly false representations designed to induce the belief that such conduct is not prohibited; or

(b) employing methods of persuasion or inducement that create a substantial risk that such an offense will be committed by persons other than those who are ready to commit it.

(2) Except as provided in Subsection (3) of this Section, a person prosecuted for an offense shall be acquitted if he proves by a preponderance of evidence that his conduct occurred in response to an entrapment. The issue of entrapment shall be tried by the Court in the absence of the jury.

(3) The defense afforded by this Section is unavailable when causing or threatening bodily injury is an element of the offense charged and the prosecution is based on conduct causing or threatening such injury to a person other than the person perpetrating the entrapment.

Article 3. General Principles of Justification

Section 3.01. Justification an Affirmative Defense; Civil Remedies Unaffected.

(1) In any prosecution based on conduct that is justifiable under this Article, justification is an affirmative defense.

(2) The fact that conduct is justifiable under this Article does not abolish or impair any remedy for such conduct that is available in any civil action.

Section 3.02. Justification Generally: Choice of Evils.

(1) Conduct that the actor believes to be necessary to avoid a harm or evil to himself or to another is justifiable, provided that:

(a) the harm or evil sought to be avoided by such conduct is greater than that sought to be prevented by the law defining the offense charged; and

(b) neither the Code nor other law defining the offense provides exceptions or defenses dealing with the specific situation involved; and

(c) a legislative purpose to exclude the justification claimed does not otherwise plainly appear.

(2) When the actor was reckless or negligent in bringing about the situation requiring a choice of harms or evils or in appraising the necessity for his conduct, the justification afforded by this Section is unavailable in a prosecution for any offense for which recklessness or negligence, as the case may be, suffices to establish culpability.

Section 3.03. Execution of Public Duty.

(1) Except as provided in Subsection (2) of this Section, conduct is justifiable when it is required or authorized by:

(a) the law defining the duties or functions of a public officer or the assistance to be rendered to such officer in the performance of his duties; or

(b) the law governing the execution of legal process; or

(c) the judgment or order of a competent court or tribunal; or

(d) the law governing the armed services or the lawful conduct of war; or

(e) any other provision of law imposing a public duty.

(2) The other sections of this Article apply to:

(a) the use of force upon or toward the person of another for any of the purposes dealt with in such sections; and

(b) the use of deadly force for any purpose, unless the use of such force is otherwise expressly authorized by law or occurs in the lawful conduct of war.

(3) The justification afforded by Subsection (1) of this Section applies:

(a) when the actor believes his conduct to be required or authorized by the judgment or direction of a competent court or tribunal or in the lawful execution of legal process, notwithstanding lack of jurisdiction of the court or defect in the legal process; and

(b) when the actor believes his conduct to be required or authorized to assist a public officer in the performance of his duties, notwithstanding that the officer exceeded his legal authority.

Section 3.04. Use of Force in Self-Protection.

(1) Use of Force Justifiable for Protection of the Person. Subject to the provisions of this Section and of Section 3.09, the use of force upon or

toward another person is justifiable when the actor believes that such force is immediately necessary for the purpose of protecting himself against the use of unlawful force by such other person on the present occasion.

(2) Limitations on Justifying Necessity for Use of Force.

(a) The use of force is not justifiable under this Section:

(i) to resist an arrest that the actor knows is being made by a peace officer, although the arrest is unlawful; or

(ii) to resist force used by the occupier or possessor of property or by another person on his behalf, where the actor knows that the person using the force is doing so under a claim of right to protect the property, except that this limitation shall not apply if:

(A) the actor is a public officer acting in the performance of his duties or a person lawfully assisting him therein or a person making or assisting in a lawful arrest; or

(B) the actor has been unlawfully dispossessed of the property and is making a re-entry or recaption justified by Section 3.06; or

(C) the actor believes that such force is necessary to protect himself against death or serious bodily injury.

(b) The use of deadly force is not justifiable under this Section unless the actor believes that such force is necessary to protect himself against death, serious bodily injury, kidnapping or sexual intercourse compelled by force or threat; nor is it justifiable if:

(i) the actor, with the purpose of causing death or serious bodily injury, provoked the use of force against himself in the same encounter; or

(ii) the actor knows that he can avoid the necessity of using such force with complete safety by retreating or by surrendering possession of a thing to a person asserting a claim of right thereto or by complying with a demand that he abstain from any action that he has no duty to take, except that:

(A) the actor is not obliged to retreat from his dwelling or place of work, unless he was the initial aggressor or is assailed in his place of work by another person whose place of work the actor knows it to be; and

(B) a public officer justified in using force in the performance of his duties or a person justified in using force in his assistance or a person justified in using force in making an arrest or preventing an escape is not obliged to desist from efforts to perform such duty, effect such arrest or prevent such escape because of resistance or threatened resistance by or on behalf of the person against whom such action is directed.

(c) Except as required by paragraphs (a) and (b) of this Subsection, a person employing protective force may estimate the necessity thereof under the circumstances as he believes them to be when the force is used, without retreating, surrendering possession, doing any other act that he has no legal duty to do or abstaining from any lawful action.

(3) Use of Confinement as Protective Force. The justification afforded by this Section extends to the use of confinement as protective force

only if the actor takes all reasonable measures to terminate the confinement as soon as he knows that he safely can, unless the person confined has been arrested on a charge of crime.

Section 3.05. Use of Force for the Protection of Other Persons.

(1) Subject to the provisions of this Section and of Section 3.09, the use of force upon or toward the person of another is justifiable to protect a third person when:

(a) the actor would be justified under Section 3.04 in using such force to protect himself against the injury he believes to be threatened to the person whom he seeks to protect; and

(b) under the circumstances as the actor believes them to be, the person whom he seeks to protect would be justified in using such protective force; and

(c) the actor believes that his intervention is necessary for the protection of such other person.

(2) Notwithstanding Subsection (1) of this Section:

(a) when the actor would be obliged under Section 3.04 to retreat, to surrender the possession of a thing or to comply with a demand before using force in self-protection, he is not obliged to do so before using force for the protection of another person, unless he knows that he can thereby secure the complete safety of such other person; and

(b) when the person whom the actor seeks to protect would be obliged under Section 3.04 to retreat, to surrender the possession of a thing or to comply with a demand if he knew that he could obtain complete safety by so doing, the actor is obliged to try to cause him to do so before using force in his protection if the actor knows that he can obtain complete safety in that way; and

(c) neither the actor nor the person whom he seeks to protect is obliged to retreat when in the other's dwelling or place of work to any greater extent than in his own.

Section 3.06. Use of Force for Protection of Property.

(1) Use of Force Justifiable for Protection of Property. Subject to the provisions of this Section and of Section 3.09, the use of force upon or toward the person of another is justifiable when the actor believes that such force is immediately necessary:

(a) to prevent or terminate an unlawful entry or other trespass upon land or a trespass against or the unlawful carrying away of tangible, movable property, provided that such land or movable property is, or is believed by the actor to be, in his possession or in the possession of another person for whose protection he acts; or

(b) to effect an entry or re-entry upon land or to retake tangible movable property, provided that the actor believes that he or the person by whose authority he acts or a person from whom he or such other person derives title was unlawfully dispossessed of such land or movable property and is entitled to possession, and provided, further, that:

(i) the force is used immediately or on fresh pursuit after such dispossession; or

(ii) the actor believes that the person against whom he uses force has no claim of right to the possession of the property and, in the case of land, the circumstances, as the actor believes them to be, are of such urgency that it would be an exceptional hardship to postpone the entry or re-entry until a court order is obtained.

(2) Meaning of Possession. For the purposes of Subsection (1) of this Section:

(a) a person who has parted with the custody of property to another who refuses to restore it to him is no longer in possession, unless the property is movable and was and still is located on land in his possession;

(b) a person who has been dispossessed of land does not regain possession thereof merely by setting foot thereon;

(c) a person who has a license to use or occupy real property is deemed to be in possession thereof except against the licensor acting under claim of right.

(3) Limitations on Justifiable Use of Force.

(a) Request to Desist. The use of force is justifiable under this Section only if the actor first requests the person against whom such force is used to desist from his interference with the property, unless the actor believes that:

(i) such request would be useless; or

(ii) it would be dangerous to himself or another person to make the request; or

(iii) substantial harm will be done to the physical condition of the property that is sought to be protected before the request can effectively be made.

(b) Exclusion of Trespasser. The use of force to prevent or terminate a trespass is not justifiable under this Section if the actor knows that the exclusion of the trespasser will expose him to substantial danger of serious bodily injury.

(c) Resistance of Lawful Re-entry or Recaption. The use of force to prevent an entry or re-entry upon land or the recaption of movable property is not justifiable under this Section, although the actor believes that such re-entry or recaption is unlawful, if:

(i) the re-entry or recaption is made by or on behalf of a person who was actually dispossessed of the property; and

(ii) it is otherwise justifiable under Subsection (1)(b) of this Section.

(d) Use of Deadly Force. The use of deadly force is not justifiable under this Section unless the actor believes that:

(i) the person against whom the force is used is attempting to dispossess him of his dwelling otherwise than under a claim of right to its possession; or

(ii) the person against whom the force is used is attempting to commit or consummate arson, burglary, robbery or other felonious theft or property destruction and either:

(A) has employed or threatened deadly force against or in the presence of the actor; or

(B) the use of force other than deadly force to prevent the commission or the consummation of the crime would expose the actor or another in his presence to substantial danger of serious bodily injury.

(4) Use of Confinement as Protective Force. The justification afforded by this Section extends to the use of confinement as protective force only if the actor takes all reasonable measures to terminate the confinement as soon as he knows that he can do so with safety to the property, unless the person confined has been arrested on a charge of crime.

(5) Use of Device to Protect Property. The justification afforded by this Section extends to the use of a device for the purpose of protecting property only if:

(a) the device is not designed to cause or known to create a substantial risk of causing death or serious bodily injury; and

(b) the use of the particular device to protect the property from entry or trespass is reasonable under the circumstances, as the actor believes them to be; and

(c) the device is one customarily used for such a purpose or reasonable care is taken to make known to probable intruders the fact that it is used.

(6) Use of Force to Pass Wrongful Obstructor. The use of force to pass a person whom the actor believes to be purposely or knowingly and unjustifiably obstructing the actor from going to a place to which he may lawfully go is justifiable, provided that:

(a) the actor believes that the person against whom he uses force has no claim of right to obstruct the actor; and

(b) the actor is not being obstructed from entry or movement on land that he knows to be in the possession or custody of the person obstructing him, or in the possession or custody of another person by whose authority the obstructor acts, unless the circumstances, as the actor believes them to be, are of such urgency that it would not be reasonable to postpone the entry or movement on such land until a court order is obtained; and

(c) the force used is not greater than would be justifiable if the person obstructing the actor were using force against him to prevent his passage.

Section 3.07. Use of Force in Law Enforcement.

(1) Use of Force Justifiable to Effect an Arrest. Subject to the provisions of this Section and of Section 3.09, the use of force upon or toward the person of another is justifiable when the actor is making or assisting in making an arrest and the actor believes that such force is immediately necessary to effect a lawful arrest.

(2) Limitations on the Use of Force.

(a) The use of force is not justifiable under this Section unless:

(i) the actor makes known the purpose of the arrest or believes that it is otherwise known by or cannot reasonably be made known to the person to be arrested; and

(ii) when the arrest is made under a warrant, the warrant is valid or believed by the actor to be valid.

(b) The use of deadly force is not justifiable under this Section unless:

(i) the arrest is for a felony; and

(ii) the person effecting the arrest is authorized to act as a peace officer or is assisting a person whom he believes to be authorized to act as a peace officer; and

(iii) the actor believes that the force employed creates no substantial risk of injury to innocent persons; and

(iv) the actor believes that:

(A) the crime for which the arrest is made involved conduct including the use or threatened use of deadly force; or

(B) there is a substantial risk that the person to be arrested will cause death or serious bodily injury if his apprehension is delayed.

(3) Use of Force to Prevent Escape from Custody. The use of force to prevent the escape of an arrested person from custody is justifiable when the force could justifiably have been employed to effect the arrest under which the person is in custody, except that a guard or other person authorized to act as a peace officer is justified in using any force, including deadly force, that he believes to be immediately necessary to prevent the escape of a person from a jail, prison, or other institution for the detention of persons charged with or convicted of a crime.

(4) Use of Force by Private Person Assisting an Unlawful Arrest.

(a) A private person who is summoned by a peace officer to assist in effecting an unlawful arrest, is justified in using any force that he would be justified in using if the arrest were lawful, provided that he does not believe the arrest is unlawful.

(b) A private person who assists another private person in effecting an unlawful arrest, or who, not being summoned, assists a peace officer in effecting an unlawful arrest, is justified in using any force that he would be justified in using if the arrest were lawful, provided that (i) he believes the arrest is lawful, and (ii) the arrest would be lawful if the facts were as he believes them to be.

(5) Use of Force to Prevent Suicide or the Commission of a Crime.

(a) The use of force upon or toward the person of another is justifiable when the actor believes that such force is immediately necessary to prevent such other person from committing suicide, inflicting serious bodily injury upon himself, committing or consummating the commission of a crime involving or threatening bodily injury, damage to or loss of property or a breach of the peace, except that:

(i) any limitations imposed by the other provisions of this Article on the justifiable use of force in self-protection, for the protection of others, the protection of property, the effectuation of an arrest or the prevention of an escape from custody shall apply notwithstanding the criminality of the conduct against which such force is used; and

(ii) the use of deadly force is not in any event justifiable under this Subsection unless:

(A) the actor believes that there is a substantial risk that the person whom he seeks to prevent from committing a crime will cause death or serious bodily injury to another unless the commission or the consummation of the crime is prevented and that the use of such force presents no substantial risk of injury to innocent persons; or

(B) the actor believes that the use of such force is necessary to suppress a riot or mutiny after the rioters or mutineers have been ordered to disperse and warned, in any particular manner that the law may require, that such force will be used if they do not obey.

(b) The justification afforded by this Subsection extends to the use of confinement as preventive force only if the actor takes all reasonable measures to terminate the confinement as soon as he knows that he safely can, unless the person confined has been arrested on a charge of crime.

Section 3.08. Use of Force by Persons with Special Responsibility for Care, Discipline or Safety of Others.

The use of force upon or toward the person of another is justifiable if:

(1) the actor is the parent or guardian or other person similarly responsible for the general care and supervision of a minor or a person acting at the request of such parent, guardian or other responsible person and:

(a) the force is used for the purpose of safeguarding or promoting the welfare of the minor, including the prevention or punishment of his misconduct; and

(b) the force used is not designed to cause or known to create a substantial risk of causing death, serious bodily injury, disfigurement, extreme pain or mental distress or gross degradation; or

(2) the actor is a teacher or a person otherwise entrusted with the care or supervision for a special purpose of a minor and:

(a) the actor believes that the force used is necessary to further such special purpose, including the maintenance of reasonable discipline in a school, class or other group, and that the use of such force is consistent with the welfare of the minor; and

(b) the degree of force, if it had been used by the parent or guardian of the minor, would not be unjustifiable under Subsection (1)(b) of this section; or

(3) the actor is the guardian or other person similarly responsible for the general care and supervision of an incompetent person and:

(a) the force is used for the purpose of safeguarding or promoting the welfare of the incompetent person, including the prevention of his misconduct, or, when such incompetent person is in a hospital or other institution for his care and custody, for the maintenance of reasonable discipline in such institution; and

(b) the force used is not designed to cause or known to create a substantial risk of causing death, serious bodily injury, disfigurement, extreme or unnecessary pain, mental distress, or humiliation; or

(4) the actor is a doctor or other therapist or a person assisting him at his direction and:

(a) the force is used for the purpose of administering a recognized form of treatment that the actor believes to be adapted to promoting the physical or mental health of the patient; and

(b) the treatment is administered with the consent of the patient or, if the patient is a minor or an incompetent person, with the consent of his parent or guardian or other person legally competent to consent in his behalf, or the treatment is administered in an emergency when the actor believes that no one competent to consent can be consulted and that a reasonable person, wishing to safeguard the welfare of the patient, would consent; or

(5) the actor is a warden or other authorized official of a correctional institution and:

(a) he believes that the force used is necessary for the purpose of enforcing the lawful rules or procedures of the institution, unless his belief in the lawfulness of the rule or procedure sought to be enforced is erroneous and his error is due to ignorance or mistake as to the provisions of the Code, any other provision of the criminal law or the law governing the administration of the institution; and

(b) the nature or degree of force used is not forbidden by Article 303 or 304 of the Code; and

(c) if deadly force is used, its use is otherwise justifiable under this Article; or

(6) the actor is a person responsible for the safety of a vessel or an aircraft or a person acting at his direction and:

(a) he believes that the force used is necessary to prevent interference with the operation of the vessel or aircraft or obstruction of the execution of a lawful order, unless his belief in the lawfulness of the order is erroneous and his error is due to ignorance or mistake as to the law defining his authority; and

(b) if deadly force is used, its use is otherwise justifiable under this Article; or

(7) the actor is a person who is authorized or required by law to maintain order or decorum in a vehicle, train or other carrier or in a place where others are assembled, and:

(a) he believes that the force used is necessary for such purpose; and

(b) the force used is not designed to cause or known to create a substantial risk of causing death, bodily injury, or extreme mental distress.

Section 3.09. Mistake of Law as to Unlawfulness of Force or Legality of Arrest; Reckless or Negligent Use of Otherwise Justifiable Force; Reckless or Negligent Injury or Risk of Injury to Innocent Persons.

(1) The justification afforded by Sections 3.04 to 3.07, inclusive, is unavailable when:

(a) the actor's belief in the unlawfulness of the force or conduct against which he employs protective force or his belief in the lawfulness of an arrest that he endeavors to effect by force is erroneous; and

(b) his error is due to ignorance or mistake as to the provisions of the Code, any other provision of the criminal law or the law governing the legality of an arrest or search.

(2) When the actor believes that the use of force upon or toward the person of another is necessary for any of the purposes for which such belief would establish a justification under Sections 3.03 to 3.08 but the actor is reckless or negligent in having such belief or in acquiring or failing to acquire any knowledge or belief that is material to the justifiability of his use of force, the justification afforded by those Sections is unavailable in a prosecution for an offense for which recklessness or negligence, as the case may be, suffices to establish culpability.

(3) When the actor is justified under Sections 3.03 to 3.08 in using force upon or toward the person of another but he recklessly or negligently injures or creates a risk of injury to innocent persons, the justification afforded by those Sections is unavailable in a prosecution for such recklessness or negligence towards innocent persons.

Section 3.10. Justification in Property Crimes.

Conduct involving the appropriation, seizure or destruction of, damage to, intrusion on or interference with property is justifiable under circumstances that would establish a defense of privilege in a civil action based thereon, unless:

(1) the Code or the law defining the offense deals with the specific situation involved; or

(2) a legislative purpose to exclude the justification claimed otherwise plainly appears.

Section 3.11. Definitions.

In this Article, unless a different meaning plainly is required:

(1) "unlawful force" means force, including confinement, that is employed without the consent of the person against whom it is directed and the employment of which constitutes an offense or actionable tort or would constitute such offense or tort except for a defense (such as the absence of intent, negligence, or mental capacity; duress; youth; or diplomatic status) not amounting to a privilege to use the force. Assent

constitutes consent, within the meaning of this Section, whether or not it otherwise is legally effective, except assent to the infliction of death or serious bodily injury.

(2) "deadly force" means force that the actor uses with the purpose of causing or that he knows to create a substantial risk of causing death or serious bodily injury. Purposely firing a firearm in the direction of another person or at a vehicle in which another person is believed to be constitutes deadly force. A threat to cause death or serious bodily injury, by the production of a weapon or otherwise, so long as the actor's purpose is limited to creating an apprehension that he will use deadly force if necessary, does not constitute deadly force.

(3) "dwelling" means any building or structure, though movable or temporary, or a portion thereof, that is for the time being the actor's home or place of lodging.

Article 4. Responsibility

Section 4.01. Mental Disease or Defect Excluding Responsibility.

(1) A person is not responsible for criminal conduct if at the time of such conduct as a result of mental disease or defect he lacks substantial capacity either to appreciate the criminality [wrongfulness] of his conduct or to conform his conduct to the requirements of law.

(2) As used in this Article, the terms "mental disease or defect" do not include an abnormality manifested only by repeated criminal or otherwise antisocial conduct.

Section 4.02. Evidence of Mental Disease or Defect Admissible when Relevant to Element of the Offense [; Mental Disease or Defect Impairing Capacity as Ground for Mitigation of Punishment in Capital Cases].

(1) Evidence that the defendant suffered from a mental disease or defect is admissible whenever it is relevant to prove that the defendant did or did not have a state of mind that is an element of the offense.

[(2) Whenever the jury or the Court is authorized to determine or to recommend whether or not the defendant shall be sentenced to death or imprisonment upon conviction, evidence that the capacity of the defendant to appreciate the criminality [wrongfulness] of his conduct or to conform his conduct to the requirements of law was impaired as a result of mental disease or defect is admissible in favor of sentence of imprisonment.]

Section 4.03. Mental Disease or Defect Excluding Responsibility Is Affirmative Defense; Requirement of Notice; Form of Verdict and Judgment when Finding of Irresponsibility Is Made.

(1) Mental disease or defect excluding responsibility is an affirmative defense.

(2) Evidence of mental disease or defect excluding responsibility is not admissible unless the defendant, at the time of entering his plea of not guilty or within ten days thereafter or at such later time as the Court may for good cause permit, files a written notice of his purpose to rely on such defense.

(3) When the defendant is acquitted on the ground of mental disease or defect excluding responsibility, the verdict and the judgment shall so state.

Section 4.04. Mental Disease or Defect Excluding Fitness to Proceed.

No person who as a result of mental disease or defect lacks capacity to understand the proceedings against him or to assist in his own defense shall be tried, convicted or sentenced for the commission of an offense so long as such incapacity endures.

Article 5. Inchoate Crimes

Section 5.01. Criminal Attempt.

(1) Definition of Attempt. A person is guilty of an attempt to commit a crime if, acting with the kind of culpability otherwise required for commission of the crime, he:

(a) purposely engages in conduct that would constitute the crime if the attendant circumstances were as he believes them to be; or

(b) when causing a particular result is an element of the crime, does or omits to do anything with the purpose of causing or with the belief that it will cause such result without further conduct on his part; or

(c) purposely does or omits to do anything that, under the circumstances as he believes them to be, is an act or omission constituting a substantial step in a course of conduct planned to culminate in his commission of the crime.

(2) Conduct that May Be Held Substantial Step under Subsection (1)(c). Conduct shall not be held to constitute a substantial step under Subsection (1)(c) of this Section unless it is strongly corroborative of the actor's criminal purpose. Without negativing the sufficiency of other conduct, the following, if strongly corroborative of the actor's criminal purpose, shall not be held insufficient as a matter of law:

(a) lying in wait, searching for or following the contemplated victim of the crime;

(b) enticing or seeking to entice the contemplated victim of the crime to go to the place contemplated for its commission;

(c) reconnoitering the place contemplated for the commission of the crime;

(d) unlawful entry of a structure, vehicle or enclosure in which it is contemplated that the crime will be committed;

(e) possession of materials to be employed in the commission of the crime, that are specially designed for such unlawful use or that can serve no lawful purpose of the actor under the circumstances;

(f) possession, collection or fabrication of materials to be employed in the commission of the crime, at or near the place contemplated for its commission, if such possession, collection or fabrication serves no lawful purpose of the actor under the circumstances;

(g) soliciting an innocent agent to engage in conduct constituting an element of the crime.

(3) Conduct Designed to Aid Another in Commission of a Crime. A person who engages in conduct designed to aid another to commit a crime that would establish his complicity under Section 2.06 if the crime were committed by such other person, is guilty of an attempt to commit the crime, although the crime is not committed or attempted by such other person.

(4) Renunciation of Criminal Purpose. When the actor's conduct would otherwise constitute an attempt under Subsection (1)(b) or (1)(c) of this Section, it is an affirmative defense that he abandoned his effort to commit the crime or otherwise prevented its commission, under circumstances manifesting a complete and voluntary renunciation of his criminal purpose. The establishment of such defense does not, however, affect the liability of an accomplice who did not join in such abandonment or prevention.

Within the meaning of this Article, renunciation of criminal purpose is not voluntary if it is motivated, in whole or in part, by circumstances, not present or apparent at the inception of the actor's course of conduct, that increase the probability of detection or apprehension or that make more difficult the accomplishment of the criminal purpose. Renunciation is not complete if it is motivated by a decision to postpone the criminal conduct until a more advantageous time or to transfer the criminal effort to another but similar objective or victim.

Section 5.02. Criminal Solicitation.

(1) Definition of Solicitation. A person is guilty of solicitation to commit a crime if with the purpose of promoting or facilitating its commission he commands, encourages or requests another person to engage in specific conduct that would constitute such crime or an attempt to commit such crime or would establish his complicity in its commission or attempted commission.

(2) Uncommunicated Solicitation. It is immaterial under Subsection (1) of this Section that the actor fails to communicate with the person he solicits to commit a crime if his conduct was designed to effect such communication.

(3) Renunciation of Criminal Purpose. It is an affirmative defense that the actor, after soliciting another person to commit a crime, persuaded him not to do so or otherwise prevented the commission of the crime, under circumstances manifesting a complete and voluntary renunciation of his criminal purpose.

Section 5.03. Criminal Conspiracy.

(1) Definition of Conspiracy. A person is guilty of conspiracy with another person or persons to commit a crime if with the purpose of promoting or facilitating its commission he:

(a) agrees with such other person or persons that they or one or more of them will engage in conduct that constitutes such crime or an attempt or solicitation to commit such crime; or

(b) agrees to aid such other person or persons in the planning or commission of such crime or of an attempt or solicitation to commit such crime.

(2) Scope of Conspiratorial Relationship. If a person guilty of conspiracy, as defined by Subsection (1) of this Section, knows that a person with whom he conspires to commit a crime has conspired with another person or persons to commit the same crime, he is guilty of conspiring with such other person or persons, whether or not he knows their identity, to commit such crime.

(3) Conspiracy with Multiple Criminal Objectives. If a person conspires to commit a number of crimes, he is guilty of only one conspiracy so long as such multiple crimes are the object of the same agreement or continuous conspiratorial relationship.

(4) Joinder and Venue in Conspiracy Prosecutions.

(a) Subject to the provisions of paragraph (b) of this Subsection, two or more persons charged with criminal conspiracy may be prosecuted jointly if:

(i) they are charged with conspiring with one another; or

(ii) the conspiracies alleged, whether they have the same or different parties, are so related that they constitute different aspects of a scheme of organized criminal conduct.

(b) In any joint prosecution under paragraph (a) of this Subsection:

(i) no defendant shall be charged with a conspiracy in any county [parish or district] other than one in which he entered into such conspiracy or in which an overt act pursuant to such conspiracy was done by him or by a person with whom he conspired; and

(ii) neither the liability of any defendant nor the admissibility against him of evidence of acts or declarations of another shall be enlarged by such joinder; and

(iii) the Court shall order a severance or take a special verdict as to any defendant who so requests, if it deems it necessary or appropriate to promote the fair determination of his guilt or innocence, and shall take any other proper measures to protect the fairness of the trial.

(5) Overt Act. No person may be convicted of conspiracy to commit a crime, other than a felony of the first or second degree, unless an overt act in pursuance of such conspiracy is alleged and proved to have been done by him or by a person with whom he conspired.

(6) Renunciation of Criminal Purpose. It is an affirmative defense that the actor, after conspiring to commit a crime, thwarted the success of the conspiracy, under circumstances manifesting a complete and voluntary renunciation of his criminal purpose.

(7) Duration of Conspiracy. For purposes of Section 1.06(4):

(a) conspiracy is a continuing course of conduct that terminates when the crime or crimes that are its object are committed or the agreement that they be committed is abandoned by the defendant and by those with whom he conspired; and

(b) such abandonment is presumed if neither the defendant nor anyone with whom he conspired does any overt act in pursuance of the conspiracy during the applicable period of limitation; and

(c) if an individual abandons the agreement, the conspiracy is terminated as to him only if and when he advises those with whom he conspired of his abandonment or he informs the law enforcement authorities of the existence of the conspiracy and of his participation therein.

Section 5.04. Incapacity, Irresponsibility or Immunity of Party to Solicitation or Conspiracy.

(1) Except as provided in Subsection (2) of this Section, it is immaterial to the liability of a person who solicits or conspires with another to commit a crime that:

(a) he or the person whom he solicits or with whom he conspires does not occupy a particular position or have a particular characteristic that is an element of such crime, if he believes that one of them does; or

(b) the person whom he solicits or with whom he conspires is irresponsible or has an immunity to prosecution or conviction for the commission of the crime.

(2) It is a defense to a charge of solicitation or conspiracy to commit a crime that if the criminal object were achieved, the actor would not be guilty of a crime under the law defining the offense or as an accomplice under Section 2.06(5) or 2.06(6)(a) or (6)(b).

Section 5.05. Grading of Criminal Attempt, Solicitation and Conspiracy; Mitigation in Cases of Lesser Danger; Multiple Convictions Barred.

(1) Grading. Except as otherwise provided in this Section, attempt, solicitation and conspiracy are crimes of the same grade and degree as the most serious offense that is attempted or solicited or is an object of the conspiracy. An attempt, solicitation or conspiracy to commit a [capital crime or a] felony of the first degree is a felony of the second degree.

(2) Mitigation. If the particular conduct charged to constitute a criminal attempt, solicitation or conspiracy is so inherently unlikely to result or culminate in the commission of a crime that neither such conduct nor the actor presents a public danger warranting the grading of such offense under this Section, the Court shall exercise its power under Section 6.12 to enter judgment and impose sentence for a crime of lower grade or degree or, in extreme cases, may dismiss the prosecution.

(3) Multiple Convictions. A person may not be convicted of more than one offense defined by this Article for conduct designed to commit or to culminate in the commission of the same crime.

Section 5.06. Possessing Instruments of Crime; Weapons.

(1) <u>Criminal Instruments Generally.</u> A person commits a misdemeanor if he possesses any instrument of crime with purpose to employ it criminally. "Instrument of crime" means:

(a) anything specially made or specially adapted for criminal use; or

(b) anything commonly used for criminal purposes and possessed by the actor under circumstances that do not negative unlawful purpose.

(2) <u>Presumption of Criminal Purpose from Possession of Weapon.</u> If a person possesses a firearm or other weapon on or about his person, in a vehicle occupied by him, or otherwise readily available for use, it is presumed that he had the purpose to employ it criminally, unless:

(a) the weapon is possessed in the actor's home or place of business;

(b) the actor is licensed or otherwise authorized by law to possess such weapon; or

(c) the weapon is of a type commonly used in lawful sport.

"Weapon" means anything readily capable of lethal use and possessed under circumstances not manifestly appropriate for lawful uses it may have; the term includes a firearm that is not loaded or lacks a clip or other component to render it immediately operable, and components that can readily be assembled into a weapon.

(3) <u>Presumptions as to Possession of Criminal Instruments in Automobiles.</u> If a weapon or other instrument of crime is found in an automobile, it is presumed to be in the possession of the occupant if there is but one. If there is more than one occupant, it is presumed to be in the possession of all, except under the following circumstances:

(a) it is found upon the person of one of the occupants;

(b) the automobile is not a stolen one and the weapon or instrument is found out of view in a glove compartment, car trunk, or other enclosed customary depository, in which case it is presumed to be in the possession of the occupant or occupants who own or have authority to operate the automobile;

(c) in the case of a taxicab, a weapon or instrument found in the passengers' portion of the vehicle is presumed to be in the possession of all the passengers, if there are any, and, if not, in the possession of the driver.

Section 5.07. Prohibited Offensive Weapons.

A person commits a misdemeanor if, except as authorized by law, he makes, repairs, sells, or otherwise deals in, uses, or possesses any offensive weapon. "Offensive weapon" means any bomb, machine gun, sawed-off shotgun, firearm specially made or specially adapted for concealment or silent discharge, any blackjack, sandbag, metal knuckles, dagger, or other implement for the infliction of serious bodily injury that serves no common lawful purpose. It is a defense under this Section for the defendant to prove by a preponderance of evidence that he possessed or dealt with the weapon solely as a curio or in a dramatic performance, or that he possessed it briefly in consequence of having found it or taken it from an aggressor, or under circumstances similarly negativing any purpose or likelihood that the weapon would be used unlawfully. The presumptions provided in Section 5.06(3) are applicable to prosecutions under this Section.

Article 6. Authorized Disposition of Offenders

Section 6.01. Degrees of Felonies.

(1) Felonies defined by this Code are classified, for the purpose of sentence, into three degrees, as follows:

(a) felonies of the first degree;

(b) felonies of the second degree;

(c) felonies of the third degree.

A felony is of the first or second degree when it is so designated by the Code. A crime declared to be a felony, without specification of degree, is of the third degree.

(2) Notwithstanding any other provision of law, a felony defined by any statute of this State other than this Code shall constitute, for the purpose of sentence, a felony of the third degree.

Section 6.02. Sentence in Accordance with Code; Authorized Dispositions.

(1) No person convicted of an offense shall be sentenced otherwise than in accordance with this Article.

[(2) The Court shall sentence a person who has been convicted of murder to death or imprisonment, in accordance with Section 210.6.]

(3) Except as provided in Subsection (2) of this Section and subject to the applicable provisions of the Code, the Court may suspend the imposition of sentence on a person who has been convicted of a crime, may order him to be committed in lieu of sentence, in accordance with Section 6.13, or may sentence him as follows:

(a) to pay a fine authorized by Section 6.03; or

(b) to be placed on probation [, and, in the case of a person convicted of a felony or misdemeanor to imprisonment for a term fixed by the Court not exceeding thirty days to be served as a condition of probation]; or

(c) to imprisonment for a term authorized by Section 6.05, 6.06, 6.07, 6.08, 6.09, or 7.06; or

(d) to fine and probation or fine and imprisonment, but not to probation and imprisonment [, except as authorized in paragraph (b) of this Subsection].

(4) The Court may suspend the imposition of sentence on a person who has been convicted of a violation or may sentence him to pay a fine authorized by Section 6.03.

(5) This Article does not deprive the Court of any authority conferred by law to decree a forfeiture of property, suspend or cancel a license, remove a person from office, or impose any other civil penalty. Such a judgment or order may be included in the sentence.

Section 6.03. Fines.

A person who has been convicted of an offense may be sentenced to pay a fine not exceeding:

(1) $10,000, when the conviction is of a felony of the first or second degree;

(2) $5,000, when the conviction is of a felony of the third degree;

(3) $1,000, when the conviction is of a misdemeanor;

(4) $500, when the conviction is of a petty misdemeanor or a violation;

(5) any higher amount equal to double the pecuniary gain derived from the offense by the offender;

(6) any higher amount specifically authorized by statute.

Section 6.04. Penalties against Corporations and Unincorporated Associations; Forfeiture of Corporate Charter or Revocation of Certificate Authorizing Foreign Corporation to Do Business in the State.

(1) The Court may suspend the sentence of a corporation or an unincorporated association that has been convicted of an offense or may sentence it to pay a fine authorized by Section 6.03.

(2)

(a) The [prosecuting attorney] is authorized to institute civil proceedings in the appropriate court of general jurisdiction to forfeit the charter of a corporation organized under the laws of this State or to revoke the certificate authorizing a foreign corporation to conduct business in this State. The Court may order the charter forfeited or the certificate revoked upon finding

(i) that the board of directors or a high managerial agent acting in behalf of the corporation has, in conducting the corporation's affairs, purposely engaged in a persistent course of criminal conduct and

(ii) that for the prevention of future criminal conduct of the same character, the public interest requires the charter of the corporation to be forfeited and the corporation to be dissolved or the certificate to be revoked.

(b) When a corporation is convicted of a crime or a high managerial agent of a corporation, as defined in Section 2.07, is convicted of a crime committed in the conduct of the affairs of the corporation, the Court, in sentencing the corporation or the agent, may direct the [prosecuting attorney] to institute proceedings authorized by paragraph (a) of this Subsection.

PART II: DEFINITION OF SPECIFIC CRIMES

Offenses Involving Danger to the Person

Article 210. Criminal Homicide

Section 210.0. Definitions.

In Articles 210–213, unless a different meaning plainly is required:

(1) "human being" means a person who has been born and is alive;

(2) "bodily injury" means physical pain, illness or any impairment of physical condition;

(3) "serious bodily injury" means bodily injury which creates a substantial risk of death or which causes serious, permanent disfigurement, or protracted loss or impairment of the function of any bodily member or organ;

(4) "deadly weapon" means any firearm or other weapon, device, instrument, material or substance, whether animate or inanimate, which in the manner it is used or is intended to be used is known to be capable of producing death or serious bodily injury.

Section 210.1 Criminal Homicide.

(1) A person is guilty of criminal homicide if he purposely, knowingly, recklessly or negligently causes the death of another human being.

(2) Criminal homicide is murder, manslaughter or negligent homicide.

Section 210.2. Murder.

(1) Except as provided in Section 210.3(1)(b), criminal homicide constitutes murder when:

(a) it is committed purposely or knowingly; or

(b) it is committed recklessly under circumstances manifesting extreme indifference to the value of human life. Such recklessness and indifference are presumed if the actor is engaged or is an accomplice in the commission of, or an attempt to commit, or flight after committing or attempting to commit robbery, rape or deviate sexual intercourse by force or threat of force, arson, burglary, kidnapping or felonious escape.

(2) Murder is a felony of the first degree [but a person convicted of murder may be sentenced to death, as provided in Section 210.6].

Section 210.3. Manslaughter.

(1) Criminal homicide constitutes manslaughter when:

(a) it is committed recklessly; or

(b) a homicide which would otherwise be murder is committed under the influence of extreme mental or emotional disturbance for which there is reasonable explanation or excuse. The reasonableness of such explanation or excuse shall be determined from the viewpoint of a person in the actor's situation under the circumstances as he believes them to be.

(2) Manslaughter is a felony of the second degree.

Section 210.4. Negligent Homicide.

(1) Criminal homicide constitutes negligent homicide when it is committed negligently.

(2) Negligent homicide is a felony of the third degree.

Section 210.5. Causing or Aiding Suicide.

(1) Causing Suicide as Criminal Homicide. A person may be convicted of criminal homicide for causing another to commit suicide only if he purposely causes such suicide by force, duress or deception.

(2) Aiding or Soliciting Suicide as an Independent Offense. A person who purposely aids or solicits another to commit suicide is guilty of a felony of the second degree if his conduct causes such suicide or an attempted suicide, and otherwise of a misdemeanor.

Section 210.6. Sentence of Death for Murder; Further Proceedings to Determine Sentence.

(1) Death Sentence Excluded. When a defendant is found guilty of murder, the Court shall impose sentence for a felony of the first degree if it is satisfied that:

(a) none of the aggravating circumstances enumerated in Subsection (3) of this Section was established by the evidence at the trial or will be established if further proceedings are initiated under Subsection (2) of this Section; or

(b) substantial mitigating circumstances, established by the evidence at the trial, call for leniency; or

(c) the defendant, with the consent of the prosecuting attorney and the approval of the Court, pleaded guilty to murder as a felony of the first degree; or

(d) the defendant was under 18 years of age at the time of the commission of the crime; or

(e) the defendant's physical or mental condition calls for leniency; or

(f) although the evidence suffices to sustain the verdict, it does not foreclose all doubt respecting the defendant's guilt.

(2) <u>Determination by Court or by Court and Jury.</u> Unless the Court imposes sentence under Subsection (1) of this Section, it shall conduct a separate proceeding to determine whether the defendant should be sentenced for a felony of the first degree or sentenced to death. The proceeding shall be conducted before the Court alone if the defendant was convicted by a Court sitting without a jury or upon his plea of guilty or if the prosecuting attorney and the defendant waive a jury with respect to sentence. In other cases it shall be conducted before the Court sitting with the jury which determined the defendant's guilt or, if the Court for good cause shown discharges that jury, with a new jury empanelled for the purpose.

In the proceeding, evidence may be presented as to any matter that the Court deems relevant to sentence, including but not limited to the nature and circumstances of the crime, the defendant's character, background, history, mental and physical condition and any of the aggravating or mitigating circumstances enumerated in Subsections (3) and (4) of this Section. Any such evidence, not legally privileged, which the Court deems to have probative force, may be received, regardless of its admissibility under the exclusionary rules of evidence, provided that the defendant's counsel is accorded a fair opportunity to rebut such evidence. The prosecuting attorney and the defendant or his counsel shall be permitted to present argument for or against sentence of death.

The determination whether sentence of death shall be imposed shall be in the discretion of the Court, except that when the proceeding is conducted before the Court sitting with a jury, the Court shall not impose sentence of death unless it submits to the jury the issue whether the defendant should be sentenced to death or to imprisonment and the jury returns a verdict that the sentence should be death. If the jury is unable to reach a unanimous verdict, the Court shall dismiss the jury and impose sentence for a felony of the first degree.

The Court, in exercising its discretion as to sentence, and the jury, in determining upon its verdict, shall take into account the aggravating and mitigating circumstances enumerated in Subsections (3) and (4) and any other facts that it deems relevant, but it shall not impose or recommend sentence of death unless it finds one of the aggravating circumstances enumerated in Subsection (3) and further finds that there are no mitigating circumstances sufficiently substantial to call for leniency. When the issue is submitted to the jury, the Court shall so instruct and also shall inform the jury of the nature of the sentence of imprisonment that may be imposed, including its implication with respect to possible release upon parole, if the jury verdict is against sentence of death.

Alternative formulation of Subsection (2):

(2) <u>Determination by Court.</u> Unless the Court imposes sentence under Subsection (1) of this Section, it shall conduct a separate proceeding to determine whether the defendant should be sentenced for a felony of the first degree or sentenced to death. In the proceeding, the Court, in accordance with Section 7.07, shall consider the report of the presentence investigation and, if a psychiatric examination has been

ordered, the report of such examination. In addition, evidence may be presented as to any matter that the Court deems relevant to sentence, including but not limited to the nature and circumstances of the crime, the defendant's character, background, history, mental and physical condition and any of the aggravating or mitigating circumstances enumerated in Subsections (3) and (4) of this Section. Any such evidence, not legally privileged, which the Court deems to have probative force, may be received, regardless of its admissibility under the exclusionary rules of evidence, provided that the defendant's counsel is accorded a fair opportunity to rebut such evidence. The prosecuting attorney and the defendant or his counsel shall be permitted to present argument for or against sentence of death.

The determination whether sentence of death shall be imposed shall be in the discretion of the Court. In exercising such discretion, the Court shall take into account the aggravating and mitigating circumstances enumerated in Subsections (3) and (4) and any other facts that it deems relevant but shall not impose sentence of death unless it finds one of the aggravating circumstances enumerated in Subsection (3) and further finds that there are no mitigating circumstances sufficiently substantial to call for leniency.

(3) Aggravating Circumstances.

(a) The murder was committed by a convict under sentence of imprisonment.

(b) The defendant was previously convicted of another murder or of a felony involving the use or threat of violence to the person.

(c) At the time the murder was committed the defendant also committed another murder.

(d) The defendant knowingly created a great risk of death to many persons.

(e) The murder was committed while the defendant was engaged or was an accomplice in the commission of, or an attempt to commit, or flight after committing or attempting to commit robbery, rape or deviate sexual intercourse by force or threat of force, arson, burglary or kidnapping.

(f) The murder was committed for the purpose of avoiding or preventing a lawful arrest or effecting an escape from lawful custody.

(g) The murder was committed for pecuniary gain.

(h) The murder was especially heinous, atrocious or cruel, manifesting exceptional depravity.

(4) Mitigating Circumstances.

(a) The defendant has no significant history of prior criminal activity.

(b) The murder was committed while the defendant was under the influence of extreme mental or emotional disturbance.

(c) The victim was a participant in the defendant's homicidal conduct or consented to the homicidal act.

(d) The murder was committed under circumstances which the defendant believed to provide a moral justification or extenuation for his conduct.

(e) The defendant was an accomplice in a murder committed by another person and his participation in the homicidal act was relatively minor.

(f) The defendant acted under duress or under the domination of another person.

(g) At the time of the murder, the capacity of the defendant to appreciate the criminality [wrongfulness] of his conduct or to conform his conduct to the requirements of law was impaired as a result of mental disease or defect or intoxication.

(h) The youth of the defendant at the time of the crime.

Article 212. Kidnapping and Related Offenses; Coercion

Section 212.0. Definitions.

In this Article, the definitions given in Section 210.0 apply unless a different meaning plainly is required.

Section 212.1. Kidnapping.

A person is guilty of kidnapping if he unlawfully removes another from his place of residence or business, or a substantial distance from the vicinity where he is found, or if he unlawfully confines another for a substantial period in a place of isolation, with any of the following purposes: .

(a) to hold for ransom or reward, or as a shield or hostage; or

(b) to facilitate commission of any felony or flight thereafter; or

(c) to inflict bodily injury on or to terrorize the victim or another; or

(d) to interfere with the performance of any governmental or political function.

Kidnapping is a felony of the first degree unless the actor voluntarily releases the victim alive and in a safe place prior to trial, in which case it is a felony of the second degree. A removal or confinement is unlawful within the meaning of this Section if it is accomplished by force, threat or deception, or, in the case of a person who is under the age of 14 or incompetent, if it is accomplished without the consent of a parent, guardian or other person responsible for general supervision of his welfare.

Section 212.2. Felonious Restraint.

A person commits a felony of the third degree if he knowingly:

(a) restrains another unlawfully in circumstances exposing him to risk of serious bodily injury; or

(b) holds another in a condition of involuntary servitude.

Section 212.3. False Imprisonment.

A person commits a misdemeanor if he knowingly restrains another unlawfully so as to interfere substantially with his liberty.

Section 212.4. Interference with Custody.

(1) <u>Custody of Children</u>. A person commits an offense if he knowingly or recklessly takes or entices any child under the age of 18 from the custody of its parent, guardian or other lawful custodian, when he has no privilege to do so. It is an affirmative defense that:

(a) the actor believed that his action was necessary to preserve the child from danger to its welfare; or

(b) the child, being at the time not less than 14 years old, was taken away at its own instigation without enticement and without purpose to commit a criminal offense with or against the child.

Proof that the child was below the critical age gives rise to a presumption that the actor knew the child's age or acted in reckless disregard thereof. The offense is a misdemeanor unless the actor, not being a parent or person in equivalent relation to the child, acted with knowledge that his conduct would cause serious alarm for the child's safety, or in reckless disregard of a likelihood of causing such alarm, in which case the offense is a felony of the third degree.

(2) <u>Custody of Committed Persons</u>. A person is guilty of a misdemeanor if he knowingly or recklessly takes or entices any committed person away from lawful custody when he is not privileged to do so. "Committed person" means, in addition to anyone committed under judicial warrant, any orphan, neglected or delinquent child, mentally defective or insane person, or other dependent or incompetent person entrusted to another's custody by or through a recognized social agency or otherwise by authority of law.

Section 212.5. Criminal Coercion.

(1) <u>Offense Defined</u>. A person is guilty of criminal coercion if, with purpose unlawfully to restrict another's freedom of action to his detriment, he threatens to:

(a) commit any criminal offense; or

(b) accuse anyone of a criminal offense; or

(c) expose any secret tending to subject any person to hatred, contempt or ridicule, or to impair his credit or business repute; or

(d) take or withhold action as an official, or cause an official to take or withhold action.

It is an affirmative defense to prosecution based on paragraphs (b), (c) or (d) that the actor believed the accusation or secret to be true or the proposed official action justified and that his purpose was limited to compelling the other to behave in a way reasonably related to the circumstances which were the subject of the accusation, exposure or proposed official action, as by desisting from further misbehavior, making good a wrong done, refraining from taking any action or responsibility for which the actor believes the other disqualified.

(2) Grading. Criminal coercion is a misdemeanor unless the threat is to commit a felony or the actor's purpose is felonious, in which cases the offense is a felony of the third degree.

Article 213. Sexual Offenses

Section 213.0. Definitions.

In this Article, unless a different meaning plainly is required:

(1) the definitions given in Section 210.0 apply;

(2) "Sexual intercourse" includes intercourse per os or per anum, with some penetration however slight; emission is not required;

(3) "Deviate sexual intercourse" means sexual intercourse per os or per anum between human beings who are not husband and wife, and any form of sexual intercourse with an animal.

Section 213.1. Rape and Related Offenses.

(1) Rape. A male who has sexual intercourse with a female not his wife is guilty of rape if:

(a) he compels her to submit by force or by threat of imminent death, serious bodily injury, extreme pain or kidnapping, to be inflicted on anyone; or

(b) he has substantially impaired her power to appraise or control her conduct by administering or employing without her knowledge drugs, intoxicants or other means for the purpose of preventing resistance; or

(c) the female is unconscious; or

(d) the female is less than 10 years old.

Rape is a felony of the second degree unless (i) in the course thereof the actor inflicts serious bodily injury upon anyone, or (ii) the victim was not a voluntary social companion of the actor upon the occasion of the crime and had not previously permitted him sexual liberties, in which cases the offense is a felony of the first degree.

(2) Gross Sexual Imposition. A male who has sexual intercourse with a female not his wife commits a felony of the third degree if:

(a) he compels her to submit by any threat that would prevent resistance by a woman of ordinary resolution; or

(b) he knows that she suffers from a mental disease or defect which renders her incapable of appraising the nature of her conduct; or

(c) he knows that she is unaware that a sexual act is being committed upon her or that she submits because she mistakenly supposes that he is her husband.

Section 213.2. Deviate Sexual Intercourse by Force or Imposition.

(1) <u>By Force or Its Equivalent.</u> A person who engages in deviate sexual intercourse with another person, or who causes another to engage in deviate sexual intercourse, commits a felony of the second degree if:

(a) he compels the other person to participate by force or by threat of imminent death, serious bodily injury, extreme pain or kidnapping, to be inflicted on anyone; or

(b) he has substantially impaired the other person's power to appraise or control his conduct, by administering or employing without the knowledge of the other person drugs, intoxicants or other means for the purpose of preventing resistance; or

(c) the other person is unconscious; or

(d) the other person is less than 10 years old.

(2) <u>By Other Imposition.</u> A person who engages in deviate sexual intercourse with another person, or who causes another to engage in deviate sexual intercourse, commits a felony of the third degree if:

(a) he compels the other person to participate by any threat that would prevent resistance by a person of ordinary resolution; or

(b) he knows that the other person suffers from a mental disease or defect which renders him incapable of appraising the nature of his conduct; or

(c) he knows that the other person submits because he is unaware that a sexual act is being committed upon him.

Section 213.3. Corruption of Minors and Seduction.

(1) <u>Offense Defined.</u> A male who has sexual intercourse with a female not his wife, or any person who engages in deviate sexual intercourse or causes another to engage in deviate sexual intercourse, is guilty of an offense if:

(a) the other person is less than [16] years old and the actor is at least [four] years older than the other person; or

(b) the other person is less than 21 years old and the actor is his guardian or otherwise responsible for general supervision of his welfare; or

(c) the other person is in custody of law or detained in a hospital or other institution and the actor has supervisory or disciplinary authority over him; or

(d) the other person is a female who is induced to participate by a promise of marriage which the actor does not mean to perform.

(2) <u>Grading.</u> An offense under paragraph (a) of Subsection (1) is a felony of the third degree. Otherwise an offense under this section is a misdemeanor.

Section 213.4. Sexual Assault.

A person who has sexual contact with another not his spouse, or causes such other to have sexual conduct with him, is guilty of sexual assault, a misdemeanor, if:

(1) he knows that the contact is offensive to the other person; or

(2) he knows that the other person suffers from a mental disease or defect which renders him or her incapable of appraising the nature of his or her conduct; or

(3) he knows that the other person is unaware that a sexual act is being committed; or

(4) the other person is less than 10 years old; or

(5) he has substantially impaired the other person's power to appraise or control his or her conduct, by administering or employing without the other's knowledge drugs, intoxicants or other means for the purpose of preventing resistance; or

(6) the other person is less than [16] years old and the actor is at least [four] years older than the other person; or

(7) the other person is less than 21 years old and the actor is his guardian or otherwise responsible for general supervision of his welfare; or

(8) the other person is in custody of law or detained in a hospital or other institution and the actor has supervisory or disciplinary authority over him.

Sexual contact is any touching of the sexual or other intimate parts of the person for the purpose of arousing or gratifying sexual desire.

Section 213.5. Indecent Exposure.

A person commits a misdemeanor if, for the purpose of arousing or gratifying sexual desire of himself or of any person other than his spouse, he exposes his genitals under circumstances in which he knows his conduct is likely to cause affront or alarm.

Section 213.6. Provisions Generally Applicable to Article 213.

(1) <u>Mistake as to Age.</u> Whenever in this Article the criminality of conduct depends on a child's being below the age of 10, it is no defense that the actor did not know the child's age, or reasonably believed the child to be older than 10. When criminality depends on the child's being below a critical age other than 10, it is a defense for the actor to prove

by a preponderance of the evidence that he reasonably believed the child to be above the critical age.

(2) Spouse Relationships. Whenever in this Article the definition of an offense excludes conduct with a spouse, the exclusion shall be deemed to extend to persons living as man and wife, regardless of the legal status of their relationship. The exclusion shall be inoperative as respects spouses living apart under a decree of judicial separation. Where the definition of an offense excludes conduct with a spouse or conduct by a woman, this shall not preclude conviction of a spouse or woman as accomplice in a sexual act which he or she causes another person, not within the exclusion, to perform.

(3) Sexually Promiscuous Complainants. It is a defense to prosecution under Section 213.3 and paragraphs (6), (7) and (8) of Section 213.4 for the actor to prove by a preponderance of the evidence that the alleged victim had, prior to the time of the offense charged, engaged promiscuously in sexual relations with others.

(4) Prompt Complaint. No prosecution may be instituted or maintained under this Article unless the alleged offense was brought to the notice of public authority within [3] months of its occurrence or, where the alleged victim was less than [16] years old or otherwise incompetent to make complaint, within [3] months after a parent, guardian or other competent person specially interested in the victim learns of the offense.

(5) Testimony of Complainants. No person shall be convicted of any felony under this Article upon the uncorroborated testimony of the alleged victim. Corroboration may be circumstantial. In any prosecution before a jury for an offense under this Article, the jury shall be instructed to evaluate the testimony of a victim or complaining witness with special care in view of the emotional involvement of the witness and the difficulty of determining the truth with respect to alleged sexual activities carried out in private.

Offenses against Property

Article 220.   Arson, Criminal Mischief, and Other Property Destruction

Section 220.1.   Arson and Related Offenses.

(1) Arson. A person is guilty of arson, a felony of the second degree, if he starts a fire or causes an explosion with the purpose of:

(a) destroying a building or occupied structure of another; or

(b) destroying or damaging any property, whether his own or another's, to collect insurance for such loss. It shall be an affirmative defense to prosecution under this paragraph that the actor's conduct did not recklessly endanger any building or occupied structure of another or place any other person in danger of death or bodily injury.

(2) Reckless Burning or Exploding. A person commits a felony of the third degree if he purposely starts a fire or causes an explosion, whether on his own property or another's, and thereby recklessly:

(a) places another person in danger of death or bodily injury; or

(b) places a building or occupied structure of another in danger of damage or destruction.

(3) Failure to Control or Report Dangerous Fire. A person who knows that a fire is endangering life or a substantial amount of property of another and fails to take reasonable measures to put out or control the fire, when he can do so without substantial risk to himself, or to give a prompt fire alarm, commits a misdemeanor if:

(a) he knows that he is under an official, contractual, or other legal duty to prevent or combat the fire; or

(b) the fire was started, albeit lawfully, by him or with his assent, or on property in his custody or control.

(4) Definitions. "Occupied structure" means any structure, vehicle or place adapted for overnight accommodation of persons, or for carrying on business therein, whether or not a person is actually present. Property is that of another, for the purposes of this section, if anyone other than the actor has a possessory or proprietary interest therein. If a building or structure is divided into separately occupied units, any unit not occupied by the actor is an occupied structure of another.

Section 220.2. Causing or Risking Catastrophe.

(1) Causing Catastrophe. A person who causes a catastrophe by explosion, fire, flood, avalanche, collapse of building, release of poison gas, radioactive material or other harmful or destructive force or substance, or by any other means of causing potentially widespread injury or damage, commits a felony of the second degree if he does so purposely or knowingly, or a felony of the third degree if he does so recklessly.

(2) Risking Catastrophe. A person is guilty of a misdemeanor if he recklessly creates a risk of catastrophe in the employment of fire, explosives or other dangerous means listed in Subsection (1).

(3) Failure to Prevent Catastrophe. A person who knowingly or recklessly fails to take reasonable measures to prevent or mitigate a catastrophe commits a misdemeanor if:

(a) he knows that he is under an official, contractual or other legal duty to take such measures; or

(b) he did or assented to the act causing or threatening the catastrophe.

Section 220.3. Criminal Mischief.

(1) Offense Defined. A person is guilty of criminal mischief if he:

(a) damages tangible property of another purposely, recklessly, or by negligence in the employment of fire, explosives, or other dangerous means listed in Section 220.2(1); or

(b) purposely or recklessly tampers with tangible property of another so as to endanger person or property; or

(c) purposely or recklessly causes another to suffer pecuniary loss by deception or threat.

(2) Grading. Criminal mischief is a felony of the third degree if the actor purposely causes pecuniary loss in excess of $5,000, or a substantial interruption or impairment of public communication, transportation, supply of water, gas or power, or other public service. It is a misdemeanor if the actor purposely causes pecuniary loss in excess of $100, or a petty misdemeanor if he purposely or recklessly causes pecuniary loss in excess of $25. Otherwise criminal mischief is a violation.

Article 221. Burglary and Other Criminal Intrusion

Section 221.0. Definitions.

In this Article, unless a different meaning plainly is required:

(1) "occupied structure" means any structure, vehicle or place adapted for overnight accommodation of persons, or for carrying on business therein, whether or not a person is actually present.

(2) "night" means the period between thirty minutes past sunset and thirty minutes before sunrise.

Section 221.1. Burglary.

(1) Burglary Defined. A person is guilty of burglary if he enters a building or occupied structure, or separately secured or occupied portion thereof, with purpose to commit a crime therein, unless the premises are at the time open to the public or the actor is licensed or privileged to enter. It is an affirmative defense to prosecution for burglary that the building or structure was abandoned.

(2) Grading. Burglary is a felony of the second degree if it is perpetrated in the dwelling of another at night, or if, in the course of committing the offense, the actor:

(a) purposely, knowingly or recklessly inflicts or attempts to inflict bodily injury on anyone; or

(b) is armed with explosives or a deadly weapon.

Otherwise, burglary is a felony of the third degree. An act shall be deemed "in the course of committing" an offense if it occurs in an attempt to commit the offense or in flight after the attempt or commission.

(3) <u>Multiple Convictions</u>. A person may not be convicted both for burglary and for the offense which it was his purpose to commit after the burglarious entry or for an attempt to commit that offense, unless the additional offense constitutes a felony of the first or second degree.

Section 221.2. Criminal Trespass.

(1) <u>Buildings and Occupied Structures</u>. A person commits an offense if, knowing that he is not licensed or privileged to do so, he enters or surreptitiously remains in any building or occupied structure, or separately secured or occupied portion thereof. An offense under this Subsection is a misdemeanor if it is committed in a dwelling at night. Otherwise it is a petty misdemeanor.

(2) <u>Defiant Trespasser</u>. A person commits an offense if, knowing that he is not licensed or privileged to do so, he enters or remains in any place as to which notice against trespass is given by:

(a) actual communication to the actor; or

(b) posting in a manner prescribed by law or reasonably likely to come to the attention of intruders; or

(c) fencing or other enclosure manifestly designed to exclude intruders.

An offense under this Subsection constitutes a petty misdemeanor if the offender defies an order to leave personally communicated to him by the owner of the premises or other authorized person. Otherwise it is a violation.

(3) <u>Defenses</u>. It is an affirmative defense to prosecution under this Section that:

(a) a building or occupied structure involved in an offense under Subsection (1) was abandoned; or

(b) the premises were at the time open to members of the public and the actor complied with all lawful conditions imposed on access to or remaining in the premises; or

(c) the actor reasonably believed that the owner of the premises, or other person empowered to license access thereto, would have licensed him to enter or remain.

Article 222. Robbery

Section 222.1. Robbery.

(1) <u>Robbery Defined</u>. A person is guilty of robbery if, in the course of committing a theft, he:

(a) inflicts serious bodily injury upon another; or

(b) threatens another with or purposely puts him in fear of immediate serious bodily injury; or

(c) commits or threatens immediately to commit any felony of the first or second degree.

An act shall be deemed "in the course of committing a theft" if it occurs in an attempt to commit theft or in flight after the attempt or commission.

(2) <u>Grading.</u> Robbery is a felony of the second degree, except that it is a felony of the first degree if in the course of committing the theft the actor attempts to kill anyone, or purposely inflicts or attempts to inflict serious bodily injury.

Article 223. Theft and Related Offenses

Section 223.0. Definitions.

In this Article, unless a different meaning plainly is required:

(1) "deprive" means: (a) to withhold property of another permanently or for so extended a period as to appropriate a major portion of its economic value, or with intent to restore only upon payment of reward or other compensation; or (b) to dispose of the property so as to make it unlikely that the owner will recover it.

(2) "financial institution" means a bank, insurance company, credit union, building and loan association, investment trust or other organization held out to the public as a place of deposit of funds or medium of savings or collective investment.

(3) "government" means the United States, any State, county, municipality, or other political unit, or any department, agency or subdivision of any of the foregoing, or any corporation or other association carrying out the functions of government.

(4) "movable property" means property the location of which can be changed, including things growing on, affixed to, or found in land, and documents although the rights represented thereby have no physical location; "immovable property" is all other property.

(5) "obtain" means: (a) in relation to property, to bring about a transfer or purported transfer of a legal interest in the property, whether to the obtainer or another; or (b) in relation to labor or service, to secure performance thereof.

(6) "property" means anything of value, including real estate, tangible and intangible personal property, contract rights, choses-in-action and other interests in or claims to wealth, admission or transportation tickets, captured or domestic animals, food and drink, electric or other power.

(7) "property of another" includes property in which any person other than the actor has an interest which the actor is not privileged to infringe, regardless of the fact that the actor also has an interest in the property and regardless of the fact that the other person might be precluded from civil recovery because the property was used in an unlawful transaction or was subject to forfeiture as contraband. Property in possession of the actor shall not be deemed property of another

who has only a security interest therein, even if legal title is in the creditor pursuant to a conditional sales contract or other security agreement.

Section 223.1. Consolidation of Theft Offenses; Grading; Provisions Applicable to Theft Generally.

(1) Consolidation of Theft Offenses. Conduct denominated theft in this Article constitutes a single offense. An accusation of theft may be supported by evidence that it was committed in any manner that would be theft under this Article, notwithstanding the specification of a different manner in the indictment or information, subject only to the power of the Court to ensure fair trial by granting a continuance or other appropriate relief where the conduct of the defense would be prejudiced by lack of fair notice or by surprise.

(2) Grading of Theft Offenses.

(a) Theft constitutes a felony of the third degree if the amount involved exceeds $500, or if the property stolen is a firearm, automobile, airplane, motorcycle, motorboat, or other motor-propelled vehicle, or in the case of theft by receiving stolen property, if the receiver is in the business of buying or selling stolen property.

(b) Theft not within the preceding paragraph constitutes a misdemeanor, except that if the property was not taken from the person or by threat, or in breach of a fiduciary obligation, and the actor proves by a preponderance of the evidence that the amount involved was less than $50, the offense constitutes a petty misdemeanor.

(c) The amount involved in a theft shall be deemed to be the highest value, by any reasonable standard, of the property or services which the actor stole or attempted to steal. Amounts involved in thefts committed pursuant to one scheme or course of conduct, whether from the same person or several persons, may be aggregated in determining the grade of the offense.

(3) Claim of Right. It is an affirmative defense to prosecution for theft that the actor:

(a) was unaware that the property or service was that of another; or

(b) acted under an honest claim of right to the property or service involved or that he had a right to acquire or dispose of it as he did; or

(c) took property exposed for sale, intending to purchase and pay for it promptly, or reasonably believing that the owner, if present, would have consented.

(4) Theft from Spouse. It is no defense that theft was from the actor's spouse, except that misappropriation of household and personal effects, or other property normally accessible to both spouses, is theft only if it occurs after the parties have ceased living together.

Section 223.2. Theft by Unlawful Taking or Disposition.

(1) Movable Property. A person is guilty of theft if he unlawfully takes, or exercises unlawful control over, movable property of another with purpose to deprive him thereof.

(2) <u>Immovable Property.</u> A person is guilty of theft if he unlawfully transfers immovable property of another or any interest therein with purpose to benefit himself or another not entitled thereto.

Section 223.3. Theft by Deception.

A person is guilty of theft if he purposely obtains property of another by deception. A person deceives if he purposely:

(1) creates or reinforces a false impression, including false impressions as to law, value, intention or other state of mind; but deception as to a person's intention to perform a promise shall not be inferred from the fact alone that he did not subsequently perform the promise; or

(2) prevents another from acquiring information which would affect his judgment of a transaction; or

(3) fails to correct a false impression which the deceiver previously created or reinforced, or which the deceiver knows to be influencing another to whom he stands in a fiduciary or confidential relationship; or

(4) fails to disclose a known lien, adverse claim or other legal impediment to the enjoyment of property which he transfers or encumbers in consideration for the property obtained, whether such impediment is or is not valid, or is or is not a matter of official record.

The term "deceive" does not, however, include falsity as to matters having no pecuniary significance, or puffing by statements unlikely to deceive ordinary persons in the group addressed.

Section 223.4. Theft by Extortion.

A person is guilty of theft if he purposely obtains property of another by threatening to:

(1) inflict bodily injury on anyone or commit any other criminal offense; or

(2) accuse anyone of a criminal offense; or

(3) expose any secret tending to subject any person to hatred, contempt or ridicule, or to impair his credit or business repute; or

(4) take or withhold action as an official, or cause an official to take or withhold action; or

(5) bring about or continue a strike, boycott or other collective unofficial action, if the property is not demanded or received for the benefit of the group in whose interest the actor purports to act; or

(6) testify or provide information or withhold testimony or information with respect to another's legal claim or defense; or

(7) inflict any other harm which would not benefit the actor.

It is an affirmative defense to prosecution based on paragraphs (2), (3) or (4) that the property obtained by threat of accusation, exposure, lawsuit or other invocation of official action was honestly claimed as restitution or indemnification for harm done in the circumstances to which such accusation, exposure, lawsuit or other official action relates, or as compensation for property or lawful services.

Section 223.5. Theft of Property Lost, Mislaid, or Delivered by Mistake.

A person who comes into control of property of another that he knows to have been lost, mislaid, or delivered under a mistake as to the nature or amount of the property or the identity of the recipient is guilty of theft if, with purpose to deprive the owner thereof, he fails to take reasonable measures to restore the property to a person entitled to have it.

Section 223.6. Receiving Stolen Property.

(1) Receiving. A person is guilty of theft if he purposely receives, retains, or disposes of movable property of another knowing that it has been stolen, or believing that it has probably been stolen, unless the property is received, retained, or disposed with purpose to restore it to the owner. "Receiving" means acquiring possession, control or title, or lending on the security of the property.

(2) Presumption of Knowledge. The requisite knowledge or belief is presumed in the case of a dealer who:

(a) is found in possession or control of property stolen from two or more persons on separate occasions; or

(b) has received stolen property in another transaction within the year preceding the transaction charged; or

(c) being a dealer in property of the sort received, acquires it for a consideration which he knows is far below its reasonable value.

"Dealer" means a person in the business of buying or selling goods including a pawnbroker.

Section 223.7. Theft of Services.

(1) A person is guilty of theft if he purposely obtains services which he knows are available only for compensation, by deception or threat, or by false token or other means to avoid payment for the service. "Services" includes labor, professional service, transportation, telephone or other public service, accommodation in hotels, restaurants or elsewhere, admission to exhibitions, use of vehicles or other movable property. Where compensation for service is ordinarily paid immediately upon the rendering of such service, as in the case of hotels and restaurants, refusal to pay or absconding without payment or offer to pay gives rise to a presumption that the service was obtained by deception as to intention to pay.

(2) A person commits theft if, having control over the disposition of services of others, to which he is not entitled, he knowingly diverts

such services to his own benefit or to the benefit of another not entitled thereto.

Section 223.8. Theft by Failure to Make Required Disposition of Funds Received.

A person who purposely obtains property upon agreement, or subject to a known legal obligation, to make specified payment or other disposition, whether from such property or its proceeds or from his own property to be reserved in equivalent amount, is guilty of theft if he deals with the property obtained as his own and fails to make the required payment or disposition. The foregoing applies notwithstanding that it may be impossible to identify particular property as belonging to the victim at the time of the actor's failure to make the required payment or disposition. An officer or employee of the government or of a financial institution is presumed: (i) to know any legal obligation relevant to his criminal liability under this Section, and (ii) to have dealt with the property as his own if he fails to pay or account upon lawful demand, or if an audit reveals a shortage or falsification of accounts.

Section 223.9. Unauthorized Use of Automobiles and Other Vehicles.

A person commits a misdemeanor if he operates another's automobile, airplane, motorcycle, motorboat, or other motor-propelled vehicle without consent of the owner. It is an affirmative defense to prosecution under this Section that the actor reasonably believed that the owner would have consented to the operation had he known of it.

Article 224. Forgery and Fraudulent Practices

Section 224.0. Definitions.

In this Article, the definitions given in Section 223.0 apply unless a different meaning plainly is required.

Section 224.1. Forgery.

(1) <u>Definition</u>. A person is guilty of forgery if, with purpose to defraud or injure anyone, or with knowledge that he is facilitating a fraud or injury to be perpetrated by anyone, the actor:

(a) alters any writing of another without his authority; or

(b) makes, completes, executes, authenticates, issues or transfers any writing so that it purports to be the act of another who did not authorize that act, or to have been executed at a time or place or in a numbered sequence other than was in fact the case, or to be a copy of an original when no such original existed; or

(c) utters any writing which he knows to be forged in a manner specified in paragraphs (a) or (b).

"Writing" includes printing or any other method of recording information, money, coins, tokens, stamps, seals, credit cards, badges, trade-marks, and other symbols of value, right, privilege, or identification.

(2) Grading. Forgery is a felony of the second degree if the writing is or purports to be part of an issue of money, securities, postage or revenue stamps, or other instruments issued by the government, or part of an issue of stock, bonds or other instruments representing interests in or claims against any property or enterprise. Forgery is a felony of the third degree if the writing is or purports to be a will, deed, contract, release, commercial instrument, or other document evidencing, creating, transferring, altering, terminating, or otherwise affecting legal relations. Otherwise forgery is a misdemeanor.

Section 224.14. Securing Execution of Documents by Deception.

A person commits a misdemeanor if by deception he causes another to execute any instrument affecting, purporting to affect, or likely to affect the pecuniary interest of any person.

Offenses against the Family

Article 230. Offenses against the Family

Section 230.1. Bigamy and Polygamy.

(1) Bigamy. A married person is guilty of bigamy, a misdemeanor, if he contracts or purports to contract another marriage, unless at the time of the subsequent marriage:

(a) the actor believes that the prior spouse is dead; or

(b) the actor and the prior spouse have been living apart for five consecutive years throughout which the prior spouse was not known by the actor to be alive; or

(c) a Court has entered a judgment purporting to terminate or annul any prior disqualifying marriage, and the actor does not know that judgment to be invalid; or

(d) the actor reasonably believes that he is legally eligible to remarry.

(2) Polygamy. A person is guilty of polygamy, a felony of the third degree, if he marries or cohabits with more than one spouse at a time in purported exercise of the right of plural marriage. The offense is a continuing one until all cohabitation and claim of marriage with more than one spouse terminates. This section does not apply to parties to a

polygamous marriage, lawful in the country of which they are residents or nationals, while they are in transit through or temporarily visiting this State.

(3) Other Party to Bigamous or Polygamous Marriage. A person is guilty of bigamy or polygamy, as the case may be, if he contracts or purports to contract marriage with another knowing that the other is thereby committing bigamy or polygamy.

Section 230.2. Incest.

A person is guilty of incest, a felony of the third degree, if he knowingly marries or cohabits or has sexual intercourse with an ancestor or descendant, a brother or sister of the whole or half blood [or an uncle, aunt, nephew or niece of the whole blood]. "Cohabit" means to live together under the representation or appearance of being married. The relationships referred to herein include blood relationships without regard to legitimacy, and relationship of parent and child by adoption.

Section 230.3. Abortion.

(1) Unjustified Abortion. A person who purposely and unjustifiably terminates the pregnancy of another otherwise than by a live birth commits a felony of the third degree or, where the pregnancy has continued beyond the twenty-sixth week, a felony of the second degree.

(2) Justifiable Abortion. A licensed physician is justified in terminating a pregnancy if he believes there is substantial risk that continuance of the pregnancy would gravely impair the physical or mental health of the mother or that the child would be born with grave physical or mental defect, or that the pregnancy resulted from rape, incest, or other felonious intercourse. All illicit intercourse with a girl below the age of 16 shall be deemed felonious for purposes of this subsection. Justifiable abortions shall be performed only in a licensed hospital except in case of emergency when hospital facilities are unavailable. [Additional exceptions from the requirement of hospitalization may be incorporated here to take account of situations in sparsely settled areas where hospitals are not generally accessible.]

(3) Physicians' Certificates; Presumption from Non-Compliance. No abortion shall be performed unless two physicians, one of whom may be the person performing the abortion, shall have certified in writing the circumstances which they believe to justify the abortion. Such certificate shall be submitted before the abortion to the hospital where it is to be performed and, in the case of abortion following felonious intercourse, to the prosecuting attorney or the police. Failure to comply with any of the requirements of this Subsection gives rise to a presumption that the abortion was unjustified.

(4) Self-Abortion. A woman whose pregnancy has continued beyond the twenty-sixth week commits a felony of the third degree if she purposely terminates her own pregnancy otherwise than by a live birth, or if she uses instruments, drugs or violence upon herself for that purpose. Except as justified under Subsection (2), a person who induces or knowingly aids a woman to use instruments, drugs or violence upon herself for the purpose of terminating her pregnancy otherwise than by a live birth commits a felony of the third degree whether or not the pregnancy has continued beyond the twenty-sixth week.

(5) Pretended Abortion. A person commits a felony of the third degree if, representing that it is his purpose to perform an abortion, he does an act adapted to cause abortion in a pregnant woman although the woman is in fact not pregnant, or the actor does not believe she is. A person charged with unjustified abortion under Subsection (1) or an attempt to commit that offense may be convicted thereof upon proof of conduct prohibited by this Subsection.

(6) Distribution of Abortifacients. A person who sells, offers to sell, possesses with intent to sell, advertises, or displays for sale anything specially designed to terminate a pregnancy, or held out by the actor as useful for that purpose, commits a misdemeanor, unless:

    (a) the sale, offer or display is to a physician or druggist or to an intermediary in a chain of distribution to physicians or druggists; or

    (b) the sale is made upon prescription or order of a physician; or

    (c) the possession is with intent to sell as authorized in paragraphs (a) and (b); or

    (d) the advertising is addressed to persons named in paragraph (a) and confined to trade or professional channels not likely to reach the general public.

(7) Section Inapplicable to Prevention of Pregnancy. Nothing in this Section shall be deemed applicable to the prescription, administration or distribution of drugs or other substances for avoiding pregnancy, whether by preventing implantation of a fertilized ovum or by any other method that operates before, at or immediately after fertilization.

Section 230.4. Endangering Welfare of Children.

A parent, guardian, or other person supervising the welfare of a child under 18 commits a misdemeanor if he knowingly endangers the child's welfare by violating a duty of care, protection or support.

Section 230.5. Persistent Nonsupport.

A person commits a misdemeanor if he persistently fails to provide support which he can provide and which he knows he is legally obliged to provide to a spouse, child or other dependent.

Offenses against Public Administration

Article 240. Bribery and Corrupt Influence

Section 240.0. Definitions.

In Articles 240–243, unless a different meaning plainly is required:

(1) "benefit" means gain or advantage, or anything regarded by the beneficiary as gain or advantage, including benefit to any other person or entity in whose welfare he is interested, but not an advantage promised generally to a group or class of voters as a consequence of public measures which a candidate engages to support or oppose;

(2) "government" includes any branch, subdivision or agency of the government of the State or any locality within it;

(3) "harm" means loss, disadvantage or injury, or anything so regarded by the person affected, including loss, disadvantage or injury to any other person or entity in whose welfare he is interested;

(4) "official proceeding" means a proceeding heard or which may be heard before any legislative, judicial, administrative or other governmental agency or official authorized to take evidence under oath, including any referee, hearing examiner, commissioner, notary or other person taking testimony or deposition in connection with any such proceeding;

(5) "party official" means a person who holds an elective or appointive post in a political party in the United States by virtue of which he directs or conducts, or participates in directing of conducting party affairs at any level of responsibility;

(6) "pecuniary benefit" is benefit in the form of money, property, commercial interests or anything else the primary significance of which is economic gain';

(7) "public servant" means any officer or employee of government, including legislators and judges, and any person participating as juror, advisor, consultant or otherwise, in performing a governmental function; but the term does not include witnesses;

(8) "administrative proceeding" means any proceeding, other than a judicial proceeding, the outcome of which is required to be based on a record or documentation prescribed by law, or in which law or regulation is particularized in application to individuals.

Section 240.7. Selling Political Endorsement; Special Influence.

(1) Selling Political Endorsement. A person commits a misdemeanor if he solicits, receives, agrees to receive, or agrees that any political party or other person shall receive, any pecuniary benefit as consideration for approval or disapproval of an appointment or advancement in public service, or for approval or disapproval of any person or transaction for

any benefit conferred by an official or agency of government. "Approval" includes recommendation, failure to disapprove, or any other manifestation of favor or acquiescence. "Disapproval" includes failure to approve, or any other manifestation of disfavor or nonacquiescence.

(2) Other Trading in Special Influence. A person commits a misdemeanor if he solicits, receives or agrees to receive any pecuniary benefit as consideration for exerting special influence upon a public servant or procuring another to do so. "Special influence" means power to influence through kinship, friendship or other relationship, apart from the merits of the transaction.

(3) Paying for Endorsement or Special Influence. A person commits a misdemeanor if he offers, confers or agrees to confer any pecuniary benefit receipt of which is prohibited by this Section.

Article 241.   Perjury and Other Falsification in Official Matters

Section 241.0.   Definitions.

In this Article, unless a different meaning plainly is required:

(1) the definitions given in Section 240.0 apply; and

(2) "statement" means any representation, but includes a representation of opinion, belief or other state of mind only if the representation clearly relates to state of mind apart from or in addition to any facts which are the subject of the representation.

Section 241.1.   Perjury.

(1) Offense Defined. A person is guilty of perjury, a felony of the third degree, if in any official proceeding he makes a false statement under oath or equivalent affirmation, or swears or affirms the truth of a statement previously made, when the statement is material and he does not believe it to be true.

(2) Materiality. Falsification is material, regardless of the admissibility of the statement under rules of evidence, if it could have affected the course or outcome of the proceeding. It is no defense that the declarant mistakenly believed the falsification to be immaterial. Whether a falsification is material in a given factual situation is a question of law.

(3) Irregularities No Defense. It is not a defense to prosecution under this Section that the oath or affirmation was administered or taken in an irregular manner or that the declarant was not competent to make the statement. A document purporting to be made upon oath or affirmation at any time when the actor presents it as being so verified shall be deemed to have been duly sworn or affirmed.

(4) Retraction. No person shall be guilty of an offense under this Section if he retracted the falsification in the course of the proceeding in

which it was made before it became manifest that the falsification was or would be exposed and before the falsification substantially affected the proceeding.

(5) Inconsistent Statements. Where the defendant made inconsistent statements under oath or equivalent affirmation, both having been made within the period of the statute of limitations, the prosecution may proceed by setting forth the inconsistent statements in a single count alleging in the alternative that one or the other was false and not believed by the defendant. In such case it shall not be necessary for the prosecution to prove which statement was false but only that one or the other was false and not believed by the defendant to be true.

(6) Corroboration. No person shall be convicted of an offense under this Section where proof of falsity rests solely upon contradiction by testimony of a single person other than the defendant.

Section 241.2. False Swearing.

(1) False Swearing in Official Matters. A person who makes a false statement under oath or equivalent affirmation, or swears or affirms the truth of such a statement previously made, when he does not believe the statement to be true, is guilty of a misdemeanor if:

(a) the falsification occurs in an official proceeding; or

(b) the falsification is intended to mislead a public servant in performing his official function.

(2) Other False Swearing. A person who makes a false statement under oath or equivalent affirmation, or swears or affirms the truth of such a statement previously made, when he does not believe the statement to be true, is guilty of a petty misdemeanor, if the statement is one which is required by law to be sworn or affirmed before a notary or other person authorized to administer oaths.

Section 241.9. Impersonating a Public Servant.

A person commits a misdemeanor if he falsely pretends to hold a position in the public service with purpose to induce another to submit to such pretended official authority or otherwise to act in reliance upon that pretense to his prejudice.

Article 242. Obstructing Governmental Operations; Escapes

Section 242.0. Definitions.

In this Article, unless another meaning plainly is required, the definitions given in Section 240.0 apply.

Section 242.1. Obstructing Administration of Law or Other Governmental Function.

A person commits a misdemeanor if he purposely obstructs, impairs or perverts the administration of law or other governmental function by force, violence, physical interference or obstacle, breach of official duty, or any other unlawful act, except that this Section does not apply to flight by a person charged with crime, refusal to submit to arrest, failure to perform a legal duty other than an official duty, or any other means of avoiding compliance with law without affirmative interference with governmental functions.

Section 242.2. Resisting Arrest or Other Law Enforcement.

A person commits a misdemeanor if, for the purpose of preventing a public servant from effecting a lawful arrest or discharging any other duty, the person creates a substantial risk of bodily injury to the public servant or anyone else, or employs means justifying or requiring substantial force to overcome the resistance.

Section 242.3. Hindering Apprehension or Prosecution.

A person commits an offense if, with purpose to hinder the apprehension, prosecution, conviction or punishment of another for crime, he:

(1) harbors or conceals the other; or

(2) provides or aids in providing a weapon, transportation, disguise or other means of avoiding apprehension or effecting escape; or

(3) conceals or destroys evidence of the crime, or tampers with a witness, informant, document or other source of information, regardless of its admissibility in evidence; or

(4) warns the other of impending discovery or apprehension, except that this paragraph does not apply to a warning given in connection with an effort to bring another into compliance with law; or

(5) volunteers false information to a law enforcement officer.

The offense is a felony of the third degree if the conduct which the actor knows has been charged or is liable to be charged against the person aided would constitute a felony of the first or second degree. Otherwise it is a misdemeanor.

Section 242.4. Aiding Consummation of Crime.

A person commits an offense if he purposely aids another to accomplish an unlawful object of a crime, as by safeguarding the proceeds thereof or converting the proceeds into negotiable funds. The offense is a felony of the third degree if the principal offense was a felony of the first or second degree. Otherwise it is a misdemeanor.

Section 242.5. Compounding.

A person commits a misdemeanor if he accepts or agrees to accept any pecuniary benefit in consideration of refraining from reporting to law enforcement authorities the commission or suspected commission of any offense or information relating to an offense. It is an affirmative defense to prosecution under this Section that the pecuniary benefit did not exceed an amount which the actor believed to be due as restitution or indemnification for harm caused by the offense.

Section 242.6. Escape.

(1) Escape. A person commits an offense if he unlawfully removes himself from official detention or fails to return to official detention following temporary leave granted for a specific purpose or limited period. "Official detention" means arrest, detention in any facility for custody of persons under charge or conviction of crime or alleged or found to be delinquent, detention for extradition or deportation, or any other detention for law enforcement purposes; but "official detention" does not include supervision of probation or parole, or constraint incidental to release on bail.

(2) Permitting or Facilitating Escape. A public servant concerned in detention commits an offense if he knowingly or recklessly permits an escape. Any person who knowingly causes or facilitates an escape commits an offense.

(3) Effect of Legal Irregularity in Detention. Irregularity in bringing about or maintaining detention, or lack of jurisdiction of the committing or detaining authority, shall not be a defense to prosecution under this Section if the escape is from a prison or other custodial facility or from detention pursuant to commitment by official proceedings. In the case of other detentions, irregularity or lack of jurisdiction shall be a defense only if:

(a) the escape involved no substantial risk of harm to the person or property of anyone other than the detainee; or

(b) the detaining authority did not act in good faith under color of law.

(4) Grading of Offenses. An offense under this Section is a felony of the third degree where:

(a) the actor was under arrest for or detained on a charge of felony or following conviction of crime; or

(b) the actor employs force, threat, deadly weapon or other dangerous instrumentality to effect the escape; or

(c) a public servant concerned in detention of persons convicted of crime purposely facilitates or permits an escape from a detention facility.

Otherwise an offense under this Section is a misdemeanor.

Section 242.7. Implements for Escape; Other Contraband.

(1) Escape Implements. A person commits a misdemeanor if he unlawfully introduces within a detention facility, or unlawfully provides an inmate with, any weapon, tool or other thing which may be useful for

escape. An inmate commits a misdemeanor if he unlawfully procures, makes, or otherwise provides himself with, or has in his possession, any such implement of escape. "Unlawfully" means surreptitiously or contrary to law, regulation or order of the detaining authority.

(2) Other Contraband. A person commits a petty misdemeanor if he provides an inmate with anything which the actor knows it is unlawful for the inmate to possess.

Section 242.8. Bail Jumping; Default in Required Appearance.

A person set at liberty by court order, with or without bail, upon condition that he will subsequently appear at a specified time and place, commits a misdemeanor if, without lawful excuse, he fails to appear at that time and place. The offense constitutes a felony of the third degree where the required appearance was to answer to a charge of felony, or for disposition of any such charge, and the actor took flight or went into hiding to avoid apprehension, trial or punishment. This Section does not apply to obligations to appear incident to release under suspended sentence or on probation or parole.

Article 243. Abuse of Office

Section 243.0. Definitions.

In this Article, unless a different meaning plainly is required, the definitions given in Section 240.0 apply.

Section 243.1. Official Oppression.

A person acting or purporting to act in an official capacity or taking advantage of such actual or purported capacity commits a misdemeanor if, knowing that his conduct is illegal, he:

(1) subjects another to arrest, detention, search, seizure, mistreatment, dispossession, assessment, lien or other infringement of personal or property rights; or

(2) denies or impedes another in the exercise or enjoyment of any right, privilege, power or immunity.

Section 243.2. Speculating or Wagering on Official Action or Information.

A public servant commits a misdemeanor if, in contemplation of official action by himself or by a governmental unit with which he is associated, or in reliance on information to which he has access in his official capacity and which has not been made public, he:

(1) acquires a pecuniary interest in any property, transaction or enterprise which may be affected by such information or official action; or

(2) speculates or wagers on the basis of such information or official action; or

(3) aids another to do any of the foregoing.

Offenses against Public Order and Decency

Article 250. Riot, Disorderly Conduct, and Related Offenses

Section 250.1. Riot; Failure to Disperse.

(1) Riot. A person is guilty of riot, a felony of the third degree, if he participates with [two] or more others in a course of disorderly conduct:

(a) with purpose to commit or facilitate the commission of a felony or misdemeanor;

(b) with purpose to prevent or coerce official action; or

(c) when the actor or any other participant to the knowledge of the actor uses or plans to use a firearm or other deadly weapon.

(2) Failure of Disorderly Persons to Disperse upon Official Order. Where [three] or more persons are participating in a course of disorderly conduct likely to cause substantial harm or serious inconvenience, annoyance or alarm, a peace officer or other public servant engaged in executing or enforcing the law may order the participants and others in the immediate vicinity to disperse. A person who refuses or knowingly fails to obey such an order commits a misdemeanor.

Section 250.2. Disorderly Conduct.

(1) Offense Defined. A person is guilty of disorderly conduct if, with purpose to cause public inconvenience, annoyance or alarm, or recklessly creating a risk thereof, he:

(a) engages in fighting or threatening, or in violent or tumultuous behavior; or

(b) makes unreasonable noise or offensively coarse utterance, gesture or display, or addresses abusive language to any person present; or

(c) creates a hazardous or physically offensive condition by any act which serves no legitimate purpose of the actor.

"Public" means affecting or likely to affect persons in a place to which the public or a substantial group has access; among the places included are highways, transport facilities, schools, prisons, apartment houses, places of business or amusement, or any neighborhood.

(2) <u>Grading.</u> An offense under this section is a petty misdemeanor if the actor's purpose is to cause substantial harm or serious inconvenience, or if he persists in disorderly conduct after reasonable warning or request to desist. Otherwise disorderly conduct is a violation.

Section 250.3. False Public Alarms.

A person is guilty of a misdemeanor if he initiates or circulates a report or warning of an impending bombing or other crime or catastrophe, knowing that the report or warning is false or baseless and that it is likely to cause evacuation of a building, place of assembly, or facility of public transport, or to cause public inconvenience or alarm.

Section 250.4. Harassment.

A person commits a petty misdemeanor if, with purpose to harass another, he:

(1) makes a telephone call without purpose of legitimate communication; or

(2) insults, taunts or challenges another in a manner likely to provoke violent or disorderly response; or

(3) makes repeated communications anonymously or at extremely inconvenient hours, or in offensively coarse language; or

(4) subjects another to an offensive touching; or

(5) engages in any other course of alarming conduct serving no legitimate purpose of the actor.

Section 250.5. Public Drunkenness; Drug Incapacitation.

A person is guilty of an offense if he appears in any public place manifestly under the influence of alcohol, narcotics or other drug, not therapeutically administered, to the degree that he may endanger himself or other persons or property, or annoy persons in his vicinity. An offense under this Section constitutes a petty misdemeanor if the actor has been convicted hereunder twice before within a period of one year. Otherwise the offense constitutes a violation.

Section 250.6. Loitering or Prowling.

A person commits a violation if he loiters or prowls in a place, at a time, or in a manner not usual for law-abiding individuals under circumstances that warrant alarm for the safety of persons or property in the vicinity. Among the circumstances which may be considered in determining whether such alarm is warranted is the fact that the actor takes flight upon appearance of a peace officer, refuses to identify himself, or manifestly endeavors to conceal himself or any object. Unless flight by the actor or other circumstance makes it impracticable, a peace officer shall prior to any arrest for an offense under this section afford the actor an opportunity to dispel any alarm which would otherwise be warranted, by requesting him to identify himself and explain his presence and conduct. No person shall be convicted of an offense under this Section if the peace officer did not comply with the preceding sentence, or if it appears at trial that the explanation given by the actor was true and, if believed by the peace officer at the time, would have dispelled the alarm.

Section 250.7. Obstructing Highways and Other Public Passages.

(1) A person, who, having no legal privilege to do so, purposely or recklessly obstructs any highway or other public passage, whether alone or with others, commits a violation, or, in case he persists after warning by a law officer, a petty misdemeanor. "Obstructs" means renders impassable without unreasonable inconvenience or hazard. No person shall be deemed guilty of recklessly obstructing in violation of this Subsection solely because of a gathering of persons to hear him speak or otherwise communicate, or solely because of being a member of such a gathering.

(2) A person in a gathering commits a violation if he refuses to obey a reasonable official request or order to move:

    (a) to prevent obstruction of a highway or other public passage; or

    (b) to maintain public safety by dispersing those gathered in dangerous proximity to a fire or other hazard.

An order to move, addressed to a person whose speech or other lawful behavior attracts an obstructing audience, shall not be deemed reasonable if the obstruction can be readily remedied by police control of the size or location of the gathering.

Section 250.8. Disrupting Meetings and Processions.

A person commits a misdemeanor if, with purpose to prevent or disrupt a lawful meeting, procession or gathering, he does any act tending to obstruct or interfere with it physically, or makes any utterance, gesture or display designed to outrage the sensibilities of the group.

Section 250.9. Desecration of Venerated Objects.

A person commits a misdemeanor if he purposely desecrates any public monument or structure, or place of worship or burial, or if he purposely desecrates the national flag or any other object of veneration by the public or a substantial segment thereof in any public place. "Desecrate" means defacing, damaging, polluting or otherwise physically mistreating in a way that the actor knows will outrage the sensibilities of persons likely to observe or discover his action.

Section 250.10. Abuse of Corpse.

Except as authorized by law, a person who treats a corpse in a way that he knows would outrage ordinary family sensibilities commits a misdemeanor.

Section 250.11. Cruelty to Animals.

A person commits a misdemeanor if he purposely or recklessly:

(1) subjects any animal to cruel mistreatment; or

(2) subjects any animal in his custody to cruel neglect; or

(3) kills or injures any animal belonging to another without legal privilege or consent of the owner.

Subsections (1) and (2) shall not be deemed applicable to accepted veterinary practices and activities carried on for scientific research.

Section 250.12. Violation of Privacy.

(1) Unlawful Eavesdropping or Surveillance. A person commits a misdemeanor if, except as authorized by law, he:

(a) trespasses on property with purpose to subject anyone to eavesdropping or other surveillance in a private place; or

(b) installs in any private place, without the consent of the person or persons entitled to privacy there, any device for observing, photographing, recording, amplifying or broadcasting sounds or events in such place, or uses any such unauthorized installation; or

(c) installs or uses outside a private place any device for hearing, recording, amplifying or broadcasting sounds originating in such place which would not ordinarily be audible or comprehensible outside, without the consent of the person or persons entitled to privacy there.

"Private place" means a place where one may reasonably expect to be safe from casual or hostile instrusion or surveillance, but does not include a place to which the public or a substantial group thereof has access.

(2) Other Breach of Privacy of Messages. A person commits a misdemeanor if, except as authorized by law, he:

(a) intercepts without the consent of the sender or receiver a message by telephone, telegraph, letter or other means of communicating privately; but this paragraph does not extend to (i) overhearing of messages through a regularly installed instrument on a telephone party line or on an extension, or (ii) interception by the telephone company or subscriber incident to enforcement of regulations limiting use of the facilities or incident to other normal operation and use; or

(b) divulges without the consent of the sender or receiver the existence or contents of any such message if the actor knows that the message was illegally intercepted, or if he learned of the message in the course of employment with an agency engaged in transmitting it.

Article 251. Public Indecency

Section 251.1. Open Lewdness.

A person commits a petty misdemeanor if he does any lewd act which he knows is likely to be observed by others who would be affronted or alarmed.

Section 251.2. Prostitution and Related Offenses.

(1) <u>Prostitution</u>. A person is guilty of prostitution, a petty misdemeanor, if he or she:

(a) is an inmate of a house of prostitution or otherwise engages in sexual activity as a business; or

(b) loiters in or within view of any public place for the purpose of being hired to engage in sexual activity.

"Sexual activity" includes homosexual and other deviate sexual relations. A "house of prostitution" is any place where prostitution or promotion of prostitution is regularly carried on by one person under the control, management or supervision of another. An "inmate" is a person who engages in prostitution in or through the agency of a house of prostitution. "Public place" means any place to which the public or any substantial group thereof has access.

(2) <u>Promoting Prostitution</u>. A person who knowingly promotes prostitution of another commits a misdemeanor or felony as provided in Subsection (3). The following acts shall, without limitation of the foregoing, constitute promoting prostitution:

(a) owning, controlling, managing, supervising or otherwise keeping, alone or in association with others, a house of prostitution or a prostitution business; or

(b) procuring an inmate for a house of prostitution or a place in a house of prostitution for one who would be an inmate; or

(c) encouraging, inducing, or otherwise purposely causing another to become or remain a prostitute; or

(d) soliciting a person to patronize a prostitute; or

(e) procuring a prostitute for a patron; or

(f) transporting a person into or within this state with purpose to promote that person's engaging in prostitution, or procuring or paying for transportation with that purpose; or

(g) leasing or otherwise permitting a place controlled by the actor, alone or in association with others, to be regularly used for prostitution or the promotion of prostitution, or failure to make reasonable effort to abate such use by ejecting the tenant, notifying law enforcement authorities, or other legally available means; or

(h) soliciting, receiving, or agreeing to receive any benefit for doing or agreeing to do anything forbidden by this Subsection.

(3) Grading of Offenses under Subsection (2). An offense under Subsection (2) constitutes a felony of the third degree if:

(a) the offense falls within paragraph (a), (b) or (c) of Subsection (2); or

(b) the actor compels another to engage in or promote prostitution; or

(c) the actor promotes prostitution of a child under 16, whether or not he is aware of the child's age; or

(d) the actor promotes prostitution of his wife, child, ward or any person for whose care, protection or support he is responsible.

Otherwise the offense is a misdemeanor.

(4) Presumption from Living off Prostitutes. A person, other than the prostitute or the prostitute's minor child or other legal dependent incapable of self-support, who is supported in whole or substantial part by the proceeds of prostitution is presumed to be knowingly promoting prostitution in violation of Subsection (2).

(5) Patronizing Prostitutes. A person commits a violation if he hires a prostitute to engage in sexual activity with him, or if he enters or remains in a house of prostitution for the purpose of engaging in sexual activity.

(6) Evidence. On the issue whether a place is a house of prostitution the following shall be admissible evidence: its general repute; the repute of the persons who reside in or frequent the place; the frequency, timing and duration of visits by non-residents. Testimony of a person against his spouse shall be admissible to prove offenses under this Section.

Section 251.3. Loitering to Solicit Deviate Sexual Relations.

A person is guilty of a petty misdemeanor if he loiters in or near any public place for the purpose of soliciting or being solicited to engage in deviate sexual relations.

Section 251.4. Obscenity.

(1) Obscene Defined. Material is obscene if, considered as a whole, its predominant appeal is to prurient interest, that is, a shameful or morbid interest, in nudity, sex or excretion, and if in addition it goes substantially beyond customary limits of candor in describing or representing such matters. Predominant appeal shall be judged with reference to ordinary adults unless it appears from the character of the material or the circumstances of its dissemination to be designed for children or other specially susceptible audience. Undeveloped photographs, molds, printing plates, and the like, shall be deemed obscene notwith-

standing that processing or other acts may be required to make the obscenity patent or to disseminate it.

(2) Offenses. Subject to the affirmative defense provided in Subsection (3), a person commits a misdemeanor if he knowingly or recklessly:

(a) sells, delivers or provides, or offers or agrees to sell, deliver or provide, any obscene writing, picture, record or other representation or embodiment of the obscene; or

(b) presents or directs an obscene play, dance or performance, or participates in that portion thereof which makes it obscene; or

(c) publishes, exhibits or otherwise makes available any obscene material; or

(d) possesses any obscene material for purposes of sale or other commercial dissemination; or

(e) sells, advertises or otherwise commercially disseminates material, whether or not obscene, by representing or suggesting that it is obscene.

A person who disseminates or possesses obscene material in the course of his business is presumed to do so knowingly or recklessly.

(3) Justifiable and Non-Commercial Private Dissemination. It is an affirmative defense to prosecution under this Section that dissemination was restricted to:

(a) institutions or persons having scientific, educational, governmental or other similar justification for possessing obscene material; or

(b) non-commercial dissemination to personal associates of the actor.

(4) Evidence; Adjudication of Obscenity. In any prosecution under this Section evidence shall be admissible to show:

(a) the character of the audience for which the material was designed or to which it was directed;

(b) what the predominant appeal of the material would be for ordinary adults or any special audience to which it was directed, and what effect, if any, it would probably have on conduct of such people;

(c) artistic, literary, scientific, educational or other merits of the material;

(d) the degree of public acceptance of the material in the United States;

(e) appeal to prurient interest, or absence thereof, in advertising or other promotion of the material; and

(f) the good repute of the author, creator, publisher or other person from whom the material originated.

Expert testimony and testimony of the author, creator, publisher or other person from whom the material originated, relating to factors entering into the determination of the issue of obscenity, shall be admissible. The Court shall dismiss a prosecution for obscenity if it is satisfied that the material is not obscene.

Glossary

accessories—parties following crime who are liable for separate, lesser offenses

accomplices—parties before and during crime who are liable as principals

actus reus—the criminal act or the physical element in criminal liability; one of the material elements in criminal liability

adversary system—the American system of law in which judges act as umpires in contests between the parties

affirm—when an appeals court upholds the decision made in a trial court

affirmative defense—defense that the prosecution need not disprove unless defendants present some evidence first

alter ego doctrine—high corporate officers are the corporation's ''brain''

appellant—the party who appeals a trial court's decision to a higher court

appellate cases—cases appealed to higher courts

appellee—the party appealed against in an appellate case

asportation—carrying away of property

assault—attempt to injure or intent to frighten without actual injury

balancing interests—securing social order while at the same time protecting individual liberty

battery—unjustified offensive touching

burden of production—the obligation to introduce evidence to avoid an adverse ruling

burden of proof—the responsibility to prove contested facts

capital felony—felony punishable by death, or in states without capital punishment, life imprisonment

carnal knowledge—the sexual contact qualifying an act for rape and related offenses

celerity—speed of punishment

claim of right—a defense to theft; the belief that property taken rightfully belongs to the taker

common law—all the statutes and case law background of England and the colonies before the Revolution based on principles and rules that derive from usages and customs of antiquity

concurrence—the requirement that *actus reus* must join with *mens rea* to cause a harmful result in order to impose criminal liability

conduct—combination of act and intention

constructive force—substitute for actual force, generally in cases where victim is unable to consent

contributory cause—a cause that contributes to death but need not be a sole cause

conversion—using property for purposes other than what owner intends

corroboration rule—that a victim's testimony alone is insufficient to convict in rape cases

criminal punishment—special meaning that criminal law gives to punishment, containing four elements: (1) pain or other unpleasant consequence, (2) inflicted for breaking a specific law, (3) administered by the state, (4) for the primary purpose of

criminal sexual conduct—gender-neutral statute directed toward a wide range of sexual violations not covered in traditional rape statutes

culpability—blameworthiness; that is, one who acts with one of the criminal mental states—purpose, knowledge, recklessness, or negligence—and can therefore be blamed for the harmful result

de minimus non curat lex—the law does not recognize trifles

defendant—the person against whom a civil or criminal action is brought

defense—evidence that defendants bring to raise reasonable doubts concerning prosecution's proof

deliberate—done with a cool, reflective mind

diminished capacity—mental capacity that is less than "normal" but more than insane

due process—constitutional requirement that statutes be clear enough to define in advance and notify citizens just what conduct is criminal

Durham rule, or **product test**—insanity test measuring capacity by determining whether crime was a product of mental disease or defect

ex post facto laws—laws passed after the occurrence of the conduct constituting the crime

excuse—defense in which defendants admit wrongdoing but claim that under the circumstances, they were not responsible for what they did

extraneous circumstances—conditions that are beyond the attempter's control and that make it impossible to complete a crime

factual impossibility—facts that make it impossible to complete a crime; not a defense to criminal attempt liability

felony——a serious crime generally punishable by one year or more in prison

felony murder—death occurring during a serious felony

Fourteenth Amendment due process clause—provision that "no state shall deprive any citizen of life, liberty or property without due process of law"

general deterrence—the utilitarian purpose of punishment; aims to prevent crime by threatening would-be lawbreakers with punishment

general intent——purpose with respect to the act and reckless with respect to the harm

general principles of criminal liability—the theoretical foundation for material

elements: *actus reus, mens rea,* causation, and harm

Hale warning—the jury instruction that says rape is easy to charge and difficult to refute

hedonism—seeking pleasure and avoiding pain

incapacitation—sometimes called special deterrence; aims to prevent crime by restraint, mutilation, and even death

inchoate crimes—crimes not yet completed, such as attempt, conspiracy, and solicitation

irresistible impulse—supplement to *M'Naghten* rule that permits insanity defense when defendants know the difference between right and wrong but cannot sufficiently control their behavior to do what is right

issue—the legal question to be decided in an appellate court

jurisprudence—philosophy of law

justification—defense that admits defendants' responsibility for harm but argues that under the circumstances, it was right to do it

legal impossibility—legal conditions that make it impossible to complete a crime; a good defense to attempt liability

M'Naghten rule, or *right-wrong test*—insanity defense based on mental disease or defect that removes defendants' capacity to know the difference between right and wrong

malice aforethought—the old common definition of the murder *mens rea*

marital rape exception—the rule that husbands cannot rape their wives

material elements—the parts of a crime that the prosecution must prove beyond a reasonable doubt, such as act, *mens rea,* causation, and harmful result

mens rea—the mental element in crime, of which there are four mental states: purpose, knowledge, recklessness, and negligence

misappropriation—getting possession of another's property

misdemeanor—a minor crime, the penalty for which is usually less than 1 year in jail, or a fine

mitigating circumstances—facts that reduce defendants' culpability but do not completely justify or excuse wrongdoing

Model Penal Code—the code developed by the American Law Institute to guide reform in criminal law

motive—the reason why defendants commit crimes

negligence—unconscious risk creation, or the mental state in which actors create risks of harm but are not aware they are creating them

nulla poena sine lege—no punishment without specific authority in law

nullum crimen sine lege—no crime without a specific law defining it as such

opinion—the reasons given for an appellate court decision

overbreadth—the principle that when statutes are so broad they include too much behavior they are unconstitutional

paramour rule—adequate provocation is provided by discovering a spouse in an adulterous act

plaintiff—the person who sues another party in a civil action

premeditate—to plan in advance

preponderance of the evidence—evidence of greater weight than that on the other side of the issue or question

presumption of innocence—criminal defendants need not prove their innocence; they are legally innocent until the state proves every material element in a crime

principle of legality—government cannot punish citizens without specific laws forewarning citizens that particular conduct will be punished in a particular manner and that statutes be clear enough that interpreting them is not left to the discretion of police, prosecutors and judges discretion

probable cause—the Fourth and Fourteenth Amendment requirement that arrests must be based on facts and not on police hunch or whim

proportionality—the Eighth Amendment prohibition against punishments grossly disproportionate to the crime

proximate cause—legal or culpable cause

punishment—penalties inflicted for the specific purpose of producing pain

rationalism—theory that reason provides the best basis for action

reasonable resistance standard—women must use the amount of force required by the totality of the circumstances surrounding sexual assault

recklessness—conscious risk creation, or the state of mind in which actors know they are creating risks of harm

rehabilitation—to prevent crime by altering criminals' behavior, usually by "treating" offenders instead of punishing them

remand—an appellate court decision to send the case back to the trial court for further proceedings

respondeat superior—employers are responsible for their employees' actions.

retribution—to pay back criminals for the harm they have done; sometimes called "just deserts"

reverse—an appellate court decision to overrule or strike down a trial court's decision

sine qua non—but-for or legal causation

stare decisis—policy of courts to stand by prior decisions and not to disturb settled points of law

statutes—rules or doctrines enacted by legislatures

statutory rape—carnal knowledge of a person under the age of consent whether or not accomplished by force

strict liability—liability without fault

substantial capacity—insanity determined by whether mental disease or defect has impaired defendants' substantial capacity to either appreciate their conduct's wrongfulness or to conform their behavior to what the law requires

superior officer rule—only the highest officers in the corporate structure can make a corporation criminally liable

surreptitious remaining—entering a structure with the intent to commit a crime inside

theft—an old word meaning larceny; now includes the consolidated crimes of larceny, embezzlement, and false pretenses.

tort—private lawsuit brought to collect money for injuries

trespassory taking—the wrongful taking required in larceny

unprivileged entry—entering a structure without right, license, or permission

utmost resistance standard—women rape victims had to use all the physical strength they had to prevent penetration

vicarious liability—the doctrine that one party is criminally liable for a third party's conduct

void for vagueness—a law so obscure that a reasonable person could not determine from a reading what the law commands or prohibits violates the due process clauses of the Fifth and Fourteenth Amendments

Wharton rule—more than two parties must be involved in conspiracies to commit crimes naturally involving at least two parties, such as rape

Index